Court Revels
1485–1559

In 1545 Henry VIII created a Revels Office within the royal household and appointed Sir Thomas Cawarden, one of the gentlemen of the Privy Chamber, as its Master. In so doing he set a precedent for the production of revels at court for the next century.

Some historians have only recently examined the revels in their historical context, but none has attempted, as W.R. Streitberger does, to study court entertainments in terms of the growth and development of the Revels organization and its adaptation to different political climates at court.

Streitberger presents evidence in the form of a calendar of court entertainments and appendices based on the primary documents; he provides an explanation of the occasion, form, and purpose of these entertainments in their historical context; and he explains the development of the Revels organization from the temporary appointment of producers at the beginning of their period into a government office by the mid-sixteenth century. Streitberger details the adaptation of the Revels organization to the very different courts of the various monarchs, and explains how their personalities, principles, and policies shaped that adaptation.

(Studies in Early English Drama 3)

W.R. STREITBERGER is a member of the Department of English, University of Washington. Among his books are *Jacobean and Caroline Revels Accounts, 1603–1642*, and *Edmond Tyllney, Master of the Revels*.

STUDIES IN EARLY ENGLISH DRAMA 3
General Editor: J.A.B. Somerset

W.R. STREITBERGER

Court Revels, 1485–1559

UNIVERSITY OF TORONTO PRESS
Toronto Buffalo London

© University of Toronto Press Incorporated 1994
Toronto Buffalo London
Printed in Canada

ISBN 0-8020-0590-X (cloth)

Printed on acid-free paper

Canadian Cataloguing in Publication Data

Streitberger, W.R.
Court revels, 1485–1559

(Studies in early English drama ; 3)
Includes index.
ISBN 0-8020-0590-X

1. English drama – Early modern and Elizabethan, 1500-1600 – History
and criticism. 2. Masques – History and criticism. 3. Theater – England –
History – 16th century. 4. Theater and state – England – History – 16th
century. I. Title. II. Series.

PR646.S77 1994   822'.2   C93-095066-6

Contents

FOR ELAINE

Preface

The aim of this book is to present evidence in a calendar and other appendices for revels, spectacles, and entertainments at court from 1485 to 1559 based on a study of the primary documents; to give some account of the occasion, form, and purpose of these revels; and to provide an explanation for the development of the Revels organization from the temporary appointment of producers at the opening of the Tudor period into a government office by the mid-sixteenth century. The choice of the terminal date for this study is not arbitrary. Sir Thomas Cawarden's death in August 1559, less than a full year into the reign of Elizabeth I, signals the end of an extensive series of accounts and documents and the end of an important era in the history of the Revels Office. Cawarden's administration was the model to which reformers looked when considering changes in the Elizabethan office.

Early Tudor revels is hardly an unexplored subject. The first attempt at a systematic study was John Payne Collier's *The History of English Dramatic Poetry to the Time of Shakespeare and Annals of the Stage to the Restoration* (1831). Substantial primary research was subsequently undertaken by C.W. Wallace, *The Evolution of the English Drama up to Shakespeare* (1912). The suspicions about the former and the deficiencies of the latter are too well known to bear repeating. Albert Feuillerat, *Documents Relating to the Office of the Revels in the Time of Queen Elizabeth* (1908) and *Documents Relating to the Revels at Court in the Time of King Edward VI and Queen Mary* (1914), edited the main accounts from 1547 to 1603, but not the subsidiary documents. During the past several decades, important new research has been published by Glynn Wickham, Sydney Anglo, Gordon Kipling, Ian Lancashire, C.E. McGee and John C. Meagher, and Alan Young.

Despite this significant body of work, when I first came to the subject in the late 1970s many of the relevant primary documents had not been surveyed and a calendar of court entertainments had not been constructed. Neither had there been an adequate attempt to study the development of the Revels organization. E.K. Chambers, *Notes on the History of the Revels Office under the Tudors* (1906), and Albert Feuillerat, *Les Bureau Des Menus-Plaisirs* (1910), gave an account of the establishment of the Office of the Revels in 1545 and of its development in the Elizabethan period, but they had only random and somewhat inaccurate generalizations to make about the earlier organization. While there is no shortage of studies of the form of early Tudor revels, many of these have tended to select aspects of the revels without regard to chronology in order to advance arguments about the Jacobean mask. Rudolph Brotanek, *Die Englishchen Maskenespiele* (1902), and Paul Reyher, *Les Masques Anglais* (1909) provided the studies from which Chambers derived some of his views on the subject in *The Elizabethan Stage* (1923). Enid Welsford, *The Court Masque* (1927), drew on these and on other sources for her influential study, as did Stephen Orgel, *The Jonsonian Masque* (1965). Sydney Anglo, *Spectacle Pageantry, and Early Tudor Policy* (1969), corrected some of the biases of earlier writers by examining the relationship between revels and spectacles and their political occasions, as did Gordon Kipling, *The Triumph of Honour* (1977), for the court of Henry VII.

My indebtedness to this significant body of research and criticism will be evident in the following pages. I have also incurred a number of personal debts in writing this book. Professors Mark Eccles, G.E. Bentley, David Bergeron, Alan Holaday, and the late O.B. Hardison, Jr., offered advice and encouragement when this study was still in the planning stages. Early in my research I benefited from the advice of Sydney Anglo, and Ian Lancashire sent me his transcripts of several of the Revels accounts. David Fowler and Alan Young read drafts of early versions of the manuscript and provided many helpful suggestions. I owe a great debt of gratitude to Gordon Kipling and C.E. McGee for their painstaking comments on several drafts of the manuscript. Their advice has been invaluable. I am also grateful for assistance and advice to J.A.B. Somerset, General Editor of the SEED series, to the late Prudence Tracy, to Virgil D. Duff of the University of Toronto Press, and to Rob Weller and Laura Utterback of the University of Washington.

An American Council of Learned Societies fellowship in 1980–1 enabled me to undertake the primary research for this study at the Public Record Office, London and Kew Gardens; the Bodleian Library, Oxford; the Surrey Record Office, Guildford; the University of London Library; the Corporation of London Record Office and Guildhall Library, London; the College of Arms; and the Folger Shakespeare Library, Washington D.C. I am grateful to the librarians, archivists, and staffs of these institutions for their unfailing generosity, particularly to Laetitia Yeandle (Folger Shakespeare Library), G.M.A. Beck (Surrey Record Office, Guildford), S. Barter Baily (H.M. Royal Armouries), R. Yorke (College of Arms), and M.M. Condon and M. Cooper (Public Record Office). I am also grateful to the Center for Research Libraries, Chicago, and the University of Washington Interlibrary Borrowing Service for the loan of microfilms of the Chamber accounts. The University of Washington Graduate School provided a grant to relieve me from teaching in spring 1985 which enabled me to bring my mass of notes into some coherent order and another grant in summer 1992 which afforded an opportunity for further research in England.

Some parts of this study have appeared before in substantially different form as notes or articles in journals. The subsidiary Revels account for Cornish's 1516 play was first announced in *Medieval and Renaissance Drama in England,* 1 (1983): 29–35. Evidence from the Chamber accounts and other financial sources was first explored in *Research Opportunities in Renaissance Drama,* 26 (1983): 31–54; 27 (1984): 21–45; and 29 (1986–7): 25–46. Articles on Henry VIII's Revels establishment and William Cornish appeared in *Medieval English Theatre,* 7 (1985): 83–100, and 8 (1986): 3–20, and one on the 1527 play at Greenwich in *The Theatre Annual,* 44 (1989–90): 21–36.

Many of the places in London and its environs which are referred to in this study may be identified on the 'Agas' map which is conveniently enlarged and indexed in *The A to Z of Elizabethan London,* compiled by Adrian Prockter and Robert Taylor (Lympne Castle, Kent: Harry Margary in association with the Guildhall Library, London, 1979). Illustrations of contemporary views and of reconstructed plans of many of the buildings referred to may be found in H.M. Colvin et al., *The History of the King's Works* (London: HMSO, 1975, 1982), volumes III, IV. A glossary of terms relating to the martial exhibitions is conveniently available in Alan Young, *Tudor and Jacobean Tournaments,* (London: George Philip, 1987), 193–5.

W.R.S.,
Seattle, 1993

Abbreviations

APC   *Acts of the Privy Council of England,* n.s., ed. J.R. Dasent (London: HMSO, 1890–1959).

Acts and Monuments   *The Acts and Monuments of John Foxe,* ed. G. Townsend (London, 1837–41; reprint New York: AMS Press, 1965).

Anglo, 'Evolution'   Sydney Anglo, 'The Evolution of the Early Tudor Disguising, Pageant, and Mask,' *Renaissance Drama,* n.s., 1 (1968): 3–44.

Anglo, 'Henry VII'   Sydney Anglo, 'The Court Festivals of Henry VII: A Study based upon the Account Books of John Heron, Treasurer of the Chamber,' *Bulletin of the John Rylands Library,* 43 (1960): 12–45.

Anglo, *Spectacle*   Sydney Anglo, *Spectacle Pageantry, and Early Tudor Policy* (Oxford: Clarendon Press, 1969).

Anglo, *Tournament Roll*   Sydney Anglo, *The Great Tournament Roll of Westminster* (Oxford: Clarendon Press, 1968).

Antiquarian Repertory   *The Antiquarian Repertory,* ed. F. Grose and T. Ashe (London: E. Jeffrey, 1807–9).

Auerbach, *Tudor Artists*   Erna Auerbach, *Tudor Artists* (London: Athlone Press, 1954).

BL   British Library, London

CPR Edward IV   *Calendar of the Patent Rolls preserved in the Public Record Office. Edward IV. A.D. 1461–1467* (London: HMSO, 1897).

CPR Edward IV and Richard III   *Calendar of the Patent Rolls preserved in the Public Record Office. Edward IV Edward V, Richard III. A.D. 1476–1485* (London: HMSO, 1901).

CPR Edward VI   *Calendar of the Patent Rolls preserved in the Public Record Office. Edward VI. A.D. 1547–1553* (London: HMSO, 1924–9).

CPR Elizabeth   *Calendar of the Patent Rolls preserved in the Public Record Office. Elizabeth I. 1558–1582* (London, HMSO, 1939–86).

CPR Henry VII   *Calendar of the Patent Rolls preserved in the Public Record Office.*
Henry VII. A.D. 1485–1509 (London, HMSO, 1914–16).

CPR Philip and Mary   *Calendar of the Patent Rolls preserved in the Public Record
Office. Philip and Mary. A.D. 1553–1558* (London: HMSO, 1937–9).

CSP Domestic, 1547–1580   *Calendar of State Papers, Domestic Series, of the Reigns of
Edward VI, Mary, Elizabeth. 1547–1603*, ed. R. Lemon and M.A.E. Green (London: Longman, 1856–71).

CSP Domestic, 1547–1553   *Calendar of State Papers, Domestic Series of the reign of
Edward VI, 1547–1553, preserved in the Public Record Office*, rev. ed. C.S.
Knighton (London: HMSO, 1992).

CSP Milan   *Calendar of State Papers and Manuscripts Existing in the Archives and Collections of Milan*, ed. A.B. Hinds (London: HMSO, 1912).

CSP Spanish   *Calendar of Letters, Dispatches, and State Papers Relating to Negotiations
between England and Spain*, ed. P. de Gayangos et al. (London: Longman, 1862–1954).

CSP Venetian   *Calendar of State Papers and Manuscripts Relating to English Affairs
Existing in the Archives and Collections of Venice and other Libraries in Northern
Italy*, ed. R. Brown et al. (London: Longman, 1864–1940).

Campbell   William Campbell, ed., *Materials for a History of the Reign of Henry VII*,
Rolls Series, vol. 60 (London: Longman, 1873, 1877).

Chambers, *ES*   E.K. Chambers, *The Elizabethan Stage* (Oxford: Clarendon Press, 1923).

Chambers, *MS*   E.K. Chambers, *The Mediaeval Stage* (Oxford: Clarendon Press, 1903).

Chambers, *Tudor Revels*   E.K. Chambers, *Notes on the History of the Revels Office
Under the Tudors* (London, 1906; reprint New York: B. Franklin, 1967).

Chronicle of Calais   J.G. Nichols, ed., *The Chronicle of Calais in the Reigns of Henry
VII and Henry VIII*, Camden Society, vol. 35 (London: J.B. Nichols and Son, 1846).

Chronicle of Queen Jane and Queen Mary   J.G. Nichols, ed., *The Chronicle of Queen
Jane and of Two Years of Queen Mary*, Camden Society, vol. 48 (London: J.B.
Nichols and Son,1850).

Collectanea   *Joannis Lelandi antiquarii de rebus britannicis Collectanea*, ed. Thomas
Hearne (London: Benjamin Wright, 1774), IV.

Collier, *HEDP*   John Payne Collier, *The History of English Dramatic Poetry to the
Time of Shakespeare and Annals of the Stage to the Restoration* (London: J. Murray, 1831; 2d ed. 1879).

Complete Peerage   G.E. Cokayne, *The Complete Peerage*, rev. ed. V. Gibbs et al. (London: St. Catherine Press, 1910–59).

Craib, 'Sir Thomas Cawarden'   T. Craib, 'Sir Thomas Cawarden,' *Surrey Archaeological Collections* 28 (1915), 7–28.

Dramatic Records   Ian Lancashire, *Dramatic Texts and Records of Britain A Chronological Topography to 1558* (Toronto: University of Toronto Press, 1984).

Feuillerat, *Edward VI and Mary*   Albert Feuillerat, *Documents Relating to the Revels at Court in the Time of King Edward VI and Queen Mary*, Materialien zur Kunde des älteren Englischen Dramas, vol. 44 (Louvain: A. Uystpruyst, 1914).

Feuillerat, *Elizabeth*   Albert Feuillerat, *Documents Relating to the Office of the Revels in the Time of Queen Elizabeth*, Materialien zur Kunde des älteren Englischen Dramas, vol. 21 (Louvain: A. Uystpruyst, 1908).

Folger Library   Folger Shakespeare Library, Washington, D.C.

Great Chronicle   *The Great Chronicle of London*, ed. A.H. Thomas and I.D. Thornley (London: G.W. Jones, 1938).

Guildford Muniment Room   Surrey Record Office, Guildford Muniment Room, Castle Arch, Guildford, Surrey.

Guistinian   Sebastian Guistinian, *Four Years at the Court of Henry VIII*, trans. Rawdon Brown (London: Smith, Elder, 1854).

Hall   *Hall's Chronicle*, ed. [Sir Henry Ellis] (London: G. Woodfall, 1809).

Hillebrand, *The Child Actors*   Harold N. Hillebrand, *The Child Actors, A Chapter in Elizabethan Stage History*, University of Illinois Studies in Language and Literature, vol. 11 (Urbana, Ill., 1926), 1–356.

HMSO   His/Her Majesty's Stationery Office.

King's Works   H.M. Colvin et al., *The History of the King's Works* (London: HMSO, 1975, 1982), III, IV.

Kipling, *Honour*   Gordon Kipling, *The Triumph of Honour* (The Hague: Leiden University Press, 1977).

Kipling, 'Patronage'   Gordon Kipling, 'Henry VII and the Origins of Tudor Patronage,' *Patronage in the Renaissance*, ed. Guy Fitch Lytle and Stephen Orgel (Princeton: Princeton University Press, 1981), 117–64.

Kipling, *Receyt*   Gordon Kipling, ed., *The Receyt of the Ladie Kateryne*, Early English Text Society, n.s., vol. 296 (Oxford: Oxford University Press, 1990).

LP   J.S. Brewer and R.H. Brodie, eds., *Letters and Papers, Foreign and Domestic, of the Reign of Henry VIII*, 2nd ed. (London: HMSO, 1920; reprint Vaduz: Kraus, 1965).

LP Richard III and Henry VII   J. Gairdner, ed., *Letters and Papers Illustrative of the Reigns of Richard III and Henry VII*, Rolls Series, vol. 24 (London: Longman, 1861).

Literary Remains   J.G. Nichols, ed., *Literary Remains of King Edward the Sixth* (Roxburghe Club, 1857).

Loseley Manor Documents   Handlist of Documents at Loseley Manor, Surrey Record Office, Guildford, Surrey.

Machyn, *Diary*   J.G. Nichols, ed., *The Diary of Henry Machyn, Citizen and Merchant Taylor of London, from A.D. 1550 to A.D. 1563*, Camden Society, vol. 42 (London: J.B. Nichols and Son,1848).

McGee and Meagher, 'Checklist'   C.E. McGee and John C. Meagher, 'A Preliminary Checklist of Tudor and Stuart Entertainments: 1485–1558,' *RORD*, 25 (1982): 31–114.

Memorials   J. Gairdner, ed., *Memorials of King Henry VII*, Rolls Series, vol. 10 (London: Longman, 1858).

MSC   *Malone Society Collections.*

PRO   Public Record Office, London.

RCHM   *Report of the Royal Commission on Historical Manuscripts.*

Reed, *Early Tudor Drama*   A.W. Reed, *Early Tudor Drama* (London: Methuen, 1926).

Rutland Papers   W. Jerdan, ed., *Rutland Papers. Original Documents Illustrative of the Courts and Times of Henry VII and Henry VIII*, Camden Society, vol. 21 (London: J.B. Nichols and Son, 1842).

Sanuto, *Diarii*   *I Diarii di Marino Sanuto*, ed. F. Stefani et al. (Venice: F. Visentini, 1879–1903).

STC   *Short Title Catalogue*

Streitberger, *RORD* (1983)   W.R. Streitberger, 'Court Festivities of Henry VII: 1485–1491, 1502–1505,' *RORD* 26 (1983): 31–54.

Streitberger, *RORD* (1984)   W.R. Streitberger, 'Financing Court Entertainments, 1509–1558,' *RORD* 27 (1984): 21–45.

Streitberger, *RORD* (1986–7)   W.R. Streitberger, 'Revels at Court from 1541 to 1559,' *RORD* 29 (1986–7): 25–45.

Wallace, *Evolution*   C.W. Wallace, *The Evolution of the English Drama up to Shakespeare* (Berlin: Georg Reimer, 1912).

Warton, *HEP*   Thomas Warton, *The History of English Poetry from the Eleventh to the Seventeenth Century* (London, 1774–81; reprint Alex Murray & Son, 1870).

Welsford, *Court Masque*   Enid Welsford, *The Court Masque* (Cambridge, 1927; reprint New York: Russell and Russell, 1962).

Wickham, *EES*   Glynne Wickham, *Early English Stages, 1300 to 1600* (London: Routledge and Paul, 1959–63).

Wriothesley, *Chronicle*   Charles Wriothesley, *A Chronicle of England during the reigns of the Tudors from A.D. 1485 to 1559*, ed. W.D. Hamilton, Camden Society, n.s., vols. 11, 20 (London: J.B. Nichols and Son, 1875, 1877).

Young, *Tournaments*   Alan Young, *Tudor and Jacobean Tournaments* (London: George Philip, 1987).

Conventions

The following conventions are employed in the transcription and presentation of documents. All scripts, with the exception of italic, are uniformly rendered in roman type. Italic type is used to represent italic script in original documents, for foreign words and phrases, for the titles of court entertainments, to expand certain archaic symbols and letters, and to expand abbreviations. Abbreviations currently in use are retained. The old long s is modernized throughout. Superscript letters are given on the base line. Editorial interpolations are enclosed within square brackets [ ]; when used with parentheses ([ ]), square brackets are simply parenthetical. Pointed brackets ⟨ ⟩ in dating are used to indicate 'between the dates of.'

PART I

Introduction

'Pastime' and 'pleasure' were the two most general terms used by contemporary writers to describe court entertainments. These terms could refer to formal spectacles such as tournaments, to state banquets, to hunting, to revels, to plays, and even to minor diversions such as table games or gambling. Payments for many minor pastimes or pleasures are recorded in the Chamber and Privy Purse accounts for the entire early Tudor period. More formal occasions at court were enlivened by professionally prepared entertainments. Musical performances of all kinds – by the permanent troupes of the royal household, by those of the aristocracy, by foreign musicians, and by a miscellany of others – were regular features at court. Acrobats, fools, singers, and dancers all took their place in the seasonal round of entertainments. Tournaments and other public exhibitions of the martial exercises were held in every reign, though much more frequently under Henry VIII, who personally participated in them. Important dynastic celebrations, such as creations, weddings, and christenings; state occasions, such as the celebration of treaties or the reception of foreign dignitaries; and the traditional major feasts – almost always at New Year's, Twelfth Night, and Shrovetide, very often at Candlemas (2 February), and occasionally at Easter – were celebrated with appropriate ceremonies, occasionally with tournaments, and almost invariably with revels. While the term 'revel' has a more specific connotation than pastime or pleasure, it is used generally in the period to refer to any single entertainment or set of entertainments held on a particular occasion.

Revels could extend for as short a period as a few hours of for as long as a few days. They were usually composed of a variety of entertainments, often given in conjunction with a banquet. Anything could be expected in a revel. In fact, spectacular display and surprise were important elements. The interplay between recognizable form and innovation which characterized the entertainments included within revels prompted contemporary observers to grasp at a variety of imprecise terms to describe them. 'Mummery,' 'disguising,' and 'mask,' for example, are used interchangeably to describe entertainments. The terms used to describe entertainments which contained substantial portions of dialogue and action were no better. 'Interlude,' 'play,' 'disguising,' 'dialogue,' 'pageant,' and (if the witness was a foreigner) 'farsa' were used indiscriminately to describe these entertainments. The terminology gets no more precise when we turn to professionals in the period. Richard Gibson, who helped produce virtually all revels, spectacles, and entertainments at Henry VIII's court from 1510 to 1534, uses every conceivable term to describe his entertainments – disguising, mummery, mask, gladness, pastime, pleasure, revel, comedy, and a number of others. Nor does he use these terms consistently. He uses 'mask,' 'meskelyn,' and 'meskellyer' to describe a type of entertainment given as part of the revels, to refer to a visor, and to refer to the persons who wore the costumes in one of these entertainments. There are occasions when he uses two different terms to describe an entertainment and others when he treats different terms, such as 'meskeller or mvmry,' as synonyms. This loose terminology is found throughout the documents and narratives of the period. Gibson and Edward Hall, Henry VIII's court chronicler, call the revels of 17 and 24 June 1520 at the Field of Cloth of Gold 'maskers' and 'meskelers,' but the herald who prepared a narrative of the events uses the term 'mommery.' Hall describes one of the entertainments produced as part of the revels at Greenwich in 1527 as a 'play' at one point and a 'disguising' at another. By mid-century the term 'mask' began to displace the earlier terms 'mummery' and 'disguising' in the accounts and narratives. But it is still not a precise term, for it is used to refer to a type of entertainment as well as to a set of costumes used in one of these entertainments, just as the term 'masker' can refer to a person performing in one of these indoor entertainments as well as to a costumed knight in a martial exhibition. The older terms, 'mummery' and 'disguising' remained in use late into the century, and show up on occasion among the bills of the artisans and suppliers of material to the Revels Office.

Such imprecision in generic terms points to a fundamental fact of the context of early Tudor revels, spectacles, and entertainments. The conception of genre was flexible and inclusive, not definitive and exclusive as ours is. Variety was the rule rather than the exception: costuming, music, poetry, dance, visual spectacle, barriers, tourneys, and dialogue were used in any number of combinations. Disguisings or mummeries often contained dramatic dialogue, occasionally barriers or tourneys, as well as music, song, dance, and pageants. Plays occasionally contained mummeries or disguisings along with song, dance and pageants. Even jousts, tourneys, and barriers held outdoors incorporated literary devices, dramatic dialogue, costuming, music, song, and pageants. There are many occasions on which several of these entertainments and spectacles were structurally or thematically related in the context of a revel.[1]

Revels were used to signal two separate yet related functions, for the royal household was at the same time a domestic and an administrative organization.[2] As a domestic organization, the household was concerned with the lodging and feeding of the sovereign and his retainers. Around these functions developed the ceremonies and entertainments associated with traditional religious and secular feasts. As an administrative organization the household was concerned with the means and methods of governing the realm. Around these functions developed the ceremonies and entertainments associated with dynastic and state occasions. The domestic and administrative functions of the household were closely interwoven in the Tudor period, and the same individuals often served the sovereign in both capacities. This lack of clear distinction between domestic and administrative functions shows itself also in the sovereign's revels. Revels and ceremonies in the household were in one sense domestic and private. The sovereign's Christmas ceremonies, such as attendance at religious services, processions to evensong, hearing sermons, and so on were the same rituals that an ordinary citizen might observe during the season, and the revels the king ordered mirrored on a more opulent scale those put on in the houses of the minor nobility. In so far as the observance of ceremony and ritual and the indulgence in revels were personal, they expressed the character of the king – his religious preference, social ideals, athletic ability, cultural refinement, wealth, and generosity. At the same time, as head of a household that governed the realm, his ceremonies, spectacles, and revels were public and so expressed the character of the state itself. Revels used to signal secular or religious feasts were in the broadest sense political, just as those which signalled dynastic and state occasions were in the narrowest sense personal.

Since by their very nature they reflected the character of the sovereign and the state, revels were planned by the king or the council. In the early Tudor period the council was a vaguely defined body of officers and advisers whose number and composition varied and whose function was to provide advice and to carry out policy. The council planned wars and defence, oversaw finances and government bureaucracy, issued proclamations, sent and received ambassadors, and administered justice from the court of Star Chamber. The early Tudor council was not well defined and was different in composition from the coterie of officers which later became known as the Privy Council.[3] There were actually two councils, one which travelled with the sovereign from palace to manor and one which resided at Westminster. The council attending the king was not always composed of the same individuals as the one at Westminster, and business initiated by one body might be continued by the other. Under Henry VIII the council began to take on a more definite form. It acquired a clerk who took minutes of meetings, though many of its confidential deliberations were not recorded. The council's power was limited, however. It had no control other than advisory over the sovereign's actions or the administrative arrangements he might make with other ministers, and before 1556 it had no seal of its own. While vaguely defined in terms of its numbers and composition, the core of the early Tudor council was composed of the chief officers of state and of the royal household. In addition to the heads of writ-issuing departments, such as the Chancellor, the Treasurer, and Privy Seal, it usually included the Admiral, the Steward, the Chamberlain, the Master of the Horse, often the Treasurer of the Chamber, the Treasurer of and Comptroller of the household, and, after 1540, the principal secretaries.

E.K. Chambers reminds us that while it seems surprising for an executive body of this stature to have concerned itself with entertainments, the early Tudor council was a more nearly direct descendant of the Curia Regis – the group of feudal lords who surrounded medieval kings – than of the more highly specialized departments of the Tudor household and the bureaucracies, such as the Chancery and the Exchequer.[4] Essentially, the council included the heads of state and the household acting collectively on everything that affected the sovereign, court, and government, and was therefore prepared to give advice in all matters. Since revels were fêtes given by the sovereign not only to his important retainers and to his household but also to foreign ambassadors, the order for such gatherings did more than confirm hierarchy at court. Revels served as a means by which monarchs could project an image of themselves and of their courts to foreign princes and by which diplomatic positions could be implied or stated. The letters sent home by foreign ambassadors, which in this period were always a mixture of news and intelligence information, pay careful attention to ceremonies, spectacles, and revels, often in painstaking detail. Munificence, a manifestation of magnificence, was regarded as one of the outward signs of power, and these public displays consequently became the most obvious means of creating an image of the sovereign's 'estate.' All of the Tudor monarchs used revels for this purpose, and early in Henry VIII's reign the steps from image-making to overt political commentary and finally to propaganda were taken.

When special fittings, such as scaffolds, degrees, or stages were needed in the Abbey or in St Paul's or in one of the palaces for coronations, weddings, christenings, or funerals, the council appointed a supervisor to oversee installation and decoration, another to coordinate the activities of musicians, yet another to arrange processions, and still others to manage more of the details. When tournaments were planned, the council appointed a supervisor to organize them. And when revels were needed, the council appointed a supervisor to produce them. Initially, the appointment of a supervisor to produce revels was no different from any of the other appointments of supervisors to manage temporary projects, and none are called by special titles. Beginning in Henry VIII's reign, the appointed supervisor was called Master of the Revels, and, in 1545, the title was confirmed by patent for life. Despite the fact that a more organized establishment for the production of revels was created in Henry VIII's reign, the council never relinquished its authority to appoint temporary supervisors of revels and to order the entertainments it thought fit for state occasions. Arrangements to produce revels at traditional feasts, unless some diplomatic purpose was to be served, were somewhat less formal. The sovereign, often in consultation with the council followed by the issuance of a Privy Seal writ or imprest from the Chamber, authorized a supervisor to produce revels.

Because they employed specially designed costumes, often used movable or fixed pageants or stages, employed dialogue, music, song, and dance, sometimes incorporated barriers or tourneys, and often included plays, devising and producing revels was a complicated matter. Post-romantic notions of the integrity of artistic works do not apply to these complex entertainments nor to the means by which they were produced. Revels were the result of collaboration by artists, costume designers, writers, composers, choreographers, artisans, and labourers in relation to whom the supervisor stood as producer and director who had financial, administrative, and aesthetic control under the king and council. The responsibility of the earlier supervisors for the content of their particular revels became a standing duty of the Masters by the early 1570s, and it is likely that this also influenced the decision in 1581 to appoint the Master as censor of plays and licenser of public theatres and acting companies.[5] While the responsibilities of the Master evolved over the course of the sixteenth century to include many other related duties, his basic function as supervisor of court revels and the means he used to produce them were established very early in the period.

Occasionally before 1516 and regularly thereafter, the supervisors or Masters contracted with writers for a text (if there was to be one) and with artists to design costumes, pageants, and properties for the revels. The Masters obtained material from the Great Wardrobe by warrant or from one of the standing wardrobes in the main palaces in and around London, bought more from London merchants using the imprests granted by the king or council, and used credit for the rest. They contracted with chief tailors, carpenters, smiths, and a host of other artisans, who sometimes hired their own crews of workmen, to produce costumes and properties. They arranged for the lease of buildings suitable for use as workshops. They consulted with the king or one of his close associates in the Privy Chamber on the appropriateness of their designs. They arranged transportation for the completed costumes and properties to court, supervised final assembly and probably approved the installation of lighting in the great halls, chambers, or banqueting houses; consulted with amateur and professional performers; coordinated script, choreography, music, and spectacle; and attended the performance with a crew, initially of workmen and later of the minor officers of the Revels, who assisted at productions. After the performance, they supervised the collection of costumes and disassembly of the properties, transported them to storage for use at a later date, and drew up an account of their expenses for which they were paid at one of the major treasuries. The early supervisors of revels were appointed for specific feasts or diplomatic occasions. When they completed their projects they returned to their ordinary posts in the household. Early in Henry VIII's reign, when the supervisor was styled Master of the Revels, his duties expanded to include arranging a variety of entertainments at court. The Master in this period was informally appointed by the king, and he also went back to other household and government duties after his projects were completed. But since he had the assistance of a deputy, who held a permanent position in the Tents, to handle ordinary production details the production of revels had a semi-permanent status in the household. Late in Henry VIII's reign, when the Master was appointed to his position by patent for life, his duties expanded to devising or selecting and to producing or supporting the production of virtually every entertainment and spectacle at court. This was a permanent appointment to a specialist who did not return to other duties after his productions; rather he was made Master of several household offices and so gave full attention to these duties throughout the year. He was assisted with ordinary production details by a staff in a complex of offices which became by mid-century a fairly extensive organization of compatible functions.

Two other court appointees, the Lord or Abbot of Misrule and the so-called Master of Ceremonies, who also received their commissions from the sovereign or council, ought to be distinguished from the Master of the Revels. As E.K. Chambers has explained, the Lord of Misrule was a traditional figure not only at court but in the households of the nobility, at colleges, and in certain boroughs and parishes.[6] He presided over a mock court and a band of revellers, and he presented a variety of entertainments during the Christmas seasons. In some houses and colleges he was elected on 1 November (All Hallows) and continued until 3 February (the day after Candlemas), but at court his reign appears to have been confined to the traditional twelve days of Christmas from the Nativity to the Epiphany. At Henry VII's court a Lord or Abbot was appointed in most Christmas seasons; at Henry VIII's court his appearances can be documented regularly from 1509 to 1521 and in 1534. The Lord of Misrule ordinarily received separate imprests and payments on his bills for his productions. There is no evidence of support by the supervisors or Masters of the Revels for the Lord of Misrule's entertainments except during the Christmas seasons of 1551–2 and 1552–3.

Sir Thomas Cawarden received orders from the council in both of these years to produce and to support the entertainments devised by George Ferrers who had been designated Master of the King's Pastimes. Except in such special circumstances, the Lord of Misrule had nothing officially to do with the entertainments produced by the supervisors or Masters of the Revels. Neither did the Master of Ceremonies. In fact, there was no official Master of Ceremonies at the Tudor court. The post was not created until the appointment of Sir Lewis Lewknor on 21 May 1603.[7] The duties later assigned to this diplomatic officer – arranging the protocol of receiving and seating dignitaries at ceremonies, spectacles, and revels – were discharged in the early Tudor period by the council and by the chief officers of the household. These duties were essentially diplomatic in nature and had nothing directly to do with the production of entertainments.

Scheduling, coordination, and support services for the many ceremonies, spectacles, and revels associated with state occasions and traditional feasts fell to the chief officers of the royal household who usually held positions on the council. Chambers' division of the Elizabethan royal household into three parts is also useful in discussing the early Tudor organization.[8] The Lord Steward's department was the domestic organization of the court. Supplying and feeding the court was accomplished by twenty offices, each supervised by a sergeant or other superior officer, assisted by a staff of clerks, yeomen, grooms, and pages. Its social centre was the Hall, under the direction of the Marshal, where meals and banquets were served under the supervision of the Butler and where entertainments were given on major feasts. The post of Butler had become hereditary in the house of Fitzalan, and the duties of this office in the early Tudor period were carried out by the king's appointee. Finance of this massive organization was vested in the Board of Greencloth – so called because of the colour of the baize used on the counting table – consisting of the Treasurer, Comptroller, and Cofferer, assisted by the clerks and clerk comptrollers of the Counting House. This board received accounts of the offices of the Lord Steward's department, took inventories, and paid bills for purchases. The entire operation was financed by one of the major treasuries – in most of the early Tudor period by the Treasury of the Chamber.

The Lord Steward was recognized as the chief officer of the royal household under the king, and so the office had been the aspiration of great nobles from as early as the twelfth century. Hereditary right to the office of Lord High Steward became merged with the Crown on the accession of Henry IV and thereafter was conferred only for ceremonial occasions. The Steward's actual duties in the household were performed by the king's appointee, called Lord Steward to distinguish him from the hereditary officer. By analogy to the French court the office designation was changed to Grand Master of the Household in 1531; however, the new title never gained favour, and the traditional one was reinstated in 1533. By the second decade of the sixteenth century, the king had ceased to host his banquets in the Hall or to hold his council there. The Eltham articles treat the problem of laxity in keeping the Hall which had caused 'lack of good knowledge, Experience and Learning how young men should order themselves.'[9] The articles specify that the Hall as well as the Chapel was to be kept at certain palaces on certain occasions. The very fact that these regulations had to be specified indicates how unimportant the Hall had become by 1526. Still, entertainments were given during the Christmas seasons when the Hall was kept through the first two decades of the century. The Lords of Misrule gave entertainments there, and it was not uncommon for plays to be put on before the Lord Steward even when the king was in residence.

By Henry VII's accession, the Courtyard where the horses were stalled and where some of the guard were stationed had also lost much of its importance. The duties originally performed by one of its chief officers, the Constable, now a hereditary and ceremonial title, were not duplicated in the household. The Marshall, the other chief officer of the Courtyard, was originally subordinate to the Constable. He sat with the Constable in the military court later known as the Earl Marshall's court and with the Lord Steward in the court of the Verge – the court governing the twelve-mile circuit surrounding the household. He also served as quartermaster, witnessed expenditures, had charge of the stable, guarded the gates, and kept order in the Hall. By the Tudor period the Earl Marshall was a hereditary and ceremonial title, and the duties he had performed were distributed among various household officers. The Knight Marshall kept order at court and presided over the court of the Verge. The rest of the household marshals oversaw precedence and order in the Hall. The Stable, where horses were stalled and some equipment relating to hunting and jousting was stored, became a distinct department headed by the Master of the Horse. In the sixteenth century, he came to be regarded as one of the chief officers of the household. In contrast to the Steward and Chamberlain, the Master of the Horse was appointed by patent. Such an appointment was legally binding. A writ describing the office holder's duties and his fees and perquisites was issued. The writ is referred to as 'letters patent' because it functioned as an open letter from the sovereign to his subjects authorizing the named bearer to perform certain services or duties. Patents were usually granted for life, and they passed through an elaborate legal process – Sign Manual, Signet, Privy Seal, Great Seal – a copy of which was enrolled in the Court of Chancery.[10] The Steward and the Chamberlain, like most of the officers of the household, were appointed by the sovereign by 'word-of-mouth,' and they held their offices not for life, as a patent holder would, but 'during pleasure' – for so long as it pleased the sovereign.

The Chamber where the sovereign lived his private life was presided over by the Lord Chamberlain assisted by a variety of minor officers. This part of the palace was provided with a number of rooms, each serving a particular purpose. The Yeomen of the Guard were stationed in the Watching or Guard Chamber to exclude improper persons from the area and to provide formal receptions on state occasions. The sovereign kept estate in the Presence Chamber, sometimes called the Dining Chamber, where he presided on formal occasions and gave audiences. Beyond the Presence Chamber was the Privy Chamber, which included a number of rooms, such as the Bed Chamber, the Breakfast Chamber, the Attiring Chamber, the Withdrawing Chamber, the Library, and the Close Stool. The queen was provided with an identical set of rooms in her Chamber separate from the king's. In the larger palaces both the king's and queen's chambers had their own staff. While the Halls were still used for major entertainments, the sovereign tended to dine in his own Chamber and to hold some of his revels there.

The Chamber was not divided into offices as the Lord Steward's department was, although three offices – the Jewel House, the Wardrobe of Robes, and the Wardrobe of Beds – were included in it. It was rather organized hierarchically. The Lord Chamberlain was assisted by a Vice-Chamberlain, a Treasurer with his own staff of clerks, the Esquires for the Body, various grooms and pages, and after 1518 by the Gentlemen of the Privy Chamber. Next to the Steward the Chamberlain was the chief officer of the household, and, like the other offices, the post of Lord Great Chamberlain had become hereditary and ceremonial, his ordinary duties being performed by the king's appointee. For a good part of the early Tudor period, the Chamber was not only the ceremonial heart of the household but the financial centre of the government. From 1491 to the early 1530s, the Treasury of the Chamber was the principal source of funding for the revels. It is little wonder that the men found to supervise the revels held positions in the Chamber or positions which brought them frequently into it.[11]

All activities which took place in the early Tudor royal household came under the general supervision of the Steward, Chamberlain, and Master of the Horse. The household regulations of 1494 make it abundantly clear that the Steward, along with his staff, and the Chamberlain, along with the staff of the Chamber, were the chief officers for ceremony and entertainment within doors: 'the Steward and the Marshall doe the King seruice in the Hall, and the Chamberlaine and Ushere doe in the Chamber' on days when the king kept estate.[12] An anonymous Gentlemen Usher's advice to his successor clearly indicates that he understood these divisions in duties and that the staff of the Chamber or the Hall provided support services for revels:

As ffor the disguyssinge it longithe not to your office but that ye wot welle it muste be redy vnder the clothe of estat quyschins and siche thinges *that* be necessary lightes in the hall

afture the quantitie of the hall and youre discrecion rowme enoughe for them. if yt be in
the gret chambre the dissgisinge then is your office to se quyschins redy laide for the kinge
vndir the clothe of estat or els at the kinges plessure on the cupbord if the king will lene
there at.[13]

The same procedure would most likely have been used for minor entertainments in either of these two divisions of the household. Plays put on before the
Lord Steward in the Hall, for example, would be supported by his staff and those
before the king in the Chamber by the Lord Chamberlain's staff. As chief officer
of what was formerly the Courtyard, most court activities outdoors fell under the
supervision of the Master of the Horse. While the preparation of tournaments was
assigned to supervisors, just as the revels were, support services and coordination
would ordinarily have come from the Master of the Horse as head of the Stable.[14]

Revels were occasionally held in the royal residences in the counties surrounding London, such as Eltham, Newhall, Nonsuch, and Oatlands, and some
were held in France. Most, however, were staged in the principal royal residences
in and around Westminster. The palace of Westminster was still the sovereign's
principal residence when Henry VII ascended the throne in 1485, but after subsequent damage by fire, particularly the fire of 1512, the residential portions of
the palace were not rebuilt. It remained the principal legal and administrative centre of the realm, housing the Chancery, the Exchequer, the common law and pre-
rogative courts, the High Court of Parliament, and, after 1548, the Commons.[15]
Henry VII's remodelling projects had left Westminster principally a site for ceremonial functions, and it remained so throughout the century. Coronation entries
and royal processions were traditionally begun at the Tower and ended at Westminster. Coronation tournaments, banquets, and some revels at the traditional
feasts continued to be held there, but Westminster did not become important as
a royal residence until after 1529. At that time Henry VIII acquired York Place,
the London residence of the Archbishop of York, which had been rebuilt by
Wolsey, and acquired properties adjacent to the site where he built a complex of
buildings. The official name given to the residence in 1536 was the New Palace
of Westminster, but by 1542 the name Whitehall, from the white ashlar stone-
work of Wolsey's great hall, was in general use.[16]

After the great fire of 1497 destroyed the old palace at Shene, Henry VII
rebuilt it and renamed it Richmount.[17] Richmond remained Henry VII's favourite
residence, but while many entertainments were held there Henry VIII did not
regard the palace as highly as his father had. In 1525 Henry VIII and Wolsey
exchanged Richmond and Hampton Court. After Wolsey's fall in 1529, Richmond again reverted to the Crown. Hampton Court became one of the principal royal residences, and Henry set about equipping it with recreational facilities

and banqueting houses which served as the setting for some of the more important revels of the latter part of the century.[18] Greenwich was Henry VIII's favourite residence, and many of his most magnificent revels were held there. Henry VII had begun remodelling the palace as early as 1500, and his son continued to make improvements.[19] Stables, an armoury, fanciful towers before the tilt-yard, tennis courts, bowling alleys, kennels, a cockpit with a gallery, and an elaborate banqueting house were all added between 1509 and 1533.

In addition to the great halls and chambers of the principal palaces, revels were occasionally held in specially built banqueting facilities. Some of these facilities were entirely temporary – chambers made of poles decorated with flowers and partitions, installed in a gallery at one of the palaces. Others were semi-permanent structures with brick or stone foundations, wooden walls, and canvas roofs. The term 'banqueting house' is applied loosely to describe these multi-purpose structures. They were used for dinners, suppers, banquets, and for revels. Very few narratives survive from the early part of the period on their construction, but it is clear that they do not conform to a particular type or style. They took as many forms as ingenuity could devise, and varied in size, shape, plan, and elaboration.[20] The banqueting house at Calais in 1520 was a polygon of sixteen sides, equipped with railed standings within, built directly above one another for spectators. The one built at Greenwich in 1527 consisted of two chambers, one for dining and one for revels, joined by a gallery. The banqueting house built at Hyde Park in 1551, was a two-storey, timber-framed building with clerestory windows and a turret. Wyngaerde's sketches of Hampton Court in 1558 show some banqueting houses and other outbuildings as fanciful, turreted structures of rectangular, circular, and polygonal form. One, which stood on the mount at the southern end of the Privy Garden, was two stories high and crowned with an ogee dome. These structures, which continued to be built throughout the century, are all ancestors of the great banqueting house built at Whitehall from 1619 to 1622 by Inigo Jones, so magnificently decorated with a ceiling by Rubens that Jones had to build a semi-permanent facility for masques in 1638 for fear of damaging the delicate ceiling with smoke from candles and torches.

Banqueting houses were expensive facilities. Edward Hall comments, for example, that 'To tel you of the costlye banquet houses [those built for the 1546 reception of the Admiral of France] you woulde much maruel, and skant beleue.'[21] Henry's council could hardly believe it either. The council at Westminster wrote to the council with the king on 13 and 15 September 1546 that they had taken an order for £4000 'for the banquett houses' on the promise not to trouble them again for a good while, 'which summs haue clerely disfurnished all *your* treasurers.'[22] Construction of banqueting houses required support services from a variety of household departments and from an army of artists and workmen. The

Works built foundations, the Wardrobe supplied hangings and material, the Tents constructed roofs and interior ceilings, the Sergeant Painter and others of the king's Painters worked on the exterior and interior of the building. Interior ceilings were sometimes painted with cosmological designs, as were the temporary palace and the banqueting house at Guisnes and Calais in 1520. Original works of art were occasionally commissioned. Hans Holbein's *Siege of Therouanne* decorated the gallery of the banqueting house at Greenwich in 1527. Portraits of Henry VIII, Edward VI, and Elizabeth I by Richard and George Bossum decorated the balcony of the banqueting house at West Horsley in 1559. Early in the century, the council appointed supervisors to oversee the construction and decoration of these facilities. Supervision of the construction of the 1551 banqueting house at Hyde Park was entrusted to Sir Thomas Cawarden as head of the organization to which the Tents and Revels belonged. The arrangement lasted only as long as Cawarden's Mastership. After 1560, banqueting houses were mainly the province of the Works, and the services of other household offices, including the Revels, were contracted as needed.

There were a number of standing departments or offices 'owtward' of the Chamber, as they are called in the *Liber Niger,* each under a master or other superior officer – such as the Great Wardrobe, the Works, the Armoury, and the Tents – which were prominently involved not only in the construction and decoration of banqueting houses but also in the production of ceremonies, spectacles, and revels.[23] In the Tudor period these offices were regarded as members of the household, but they were operated quite differently from ordinary household departments. Officers in these departments were appointed by patent for life, in contrast to most of the officers of the household who were sworn in by one of the chief officers and held their appointments during the sovereign's pleasure. Each officer's annual wage was specified in his patent and was paid by the Exchequer or by the Treasurer of the Chamber rather than by the Cofferer of the Household. Since their offices were located away from the palace, traditional allowances were also handled differently. Officers of the household were allowed lodging at court, apportioned according to rank; diet, their dinner and supper at an appointed table in the Hall or Chamber; 'bowge of court,' the bread, beer, wine, candles, and fuel issued to all who boarded at the palace; and livery, an issue of cloth from the Great Wardrobe to make clothing. Officers in the standing departments submitted accounts which included standard payments in lieu of some or all of these traditional allowances: rent of office space, workrooms, yards, storage facilities, and personal quarters; payment for diet and board wages for their actual days of service; cash payments for livery and also for standish – paper, ink, and writing implements. There were also traditional rewards or perquisites which they received which did not appear in their accounts, and rewards that they had to pay, to the auditors and clerks at the Exchequer for example, which they charged to the government.

The Office of the King's Works was principally concerned with building and maintaining the royal residences, but it also assisted the various producers of revels and supervisors of other special events.[24] The Works fitted St Paul's or the Abbey or one of the palaces with galleries, halls, stages, seatings, standings, and other devices for coronations, weddings, christenings, and funerals. They constructed the seatings, standings, and other paraphernalia needed for the sovereign's spectacles. They built the observation towers, standings, lists, and other carpentry work for tournaments and martial exhibitions. They built foundations, walls, and supports for temporary banqueting houses. And they fashioned the seatings, standings, stages, raised platforms, and other equipment needed for revels and entertainments in the great halls or chambers of the palaces.[25] There is much documentary evidence of Works involvement in these activities from 1560 to 1640.[26] Construction of stages, scaffolds, and other devices for triumphs, plays, masks, revels, dances, banqueting houses, martial exhibitions, and baitings occur in the accounts of the office in virtually every year. Further, under Inigo Jones, Surveyor of the Works in the Stuart period, the elaborate court masks were produced more directly by the Works than by the Revels, whose function was then more often to supply lighting and small properties.[27] Far fewer accounts survive from the earlier period, but available evidence shows that the Office of the Works was involved in some if not all of the major productions from the opening of Henry VII's reign.[28] Charges for construction by the Works never occur in the Revels accounts. The Masters simply drew on the services of the Works as they did on other household departments, and consequently these expenses are never included in the estimates of the total costs of court revels.

Detailed plans of the construction of the stages, the seating and standing arrangements built in the great halls, chambers, and banqueting houses for court revels are unfortunately lacking, but hints from descriptions of modifications made to the royal palaces and manors suggest that these were adapted as need dictated. The cockpit at Greenwich, for example, was constructed by the Works as a permanent facility in 1533 with 'iiij ryngs ffor men to sytt upon' as well as a place in the gallery over the bowling alley for the queen to observe the sport.[29] These 'rings' had been used in the banqueting house at Calais in 1520. Raised seatings which were sloped and railed were used in the banqueting house at Greenwich in 1527. Hall makes a point of describing the cleverness of their construction which allowed everyone a good view of the festivities.[30] There is little doubt but that more details of the construction techniques used by the Works would help to illuminate our sketchy understanding of the facilities which were built for court entertainments.

There were a number of wardrobes attached to the royal household. The largest was the Great Wardrobe, which was charged with the purveyance of cloth, furs, and furniture for the government. Each royal residence also had a wardrobe under the supervision of a keeper, the largest of these being at Westminster. The Yeoman of the Robes, an officer in the Chamber, was charged with the king's personal wardrobe. He ordered material from the Great Wardrobe but also purchased items on the open market not only for the king's ordinary clothing but also for garments for ceremonies through the year. He also stored the materials and the garments made from it by the king's Tailor in one of the privy wardrobes.[31] These minor wardrobes as well as the Great Wardrobe provided garments for the revels throughout the period, and under Sir Thomas Cawarden were a main source of material as well as of garments. Thomas Blagrave, Clerk of the Revels, comments on this in his 'Platte of Orders':

oute of the privye or speciall wardrops of her Maiesties seuerall houses or the tower or greate wardrop of suche store as hath layen longe and decaied or now growen vnmete for the first purpose or to serve the present vse any lenger may be deliuered over to be ymploied to the best and ferthest stretche of this turne (as was in Sir Thomas Cardens tyme as well oute of the hole pece as in hanginges and garmentes and other sorte) but not any other thing which is not alredy there of olde store to come from thence by any new provision[32]

By virtue of its function as supply organization to the household, its great store of cloth, furs, furniture, its staff of tailors, purveyors, and clerks, and its experience in purchasing, storing, delivering, and accounting for such material, the Great Wardrobe was the chief provider of material for ceremonies, spectacles, and revels. Preparations and expenses, particularly for coronations and funerals for which the entire household was issued livery, were enormously elaborate. But even minor ceremonies such as the feasts of St George, the Maundy, the traditional keeping of estate in the Great Hall or Chamber, and the processions to evensong or Mass on holidays were provided with the requisite hangings, pennons, heraldic decorations, gift gowns, and furs.[33] Often enough the Great Wardrobe supplied part of the cloth and other furniture for tournaments and revels which were not charged as part of actual expenses in the accounts of the producers and supervisors. The stable administrative structure of the Great Wardrobe was used occasionally in supervisory or accounting capacities for ceremonies, spectacles, and revels. For example, separate Works and Wardrobe accounts were filed for the funeral of Queen Mary, showing clearly that they contributed services along the traditional divisions of their offices. The Office of the Works was responsible for the carpentry projects and the Wardrobe for the hangings, banners, and heraldic decorations. But Elizabeth I's coronation was handled entirely on the Wardrobe's account even though an officer of the Works directed over £700 of the preparations.[34] This was no doubt an attempt to balance budgets in both offices at the beginning of the new reign, but it shows not only the interdependence of these departments in practice but also the capacity of the Great Wardrobe to take on administrative duties with relative ease. The revels bills for Christmas 1508, for example, were paid to the Keeper of the Great Wardrobe in 1509 rather than to the supervisor of the production.[35]

The Armoury, the Ordnance, and the Stable were offices which contributed services mainly to the tournaments and martial exhibitions. The Stable was part of the royal household proper under the supervision of the Master of the Horse. Here the king's and the guard's horses were stalled, and bits, reins, spurs, saddles, and other equipment stored and made ready for the jousts. The Ordnance was rarely involved in ceremonies, spectacles, and revels unless some firearms or explosives were required, as they were on occasion for sieges in the tilt-yard. The rare sieges on water and the frequent peals of ordnance from ships or from the Tower for the reception of dignitaries could also be handled by the Navy or the Tower. Since the Armoury, with its staff of armourers, assistants, and clerks, all under the supervision of a Master, supplied not only the implements needed for war but also the practice weapons, spear shafts, tips, bows, arrows, swords, pikes, and other equipment used in tournaments and martial exercises, it was often involved in the production of spectacles, particularly in Henry VII's and Henry VIII's reign. In fact, the Masters of the Armoury were usually appointed to supervise the preparation of tournaments in this period.[36]

Significant studies have been made of the Office of the Works and Wardrobe, but there has been very little written on the Tents, an ancient office which performed important functions within the royal household until its absorption by the Works at the end of Charles II's reign.[37] As early as the reign of Henry I a 'Cortinarius' was attached to the household; by the fourteenth century he was styled Royal Pavilioner; by the fifteenth, Sergeant; and in the mid-sixteenth, Master of the Tents.[38] The medieval Pavilioner was an official in the Wardrobe, but by the beginning of the Tudor period the Sergeant of the Tents was appointed by patent to preside over a standing department. The Sergeant had the permanent assistance of a boy or *garçon*, and purchased material and hired labourers as necessary to complete his duties. By 1545 a permanent office was created under the direction of a master with the assistance of a clerk, clerk comptroller, a yeoman, and a groom.

An itinerant court found tents, hales, and temporary houses absolutely essential. Even after the court became more or less settled in palaces and manors in and around Westminster there were still wars to be fought, tournaments to be held, receptions to be organized, banqueting facilities to be built, and progresses to be supported, all of which required the services of the Tents. In the field, the essential offices of the royal household were duplicated on a smaller scale, and each office had its own tents and hales assigned to it as well as mules to carry them. The Lord Steward's department, with its offices of the Kitchen, Larder, Boilinghouse, and others, was set up in canvas and wood, as were the rooms of the Chamber, and even the Stable had special tents for the king's horses.[39] Tents made for the king and high court officers were elaborately constructed of canvas stretched over timber frames or made entirely of wood; fabricated to include windows; painted, often to resemble brickwork; and decorated with insignia, rich tapestries, and hangings. The duties of the Tents were to fabricate these temporary houses, to maintain them during the year, and to set them up when and where needed. The involvement of the Tents in the preparation of ceremonies, spectacles, and revels varied from setting up simple pavilions for receptions and tournaments to the construction of banqueting houses, from supplying a few tents for a summer progress to housing hundreds of courtiers and soldiers for an international spectacle. At the Field of Cloth of Gold in 1520, for example, the English court setup near Guisnes consisted of about four hundred tents.[40] There was not much difference between the material, construction methods, and techniques used in the Tents and those used in the Revels. Stretching canvas over a frame for a pageant and decorating it for the revels was similar to the procedures used in constructing the tents. Contracting with painters, ironworkers, glaziers, carpenters, and joiners was also similar, as were the methods of airing, storing, and repairing the equipment. Early in Henry VIII's reign, the Tents were used to provide an administrative establishment for the production of revels. The functions associated with the Tents and the Revels were in practice connected from about 1513 and formally connected in 1545 with the appointment of Sir Thomas Cawarden as Master of both offices. Even when the patents to the Masterships of the Revels and Tents were separated in 1560, there continued to be a close administrative connection. The two offices shared storage facilities until 1607 and the services of a clerk and a comptroller until 1642.

The Office of the Toils takes its name from the ancient 'toil,' a large piece of canvas bordered with ropes, joined together with other such pieces and staked so as to form an enclosure into which game animals were driven. The duties of this office were to procure material, to fabricate, store, and repair the toils, and to set them up whenever and wherever needed. The Toils was not an office ordinarily involved in the production of revels, although on one occasion a toil was supplied for use as a tilt in a mock joust. Hunting, however, was one of the pastimes or pleasures often accorded to ambassadors and other visiting dignitaries. This and the fact that the material used by the Toils was virtually identical to that employed in the Tents explain its incorporation into the Tents-Revels organization during the eight-year period from 1552 to 1560.

Court revels depended heavily on visual impact, not only in costuming but also in pageants, scenic devices, masking headpieces, and other theatrical properties. The supervisors and Masters of the Revels contracted the design and execution of these visuals to artists. Generally the services of a chief artist were contracted. He often employed a crew of painters, sculptors, joiners, carvers, stainers, and colour grinders. The chief artist drew designs for pageants, mounts, banqueting houses, costumes, masking headpieces, and properties based on the device given to him by the supervisor or Master of the Revels. He occasionally made patterns for costumes, built models for banqueting houses, fashioned headpieces and properties for masks and plays, cast moulded works for pageants and mounts, and drew designs for painters to follow. The artist showed up for work with his crew of workmen at the appropriate stage of preparations, completed his projects at that stage, and occasionally came along to court to put the finishing touches on pageants or mounts that were transported from the work site by barge. Afterwards he drew up an account of his expenses and submitted it for payment to the supervisor or Master of the Revels. In his 'Platte of Orders,' Thomas Blagrave recommended that the office adopt the procedure of having an artist render in colour 'patterns' and 'plats' of masks and other entertainments both as a means of estimating the cost and methods of producing them as well as recording what had been done. None of these designs have survived, an unfortunate fact, for many of the early Tudor revels employed the services of artists with international reputations.

Beginning in Henry VII's reign, foreign artists came to England in increasing numbers. So many had found patronage at the English court that in 1545 Secretary Paget wrote to the deputy of Calais not to allow any more of them entry, for the court was at its wit's end to know what to do with them all.[41] Flemish artists were in fashion in Henry VII's reign, but the continued patronage of artists of the stature of Lucas Hornebout and Levinnia Benninck kept northern influence alive at the English court into the 1570s. Italian and French painters began to receive patronage in Henry VIII's reign. Continental styles in painting and design had become so entrenched by the 1540s that the court's Sergeant Painters from 1544 to 1571 were not Englishmen but an Italian and a Frenchman. So many artists of significant stature were employed at court that titles for their appointments were difficult to find.

The king's Painter held his office by patent from at least the time of Edward IV.[42] By Henry VII's reign, foreign artists who began to receive patronage were also called king's Painters.[43] Some of the confusion was cleared up in 1527 when the title of Sergeant Painter was used to distinguish the patent holder from others who received annuities as king's Painters. Not much can be made of the distinction between the patent holder and others of the king's Painters in terms of the kind of projects they undertook. The Sergeant Painter as well as the king's Painters were employed by the Works, the Great Wardrobe, the Tents, the Navy, and by the supervisors or Masters of the Revels on projects as simple as painting rails and posts in the privy gardens of the royal palaces and as complicated as illuminating manuscripts, painting portraits, decorating banqueting houses, and designing for revels.[44] Richard Rowangre, an artist of unknown nationality and training, was employed as a heraldic painter and carver for several royal funerals as well as for work on revels in 1508 and 1514 and on the Greenwich banqueting house in 1527.[45] John Browne, Sergeant Painter in 1527, was employed on many revels projects from about 1511 to his death in 1534. Hans Holbein, German artist in the king's service from about 1526, worked on the interior ceiling and painted the *Siege of Therouanne* for the gallery of the Greenwich banqueting house in 1527. Nicholas Lizard, a Frenchman who held the patent as Sergeant Painter from 1554 to 1571, was employed on revels productions in the early 1540s. Lucas Hornebout, a member of the Ghent Painter's Guild and son of Gerard, court painter to Margaret of Austria, was in Henry VIII's service from 1528 and was employed in revels productions in 1543. Anthony Toto del Nunziata, who studied under Pietro Torrigiano, a fellow student of Michaelangelo, was employed in revels projects during his tenure as Sergeant Painter from 1544 to 1554. Nicholas Bellin of Modena, *valet de guarderobe* to Francis I and *sculpteur et faiser de masques* at Fontainebleau, designed garments and properties for revels from 1546 to 1553, and executed the moulded work for Edward VI's coronation mount. Robert Trunckwell, 'straunger,' worked under Bellin's supervision on the Tower of Babylon for a play at court in 1548 as well as many other revels projects, including the design of several banqueting houses from 1546 to 1559. The list is sufficient to indicate that visual design in early Tudor revels was heavily influenced by Italian, French, and Flemish styles.

This complicated array of personnel and departments within and without the royal household was mobilized and coordinated by the Revels organization. The earliest observations on the origin of this organization are contained in a document entitled 'Of the first Institution of the Revels':

the Prince beinge disposed to pastyme would at one tyme appoynte one persone, at sometyme an other, suche as for creditte pleasaunte witte and habilitye in learnynge he thought meete to be the *Master* of the Revelles for that tyme, to sett fourthe suche devises as might be most agreable to the Princes expectacion/ The workes beinge fynyshed It is thought that the Princes Tayler havinge the oversight of the workemanshippe brought in the Bill of charges and was payed for it wherevpon is gathered that Iohn Houlte yeoman of the Revelles vsed to saye Concerninge allowaunce of charges in the office of the Revelles it hath bene but a Taylers Bill.[46]

The principal subjects of this document are the administrative and financial problems of the Revels Office in the early 1570s. Its usefulness as a history is affected by a reliance on hearsay and anecdote: 'it is alledged by some,' 'it shoulde seeme by reporte,' and 'some thinke' preface virtually every statement about the early Revels organization. The claim that the early supervisors of revels were appointed temporarily can be confirmed with evidence from Privy Seal writs and from entries in the Chamber accounts, although there is no evidence that they were called Masters before 1510. Many of the rest of the statements in 'The First Institution' are inaccurate or exaggerated. John Holt's anecdote, for example, applies to the operation of the Revels organization during the early 1540s when his predecessor, John Bridges, king's Tailor and Yeoman of the Revels, produced several inexpensive entertainments. The generalization is inadequate to describe the arrangements for the production of revels in the earlier Tudor period when Henry VII attempted to match the splendour and sophistication of continental courts or when Henry VIII dazzled the European community with his magnificent spectacles.

By the mid-sixteenth century the Revels Office had become part of an extensive organization whose function was to devise or select and to produce or to contribute services to the production of tournaments, spectacles, revels, plays, and other entertainments at court. In about 1573 or 1574, when 'The First Institution' was written, that organization had been broken up for more than a dozen years, and its former functions were being performed by separate offices: the Tents, the Toils, the Revels, and the Works. While the writer of 'The First Institution' had keen insights into the problems of the office in the early 1570s, he had no awareness of the elaborate revels of the first three decades of the century, little understanding of the organization which grew up to produce them, and only an imperfect conception of the extent to which the later office was influenced by earlier practices. The story of how the Revels organization grew into a department of the Chamber 'owtward' by 1545 and how it acquired its various responsibilities begins at the opening of Henry VII's reign.

1

Early Arrangements, 1485–1503

The origin of the duties associated with the production of Tudor revels is traceable to the beginning of Henry VII's reign. Richard Pudsey, Henry VII's first supervisor, produced disguisings at court under the authority of temporary appointments from 1485 until at least 1491. What qualities recommended him to the position are not evident from the records, unless he was the same Pudsey, 'piper in the bagpipe,' who was paid 6s. 8d. for a performance on 16 May 1493.[1] He is described in a Privy Seal writ of 18 November 1485 as the Sergeant of the Cellar, a position, like those held by the supervisors later in the reign, which brought him frequently into contact with the king.[2] Since the production of disguisings was a temporary duty, Pudsey was employed at court, as his successors were, in a variety of capacities. On one of his official missions to the north, for example, where he was robbed of his horse and other property 'to his grete hurte & hinderaunce,' he was paid 20 marks in compensation. Despite such minor setbacks, Pudsey prospered in the king's service, receiving a number of grants of land, licences for export, and offices at court.[3] When he received a grant of the manor of Hampton in Warwickshire on 16 November 1496 he was an Esquire for the Body, and by 27 March 1500, when he leased lands in Somerset, he is described as Knight for the Body.[4] Scattered among the numerous rewards and payments he received by Privy Seal are a few for the production of disguisings during the Christmas seasons of 1485–6, 1486–7, and 1490–1. Circumstantial evidence suggests that he also produced them for the Christmas seasons of 1487–8 and 1488–9.

Records from this period also show that spectacles, such as tournaments, and ceremonies were handled in the same way as the disguisings. The king or council appointed a supervisor to oversee their production. The great event of the first year of Henry's reign was the coronation on 30 October. A tournament, scheduled for the Sunday following but postponed until 13 November, was prepared by Sir Richard Guildford, Master of the Armoury, who received an imprest of 100 marks on 23 October and the balance of £50 2s. 2d. on 9 December.[5] We have no information about the revels held on the occasion.[6] Our only source, Bernardus Andreas's *De Regalibus Conviviis et Torneamentis in ipsa coronatione regio luxu celebratis*, survives as a fragment of a few lines.[7] We also have little information about the wedding festivities of Henry and Elizabeth of York. Bernardus Andreas simply states that the marriage, which took place on 18 January 1486, was the subject of general rejoicing and magnificent festivities. A few Privy Seal writs for the purchase of jewels survive, and Piers Curteis – Gentleman Usher to the King, formerly Keeper of the Great Wardrobe to Edward IV and Richard III and soon to be reappointed by Henry VII – procured material for the wedding, as did Richard Doland, Clerk of the Works, but there is no record of the festivities.[8]

There is no reason to doubt Andreas's word, for the Christmas season in 1485–6 was lavishly celebrated with revels. A variety of material was ordered from merchants and artisans, and in addition Piers Curteis procured material.[9] His selection was probably a matter of convenience, since he had been appointed to this duty for the wedding in January. It is probable that some of the material was supplied to Richard Pudsey to produce the disguising on Twelfth Night, but not all of it, for Pudsey was issued a Privy Seal writ 'for *cer*tain special consideracions' in November 1485, probably as an imprest for his disguising and another for £10 on 3 March 1486 for material that he bought and for his labour.[10] No narrative of Pudsey's production survives, but among the material ordered for Twelfth Night was a gilt flower made by the same silversmiths and goldsmiths who supplied material for other ceremonies during the season. The flower, suggesting some emblematic device on the theme of the union of the houses of Lancaster and York, figured prominently in the imagery of Henry's early reign, but it is uncertain whether it was used in the disguising or for decoration in connection with other ceremonies.[11]

Prince Arthur was born on 20 September 1486 at St Swithen's Priory. He was christened the following Sunday at Winchester Cathedral. While Privy Seal writs survive to document work in the cathedral for the ceremony and on the queen's and prince's lodgings, and while a narrative survives for the ceremony, mentioning the 'ij pipes of wyne' set up in the churchyard that every man 'myght drynke ynow,' the formal entertainments are not well documented.[12] Warton records a play, *Christi Descensus ad Infernos*, performed on Sunday at dinner by the boys of the Chapel of St Swithun's Priory and Hyde Abbey, though it is not clear whether the performance was supported with material and production assistance by the royal household.[13] There may also have been a tournament. Sir Richard Guildford was paid £16 19s. 10d. on 21 September 1486 for having prepared a joust.[14]

After the christening, the court moved to Greenwich, where All Hallows and
Christmas were celebrated. The anonymous author of the narrative of these feasts
notes that Christmas was less elaborate than All Hallows: 'likewise the king kept
his Cristemas at the same place Aforsaide howbeit he was not Accompanyed with
lordes as he was at halhalontyde' and 'kept ther non Astate In the halle.'[15] While
Christmas 1486–7 may have been less ceremonious than All Hallows, disguisings
were produced. The Privy Seal writ issued to Pudsey on 22 November 1486 was
for 'thordaynyng and preparing of disguysinges for our disportes ayenst the ffest
of Cristemas nowe approching' and the one issued on 23 March 1487 for the balance of payment was for 'suche costes and expenses he hath made an doon but late
by oure comaundement by certeyn Disguysinges for our pleasur and for Rewarding of players.'[16] No narratives of these disguisings have survived, but the wording of the Privy Seal writ provides the earliest evidence from the period of a
connection between players and a court-appointed supervisor of disguisings.
There is no mention of the names of these players nor any indication that they
belonged to an organized company. This single reference in the Privy Seal writs
indicates that paying players was not part of Pudsey's ordinary duties; rather, it
suggests that these players were used in connection with his disguising as, for
example, Walter Alwyn did in 1494.

Henry kept All Hallows 1487 at St Albans before making a triumphal entry
into London on 3 November in preparation for the great state occasion of the
year, the coronation of the queen scheduled for 25 November. The coronation festivities began on 23 November with a river procession from Greenwich to the
Tower and continued on the 24th with a procession from the Tower to Westminster. The spectacles – the river pageants, including a bachelor's barge 'gar-
nysshed And Apparielde passing al other Wherin was ordeynede A great Red
dragon spowting flamys of fyer into temmys,' and the pageants for the London
procession on the 24th, including singing children costumed as virgins and angels
– were civic preparations.[17] Royal preparations were also extensive. Piers Curteis,
now Keeper of Henry's Great Wardrobe, supplied furs and other material for the
ceremony.[18] For the feast, a banqueting hall was prepared. No details of its design
survive, but the banquet itself was compared to the one served to Cardinal Morton for his installation at Canterbury in January 1487, described by the anonymous author of the narrative as 'the best orderde And serued fest That euer I Sawe
that myght be comparede to.' No revels are recorded at the banquet, and while
Sir Richard Guildford was issued an imprest of 100 marks on 5 October to prepare a joust, neither a narrative nor a Privy Seal writ for the final payments survives.[19]

The festive Christmas season of 1487–8 included 'many And dyuers playes.'
On Christmas Eve Henry and his nobles attended high mass followed by even-

song, and on Christmas Day he dined in state in his Great Chamber. The Knights of the Garter attended court on New Year's Day attired in their livery of white cloth with garters, which they again wore for the feast of St George in April, and 'on Newres day at nyght ther was A goodly disgysyng.'[20] On Twelfth Night after mass and evensong, Henry kept estate in the Hall where 'At the Table In the medell of the hall sat the Deane And thoo[se] of the kinges chapell whiche incontynently after the kinges first course sange A Caroll,' and minstrels played after the second course. We cannot be certain that Pudsey produced the New Year's disguising, but there are no other likely candidates.[21]

Henry spent Easter, Whitsuntide, and All Hallows in 1488 at Windsor, keeping the feast of St George (23 April) on 27 April in his 'propre persoune' attended by the Knights of the Garter in the livery they had worn on New Year's Day.[22] There was also a procession and ceremony, but no record of revels, for Henry's receipt of the Cap and Sword of maintenance from the Pope at Whitsuntide.[23] The king kept Christmas 1488–9 at Shene with his nobles, but no narratives of the entertainments survive. Pudsey was issued £10 in Michaelmas term, possibly as an imprest for Christmas revels, and he was rewarded £10 on 20 February for 'service vnto vs hertofore doon in sundry wises,' the right amount paid at the right time of year to suggest that he may have produced a disguising.[24]

Princess Margaret, born on 29 November 1489, was christened on the 30th, the same day that Arthur was created Prince of Wales.[25] The only record of entertainments that has survived from this double occasion is the Thames water reception for the Prince. He was conveyed by royal barge from Shene for the ceremony and was greeted at Chelsea by the mayor and guilds of London and then at Lambeth by the Spanish ambassadors, attended by merchants who provided a welcome by shooting off a number of guns and then 'casting apples as it had bene In fighting on the see with targes.'[26] The king intended to keep Christmas 1489–90 at Westminster, but because of an outbreak of 'meazellis soo strong and in especiall amongis the ladies and the gentilwemen that sum deid of that sikeness,' the court removed by water to Greenwich. The king dined with the French ambassadors on Christmas, with the Spanish ambassadors on Twelfth Night, and gave gifts on New Year's, but the anonymous herald who narrated the events writes: 'I saw no disguysyngs and but Right few pleys but ther was an abbot of misrule that made muche sport and did Right well in hys office.'[27] By Candlemas the court had removed from Greenwich, for the king went in procession from the Chapel to Westminster 'whiche hallis and alsoo the king[es] chambres wer that day as Richely beseen and hanged as ever I saw them' and 'at nyght the kyng the qwene and my ladye the kynges moder came in to the Whit hall and ther had a pley.'[28] Neither the subject of the play nor the company performing it is identified. No narrative evidence survives to document the Christmas of 1490–1, but notes in one of the Exchequer 'rough entry' books for Michaelmas show that Pudsey was paid £40 to put on 'Disguysyngs agens Christenmas.'[29]

The records clearly indicate how Pudsey's disguisings were financed. For the first six years of Henry VII's reign, the Exchequer was the chief instrument of national finance. It paid the bills for court disguisings, relying on procedures every bit as cumbersome as those used to finance the navy or royal building projects.[30] The supervisor was issued a Privy Seal writ for an imprest – an advance of money on account – to begin his work. He was issued another writ for the balance of his purchases and expenses and as a reward for his services after he had completed the project. For example, Pudsey was issued a Privy Seal writ for £20 on 18 November 1485, and then on 3 March 1486 he was issued another for £10 in repayment for certain material he provided and for his labour.[31] For his Christmas productions in the following year he was issued an imprest of £40 on 22 November 1486, and then one for £7 on 23 March 1487 for his labour and for rewarding players.[32] While a variety of treasuries were later to pay bills for revels, the basic financial arrangements remained constant. The supervisors continued to receive imprests and, after their productions were completed, they were paid the balance of expenses on their accounts. This arrangement was identical to the one used for other entertainments, spectacles, and ceremonies at court – the entertainments of the Lords of Misrule, for example, and the supervisors of the tournaments. The records also clearly indicate that Pudsey's responsibility was limited to disguisings at certain feasts. Since he was not in charge of the many other entertainments at court, we must regard him and, indeed, his successors in Henry VII's reign, as early, limited versions of the later Masters of the Revels.

i

Lack of reliable records and narratives makes it difficult to adequately document the revels from 1491 to 1493.[33] Part of Henry VII's plan to solidify control over his divided country involved replacing the Exchequer with his own, more accessible household Chamber as the dominant treasury.[34] This he accomplished by 1491, and thereafter most major government payments, including those for disguisings, were made from the Chamber, the accounts of which he personally reviewed.[35] Under the leadership of John Heron, Treasurer of the Chamber from 1492, the Chamber continued as the principal treasury throughout the early part of Henry VIII's reign.[36] The Chamber relied on a much simpler accounting procedure than that of the Exchequer. The Treasurer kept a book organized chronologically in which he simply listed each of his payments. Expenditures for minor entertainments costing a few shillings are listed side by side with major expenses running into the hundreds or even thousands of pounds.

The last recorded disguising was produced by Pudsey at Christmas 1490–1, and the next available record shows that Walter Alwyn produced the Christmas pageant-disguising of 1493–4. Several important state occasions during the intervening years would normally have required major spectacles or revels. Prince Henry was born on 28 June 1491, and Princess Elizabeth, who was to die three years later, on 2 July 1492. The only recorded joust during this period was the ill-fated tournament of May 1492 in which Sir James Parker was killed. The tournament was under royal sponsorship, for Sir Richard Guildford prepared it, and the Clerk of the Works was paid £24 2s. 10d. for constructing the lists at Shene.[37] Disguisings may have been produced during this period as well, for evidence from the Chamber accounts shows that other entertainments were held. William Ringley was issued imprests of 100s. as Lord of Misrule for both seasons, Oxford's and Northumberland's players performed, William Newark, Master of the Children of the Chapel, was paid 20s. for making a song on 6 January 1493 which he presumably sang with the Children, and 'My Lorde Privy Seall fole' was rewarded for a New Year's appearance.[38] There was cock-fighting at Westminster for Shrovetide 1493, and a bull-baiting was held in September.[39]

The revels at Westminster for Christmas 1493–4 were elaborate. On New Year's day, 'iiij pleyers of Essex' and the 'pleyers of Wymbone Mynystre' were rewarded for performances, and on 2 January unidentified performers were paid for 'pleying of the mourice daunce.'[40] On Twelfth Night, French players, in their first recorded appearance at court, were paid 20s. for a performance, and the King's Players, in their first appearance, were paid 53s. 4d. The major entertainment was a disguising produced by Walter Alwyn featuring William Cornish in a leading role. Alwyn, of whom we know very little, was issued a Chamber payment of £13 6s. 8d. on 16 November for the 'revells at Estermes (sic).'[41] While revels were occasionally held in the spring around Easter or Whitsuntide, it seems likely that this payment, coming as it does in mid-November, was an imprest for the Twelfth Night revels, for he was paid £14 13s. 4d. on 15 February 'in full payment for the disguysing made at Christenmes.'[42] The payments of roughly £28 do not represent its full cost. The Wardrobe may well have supplied some of the material and furniture, and Richard Doland, Clerk of the Works, certainly built the scaffolds in the great Hall at Westminster. Doland was paid £28 3s. 5 3/4d. for constructing 'super factura certorum spectaculorum sive theatrum vulgariter scaffolds infra magnam aulam Westmonasterii ut ludi sive la disguysyngs nocte Ephiphanie populo exhiberentur.'[43]

The narrative describing this disguising is unusually detailed. The mayor and aldermen of London were entertained at dinner at Westminster, and after the mayor had been knighted by the king in his Chamber they were all invited by the Lord Steward to stay for the 'dysportys as that nyght shuld be shewid.'[44] The Hall was hung with arras, and Doland's scaffolds were built to provide spectators with good views of the performance. At about 11 p.m. the king and queen came into the Hall accompanied by the ambassadors of Spain and France. The King's Players performed an interlude which was interrupted by 'oon of the kyngys Chapell namyd Cornysh' who came riding into the Hall on horseback costumed as St. George and leading 'a ffayer virgin attyrid lyke unto a kyngys dowghtyr,' who, in turn, led 'a Terryble & hughe Rede dragun,' which 'spytt ffyre at hys mowth.' Cornish led the maiden and the dragon before the king and 'uttyrd a certain speech made In ballad Royall, afftyr ffynysshyng whereof he began This antempn of Seynt George, *O Georgi deo Care*, whereunto the kyngys Chapell which stood ffast answerid *Salvatorum Deprecare, ut Gubernet Angliam*, And soo sang owth alle the hool antempn wyth lusty Corage.' During the song, Cornish left with the dragon, and 'the vyrgyn was ladd unto the Queenys standyng.' After the song, twelve disguised gentlemen preceded by a 'small Tabret & a subtyle ffedyll' entered, leading disguised ladies 'by kerchyffs of pleasance.' The gentlemen leaped and danced the entire length of the Hall while the ladies 'slode aftyr thym as they hadd standyn upon a frame Runnyng, with whelys, They kept theyr Tracis soo demwyr & clooss that theyr lymmys movid all at oonys.' The gentlemen disguisers then unmasked before dancing for an hour, performing 'lepys Ganbawdys & turnyngys' above ground 'which made that theyr spangyls of goold & othyr of theyr Garnysshys ffyll ffrom theym Ryght habundantly.' The ladies, however, 'kept theyr ffyrst maner soo demuryly as they hadd been Imagis.' After the dances, the disguisers left the Hall, but the gentlemen returned, still in disguise, carrying dishes for the king's banquet. At the end of the evening the king and queen were conveyed into the palace 'wyth a grete sort of lyghtis.' Another description of this disguising, often reprinted, but much briefer, mentions 'A playe' and 'A pageant of St george with A castle And Also xij lordes knightes and Esquyers with xij ladies dysguysed which dyd daunce.'[45]

Narrative and dramatic elements had been incorporated into court entertainments as early as Lydgate's mummeries, but in Alwyn's St George disguising a dramatic fiction appears to unify the entire revel. The interlude performed by the King's Players appears to have served as an introduction which set up the narrative context for the introduction of the main pageant. The poetry, music, and song used in conjunction with the pageant furthered the dramatic action, which was finally concluded by the dance of the disguisers. We can only speculate that the interconnections among the various parts which made up this revel were thematic as well as structural. Hints from the narratives make it possible to undertake a conjectural reconstruction. Henry had observed St George's day since his accession with a feast at court and a chapter of the Order of the Garter. He was as careful to enlist this favourite British tradition and myth as he was to use the imagery of the joined roses in his dynastic propaganda. The Twelfth Night revel appears to link Henry's devotion to St George and his hopes for governing a divided nation.

The source for Cornish's pageant was probably the first story of St George from the *Legenda Aurea* which had been reissued that year by the king's printer, Wynkyn de Word.[46] In this story, the city of Silene in Libya was besieged by a venomous dragon who required two sheep a day as tribute. When the sheep ran out, children were taken by lot to be fed to the dragon until, eventually, the king's daughter was chosen. Under threat from his subjects, the king consented to sacrifice his daughter. St George saved the princess by mesmerizing the dragon with the hilt of his sword in the shape of a cross and wounding it with his spear. He then ordered the princess to 'Deliver to me your girdle, and bind it about the neck of the dragon.' The dragon then followed the princess, 'as it had been a meek beast and debonair,' into the city, where St George promised to kill it on the condition that the populace become baptized. St George then slew the dragon, cut off its head, and had its body carried to the fields in four ox carts. It is possible the interlude by the King's Players consisted in dramatizing the story up to the threatening behaviour of the subjects and the king's anguish in having sacrificed his daughter. The pageant-castle may have functioned as the scenic backdrop for the king's castle.

Cornish interrupted the play at this point with his pageant, and delivered a speech in rhyme royal.[47] The speech was followed by Cornish's anthem celebrating St George as patron of England. When the Gentlemen of the Chapel joined in the song, Cornish led the dragon out of the Hall and the virgin was led to the queen's standing. The king and queen were thus incorporated as silent characters to whom parts of the dramatic action are referred. If this blurs the distinction between art and life, it does so as formal spectacle in the way that Lydgate's mumming at Hertford did in having complaints from husbands against wives read by a presenter impersonating the king's advocate who replied on behalf of Henry VI. The song in the 1494 St George revel is followed by the dance of the disguisers. From the fact that the gentlemen who performed the dances also served dishes for the banquet afterward, it seems clear that they were not professionals, but rather members of the court. So were the ladies, for as the herald reports, 'soom of theym cowde speke quyk & delyver Inglysh yf there were fferre attemptid (as soom of theym were there then Reportid).' The description of the elaborate leaping dances by the men and their later athletic dances is a fitting conclusion to the drama which had just been played out. The dancers may have impersonated the king's subjects or courtiers expressing joy over the deliverance, the conversion, and their optimism about the future with St George as their patron. This description of the plot and theme of the revel is speculative, but enough evidence survives from the narratives to indicate that a dramatic fiction had been integrated into a revel, and that innovations which have been thought to date from later in the period had been introduced at least by 1494.

The records documenting the 1494 Twelfth Night celebration provide a startling glimpse into the revels at Henry's court. In overall arrangement, the celebration accords reasonably well with the Twelfth Night orders in the Northumberland Household book.[48] The king and ambassadors made their formal entry into the Hall. A three-part revel was presented followed by a banquet, and, finally, the king and queen took their formal departure from the Hall, lighted by torches. Aside from the general structure, there are many surprises. This is the first notice of an appearance by the King's Players, who were to perform at court during the Christmas seasons and at other times throughout the rest of the reign; the first evidence of the use of a pageant in a court disguising; the first notice of the involvement in a revel of William Cornish; and the first and most detailed description of the dances used in a disguising to survive from the entire early Tudor period. This pageant-disguising shows that the technology, organization, and artistic sensibility were in place to produce remarkably elaborate and sophisticated revels. While Alwyn's revel provides us with the first clear evidence of this capability, the payment to Pudsey in 1487 for rewarding players in conjunction with his disguising suggests that it was probably not a wholly new development. Also, the comparisons made by the anonymous writer of the narrative show that he was familiar with pageants and their effects. The dance steps of the ladies, for example, made them appear as if they were carried on a wheeled pageant.

ii

Another disguising was produced by one 'Peche,' possibly Sir John Peche, in late spring of 1494, probably for Palm Sunday or Easter, but we have no other information about it.[49] Virtually all of the disguisings from Christmas 1494–5 through June 1501 were produced by Jaques Haulte, son of Martin Haulte, Usher of the Chamber to Elizabeth Woodville.[50] By January 1479 he was an Esquire for the Body and still held that office on 3 July 1482, when he received the reversion to the office of Keeper of the Exchange and Mint at the Tower and custody of the coinage of gold and silver in the realm.[51] Richard III granted him the manor of Mote in 1484 for his service against 'the rebels,' but he seems to have committed himself to Henry's cause, for barely a month into the new reign he received a life grant of the office of Steward of Hanslap, Northampton, and on 21 April 1496 he was granted the offices of Bailiff of the Lordship of Donnyngton, Berkshire, and Warden of the hospital, with an annual grant of £6 13s. 4d. to keep the castle and park.[52] Haulte served at Henry's court in several capacities between 1492 and 1501 in which year his name disappears from the Chamber account.[53] On 4

September 1508, 'sore vexed and trobled wi*th* mortall infirmitie' Haulte made his will. He was buried in the 'quere of St. Aphie in Estgrenewiche,' and, after bequeathing ordinary sums for forgotten tithes and obligations, expenses, and debts, he left all to his executors 'Sir Rauf Varney Maister Iannys Leyson and Maister John Sutton.'[54] The will was probated on 19 July 1509, but Haulte was dead by 1 October 1508, when a grant of the office of Keeper of the manor and park of Donnyngton was granted to Wistan Broun 'in the room of James (sic) Hawte deceased.'[55]

Haulte's name first appears in the Chamber account on 24 January 1492 as a procurer of gaming and sporting equipment for the king – tables, chessmen, tennis balls, and the like. These and other related privy expenditures were taken over by Hugh Dennes in 1494 around the time that Haulte received his first appointment to produce disguisings.[56] Like other appointees in the early Tudor period, Haulte was employed in other capacities. In 1497, probably in connection with his duties in the Chamber, he arranged for the king's tennis play, and in the same year he supervised the building projects at Woodstock.[57] No narrative descriptions survive for the disguisings Haute produced over the six-year period from 1494–5 through 1499–1500, but evidence from the Chamber accounts indicates that the Christmas seasons were celebrated very much as they had been since the beginning of the reign.

Several important dynastic events occurred during this period. The most important tournament of the reign before 1501 was held in November 1494 to celebrate the creation of Henry as Duke of York, but there is no evidence of revels.[58] Haulte's disguising for Christmas 1494–5 was funded by an imprest of £20 on 29 November, and the balance of £13 10s. 6d. was paid on 13 February.[59] For the following Christmas, 1495–6, two disguisings were produced. Haute received an imprest of £20 in two instalments on 27 November and 23 December and a final payment of £6 17s. 6d. in January for his disguising. In addition, 'lorde Suf*folk* lorde Essex my lorde Will*i*am and other' were paid for a disguising between 7 and 9 February 1496.[60] No narrative description survives, but it is likely that the disguising was devised by or under the direction of these individuals. It was not a gift to the king, for while the amateurs may have born some of the charges themselves, £40 was issued from the Chamber to pay for it. The separation of payments in the Chamber accounts to Haulte and to Essex and Suffolk suggests that Haulte may have provided production assistance, as Richard Gibson was to do for Essex in 1510.[61] This disguising was probably produced for Candlemas, the same occasion for which Medwall's *Fulgens and Lucrece* may have been performed at Morton's. Spanish and Flemish ambassadors were present at court from 1 to 24 February of that year to negotiate the projected marriage of Prince Arthur to Katherine of Aragon.[62]

Haulte produced what appears to have been a rather small disguising for Christmas 1496–7 at a cost of £18 17s. 8d. The betrothal of Prince Arthur and Katherine of Aragon by proxy at Woodstock in August 1497 would ordinarily have justified revels, but perhaps the king was waiting for final confirmation from Spain. Haulte produced a somewhat more expensive disguising for Christmas 1497–8 at a cost of £27 14s. 2 1/2d. The new marriage treaty was finally ratified by the Spaniards in February 1498, and in late summer the prince began to be accorded the dignities appropriate to an heir apparent. He was entertained with a pageant and a play of the Assumption at Chester on 4 August, and was given a royal entry into Coventry on 17 October.[63] Haulte produced the single most expensive disguising of the early part of Henry VII's reign for Christmas 1498–99 at a cost of £52 18s. 6d.[64] That season also marks the first performance at court by the Prince's Players, and they performed again in February, probably for Shrovetide.[65] Arthur was being publicly 'brought out' in preparation for his wedding. This is the first clear use of the patronage of a playing company to achieve status at court, although evidence from the Chamber accounts suggests that it was a tactic used by the great nobles from at least as early as 1492. A papal dispensation was sought for another proxy marriage at Bewdley on 19 May 1499 which may have been celebrated by barriers at Greenwich. The proxy marriage was repeated again the following fall when Arthur reached fourteen years of age. It seems likely that the Christmas revels of 1499–1500 and 1500–1 were deliberately scaled down in anticipation of the spectacular celebrations planned for the royal wedding in November 1501. No record of an imprest to Hault is recorded in the Chamber account for 1499–1500, but a payment of £8 10s. 6d. was made to him for a disguising on 14 February 1500.[66] There is no record of a disguising at all in 1500–1.

iii

In the spring of 1500 the council commissioned Jaques Haulte and William Pawne to be appointed to 'devise and prepare disguisings and some morisks after the best maner they can' for the upcoming royal wedding of Prince Arthur and Katherine of Aragon.[67] This commission provides the first clear evidence that Henry's supervisors devised as well as produced the disguisings, but the absence of payment for such services in earlier and later records suggests that this was a matter of course. After his six years of experience, Haulte would have been the council's natural choice to devise disguisings, but why Pawne was chosen is not immediately clear. He was Surveyor of the Works at Calais from about 1495 to 1501, and Master of the Works at Tournai from the fall of 1515 to 1519.[68] Pawne was directed to certify the king of the reparations in progress at Calais in 1499,

and on 12 March 1501 he was given a commission as Master of the Works to pur-
vey material and labourers for the project. His name drops out of the accounts
there in 1501–2, as he had obviously been called to London to carry out the
council's directive. He does not appear to have been involved in the production
of disguisings or morris dances for the wedding festivities, but it is possible that
he oversaw the Works projects. The Works account for the tournament shows the
tilt-yard was laid out on the north front of the Great Hall at Westminster. Scaffolds, lists, and a viewing platform for the king and queen were also constructed, the latter of which, covered with sail cloth, doubled as an armoury.[69] There
would normally have been modifications made in the church for the wedding and
in the prince's and Katherine's lodgings, and these would have been undertaken
by the Works. It is possible that Pawne supervised these projects as well as the
alterations in the lodgings of the ambassadors, as he was to do again for the Scots
ambassadors who attended the betrothal in London of Princess Margaret to James
IV of Scotland in the following year.[70]

Haulte was paid 22s. 8d. 'opon his bill' on 30 September 1500 and 53s. 7 1/2d.
'opon ij billes' on 30 June 1501, the same day that John Atkinson was paid £20
'for certain stuff to be bought for Jakes Haute,' all in connection with the wedding festivities.[71] By 16 July 1501, Haulte's name disappears from the accounts
and Atkinson begins to receive imprests in his own name. We do not know the
reason for this change of administration. In any event, the rest of the productions
both for Arthur's wedding in November 1501 and for the betrothal of Margaret
in January 1502 were supervised by Atkinson, who contracted some of the
pageants and disguisings to William Cornish, Gentleman of the Chapel, and to
John English, one of the leading members of the King's Players. Atkinson is a
common enough name, but this is probably the John who received a life grant
from Richard III on 22 March 1484 of the office of Yeoman Keeper of the King's
Armoury in the Tower and elsewhere and a life annuity of 10 marks on 25 March
1485. By 27 February 1501 he had been appointed Henry's Clerk of the Ordnance.[72] Atkinson's experience in the Armoury would have brought him into contact with the fashionable pageantry, costuming, and literary devices associated
with tournaments; thus, he would have been well qualified to supervise a wide
range of the preparations for the wedding ceremonies, spectacles, and entertainments.

It was not until November 1501, after many delays which are reflected in the
council's plans for her reception, that Katherine of Aragon arrived in England.[73]
The London civic pageants staged for her entry were among the most distinguished of the entire century.[74] The great tournament at Westminster which was
held between 18 and 25 November 1501, with its pageant-tree of chivalry, allegorical costuming, pageant-car entries, and dramatic action, brought England a

long way toward catching up with continental practices in the genre. Henry VII had met with Archduke Philip in early 1500 in Calais at a conference attended also by the acknowledged master of chivalric productions, Anthony Comte de la Roche, known as the Grand Bastard of Burgundy. As Gordon Kipling has suggested, it is likely that contact with members of the Burgundian court influenced planning for the entertainments to celebrate the royal wedding.[75]

The challenge for the tournament was issued by the Duke of Buckingham, who with four companions would honour the marriage of the Prince. The combats were to include jousts at tilt, jousts with sharp spears in open field, a tourney on horseback with rebated swords, and foot combats at barriers with swords and spears. The challenge was to be proclaimed and answered at Westminster, where there was to be set up a pageant of three trees. For the actual tournament, the challenge was simplified to include only one tree and shields were hung on the surrounding fence. The presence of the tree of chivalry is especially important, since it is the first in England of many more to come in the Tudor period.[76] On the continent, the tree had become a classic symbol of the challenge to feats of arms, a stage setting suggesting the romance which had come to characterize the Burgundian tournament.

The field for the tournament was laid out in front of Westminster Hall. The tree was set up at the north end, and the royal platform was erected on the south. The field was surrounded by double stages or viewing scaffolds. On the first day of the tournament, according to the model set by the Comte de la Roche in the *Pas de l'Arbre d'Or* of 1468, the challengers rode in on richly barded coursers and used portable pavilions. The Duke of Buckingham, as the Prince's champion, entered the lists in a square pavilion of white and green silk decorated with rose leaves, which was either wheeled or held aloft by his attendants.[77] When the pageant opened, the Duke rode out fully armed wearing the emblems of Arthur and Katherine. The answerers were expected to contribute fantastic pageants to the romantic setting of the tournament. The Marquis of Dorset, as chief answerer, entered within a pavilion of cloth of gold striped with black velvet. His thirty footmen were led by a hermit clad in black as 'guyder of the said Tent.' William Courtenay rode in a red dragon led by a giant. Guillaume de Rivers entered within a ship. The Earl of Essex rode on a green mountain set with trees, herbs, stones, and beasts, on top of which was a young lady. A red dragon led by a wild man pulled this pageant into the lists. Sir John Peche made his entry in a pavilion of red silk. The answerers filed in procession around the lists until they came before the king's standing. Here they exited their pavilions and wheeled pageant cars, and rode to the lists to answer the challengers. The jousting continued on the second day of the tournament, but with less spectacular entries. For the third day, the tilt was removed and the ground was resurfaced for running *volant* with sharp spears, a very dangerous event and one which was to be abandoned by mid-century. For the barriers, the challengers took up their positions near the king's standing. The answerers rode into the lists within a great pageant – a ship 'with all maner of tacklynges and marinurs in her,' firing off 'serpentyns/ and othir gunneshote.' This ship anchored near the barriers, where the answerers immediately disembarked and engaged the challengers with spears. On the last day of the tournament, Thursday, 25 November, the challengers, mounted on horses garnished with spangles, bells, and other devices 'aftir [the] most nuest fachon,' rode in procession grouped around a great pageant car drawn by four marvellous beasts. Two lions, a hart with gilt horns, and an ibex, each operated by two men, 'ther legges, aloonly apperyng, beyng aftir the colour and simylitude of the beastes that they were in,' drew the pageant car. Within the pageant was a young lady who was set on the king's platform and collected again after the day's events.

The importance of this event in the annals of the English tournament has not been underestimated by modern historians. It was also an important event in the history of the revels, for this tournament was punctuated by four great banquets held between 18 and 28 November, each celebrated with plays, pageants, and disguisings, some of them thematically and structurally connected to the tournament. It is the first certain record of the extensive use of massive indoor pageants, and it is the first certain instance of an interconnection between tournament and revel.

The initial banquet was held on 19 November at Westminster. The revels included a 'moost goodly and pleasaunt disguysing' presented with pagents.[78] The first of the three pageants was a castle drawn into the Hall by four heraldic beasts – a golden and a silver lion, a hart with gilt horns, and an ibex. 'Within everych of the which iiijor bests were ij men – oon in the fore parte and anothir in the hynde parte – secretly hide and apparellid, no thing seene but their legges, and yet thoes were disguysid aftir the proporcion and kynde of the bests that they were in.' These were the very same beasts which were to draw the challengers' pageant into the lists on 25 November. Within, at the windows of the castle, were eight disguised ladies. In its four turrets were children disguised as maidens 'syngyng full swettly and ermeniously,' as the pageant was drawn through the hall before the king. The second pageant, a ship 'sett uppon whelys without any leders in sight, in right goodly apparell, havyng her mastys, toppys, saylys, her taclyng, and all other appurtenauns necessary unto a semely vessel,' was drawn into the Hall and anchored near the castle. This was probably the same ship which was to draw the answerers to the barriers later in the tournament. In addition to the masters and their company, who 'in their countenans, spechis, and demeanour usid and behavyd themsilf after the maner and guyse of marynours,' the ship carried a young lady, 'in her apparell like unto the Princes of Hispayne,' and Hope and

Despair, ambassadors of the Knights of Love. Using a ladder to descend from the ship, the ambassadors approached the ladies of the castle as 'wowers and brekers of the mattir of love.' When the ladies gave 'their finall aunswere of uttirly refuse,' the ambassadors warned that the response would provoke an assault by the knights. A third pageant, a mountain which bore eight knights with their banner displayed 'naming themselves the Knightes of the Mounte of Love' was drawn into the Hall and conveyed next to the ship. The knights descended and 'with moch males and curvagyous myend' assaulted the castle. The ladies eventually yielded and descended to perform dances with the knights, during which time the pageants were removed from the Hall. After the disguisers had completed their performances, Prince Arthur and Lady Cecil performed two baas dances. This was followed by Katherine and one of her ladies. 'Thirde and last cam doun the Duke of York, havyng with him the Lady Margaret his sister on his hond, and dauncyd two baas daunces. And aftirward he, perceyuyng himself to be accombred with his clothis, sodenly cast of his gowne and daunced in his jacket with the said Lady Margaret in so goodly an pleasaunt maner that hit was to the King and Quene right great and singler pleasure.'

The St George disguising of 1494 incorporated play, pageant, music, song, and choreographed dance. Each part, however, was a separate element, and one gave way to another as the action moved from verisimilar representation to visual symbol, poetry, song, and dance. In the 19 November 1501 revel, drama, pageant, and disguising are fully integrated. Pageants serve for entries and as scenic properties for dramatic action. Drama serves not as a frame or introduction to the pageant and disguising, but is realized in dialogue and mock assault. The dance, used to resolve the conflict between the ladies and the knights, is performed by principals in the dramatic action. The 1494 St George disguising drew its inspiration from the folk mumming, in which St George was a traditional figure, and from the saint legends preserved in the *Legenda Aurea*.[79] The 19 November 1501 revel draws on romance literature – like the tournament itself – on allegorical drama, and on continental court revels. The introduction of romance into the revels made the structural and eventually thematic connections to tournaments naturally attractive. Romance literature influenced the course of the revels and spectacles at Henry VIII's court until the late 1520s, and was revived on occasion throughout the century. Romance opened a vast array of characters to be impersonated and simple plots to be enacted which were later adapted not only to express the diplomacy of the court but also the ideals and anxieties of monarchs and courtiers.

In continental revels, knights storming castles guarded by ladies had symbolized the assault of lust on chastity. The assault was usually represented by an attack with swords defended with flowers, and the success of the ladies represented the triumph of virtue over vice, of chastity over lust, of civility over barbarity. In a wedding revel, as Gordon Kipling has pointed out, the ladies do not represent chastity but more probably indifference, while the knights represent love.[80] The knights' victory in the revel suggests acquiescence to the legitimacy of matrimony where individual romantic relations have a higher significance of uniting two nations. This is certainly the visual impact of the revel. The princess of Spain is not one of the ladies of the castle, but carried on the ship with the ambassadors of the knights, and the dancers, disguised half in English and half in Spanish costumes, clearly represent the harmony of the two nations. The dances which followed the disguising also reinforce this symbolic union. Arthur's dance, followed by Katherine's, and then by Henry's and Margaret's, provided a transition between the artifice of the pageant-disguising and the real event being celebrated. Literary context, dramatic action, and symbolic visuals lead to a climax in which the real heir apparent of England and his Spanish bride dance in harmony.

The second revel, held at the banquet on 21 November, included an interlude and a disguising with two pageants. The first, an arbour carrying twelve disguised gentlemen, was brought into the Hall and positioned so that its gate faced the king. The gentlemen descended through the gate and performed 'dyvers and many daunces.' A trumpet was sounded and a second pageant entered, a lantern carrying twelve disguised ladies. The pageant, which was 'made of so fyn stuf, and so many lights in hit, that these ladies might perfectly appiere and be known through the seid lanterne,' was brought before the king, and the ladies descended and danced alone. In the concluding dance of the disguising, the ladies and gentlemen danced together. Gordon Kipling has pointed out that the luminous palace is a common image in dream allegory poetry which has precedents in Burgundian disguisings and that these two pageants and disguising are in the tradition of Lydgate's allegories, *The Complaint of the Black Knight*, and *The Temple of Glass*.[81] The conclusion unites the masculine character of the arbor and the feminine character of the brilliant lantern, emblems of love and constancy, in a harmonious dance.

An award banquet was held at Westminster on 25 November to conclude the tournament. The Duke of Buckingham received a diamond, Dorset received a ruby, and the rest of the contestants were awarded jewels or gold rings. The pageant-disguising held at this banquet relied on music, song, dance, and visual symbols. Disguised gentlemen and ladies entered the Hall on two separate pageant mountains bound together with a golden chain. One was decorated with trees, herbs, flowers, and fruits; the other was arid, studded with minerals 'right subtily pictured/ and empainted as ever hath been seen.' Twelve disguised gentlemen sat about the fertile mount playing lutes, harps, tabors, and recorders, while twelve ladies on the arid mount played 'clavycords, dusymers, clavysymballes, and such othir.' A maiden dressed as the Spanish Infanta reigned over this pageant. The disguisers descended from their pageants, danced alone at first and then together to conclude this tableau of concord between the two nations. Walter Ogilvie thought that this was the best of the disguisings presented on the occasion and that in the singing he heard 'almost angelic voices.'[82]

The last revel, held at the recently rebuilt Richmond Palace on 28 November, featured a pageant tower or tabernacle built in the form of a chapel with many windows and lights.[83] In its lower storey were eight costumed gentlemen; in its upper, eight ladies. Around its base were mermen and mermaids, and in 'every off the sayde mermaydrs a Chylde of the Chapell, syngyng ryght suetly,' the first confirmed appearance of the Children of the Chapel in a court revel. Three wildmen drew the pageant before the king. The disguised gentlemen loosed rabbits in the Hall, to the delight of spectators, and then performed a dance. The ladies released doves which flew about the Hall, again to the surprise and delight of the audience, and then the ladies descended and danced with the gentlemen to conclude the disguising. The innovations evident in these wedding entertainments – spectacular visual display; dramatic integration of music, dialogue, dance, scenery, and costume; surprise; and concluding dances by royalty – were to be important features in the revels for several decades.

Attributing the production of the wedding disguisings is not altogether a straightforward matter. Since disguisings were complex entertainments, production could be subdivided along obvious lines – device, visual design, musical arrangement, choreography, script (if there was to be one), and artistic direction. There is no evidence from the Tudor period that production was ever this neatly parcelled out, but in later, more well-documented cases, we do find occasions on which artists worked on designs and models based on the Master's 'device,' writers contributed scripts for dramatic portions, and, on one occasion, bells were ordered to teach dance steps for a morris. The disguising produced by Suffolk and Essex in 1496 was probably devised, directed, and at least partly produced by servants of the peers with production assistance from Haulte. But nothing quite like the extraordinary arrangements for production in 1501 had been used before. Atkinson was certainly the supervisor in charge of the 1501–2 revels, but, as the Chamber payments show, he was coordinating and supervising productions for the ceremonies and receptions as well as for the disguisings. On 8 September, for example, he was paid £26 'for the tentt,' probably the one used in connection with Katherine's reception, and he may well have been the payee on a separate account for the fountain used at the wedding.[84] Because of the range of his responsibilities, the services of William Cornish and John English were contracted to help prepare pageants and disguisings. Stylistic evidence connecting the 19 November disguising to Cornish's known practice at Henry VIII's court suggests that he may well have devised it himself. The fact that English was responsible for the production of the disguising on 21 November and again in January suggests that he may have provided the device for it. It is virtually certain that the two men produced at least these two of the four disguisings and that they provided artistic direction for them.

William Cornish received Chamber payments of £10 on 6 and 22 August and again on 8 September for his 'disguising.' On 20 September a payment of £10 was issued to 'Cornyshe for his pagent,' and on 3 November a final payment of £20 was issued to him for 'iij pageanttes.'[85] Sydney Anglo has attributed the 19 November revel to Cornish, arguing that it was the only one to employ three pageants, and its structure anticipates Cornish's later work at Henry VIII's court.[86] Cornish was also hired to help prepare the tournament and to produce a play at Greenwich for Margaret, Queen of Scots, in May 1516, and the documents associated with that event shed some light on his role in 1501.[87] The fact that Cornish received direct payments for his work both in 1501 and in 1516 shows that his appointment was considered official. While this indicates that he had some authority over his productions, it does not mean that he worked independently of Atkinson in 1501. In fact, Cornish submitted a bill for the production of his play in 1516 to Gibson who, in turn, charged for this material in one of his Revels accounts. It is likely that a similar procedure was followed in 1501, and this is illustrated better by the payments to John English.

There is compelling evidence to attribute the direction of the 21 November revel to John English. Gordon Kipling has pointed out that the lantern pageant used on 21 November was revived three months later for the revels celebrating the betrothal of Princess Margaret and James IV of Scotland, which English and Atkinson certainly produced.[88] On 31 August Atkinson received a payment of £6 13s. 4d. 'for John English.' On 8 September and again on 3 November English himself received payments of £6 13s. 4d. 'for his pageant.'[89] As the direct Chamber payments indicate, English, who is listed as a joiner in the preparations for one of the pageants for the 1508 disguising, had some authority over his production, but one of the payments also indicates that part of the money came through Atkinson.

Cornish received exactly three times as much money from the Chamber as English did, and since one of these payments was apparently added only in the last few months before the revels took place, a division of responsibility is suggested.[90] Atkinson received payments totalling over £300 for the pageant-disguisings and for other projects from July through the end of October. Because the amount billed through Atkinson's open account or drawn in material from government departments cannot be established we cannot be certain of the final cost of any of the pageant-disguisings. But the combined evidence makes it virtually certain that Cornish was responsible for the pageant-disguising on 19 November and English for the one on 21 November and makes a suggestive case for Cornish's responsibility for those on 25 and 28 November.

Just two months later, in January 1502, Princess Margaret was betrothed to James IV of Scotland. The event was celebrated in London on 25 January with a tournament and an elaborate revel which included a pageant, a disguising, and a morris dance. After the award banquet held to conclude the tournament on 25 January, the revels began. 'Incontinent after the Pryses were giuen, there was in the Hall a goodly Pageant curiously wrought with Fenestreallis, having many Lights brenning in the same, in Manner of a Lantron out of which sorted divers Sortes of Morisks, Also a very good Disguising of Six Gentlemen and Six Gentlewomen which daunced diuers Daunces.'[91] As the Chamber payment makes clear, Atkinson produced this revel with the help of John English, who revived the lantern pageant of 21 November 1501.[92] The King's Players, who had performed in conjunction with the 21 November disguising, performed again on 25 January, probably in connection with the revel. The dances which 'sorted' from the pageant may have been choreographed by the 'one Lewes' who was paid 53s. 4d. on 4 February 1502 for a 'mores daunce.' Morris dances were in vogue at Henry VII's court. Their popularity in the revels can be seen from the fact that Chamber payments are occasionally made to make disguisings for them. The spectacular nature of the costuming traditional in the morris and the athletic nature of the dance are appropriate as expressions of joy or as antic precursors to the more refined dances performed in the disguisings.[93] Princess Margaret left on her progress to Scotland on 27 June 1503. She was accorded a reception at Dalkeith and pageants at Edinburgh when she arrived on 13 August. Her wedding to James IV was celebrated in Edinburgh with a tournament, revels, and plays.[94] Three of the King's Players, led by John English, accompanied her on her journey and performed at least twice at the Scots court.

The organization, preparation, and expense of the spectacles and revels held from November 1501 to January 1502 were on a scale with their ambition. Politically, Henry was making a major foreign policy bid in connecting his dynasty by marriage to Spain and to Scotland. The expense alone, excluding the reception, the tournaments, and the contribution of other government offices, was astronomical by the standards of the rest of the reign.[95] Atkinson, Cornish, English, and Adam received over £566 in payments for their parts of the preparations. The demands on the royal household for ceremonies, spectacles, and revels led to the extraordinary arrangements used for their production. There are no other documented instances in Henry VII's reign – although there are many in Henry VIII's – in which an appointed supervisor engaged the services of semi-professionals like Cornish and English to help with productions. The arrangement appears forced by the pressure of immediate needs. Its effect was to encourage the development of administrative procedures for coordinating services among household officers and appointed officials, systems of sub-contracting, finance, and accounting. These procedures show up clearly in the better-documented revels toward the end of the reign.

iv

Only modest entertainments were held at court after the revels of January 1502. Queen Elizabeth received an imprest of £10 from the Chamber 'for the kinges Disguysing' at Christmas 1502–3.[96] This is the only evidence from the reign in which a member of the royal family was involved in the production of revels at a major feast. The queen, of course, kept her own court. Her household was a duplication on a smaller scale of the king's. She had her own Steward, Chamberlain, Master of the Horse, her own finance, and all of the accoutrements appropriate to a person of her rank. Her Privy Purse accounts, which survive only for the last year of her life, reveal that she kept an extraordinarily active court and that she had revels produced. Payments for entertainments of all kinds are recorded at Westminster and during her progresses throughout the countryside.[97] Many of the entertainments given in the king's court were also shown in hers. She rewarded the Children of the Chapel for their St Nicholas Bishop on 5 December 1502 at Westminster, the Lord of Misrule on New Year's Day, and she commissioned entertainments of her own. She paid 13s. 4d. to 'Cornisshe for setting of a Carralle vpon Cristmas day,' and issued rewards to minstrels, musicians, and fools on New Year's. She also paid rewards for performances before her while on progress. On 16 October, probably at Ewlme, Oxfordshire, where she had lost money playing dice on 13 October, she paid 3s. 4d. to 'my lady Bray for money by hure geven in rewarde to a disar that played the Sheppert.'[98] This 'Disar' [OF *disour*] was probably a story-teller, like William Tyler, late servant to the Earl of Oxford, whom she rewarded on 4 January 1503, and this October performance may have been one of the popular ballads in which the story-teller impersonated a shepherd. In addition to these payments which show a continuing interest and involvement in entertainments of the type found at the king's court, she was actively involved in sponsoring and producing disguisings.

On 11 June 1502, the queen paid 56s. 8d. to 'William Antyne Copersmith for spangelles settes square peces sterrys dropes and pointes after silver and gold for garnisshing of iakettes against the disguysing.'[99] Whether this payment refers to the coming Christmas of 1502–3, for which she was issued the imprest from the Chamber to produce the king's disguising, or to the previous year for which she made a payment on 9 December 1502 for 'iiij Cotes of White and grene *sarc*enet for iiij of the king*es* mynstrell*es* against the disguysing in the yere last passed' is not certain, but at least two disguisings were produced in this period.[100] There was also a payment made by the Chamber between 2–4 January for 'Dauncyng of mores Daunce.'[101] Who produced this or whether it was connected with the queen's disguising is not clear.

Another disguising was produced at court for Palm Sunday. Lewis Adam, probably the same Lewis who was paid for a morris dance in February 1502, was paid £10 on 12 April 1503 for making 'Disguysinges.'[102] This is the last disguising on record for several years. The magnificence of the revels of 1501 and 1502 and the political hopes they represented were undercut by the death of Prince Arthur in April 1502, less than five months after his wedding.[103] Arthur's death was followed by the queen's less than a year later. She died as a result of childbirth on 11 February 1503 at 38 years of age.[104] After these personal losses, the king did not order revels and spectacles on the scale of those produced in 1501 and 1502 again for several years.

2

Later Arrangements, 1504–1509

Playing companies and, occasionally, Lords of Misrule graced the Christmas seasons from 1504 to 1506, but there were no disguisings. Henry was created Prince of Wales on 23 February 1504, but no record of entertainments survives for this occasion nor for the tournament which was held in July 1505.[1] Interest in revels and spectacles on a grand scale was not revived until 1506. In January of that year an event occurred which was to shape the course of diplomatic negotiations for the remainder of Henry's reign. When Philip of Burgundy and his queen, Joanna of Castile, were unexpectedly forced ashore in England during a storm Henry turned the accident to his advantage by arranging to have Philip installed as Knight Companion of the Garter and to have Prince Henry installed in the Order of Toison D'Or.[2] The king provided spectacles and revels appropriate to the occasion. Hunting, hawking, tennis play, and banquets were held, and a tournament was prepared at Greenwich by Edward Guildford, who had succeeded his father as Master of the Armoury.[3] Negotiations were begun to marry Princess Mary to Philip's son, Charles, inheritor of Austria, Burgundy, and Castile. A treaty for this was concluded in 1507, and the betrothal took place at St Paul's at Christmas 1508. The opportunity for a match to complement those already made with Aragon and Scotland promised to bring England into the mainstream of European affairs. This, and the opportunity to entertain a prince of Philip's stature, rekindled in Henry a desire to promote the magnificence of his court, and the rest of his reign is filled with fashionable tournaments and revels.

Jousts were held again from 14 to 21 May 1506, just a few months after Philip's departure, and a maypole was set up at Westminster on the 22nd.[4] There is no record of pageants used in the lists, but the reference to a ship in the articles of challenge suggests that such a pageant may have been erected at Greenwich. The challenge, a literary narrative of the type fashionable in Burgundy from the fifteenth century, came in the form of a letter addressed to Princess Mary from Lady

May. Lady May had heard that 'not long agone' Dame February, servant of Lady
Winter, was honored 'by the reason of exercises of feats of arms.' The rumour of
these jousts honouring Philip of Burgundy prompted her to seek the permission
of her mistress, Lady Summer, to request that Princess Mary allow her servants
to defend her honour. Lady May had been sailing the stormy seas of March and
April 'in this ship' seeking England, 'this most famous stream of honour, fountain of all noblesse.' Lady May was sure that with Princess Mary's license her servants would honour her as they did Dame February. As in 1498, when in
preparation for his wedding Arthur's status was being emphasized by the appearances of his playing company and by elaborate disguisings at court, Princess Mary
was now given centre stage in court spectacles in preparation for her betrothal to
Charles. This first recorded fictional narrative challenge for a joust in England was
the precursor of many more to come. Burgundian-style tournaments, essentially romances using fictional narratives for challenges, and often employing
pageantry, scenery, costume, music, and, of course, the drama of the combats,
dominated the rest of the reign and several years of the next.[5]

Despite its acquisition of fanciful elements, such as elaborate horse bards and
entrances in portable pavilions which had been used even in England from the
late fifteenth century, the tournament in Henry VII's reign was still regarded as
a proving ground for martial prowess.[6] By 1501, military exercises began to be displaced by an emphasis on spectacular display in the context of romance literature.
The knights in the great 1501 wedding tournament entered the lists in a complete
set of pageant cars, and hung their shields near a tree of chivalry much as the
Grand Bastard of Burgundy had done in Bruges at the *Pas de l'Arbre d'Or* over
three decades before. Throughout the rest of the reign the tournament acquired
more fictional and dramatic elements. The 'Justs of the Months of May and June'
in 1507 combine the spectacle and pageantry of Arthur's wedding tournament
with the literary and dramatic elements of the 1506 jousts of May.[7] The challenge
takes the form of a letter from the Queen of May under her signet at the 'Castle
of Comfort in our City of Solace.' As in the jousts held the previous year, Princess
Mary is the principal focus of this tournament. She may have even appeared as
the May Queen in a green, flower-decked dress, while her four champions defended her honour in green costumes wearing her badges around their necks. There
are other poorly documented tournaments in the reign, but given the fact that the
style dominates the first few years of Henry VIII's reign, we can only conclude
that they were refinements of the developments at Henry VII's court. The tournament, characterized by literary influence, fictional challenges, costumed
knights, spectacle, pageantry, and dramatic action, was a fully developed form in
England by at least 1507.

Revels in the Christmas season of 1508–9 centred on the betrothal ceremony of Princess Mary and Archduke Charles at St Paul's on 25 December. William Wynnesbury, the first named Lord of Misrule in several years, was issued an imprest of 66s. 8d. on 19 December and an identical payment on 7 January. Buckingham's players 'that playd in the Hall at Grenewyche' received 6s. 8d. on 2 January. The players of the Chapel were paid 53s. 4d. for performing 'afore the King vpon xij*th* nyght,' and the King's Players received 40s. on 7 January, probably for a performance on Twelfth Night as well. Of the tournament, probably prepared by Edward Guildford, we have little information other than that it included a tourney. Henry Wentworth was appointed to supervise the preparations of three pageants – a castle, a tree, and a mount – and a disguising. Wentworth was a Gentleman Usher of the Privy Chamber whose name first appears in the Chamber account on 20 December 1507 as payee for £13 6s. 8d., followed by another 100s. on 31 December, 'towarde the making of a disguysing for a moryce daunce.'[8] Even at the modest cost of slightly over £18, this was the most expensive disguising held at court since the queen's death four years before. It was successful enough, for Wentworth was to continue to produce disguisings through the first year of Henry VIII's reign. In making this appointment, Henry followed his earlier practice of appointing men whose duties brought them into contact with him on a regular basis, obviously a measure designed to permit him to oversee their plans. By this means he effected personal control of his revels and of the image he projected in them: the reserved patron and magnanimous host.

Available evidence indicates that Wentworth's pageant-disguisings on 25 December 1508 were structurally much like earlier ones at Henry VII's court. From the sketchy narrative we learn that 'ludi Maurei quas *morescas* dicunt, et saltantium juvenum generosa virensque propago, simul et comediarum tragediarumque hystrionica et ludicra queque spectacula previsa sane prius ac sumptuose preparata.'[9] The King's Players were not paid for a performance until Twelfth Night, but 'Master Kyte Cornysshe and other of the chapel' were paid £6 13s. 4d. for playing before the king at Richmond on 25 December.[10] It seems clear that William Cornish, John Kyte, and other members of the Players of the Chapel performed some of the plays mentioned in the narrative and may have performed in the pageant-disguisings. We can only conjecture that the plays, pageants, and dance were structurally and thematically integrated. We can also only speculate about the relation between the tournament and the revels. We know from Wentworth's Revels account that the pageants were equipped with wheels. Like the tournaments of 1506 and 1507, this one may well have used a fictional challenge, costuming, and dramatic action, and Wentworth's pageants may have doubled in the tiltyard and in the Hall at Richmond. The series of revels in 1501 shows that pageant-disguisings intended to celebrate royal marriages could take a variety of forms, from tableaux of international amity – as the chained mountains of

25 November – to dramatic action and literary allusion which related the couple in a personal, national, and international union. The castle had been a traditional emblem of Castile, the country of the bridegroom, but it had also contained the indifferent ladies on 19 November 1501. The tree with its hawthorn leaves had been a symbol of England in the 1507 tournament, but it is also associated with the Burgundian tree of chivalry which had been adapted in England as early as 1501. The mount had been used to symbolize nations, as it did in 1501, but it had also carried the Knights of the Mount of Love. How the three pageants were used in the revel is not certain. The disguising was probably danced by members of the court, but since Cornish and others of the Chapel played on that night, it is likely that music, and song were included in the plays and possibly also in the pageant-disguising as well. A morris dance was also included, but how it functioned can only be guessed.

i

Wentworth submitted a Revels account for his work at Christmas 1508–9, the only one to survive from the entire reign, entitled the 'Boke of the disguisinges ffor the comyng of thambassadours of fflaunderes.'[11] While there are many questions this account does not answer for us, it does illuminate procedures and methods of production, and makes possible some clearer conceptions of Wentworth's role in this revel. He worked on the preparations from 27 September to 17 December 1508, a total of eighty days, for which he charged 7d. a day for himself. He also worked from 8 to 22 January 1509 at an additional *per diem* of 8d. a day to cover the higher costs of living in London. He received material from the Great Wardrobe and purchased more from mercers for the pageants and costumes. He hired tailors to make the costumes; embroiderers; basket makers, probably to make the headpieces for the disguisers; and subcontracted work on the pageants to painters, joiners, and ironworkers. Wentworth had a personal servant to assist him who was paid 4d. a day. However, Wentworth's bill shows the purchase of a wide range of material, indicating that he personally supervised all phases of the preparations. Artisans and labourers were hired as necessary to complete the projects, some for as short a period as a few days, others for as long as two months. The work was completed in two large buildings, rented for the purpose. Wentworth hired one house 'at the Crane in the vintere for ij pagiauntes there made by the space of xvj wekes' and another at 'the bishop of harfordes place' for 'a pagiant cauled the mount by the space of xij wekys.'[12] The Vintry was located near the Tower. Its attraction to a producer of pageants was its proximity to a wharf, for the usual means of transporting pageants and other properties for revels was by barge from London to one of the royal palaces located on the river. The Bishop of Hertford's building in Blackfriars offered similar advantages of a house large enough to construct a pageant and ease of access to a wharf on the Thames bank. Both of these buildings were to be used on other occasions during Henry VIII's reign. From the amount of canvas listed in the mercers' parcels it appears that the construction of the pageants was the standard canvas stretched over timber frames still in use in the Elizabethan period. Three joiners, John English among them, constructed the mount at the Bishop of Hertford's building. Seven joiners worked on the castle and tree at the Vintry, some for as many as forty-two days.

Painting was contracted to Richard Rowangre, an artist who was employed on royal projects from as early as Prince Arthur's funeral in 1502 to as late as the great banqueting house at Greenwich in 1527.[13] Later in the century, the Revels accounts specify payments to artists of Rowangre's stature for designing costumes, properties, and banqueting houses. The bill which he submitted to Wentworth included charges for eleven painters and five colour grinders whose job would have been to paint and decorate the pageants and other properties according to his designs, including making the rose, marigold, and hawthorn leaves for the pageant tree, and probably the axels, hubs, and other ironwork for all three of the pageants.[14] Ironworkers and wiredrawers were hired later in the century to fashion the chandeliers used to light performances, but at this early date lighting appears to have been the province of the household staff.

At one point during the preparations, the king wished to inspect the costumes and properties. Wentworth loaded 'ij standards and ij gret cofers' on barges and transported them to Richmond 'to thentent he myght se the disguising stuff.'[15] The king must have approved, for there is no record of major alterations. On the day of the performance, all of the material was transported to Richmond by barge. Painters and joiners attended to assemble and finish the pageants. The production was not without its last-minute problems. Wentworth's servant was sent to London by horse on the day of the revel to obtain another costume. Afterwards, the properties were disassembled and costumes collected and returned to London under Wentworth's supervision. There he worked from 8 to 22 January cleaning and storing material and making up his accounts. Material was stored in the Prince's Wardrobe, probably the building in the parish of St Andrew on Warwick Lane. Material continued to be stored here and occasionally pageants were built as well through the first four decades of the century.

Wentworth's bill of £60 17s. 11d. does not reflect the total cost of his productions. Material was received from the Great Wardrobe for which Wentworth only charged for carriage. The Works, as it had done in the past, probably supplied the scaffolds. No payment for this pageant-disguising was issued to Wentworth from the Chamber during Henry VII's reign, but this exact amount was paid to Sir Andrew Windsor, Keeper of the Great Wardrobe on 2 September 1509 for disguisings before the ambassadors of Flanders.[16] Such a procedure was not altogether unknown and was no doubt an attempt to balance budgets at the change of reigns.

Wentworth's account does not contain a narrative section which describes the pageant-disguisings in detail; it does not mention who devised them; it does not mention who the performers were; and it does not mention how the plays and other spectacles and entertainments were coordinated. That he devised the pageant-disguisings can be inferred from the fact that no other individuals are named as payees in the Chamber accounts for this service. That he provided high-level coordination for the various spectacles and revels is doubtful. Coordination of the various entertainments was probably handled at high levels of the household administration and ultimately by the council and by the king who personally inspected and approved Wentworth's work. That Wentworth's supervision was limited to the pageant-disguisings is clear from the fact that he did not charge to make outfits for the participants in the tournament, and he did not charge to make costumes or properties for the plays.

ii

Plays were scheduled at court as part of the revels from the beginning of Henry VII's reign. Some were shown in conjunction with disguisings but most were scheduled as separate entertainments, mainly on feast days but also on other occasions. Invitations to playing companies to perform at court were extended more frequently by Henry VII than by any Tudor monarch other than Elizabeth I. There are well over fifty performances by foreign troupes, by civic companies, by troupes patronized by the nobility, by the royal companies, and by the Players of the Chapel recorded in the Chamber accounts from 1491 to 1509. Between 1485 and 1491 narrative evidence shows that 'many And dyvers playes' were expected entertainments at Christmas. Even in years when disguisings had to be cancelled, plays were staged. The measles outbreak in 1489–90, for example, prompted a disappointed commentator to mention that no disguisings and only a few plays were shown. Such extensive use of playing companies as part of the revels at court raises a number of questions. Definitive answers can be given to only a few, but they are worth asking nonetheless. What appeal might plays have had to schedule them so often? Why did the king create the royal companies and how did their performances compare to the many others at court? Since the king's supervisors of the revels – like Pudsey, Alwyn, Haulte, Wentworth – were charged only with the disguisings, how were these plays selected and produced?

Plays had been performed at the Yorkist court, but Henry VII was the first English monarch to patronize companies of players.[17] In doing so he set a precedent for the rest of the Tudor and Stuart periods. The *Lusoribus Regis, alias in lingua Anglicana, les pleyars of the kings enterludes* first appeared in 1494, and although the company may date from a slightly earlier period the evidence suggests that from 1493 to 1495 the king was particularly determined to acquire a reputation as a patron of the arts.[18] The company performed regularly at court on state occasions and during the Christmas seasons beginning at Twelfth Night 1494 and continuing to the end of the reign. They were paid an annual salary of 20 marks, livery, and rewards for performances. The company was initially composed of four players – John English, Richard Gibson, Edward Maye, and John Hammond. Maye appears only in the 1494 list By 1504 John Scott and William Rutter were added to the company, bringing the total to five members.[19] English may have been the driving force behind the troupe early on. He led the company to Edinburgh, for example, to perform at the Scots court for the wedding festivities of Princess Margaret and James IV in 1503. On the first Sunday after the marriage 'After Soupper, the Kynge and the Queene being togeder in hyr Chamber, John Inglish and hys Companyons played and then ichon went his way,' and on one of the preceding days the troupe acted a 'morality' before the king and queen.[20] From 1505 to 1509, payments to the company were made to Richard Gibson and his fellows, suggesting that Gibson was providing the leadership. After 1510 English apparently again headed the company.

None of these men, so far as we know, were professional actors, certainly not the two chief members of the troupe. English was employed to purchase silks for the coronation of Henry VII in 1485. John Atkinson contracted his services in helping to produce pageants and disguisings in November 1501 and in January 1502. In December 1508 Henry Wentworth employed him as a joiner to work on pageants.[21] Gibson was Yeoman Tailor and Porter of the Great Wardrobe who became Sergeant of the Tents and Sergeant at Arms under Henry VIII. His later career will be discussed in the next chapter. As Gordon Kipling has pointed out, the King's Players scarcely travelled at all during Henry VII's reign, and comparison to the travelling troupes of the aristocracy is inappropriate.[22] They were essentially a household troupe whose job it was to present several plays at court each year. The company was scheduled more frequently than any other at court, and it appears that this was one of the king's means of preserving his image as patron. However, it is easy to imagine how the King's Players might dominate the revels schedule not simply through the frequency of their appearances but also through elaborate productions. The size of the rewards they received in comparison to visiting companies suggests recompense for more than performance. Four to ten marks was a sizeable sum of money, particularly if coupled with the non-chargeable services of household departments, such as the Works, Great Wardrobe, and privy wardrobes. There are occasions when the Chamber paid

about twenty to thirty marks for disguisings on major feasts. Given this circumstantial evidence and the fact that Gibson (a professional tailor in the Wardrobe
who went on to become the Henry VIII's principal costume designer and producer of pageants, disguisings, masks, plays, and tournaments) and English (a
joiner who produced or helped to produce pageant-disguisings in 1501, 1502,
and 1508) were both members of the company, the King's Players would have easily been able to mount productions as elaborate as those indicated by the texts of
Lucrece and *Magnificence*. In an age which valued spectacle as integral even to martial exercises, the appeal of the royal companies at Henry VII's court may be
understood at least partly in these terms. Such productions, along with prefer-
ential scheduling on the most important feasts, was sufficient to dominate the
myriad of plays produced at his court and so maintain the king's image as chief
patron of his revels.

The creation of these companies, particularly the King's Players, pioneered the
development of courtly drama. By the end of Henry VII's reign they had established a sixteen-year tradition of dramatic performances. Regrettably, not a single play title can be associated for certain with the company.[25] During the first
decade of Henry VIII's reign, the King's Players underwent a radical restructur-
ing, probably as part of the same movement which overturned the hegemony of
style in revels and spectacles of his father's court. This new style, centring on the
work of William Cornish and members of the Chapel Royal, also had its beginning at Henry VII's court.

The name of William Cornish is associated with court entertainments from as
early as 1493. Clear evidence documents his career from July 1504 to 1524, first
as a Gentleman of the Chapel, then as Master of the Children of the Chapel, and,
finally, as deviser of court entertainments. The details of his earlier career, par-

ticularly between 1502 and 1504, are difficult to sort out. The surname is not uncommon, and there were at least three men named William Cornish living in London and Westminster between 1493 and 1524. A William is listed third among surviving children in the will of John Cornish in 1474. It is not certain that this William was the famous composer and dramatist, but it is an attractive hypothesis, for it would have made him over fifty years of age at his death in 1524.[26] A William Cornish also became Master of the song school at Westminster Abbey in 1479, a post he was to hold until 1490–1.[27] Most scholars identi-fy him with the Cornish who began to receive rewards at court in 1493 – also an attractive hypothesis, for this was the first such appointment at the Abbey and to a position where Cornish's skill was likely to have caught the attention of the king, and the end of his Mastership at the Abbey accords well enough with the begin-ning of his career at court. The initial reward of 100s. which he received in Michaelmas 1493 was for an unspecified service, but on 12 November of that year he was rewarded from the Chamber for presenting a 'prophecy,' and, on Twelfth Night 1494, he appeared in the lead role as St George in the king's disguising.[28] It seems clear that he was the William who received a grant of property in 1494, and he may also have been the William who received a commission to impress sol-diers and sailors in early 1496.[29] He is first associated with the Chapel in 1494, and confirmed as a Gentlemen of the Chapel in a Chamber payment of Septem-ber 1496.[30] He was paid from the Chamber again for an unspecified service on 13 March 1500, and in 1501 for helping to produce the pageant-disguisings for the wedding celebrations of Arthur and Katherine.

Conflicting evidence survives from the years between 1502 and 1504. The accounts of St Margaret's parish, Westminster, show that a William Cornish died by 1502, and his name apparently is included in the Bede Roll of the Fraternity of St Nicholas.[31] It has been suspected that this William was a Gentleman of the Chapel from 1493 to 1502 and that he was father to William Cornish the famous composer.[32] The suspicion is based partly on the accounts of St Margaret's and partly on the Fayrfax Manuscript (ca. 1500), which contains songs by composers mainly from Henry VII's reign, some of which are attributed to William Cornish 'iun.'[33] The songs contained in Henry VIII's Manuscript, prepared at least fifteen years later, are attributed to William Cornish, W. Cornish, and Cornish.[34] The implication is that after the elder Cornish's death there was no need to distinguish the work of the two Cornishes. However, there is no evidence to show that the William Cornish who died by 1502 was a Gentleman of the Chapel. Further-more, the scribe who wrote the Fayrfax Manuscript does not distinguish between William and William Junior, and neither does the scribe who wrote Henry VIII's Manuscript. These are two distinct styles of attribution by two separate scribes working at least fifteen years apart. The evidence does not necessarily warrant the conclusion which has been drawn from it, for payments to Cornish continue to be made at court. In December 1502 he received a reward from Queen Elizabeth for setting a carol to music, and there are two Chamber payments for unspecified services made on 31 December 1503 and on 13 January 1504.

It has also been suggested that John Cornish was a member of the Chapel. His name appears on the Lord Chamberlain's 23 February 1504 list of livery to be issued to eighteen Gentlemen of the Chapel for the funeral of Queen Elizabeth. William's name is missing.[35] There were at least three, possibly four, men named John Cornish flourishing around this time. The eldest son of the John Cornish who died in 1474 was also named John. In 1498, a John Cornish received a commission for gaol delivery in Winchester city, and another John, a merchant from Wales, received a pardon for outlawry.[36] Finally, a song by John Cornish is included in Ritson's Manuscript.[37] This latter piece of evidence, coupled with his name on the list of the Gentlemen of the Chapel, has led to suggestions that he was a member of the Chapel, that he died in 1504 (since his name never appears again on the Chapel lists), and that he was responsible for the 1501 wedding disguisings.[38]

The evidence is certainly muddled, but a few conclusions can be drawn. The Chamber payment for the wedding disguisings of 1501 specifically names William Cornish, and so the suggestion that John was responsible for these revels can be discarded. If there were more than one member of the Chapel named Cornish, we might expect to find a consistent attempt to distinguish payees by their first names in the Chamber accounts. But we do not, and there are no payments to John at all. Further, the provenance of Ritson's Manuscript is the west country, possibly Exeter, not the court. In style, it is the oldest of the three main early Tudor musical manuscripts, and represents the end of the tradition of the medieval carol. Its compositions are not consistent with music performed at court. There were several branches of the Cornish family living in the west country, and John Cornish the composer was more likely from Winchester or Exeter than from London. It appears that the name John in the 1504 list of Gentlemen is an error for William, for in July of that year William wrote his *Treatise bitwene Trowth and enformacion* from the Fleete prison, and in the title refers to himself as 'Chapelman' to Henry VII.[39]

Until we have more biographical evidence about his early career, the most plausible argument is that William Cornish the composer and dramatist was born probably before 1474, and that he was probably Master of the Choristers at Westminster Abbey between 1479 and 1490–1. His career at court dates from at least September 1493, when he assumed a major role almost immediately in solo performances and disguisings, and, in 1501, devising pageants. He was in prison for an unknown offence in July 1504. He performed as a player with other members of the Chapel in 1508, and he was probably the driving force behind the Players of the Chapel from 1505 to 1512. He was appointed Master of the Children of the Chapel by 1509, and by 1517 he had transformed the Children into an acting company. He was responsible for devising revels at Henry VIII's court, probably as early as 1514 but certainly by 1516. He retired by the spring of 1523 and received a grant of the manor of Hylden, Kent, and, in addition to the one he owned at Malmsbury, a corrody at Thetford Priory. He died before 14 October 1524 and was survived by his wife and several children, among them a son named William.[40]

The Chapel Royal, the ancient choral organization of the royal household, was charged with keeping the Chapel and with singing at mass and at court ceremonies. In the early Tudor period it was composed of a dean, six chaplains, twenty clerks, from eight to ten children, and two yeomen, chosen from among the Children whose voices had changed. The adult members were called Gentlemen of the Chapel, one of whom received an appointment as Master of the Children and whose duty was to recruit, govern, and teach promising boy singers.[41] In addition to composing, arranging, and performing music and songs at mass, the Chapel gave musical performances before the court on feast days throughout the year, particularly during the Christmas season when the king had 'a songe bifore him in his hall or chambre vpon Alhallowin day at the latter graces by some of these Clerkes and Children of the Chappell in remembraunce of Christmasse and soe of men and children in Christemas throughout: But after the songe on Alhallowin day is done, the Steward and Threasurer of the houshold shalbe warnd where yt liketh the kinge to keepe his Christemas.'[42] The performance on 1 November in which the Children customarily sang *Audivi Vocem* formally began the planning for ceremonies and revels at Christmas, a practice which continued throughout the Tudor period. They were also rewarded for their St Nicholas Bishop ceremony on 6 December and sang *Gloria in Excelsis Deo* before the king on Christmas Day.[43] The Gentlemen gave a required performance on Twelfth Night. After the Steward's cry of 'Wassail!' the Gentlemen stood in the Hall and responded with a song.[44] There were other unspecified performances during Christmas for which the Gentlemen ordinarily received £13 6s. 8d. for their annual reward, except in 1501 when they received £10.[45] Both the Gentlemen and the Children also received rewards for special performances at court. Some of these were solo or small group performances, others were in court disguisings.

The earliest evidence of participation by members of the Chapel in a secular entertainment is from Twelfth Night 1494, when Cornish and others took part in the St George disguising. Eleven years later, on 11 January 1505, a group of the Gentlemen performed at court as the Players of the Chapel.[46] This newly-formed playing company probably owed its development to Cornish, who had received rewards for separate performances from 1493, and beginning in 1500 he had been rewarded for performances on the same dates as other members of the Chapel. On 13 March 1500, for example, Cornish was rewarded 40s. for a performance while the Gentlemen received 40s. On 13 January 1504, Cornish was rewarded 40s., John Sidborough 20s., and the Gentlemen received their traditional annual reward of £13 6s. 8d. While we do not know whether these performances were musical or dramatic, they provide suggestive evidence of collaboration. The players of the Chapel performed again on 10 January 1506, when they were described as a company of four; on 7 January 1508, when they were rewarded for a performance on Twelfth Night, their number, like the King's Players, had increased to five. After their first payment of 100s. in January 1505, their reward was raised to £6 13s. 4d. The payment of 53s. 4d. to 'diuerse of the Kinges Chapell' for playing before the king on Twelfth Night 1509 gives us a quasi-dramatic tradition of performances by Cornish and the Gentlemen from 1494, suggestive evidence of collaboration from 1500 to 1504, and an unbroken series of performances by an identifiable company from January 1505 until the end of the reign. The company was not patronized by the king in the same sense that the King's Players were. The Players of the Chapel did not receive annual wages and livery as players, but they were certainly encouraged.[47] They already were paid a variety of fees and wages as members of the Chapel, and they received handsome rewards for their performances.

Identifying the original members of the company is a matter of speculation. The 1508 Chamber payment gives us the names of two of its members: William Cornish and John Kyte. Kyte entered the Chapel before 1509, became sub-dean, and participated with Cornish in court revels until his appointment as Bishop of Armagh in 1513. Circumstantial evidence connects other members of the Chapel to the company. Other than Cornish, only four members of the Chapel were prominent enough to receive separate rewards for court performances. William Newark, Master of the Children, was rewarded for making a song in 1493, and on 31 December 1500 he was paid 53s. 4d. probably in connection with the Children's St Nicholas Bishop ceremony. It was during his Mastership that quasi-dramatic performances by the Children are first recorded. John Sidborough, who entered the Chapel before 1504 was rewarded with 20s. along with Cornish and the Gentlemen on 13 January 1504 for an unspecified performance, and again on 31 March 1504 for a song. It seems that these extra performances by members of the Chapel led to the development of an organized playing company at court, and the most likely candidates for the original four members are Cornish, Kyte, Sidborough, and Newark.

Members of the Chapel were free to take outside engagements when their services were not required at court. The Chapel sometimes sang mass, for example, before the annual dinner of the Fraternity of St Nicholas.[48] Cornish received a 10s. reward on St Edward's Day in 1523 for a performance with the adult choristers of Westminster Abbey, and on occasion he had lent garments to the Church-wardens of St Margaret's in Westminster, probably for performances by the parish choristers. John Sidborough was an active member of the parish of St Mary at Hill, Billingsgate, London. He signed the churchwardens' account for 1513–14, arbitrated a dispute between the parish and a bell founder with John Kyte's help in 1510, held voice trials for the appointment of a new lay clerk in 1513, and invited his colleagues in the Chapel to sing at St Mary's on numerous occasions.[49]

On 11 June 1510 the 'singers of the King's chapel' performed at St Mary's, after which they were entertained with food and wine at Sidborough's house. In 1511 members of the Chapel sang there twice. On the first occasion, Kyte and Cornish were entertained at a fish dinner in 'Mr. Aldermans place' after the per-formance, and on the second, Kyte and Henry Prents were feasted at Sidborough's house. Sidborough is last mentioned in the accounts of St Mary's on 14 January 1545, but the Chapel continued to perform there until 1554.[50] The evidence asso-ciates Kyte, Cornish, Sidborough, and Prents in some of the Chapel's extra-curricular activities. Assuming that Newark was one of the original members of the players in 1505, his death by 1509 would have necessitated a replacement. The most likely candidate is William Crane, who entered the Chapel before 1509 and who succeeded Cornish in 1523 as Master of the Children. Along with Cor-nish, Kyte, and 'Master Harry,' Crane performed in many of the revels early in Henry VIII's reign. There was a fifth member by 1508. This was probably Harry Prents, who entered the Chapel before 1509 and who was associated with Sid-borough in performances at St Mary's in 1511. He is the best candidate for the 'Master Harry' who begins to appear in court revels after Kyte's retirement to his Bishopric in 1513.[51]

Like the personnel of the King's Players, members of the Chapel were not pro-fessional actors. Their main duties were in the Chapel, and their playing company disbanded after each performance. But the Chapel was composed of talented musicians, composers, or singers in contrast to the bureaucrats and artisans that composed the King's Players. While they were not professional actors, they were all professional performers, and differences in education and talent must have shown up in their performances. Their background prepared them to provide the most desirable ingredient in court entertainments: variety. They were familiar with foreign languages; they could compose music, play and sing it; and could write scripts and design pageants. And it was probably the variety of their talents which was responsible for their eventual leading roles in court revels. The two acting companies were not competitors, however. They appear side by side in the court schedule of plays from 1505 until the Players of the Chapel were disbanded. Their last performance was on 2 June 1512 at Henry VIII's court, not coincidentally in conjunction with the last Burgundian-influenced tournament of the reign. A change in emphasis in all forms of spectacles and revels was effected between 1510 and 1515. The chief members of the Players of the Chapel and the King's Players found employment in the new order and continued to contribute to the development of court revels and entertainments throughout their careers. Cornish prepared scripts, composed songs, devised revels, designed pageants, wrote plays, and also produced court entertainments and spectacles. Gibson designed costumes and outfits for tournaments, revels, and plays, and supervised production. Even if they had not already done so, these two companies would earn a place in the annals of English theatre, for under Henry VII's patronage and encouragement they transformed the medium of the travelling player, giving his all with a few boards and a passion, into a form of court spectacle, one which was to leave an indelible mark on English drama and letters by the end of the century.

No text of a play presented at court survives from the early Tudor period, but several plays which were performed in great households suggest that some shared features in common with the disguisings. Some plays clearly were produced as complex entertainments. Dramatic dialogue was the principle component, but this was supplemented by the addition of other elements, such as music, dance, mumming, disguising, and morris dances. Sir Henry Guildford, for example, devised an 'interlude' which contained a morris dance for Twelfth Night 1514.[52] Medwall included a mummery in *Fulgens and Lucrece*.

Fulgens and Lucrece, a two-part drama meant to be performed at a banquet, is associated with Cardinal Morton's household.[53] Scholars have noted that *Lucrece* is a conventional play, and that Medwall may have been familiar with *Wisdom* and other plays of the same tradition, for dancing, disguising, and music are common to them.[54] The incorporation of music, dance, and a mumming allies part of the dramatic experience with that of the court disguising. At one point in part two, Publius Cornelius asks Lucrece if she would like to 'see a bace daunce after the guyse/ Of Spayne, whyle ye have no thyng to do?/ All thyng haue I purvaide that belongyth therto.'[55] When ordered to bring in the minstrels, B delivers his famous line of Flemish: '*Spele up tamboryne, ik bide owe frelike!*' which is followed by the stage direction: *Et deinde corisabunt*. The baas dance, which had emigrated from Spain to Burgundy by the late fifteenth century, and thence to England, distinguishes this stately manner of dancing as aristocratic.[56] The elegant baas dance, like the ones which were performed by members of the royal family at the conclusion of the pageant-disguising on 19 November 1501, marks a distinction between courtier and commoner. It is the kind of show we might expect from the patrician, Publius Cornelius. The elaborate costuming, also like that found in court disguisings, is peculiar enough to require a dramatic discussion. Lucrece asks

'Be these godely creatours?/ Were they of Englonde or of Wales?' B replies: 'Nay, they be wylde Irissh Portyngales/ That dyde all these pleasures.'[57] The mummery, with its costuming, music, and dance, is made by Medwall to serve the interests of character development and theme. Skelton's *Magnificence*, a play obviously written for an aristocratic audience but which we cannot certainly attach to the court, presents us with another example of the adaptation of music and dance. It has been dated between 1516 and 1523, but topical references and parallels indicate that the play probably refers to events at court ca. 1519.[58] *Magnificence* is an adaptation of the morality structure to a secular issue. It is a political allegory, the first known to satirize folly at court, in which the chief character, Magnificence, must work out a secular version of salvation, alternately tempted and counselled by court virtues and vices. Skelton includes not only quite a bit of humour but also costuming, music, and dance. One of the stage directions for Folly reads: *'Hic ingrediatur Foly, quatiendo crema et faciendo multum, feriendo tabulas et similia.'*[59] Folly plays on instruments before joining with Fancy in a poetic duet. Another stage direction, which brings in Courtly Abusyon, reads: *'Hic ingrediatur Courtly Abusyon cantando.'* After singing some of the Flemish song, *'Rutty bully ioly rutterkyn, heyda!',* Courtly Abusyon is asked by Cloaked Collusion, *'De que pas este vous? ... / Say vous chaunter Venter tre dawce?'*[60] Courtly Abusyon replies in French, *'Wyda, Wyda* [Oui, Oui].' Like Medwall's *Lucrece,* in which Publius Cornelius's mummery is both entertainment and a dramatic means of developing character and theme, Skelton's music and songs develop the characters of Cloaked Collusion and Courtly Abusion by showing that these courtiers were familiar with fashionable court tunes.

Not enough plays survive from the period to allow us to be overly confident in discussing their form or the manner of their presentation. But the elaborate costuming, music, song, and dance found in *Lucrece* and in *Magnificence* appear also in other plays. While it is clear that Medwall and Skelton took pains to ensure that the music, song, dance, or mummings reinforced the dramatic portions of their plays, they could be regarded as detachable. In the preface to his *Four Elements,* Rastell allows a disguising to be brought in 'yf ye lyst'[61] It is likely that many plays at court were staged without the variety of music, dance, song, and disguising. Nevertheless, variety was still considered an important ingredient in the court play as late as the early seventeenth century. Among the papers of the Duke of Northumberland are orders for the entertainments at court of the Muscovite ambassador and the Duke of Bracciano in 1600–1, in which it is noted: 'To Confer with my Lord Admirall and the *Master* of the Revells f[...] taeking order generally with the players to make choyse of [...] play that shalbe best furnished with rich apparell, have great [...] variety and change of Musicke and daunces [...] and of a Subi[...] that may be most pleasing to her maiestie.'[62] It appears

quite clear that during Henry VII's reign, some plays, like the disguising, had
attracted music, song, dance, and elaborate costuming, and developed into a
minor form of court spectacle.

Other than William Cornish, and possibly John English, the names of only two
dramatists surface from the period to whom we can attribute the several score of
plays produced at Henry VII's court: Henry Medwall and John Skelton. Medwall,
the first English playwright with whom we can associate play titles, was employed
in Cardinal Morton's household between 1491 and 1500.[63] John Bale had seen
only *Nature* but referred to it as one of many of Medwall's works, and Pitseus
laments the fact that the rest of his writing had disappeared.[64] If Collier is correct,
a morality by Medwall was performed by the King's Players at court in 1514, but
his only two surviving plays from Henry VII's reign were probably performed in
Morton's household, not in Henry VII's court.

John Skelton – priest, poet, laureate, translator, dramatist, satirist, tutor, royal
orator – who received employment at the courts of Henry VII and Henry VIII,
was the author of several interludes. In *The Garland of Laurel*, for example, Skelton mentions 'Of Vertu also the souerayne enterlude' and 'His commedy,
Archademios.' Both plays are lost Lost now as well is *The Nigramansir*, supposedly performed at court in 1504. Warton claims to have seen the text in the late
eighteenth century:

I cannot quit Skelton … without restoring to the public notice a play, or Morality, written by him, not recited in any catalogue of his works, or annals of English typography; and,
I believe, at present totally unknown to the antiquarians in this sort of literature. It is, *The*
Nigramansir, a *morall* Enterlude *and a pithie written by Maister* Skelton *laureate and plaid*
before the king and other estatys at Woodstoke on Palme Sunday. It was printed by Wynkin
de Worde in a thin quarto, in the year 1504. It must have been presented before king
Henry the seventh, at the royal manor or palace, at Woodstock in Oxfordshire, now
destroyed. The characters are a Necromancer, or conjurer, the devil, a notary public,
Simonie, and Philargyria, or Avarice. It is partly a satire on some abuses in the church; yet
not without due regard to decency, and an apparent respect for the dignity of the audience. The story, or plot, is the tryal of Simony and Avarice: the devil is the judge, and the
notary public acts as an assessor or scribe. The prisoners, as we may suppose, are found
guilty, and ordered into hell immediately. There is no sort of propriety in calling this play
the Necromancer: for the only business and use of this character, is to open the subject in
a long prologue, to evoke the devil, and summon the court. The devil kicks the necromancer, for waking him so soon in the morning: a proof, that this drama was performed
in the morning, perhaps in the chapel of the palace. A variety of measures, with shreds of
Latin and French, is used: but the devil speaks in the octave stanza. One of the stage-direc-
tions is, *Enter Balsebub with a Berde.* To make him both frightful and ridiculous, the devil

was most commonly introduced on the stage, wearing a vizard with an immense beard. Philargyria quotes Seneca and St Austin: and Simony offers the devil a bribe. The devil rejects her offer with much indignation: and swears by the *foule Eumenides*, and the hoary beard of Charon, that she shall be with Mahomet, Pontius Pilate, the traitor Judas, and king Herod. The last scene is closed with a view of hell, and a dance between the devil and the necromancer. The dance ended, the devil trips up the necromancer's heels, and disappears in fire and smoke.[65]

Skelton's *Magnificence* cannot be certainly attributed to the court, but an eight stanza poem in rhyme royal, 'a Lawde and prayse made for o*u*r Soureigne Lord the kynge,' survives among Gibson's Revels documents. The handwriting of the text may be Skelton's own, but the title which appears as an endorsement is not in the same hand. The subjects treated in the poem include the uniting of the white and red roses in Henry VIII, the legitimacy of his claim to the throne, the chaos of the fifteenth century and now the return of the age of Astrea, the promises made by Henry to redress wrongs committed by his father's ministers, particularly Empson and Dudley who were executed on 17 August 1510, and, finally, praise of a king who embodies the characteristics of Adonis, Priam, and Mars.

The circumstantial evidence of its inclusion among Gibson's papers suggests that *A Lawde* may have been recited before the king in one of his revels held early in the reign. The composition of the poem has been dated shortly after the coronation on 24 June 1509, but the topicality of its issues suggests that it could have been recited before the king as late as the end of 1510.[66] That Skelton did present plays and possibly revels both at Henry VII's and Henry VIII's courts seems likely, but without additional evidence it is difficult to assess the extent of his role.

While we know the names of many of the companies which performed plays at court and can guess who wrote a few of them, we do not know who scheduled or produced them. Selection and scheduling, which would later become the province of the Revels Office, was probably handled by the chief officers of the household and ultimately approved by the king. Production services would also later be handled by the Revels Office, but Wentworth's account does not mention plays and there are no payments to producers of plays in the Chamber accounts. The absence of such information suggests that they were produced by the companies themselves. Support services for lighting and other ordinary equipment were probably supplied initially by the Hall or Chamber staff. The many plays at court by the companies of the aristocracy and the towns were probably presented mainly with whatever costumes and properties they owned, although it is likely that some support was offered by the royal household. Given their status, the frequency of their appearances at court, and the known involvement of the chief members of these troupes in producing major revels at court, it is likely that the performances of the King's Players and the Players of the Chapel were given elaborate productions.

iii

Evidence from Henry VII's reign indicates that the production of court revels was decentralized. Final control over the scheduling of revels, over the appointment of supervisors, and even on occasion over the aesthetic details of particular productions was in the hands of the king and the council. They appointed supervisors for different projects – some to prepare ceremonies, some to prepare tournaments, some to prepare disguisings, and some to prepare the entertainments of the Lords of Misrule. The most important of all of these individuals, in terms of the production of revels at court, was the supervisor of the disguisings, for it was his duties which were shortly to be subdivided to create the beginnings of an organization. That these early supervisors did not exercise the duties of the later Masters of the Revels is clear from an examination of the evidence in relation to the statements made in 'The First Institution.'

The comment by the writer of 'The First Institution' that the early 'Masters of the Revels' were chosen for their 'creditte' has led to the assumption on the part of some modern scholars that they were selected from among high-ranking courtiers.[67] This was not the case at Henry VII's court. None of his supervisors had 'creditte' in the sense of status at court. They were all lower-level household officers: Sergeant of the Cellar, Surveyor of the Works, Yeoman Keeper of the Armoury, Clerk of the Ordnance, Esquire for the Body, and Gentleman Usher of the Privy Chamber. No doubt all were appointed because of their particular expertise, but in some cases the king clearly had other motives as well. His appointment of men within his Privy Chamber, for example, may be understood in terms of Bacon's observation that Henry VII kept his distance, 'which indeed he did towards all.' This observation has been taken by recent revisionist historians to be the hallmark of the king's style of government.[68] It was the means by which he insulated himself in his Privy Chamber to concentrate on personal management of the government. This was a king who made his household Chamber into the national treasury and who reviewed and signed the most important financial accounts himself. Henry insulated himself by appointing during pleasure men of lower social stature to posts in the household and government, by which means he suppressed faction in his court. Henry's appointments to produce revels and spectacles followed this pattern. None of his appointees were titled, and none wielded influence at court.

How much 'pleasaunte witte and habilitye in learninge,' as the writer of 'The First Institution' puts it, the early appointees had is a matter of speculation. Documentary evidence clearly shows that they oversaw the practical aspects of production. The often ambiguous wording of the Privy Seal writs and Chamber account entries does not convincingly demonstrate that they devised their own disguisings. Pudsey 'ordained' or 'prepared' disguisings; Alwyn, Peche, and Haulte were paid 'for' disguisings. 'Ordain,' 'prepare,' and 'for' are clearly ambiguous words which could easily refer only to production duties. More convincing are the payments to Lewis Adam and to Henry Wentworth who 'made' disguisings, and in 1500 the council commissioned Haulte to 'devise' disguisings. In contemporary documents the term 'advice' is most often used to describe aesthetic consultation, and the term used to describe an actual composition is 'made' – as in the 'pastym that master kornyche maad' for the 2 September 1519 revel. The term 'device' can refer to a developed artistic composition, but most often it refers to an aesthetic conception or design, the details of which were left to artists or writers hired on the project. At Candlemas 1557, for example, Robert Trunckwell was paid for 'woorking and framinge to dyuers patrons of Maskes devysed by the Master,' and in 1559 he was working on a model for a banqueting house according to the device given him by Sir Thomas Cawarden.[69] Trunckwell was an artist, working out the artistic details of designs given to him by the Master. However, such terminology in the early Tudor period was elastic, and it is probably best not to put an undue amount of pressure on the descriptions of services entered into financial accounts. More important evidence is the presence or absence of payments from one of the treasuries.

If someone other than the king's appointee devised or directed a disguising we would expect to find payment or reward among the Privy Seal writs or Chamber account entries. We find this in two instances. One example is afforded by the records of 1496 when Suffolk and Essex presented a disguising at court. The most important and well documented of these occasions is the wedding of Arthur and Katherine in 1501. Device, artistic direction, and production duties were parcelled out among several individuals. Unless some special purpose of the king or council was to be served, it was probably ordinary procedure for the king's appointees to provide the device and the artistic direction for their revels. The fact that Wentworth carried his costumes and properties to Richmond indicates that he had charge of artistic direction subject to the king's approval. It is clear from the records of the 1501 and 1508 entertainments that the sovereign and council had ultimate control. This continued into Henry VIII's reign. The king often gave specific directions to Richard Gibson about the kind of costumes or revels he wanted, and on occasion, as his father had done in 1508, personally reviewed and approved them.

The writer of 'The First Institution' refers to a two-part division of duties between a temporarily appointed 'Master' and 'the Princes Tayler havinge the

oversight of the workmanshippe [who] brought in the Bill of charge*s.'*[70] The writer imagines the situation that existed at Henry VIII's court in which a high-ranking courtier who was acquainted with the king's preferences for revels had the
assistance of a yeoman-level deputy who handled the practical aspects of production. This was a centralized organization in which the production for all revels and spectacles – pageants, properties, and costumes for tournaments, plays,
disguisings, and masks – was handled by the deputy under the supervision of a
Master who also coordinated other entertainments at court. It was an organization much more nearly like the Revels Office which was created around mid-century. The records indicate that no such formal division of duties existed in Henry
VII's reign. Wentworth's account shows that he contracted the services of artists,
tailors, and artisans, drew on the resources of the household and bought other
material himself only for the pageant-disguisings. He did not have the services of
an inferior officer at his disposal for production duties. Rather he employed a servant to help with production, but he took care of many details himself.

    While Richard Gibson referred to Henry Wentworth as *Master of the Revels* in
his 1510 Revels account – the first confirmed use of the title in the Tudor period
– the title does not appear in Wentworth's own Revels account nor in any other
document from the period. Gibson was probably employing one of the grand
titles fashionable at Henry VIII's court when the Master of the Revels devised or
oversaw the device of the revels, drew on the services of a deputy for production,
and arranged or helped to arrange the schedule of revels at court. While Wentworth and his predecessors did devise and supervise the production of disguisings,
they did not exercise all of the duties later associated with the Masters.

    Wentworth's account also confirms that cooperation practised among the var-
ious offices of the household continued throughout the reign. As early as 1485–6,
Piers Curteis, Keeper of the Great Wardrobe, procured material for the coronation, the wedding, and the Christmas revels. And as late as 1508–9 Wentworth
drew on the resources of the Wardrobe – without paying for it – to furnish his
revels. Provisioning ceremonies and state occasions was an ordinary obligation of
the Great Wardrobe, and earlier in the Middle Ages it had been used to furnish
material for the revels. The relationship was so close that it has been suspected,
on circumstantial evidence, that the Wardrobe provided a home for the production of revels in Henry VII's reign.[71] Richard Gibson was Yeoman Tailor of the
Wardrobe. But he was probably the chief producer of plays by the King's Players
because of his involvement in the company, not because he held an official position in the Wardrobe. The Wardrobe certainly supplied material for disguisings,
and in 1509 Sir Andrew Windsor acted as paymaster for Wentworth's disguisings.
Such a procedure was not unique. The Wardrobe was used on at least one occasion to pay the bills even of an ancient office like the Works at a change of reigns.

This was no doubt the reason for the payment to Windsor, but the Wardrobe did not provide an ongoing administrative structure for the production of revels in Henry VII's reign. The producers of revels ordinarily received their imprests and payments on their bills directly from the Chamber. These instances of collaboration between a Keeper of the Wardrobe and a producer of the revels in Henry VII's reign were predecessors of the close relationship between these offices which was to persist throughout the Tudor and early Stuart periods. The Great Wardrobe continued to provide material for the revels by warrant from the sovereigns until the early seventeenth century.

Providing support services for court functions was one of the standard duties of the Works. Clear evidence of support by the Works for spectacles and revels surfaces in the early 1490s. Richard Doland, Clerk of the Works, built the lists at Shene for the tournament supervised by Sir Richard Guildford in May 1492, and he also built the scaffolds in Westminster Hall for Alwyn's disguising at Twelfth Night 1494. Later in the period there is certain evidence of the regular contribution of services by the Works for revels. It was not until the mid 1570s that the Revels Office began to be charged for material from the Wardrobe; they were never charged for services by the Works. The amount of money issued to the early supervisors by Privy Seal, or to later appointees from the Chamber, does not provide certain evidence of the total cost of revels productions. It is likely that these early supervisors, like those later in the period, ordinarily had help from the Wardrobe and the Works. The renewal of Pudsey's, Hault's, and Wentworth's appointments over a number of years was obviously a factor in establishing a working relationship among household departments for the production of revels.

Wentworth's account shows that the procedures for organizing and coordinating a work force capable of producing complicated entertainments had evolved by the end of Henry's reign and that a small storehouse for revels properties had been created. While many of the procedures had been established, the production of revels was not formally organized. The various supervisors held positions in the household. Their appointment was an extra duty, and after rendering their accounts they went back to their ordinary posts. For the next series of revels and spectacles the court went through the same cumbersome procedure. The king or council appointed supervisors, ordered them to devise and prepare tournaments, spectacles, and disguisings, and set in motion the complicated paperwork necessary to issue imprests from the Exchequer or from the Chamber to begin the work. Despite the clumsiness of the appointment procedure, the king tended to appoint the same individual for a period of years. Pudsey produced the disguisings from 1485 to 1491, Haulte from 1494 to 1501, and Wentworth from 1507 to 1510. Such renewals of appointment must have had the effect of imposing certain styles on the disguisings in particular periods of the reign. This is suggested by Haulte's replacement in 1501 which coincided with the Burgundian-influenced revels for Arthur's wedding, and by Wentworth's replacement in 1510 which coincided with the beginnings of a change in the style of revels at Henry VIII's court.

3

The Master and His Deputy, 1510–1515

At the beginning of the new reign, a number of changes transformed Henry VII's arrangement for producing revels into a semi-formal organization. The change in production arrangements is associated with the beginnings of a change in style. Henry VII's distinctive spectacles and revels were modified by 1515 to reflect the personality, government, and court of the new king. Tournaments began to be held without pageants and the participants to appear as themselves rather than as characters from romance. New forms and other modifications were introduced in the revels emphasizing participation by the king, his friends, and guests. Plays, so prevalent at Henry VII's court, were scheduled less frequently. A centralized organization was created to produce both revels and spectacles in which supervision and production functions were separated, the one placed in charge of a high-level courtier who was personally close to the king and the other placed in charge of a yeoman-level deputy. Henry Wentworth continued his involvement in the production of revels until he retired, or perhaps was retired, in November 1510. Plans for reorganization were being made as early as January of that year when some of Wentworth's practical and administrative duties were being taken over by Richard Gibson and some of his aesthetic control by the king's personal friends.

We do not know who supervised the preparations for Henry VIII's coronation festivities, but duties in connection with them fell to several officers. Imprests were issued in May 1509, and payments for left-over bills were made from the Chamber in July and September, the bulk of which, totalling some £5,332, were paid by Sir Andrew Windsor, Keeper of the Great Wardrobe. He would normally have supplied much of the material for the ceremonies, just as his predecessor, Piers Curteis, had done for Henry VII's coronation. Windsor paid the bills for some of the revels as well.[1] The payment on 2 September 1509 for the disguisings before the Flemish ambassadors the previous Christmas indicates that Windsor was acting as paymaster for left-over revels bills from the previous reign, and it is probable that the expenses of the coronation tournament and pageants were also handled on his account.[2]

While we have no evidence of revels for the coronation in June 1509, the tournament held at Westminster exhibits all of the characteristics of those produced since 1501, with the addition of a preliminary exhibition, suggesting that any revels would also have been heavily indebted to those produced at Henry VII's court. The tilt gallery was decorated to resemble a castle, complete with towers and with a crown atop the roof. Its walls, on which the shields of the combatants were hung, were decorated with royal badges and a vine, 'the leaues and grapes thereof, gilded with fine Golde,' amid which fountains of red, white, and claret wine spouted from gargoyles.[3] The exhibition began when trumpets announced the entry of young gentlemen 'gorgeously appareled' who demonstrated feats of horsemanship. Following this, a pageant, resembling a castle or turret of cloth of gold, covered with roses and pomegranates, within which was the Lady Pallas holding a crystal shield, was carried in by the 'strength of menne.' Followed in procession by the challengers, accompanied by one hundred attendants clothed in velvet with hose and bonnets to match, the pageant was paraded about the lists and taken before the royal gallery where Pallas introduced the challengers as her 'scholers.' The answerers entered the lists preceded by about sixty mounted gentlemen, drummers, fifers, and footmen clothed in velvet and silk, led by a mounted gentleman carrying a golden spear which he presented to the queen, explaining that his knights had come to do feats of arms for the love of ladies. He offered to wager the golden spear against Pallas's crystal shield on the outcome of the event.

On the second day of the tournament there was a tourney with swords on horseback. Pallas's scholars entered in garments of white and green velvet embroidered with gold roses and pomegranates. On their helmets were wings of 'flatte Golde of Damaske.' The answerers entered with horse bards and bases of green satin embroidered with bramble branches of gold, followed by a group of men dressed as foresters. A pageant, like a forest with bushes, ferns, trees, and deer, enclosed with a white and green fence, was brought before the queen. The deer were flushed out, pursued and killed by greyhounds, and then presented to the queen and her ladies.[4] The gentleman who had carried the spear on the previous day explained to the queen that his knights were servants of Diana who had heard about Pallas's knights while they were hunting, and intended to do combat 'for the loue of ladies to thutterance.' The queen sent to the king for advice, who himself got into the dramatic spectacle by observing that since a grudge existed between the two parties he would not allow an open combat but a tourney in which the number of strokes would be limited to twelve.[5]

While many of the features of the coronation tournament are familiar from practices at Henry VII's court and while more like it were to be produced, an indication of change is signalled on 12 January 1510 when the king made his first of many personal appearances in the lists. He and his close friend, William Compton, went in disguise, 'vnknowen to all persones, and vnloked for,' to a joust held at Richmond.[6] The contest was apparently running *volant*, without lists, and when Compton was almost killed by Sir Edward Neville the king had to reveal himself to assure spectators that he was not injured. This was not a formal court spectacle, but it is the first evidence of the king's intense interest and personal participation in the martial exhibitions. Despite several close calls, Henry appeared as chief challenger or as answerer in virtually every major tournament and other martial exhibition until 1527. Even allowing for the excessive praise of a chronicler like Hall, it is clear that Henry was a talented athlete whose performances in the lists regularly impressed foreign ambassadors. The king's participation lent the kind of drama which was to mark his tournaments with a personal style.

A similar change was signalled indoors. The king surprised Katherine by appearing unannounced in her Chamber at Westminster with ten of his companions dressed as Robin Hood's men and a woman as Maid Marian, 'whereof the Quene, the Ladies, and al other there, were abashed, aswell for the straunge sight, as also for their sodain commyng, and after certain daunces, and pastime made, thei departed.'[7] Like the tournament Henry took part in eight days earlier, this was not a formal occasion. But Henry's personal participation lent a similar kind of drama to this disguising, marked it with a personal style, and transformed its effect. As is clear from Hall's account, the surprise at the king's presence and his breach of ordinary decorum made the spectators into participants: the queen and her ladies were 'abashed' at the 'straunge sight' and at the 'sodain commyng.' This informal entertainment, the first recorded in Gibson's account for the year, also signals a change in the supervision of revels. It was organized by one of the king's friends, Edward Guildford, Master of the Armoury, who performed as one of the merry men. Guildford issued material for the disguising to Richard Gibson who made the costumes. Guildford himself probably supplied the bows, arrows, and staves from the Armoury. There is no record of payment for Guildford's services, though Gibson included his own costs in the first Revels account that he later filed.

Henry Wentworth was still, at least nominally, in charge of the production of revels, but even before he retired, the king and his friends – with a little help from Gibson – were devising and producing revels on their own. The deviser and supervisor of the great revel held in this season, the Shrove Sunday [28 February] mummery and disguising in the Parliament Chamber at Westminster was the Earl of Essex, supported in part by production assistance from Gibson and Wentworth.[8] Essex was Henry VIII's cousin and one of his high-ranking courtiers. He was a

participant in many other ceremonies and martial exhibitions at Henry VII's court
and participated in virtually all of the revels in the early years of Henry VIII's the
reign.[9] The presentation of a formal revel by courtiers was not new. Essex, Suffolk, and others of the nobility presented one in 1496, although we do know
whether they performed in it. This 1496 disguising was unique at Henry VII's
court, but there were to be quite a few such instances at Henry VIII's court.
Essex's revel began at a banquet from which the king departed and then returned
in a disguising, Henry and Essex costumed as Turks and their companions as Russians and Prussians, led by torchbearers disguised 'lyke Moreskoes, their faces
blacke.' The king then 'brought in a mommerye' in which the court was invited
to participate before the mummers departed to change costumes for the dance.[10]
After Henry began the general dancing, he departed again only to return in a second disguising, which included dances by six disguised gentlemen and six ladies
– including Henry's sister, Mary, and her companions dressed as 'nygrost or blacke
Mores.' Gibson made some of the costumes and supplied a few of the properties,
but it is clear from his account that he did not have full knowledge of the details.
He notes that the revel was 'made by the Advyse of the erll of essex & so ouersene
& stondys At the Accownte by hym' and his servant, John Smith. Wentworth supplied a few costumes from the king's store and collected those made by Gibson
afterwards: 'all Abyllmentes [were] dellyured to the erll of essex & master harry
Wentworth then master of the Revylls.'[11]

    In March, the king received ambassadors from Aragon and Castile, whom he
entertained on the 17th with running at the ring.[12] There is no mention of Wentworth's participation, but Gibson made the gold embroidered base and demi-trap-
per for the king's horse, set with 1,150 gold badges in the form of sheaves of
arrows and castles, some of which were given as gifts to the ambassadors. This is
the first instance in which it becomes clear that the king intended to centralize
the design and production of costumes for both the tournaments and the revels
under the supervision of a single individual. Support services for the martial exhibitions were later to become a standing duty of the Revels Office and was continued well into the seventeenth century.

    On 8 November 1510 the king removed to Richmond and issued a challenge
that he and his friends, Charles Brandon and William Compton, would answer
all comers in a joust to be held on the 13th and a tourney with swords on the
14th to entertain the imperial ambassadors.[13] Revels were held to conclude this
tournament. On the night of the 14th, after a banquet, guests were ushered into
the queen's Chamber, where the revels were to be held. Fifteen gentlemen disguised as 'Alamains,' including the king, 'came in with a mommery, and after a
certayne tyme that they had played with the Quene and the straungers, they
departed.'[14] Six minstrels entered playing instruments followed by thirteen gen-

tlemen in 'Alamain' costumes bearing torches. Finally, six gentlemen entered in outfits of white and green satin of 'a straunge facion' set with castles of gold, and six ladies costumed in Spanish garments of crimson satin. After dancing, they removed their visors to reveal that the six disguised gentlemen were Essex, Henry Guildford, Charles Brandon, Sir Edward Howard, Sir Thomas Knyvet, and the king himself, most of whom had participated in the tournament on 13–14 November. In its structure and surprises, this revel resembles the one devised by Essex for Shrove Sunday earlier in the year.

Both the revel of 28 February and that of 14 November 1510 incorporated a 'mummery' along with disguisings. Given the wording of the narratives, it appears that the game of 'mumchance' is meant, a pastime in which mummers silently play at dice with some of the guests. The main innovations were the king's active participation and the surprise revelation that some of the performers were members of the royal family and others participants in the tournament. The elements of breaching ordinary decorum, concealed identity, and surprise, first evident in the informal Robin Hood disguising, are here incorporated into formal court revels. But these innovations are not without point. The subjects of the revels were specifically chosen to complement diplomacy. Essex's revel used a double disguising of Turks, Russians, Prussians, and Moors to entertain ambassadors 'out of diuerse realmes and countreis.' The November revel for the imperial ambassadors provided 'Alamains' surrounding principal disguisers in Henry's colours dancing with ladies in Spanish garments, suggesting amity among England, Spain, and the Empire. Like the revels at his father's court, the interests of prestige diplomacy were being served, but the manner of their presentation, emphasizing participation by the king and his friends, personalized diplomacy in a manner calculated to overwhelm.

The 1511 Twelfth Night revel was devised by another of the king's friends, Sir Henry Guildford.[15] It was a pageant-disguising which was conceived as a spectacle. The pageant, the first of the reign to be used indoors, was a 'mountayne, glisteringe by night, as though it had bene all of golde and set with stones' atop of which was a golden tree with roses and pomegranates, the emblems of England and Spain. It was constructed by Gibson in London and transported to Richmond by barge. This provides the earliest evidence that in addition to designing and producing costumes Gibson was supervising the construction of pageants. Gibson notes that concealed within the pageant were the king's young gentlemen 'as hynsmen,' disguised as knights in green, white, and black, and 'a ladye, appareiled in cloth of golde.'[16] They came out of the pageant 'and daunced a Morice,' after which the pageant, which was drawn 'with vyces,' was removed from the Hall to make way for the banquet. Gibson had ordered bells to teach them the dance steps. Guildford's employment of an indoor pageant of the kind in use since at least as early as 1501 was to be repeated in many of the revels up to 1517 and thereafter on occasion throughout the reign. The production must have been successful, for Guildford was to become styled 'Master of the Revels,' a title which signals a change in conception of the supervision and production of revels at court.

i

Henry Guildford, son of Sir Richard Guildford (d.1506) – Master of the Armoury, Comptroller of the Household, and half-brother of Edward Guildford, also Master of the Armoury – was twenty years old at the accession of Henry VIII and one of the king's close, personal friends who rose rapidly in public service. He was an Esquire for the Body, a position he continued to hold even after he was knighted by King Ferdinand on 15 September 1511. Henry knighted him also on 30 March 1512.[17] He was the king's Standard Bearer from 28 May 1513, Master of the Horse on 6 November 1515, and Comptroller of the Household by 1522.[18] He was a member of the council who participated in the negotiations and signed most of the treaties of the reign. While he was not particularly active in the lists, he did sign the articles of challenge for the second day of the tourney on 13 February 1511, and he supervised the jousts at Greenwich in the summer of 1517 when his half-brother, Sir Edward Guildford, was Marshall.[19]

Guildford participated in many of the revels at Henry's court during the first eighteen years of the reign, and certainly was the most distinguished public figure ever to hold the Mastership of the Revels on a regular basis. His appointment not only elevated the status of revels at court, but was also an important practical innovation. As a personal friend of the king's, he could participate not only in planning revels but also in the informal discussions about them and would know at first-hand the sometimes changing aims and preferences of the king and council. He could also more easily coordinate his revels with other court activities. His constant association with officers at high levels of administration in the household and in the government provided an appropriate complement to Gibson's coordination of business at a more practical level, and integrated the production of revels into the structure of the household in a way that it had never been at Henry VII's court. No patent has been discovered for Guildford's appointment as Master of the Revels. It was probably an informal title, but in view of the fact that we can document his supervision of revels from as early as January 1511 and as late as November 1527, he was de facto Master.

Guildford's title was not ceremonial, nor was his supervision, early on, relegated to high-level administration. He is credited with devising or supervising most of the major entertainments from 1511 to 1517, in 1522, and in 1527. He signed

Revels and other accounts relating to them, and was paid on occasion for his personal attendance on business related to the production of revels. Further, there is evidence to show that his duties extended beyond the production of disguisings and masks. He was in charge of the construction of the banqueting house at Greenwich in 1527, and in a letter from Brussels on 4 February 1516, Knight wrote to Wolsey that Guildford had sent letters to Hans Nagel, the actor, to come to England with his company to play before the king at Christmas. Agreement was apparently never reached, for there is no record that he performed at court.[20] The document provides the first evidence of a Master of the Revels functioning in a manner the title implies. Guildford was not assigned to produce certain disguisings, as Wentworth and his predecessors were, but was responsible, as the later Masters were, for arranging a more diverse schedule of entertainments than Gibson's surviving Revels accounts or any of the narratives document. Guildford's entertainments contributed in no small way to the international reputation for magnificence that the English court achieved. Reports from the foreign ambassadors who witnessed Guildford's productions are hyperbolic in their enthusiasm, and Erasmus sent two letters to Guildford in 1519 praising the English court.[21]

Guildford was to have as his deputy the man who had been actively helping to produce revels and tournaments from at least January 1510. From the time his name shows up in the Revels accounts in 1510 until his death in 1534 Richard Gibson was actively involved in the production of every major tournament and revel at court of which we have record. What qualities recommended him to this position can be documented only in part. Gibson was one of the original King's Players, and he still held a position with the troupe in 1509 when he marched in Henry VII's funeral.[22] Earlier in the reign he had received two grants during pleasure, one on 22 January 1501 of the office of Yeoman Tailor of the Great Wardrobe (succeeding Christopher Sandis, who had held the post from 30 December 1485), and another on 22 May 1504 of the office of Porter of the Great Wardrobe (after the death of Thomas Swanne, with wages of 4d. a day from the Exchequer); both of these grants were renewed by Henry VIII on 6 June 1510.[23] Gibson acquired other offices and perquisites later in the reign. A life annuity of £3 18s. 4d. was granted him in 1516 in addition to one he held from Henry VII, and another for £10 was granted on 18 May 1517.[24] By 1526 he had become a royal Sergeant at Arms, and in that year he was named one of the commissioners of sewers from East Greenwich to Gravesend. He also served on the commission appointed on 3 December 1528 to investigate the number of foreign artificers within two miles of the city of London, and in the parliament held at Blackfriars on 3 November 1529, he was named as one of the burgesses for Romney, one of the Cinque Ports.[25]

Gibson's position as tailor in the Great Wardrobe is not in itself sufficient to explain the fact that he began to make Henry VIII's jousting outfits and began to support the production of revels by January 1510. In order to have gained the king's confidence this early in the reign, Gibson must have acquired experience in costume design and production during his career with the King's Players at Henry VII's court. Wentworth, whom Gibson calls Master of the Revels in his account, was not the person to whom directions were given for the tournament and revel of 13–14 November 1510. Rather, Gibson was summoned into the king's presence on 8 November where he was given directions and was issued material and jewels by William Compton and the Yeoman of the Robes. While Wentworth was 'Master,' his participation was limited to providing garments from the store, and from the fact that three yards of crimson satin used in making the 'Alamains' costumes for the disguising were given to him 'by *the* kyng*es* gyvft,' we may conclude that he may have played one of these parts in a farewell appearance.[26] On the following day he retired. On 15 November 1510, Gibson notes that he had taken charge of 'ye kyng*es* stoor ye ij*d* yer,' and acknowledged receipt of two war chests and a standard formerly in Wentworth's charge, containing revels properties and garments.[27] Gibson appended the first surviving inventory of properties to his account for this year, something done later in the period only at a change of administration or at the beginning of a new reign. Part of the material was kept for the revels and part given to the King's Players, the first evidence from the reign of material support for a royal company.[28]

Gibson continued his duties as mid-level supervisor in costume design and in the production of revels and tournaments. His authorization to do so probably came from renewed word-of-mouth appointments until the first Anglo-French War of 1512–14. The war in France had a significant effect on the subsequent administration and organization for the production of revels, for during its course production duties became attached to a permanent household department. At the opening of the reign, Gibson received his instructions and his material from high-ranking courtiers. Within a year he was receiving material and instructions in the presence of the king or ordering material himself from the Wardrobe. Early on, his accounts were declared for him, but by 1 June 1512 Gibson was receiving direct payments from the Chamber.[29] This recognition by the king, his receipt of payment from the Chamber and material from the Wardrobe, and his charge of the storehouse containing properties for the revels all put an official stamp on his position as 'deputy' to the Master of the Revels. It remained only to find a place in the household for the developing organization.

By February 1513, Gibson became 'deputy' to the Sergeant of the Tents. The methods used to construct and to maintain the equipment for the Tents were similar to those used to construct pageants and to maintain revels costumes, as were the procedures for contracting the services of artists and artisans and for airing, repairing, and storing material. Perhaps as important, the period during which the workload was heaviest was reversed. Except when the army was in the field – and it was usually not in winter – the Tents were busiest in the spring, summer, and early fall. While there are exceptions, revels were produced mainly from December through February or March. Attaching the production of revels to the Tents was an intelligent administrative innovation. A permanent officer with the proper background could handle both offices, eliminating the need for separate appointments and the inefficiency that inevitably resulted from the need to coordinate services. Gibson was just such a man. His offices in the Great Wardrobe, his fifteen years of acting experience with the King's Players, his experience in costume design, and his obvious accounting skills, made him an ideal choice.

Gibson filed an account in October 1513 as 'deputy' to Sir Christopher Garnesche, 'Sergeant of the Tents,' and he is styled 'Yeoman' in a book of payments dated 29 October of that year.[30] He is also called 'Yeoman' by Hall, who narrates a French attack on the English tents at Newnam bridge, outside of Calais, in early July 1513.[31] English archers fended off the attack which roused such a commotion that the alarm was sounded. Henry, who was in the city, came to the walls, and Gibson explained to him what had happened. The title 'Yeoman' had only recently come into use in the Tents. Thomas Walshe and William Tournell, Sergeants of the Tents in Henry VII's reign, were granted 4*d.* a day under the terms of their patents for a boy or garçon to mend the tents. In other documents he is called 'Groom' and, on one occasion, 'Yeoman.'[32] This was the only other permanent staff position in the office, though it was not granted by patent. Other labour was done by contract, or by impressing workmen during wartime. Tournell's successor, John Morton, only had the assistance of a Groom. The change in structure is associated with the appearance of Garnesche, who did not hold a formal patent to the office. He was no doubt acting as wartime Sergeant in France, for Morton did not surrender his patent as Sergeant until 1518 when Gibson, who got into the organization as wartime Yeoman, succeeded him.[33] Gibson's duties in the Tents occasionally kept him working between London and Calais. He had a house there as early as 1512, no doubt to use as headquarters for the Tents. His account for 1514 shows that he had rented a house from Sir Richard Whettehill, which he maintained for at least five years.[34] Whether he kept this particular house or rented a new one by 1532 is not clear, but he is listed as one of the inhabitants demanding expenses for the French king's train in that year at Henry's meeting with Francis I.[35]

The appointment of a Yeoman as a mid-level supervisor who functioned as deputy to the Sergeant of the Tents as well as to the Master of the Revels was a key step in reorganizing these compatible functions and led to their formal combination in 1545. While the Tents and production of revels were functionally and administratively compatible, their status at court was different. The Sergeant of the Tents was not a courtier. It was only during the 1512–14 war that a person of Garnesche's stature was temporarily appointed to the office. Revels, on the other hand, ordinarily reflected – in fact, helped to create – the king's image, and Henry was anxious to exploit revels for this purpose. The thrust of the changes initiated at the opening of the reign was precisely to elevate the status of revels by appointing a Master who attended on the king and sat on the council and to relegate production duties to a household office.

Gibson ordinarily received his instructions from the king or from Guildford, his issue of material from one of the wardrobes by the king's warrant, and his imprests from the Chamber. All of the practical aspects of production were under his supervision. He rented houses large enough to serve as workshops, contracted the services of the Works and other household departments, hired artists and artisans to fabricate costumes, pageants, and properties, arranged for transportation, attended the productions, cleaned, stored, and cared for the inventory; kept records; and filed the most descriptive series of accounts to have survived from the early Tudor period. He was responsible for making the jousting apparel for the king and his companions, the trappers and bards for their horses, and the pageants for martial exhibitions. He also decorated banqueting houses, made costumes and properties for certain plays performed before the king, and, of course, supervised the construction of all of the pageants, costumes, and properties for the revels. His position in the Tents made him responsible for housing the army in the field, for setting up pavilions for tournaments, receptions, and conferences, and for helping to construct banqueting houses.

ii

In one of his rare appearances in the lists, Sir Henry Guildford answered the challenge in the tournament held at Westminster on 12–13 February 1511 to celebrate the birth of Prince Henry. As Master of the Armoury, Edward Guildford probably oversaw many of the preparations, and Gibson produced the main pageant as well as the outfits of the king and his companions. This, one of the greatest spectacles of the early part of the reign, drew on devices familiar from Henry VII's tournaments and from the coronation tournament. Burgundian-style fictional challenges, allegorical impersonation, and pageant-car entries were employed.[36] The challengers, all with allegorical names – 'Couer Loyal' (Henry), 'Valiant Desire' (Sir Thomas Kynvet), 'Bon Voloire' (Sir William Courtenay), and 'Joyous Panser' (Sir Edward Neville) – entered the lists in elaborate outfits by Gibson and within a 26' x 16' x 9' pageant which had also been constructed by Gibson at Blackfriars.[37] It was made to resemble a forest with trees of various kinds inhabited by birds and animals, presided over by foresters with horns and bows. In its midst was a castle made of gold paper in which was a lady making a garland for the prince. The pageant, mounted on wheels, was drawn into the lists by a gold lion and a silver antelope upon which were mounted ladies clad in russet and blue damask and led by four wild men, costumed in shredded material to resemble hair or wool. When the pageant was brought before the queen, the foresters blew their horns and the challengers rode out fully armed to deliver small shields to the heralds.

On the following day the challengers entered singly, preceded by trumpets, heralds, and gentlemen. The knights were enclosed within portable pavilions, made by Gibson, of the type familiar in Henry VII's reign, the king's surmounted by a crown and the others by golden balls. The narratives do not describe the pageants used by the answerers on the first day of the tournament, and list only five of the thirteen used on the second day. Two examples will suffice. Sir Henry Guildford entered within a pageant castle of russet sarcenet set with his posy in gold letters, and Charles Brandon entered within a tower, led by a jailor with a key in his hand who unlocked the gate of the pageant before the queen. Brandon rode out disguised in a long habit of a religious person with a pilgrim's hat and staff. His face was hidden by a flowing beard which came down as far as his saddle. A pair of golden beads adorned the hook of his staff, and a letter, requesting the queen's permission to enter the tournament, was attached to its tip. When the queen granted permission, Brandon cast off his disguise to reveal his armour.[38] This tournament, in which the king won the prize as challenger by breaking twelve lances and scoring nine attaints on the body and one on the head in twenty-eight courses, is described by the writer of *The Great Chronicle* as the most excellent joust ever seen in England, principally because of the splendour of the pageants, and 'the excellency/ of the kyngis persoon, which nevyr beffore that day as I thynk was seen In propyr persoon.'[39]

This was one of the last great spectacles which employed massive pageants in the tilt-yard. Only a few more were produced, and by 1515 they were virtually abandoned. In April 1511, Henry issued a challenge for a joust to be held at Greenwich during the first three days of May. Like those late in Henry VII's reign, it was organized around a literary device and employed costuming. On 1 May the king and his companions went off into the woods to 'fetch May.' On their return they encountered a ship pageant with full rigging and sails.[40] In the course of the dialogue between the king and the ship's master, it was established that the ship was called 'Fame' and its cargo was 'Renoune.' Henry and his companions bought the cargo and undertook to defend it against pirates. After a peal of artillery fire, the ship sailed before the knights into the tilt-yard. In the joust, which began in the afternoon and continued for the next two days, Henry and his companions defended the cargo in the lists against those who sought to 'medle' with the merchandise. The last joust held before the outbreak of war with France and the last to employ pageant entries into the lists was held at Greenwich on 1 June 1512.[41] Four ladies costumed in white and red silk, riding on horses trapped with the same material fretted with gold, entered the lists before a pageant. The pageant was a fountain decorated with russet satin and set with eight gargoyles spouting water, in the midst of which sat the king in full armour. Following this came a lady clad in black silk set with silver drops riding a horse trapped in the same material. A horse litter followed, in which Charles Brandon was carried in full armour. After the entry the king and Brandon took their positions in the lists to await all comers. The answerers made their entries to the sound of trumpets, but Hall describes only Sir Thomas Knyvet's black pageant, called 'the dolorous Castle.' Richard Gibson prepared most of the garments for this tournament, and at least the king's pageant, which was broken and returned to the storehouse.

The change in style of tournaments is associated with events in the 1512–14 war. The war transformed Henry from a talented and promising athlete into a successful warrior. Gibson's pavilions, which had dazzled spectators at the Westminster tournament in February 1511 were altered to serve at Calais and Therouanne during the war.[42] Henry's entries into Calais, Therouanne, Lille, and Tournai in 1513 were not imaginative games but ceremonies celebrating real victories. His appearances in the lists afterwards were seldom in the guise of figures such as 'Couer Loyal' from the landscape of the imagination, but as he now regarded himself, and as he was regarded abroad, the warrior Prince of England. This is the image Henry continued to enhance until his retirement from the lists after 1527. The new style is first observable in the king's tournament and revels held in France in 1513.

Henry was in France from late June until 22 October 1513. In September, the king received an invitation from Charles, Prince of Castile, and his governess, Margaret, Duchess of Savoy, to attend a reception and entertainment at Lille. Henry accepted and entered the city attended by Buckingham, Dorset, Essex, Lisle, 'the Master of hys horse Sir Henry Guylforde and the hensmen,' and others. The king's apparel and bard were 'cloth of syluer of small quadrant cuttes trauersed and edged with cutt cloth of golde, and the border set full of redde roses, his armore freshe and set full of iuels.'[43] Henry was given the keys to the town before he was received by the Emperor and a number of nobles from Flanders, Brabant, Holland, and Hainault. Three days were spent at Lille, from 18 to 20 September, and 'great was the chere with bankettes, playes, commodies, maskes and other pastymes that was shewed the king in the courte of Burgoyne.' In return for the hospitality shown to him at Lille, Henry invited Margaret of Savoy, the Prince of Castile, and various ambassadors to Tournai on 18 October. The tournament was prepared by Sir Edward Guildford, and the king and Lord Lisle, who appeared as chief challengers, significantly impressed all who saw them perform.[44] Gibson, who was in France during this period as Yeoman of the Tents, was issued green velvet and cloth of silver from the king himself in the Staple Chamber at Calais, probably to be made into Henry's outfit for the jousts. The bases and trappers of purple velet for the king's and Lisle's horses were set with *S.S.* in fine gold bullion. He apparelled the king's twenty-five attendants in purple velvet and cloth of gold and made a tent of cloth of gold to serve as an armoury in the lists. The romance in this tournament did not come in the form of pageants but in Henry's impressive performance and chivalrous behaviour. After his courses, Henry and Lisle took off their helmets and 'did great reuerence to the ladies,' and this courtesy was continued at the banquet held in the evening. One hundred dishes were served, and during the dancing which followed, Henry and eleven companions accompanied by four minstrels costumed in yellow damask entered in disguise. One of the participants was Sir Henry Guildford, who may have devised the entertainment which concluded with the maskers casting off their rich garments 'amongest the ladies, take who could take.' There were no pageants used in this entertainment, which Hall calls a 'maske.' The only action Hall records was passing the 'time at their pleasure.'

Disguise continued to be used in the lists on occasion, but the inspiration was often political. Less than a year after the joust at Tournai, for example, Henry and Charles Brandon, recently created Duke of Suffolk (very probably in anticipation of his proposed match with Margaret, Duchess of Savoy), appeared as chief challengers in the May 1514 tournament. There were no pageants, but there was costuming and drama. The king was dressed 'in a scopelary mantel, and hat of clothe of syluer and like a whyte armite, and the duke apparelled like a black armite all of blacke veluet, both ther berdes were of Damaske syluer.' When they appeared before the queen, they removed their disguises – which they gave to the ladies as gifts – revealing Henry in black armor and Suffolk in white, both holding black staves on which was written *who can hold that wyl away.'* The 'posye,' says Hall, 'was iudged to be made for the duke of Suffolke and the duches of Sauoy.'[45] This is the first time a tournament at court was used not simply for the purpose of prestige diplomacy but to advance a specific diplomatic position – that Suffolk was indeed a match for the Duchess. While there are a few more instances of disguise used in tournaments, the new fashion which begins to emerge in the 1513 Tournai jousts emphasized rich apparel and elaborate horse trappers and caparisons set with gold and jewels on which the *impresa* of the combatants were embroidered. These tournaments were no less grand than earlier ones. They tended to be thematically organized and featured English champions who defended propositions drawn from the courtly love tradition or from diplomatic negotiations then in hand. Connections between tournaments and revels were made thematically through the use of *impresa*. Such connections were much easier to make given the new organization for production: as Master of the Armoury Edward Guildford would have been involved in the preparations for the tournaments, as Master of the Revels Sir Henry Guildford would have been involved in the preparations for the revels, and as deputy to the Master Gibson was involved in the production of all tournaments and revels.

Pageants did not disappear immediately after the jousts at Tournai, for Gibson was occupied between 19 March and 9 May 1515 building a pageant called the 'Pallys Marchallyn,' probably intended for the jousts to be held at Greenwich in May of that year. The pageant was 36' x 28' x 10', composed of four sections joined together. The timbers were bolted together with iron 'that the intent was of an oweres Raysyng or takyng downe.' There were also to be ten towers 'in battylyd, kestyd, in bowyd, dormanddyd,' as well as other work to be performed by joiners, carpenters, and carvers so that the pageant could carry 'vn bardyd koarsars a kyng, a dewke, a markes, and an erll,' armed and attended.[46] It was to be 'hyllyd with rich clothes of gold and silks,' prepared by Leonard Friscobald and Anthony Cavalero, Italian dealers in fabric, according to Gibson's directions in consultation with Richard Smith, Yeoman of the Robes, from whom other material was to be obtained.[47] But this pageant was abandoned, and the entire spectacle was reorganized into an elaborate May celebration. It may be, as Marie Axton suggested, that the reorganization was associated with Henry's reconciliation with Charles Brandon who had married Mary, the king's younger sister, without permission.[48]

For this May celebration, 'outlaws' invited the king, queen, and ambassadors to dine with them in the woods outside of Greenwich. Bowers were prepared in the form of a great hall, great chamber, and an inner chamber all covered with flowers and herbs and filled with songbirds. After an archery exhibition by the king's guard costumed as Robin Hood's men, including whistling arrows, the king and queen were invited to a dinner of venison, served to the music of flutes, organs, and lutes. On the return journey, the royal train encountered a procession and pageants. Lady May and Lady Flora, drawn in a chariot by five horses, each of which 'had hys name on his head, and on euery horse sate a ladye *with* her name written,' escorted the royal party to court while an estimated 25,000 spectators looked on.[49] The May festival of 1511 with its ship pageant carrying a cargo of *'Renoune'* was thematically related to the joust that afternoon. In 1515 the preliminary entertainment and pageants are divorced from the jousts, probably a result of the decision to abandon the 'Pallys Marchallyn' pageant and whatever romantic fiction was planned for it. The May procession, Robin Hood disguise, archery exhibitions, and music and song at the banquet held in a pastoral bower

are grounded in native, not continental, tradition, and the joust held that afternoon is notable for its absence of a fictional challenge and costuming. The king,
Suffolk, Dorset, and Essex, appareled in green velvet and cloth of gold, ran against
sixteen answerers 'all appareyled richely after their deuises.' Gibson produced the
entire extravaganza, from the pageants to the costumes of Robin Hood, Little
John, Friar Tuck (played by William Wynnsbury, veteran Lord of Misrule at many
court Christmas celebrations), Maid Marian, Lady May, the jousting apparel of
the king and the other challengers, and for the 125 yeomen attendants, eleven
ladies, and the Children of the Chapel.[50]

iii

The movement away from pageantry in the lists, evident in the tournaments
between 1509 and 1515, was not duplicated indoors. While other innovations
were introduced, pageants continued to be employed, particularly on important
diplomatic occasions. The tournament of 11–12 February 1511 was concluded
by one of the most spectacular revels held in the early part of the reign. The
pageant-disguising *The Golldyn Arber in the Arche Yerd of Pleyser*, produced by
Gibson on the evening of 13 February, employed many of the devices familiar
from Henry VII's court.[51] The White Hall at Westminster was furnished with
seating and decorations, no doubt by the Works. After a banquet followed an
interlude which included songs performed by the Gentlemen of the Chapel, two
of whom were costumed as shipmen. This was followed by a dance from which
the king withdrew. Later, four torch bearers entered to the sound of trumpets,
leading a massive pageant which was moved about on beer-cart wheels. The
orchard was decorated with various trees and flowers, and a vine of silver bearing
golden grapes. Six ladies in garments of white and green satin set with yellow letters of H and K, and six gentlemen, including the king, Knyvet, and Neville,
dressed in garments overlaid with their poesies and to which were fixed letters in
gold bullion, were positioned on the pageant. Henry's costume contained 887
pieces of gold in the shapes of the letters H and K, hearts, and sets of the letters
of his allegorical name in the joust, LOYAL. Knyvet's costume contained 893
pieces, including his name, VALIANT DESYR, and one additional DESYR set
on his codpiece. Along the sides of the pageant were eight minstrels and on its
front steps several individuals in costume, including John Kyte, William Cornish,
and William Crane of the Chapel. Atop were six Children of the Chapel who sang
as the pageant was wheeled about the Hall.

The thirty people carried on the pageant made it 'mervelvs wyghtty to remevf
and karry as yt dyd vp and down the hall and tvrnyd rovnd.' It was heavy enough
to begin with. Gibson charges in his account for repairing the broken floor at the

Bishop of Hertford's place in London where it had been constructed. William Cornish played several parts in the entertainment, for Gibson prepared at least two garments for him and only one each for John Kyte and William Crane. The first was a gown and bonnet of blue satin set with yellow satin letters for 'oon of hys partes.' There was another 'playyng gown' of green sarcenet set with letters in white satin. Possibly one was for the play performed by the Gentlemen earlier in the evening and possibly the other as presenter for the pageant-disguising. When the pageant was brought part way into the Hall it was concealed by a 'great cloth of Arras,' while a gentleman came forward to explain the meaning of the show, which, according to Hall's narrative, was 'howe in a garden of pleasure there was an arber of golde, wherin were lordes and ladies, moche desirous to shew pleasure and pastime to the Queen and ladies, if they might be licenced so to do.' When the queen consented, the cloth was removed and the pageant was brought further into the Hall. The disguised lords and ladies descended from the pageant and danced with each other, and even the minstrels joined in.

The narratives of this revel make it difficult to pinpoint the theme precisely, but the inspiration for the garden is quite clearly from romance. The presenter's explanation makes it certain that the garden itself is a *hortus deliciarum* which could be used to symbolize court life.[52] The allegorical costumes worn by the king and his companions connect the revel to the tournament, and their discovery of a golden arbour may symbolize the discovery of something of importance amid this garden of pleasure – perhaps the values set forth in the *impressa* which had been championed earlier in the lists, the mottos for which were now embroidered on the costumes of the king and his companions.

Structurally, the revel is similar to those held at Henry VII's court, but there are important differences. The participation and surprise appearances and disappearances by the king, which he had introduced in earlier disguisings, also marked this revel with his personal style. Another, such as the use of a curtain to screen the pageant from view was wholly new. This unveiling was to be incorporated into several pageant-disguisings in the future. The method used to distribute souvenirs, however, proved to be frustrating to Gibson. He notes that the pageant, which was moved to the end of the Hall to make room for dancing, was attacked by 'rude' people and torn to shreds for souvenirs, 'and the poor men that wer set to keep yt ther hedes brokyn ij of them, and the remnant put ther from wyth foors so that noon but the baar tymber cvm near to the kynges ews nor stoor.' The king had planned to allow the ambassadors to take some of the gold letters from his costume as souvenirs and had arranged that they should pluck them from the garments at an agreed place and time. Seeing this, souvenir hunters attacked the king and Knyvet, stripping Henry to his hose and doublet, and Knyvet, trying vainly to battle them off from a position on one of the scaffolds, was similarly plundered. Gibson carefully notes all of these losses in his accounts.[53]

Apparently the spectators had been primed for this at the tournament, for Gibson also notes that saving the pavilions to the 'kyngs ews' was no easy task and 'profyd with meche payn.' Souvenir distribution was not discontinued as a result of this incident in 1511, merely choreographed more carefully. Souvenir scrambling was an established part of the revels at Henry VII's court as well.[54] But souvenir distribution combined with the various disguises of the king and his courtiers and the spectacular pageants which suddenly appeared or disappeared all conspired to transform audiences into performers, spectators into actors. The cost of producing this tournament and revel was enormous. John Daunce, who acted as paymaster for the event, received a Chamber payment for £4371 11s. 2d. in April 1511, but it is not certain that even this figure represents the total cost.

The New Year's 1512 pageant-disguising, produced by Gibson under Guildford's direction in the banqueting hall at Greenwich, also drew on devices familiar from Henry VII's court.[55] The pageant, called *Le Fortresse Dangerus*, was built like a castle with towers and bulwarks and fortified with ordnance. It included a dungeon on which a banner was 'dyssplayed with a schevf of arrows betyn therein.' It was built of timber and old sails – possibly those used for the ship in the May jousts – at Sir Edward Borrow's house in London, and then transported by barge from Paul's wharf to Greenwich. It appears to have been constructed so that it could be moved about by attendants rather than equipped with wheels, for Hall notes that it was 'caried about the hal.' Six ladies clothed in russet satin covered with leaves of gold were stationed within the castle. It was assaulted by the king, Brandon, Knyvet, Essex, Henry Guildford and two other lords dressed in coats of half russet satin spangled with gold and half cloth of gold, their russet satin caps set with gold bullion. These garments were all tailored under Gibson's supervision in the Prince's Wardrobe, for he includes payments for certain repairs made there in his account. The ladies, of course, eventually yielded the castle to the knights and danced with them, but after, when they reentered the castle, it 'sodainly vanished' out of sight. This spectacular finale must have been accomplished with the use of another curtain, for Gibson notes in his account that the rope used for the 'travas' in the Hall was stolen.[56]

There was obviously more to this entertainment than is recorded in Hall's narrative or in the Revels account, for William Cornish, John Kyte, William Crane, and other Gentlemen of the Chapel participated. Gibson made costumes of russet and yellow damask for the Gentlemen; Kyte was appareled in green satin, and Cornish and Crane in white satin 'for hys part.' Whether a play by the Gentlemen preceded the disguising is not certain, but we might imagine that this one was structured like several earlier disguisings which did include a play and, given the number of Gentlemen involved, that there was a musical component. The narrative evidence is not full enough to be precise about the theme of this revel. The castle, which could be used to figure virtually anything, is ubiquitous in medieval literature, and the assault or siege is associated allegorically with the *psychomachia*. It is probable that this castle was assaulted to free prisoners from its dungeon. In his tale of Sir Gareth of Orkney, Malory mentions a 'Castell Daungerous' which was besieged by the Red Knight, and later refers to another castle in which the Brown Knight 'wythoute Pyte' had imprisoned thirty widows.[57] The gift-giving appears to have been exciting, but the general melee of February 1511 was not repeated. Six of the russet satin garments were 'in the hall cast off at large' and the king gave over four ounces of gold 'off his jacket' to lords and ladies. The Gentlemen of the Chapel received seven garments. John Kyte was given his gown and hood, William Cornish his gown and bonnet, Guildford the banner, and much was given to others. The remainder was delivered to Guildford on 9 March and then to the Yeoman of the Robes to be made into footmen's jackets. The pageant did not survive the evening, and was sent by Gibson to the Wardrobe as broken store. The structure of this pageant-disguising is similar to those produced at Henry VII's court from at least as early as 1501. There is nothing in this pageant-disguising, other than the fact that the king personally participated, to indicate the innovation which was introduced in the Twelfth Night revels.

Henry's interest in participating in revels is nowhere more evident than in the introduction of the mask on Twelfth Night 1512. Hall describes the event:

the kyng with a .xi. other wer disguised, after the maner of Italie, called a maske, a thyng not seen afore in Englande, thei were appareled in garmentes long and brode, wrought all with gold, with visers and cappes of gold & after the banket doen, these Maskers came in, with sixe gentlemen disguised in silke bearyng staffe torches, and desired the ladies to daunce, some were content, and some that knewe the fashion of it refused, because it was not a thyng commonly seen. And after thei daunced and commoned together, as the fashion of the Maske is, thei tooke leaue and departed.[58]

The controversy among historians of the drama over this revel has centred on its exact form and on its relationship to the development of the mask in England.[59] The generally accepted view is the one expounded by Sydney Anglo, who pointed out that Hall's conception of the innovation is twofold: dancing and commoning, or informal conversation, between disguised and undisguised persons; that there is nothing in these elements which contributed to the development of drama in the mask; and that this mask was not the primary ancestor of the later, Jacobean mask.[60] Pageant-disguisings had already been presented at Henry VII's and Henry VIII's courts which more closely resemble the Jacobean mask. The ancestors of the later masks are the Tudor revels themselves which subsumed a variety of forms, including the pageant, the mummery, the morris, the tourney, barriers, the disguising, the play, and the mask. The confusion about the relationship between the mask introduced in 1512 and the later mask is traceable to the fact that contemporary writers were notoriously inexact in their use of generic terms. 'Disguising,' 'mask,' and 'mummery' are used on occasion to denote specific kinds of entertainments, but they are also freely applied to revels in general. Gibson, who produced most of these revels, uses the term in a variety of ways.[61] The term 'mask,' which Gibson used to designate the type of revel held on Twelfth Night 1512, became generally applied to court revels, for the most part replacing the terms 'disguising' and 'mummery.' The term was still not a precise one in the later Tudor period, for it continued to be used throughout the century, even in the Revels accounts, to refer to a kind of entertainment, to designate persons performing in revels, and to identify a single costume or set of costumes used in them.[62]

The Italian mask of 1512 was a straightforward affair. No pageants were used. No formal dancing by disguised persons is mentioned. But this mask did have an impact on the revels at Henry's court. It was a form very much in keeping with the spirit of other changes during the first few years of Henry's reign. In 1513 the king began to appear in tournaments without disguise. Between 1510 and 1513 he also began to appear in pageant-disguisings as a dancer and actor. Beginning with the mask of 1512 he began to participate in revels more informally. There are probably many reasons for this. Revels depended on variety, and variety in the disguising depended on elaborate costuming and intricate dancing. Gibson had time to make costumes, but it is unlikely that the king and his courtiers could be counted on to learn the dances necessary to bring more than a few disguisings off. Time for this must have run short on occasion, particularly in the midst of diplomatic negotiations. To be successful, the mask required only the dances which fashionable courtiers and ladies might be expected to perform. Henry could indulge his love of dressing up, of 'abashing' the ladies, and of surprising the court by performing as himself. The mask also did not require the design and construction of elaborate pageants. It was a less expensive and less complicated revel. The king could order garments from Gibson, and perform without much preparation, as he was to do at Tournai in the following year.

In an Italian mask, such as the one represented in Shakespeare's *Romeo and Juliet*, disguised gentlemen crashed parties to dance and to flirt with ladies. There was an element of tension and suspense here which could and did lead to violence.[63] Henry's mask used this tension and suspense to create a court drama. The ladies who refused to participate, as Hall notes, 'knewe the fashion of it.' They must have felt the same threat to social decorum that was responsible for several centuries of prohibitions against mummers. The denouement of Henry's little drama provided reassurance. The surprise unmasking revealed that the king and his courtiers had been impersonating maskers, only playing with a risqué form. Despite the initial reaction of the court, the mask was to be used on a number of occasions. The dancing of disguised and undisguised persons, the 'commoning,' and the mood of unpretentious joviality at the unmasking – discovering that chief officers of state, ambassadors from foreign courts, noted courtiers, and even the king himself were in disguise – transformed spectators into participants and life into art. The king's personal preference for role playing and for participatory revels was thus imposed on his court. The introduction of the mask expanded the choices available to producers of court entertainments, but it did not alter the structure of subsequent revels at court. Pageant-disguisings of the kind familiar from Henry VII's reign continued to be produced, such as the one for Twelfth Night 1513.

Guildford's pageant for the occasion was called *The Ryche Mount,* described by Gibson as 'a rock or mountain of gold and precious stones, set with herbs of divers kinds, and planted with broom to signify Plantaganet, and also with red and white roses; on the top a burning beacon; on the sides fleurs de lis.'[64] He spent twenty-seven days constructing the pageant at Sir Edward Borrow's house in London, transported it by the Lord of Northumberland's barge from Paul's wharf on the 6th of January, installed it in the Hall at Greenwich, and returned it to London on the 7th. There is no record of a play in conjunction with the disguising. The pageant was drawn into the Hall before the queen by two mighty 'woodowssys or wyld men.'[65] Mighty they must have been, for there were twenty-eight people in the disguising: four wild men, six lords, six ladies, two knights, minstrels and four others. The king was one of the six disguised lords who sat on the pageant around the beacon. When they descended and danced before the queen, the mountain 'sodainly' opened and the six ladies costumed in crimson satin gowns embroidered with gold and pearls and French-style hoods emerged and danced alone. The lords and ladies danced together before reentering the pageant, which was closed and withdrawn.

This is the second mountain pageant which Guildford had prepared within a two-year period. The first, in 1511, was a golden mountain with roses and pomegranates signifying England and Spain. The mountain was the visual symbol of the dynasty and the disguised dance of the 'King's Henchmen' a tribute to Henry's court. A disguising oriented toward raising nationalistic feelings might be expected in 1513 in view of the fact that the court had been busily preparing for war since spring. No doubt this pageant of the 'ryche movnt' decorated with the floral emblems of Plantagenet, York, and Lancaster was meant to call attention to the genealogy and prowess of the Tudor dynasty. The standard finale of bestowing garments concluded the evening. Souvenir hunters plundered the king's and Brandon's costumes, for Gibson notes that over four ounces of gold was 'given or for pleasure suffered to be taken.'

For Twelfth Night 1514 Guildford devised an 'interlevt in the weche contaynet a morreske' which was shown at Richmond. This is one of the few occasions early in the Tudor period on which an interlude – together with music, dance, and spectacle – was used as the principal entertainment on a major feast Gibson does not mention the actors in his Revels account, but he made their costumes and transported them to the palace by barge. He notes that there were six people in addition to two ladies called 'venvs' and 'bewte.'[66] The gentlemen performers were costumed in white jackets and black gowns; the minstrels and a fool were appareled in yellow sarcenet painted with hearts and wings of silver by Richard Rowangre, the same artist who worked on Wentworth's disguising in 1508. Collier attributed the interlude to Cornish based on a document he claimed to have discovered: 'a singular contemporaneous paper folded up in the roll [of the Revels account] and in a different handwriting, giving an account of the nature of the exhibition before the king on this occasion. Two interludes were performed, one by Cornish and the Children of the Chapel, and the other by English and the King's Players.' He extracts the following from the document:

Venus dyd synge a songe with Beawte, which was lyked of al that harde yt, every staffe endyng after thys sortte:

> Bow you down, and doo your dutye
> To Venus and the goddes Bewty:
> We tryumphe hye over all,
> Kyngs attend when we do call.

Inglyshe, and others of the Kynges pleyers, after pleyed an Interluyt, which was written by Master Midwell, but yt was so long yt was not lyked: yt was of the fyndyng of troth, who was caryed away by ygnorance & ypocracy. The foolys part was the best, but the kyng departed befor the end to his chambre.[67]

It is possible that Guildford asked Cornish to write the script for this revel, as he was to do regularly beginning in 1516. Revels accounts are complicated financial documents, and it is a serious error to assume that any one of the yearly accounts includes information on all of what we might consider important details. Collier was the only scholar to see this document, which he thought to be in Cornish's handwriting. It has since disappeared. Wallace used it as pivotal evidence to suggest that Cornish and the Children went on to prosper with their new drama while Medwall and the old morality were consigned to the 'doom of disregard.'[68] Boas and Reed did their best to discredit Collier's transcript.[69]

The New Year 1515 revel may have been devised by Charles Brandon, for Gibson acknowledges receipt of a quantity of material from Lewis Wynwood, servant to the Duke of Suffolk. Gibson made a total of eighteen costumes for the entertainment: eight for the principal disguisers, eight for the minstrels and drummers, and two for unidentified performers. Suffolk, Nicholas Carew, the king, and one other person, probably Guildford, entered the queen's Chamber at Greenwich in Portuguese costumes. They were accompanied by four ladies in Savoyan costumes with whom they danced 'a greate season' before revealing themselves. Hall notes that this 'straunge apparell pleased muche euery person' and so delighted the queen that she kissed Henry after he unmasked.[70] This disguising provides yet another example of the interest in participatory revels at Henry VIII's court. Its effect depended not simply on the costumes, music, and dancing. It was a portable disguising, taken as a surprise to the queen's Chamber. In part it depended for its effect on this surprise and on the revelation of the identity of the performers. Suffolk may have conspired with the queen's Steward and Chamberlain, leading her to believe that this would be an ordinary Christmas disguising. Given her reaction after Henry unmasked, the queen appears to have been as surprised and delighted as the rest of the court.

The play produced on Candlemas Night by John Harrison may have been the queen's attempt to return the favour, for at £28 13s. 6d. it must have been an elaborate production.[71] The play was probably connected to the joust held at Greenwich on the following day, 3 February, in which the king and the Marquis of Dorset appeared as chief challengers, facing fourteen answerers who were richly appareled, 'everyman after his awne deuice' in embroidered velvet and cloth of gold.[72] The king's richly embroidered base and trapper and his apparel, made by Gibson, were given away. No pageants are mentioned, and if Gibson supported Harrison's play, which is possible, his account has perished.

Guildford's pageant-disguising, *The Pavyllyon vn the Plas Parlos*, presented before ambassadors and visitors from France, Spain, and Germany on Twelfth Night, just a week after the surprise disguising in the queen's Chamber, was an extraordinarily elaborate event.[73] The pageant was constructed by Gibson in London and transported from Paul's wharf to Richmond. Preparations required Guildford's personal attendance for fourteen days, for which Gibson charged £7 in his accounts 'for the master of the Reuelles.' This pageant, a pavilion of crimson and blue damask surmounted by a gold crown and a rosebush, was mounted on a stage. There were brickwork towers at each corner supporting a 'lord' dressed in purple satin embroidered with the gold letters H and K. Six minstrels played on the stage, and at its foot stood two armed knights. William Cornish, William Crane, 'Mr Harry,' and one or more Children of the Chapel entered to explain the meaning of the pageant. There are discrepancies between Hall's and

Gibson's descriptions of the disguising, but it appears to have consisted of a tourney held by four knights who were attacked by four or six 'wodwos,' or wild men, 'apparayled in grene mosse, made with slyued sylke, with Vggly weapons and terrible visages.' When the knights drove the wild men from the hall, four ladies descended from the pavilion and danced with the victorious knights. Finally, they returned to the pavilion which was conveyed out of the Hall, but not before it 'with press was spoiled.' Wild men had been employed to draw or carry pageants before, but this is the first time a battle between knights and these mythical creatures became a principal focus, and it is the first time an actual martial exhibition was used as part of a revel. Nothing like it is recorded at Henry VII's court. There are a number of perilous places in Malory – a chapel, lake, rock, castle, siege – but none involve battles with wild men, and while Chretien's *Yvain* contains the most famous example of a wild man in romance it was probably not the source. Battles between knights and wild men had been depicted on the continent from as early as the fourteenth century, and the inspiration for this revel is probably diffused in romance literature and iconography.[74]

Guildford devised or supervised at least eight of the nine major revels produced between January 1511 and January 1515, and his record is sufficient to earn him a place of distinction among the Tudor and Stuart Masters of the Revels. The structure of many of Guildford's revels are reminiscent of those produced at Henry VII's court, but they were modified to emphasize participation by the king, his friends, and ambassadors. Movable pageants characterized all five of his disguisings in this period, but they were used in new ways – some of them 'sodainly' appeared or disappeared with the use of curtains. The extent to which music and song were integral to his productions is suggested by the inclusion of Cornish, the Gentlemen, and the Children of the Chapel in at least three, and probably four, of his revels. Mock sieges had already been used at Henry VII's court, but Guildford's *Pavyllyon* was the first to use a tourney indoors. Guildford did not ignore the king's love of disguise and role playing, for he was written into three of the five major pageant-disguisings in this period, delighting spectators by assaulting *Le Fortresse Dangerus* in 1512, dancing in *The Golldyn Arber* in 1511 and in *The Ryche Mount* in 1513. Guildford transformed the pageant-disguising spectacles of Henry VII's court into participatory revels. The themes for these revels were drawn from romance. Medieval literature and drama inspired the assault on *Le Fortresse Dangerus* in 1512. The atmosphere of medieval romance pervades *The Pavyllyon vn the Plas Parlos* of 1515 and *The Golldyn Arber* of 1511. Dynastic and nationalistic spirit was celebrated in the golden mountain of 1511 and in *The Ryche Mount* of 1513. Guildford also devised an interlude of *Venvs and Bewte* with a morris dance for Twelfth Night 1514 as a principal revel, suggesting a classical theme probably mediated through a medieval adaptation. The mask was also introduced in 1512, a revel calculated to emphasize less formal participation by the king, his friends, and ambassadors. And even portable disguisings were put on by the king and his friends to surprise the queen. Guildford, who would have become intimately familiar with the pageantry for tournaments in his father's household, had the imagination to adapt the devices pioneered at Henry VII's court and to introduce innovations which suited the personal style of the new king and his court.

The number of innovations in the planning and production of revels from 1510 to 1515 had the effect of creating a semi-formal, centralized organization. Costs were not necessarily reduced, but this was clearly not Henry's aim. The fact that Gibson held a permanent position in a compatible household department regularized ordinary production procedures and gave the organization a permanent home. It became possible to develop a significant inventory, to keep usable records, and to establish semi-formal networks not only with other government offices but also with suppliers of material, with artisans, and with labourers. The decision to appoint a Master of the Revels from among high-ranking courtiers who were personally close to the king gave Henry access to planning and also contributed status to the revels. His Master served only during pleasure, which provided some flexibility, but the fact that Sir Henry Guildford continued to serve as Master during the early part of the reign had the effect of imposing a particular style on the revels as well as of contributing stability to the new organization.

iv

The corollary of the emphasis on participatory revels early in the reign was a decline of interest in separate performances of plays. A comparison between the rewards paid by the Chamber during the thirteen-year period from 1509 to 1521 to those made during the preceding fifteen years reveals significant differences in the revels schedules at Henry VII's and Henry VIII's courts. The number of plays scheduled at the opening of Henry VIII's reign accords well enough with practices at his father's court, but as the decade wore on far more tournaments and revels and fewer plays were scheduled. The rewards paid by the Chamber for plays reveal a shift in the percentages of plays performed at Henry VIII's court by the royal companies and by invited companies and a change in the structure of the two royal companies.

Between 1495 and 1509 there were over fifty performances by playing companies, an average of about 3.3 a year. Close to half of these performances were given by the King's Players and by the Gentlemen Players of the Chapel. About one seventh were given by companies patronized by the nobility, a couple were given by foreign companies, and the rest by miscellaneous local and unnamed companies. During the period from 27 December 1509 to 6 January 1521 there were thirty-three separately scheduled performances by playing companies, an average of about 2.5 a year. The significance lies less in the average decline of almost one performance a year than in the distribution of invitations made to the royal and to outside companies. Of these thirty-three rewards only one was made to a company patronized by the nobility. A performance by the Earl of Wiltshire's company was cancelled on 26 December 1514. They performed a year later on 1 January 1516. This single performance by Wiltshire's company stands in contrast to the comparatively generous number of such invitations at Henry VII's court. Whether the virtual exclusion of such companies was an attempt to limit the presence at court and therefore the prestige of powerful barons is not clear. Probably this was part of the reason, but the new emphasis on participation in revels appears to have made spectator entertainments, like plays, somewhat less desirable.

If performances by companies patronized by the nobility were scarce, so were those by local and civic companies. Unnamed players were paid for performances in the Hall on 27 and 30 December 1509 and four players from Suffolk were rewarded on 29 December 1511 for performing before the Lord Steward in the Hall. It is unlikely that the king saw any of these plays. The small number of such invitations in comparison to those at Henry VII's court and the fact that they were concentrated between 1509 and 1511 suggests that practices from the old reign were simply carried over. Changes were effected within a few years. No more invitations were made to civic or local companies between 1512 and 1521, but the Lords of Misrule presented their entertainments at court in ten of the twelve years from 1509 to 1521, a practice continued from Henry VII's court. William Wynnsbury, who played Friar Tuck in the May Day Festival of 1515, was Lord of Misrule in 1508–9, 1509–10, 1512–13, 1513–14, and 1514–15; he may also have been the unnamed Lord appointed in 1510–11 and 1511–12.[75] No narratives survive, but given the amounts of his imprests, payments, and rewards (which on occasion mention his 'revels') they were probably elaborate. This may be the explanation for continuing appointments of the Lords of Misrule, and suggests that the pattern we find in the king's Chamber where participatory revels were preferred to plays was echoed in the Hall. However, when the Chamber accounts resume in 1529 there are no payments to the Lords of Misrule, and we have evidence of only one other such appointment in 1534. The explanation may be that the Hall had declined to such an extent by the time the Eltham orders were issued (drafted in 1519 and issued in 1526) that a point was made about that fact that the Hall was seldom kept and special regulations were made to insure that it was on specific occasions.

The rest of the twenty-nine Chamber rewards paid to playing companies between 1509 and 1521 went to the King's Players (eighteen) and to the Chapel Royal (eleven). Together they performed about 90 percent of the separately scheduled plays in comparison to the approximately 50 percent they performed at Henry VII's court. Even more noteworthy than the dominance in scheduling is the change in composition of these two companies.

The Gentlemen Players of the Chapel were rewarded for performances on 6 January 1510 (in the Hall), on 6 January 1511, on 22 February (Shrove Sunday) 1512, and on 2 June 1512 (in conjunction with the last Burgundian-influenced tournament of the reign). They received no more rewards after this date, indicating that the company was disbanded. At about the same time, Cornish and other Gentlemen members of the Chapel began to perform in the dramatic components of some of Guildford's revels. By 4 January 1517 William Cornish had organized the Children of the Chapel into a playing company which received rewards for performances on that date, on 6 January 1519, on 7 March 1519, on 6 January 1520, on 1 April 1520 (for two interludes), and on 6 January 1521. These plays by the Children established a tradition of royal performances which would continue throughout most of the century. The fact that Cornish and the Children accompanied the king to France for his interviews with Francis I and Charles V in 1520 suggests the status of the company, especially when it is recalled that in 1513 Henry took the King's Players with him to France.[76]

The King's Players also underwent a major alteration. The King's Players who began to perform in 1494 and who were the most frequently scheduled acting company at Henry VII's court continued to perform early in Henry VIII's reign. They were rewarded for performances on 6 January 1510, 6 January 1511, 6 January 1512, 6 January 1513, and 6 January 1514. Three years after the disappearance of the Gentlemen Players of the Chapel, the King's Players were restructured and split into two groups. On 6 January 1515 a £4 reward was paid to the King's 'olde' Players and a reward of 66s. 8d. was paid to the King's Players.[77]

The 'olde' Players probably included the men who had been in the company since Henry VII's reign. This was a household troupe who scarcely travelled at all, and the positions of some of its members in the household indicates that they were capable of producing spectacles on a grand scale. Even after Richard Gibson left the company by 1510 to help produce the king's revels and tournaments, he was instrumental in supporting the company. In the first surviving inventory of Revels properties made by Gibson in 1510, some of the costumes formerly used in disguisings were delivered to John English for the company 'by the kynges commandment for to play be foor the kinges graac.'[78] It is quite clear that elaborate costuming and probably elaborate properties characterized the productions of the King's old Players.

The King's new Players were created as a travelling company, for records of their activities survive from the provinces.[79] However, they performed at court every year, often on the same bill with the 'olde' Players. Both companies were rewarded in early January in every year from 1515 to 1521 with the exception of 1518 when only the new Players received a reward. This anomaly can be explained by the 'Swetyng sicknes' which raged so fiercely from July through December 1517 that 'many died in the kynges Courte' and there was consequently 'no solempne Christmas.'[80] Chamber accounts do not survive to document the Christmas seasons from 1522 to 1528, and by 1529 only the new Players received rewards, indicating that the old Players retired or disbanded sometime between 1522 and 1528.

One explanation for this change, like the change in the playing companies in the Chapel Royal and like the changes in the revels and tournaments, was an attempt by the young king to impose his own personal style on his court. That meant transforming the style of entertainments and revels his father had produced. This was accomplished by redeploying the expertise that went into creating the kind of entertainments associated with the Gentlemen Players of the Chapel and the old King's Players in the king's new revels. Gibson was employed to design costumes for revels and tournaments, to supervise the construction of pageants, and to produce revels while Cornish, who was eventually to devise and help produce some of the revels, was now performing in them along with Kyte, Crane, and other Gentlemen of the Chapel. Another possible motive for the change in the organization of the King's Players may have been to enhance the king's image in the provinces which were now dominated by the playing companies of the nobility.[81] Such a tactic was not new to Henry. He had patronized travelling companies – the Lord Warden's Players and the Prince's Players – at his father's court.[82]

Henry VII had imposed a personal style on his revels in which he projected an image of himself and of his court. From the evidence which survives, that image was of a serious and dedicated monarch whose personal interests were virtually identical to his public obligations. There were, of course, delightful spectacles in Henry VII's revels. Loosing rabbits and doves into the hall in November 1501 must have provoked spontaneous responses from the court. But, by and large, there was a clear separation between performance and audience, and by implication between the king and his court. Henry VII maintained personal control of his government and suppressed faction by appointing men of relatively low rank to important household and government posts. He controlled the image he projected in the revels in the same way. In contrast, Henry VIII surrounded himself with influential individuals. His appointments of personal friends to the Privy Chamber and to important posts encouraged faction at court. His appointments to produce revels gave him the same access to his supervisors as his father had, but

it is quite clear that he did not control his image in the same manner. Henry genuinely enjoyed participating in revels. More often than not, the characters he portrayed were indistinguishable from his friends or from ambassadors until the
surprise unmasking. He was content to delegate authority to such an extent that
Wolsey from 1518 to 1528 and Cromwell from 1535 to 1540 were more closely
identified with policy than he was.[83] And the result was that during Wolsey's
administration many revels were calculated to glorify the cardinal's role in diplomacy.

Many of Henry's early revels and spectacles are genuine expressions of a personal interest and enthusiasm which sometimes conflicted with the responsibilities or expectations of his public role as king. The most obvious ongoing example
of this conflict between 1510 and 1527 was his interest in the martial exhibitions.
Despite a number of near serious injuries and repeated warnings from his counsellors, Henry continued to participate in tournaments. While Henry's many disguises in the revels may indicate a tension between private interests and public
duty, the variety of roles he played – Turk, masker, Couer Loyal, shepherd, king,
Hercules, and the others – should be placed in the context of developing notions
of the Renaissance courtier.

Hall's account of Henry's activities during the summer progress of 1510, even
if somewhat exaggerated, serves to illustrate his energy and range of accomplishments. The king spent time

exercisyng hym self daily in shotyng, singing, daunsyng, wrastlyng, casting of the barre,
plaiyng at the recorders, flute, virginals, and in setting of songes, makyng of balettes, &
did set. ii. goodly masses, euery of them fyue partes, whiche were songe oftentimes in hys
chapel, and afterwardes in diuerse other places. And whan he came to Okyng, there wer
kept both Iustes and Turneys: the rest of thys progresse was spent in huntyng, hawkyng,
and shotyng.[84]

At about this date, between 1508 and 1516, Castiglione was writing about the
courtier's range of accomplishments and the various roles he was required to play
at court – warrior, diplomat, athlete, dancer, musician, poet, lover. And when he
turns his attention to revels, Castiglione specifically indicates that performances
at court are perfectly appropriate for courtiers.[85] In fact the king's disguises fit in
well with Castiglione's idea of the effect 'disgracing' has on image making. Even
before the book was published, the courtier's broad range of accomplishments and
role playing were already being enacted at the English as well as at other courts.
Henry, just as Francis I a little later, exhibited the same pan-European notions
about the accomplishments required to serve at court that Castiglione did. The
image that Henry projected in his revels both modeled and mirrored the multi-

faceted personality of the new courtier, and by so doing incorporated and helped to shape the latest fashions in court style.

4

The Revels Organization, 1516–1526

i The 'avyes of Wyllyam kornyche'

Some of the revels between 1510 and 1515 were pageants and disguisings of the kind familiar from Henry VII's reign; others were newly introduced. These revels incorporated all of the forms that amateurs could devise, but by 1515, the initial enthusiasm for revels and spectacles, ideas for new ones, and the time to arrange them ran short. Henry's success in France in 1512–14 gave England stature in European affairs, and the king took the opportunity to develop a foreign policy which ensured its continuance. His important courtiers, like Sir Henry Guildford, were assigned to more taxing administrative posts. The decade from 1516 to 1526 was filled with conferences and treaty negotiations with France and the Empire, and Henry was to use his revels and tournaments in these negotiations not only as a tactic of prestige diplomacy but also to advance his political positions. In order to serve these ends, formal spectacles which relied on visual allegory and which included sustained dramatic components were required. The king, high-ranking courtiers, and ambassadors continued to perform in some of the revels and to surprise the court with new twists on old conventions. These participatory revels, however, were supplemented by more formal spectacles. To devise and to help produced some of them, Sir Henry Guildford relied on the services of William Cornish.

Cornish and members of the Chapel were involved as performers in some of the revels from as early as 1494, and beginning in 1511 we have considerable evidence of fairly regular participation. Cornish, William Crane, John Kyte until his retirement in 1513, after him 'Master Harry,' and varying numbers of the Gentlemen and Children performed in *The Golldyn Arber in the Arche Yerd of Pleyser* on 13 February 1511, *Le Fortresse Dangerus* on 1 January 1512, *The Pavyllyon vn the Plas Parlos* on 6 January 1515, in the May Day celebration of that year, and possibly in the interlude of *Venvs and Bewte* in 1514. While Cornish may have been instrumental in the production of some of these earlier revels, beginning in 1516 contracting his services for politically significant revels became routine. At about the same time, Cornish also transformed the Children of the Chapel into an acting company which specialized in royal performances.

By 1515 Sir Henry Guildford became Master of the Horse, an appointment which placed the Stable under his jurisdiction. Along with the Armoury (under the supervision of his half-brother, Sir Edward) these were the main offices and storehouses supplying the jousts and martial exhibitions. The supervision and production of tournaments and revels were now more centralized than ever before. There is evidence of Guildford's direct involvement in supervising the production of the 7 July 1517 tournament and several revels – *Troylus and Pandor* on Twelfth Night 1516, *Gardyn de Esperans* on Twelfth Night 1517, and *Schatew Vert* on 4 March 1522. However, his general practice now appears to have been to provide high-level supervision, relying on Gibson to design and make costumes for masks, mummeries, disguisings, and to supervise the production of pageants, and on Cornish, whose duties ranged from making repairs and preparing spectacles to procuring material, devising pageants, writing texts, and performing in revels. All of this work would have been subject to Guildford's approval, and the bulk of production duties were still Gibson's responsibility; but Cornish submitted bills for his work, on occasion to Gibson and on others to the Chamber, indicating that he functioned with some independence. His contribution to court entertainments was an important one, for Cornish certainly helped to devise and produce six – and strong internal evidence argues for his involvement in three more – of the major spectacles and revels mounted between 6 January 1516 and 15 June 1522. In addition, he presented plays with the Children of the Chapel before the king and court on at least eight separate occasions between 4 January 1517 and 6 January 1521. In short, about one-third of the revels and over half of the plays at court in this period bore the marks of his style. No other individuals, with the exception of Guildford and Gibson, had such an impact on the revels at Henry VIII's court early in the reign.

The first certain evidence of Cornish's responsibility for a revel in Henry VIII's reign dates from Twelfth Night 1516, which according to Gibson's account was produced 'as well by the avyes of wyllyam kornyche as by the avyes of the master of the revelles.'[1] 'Advice' suggests that Cornish acted as aesthetic consultant, but it is clear from the documents that he did much more. He wrote the comedy, directed the performances of the Children of the Chapel, and acted in it himself. He also acted the part of the herald in the disguising and wrote the speeches for part of it. Cornish's 'avyes' in 1516 initiated a period in which it became common for the Master to contract the device of his revels to a semiprofessional, and in the period from 1516 to 1522 that was invariably William Cornish.

Gibson received a £10 imprest from William Compton to begin work on this project, the first recorded instance in which the Chamber was bypassed to provide funding for the revels. The money must have come from the king's Privy Purse, and the full bill was paid by the Chamber in February 1516.² This four-part entertainment began with a comedy of *Troylus and Pandor*, written and performed by Cornish and the Children of the Chapel. Cornish played the part of 'kallkas.' The Children played the parts of 'kryssyd,' who was 'inparylled lyke a wedow of onour' in black sarcenet, 'Eulyxes' and 'dyomed and the grekes inparylld lyke men of warre.' While it is not entirely certain, it appears that the pageant castle, built of timber according to Cornish's instructions and installed in the Hall at Eltham, formed the backdrop both to the play and to the disguising, for Gibson notes that at the conclusion of the play, a herald appeared, played again by Cornish, to proclaim that three strange knights had come to do battle with the knights of the castle. Three armed men came from the castle and fought at barriers with the challengers, first with spears, then with swords. When the knights departed, a queen accompanied by six ladies emerged from the castle and delivered speeches 'after the devyse of Mr. Kornyche.' Seven minstrels stationed on the walls and towers of the castle played while the six ladies danced with six disguised lords, apparelled in white and green satin set with the letters H and K. While there is considerable evidence of speaking parts for women characters in plays before this time (which parts would have been performed by boys), there is not much to suggest that the women who performed in disguisings had such parts. The ladies of the castle in the disguising of 1501 did give an answer when they refused the ambassadors of the Knights of Love, but Cornish's disguising in 1516 provides the first notice of 'speeches' assigned to a woman character.

According to Gibson there were fifteen people in the play and thirty-four in the disguising. Cornish could have been influenced by any of the rich tradition of the Troilus story.³ It seems clear that this comedy of *Troylus* was connected to the rest of the revel by setting up some irresolvable paradox, possibly having to do with the issue of faith and courtly love.⁴ Gibson made a costume for the character 'Fayth,' but whether she appeared in the comedy or was one of the pageant queen's ladies is not certain. The lack of resolution was probably referred to the combat at barriers, as was to be done again in the 1527 *Love and Riches*. The barriers, which we might imagine being fought by knights costumed as Trojans and Greeks, probably did not resolve the issue either, for the queen of the pageant then delivered speeches which had been written by Cornish and which probably provided some insight into the matter. All of this was linked to Henry's court in the dance of the six lords and ladies dressed in the king's colours and letters. This is the first revel for which we have certain evidence that the Children of the Chapel played lead dramatic – as opposed to singing – roles. It is also the first revel at Henry VIII's court which clearly exhibits the kind of dramatic shape we find associated with the *Knights of the Mount of Love* in 1501.

Cornish's next project was to assist Gibson in producing both the jousts and entertainments at Greenwich in May 1516 for Henry's elder sister, Margaret, Queen of Scots.[5] The elaborate spectacle involved two days of jousts in which the king, Essex, Suffolk, and Nicholas Carew challenged all comers.[6] On the first day, the king and his companions were costumed by Gibson in blue and black velvet embroidered with honeysuckle vines and leaves made of flat gold of damask. On the following day, they were dressed in blue velvet with rose leaves of cloth of gold bordered with letters of gold bullion. The twelve answerers were in white satin traversed with cloth of gold. After the prescribed courses, Henry and his company ran *volant* out of the lists. Cornish was paid £136 10s. from the Chamber accounts for making repairs and for paving urinals at Greenwich in preparation for this event, and he also produced a play.[7] Gibson supported the production of this play, probably acted by Cornish and the Children of the Chapel at the banquet on the evening of the 20th, and prepared a second account for leftover charges for the jousts and for the 'Costys of the play layd out by master wyll*ia*m Cornysshe.'[8] Cornish ordered costumes and properties from Gibson, who, in turn, had them made by other sub-contractors – tailors and painters – and purchased only the material necessary to finish details for the production. By May of 1516 Cornish is not simply flattered with credit for his advice in helping to devise entertainments but is recognized by Gibson as an authorized payee for this kind of work.

Cornish and some of the Children of the Chapel performed again in the pageant-disguising, *Gardyn de Esperans*, on Twelfth Night 1517. Richard Gibson produced this revel under the direct supervision of Sir Henry Guildford.[9] The pageant, constructed in London and transported to Greenwich by barge, was 'rayllyd with bankys all set with goodly flowers artyfycyall' and a profusion of other plants. In its centre was a pillar supporting six 'partyd antyks' set with precious stones and decorated with roses and pomegranates. Six knights and six ladies strolled in the garden. Hall does not mention that Cornish performed in the revel, but obviously he did. Cornish 'inparralled like a straunger in a gown of red sarcenet' rode into the Hall to explain the pageant. In another part of the show, for which there is no narrative evidence, he was costumed in a black gown and a green coat, and two of the Children of the Chapel were costumed in purple satin garments. The pageant was brought into the Hall, the knights and ladies descended and danced, and then the pageant was removed. Neither Hall's narrative nor Gibson's account are sufficient to determine the structure, let alone the theme, of the entertainment, but the fact that Cornish appeared in at least two and possibly three roles and that some of the Children of the Chapel were involved suggests that he may have helped in devising it.[10] Gibson's careful husbandry of the inventory included returning even broken pageants such as this one – no doubt the victim of souvenir hunters – to the storehouse.

Cornish appears to have been involved, along with Gibson, in the production of the 'costly Iustes' for the Flemish ambassadors at Greenwich on 7 July 1517. Sir Edward Guildford was Marshal for the tournament and Sir Henry Guildford supervised the preparations. Gibson provided the elaborate outfits for the challengers as well as the king's 125 attendants. The king and fourteen knights and gentlemen appeared as challengers. Their bases and trappers were of white satin and white velvet with flat silver of damask on the right side and their own colours on the left. The splendour of the outfits was noted by several of the ambassadors in attendance, one of whom mentioned that the goldsmiths of London had been working on the project for four months and that the harnesses alone had cost the king a mint. Henry's own outfit included a coat of cloth of silver and black tinsel. His base and bard were embroidered with letters of gold bullion and set with pearls and precious stones. On his head he wore a lady's sleeve set with diamonds. The answerers – Suffolk, Dorset, and eight others – were equally magnificent. Their apparel was embroidered with gold letters C and M, for Charles Brandon and Mary, the king's younger sister, widow of Louis XII of France, now married to Suffolk. Sir Edward Guildford notes that 506 spears were broken, and one of the ambassadors described the courses between Henry and Suffolk as an epic contest between Hector and Achilles.[11]

Gibson's account for the entertainments connected to these jousts does not survive. Hall mentions 'many riddeles and muche pastyme' at the banquet, but does not describe them. Reports by the ambassadors who attended are not entirely consistent, but a stage was apparently built in the centre of the Hall on which a company of boys sang or played on instruments. Dishes were served to the king's table by elephants, lions, panthers, and other animals, marvellously designed, and new 'representations' were produced to the sound of music. The payment to Cornish over a year later on 8 August 1518 for two pageants which were shown before the king and others on 6 July 1517 probably refers to these 'representations.'[12] The entertainment seems similar to the banquet planned for Charles V at Calais in 1520.[13] The revel was concluded with dancing which lasted two hours, during which time Henry impressed the ambassadors with his energy.

The Anglo-French proxy marriage and treaty of peace of October 1518 was celebrated with several spectacles and entertainments, including two days of jousts, a mummery and disguising at Wolsey's, and a political allegory. While it can be argued that plays, like Medwall's *Fulgens and Lucrece*, in which theme complemented the subject of diplomatic negotiations, were written as early as the 1490s, this political allegory, which can be attributed to Cornish on internal evidence, is the first court disguising to take a particular diplomatic negotiation as its main subject. The agreement for the surrender of Tournai and for the marriage of Princess Mary to Francis I's infant son was concluded in July of that year. At a mass celebrated by Wolsey at St Paul's on 3 October an oration by Richard Pace, the king's Secretary, delivered before the king, the French ambassadors, and the Papal Legate, the treaty and marriage were hailed as the key to peace in Christendom.[14] Sir Edward Belknap, who was to supervise the building at Guisnes and Calais in 1520, was in charge of this service and of the wedding preparations. He constructed 'a hautepace of tymber of .xii. fote broade, that the kyng & the Ambassadors might be sene' from the west door to the choir door of the church, equal with the highest step.[15] That evening Wolsey hosted a revel, which was produced by Gibson at the king's charge. Six minstrels preceded by three gentlemen costumed in crimson gowns with gold cups in their hands entered the Chamber to begin the entertainments. One cup contained dice, another cards, and a third angels and royals. 'These gentlemen offred to playe at momchaunce, & when they had played ye length of the first boorde, then the mynstrels blew vp, & then entred into the chambre .xii. ladyes disguysed' and twelve gentlemen in disguise accompanied by twelve torch bearers all in green satin and cloth of gold with masking hoods.[16] After a dance, they unmasked to reveal that the company included Henry, his sister Mary, Suffolk, Guildford, and others of the king's friends. Gibson's account for this revel does not survive, but he was paid £230 4s. 4d. by the Treasurer of the Chamber in October for producing it.[17] He also prepared the jousts held on the 6th and 7th, which were under the supervision of Sir Edward Guildford, as well as the entertainments following the banquet on the 7th, including comedies with 'pageants of such sort as are rarely seen in England.' We can only take Hall's word for this, for the king's mummery and disguising depends on devices at least a decade old. However, the pageant-disguising, which used a political allegory on the theme of a Christian alliance made possible by the Anglo-French treaty, was a genuine innovation.

Several characters costumed as Turks entered playing drums to begin the action. A rider, named Report, entered on a winged horse. This horse, who spoke, explained that he was 'the horse Pegasus, who having heard of this peace and marriage, flew to announce it to the whole world,' and then introduced two children to sing a song about it. After the song, Pegasus announced the entry of the pageant. A curtain was lowered to reveal the pageant, a rock 'ful of al maner of stones, very artificially made' within which was a gilded cave, its entrance hung with silk curtains. Inside were nine women, like goddesses, holding candles. Nine identically-dressed youths sat around the pageant, within which musicians were concealed. Five trees sprouted from the top of the rock: an olive, bearing the pope's arms; a fir with the arms of the emperor; a lily with the arms of France; a rose with the arms of England; and a pomegranate with the arms of Spain. In the midst of these trees was a lady dressed as a queen with a 'Dolphin' in her lap.[18] Report then came forward to explain the pageant: 'That rock is the rock of peace; the Queen and the Dauphin thereupon signify the marriage.' He also explained the significance of assigning these particular trees to the monarchs, concluding that 'as all these personages rejoice at this peace, as also does the whole world, I planted the trees on the rock of peace.' A Turk stepped forward to object and issued a challenge. Fifteen Turks and fifteen knights then fought a tourney, after which the pageant was drawn about the Hall. Musicians played before it was returned again, when the youths and damsels descended and danced. The subject and theme of this entertainment clearly underscores the political point of the Anglo-French league and its implications for an alliance among Christian nations against the Infidel. The revel, which lasted until 2 a.m., concluded with gift giving. Henry presented fifty-two large silver drinking vessels to the French visitors and gave his robe of ermine and gold brocade to the Admiral of France.

The narrative derives from a report by an Italian observer. Hall's description is very brief, and Gibson's account does not survive.[19] The revel is very much like those supervised earlier by Guildford in which Cornish participated. Even the structural devices, such as the curtain to conceal the pageant, had been used as early as February 1511 in another revel supervised by Guildford and acted by Cornish. Cornish had played the part of St George, who rode a horse in 1494, and the presenter who rode a horse in the Twelfth Night pageant-disguising in 1517. The text he wrote for the pageant-disguising in connection with the comedy of *Troylus and Pandor* and the barriers for Twelfth Night 1516 employed a personification of Faith, and the allegory here in 1518 anticipates the political allegory he certainly wrote for the entertainment of Charles V in June 1522. The evidence is sufficient, as Sydney Anglo has argued, to suggest the attribution.[20] The imagery used for most of this revel was by now traditional. The trees symbolizing nations had been used previously in revels, and decorating them with arms is reminiscent of the trees of chivalry in English tournaments from 1501. The trees all implanted on the rock of peace symbolize the new treaty, and the tourney with the Turks a gesture in the direction of its ideal significance. The use of a personified Report and of Pegasus with a speaking part is new. The concept had been used in one of the pageants at Paris for Philip of Austria in 1501 when a personification of Paris rode Pegasus, suggesting that the fame of the city would spread around the world.[21] Here Cornish made all elements of the revel – allegory, pageant-disguising, tourney, dance – subservient to a political theme.

Gibson produced two major entertainments for the French hostages, residing at Henry's court as security for the delivery of Tournai, in March and in September 1519. Cornish was involved in devising the second in this series of revels, and may have worked on the first as well. Gibson prepared apparel for the jousts on 3 and 8 March 1519, and a 'goodly comedy of Plautus' and a disguising or 'maskalyn' after 'the maner of the contrey of ettaly' on the evening of the 7th.[22] Preparations for the revel on the 7th were elaborate. The king 'caused his greate chambre at Grenewiche to be staged, and great lightes to be set on pillers that wer gilt, with basons gilt, and the rofe was couered with belwe sattin set full of presses of fine gold and flowers: and vnder was written, *iammes*, the meanyng wherof was, that the flower of youth could not be oppressed.'[23] Gibson does not include this material in his account, and probably contracted the stage to the Office of the Works, the ceiling design to a painter, and the lighting to a wire drawer.

It is not certain which company acted this comedy of Plautus, the first recorded classical play at court, and one which appears to have been performed on a fixed stage. It is likely also that it was performed in Latin, for translating reasonably familiar Latin into difficult English would not help a French audience. Cornish and the Children of the Chapel were paid for presenting a play on this date, but it is not certain that the payment was for this one.[24] Of course, the Children were trained in foreign languages to sing with the Chapel at mass, and while we may imagine that they might easily have performed classical plays, we have no substantiating evidence. It is possible that Wolsey's Gentlemen, who certainly presented Plautus's *Menaechmi* in Latin on 3 January 1527, were the performers.

Gibson lists the costumes for the 'Italian' mask in his main account. Eight ladies apparelled in black velvet, hooped gowns, and with gold headpieces like Egyptians, passed around the Hall in procession before eight gentlemen entered in long taffeta gowns set with gold bullion over coats of black velvet. The men danced with the ladies, and then suddenly threw off their gowns to reveal their gold-embroidered black velvet coats. At the conclusion, the maskers removed their visors to reveal that the king, Suffolk, and the king's sister Mary were among the company. In the narrative description of the revel no dancing of disguised persons with the audience is recorded. However, in his description of the September entertainment, Hall still takes dancing and 'commoning' as well as surprise revelation of identities to be key elements in the mask. In the joust on the day following the March entertainment, the king and his eight young companions had gold-embroidered black velvet bards and bases. Since Gibson does not list separate garments for the joust, it is likely that the doffing of the gowns in the mask revealed the coats to be used by the challengers. This revel, with its comedy and mask anticipating the jousts, appears to have been a celebration of the prowess of youth.

The second entertainment for the French hostages, consisting of an interlude and a double mask, was held on 3 September at Newhall, Essex.[25] The king sent

for Gibson and ordered Sir William Compton to make out letters of credit to
mercers for the needed material. Henry devised his own costume. He must have
been satisfied, for although he continued his practice of giving costumes used in
the revels as gifts – on this occasion, twenty-two suits of apparel – he kept his
own. Cornish 'maad' the 'pastym,' performed by the Children of the Chapel, and
Gibson contracted John Browne, the king's Painter, to paint their costumes of
Summer, Lust, Winter, Moon, Sun, Rain, and Wind. The play was probably performed before the banquet, for afterward, as Hall notes, 'with noise of minstrelles
entered into the chamber eight Maskers with white berdes, and long and large garmentes of Blewe satten pauned with Sipres, poudered with spangles of Bullion
Golde, and they daunsed with Ladies sadly, and commuued not with the ladies
after the fassion of Maskers, but behaued theimselfes sadly. Wherefore the quene
plucked of their visours, and then appered the duke of Suffolk, the erle of Essex,
the Marques of Dorset, the lorde Burgainy, sir Richard Wyngfeld, sir Robert Wyn-
gfelde, sir Richard Weston, sir Wyllyam Kyngston: all these wer somwhat aged,
the youngest man was fiftie at the least. The Ladies had good sporte to se these
auncient persones Maskers.' After the departure of the first group, the king, the
Earl of Devonshire, four of the French hostages, and six other lords came in disguised in green and yellow outfits with gold and silver scales: 'euery Masker toke
a ladie and daunsed: and when they had daunsed & commoned a great while their
visers were taken of, and then the ladies knew them.'

This mask is clearly different from the one introduced in 1512. As Wallace
observed, the two sets of maskers relate in somewhat the way later anti-masques
and masques do. More importantly, the parts of this double mask are clearly related by the theme of youth and age. More important still is the fact that this double mask appears to take its cue from the larger theme relating the two revels for
the hostages.[26] The joust, comedy, and mask in March focused on the irrepress-
ibility of youth; the one in September on youth and age. The use of the comedy
of Plautus, whose plays often celebrate the energy of youth, in March suggests that
Cornish's 'pastym' of Summer and Winter in September may well have had as its
subject youth and age rather than, as Wallace suggested, the seasons themselves
as in Rastell's Four Elements. This, one of the more interesting sets of revels from
the period for its thematic links not only of the plays but of the jousts and masks,
was to be repeated later in the reign.

Cornish attended the king at the Field of Cloth of Gold in 1520 where his
main duties were probably to arrange and conduct the Children in singing at the
elaborate masses and ceremonial banquets, but he also was charged to devise
pageants. After his return from France he devised at least one and possibly two
more revels for the king before his retirement in the spring of 1523. The revels
with which his name is associated from 1494 to 1522 share similar characteris-

tics. They almost all employ allegorical pageants which are used as scenic devices for dramatic action: castles in 1494, 1501, 1512, and 1522; gardens in 1511 and 1517; mounts or rocks in 1501, 1508, and 1518. Most of these revels employ a three- or four- part structure consisting of a play as prologue, a pageant-disguising with some dramatic action or martial exhibition thematically connected to the play, and a concluding disguised dance. Several of them use presenters or prologues, often played by Cornish himself, who interpreted the allegorical import of the revel. One introduces barriers in an indoor revel for the first time. Most of Cornish's revels draw their inspiration from medieval literature, principally from romance. Assaults on castles, pavilions in perilous places, and gardens of pleasure are commonplace allegorical settings in romance. Even when he departs from romance, as in *Troylus and Pandor* in 1516, he chooses a classical story mediated through medieval sources and allied to romance. They are, in fact, specifically linked to the chivalric ideal, or, like his surviving songs, to the courtly love tradition. The 1522 political allegory of *Friendship, Prudence, and Might* was to be unique in its departure from the trappings of romance. Here, instead, Cornish was to adapt medieval allegory – itself adapted from classical allegory – to political purposes. The main literary influence in court revels from 1516 to 1522, then, was medieval romance. We have notice of only one play by Plautus at court in March 1519, and that probably owed its existence to Wolsey's influence.

The most distinctive feature of Cornish's revels, and the one that made them particularly suitable to diplomatic and political commentary, was the adaptation of dramatic action to the pageant-disguising. We find this as early as 1494, when Cornish's pageant-disguising interrupted a play being performed by the King's Players, and we continue to find evidence of plays in conjunction with the revels in which Cornish performed up to 1515. By 1516, and probably before, he was writing his own texts for the dramatic portion of his revels as well as speeches for characters in the pageant-disguising. Of course, drama had been used to present court mummeries from Lydgate's time, and presenters had been used to explain the action, costuming, and visual symbols, but by 1522 Cornish's extensive use of drama to connect the parts of his revels led to the production of pageant-disguisings close to what we might call plays.

Henry's political ambitions required revels scaled to the purpose not only of prestige diplomacy but also of overt political commentary. The number of revels he ordered between 1516 and 1520 encouraged the development of an organization in which the delegation of production responsibilities became essential. Sir Henry Guildford continued personally to produce some of the revels and to make arrangements for the court's entertainment, but he also supervised at a high level the production of revels by Gibson and Cornish. Gibson produced masks simply on the advice of Guildford or of the king. In its simplest form, the mask as practised at the English court required only costuming. The success of this kind of revel depended on ordinary dancing, 'commoning' among disguised and undisguised persons, and the surprise revelation of the maskers' identities. Even in its more complicated form, which was introduced by September 1519 with the double mask of youth and age, it required only costuming and an idea for a theme. The comparative informality of the mask and the fact that it lacked a text made it less suitable for the grand displays needed for prestige propaganda and political commentary. These latter interests were served mainly by Cornish's more dramatic revels.

ii   The Growth of the Revels Organization

The jousts held on 21, 27, and 28 October 1519 for the wedding of the Earl of Devonshire, for which Gibson made outfits for the king, Sir William Kingston, and William Carre at a cost of £200 4s. 9d., preceded a two-year period which was to be the busiest in the early revels organization.[27] Gibson produced a 'Meskeller or mvmry' at Greenwich on New Year's Eve for fourteen people, six in russet coats with Portuguese caps and six in yellow Venetian garments with Turkish bonnets, with two torch bearers in long gowns and hoods.[28] On 5 January 1520 the king and nineteen gentlemen went in 'meskellyng apparel' by water to Wolsey's. Gibson supplied these garments from the store and made only one additional long, black sarcenet gown and five black velvet bonnets, which he delivered to Greenwich on the evening of the 5th. The king ordered a pageant and a disguising for the 6th at Greenwich. On such short notice and for the small cost of 22s., Gibson must have refurbished one of the pageants in the storehouse. He charges only for wages of labourers for the day and night and for carriage and boat hire and does not mention making costumes, although he could at this point supply any number of them from the inventory. On the following day he was ordered to furnish yet another entertainment, a 'meskeller' on 8 January at Greenwich. The entertainment appears to have been a mask of six ladies and six gentlemen. Six great cloaks of crimson sarcenet, six yellow satin coats with large sleeves bordered with crimson satin with bonnets and hoods to match, and six long crimson gowns rolled with yellow sarcenet, again with bonnets and hoods to match, were made. Much of this material was bought by Gibson, and he must have employed a number of tailors to produce costumes like these on such short notice. Given the great cloaks made for the men, it may have been a mask modeled on the surprise in the entertainments for the French hostages on 7 March and 3 September, in which doffing part of the masking attire revealed surprises about the identities of the wearers.

    In February, Gibson produced a pageant and two jousts.[29] On 1 February the king and queen were 'surprised' on their return from evensong before the queen's chamber at Greenwich. A trumpet sounded, and four gentlemen entered in a disguise of long garments of blue damask bordered with cloth of gold. They had with them a 'tryke' or 'spell wagon,' on the corners of which were four headpieces of 'armytes,' each with a different device. A lady sat in the middle of this pageant under a canopy, and she delivered a challenge to the king. The four gentlemen would 'for the love of their ladies' answer all comers at a joust appointed for Shrovetide. The king ordered Gibson to prepare apparel for himself and for the four challengers: Sir Richard Jerningham, Sir Anthony Browne, Sir Giles Capel, and Henry Norris. Gibson prepared the pageant as well as the king's saddle, trapper, and base made of russet velvet lozenged with cloth of silver of damask, each of the lozenges wrapped in cloth of gold and in each lozenge a branch of 'elegantine' embroidered in gold damask. He also attired the king's four gentlemen waiters in russet and white damask, and the two attendants and George Lovekyn, Clerk of the Stable, and four master armourers were apparelled in white and yellow sarcenet. Gibson lists the joust apparelled as above for 12 February, which may have been a practice, and another on 19 February in which the king answered the challenge of the four gentlemen.

The number of masks, disguisings, and pageants produced in 1519 and 1520 indicates that the inventory of costumes and pageants Gibson so jealously guarded was of sizeable proportion. Guildford, Gibson, and Cornish were now to accompany Henry to France for his meetings with Francis I and with Charles V. There they would be asked to undertake the most difficult productions of their careers, not only because of the variety of their duties but because they were so far from home. They contributed in no small way to the grandeur of the events held in France, and their work was a testimony to the skill and ingenuity which had developed at the English court. The enthusiastic reception of the English buildings, revels, and performances and the personal meetings with Francis I and Charles V sent Henry home at the end of the summer of 1520 with self-confidence from success in a daring diplomatic endeavour. Henry's court in the years immediately following was filled with revels and spectacles, mostly furnished with the massive inventory of rich material used in the entertainments in France. The preparations for these international conferences, later imitated at home on a smaller scale, perhaps illustrate more clearly than any other examples how it was that the production of revels eventually became part of a large bureaucracy. The variety of facilities and support required to stage successfully such spectacles drew on the resources of the standing departments of the royal household and on the services of a number of artists, artisans, and labourers who were temporarily hired on the project.

Gibson was in France in his capacities both as Sergeant of the Tents and as deputy to the Master of the Revels. He was responsible for setting up over four hundred tents for the English camp at Guisnes, for covering the roof of the temporary palace with canvas, for setting up the pavilion between Guisnes and Ardres for the meeting of Henry and Francis I, for the pageant tree and other temporary structures for the jousts, for setting up the pavilion for the meeting of Henry and Charles V at Gravelines, for the banqueting house at Calais, and for producing costumes for the revels. Gibson was in Calais in late May where he consulted with the king, probably on all aspects of the buildings and entertainments, and he was issued material for these purposes in the king's presence. At Guisnes, Gibson's duties included marking out the place for the first meeting of Henry and Francis I, which was to occur in a valley between Guisnes and Ardres. Gibson marked the spot with four pennons; but this was unacceptable to the French Marshall who threw them down 'in rigorous and cruel maner.' An argument ensued between Gibson and Chastillion which was apparently straightened out by the Earl of Essex, for the pavilion of crimson and cloth of gold for the monarchs' first meeting was set up in the centre of this valley.[30]

The conference was filled with lavish ceremonies, spectacles, athletic events, and revels. Preparations for the tournament were on a scale which dwarfed every other spectacle of the period. Sir Edward Guildford had charge of the provisions. Fifteen hundred spears, one thousand swords, five hundred two-handed swords, one hundred heavy swords for the tourney on horseback, and four hundred for foot combats were transported to France.[31] An armoury was set up at Calais. A steel mill was dismantled at Greenwich and shipped to Guisnes, and four forges were constructed. What could not be shipped was procured in Flanders and Germany by the king's agents. Gibson's Tree of Honour was the centrepiece for the martial exhibitions. The tree itself was massive – some 130 feet around – for which Gibson used two thousand artificial cherries made of crimson satin, leaves of green damask and withered leaves of gold, flowers and fruits of silver and gold, and a timber framework for the trunk.[32] It was set on a square mount which was railed to provide places for the heralds, and it was here that the contestants hung their shields. The apparel Gibson prepared for the tournament was as lavish. The *impresa*, for example, were made of pure gold, more spectacular than the jousts and tourneys themselves, which were somewhat disappointing due to the bad weather.[33]

The temporary construction projects were under the general supervision of Sir Edward Belknap, brother-in-law of Henry Smith, Clerk of the Works. Belknap had earlier supervised the construction of the 'hautepaces' at St Paul's for the Anglo-French negotiations and the proxy marriage of Princess Mary in 1518. There was literally an army of workmen under his supervision in France. His brother-in-law had impressed them by the hundreds, and the result of their efforts was an international spectacle of historic significance.[34] The English temporary palace at Guisnes, made of timber and canvas over a brick foundation, some three hundred feet in length and two stories in height, with clerestory windows, was the marvel of the event. Du Bellay thought it one of the most beautiful in the world, and other writers compared it to the fanciful palaces in Ariosto's *Orlando Furioso*.[35] Richard Gibson was in charge of covering the roof of the building. Work had begun in March on the temporary palace, but Gibson was delayed in England with other preparations. The commissioners in charge of the project became anxious because the roof had to be completed before the interior artwork was begun:

And Richarde Gybson who shuld cover the rofes with seared canvas ys not yet commen, and yt is highe tyme hys warkes wer in hande, for yt muste be paynted on the owte syde, and aftir curiously be garnissed under wit[h] knottis and batons guyltt and other devises, whiche busynes is committed to John Rastell, Clement Urmeston and other. Theis warkes be of greate and importunate charges, and we be in doubte how they shall overcumme the same by the daye appointed.[36]

Gibson completed his work in time for the artisans to begin theirs. John Rastell, who was to figure prominently in court entertainments during the decade of the 1520s; Clement Urmeston, who went on to decorate more palaces and banqueting houses until the early 1530s; John Browne, the king's Painter; 'maistre Maynn' (Giovanni da Maiano?); and 'maistre Barkleye' (Alexander Barclay?) were responsible for the interior ceiling, wall designs, and lighting.[37] The revels are not well documented, and Gibson uses the term 'mask' to refer to a set of costumes in his account. It appears that at least seven 'masks' were made by Gibson, for in one of his accounts, garments for the 'vijth meskeller' at Ardres in the French court are mentioned.[38] How many of these were devised by the king is not clear, but in the same memorandum indicating that Cornish was to be charged with the pageants, devising the 'mummeries' was to be left to the king.[39] On the evening of Sunday, 17 June, Henry was invited to the French camp at Ardres, and Francis to the English camp at Guisnes. Henry brought thirty attendants with him to the banquet hosted by the French queen.[40] A group of ten young lords was costumed by Gibson as Russlanders with cloaks of crimson velvet lined with cloth of gold, doublets of the same material, their hose and shoes of Eastland fashion, purses and girdles of seal skin, with visors and hats made in the town of Dansk. A second group of ten maskers was costumed in blue satin gowns of 'the auncient fashion' embroidered with 'reasons of golde that sayd, *adieu Iunesse.*' These maskers wore violet standing caps and girdles of silk with purses of cloth of gold and visors, 'their faces of like auncientie.' Obviously the first two masks formed an antithetical pair of youth and age, much like the entertainments of the French hostages in September 1519. The third group of maskers, which included the king himself, was costumed in princely gowns of cloth of gold and face visors with beards of 'fine wyer of Ducket gold.' The accompanying drumslades and minstrels, who played all during the company's progress through the town, were costumed in yellow, white, and russet damask. The maskers danced with ladies and, at the queen's insistence, revealed their identities before the banquet.

Jousting occupied the first part of the following week, with a tourney on horseback with swords on Wednesday and Thursday and barriers on Friday, but they were plagued by bad weather. On the last night of the interview, Sunday the 24th, prizes for the tournament were awarded at banquets. Henry took four companies of maskers to Ardres this time, consisting of twenty ladies and twenty gentlemen.[41] Ten of them were costumed by Gibson in coats of crimson satin embroidered with quatrefoils of cloth of silver and gold. Their visors were decorated with beards of gold wire. Ten of the ladies were apparelled in Genoese fashion with white satin gowns embroidered with crimson satin and damask gold, and they wore square bonnets of damask gold. The other ten ladies were apparelled as Milanese in cloth of silver with bonnets of crimson satin and cloth of gold. The remaining men were costumed as heroes. The king as Hercules, who led the group, wore a shirt of silver damask on the borders of which was written: 'en femes et infauntes cy petit assurance.' He had a hood with a garland of green leaves cut from damask, a club covered with green damask with 'prickes,' and a lion's skin of cloth of gold over his shoulder. The classical heroes were costumed as 'Hector, Alexandre, and Iulius Caesar' who wore Turkish garments and bonnets of cloth of gold and silver. There were also Princes of Jewry – 'Dauid, Iosue, and Iudas Machabeus' – and Princes of Christendom – 'Charlemaine, Arthur, & Godfry de Boulloigne.' The inspiration for this mask was the 'Nine Worthies,' a tradition dating to the fourteenth century.[42] Revels in which mythological, legendary, or historical characters are impersonated do not become common at court until mid-century. There is only one example of such impersonation at Wolsey's court in 1528, but that was part of a larger revel which employed a pageant car and included a play. While the king's revel at Ardres appears to have been a mask similar to the kind used in 1519, it is based here on a literary theme.

Henry removed to Calais on 25 June to await the arrival of Emperor Charles V. Gibson arranged a pavilion for the meeting of the two monarchs at a spot equidistant from Calais and Gravelines on 10 July. The English entourage was entertained at Gravelines by the emperor on the evening of the 10th, and on the following day the monarchs removed to Calais. Charles V was lodged in the Staple Hall where Henry and about fifteen of his companions visited him in masking apparel that evening.[43] The following evening was to feature a great banquet with revels for the two monarchs. Near the Exchequer at Calais, a banqueting house was erected, made of ship masts and canvas in the shape of a polygon of sixteen sides. Its height is calculated to be about 22 feet and its diameter is estimated between 60 to 150 feet.[44] In the centre was a timber column made of eight masts tied together with iron bands. It rose high enough above the walls to use rope to form a pavilion. The roof was made of double canvas, painted blue. There were three 'loftes' inside instead of seatings, one situated above the other around the sides and terraced or graded so that spectators 'that stode behynd myght see over the hedes that stode before, it was made so highe behynd and low before.' Other accounts indicate that these galleries were built in horseshoe fashion about ten feet above each other, and that the floors were about eight or nine feet deep, each fronted by a parapet about waist-high. Stages of timber were built for organs, for musicians, and for pageants. Special banquet tables were built for Henry and Charles.[45] A map of the world, displaying the four elements, was painted on the interior ceiling. The roof was illuminated by cornucopia candlesticks fixed around the outside of the banqueting area and by great branches, or chandeliers, hanging from the ceiling interspersed with silk-clad wicker figures bearing torches in their hands.

The construction and decoration of this structure is attributed to the same team of artists and artisans who had recently completed the temporary palace at Guisnes.[46] Gibson, for example, probably covered the frame with canvas and provided some of the decorations as well as the costumes for eight companies of maskers for the revels. Since the king only took masks or mummeries to Ardres, it was here at Calais that Cornish's pageants, probably much like those which served at the banquet in July 1517, were most likely employed. The inclement weather which had plagued the meeting with Francis, interrupting the tournament and forcing the French to dismantle their pavilion at Ardres, now tore the roof from the Calais banqueting house. The banquet and revels for Charles were rescheduled in the Exchequer at Calais, 'but because the rome was small, the shew was the lesse.' It is difficult to determine from the records what kind of revels were held. Gibson again uses the word 'mask' to describe a set of costumes. He prepared costumes for eight companies of maskers, each company composed of twelve persons.

Nothing on the scale of the building projects, tournaments, and revels in 1520 had been attempted before in England, let alone so far from home. Doubtless the intelligent administrative decision to centralize many of the production duties associated with revels and tournaments in the Tents by 1513 made this much easier than it otherwise would have been. Still, many of the preparations were under the charge of a hierarchy of temporary appointees, who contracted the services of artists, artisans, and labourers, and the services of the Great Wardrobe, the Armoury, the Works, and the Tents. When festivities of the diplomatic importance of those in France in 1520 were mounted in England – as they were on a smaller scale for the reception of Charles V in 1522 and for the second Anglo-French treaty in 1527 – a similar hierarchy of temporary appointees, contract artists, and services of the household offices was used. The repeated association of these offices with the preparations for major diplomatic festivities led to the administrative decision to locate responsibility for many of these preparations in the Revels Office by mid-century.

Alterations in the method of financing revels after 1516, the delegation of production responsibilities, and the reliance on a well-stocked inventory had the effect of increasing efficiency in revels productions. Wallace observed that in 1520 Henry came back from France 'maskelling-mad,' ordering six of these revels between November 1520 and February 1521, occasionally on only a day's notice.[47] Gibson was able to comply because of the large inventory which had developed in connection with the revels in France. Storing material used in the revels and refurbishing it for subsequent productions had been characteristic of procedures from as early as Wentworth's time, but due to the lack of a developed administrative structure it is unlikely that any systematic use of the inventory was effected. Gibson mentions reusing material from the inventory as early as 1510, but it was not until 1518 that the practice was becoming common. This is plain from Gibson's careful identification of the garments he altered, even to the point of identifying the earlier production in which they were used. Late in 1520 the inventory of revels properties was so extensive that the court celebrated throughout the winter season at a fraction of the cost of earlier years. Such concerns about economy and efficient measures to deal with the inventory were to become characteristic of the Revels Office later in the century.

The king kept Christmas of 1520–1 at Greenwich 'with muche noblenes & open court.'[48] Gibson furnished six masks and a joust mainly from his inventory. He prepared an account of all material he had received up through 3 November 1520 and explains only in a summary how it was used from that date through 12 February 1521.[49] For the 'maskeller' at Greenwich on 3 November 1520, six people were costumed in friars' habits of russet damask and six in garments from the king's store which are not described. For the revels held on 9 December the friars' habits used on 3 November were altered into mariners' frocks and hoods. On 3 January 1521, a revel was held at York Place. For this mask at Wolsey's, Gibson made eight garments of crimson velvet and cloth of gold which he altered from seven cloaks and eight doublets used at the 'maskeller' given at Ardres on 17 June and from seven half coats used at the 'maskeller' given at Calais on 12 July 1520. The eight gowns made for women in this mask were altered from three blue and purple gowns, two russet gowns, and six mantles of crimson gold material, all from the king's store. The capes and hoods were made from the linings of sleeves and cloaks of previously used garments. On 1 or 4 January another revel was held at Greenwich for which Gibson made eight 'reyster's coats' of cloth of gold and tinsel satin, the body and sleeves of gold material tufted with white sarcenet. These were made from seven gowns of estate from one of the 'maskellers' at Ardres. These translated garments were also used by the king and the Earl of Devonshire who participated in the disguising. For Shrovetide there was a joust and tourney on 11 and 12 February in which the king challenged all comers. The bases, bards, and coverings, as well as the outfits for the tournament, were prepared by Gibson, partly from new material and partly from material left from the jousts at Guisnes. There were also two masks. The first, on 11 February in the 'place of pleasure at a banquet,' featured six friars whose habits were translated by Gibson from material in the store and eight other garments of blue satin from costumes used at one of the 'maskellers' at Guisnes.[50] For the mask on the following night, eight coats and hoods were made from five ladies' garments and six jackets which had been used in the pageant-disguising on 7 October 1518 celebrating the Anglo-French Treaty, and from eight satin mantles which had been used at one of the 'maskellers' at Guisnes. The practice of altering garments effected great economy in the revels for this season. Gibson's entire bill for six masks and the martial exercises was only £167 15s. 5d., the bulk of which was spent on the tournament.[51]

Study of the revels after 1521 is hampered by a lack of financial documents and by sketchy narratives.[52] John Heron, the bulwark of the Chamber system, retired in 1521, an event which signalled general disorder in the financial records for two decades. The increasing complexity of revels productions had already led to the preparation of large summary accounts to which a number of subsidiary accounts were attached. As the accounts became more complicated, they lost their narrative quality.[53] Hall's frequent generalizations about the plays, masks, and disguisings during the Christmas seasons suggest that he had access neither to eyewitness reports nor to Revels accounts, for when he did have this information he invariably gave details. Only the great diplomatic spectacles and revels are well documented.

The Christmas season of 1521–2 inaugurated a year filled with spectacles to celebrate the Anglo-Imperial alliance and the reception of Charles V. Hall mentions without giving details that 'This yere many goodly and gorgious Mommeries were made in the court to the great reioysing of the Quene and ladies and other nobles.'[54] Gibson prepared revels for 29 December and 1 January by translating garments from the seasons of 1513–14 and 1515–16.[55] Other than the fact that they were both 'maskellers,' few other details survive. Henry participated in at least one of them, for Gibson records making a 'sparver' of russet sarcenet for him. The spectacles and revels for the imperial ambassadors, in England to negotiate an alliance, were held in March. They included a joust at Greenwich, a play and mask at Wolsey's, and a pageant-disguising held at York place.

Suffolk led one group of the combatants on 2 March 1522 in the joust focusing on the theme of the pain of love. Henry led the other group, his horse bard of cloth of silver embroidered with letters of gold **L** under which was a wounded heart and a golden scroll inscribed *'mon nauera,'* which when put together read *'ell mon ceur a nauera, she hath wounded my harte.'* Sir Nicholas Carew's motto was: 'in prison I am at libertie, and at libertie I am in prison.' The Earl of Devonshire's and Lord Roos' mottos were 'my harte is betwene ioye and pein.' Bound hearts were the emblems of Sir William Kingston and Thomas Knyvet, Nicholas Darrel used a broken heart, and Sir Anthony Browne, broken spheres of the world set over broken hearts with the motto *'sance remedy.'* Gibson made the bases, bards, and trappers, which he returned to the storehouse afterwards, and the girths, stirrups, and spurs were returned to the Clerk of the Stable and the Master of the Horse.[56] On 3 March, Wolsey 'made to the kyng and the Ambassadors, a great and a costly banket, and after that, a plaie and a Maske.' The play was performed by Wolsey's Gentlemen, but Gibson furnished the costumes for it and for the mask by translating garments from the store.[57] Few narrative details survive. We do not know the title of the play, and of the mask we know only that the costumes were half russet satin and half yellow. The revels at Wolsey's are better documented.

The pageant-disguising, *Schatew Vert,* was produced by Gibson under the supervision of the 'hy Kountrolleler Mr. Sir Harry Gyllforthe' and featured performances by the Children of the Chapel.[58] Gibson began work on 20 February to construct the pageant, which required a great amount of timber as well as modifications to the Hall: 'the bord spent vn the stayers in to the havt plaas set vn the wyndow and spred from the jams of the saam and all so bord and tymbyr instrements.'[59] It was transported by barge to York Place and back again, being unloaded at the 'Krane in the Ventre,' a site used for this purpose from at least 1508, and then loaded on five carts for transport to the Wardrobe. The pageant castle was erected at the far end of the chamber, its three towers, each with a banner – three rent hearts, a lady's hand gripping a man's heart, and a lady's hand turning a man's heart – painted green, and its battlements covered with green tinfoil. Within, eight ladies were imprisoned: Beauty, Honour, Perseverance, Kindness, Constancy, Bounty, Mercy, and Pity. Sixteen of the ladies' garments used in the revel were made by translating garments from the storehouse. Since their names were embroidered on their headpieces, these were probably non-speaking parts. They were played by ladies of the court who all kept their costumes after the performance, including the king's sister Mary, and Anne Boleyn. Although he names only seven, Hall reports that there were eight ladies on the battlements of the castle, costumed like women 'of Inde': Danger, Disdain, Jealousy, Unkindness, Scorn, Strangeness, and *'Malebouche.'* These parts were played by the Children of the Chapel, who kept the first eight ladies in prison.

A company of eight lords – Amorous, Nobleness, Youth, Attendance, Loyalty, Pleasure, Gentleness, and Liberty – were led by one costumed as Ardent Desire in crimson satin with 'buryning flames of gold' who entered and demanded surrender of the castle. When Scorn and Disdain refused, the lords assaulted the castle 'at whiche tyme without was shot a greate peale of gunnes.' The lords used oranges, dates, and other 'fruites made for pleasure.' The Children defended with rose water, comfits, and at least three of their hats, for Gibson complains that they were lost 'by casting down out of the castle.' The lords prevailed, of course, rescued the ladies, and led them in a dance before unmasking. A banquet concluded the revel. Given the fact that the Children of the Chapel were involved in the revel and that Cornish devised the political play in June of this year, it is likely that he was involved in the production of this one. The lyrics of Cornish's 'Yow and I and Amyas,' about a knight named Desire who appears at a castle searching for Lady Pity and is answered at the gate by Lady Strangeness, sound very much as if they were made for a disguising like this one.[60] The inspiration for the revel must be the *Roman de la Rose* in which the castle – the fortress within which the rose is guarded and the tower within which *Bel Acueil* is imprisoned – is the object of a siege by the god of love and his vassals.[61] Further, the joust held on 2 March 1522 with its focus on the theme of desire connects thematically with *Schatew Vert.* Marie Axton singles out this, the first revel in which Anne Boleyn performed, as a paradigm of the Desire and Beauty theme which underlies some of the masks and entertainments produced at Leicester's instigation in Elizabeth I's reign.[62] Axton rightly points out that Henry was not costumed as Ardent Desire in this revel, but as one of the eight lords. Hall mentions that the king was chief of this company of lords, but whether he intends to identify Henry as Amorous, the first in his list or Loyalty, as Axton seems to prefer because of what she regards as the king's discretion, is not clear. Certainly, Henry's *impresa* in the joust on that day does not argue circumspection.

The Emperor Charles V himself came to England to sign the treaty. Wolsey met him at Dover on 25 May and he was visited there by Henry. The two monarchs, together with the nearly 2000 attendants of the emperor, journeyed to Greenwich where they were received by the queen on 2 June.[63] A tournament was held on 4 and 5 June in which the king and the emperor participated. Gibson set up special pavilions and tents, which took thirteen carts to carry, for the 'parellments' of the sovereigns in these martial exercises.[64] In the joust held on the 4th, Henry appeared as chief challenger. Gibson made new horse bards for the king and the Earl of Devonshire of cloth of gold embroidered with mountains and hearts and other works made from cloth of silver, and supplied great plumes for their helmets. Suffolk led the answerers. He and Dorset had bards of russet velvet embroidered with knights on horseback riding up mountains of gold with broken spears in their hands. The upper parts of the bards were 'powdyred with clowds' and ladies were pictured coming out of the clouds, casting darts at the knights. Hall records that Henry ran eight courses and broke eight spears, and that after the prescribed courses the party ran *volant*. The emperor watched the jousting along with the queen in the gallery, but on the following day he personally participated in the tourney on horseback.

Two revels punctuated the tournament.[65] On the evening of the 4th there was an banquet and a 'maskeller.' During the course of the banquet, while the ladies were dancing, 'sodainly came to the chamber' six noblemen apparelled in crimson velvet with cloth of gold and mantles of taffeta rolled about their bodies with Portuguese hoods, Milan bonnets of cloth of gold and black velvet buskins. These maskers danced with the ladies awhile before another group of maskers entered accompanied by drummers. Among the maskers were Henry, Suffolk, the Prince of Orange, and the Count of Nassau, costumed in long gowns and hoods of cloth of gold, all of which costumes were given as gifts to the wearers after the entertainment. The first group withdrew, leaving the remaining group to dance with the ladies before unmasking. On the evening of the 5th there was another banquet and mask in the Hall, which was 'full of great lightes, set on gylte braunches.' When everyone was seated, eight men entered in masking gear with visors and garments of black velvet bordered and embroidered with cloth of gold, and with satin mantles. Half of the maskers were English and half 'straungers.' They took out ladies and danced, when 'sodainly' eight other maskers appeared costumed in rich tinsel and cloth of gold with mantles and hoods of crimson satin. According to Hall, 'these lustie Maskers entered, and reueled lustely' before a round of spices and wine. There is no indication of the theme of this double mask. All of these entertainments were prologue to the great royal entry into London on 6 June. Preparations had been under way since 28 March on the nine pageants, organized on the general theme of the royal houses of Spain and England personified in Charles V and Henry VIII.[66] Despite the fact that the royal entry was a civic production, Gibson was required to furnish at least the tent of cloth of gold for Henry and the emperor to change into their ceremonial regalia.

The Anglo-Imperial alliance was concluded on 16 June, and on the evening of the 15th a revel was held at Windsor, consisting of a political allegory, pageant, and mask. Gibson produced the revel and credits Cornish with devising the revels.[67] Gibson made three foresters' coats and hoods, four hunters' jackets, procured 'chequered kendall' hose for the 'keeper' of the horse, and used 240 ells of canvas for wild men's garments, for covering the pageant, and for making a stuffed body, as well as the costumes for the mask. No descriptions of the pageant survive, and we can only guess how the stuffed body was used, but Gibson notes that the pageant took nine days to construct and was transported to Windsor by barge. Such a pageant, made of timber and canvas, could have been moved about the Hall, probably by the 'wodos,' or wild men, who had been employed in pulling pageants in the past. While the fragmentary narratives do not give us all of the details, Cornish, who may have performed in this with the Children, was adapting from medieval psychological allegory for political purposes.[68]

Martin de Salinas, in a letter to the Treasurer of Salamanca, describes the action as consisting of three main characters named Friendship, Prudence, and Might, who agreed that together they could perform great deeds. Friendship was to promote amity, Prudence to supply good counsel, and Might to carry out their plans.[69] Several blacksmiths entered with hammers and an anvil along with a 'keeper' of a wild horse. The trio made a bridle for the horse, which the 'keeper' thought tame enough, except that it held its head too high. Friendship then attached a curb to the horse's head. Hall, who calls this entertainment at one point a play and at another a disguising, gives a slightly different account.[70] He says that Amity sent Prudence and Policy to tame the horse but that Force and Puissance had to bridle it. Hall identifies Amity with the king of England and with the emperor, but both he and de Salinas agree in identifying the horse with Francis I. Despite the differences in the narratives, it is clear that the play expresses the purposes of the Anglo-Imperial alliance in checking the power of France. Hall notes that the play was followed by a 'sumptuous Maske of .xii. men and .xii. women' clad in cloth of silver and gold loose-laid on crimson satin with points of gold. Their bonnets, hoods, and buskins were also of gold. De Salinas gives the number of maskers as eight men and eight women, who danced a *pabana* before the banquet.

We have no detailed record of entertainments at court from June 1522 to early 1524, not even for the Christmas seasons of 1522–3 and 1523–4. There were, of course, disappointing military operations in the war with France as well as on the Scottish border until late in 1523, but this is insufficient to explain the supposed lack of entertainments. Henry had revels produced at court during the war of 1512–14, and, according to Hall, kept the Christmas seasons of 1522–3 at Eltham and of 1523–4 at Windsor. When the Scottish ambassadors who attended the mask on 29 December 1524 registered surprise at the fact that entertainments were scheduled during wartime, they were informed that 'the kyng and his courte, vsed them still all the warre tyme, as thei dooe now, for thei set not by the French kyng one bene.'[71]

One of the most elaborate spectacles of the decade, the *Castle of Loyalty*, put on to entertain the Scottish embassy, was produced during the Christmas season of

1524–5. The event, which began on 29 December and ended on 8 February and included a formal challenge, a joust, barriers, a tourney, assaults on a fortress, banquets, and masks, was the focal point of the entire season.[72] Before Christmas, Lord Leonard Grey, who was appointed supervisor of the martial exhibitions, and his fifteen challengers sent 'Chasteau Blanche,' a role played by Windsor Herald, into the queen's chamber in the presence of the king to declare the challenge.[73] He had with him a coat of arms of red silk 'beaten with a goodly Castle, of foure Turrettes siluer, and in euery turret a faire lady, standyng gorgiously apparled.' After a trumpet sounded, 'Chasteau Blanche' elaborated the romantic fiction for the tournament: 'the kyng our souereigne Lorde' had given the Castle of Loyalty to four maidens of his court to dispose of at their pleasure, who in turn entrusted it to a captain and fifteen gentlemen to defend. The herald then declared to 'all kynges and princes, and other gentlemen of noble corage' that a mount and a unicorn – which was built by Richard Gibson – would be erected near the castle, and that whoever touched one of the shields would be answered in the appropriate combat by one of the defenders.

The castle itself was constructed in the tilt yard at Greenwich, probably by the Office of the Works, twenty feet square and fifty feet high, 'of great timber, well fastened with yron, the embatelmentes, loupes and euery place where men should entre wer set with greate rolles, and turned assone ... so that to semyng no man could entre.' Drawbridges over fifteen-foot ditches and a steep earthen pale led to the north and south entrances. On the west was a great bank with a steep twenty-four-foot ditch. The fort appeared so strong that some said 'it could not be wonne by sporte, but by ernest'[74] Henry intended to assault it himself – and would have, if his carpenters had built adequate siege equipment.

The joust, which employed disguise and dramatic impersonation, was held on 29 December. Six gentlemen rode from the castle to the tilt to await answerers. Two ancient knights clad in purple with beards of silver were led into the lists by two ladies on horseback. They presented a petition to the queen to answer the challenge, for while they were aged, their desire and good will encouraged them. When the queen consented, they threw off their disguises to reveal the king and Suffolk outfitted with bards of gold embroidered with purple, silver, and black.[75] Six courses were run, in which the king broke six spears. That evening the king and the Scottish ambassadors went into the queen's Chamber, 'where after that the Lordes and diuerse Ladies had daunced, there came in a Maske of .xvi. all appareled in clothe of Golde, riche tynsell and crimosyn veluet, cut, slit, and tied very curiously, their buskins and shoen wer gold, cappes and whoodes all gold.' Among the maskers were the king and Suffolk who, after taking out the ladies and dancing 'a greate season,' revealed their identities before wine and spices were served. Hall makes a point that the costumes were 'all gold, riche and not counterfeted.'[76] Gibson, who made the costumes both for the joust and for the mask, altered previously used garments and employed 'broken' cloth of gold from the storehouse to embellish the black velvet sleeves of six of the garments. His total charge was £12 4s. 11 1/2d.[77]

On 2 January the castle was assaulted by four knights from without and defended by two from within with pike, target, and sword. The castle was taken in the best 'battle of pleasure' ever fought, according to Hall, but the following day's assault was marred by injury.[78] After the combatants were disarmed, some young persons began to throw stones, 'and many honest men whiche threwe not wer hurt.' Fighting at barriers with swords, in which the king himself participated, took place on 5 January. On 8 February a tourney on horseback was fought with swords. The king participated, leading a party of twenty knights against Sir Anthony Browne and his company. On this occasion Henry's base and bard, furnished by Gibson, were made of cloth of silver and black velvet 'ruffed and not plain, and ouer that was a worke of purple veluet, embraudered richely with gold, cutte in knottes or foldes fastened, so that it bossed out and frounced very stately to behold.'[79]

Sieges or assaults on fortresses were common on the continent as backdrops for tournaments, but few are recorded in England.[80] The Castle of Loyalty is the first example of such an exhibition at Henry's court, no doubt authorized by the king to experiment with a fashionable form. The fact that it was introduced before ambassadors clearly indicates Henry's continuing interest in spectacles of dazzling proportion, but the form never became popular in England. There are many examples of mock sieges in court revels, but only a few of these more earnest assaults were produced later in the century.

This was also one of the last tournaments in which Henry participated. Perhaps advancing age was an issue, but the king was becoming increasingly concerned with producing a male heir, and around this time there were a few serious accidents which must have made it clear that retirement was appropriate. On 10 March 1524 Henry had a new harness made of his own design and a new set of armour 'suche as no armorer before that tyme had seen.'[81] Suffolk, against whom the king was to run a few courses apparently also had new armour, for he could not see well. The king neglected to close his visor, and he was struck on the brow by the duke's spear, driving the headpiece back and filling it with splinters. Henry assumed blame for the accident, and to show spectators that he was unhurt he ran six more courses. Suffolk was so shaken by the incident that he vowed never again to run against the king. Henry was undaunted, for he participated in the Castle of Loyalty tournament at Christmas in 1524–5, and again in a joust at Greenwich on 13 February 1526. But if the accident in 1524 could be brushed aside, the results of the one in 1526 could not. The king led a party of twelve against the

Marquis of Exeter and eleven companions, and in an accident reminiscent of Henry's in 1524, 'by chaunce of shiueryng of the spere, sir Francis Brian lost one of his iyes.'[82] Henry kept up appearances at the banquet that evening by doing 'seruice to the Quene and ladies hymself,' but it is clear that the incident had an effect. Of the six tournaments held at court from the Christmas season of 1526–7 through the following year, Henry is named as a participant in only one, on 5 March 1527.[83] He withdrew from active participation around this time, for he is not named in the two most diplomatically important jousts held in May and November 1527. He continued to practise privately, however, and sustained at least one more injury in 1536. While the king's withdrawal from the lists altered the spirit of these spectacles, it did not immediately diminish the magnificent displays associated with them.

The documents which survive for the period between 1525 and 1526 do not give an adequate account of revels and spectacles. On 18 June 1525 the king created Henry Fitzroy, his bastard son by Elizabeth Blount, Earl of Nottingham and Duke of Richmond and Somerset in an elaborate ceremony in which a number of other creations were made. Hall notes that 'at those creacions, were kept greate feastes and disguisynges.'[84] The charges were almost certainly borne by the king, but Gibson's account does not survive, and Hall does not give details. In December 1525 there were a great many deaths in London, and 'the king for to eschew the plague, kept his Christmas at Eltham with a small nomber, for no manne might come thether, but suche as wer appoynted by name: this Christmas in the kynges house, was called the still Christmas.'[85] One of Gibson's Revels accounts survives from early 1526, but it does not relate to a specific entertainment. It is a day-book – a running account of material and wages paid for a particular period – and an outline of a partial account beginning imperfectly.[86] As with all day-books, it does not supply dates of entertainments themselves, only the day on which work was begun or terminated. Since the account begins imperfectly, it is difficult to say whether the dates it does contain are beginning dates, terminal dates, or the period of the day-book. The day-book contains a few items which could relate to a joust, probably the 13 February joust in which Sir Francis Brian was injured. Gibson also mentions barriers fought by six lords who were furnished with equipment from the king's store. Whether the barriers were fought outdoors or were part of an indoor entertainment is not clear. Some of the items for example, the 108 feet of timber, 327 feet of elm board, 220 ells of canvas 'for Greenwich,' and many of the minor purchases suggest the construction of a pageant. Costumes for at least two masks are listed. One is for sixteen people: eight ladies were costumed in gowns of cloth of gold with purple velvet bonnets, and hired wigs; eight men were costumed in sarcenet coats, black satin mantles bound with velvet, black velvet buskins and bonnets, and gold beards. A second mask was for six gentlemen in gowns of cloth of silver and gold on one side and black tinsel satin on the other with black velvet buskins, great hoods of black tinsel satin, and silver beards for their visors. Exactly how much of this material was deployed over the season is not clear. The king may have given entertainments in January and February, which was his usual custom, in addition to the joust on Shrove Tuesday, and some of the material may have been used for the entertainments at Eltham during Christmas.[87] The king also kept a solemn Christmas at Greenwich in 1526–7 'with greate plentie of victaile, Reuels, Maskes, disguysynges, and bankettes.' There was a joust on 30 December with spears and swords, and another on 3 January in which four hundred spears were broken. After the latter, the king and fifteen of his companions went by barge to Wolsey's for revels.[88]

The development of the Revels organization after 1516 is attributable to Henry's negotiations with France and the Empire for a major role in European politics. The simple fact that so many revels were needed forced the development of an organization sophisticated enough to produce them – stable enough to provide administrative continuity and flexible enough to adapt and innovate. The separation of duties and delegation of responsibilities was an important step in professionalising revels productions. Guildford personally devised and supervised some of the revels and made arrangements for the court's entertainments, but he also provided high-level supervision for the productions of Cornish and Gibson. Cornish devised some of the more formal revels, which employed pageants and which relied on the adaptation of the play, while Gibson, in consultation with Guildford or the king, produced Cornish's revels as well as costumes for masks and plays, outfits for jousts, and pageants. This advance in production methods coupled with alterations in finance and the development of a large inventory of costumes and properties characterized the period. The Revels organization came into its own, conscious of itself as an important establishment in the royal household and concerned with the economical and judicious use of its expensive properties.

Because he thought that Cornish's talent was chiefly responsible for the success of Henry's revels and because he overestimated the impact of the second Anglo-French War (1523–6), Wallace dated the decline of court revels from 1523.[89] The combined evidence of narratives, reports, and accounts is sufficient to show that there was no decline in frequency of court revels and spectacles and no decline in their magnificence in this period. Hall, our main narrative source, makes clear that many entertainments were produced for which we have neither financial records nor detailed narratives. There were banquets, plays, masks, and other pastimes held at court in every Christmas season and on important state occasions. The evidence shows that magnificent revels and spectacles were still being produced. During the decade, the siege was used in a tournament, plays on contemporary diplomatic history were incorporated into the king's revels, and Wolsey made extensive use of classical elements in his. The Revels organization grew in this period to meet the demands imposed on it.

5

End of an Era, 1527–1534

i   Wolsey's Influence

The revels and spectacles of the decade of the 1520s rivalled any produced earlier in their scale and magnificence. In some measure their grandeur was due to Wolsey's statesmanship. Wolsey, who recognized the importance of the relationship between spectacle and political power as well as if not better than the king did, exploited it consistently. He was occasionally compared to the Pope in the elaboration he used in performing religious services, and in 1520, at the Field of Cloth of Gold, his retinue exceeded the combined entourages of the Archbishop of Canterbury and the Dukes of Suffolk and Buckingham.[1] His stature in these negotiations is apparent from the fact that he alone of the English embassy resided at the king's great temporary palace, where he hosted entertainments for French nobles and clerics, and, in turn, was himself entertained by the French queen at Ardres.[2] Wolsey's court was as likely a place as Henry's to find revels associated with negotiations of diplomatic moment, and from 1518 to 1529 his court rivalled the king's in the prestige and power such magnificence implied. Wolsey, whose diplomatic negotiations brought him frequently into contact with foreign courts and ambassadors, held revels with a distinct continental orientation. Further, the revels at Henry's court which celebrated negotiations of diplomatic moment during Wolsey's administration were influenced, and in some cases shaped, by the cardinal's role in those endeavours. Wolsey's prominence in government affairs and his lavish ceremonies and entertainments engendered considerable hostility. In recording events of the decade, Hall never misses an opportunity to expose what he regards as Wolsey's overreaching and extravagance, as in his description of the season of 1525–6 when the king kept a 'still' Christmas at Eltham because of the plague while the cardinal kept an open court at Richmond 'with plaies and disguisyng in most royall maner.'[3]

Beginning in 1518, Wolsey's diplomacy was celebrated with revels in which his negotiations were viewed as the key to political stability in Europe. The treaty of 1518, for example, was celebrated with *Report and Pegasus*, an allegorical revel showing that the Anglo-French league and marriage would create a unified Christian Europe strong enough to balance the power of the Turk. In October 1518, Wolsey hosted a disguising for the French embassy, in which the king participated. In January 1520, the king and nineteen of his companions costumed in masking apparel, were entertained with a banquet and revels at Wolsey's, and in January 1521 another revel was held there. A year later, the cardinal hosted some of the main revels in connection with the Anglo-Imperial treaty negotiations. On 3 March 1522 the king and the imperial ambassadors attended a banquet, a play performed by the Cardinal's Gentlemen, and a mask at Wolsey's court, and on the following evening another banquet and pageant-disguising – *Schatew Vert* – was produced there by Gibson under Sir Henry Guildford's supervision at the king's charge. Cornish's political allegory in June of that year celebrated the importance of the Anglo-Imperial treaty in checking the power of France. The height of Wolsey's power in international negotiations came in connection with the negotiations for the second Anglo-French treaty in 1527 and early 1528.

It was not simply the fact that Wolsey used spectacle to enhance his power that makes him important in the history of court revels, for under his auspices innovations quite different from those at Henry's court were introduced into England. The magnificence of the cardinal's court was naturally compared to the king's, and Henry noticed that in such comparisons Wolsey sometimes came off better. The cardinal's architectural projects at Hampton Court and York Place were without question more important than the king's, and led eventually to the exchange with the Crown of the former and the confiscation of the latter after Wolsey's fall.[4] Even as early as 1518, Wolsey's Chapel was better than the king's. Pace wrote to Wolsey that 'yff itt were not for the *per*sonall loue that the kingis highnesse doith bere vnto *your* grace, suerly he wolde haue owte off *your* chiapell, not chyldren oonly, but also men. for hys grace haith playnely schewydde vnto cornysche, that *your* grac*es* chiapell is better than hys, and prouidde the same bi thys reason, that yff any maner of newe songe schulde be brought vnto boith the sayde chiapellis to be sunge improuiso, then the sayde songe schulde be bettre, & more suerly handylde bi *your* chiapell than bi hys grac*es*.'[5] After the death of the Earl of Northumberland, Wolsey appropriated his chapel, noted for its distinguished musical and dramatic tradition. It was the talent which Wolsey had recruited, as well as the intimate acquaintance with continental courts, which underlies the innovative revels at his court.

Chambers did not exaggerate when he credited Wolsey with the encouragement of classical comedy in England.[6] The cardinal's revels included far more in

the way of classical elements than did the king's, and classical plays were incorporated into larger revels which exhibit marked continental influence. This is
illustrated by the revels at Hampton Court on 3 January 1527. Spinelli's letter
describing the event and Cavendish's generalized account illuminate the proceedings.[7] Wolsey was banqueting the papal legate, the Venetian and French
ambassadors, and some of the leading English nobles on this occasion. Henry had
spent the day in jousting, and 'That same night, the kyng and many yong gentlemen with hym came to Bridewell, & there put hym, and .xv. other, all in
Maskyng apparell, and then toke his Barge, and rowed to the Cardinalles place,
where wer at supper a great compaignie of lordes and ladies, and then the Maskers
daunced, & made goodly pastyme, and when they had well danced, the Ladies
plucked away their visors, & so they were all knowen, and to the kyng was made
a great banket.'[8] The king's arrival was signalled by cannon shot, and he and his
band of maskers, costumed as shepherds with beards of gold and silver wire,
entered the hall accompanied by a number of drums and fifes. The maskers played
at dice or mumchance with the cardinal and some of the ladies before revealing
their identities and joining the banquet. Henry's entrance was, by this time, an
ordinary if not tired invention in the annals of court revels, but Wolsey's entertainments were startlingly fresh. After the banquet, the company moved to a separate chamber to view a performance in Latin of Plautus's *Menaechmi* by the
Cardinal's Gentlemen. From Spinelli's description it appears that it was performed, like the Plautine play of March 1519, on a fixed stage, and the use of the
word 'scena' indicates some form of scenery rather than a bare platform.[9] After the
performance, the actors presented themselves before the king to recite Latin verses
in his honour before the company moved back to the banqueting hall. They
returned to the chamber later to see a pageant-disguising, apparently performed
on the same stage but set with different scenery. A character costumed as Venus
accompanied by six ladies entered to begin the disguising. A trumpet sounded to
signal the entrance of Cupid who was pulled in a chariot by three naked boys, and
who led by a silver rope six old men costumed as pastoral characters. Cupid introduced the men to Venus, and complained that they had been wounded by love
for the six ladies. Venus ordered the ladies to requite the gentlemen's affections,
and each of the old men danced with his beloved, described by Spinelli as '*una
molto bella danza.*' The revel was concluded later in the evening with dancing led
by the king.

While there are some similarities, the elements of Wolsey's revel are quite different from those at Henry's court. Henry's revels were principally oriented toward
a celebration of chivalric virtue and courtly love for which the main inspiration
was medieval romance. As Anglo has observed, Wolsey's revels are reminiscent of
Italian court entertainments which included classical plays, particularly plays by

Plautus, *intermezzi* of mythological and classical characters, brief dialogues, and choreographed dances.[10] The play by Plautus performed in March 1519 at Henry's court was part of a larger revel for French hostages in connection with the first Anglo-French treaty negotiations. It is likely that Wolsey influenced the planning, and the play may have been performed by the Cardinal's Gentlemen. They certainly performed a play, which may have been classical and performed in Latin, in connection with the revels for the imperial ambassadors on 3 March 1522. Many of the revels at Henry's court had centred on identity. The first part of the double mask in September 1519 turned on the revelation of the old courtiers as maskers. The revel of January 1527 also centres on identity. The *Menaechmi* is a play about love in which confusion of identity is the main plot device. The thematic connection to the pageant-disguising is the identity of the old pastoral characters as lovers. The revel reflects the diplomatic issues under negotiation with France which were to be specifically celebrated in May and November. Among other things, the French ambassadors were renegotiating the marriage treaty of 1518. They proposed to match Mary with the Duke of Orleans, second son of Francis I. According to Hall, 'many a man marueled' about this, and said 'she was mete for himself [Francis I].' There is little question about the classical and continental orientation of Wolsey's revels up to the early part of 1527, and diplomatic events later in that year provided the opportunity for more innovations.

The well-documented revels for the Anglo-French treaty in May and November 1527 are only properly understood in the context of Wolsey's diplomacy. Wolsey's revels of 3 January 1527 were prologue to the arrival of a French embassy in February to negotiate a treaty whereby England and France would oppose the Empire which the marriage would solidify. The treaty was concluded on 30 April and was celebrated by a tournament and an elaborate entertainment on 6 May. Sir Nicholas Carew, Sir Henry Jerningham, Sir Anthony Browne, and Nicholas Harvey appeared as challengers, a role almost invariably occupied by the king in the past. Gibson made their bases and bards, the right side of 'ryche tyssue embraudered with a compasse or roundell of blacke veluet and in the compas a right hand holding a sworde, and about the sword were pennes and peces of money of diuerse coynes, all embrawdered, vnder the hand was embraudered *Loialte,* and on that side of the bard was written in embraudery, *Bi pen, pain nor treasure, truth shall not be violated.*[11] The other side was of cloth of gold and silver. The Marquis of Exeter led the band of fourteen answerers. The right side of their bards and bases were of cloth of gold 'cut in cloudes engrayled with Damaske golde, the otherside cloth of syluer set with moyntaynes full of Oliue braunches, made of gold all mouyng.' Despite the rain, three hundred spears were broken in two and one-half hours 'with little missyng.' Gibson's day-book, which documents his preparations for a joust on 5 March in which the king participated, also contains the 'prepayerments' for apparel for these jousts in May.[12] Fifteen tailors were employed up to 5 March for the first joust, and then on 25 April four more tailors were hired to complete the work for the joust held on 6 May, indicating that much of the preparatory work was done in connection with the earlier joust.

A banqueting house was constructed beside the tilt at Greenwich for the entertainments and revels following the joust.[13] Not only some of the details of the design of this temporary building but also the system of delegating and contracting the work on the entire project was reminiscent of the Field of Cloth of Gold in 1520. Construction of the banqueting house was under the supervision of Sir Henry Guildford and Sir Thomas Wyatt, assisted by a number of contract supervisors, artisans, and labourers. Guildford's and Wyatt's account book as well as a number of Gibson's accounts document details of the building and its construction.[14] Gibson notes that as early as 14 January he was commanded by the king to begin work on this 'hovs kalled the long hovs' which was 'ordayned and maad for pastyme and to do solas to strangers.'[15] It was to be 'fvrnyshed of werke of plessyer for reuells of dysguysyng and meskelyng ... in goodly hast.' Labourers, painters, carpenters, and, by 18 January, tailors worked on the building until 11 March. They resumed work on 3 April and continued until the evening of the entertainment in May. On 6 February, three weeks after Gibson's crew began work, Guildford and Wyatt began to disburse payments to labourers, artisans, and craftsmen including four Italian painters – Vincent Vulpe and Ellys Carmyan who worked from 6 February to 4 May at 20s. a week, and Nicholas Florentyne and 'Domyngo' who worked from 11 February at 2s. and 1s. 4d. a shift, day and night.[16]

The banqueting house was 'of an hundreth foote of length and xxx. foote bredth' with clerestory windows; 'the Iawe peces and crestes were karued wyth Vinettes ... and richely gilted with gold and Bise.'[17] It consisted of two chambers connected by a gallery, one to be used for dining and the other to be used for revels. Tables in the dining chamber were arranged in horseshoe fashion. Dinner was served from cupboards, one of seven stages, thirteen feet long, containing vessels of gold and silver set with precious stones, and another of nine stages containing vessels of silver 'so high and so brode that it was a maruaile to beholde.' The walls were covered with tapestries depicting the history of David. Candlesticks of 'antyke woorke whiche bare litle torchettes of white waxe' were fixed on the walls. These candlesticks of iron work were in the charge of Clement Urmeston, who probably also provided the hanging branches for lights, set with 230 'antique cuppis' with an hundred 'antique knoppis pomander ffacion,' the cups garnished with 1,900 leaves of lead. The eighteen beams supporting the lights were decorated with four hundred roses and five hundred antique leaves made of gilt lead.

Urmeston also made a 'pagiant of Light*es*' with twenty images holding candle-sticks. This pageant was apparently like the pageant figures of men and women used at the Calais banqueting house in 1520 and like the pageant of dancing lights he was to make for the November 1527 entertainment.[18] Obviously, indoor entertainments require significant illumination, but we find little information about it in Gibson's accounts. For important state occasions it appears that he contracted this work to wire drawers, like Urmeston, artisans who specialized in fashioning the chandeliers, candelabra, and torches necessary to illuminate such performances.[19]

At the end of the dining chamber, leading to a gallery and then into the rev-els chamber, was a triumphal arch with three entrances. The two outer entrances were used for service. The centre was between two cupboards, stocked with wine, over which was a balcony for musicians. The arch itself was decorated with gar-goyles, serpents, armorials, and busts of emperors, possibly the beasts made by Gibson beginning on 11 March, and the antique heads painted by Giovanni da Maiano.[20] George Lovekyn supervised the production of the arch and charged £292 9s. 8d. in Guildford's and Wyatt's account for the work, which included sewing the carpets for the floor of the disguising chamber.[21] Painting the arch itself was in the charge of John Browne and Vincent Vulpe at a cost of £282 15s. 4d. Lovekyn paid for twenty-four ells of canvas for lining the rear sides of the arch. A 'maister hans' (probably Hans Holbein) was paid £4 10s. in Lovekyn's account for 'the paynetyng of the plat of Tirwan' in which 'the very maner of euery mans camp, [was] very connyngly wrought.'[22] Beyond the arch was a gallery 'richely hanged,' at the end of which was a door 'made with masonrie embatayled with Iasper,' and beyond the door was the revels chamber 'raised with stages .v. degrees on euery syde, & rayled & counterailed borne by pillars of Azure, full of starres & flower delice of gold, euery pillar had at the toppe a basin siluer, wherein stode greate braunches of white waxe, the degrees werre all of Marble coler, and the railes like white marble.'[23] Gibson's Revels account confirms Hall's description of the pillars, the basins of which were silvered by John Browne. The seating arrange-ments here appear to be amphitheatre style, each row behind and above the pre-vious one, in contrast to the Calais banqueting house, which had galleries.

Like the temporary palace at Guisnes and the Calais banqueting house, the Long House had two roofs, one exterior roof and one interior decorative ceiling. Gibson prepared the outer roof and supplied the 464 ells of linen and gold and silver cloth for the inner ceiling.[24] The inner ceiling of the dining chamber was of 'purple cloth ful of roses and Pomgranettes.' The inner ceiling of the revelling chamber was 'conninglie made by the kynges Astronimer, for on the grounde of the rofe, was made the hole earth enuironed with the Sea, like a very Mappe or Carte, and by a conning makyng of another cloth, the zodiacke with the .xii.

Signes, and the fiue circles or girdelles and the two poles apered on the earth and water compassing the same, and in the zodiak were the twelue signes, curiously made, and aboue this were made the seuen planettes, as Mars, Jupiter, Sol, Mercurius, Venus, Saturnus, and Luna, euery one in their proper houses.'²⁵ Hall suggests that Nicholas Kratzner designed the ceiling, but Gibson's payments reveal that it was executed by Master Hans in collaboration with 'Master Nikolas' who was paid 4s. a day from 8 February until 3 March. The payments include 'party golld fyn syllver fyen golld: spent vn the greet rovf by master hans and his paynters for the lynes and regements the stars and syche.'²⁶ Nicholas Kratzner was a native of Munich, born about 1487, educated at Cologne and Wittenberg, and a reader in mathematics at Oxford who also lectured on astronomy. By 1520 he was being paid for devising 'Horologes' for the king, to whom his two manuscript works on astrology are dedicated.²⁷ In addition to the two cloths used for the ceiling, there were two other cloths; and since Master Hans was paid for four cloths, he and his painters were probably also responsible for the two that were hung at opposite ends of the chamber. These were ready by 11 March, when ten men were paid to hang them for the king's inspection and take them down again.²⁸ In the middle of the revels chamber was an arch which stretched from side to side. It was constructed of imitation masonry work, and its pillars and garnishings were painted gold and bice. Over the gate of the arch were busts of 'Hercules, Scipio, Iulius, Pompei and other such conquerors,' so impressive that Spinelli marvelled that it could have been built in such a short time.²⁹

On the evening of 6 May, after a great banquet in the dining chamber and after pausing to view Holbein's painting in the gallery, the company went into the revels chamber. Ladies were seated on the left and the ambassadors and invited male guests on the right. Henry, his sister, and the queen were seated on a royal dais in the center. Hall says that the entertainment began with the entrance of a person costumed in cloth of gold with a blue silk mantle on which was embroidered eyes of gold and wearing a gold cap set with garlands of laurel and gold berries. This character delivered a Latin oration in praise of Francis I, Henry VIII, and Wolsey. Eight members of the Chapel entered singing accompanied by 'one richly appareled: and in likewise at the other side, entred eight other of the saied Chappel bryngyng with them another persone, likewise appareled.'³⁰ These two persons played a dialogue, debating whether riches were better than love. In Spinelli's account, the eight choristers entered with a youth costumed as Mercury in a blue mantle who, after the singers had withdrawn, gave his oration.³¹ Mercury also announced that Jupiter had heard debates between Love and Riches and, unable to decide between the arguments, appointed Henry as judge. When Mercury departed, eight young choristers entered, four led by Love and four by Riches. Between them walked Justice who came before the king and outlined the dispute in English. Love stated his case, supported by four choristers, and Riches answered, supported by his choristers. The debate resulted in a deadlock, and it was decided to refer the matter to combat. Six armed knights entered, three as champions for each party, and took their positions at the arch. A gilt bar descended in the arch to form a barrier at which the knights fought one on one. After this, an old man with a silver beard entered to declare that 'loue & riches, both be necessarie for princes (that is to saie) by loue to be obeied and serued, and with riches to rewarde his louers and friendes, and with this conclusion the dialogue ended.'[32] This is the only revel in the period between 1523 and 1541 for which we have evidence of the Chapel's participation. Spinelli's description of them as 'young' choristers suggests the Children only, but the narrative shows that there were eighteen choristers at least, and, since there were only twelve Children at this time, some of the Gentlemen may have participated.

The dialogue builds on the chivalric theme of the joust held that afternoon. The answerers used emblems of olive branches and the challengers displayed mottos declaring loyalty and proclaiming that truth would not be violated by 'pen, pain nor treasure.' The theme of peace, relevant to the treaty negotiations, is grounded in a chivalric dedication to truth and honour. In *Love and Riches* the stalemate between seemingly incompatible positions yields neither to debate nor to arms. The failure of debate and combat is resolved by the old man who bases his insight on chivalric virtue – truth and honour grounded in the allegiance of retainers and the munificence of their lords. The seemingly incompatible positions are held in balance by wisdom, which acknowledges the importance of both, just as the seemingly incompatible diplomatic positions of England and France are by the treaty. The harmony of apparent opposites at higher levels of human insight is a theme which appears similar to that of Cornish's *Troylus and Pandor* in 1516.

The authorship of *Love and Riches* is not certainly established. Wallace attributed it to John Heywood based on its similarities to the *Play of Love* and especially to the *Play of the Weather,* in which Jupiter appears as Prime Mover.[33] Hillebrand felt that Rastell, who at least was employed on the project, and even Crane – none of whose original compositions or arrangements survive – are better candidates than Heywood.[34] Reed attributed the dialogue to Rastell based on the payments to him in the bill he submitted to Guildford for 'dyuers Necessaries bought for trymmyng of the Pageant of the ffather in hevun.' Like Wallace, Reed associated the Father in Heaven with Jupiter in *Love and Riches* and cited a payment from the account for writing a dialogue as part of his argument for Rastell's authorship.[35] Anglo, who also attributed the dialogue to Rastell, rejected Reed's identification of Jupiter with the Father but argued that Guildford's payments to Rastell are for three separate projects: moulded royal beasts, a display pageant – a fixed *entremet*, very much like the Father in Heaven pageant he had made for the 1522 reception of Charles V – and for the dialogue of *Love and Riches*.[36] However, Guildford's account is for fittings in the banqueting house, not for the revels. It is unlikely that any of the payments in this account are for *Love and Riches*. The payment to Rastell's assistant, John Redman, for writing 'the screptur,' 'the dialogue,' and for making the 'Rhyme' in English and Latin is for scribal work. Like those used in Rastell's 1522 pageant, this scripture and dialogue may be associated with a display pageant made for the banqueting house.[37] Crane and Rastell are the best candidates for authorship, but the evidence is insufficient to certainly attribute the work.

After *Love and Riches*, a pageant-disguising featuring Princess Mary was introduced. Its theme was the marriage alliance. Hall and Spinelli both mention that a curtain or painted cloth was let down to the ground to reveal 'a goodly mou*n*t, walled with towers and vamures al gilt, with all thinges necessarie for a fortresse, & all the mount was set ful of Christal coralles, & rich rockes of rubie cureously conterfaited & full of roses & pomegranates.'[38] The curtain appears to have been painted with a scene. This is the third confirmed use of a curtain in Henrican revels – the first two were used in 1511 and in 1518 – and its purpose here is to suddenly reveal the scene of the cave. Both narratives of the cave, which could be entered by four steps, are vague. Gibson's account is not much help other than to show that the cave was decorated with flowers.[39] On or around the rock were eight youths costumed in cloth of tissue and silver 'cut in quatre foyles, the gold engrailed with siluer, and the siluer with gold, al loose on white satin, and on ther heddes cappes of blake veluet set with perle and stone, they also had mantelles of blake saten.'[40] Princess Mary and seven ladies costumed in 'romayne fashion,' in cloth of gold and crimson tinsel with bonnets of crimson velvet set with pearls and stones, came out of the cave and danced alone before the king. The youths also danced alone before joining the ladies for another dance. As Anglo has observed, elaborate choreography is suggested.[41] During the final dance, six maskers with visors and silver beards, apparelled in cloth of silver and black tinsel satin with hoods of cloth of gold 'after the fashion of Iseland,' entered and took the ladies out to dance. Finally, eight more maskers, among them the king and the French ambassador, entered in cloth of gold and purple tinsel satin 'greate, lo*n*g & large, after the Venecians fashion' with visors and beards of gold to dance with the ladies until they were unmasked.

The next day, 7 May 1527, imperial forces sacked the city of Rome, an event which opened the way for Wolsey's starring role in political negotiations which were to have specific religious overtones. Henry and Wolsey regarded themselves as champions of orthodox Christianity against the heretic Luther, and now the means of connecting politics and religion presented itself in the desecration of the

Holy City. Wolsey spent the months from July through September 1527 in France conducting negotiations related to the tensions between Francis I, Charles V, and the Pope. The cardinal was entertained while in France with plays about the sack of Rome and by a series of civic entries celebrating his role as peacemaker.[42] On his return to England, plans were made to celebrate Henry's ratification of the Anglo-French treaty and the reciprocal installation of Henry into the Order of St Michael and Francis I into the Order of the Garter. A tournament and an evening of revels were scheduled for 10 November. The event was prepared at the king's charge, but deference to Wolsey is apparent in the planning, particularly in securing the services of the Children of St Paul's School, who performed a play on the same theme as those which had been presented in France.

The Greenwich banqueting house was renovated for the entertainments. Preparations were again under the supervision of Guildford, who delegated work to Gibson, George Lovekyn, and others. Lovekyn had charge of renovating the two arches in the banqueting house and of building a fountain, a portal, and other new work in the revels chamber. Gibson had charge of constructing a pageant of an arbour, of decorating the chambers, and of providing garments for the play and masks. John Browne, Vincent Vulpe, Ellys Carmyan, and Giovanni da Maiano were all employed again, and Clement Urmeston was hired to provide the lighting. He prepared seventeen branches decorated with coats of arms and a pageant of 'dancing lights' which must have been like those used at Calais in 1520, for tailors were hired to make coats and caps for the human figures associated with them. Work began on 10 October, and the renovations were completed by 10 November. Bills for the work, which totalled only about £140 in contrast to the £800 spent in May, confirm that the preparations were essentially renovations.[43] The celebration included a joust held on the afternoon of 10 November and entertainments in the evening. Gibson's account does not survive, and Hall simply mentions that twelve challengers faced twelve answerers.[44] That evening a banquet of ninety dishes was served in the dining chamber of the Long House, and a play and disguising were held in the revels chamber.

After the play, there were four masks, of which Hall describes only the king's, which involved the disguised ladies of the pageant-fountain. This fountain of white marble, three levels high, stood on balls of gold supported by 'rampyng beastes wounde in leues of golde.'[45] The first level had golden gargoyles spouting water. The second was environed with gold winged serpents which gripped the next level. On top was a 'fayre lady out of whose brestes ran aboundantly water of merueilous delicious sauer.' About this fountain were benches of rosemary 'fretted in braydes layde on gold,' the sides of which were covered with roses as if they grew naturally. On these benches sat eight ladies dressed in 'straung attier' – outfits of cloth of gold 'embrodered and cut ouer siluer.' On one side of this fountain was a hawthorn tree 'all of silk with white flowers' surmounted by the arms of England and encircled with the emblem of the Order of St Michael. On the other side was a mulberry tree 'ful of fayre beryes all silke' surmounted by the arms of France and encircled with the emblem of the Order of the Garter. The pageant, symbolizing France and England, was a visual tribute to the alliance, the installation of the two kings into the orders, and formed a backdrop to the revels. Montgomery, Suffolk, Exeter, Edward Neville, the king, and three others costumed in cloth of gold, purple tinsel satin, and mantles of crimson satin danced with the ladies of the fountain.[46] Gibson, who altered the garments used in the May revels, notes that their visors were equipped with beards 'towskyd withe uppar lyppis flossyd.'[47] From the other costumes Gibson made, it appears that the other three masks included one of six 'men at arms,' one of six 'black maskelers,' and one which is called the 'great mask,' probably the one in which Princess Mary and seven other ladies appeared. For this latter mask Gibson altered at least one garment of cloth of silver and gold 'that was of the Remayns of Ladyes garments at Ard the xijth yer the vijth maskeller in the ffrenche kort.'

Cavendish who attended the revel as Wolsey's personal assistant described it as consisting of a banquet, barriers, two masks of ladies and gentlemen, and an 'interlude made in Latine.'[48] The most noteworthy part of the revel was the play. Hall records that it was performed

in maner of Tragedy, the effect wherof was that ye Pope was in captiuitie & the church brought vnder the foote, wherfore S. Peter appeared and put the Cardinal in authoritie to bryng the Pope to his libertie and to set vp the church againe, and so the Cardinall made intercession to the kinges of England and of Fraunce, that they tooke part together, and by their meanes the pope was deliuered. Then came in the Frenche kynges children and complayned to the Cardinal how the Emperor kept them as hostages and would not come to no reasonable point with their father, wherfore thei desired ye Cardinal to helpe for their deliueraunce, which wrought so with the kyng his master and the French kyng that he brought the Emperor to a peace, and caused the two yong princes to be deliuered.[49]

The play was more complicated than Hall indicates, for Gibson lists costumes for thirty-eight characters in his account.[50] There was an orator 'in aperell of gold'; a poet 'in aperell of cloth of gold'; Religion, 'ecclesia,' and 'veritas lyke iij novessis In garmentes of sylke and vayelles of lawne and sypers'; 'Errysy,' 'ffalse interpretacion,' and 'Corrupcio scriptoris lyke laddys of beeme inpereled in garmentes of sylke of dyvers collors'; Peter, Paul, and James 'in iij abettes of whyghte sarsenet/ and iij red mantylles/ and heris of sylvar of damaske and pellevns of skarlet'; a Cardinal 'in hys aparell'; two Sergeants 'in ryche aparell'; 'The dolfyn and his brother/ in cottes of velvit inbravdrid withe gold and capis of satyn bownd with velvett'; a Messenger 'in tynsell satyn'; six Men in gowns of green sarcenet and six Women in gowns of crimson sarcenet; War 'in ryche cloth of gold and fethers and armyd'; 'iij Alamyns in aparell all cvt and sclyt of sylke'; 'Lady pees in ladys aparell all whyght' and rich; Lady Quietness; and Dame Tranquillity, richly 'besyn in Ladis aparell.' The most surprising costumes were for 'The herrytyke Lewtar lyke a party frer in rosset damaske and blake taffata' and 'Lewtars wif lyke a frowe of spyers in almayn/ in red sylke.'

The play appears clearly to have been written by John Rightwise, educated at Eton and Cambridge and appointed Surmaster of St Paul's School in 1517 under William Lyly, whom he succeeded as High Master in 1522. Gibson made payments in his account for boat hire for the Master (Rightwise), the Usher, and the Children of Paul's to and from Greenwich in connection with the 10 November 1527 revel, for the Childrens' costumes, for 'fyar in tyme of Learnyng of the play,' and for bread, ale, and beer for thirty-eight children.[51] Evidence suggests that Rightwise presented other entertainments in connection with the reception of the French embassy in 1527. A reward of 40s. is recorded in the records of the City of London on 29 October 1527 for his 'payn & labor that he toke in makyng of the proposicion to the ffrenshe Ambassadors,' possibly some civic entertainment presented by the city on that occasion.[52] The dramatic tradition at St Paul's stretched back to 1378, and while this is the first certain evidence of a performance by them at Henry's court, Rightwise is credited with making 'the tragedy of Dido out of Vergil' and performing it with the scholars of his school before Cardinal Wolsey 'with great applause.'[53] The date of this performance is unknown, but it is certain that the Children acted Terence's *Phormio* on 7 January 1528 at Wolsey's, and it appears fairly certain that Rightwise was the author of the politico-religious play which followed it that evening. In his undated petition to the king for aid, probably written around the time of his removal as High Master of St Paul's school for neglect of duty, he reminds the king that he had 'caused commedies and/ ... [s]uche like pleasures to be plaide as well be fore your/ [am]bassiters and other straungers for ther intertaynment.'[54] On 21 January 1531 he was paid £13 9s. from the king's Privy Purse for an unspecified service. While this reward may have been a response to his petition, this was the Christmas season in which the king kept estate in the Hall shortly after Wolsey's death. Given the timing, the amount of the payment, and Rightwise's association with Wolsey, it is possible that the reward was for an entertainment. The evidence is not as full as we could wish, but it is enough to suggest that Rightwise was the deviser of more entertainments for the City of London, for Wolsey, and for the king than we can fully document.

Rightwise's play for 10 November has been described as anti-Luther and anti-Protestant in subject.[55] It includes anti-Protestant material, but as Wallace has pointed out it was written at Wolsey's instigation in order to glorify his role in the Anglo-French negotiations, and Anglo has explained how the play accords with contemporary events: the city of Rome had been sacked by imperial forces on 7 May. Pope Clement was prisoner of Emperor Charles V. The treaty of Madrid, forced by Charles V on a defeated Francis I, provided for the imprisonment of his sons as surety for peace. The Anglo-French alliance, negotiated by Wolsey in the summer of 1527, was designed to bring the Empire to terms on these issues.[56] While this is not the first court play to dramatize contemporary political events, it is the first to mix historical, contemporary, and allegorical characters to do so. It is the first court play to focus on the interrelationship between politics and religion. And, it is the first original court play of which we have record to be performed in Latin. The play, which ought to be renamed *Cardinalis Pacificus* to reflect its real theme, is a curious hybrid that incorporates characters from popular dramatic tradition, exhibits the influence of Humanist school drama, and anticipates the history play of the following decade.

While written in Latin, the narratives indicate that *Cardinalis Pacificus* was not constructed on a classical model. Rather, it employs classical trappings to field contemporary as well as familiar dramatic characters from the court, civic, and popular traditions. There are some obvious points of contact with the morality and with the saint and biblical plays, but *Cardinalis Pacificus* owes as much, if not more, to the civic entry pageant which had for some time mixed allegorical characters, contemporary figures, and historical personages and which had set events in the context of universal history. Anglo has argued that it is reminiscent of the plays and pageants presented before Wolsey at Boulogne, Abbeville, and Amiens during the previous summer.[57] Some of the same characters were employed, as well as the notion of an apocalypse in history keyed to the cardinal's attempt to bring peace to western Europe and to restore the church. The play proceeds by narrowing the scope of contemporary history to identify a threat to Christian civilization. That threat is no longer the Turkish empire, as it was in the allegorical court play of 1518 – and as it continued to be in the writings of Humanists such as More and Vives – but the policies of Charles V.[58] He is the tyrant whose intransigence is responsible for the imprisonment of Francis I's sons, whose toleration of Lutheranism has weakened the church, and whose army had recently committed sacrilege in the sack of Rome and imprisonment of the Pope.

Hall tells us that the Children of Paul's performed this play in the manner of a tragedy. The conclusion is not tragic, for the play projects the willingness of Gattinara to negotiate, and the consequent release of Francis I's sons, the liberation of the Pope, and the restoration of the church. Dramatic tension in the play, however, is more like that in tragedy than in the morality, where the protagonist is torn by opposing virtues and vices. Wolsey is a hero caught between his obligations as an ecclesiastic and his duty as a statesman. He must oppose Katherine of Aragon's nephew, England's sworn ally, and risk plunging Europe into another war. Wolsey's political and ecclesiastical positions as Lord Chancellor and as cardinal endow his actions with both political and spiritual significance. In the con-. text of temporal history he – and Henry VIII – oppose the Empire spiritually by supporting the church with writings against Luther and politically by the new treaty with France. The free use of dramatic time allows the introduction of Peter, James, and Paul to focus on the historical continuity of the papacy and, thereby, to place Wolsey's efforts in the context of universal history. The cardinal becomes an instrument who accepts an apostolic appointment to espouse Veritas, support Religion, restore Ecclesia, and establish Peace and Tranquility. Hall, of course, does not let slip the opportunity to turn the spectacle against Wolsey by noting that at 'this play wisemen smiled & thought that it sounded more glorious to the Cardinal then true to the matter in dede.'

An original play performed in Latin only a few years after the first notice of a classical play at court is a noteworthy development in itself, but in its intermixture of genres and in its politico-religious theme, the play is even more remarkable in anticipating the propaganda drama of the next decade. It does so by attempting to harmonize Wolsey's dual roles and by glorifying his place in universal history. In this, the play looks forward to Protestant historiography, in which Henry VIII or Edward VI or Elizabeth I are imagined as instruments in fashioning a state in which it becomes possible to restore the ancient sincerity of the apostolic church.[59] The ideology of power reinforced by an idealized image, begins to develop in conjunction with leaders who find conflict between their secular and spiritual roles. This is quite a different matter from the tension between private satisfaction and public duty which we find in some of the king's earlier disguises. While Henry VIII played many roles in his revels, there is no indication of an attempt, nor any indication that a need was felt, to harmonize these roles. The conflict, resolved in *Cardinalis Pacificus* by Wolsey's apostolic appointment, seconded by the power of Henry and Francis, anticipates changes in royal ideology after the Reformation. Like it or not, monarchs will then have to confront the problem of a divided public role and seek the means of harmonizing it through a manipulation of the royal image in the revels and elsewhere. Henry VIII did not have difficulties with this. The frontispiece of Cranmer's Bible in 1539 depicts Henry handing the Word of God to his bishops and nobles. The head of the secular hierarchy is depicted as the obvious means by which God's Word is mediated to the lower orders of both ecclesiastical and temporal hierarchies. The Reformation was too new and too dependent on Henry's personal commitment for this idea to promote serious difficulties. It did produce difficulties for his successors.

Wolsey's last recorded revel was held on 7 January 1528 to celebrate the Pope's escape to Orvietto in December 1527. On 5 January the papal legate, English bishops, and ambassadors, went in procession to St Paul's for a thanksgiving service, followed by an address to the crowd outside the cathedral by Wolsey.[60] Two days later the cardinal invited the ambassadors to a banquet and revels, which included a performance of Terence's *Phormio* followed by a politico-religious play.[61] For the occasion a banqueting chamber was decorated with a large garland inscribed in gilt letters *Terentii Phormio*. On both sides of the chamber were banners, on one of which was written in Gothic letters, *Cedant arma togae,* and on the other, *Foedus pacis non movebitur.* Beneath the garland was inscribed a reference to Wolsey's style, particularly appropriate to the role he had played in freeing the Pope: *Honori et laudi Pacifici.* Other mottoes on the theme of peace decorated the sides of the chamber. Spinelli was impressed with the performance of *Phormio* by the Children of Paul's. Afterwards, three 'girls,' representing Religion, Peace, and Justice, came forward to explain that they had been expelled from Europe by War, Heresy, and Ambition. After this, the boy who had played the part of the Prologue in *Phormio* entered to deliver a Latin oration celebrating the release of Pope Clement. The play portrayed Wolsey in his diplomatic role as protector of the Church and promoter of peace. Given the fact that the Children of St Paul's performed on the occasion, and that the play on the delivery of the Pope is close in theme and contains three characters identical with those in *Cardinalis Pacificus,* it is probable, as Anglo has argued, that Rightwise was the author.[62] This is the last recorded revel held by the great cardinal before his fall in the following year, and marks the height of his power in international politics.

Wolsey was as skilled in the use of propaganda for political and diplomatic purposes as he was in furthering his own career. He anticipated the uses which his successor, Cromwell, was to make of polemical drama in the next decade, but ironically, he was undone at least partly by the hostility which his lavish spectacles and propaganda engendered.[63] In 1521 an anonymous writer complained that this 'butcher's cur' had wasted the royal treasury through his extravagance.[64] After years of such suggestions, Wolsey became hypersensitive even to supposed references to his influence in government. John Roo's Gray's Inn play, produced at Christmas 1526–7, was highly praised by Hall, who explains the plot and theme:

the effecte of the plaie was, that lord gouernance was ruled by dissipacion and negligence, by whose misgouernance and euill order, lady Publike weele was put from gouernance: which caused Rumor Populi, Inward grudge and disdain of wanton souereignetie, to rise with a greate multitude, to expell negligence and dissipacion, and to restore Publik welth again to her estate, which was so done. This play was so set furth with riche and costly apparel, with straunge diuises of Maskes & Morrishes that it was highly praised of all menne, sauying of the Cardinall, whiche imagined that the plaie had been diuised of hym.[65]

Wolsey jailed Roo and Thomas Moyle, one of the actors, and threatened the others. Hall defends the play, saying that Roo had compiled most of it some twenty years before and that 'it was neuer meante to hym [Wolsey].' Hall sides, characteristically, with those 'wise' men who 'grudged to see hym take it so hartely' and suggests that the cardinal was dissembling when he claimed that he took action only because the king was displeased.

Public opinion in England of Wolsey as an extravagant overreacher with French sympathies combined with the suspicion of his role in international politics held by European princes and by the cardinals in Rome. When Wolsey's French-oriented foreign policy backfired, Henry was forced to take the most prudent political course by removing him. The unpopular French alliance, the defeat of French forces in Italy in 1529, the treaty concluded between the Pope and Emperor Charles V, and that between Charles V and Francis I rendered impotent England's position in European politics. It left Henry without political leverage in the matter of his divorce and led to the Pope's humiliating summons to appear before the court in Rome.[66] The outcry against Wolsey led to his being sent to York, where he was arrested on 4 November, the strain hastening his death on 29 November 1530.

There is little question that Wolsey's fall had an impact on the development of court revels in England. The cardinal's revels and those which celebrated his diplomacy at Henry's court were on the leading edge of the introduction of classical and continental elements as well as of the innovative adaption of medieval drama to international politico-religious events. All of this was lost. Henry's focus on domestic policy in conjunction with the divorce, a consequence of England's waning power in European politics, effectively put an end to the grand displays connected to events of diplomatic moment. The king's next international interview with Francis I in 1532 was scaled to the domestic substance of the negotiations, and the revels at home found little inspiration in the nasty business of divorcing Katherine, marrying Anne Boleyn, and promulgating the Reformation.

ii   The End of an Era

Only imperfect Revels accounts survive for the Christmas of 1527–8 and none for the rest of the period to 1534. Narratives provide only generalizations, but enough to establish that the king did hold revels in these years. Unspecified entertainments were held at Richmond and Greenwich in 1527–8.[67] Hall records that in 1528–9 'the Kyng kept his Christmas at Grenewiche, with much solempnitie

... shewed great pleasures, bothe of Iustes, Tornay, Bankettes, Maskes and disguisynges,' but he provides no details other than to explain that they were held
'more to quicken his [Henry's] spirites and for recreacion.'[68] The Chamber
accounts document appearances by playing companies at a level close to that at
the beginning of the reign.[69] The King's Players were paid £6 13s. 4d., the same
amount was paid to William Crane and the Children of the Chapel, and £4 was
paid to the Princess's 'new' Players for performances.[70] In 1529–30 'the kyng
remoued to Grenewiche and there kept his Christemas with the quene in great triumph: with great plentie of viaundes, and diuerse disguisynges and Enterludes.'[71]
Some of these interludes were given by the King's Players, the Princess's Players,
and by Crane and the Children of the Chapel, all of whom were rewarded for performances before the king on New Year's Day. Another was given by 'certain players of coventry' who were paid 20s. for a performance at Christmas, probably in
the Hall.[72] The Master of the Bears was also rewarded on 31 December, probably for a baiting on that day.

    After Wolsey's death in 1530, 'the kyng remoued from Hampton court to
Grenewiche where he with quene Katherine kept a solempne Christmas, and on
the twelfe night he satte in the halle in his estate, where as were diuers Enterludes,
riche Maskes and disportes, and after that a great banket.'[73] We have no details
about these revels, but plays were performed, again, by the King's Players, the
Princess's Players, and by Crane and the Children of the Chapel, all of whom were
rewarded on New Year's Day. John Rightwise was also paid £13 9s. on 21 January,
suggesting that one of the Christmas entertainments may have been written and
produced by him.[74] The Gentlemen of the Chapel received their traditional
reward of £13 6s. 8d. in each of these years on New Year's Day, but the justifica-
tion was for their 'pains taking' at Christmas.[75] It is difficult to know exactly what
this painstaking included beyond the songs they usually performed in conjunction with traditional ceremonies.[76] The evidence clearly shows that revels were
held at Henry's court in every Christmas season and that plays were performed
at least from 1528 to 1531. Since the Chamber accounts do not survive from
1522 to 1528 nor from 1532 to 1538, we can only surmise that dramatic performances were also regular features of the Christmas entertainments in those
years.

    We have no evidence of the plays performed by these companies, and, in con-
trast to abundant evidence of the Chapel's participation in revels earlier in the
reign, there is only one recorded instance in this period. Few firm conclusions can
be drawn, because of the absence of Revels accounts and because we know so little about the Master of the Children. When Cornish retired from the Chapel at
Easter 1523, he was immediately succeeded by William Crane.[77] Crane functioned
as Master during pleasure until his formal appointment by patent on 12 May

1526, which raised his annuity from 40 marks to £40 and increased the number of children from ten to twelve.[78] Crane had been a Gentleman of the Chapel from at least 3 June 1509, and spent twenty-two years of his thirty-six-year career as Master of the Children. He retired in 1545 and died before April 1546.[79] Married and the father of at least one daughter, Crane was a merchant of considerable wealth. His position at court and at least occasional familiarity with the king helps to account for his thriving business interests. He received several grants of buildings in London, licenses for the export and import of goods, and contracts during the wars of 1512–14 and 1523–6 to outfit the king's ships.[80] While records are adequate to document his business enterprises, none of his musical, literary, or dramatic compositions have been discovered. Circumstantial evidence associates him with the old Players of the Chapel between 1509 and 1512, and documentary evidence confirms his appearance in at least three major court revels between 1511 and 1516. Because the position he occupied required such services, we can only infer that he was a talented musician and skilled enough in drama to merit the appointment as Master of the Children. Whether Crane wrote plays for the Children or texts for the revels as his predecessor had done cannot be determined. It is certain that, during his Mastership, he performed plays with the Children before the king in every Christmas season for which documentary evidence survives and he participated in the May 1527 performance of *Love and Riches*.

The queen's absence from court because of the divorce proceedings and the king's open association with Anne Boleyn made Christmas 1531–2 a dismal affair. Despite the fact that 'the Kyng kepte his Christemas at Grenewyche with great solempnitie ... all the men sayde that there was no myrthe ... because the Queene and the Ladies were absent.'[81] Henry was occupied this year in solidifying an international position made unstable by his divorce, by his projected marriage to Anne, and by Wolsey's death. His trip to France in 1532 was aimed at winning the support of Francis I against Charles V, whose aunt Henry was divorcing. The king arrived at Calais in October and met with Francis on the 21st. On the 25th they journeyed to Calais, where Francis was lodged at the Staple Hall.[82] Entertainments were modest – nothing on the scale of the 1520 meeting. There were a few banquets and ordinary entertainments: bull- and bear-baiting, and dancing. On 27 October there was a mask of ladies, led by Anne herself, who took Francis out to dance:

After supper came in the Marchiones of Penbroke, with .vii. ladies in Maskyng apparel, of straunge fashion, made of clothe of gold, compassed with Crimosyn Tinsell Satin, owned with Clothe of Siluer, liyng lose and knit with laces of Gold: these ladies were brought into the chamber, with foure damoselles appareled in Crimosin sattyn, with Tabardes of fine Cipres: the lady Marques tooke the Frenche Kyng, and the Countes of

Darby, toke the Kyng of Nauerr, and euery Lady toke a lorde, and in daunsyng the kyng of Englande, toke awaie the ladies visers, so that there the ladies beauties were shewed, and after they had daunsed a while they ceased, and the French Kyng talked with the Marchiones of Penbroke a space, & then he toke his leaue of the ladies, and the kyng conueighed hym to his lodgyng: the same night the Duke of Norffolke feasted all the nobles of Fraunce, beyng there in the castle at Caleis, with many goodly sportes and pastymes.'[83]

We have no record of the entertainments at Norfolk's feast, so we do not know who produced them. Gibson had rented a house in Calais around this time which probably served as an office. He did produce Anne Boleyn's mask, but this appears to have been a slight affair, for the bill, which was paid from the king's Privy Purse, was only £11 3s. 1d.[84] Gibson's larger account, covering the total charges for all of the entertainments, does not survive, and neither does the Chamber account for this period.

Hall records that Henry kept the Christmas seasons of 1532–3 and 1533–4 at Greenwich, but gives no details of the entertainments.[85] The great spectacle of 1533 was Anne Boleyn's coronation.[86] Gibson's account does not survive for the 'iustes at the Tilte' for the event, but in comparison to the martial exhibitions earlier in the reign it appears to have been unspectacular. Hall notes that 'there wer very fewe speres broken, by the reason the horses would no[t] cope.'[87]

Beginning with Wolsey's death in 1530 and with the divorce proceedings against Katherine, revels oriented toward foreign policy and calculated to astonish ambassadors by lavish display were no longer needed. The 1533–4 Christmas season marks the end of an era in Henrician revels, one that had dragged on for several years past its time. In conjunction with the change in political climate, the men who had been responsible for producing the great revels and spectacles of the early reign began to die off.

Sir Henry Guildford, Master of the Revels from 1511, died in 1532. By this time the Revels organization was well-established, and the loss of an experienced man such as Guildford might be sustained. But within two years every key individual who had a part in the great international spectacles was dead. John Browne, Sergeant Painter, who was chief artist for most of the revels, spectacles, and ceremonies from early in the reign, died in 1532.[88] Brown's death left the Revels organization without its most experienced artist and designer. John Rightwise, author of political plays and classical adaptations for Wolsey and for the king, and producer of classical plays by the Children of Paul's, was removed in 1531 as High Master of Paul's School for neglect of duty. He petitioned the king, reminding him of his service, but died about a year later, in 1532, leaving the Revels organization to look elsewhere for playwrights.[89] It is unlikely that they would have found one in John Rastell. Rastell had been employed in at least three of the great spectacles of the 1520s, and while his employment on these projects appears to have been limited to visual design for ceilings and pageants, he was a playwright with a wealth of experience in staging and printing of drama and a man with literary connections to the most important writers of the time. After 1529 Rastell committed himself to the Reformation with an earnestness which led to his ruin.[90] His association with John Gough in the printing of Reformation propaganda and his work as a messenger for the Bishop of Coventry apparently contributed to the losses in his legal and in his printing businesses, of which he complains in a letter to Cromwell in 1534. He was imprisoned in 1535 for his opposition to the royal proclamation on tithes and offerings in the city of London, and died shortly before 25 June 1536. Clement Urmeston, lighting designer, attempted to attach himself to Cromwell's service by writing treatises on social problems which were ignored, and he died in obscurity.[91] Sir Henry Guildford's half-brother, Sir Edward, who as Master of the Armoury had supervised the preparation of tournaments from as early as 1506 and at least one revel, died in 1534.

Perhaps the most devastating loss of all was that of Richard Gibson who died between 4 and 28 October 1534 and was buried in St Thomas the Apostate in London, where he was then a parishioner. Gibson exercised the same care in describing the items he bequeathed to his family and friends as he did in describing the costumes and properties he made for the revels.[92] His garments of velvet trimmed with fur, harnesses, and saddles, one that he 'hadd at Caleys,' he left to his friends. To his son William, he left his mace of gold and silver, 'called the Sergeant of arms mase, which I have used to bere afore our Soueraigne lord the King.' He also left legacies to two daughters, Mary and Philipe, and to three other sons: Richard, Giles, and an unnamed son, a priest, to whom he left a black gown.[93] Alice, Gibson's 'entirely welbeloued wife,' daughter of Sir William Bayly, 'late Mayor & Alderman of London,' and his son, William, were named as executors of the will. After specific bequests, including a silver cup given to the Merchant Tailors Guild, his property was to be divided between his wife and children, according to the 'laudable vse & custome' of the city of London. His lands in Kent were left to his wife during her lifetime and then to William, who was charged to care for his sisters. Alice, as Gibson's widow, received an annuity of £13 6s. 8d. from the king in April 1535 in survivorship with Randolph Allet, Sewer of the Chamber.[94] Gibson had four decades of experience in performance, design, and production of revels, spectacles, and entertainments at court. Every important tournament, pageant, disguising, mask, play, and banqueting house from 1510 was produced with his assistance. Gibson was to the Revels organization what John Heron was to the old Chamber system, a key figure who was chiefly responsible for the proper functioning of a complicated organization and who left detailed records of his office. While we know more about the operation of the Revels Office later in the century, we know less about the revels themselves because nothing like Gibson's accounts were kept.

The change in revels productions after Wolsey's fall in 1529 was chiefly the result of the king's shift from international to domestic policy. The fall of the great cardinal, Henry's alienation of Katherine's affection after twenty-five years of marriage, and the vulgarity of his justifications to legitimize his paramour were events that could be neither celebrated nor forgotten with revels. The magnificence of the spectacles and revels produced in the decade of the 1520s was being undercut by the historical events which spelt their end. In addition, the deaths between 1532 and 1534 of the men associated with great productions of the early reign contributed in its own way to the reduction in scale of productions in the later part of the reign. The loss of their talent and expertise turned the Revels organization into a minor household function carried out by undistinguished individuals who have left only a few clues of their activities.

6

The Yeomen of the Revels, 1534–1543

Henry Machyn referred to Richard Gibson as 'sergantt of armes, and of the reywelles, and of the kynges tenstes [sic].'[1] None of Gibson's patents have survived, but his offices were distributed to successors within a few months of his death. Thomas Buckeworth became Sergeant of Arms following Gibson's death on 28 October 1534. John Malte, the king's Tailor, became Yeoman Tailor of the Great Wardrobe on the same date. John Parker, Yeoman of the Wardrobe of Robes, succeeded as Sergeant of the Tents on 8 December 1534 with wages of 12*d.* a day and 4*d.* a day for a Yeoman under him.[2] The first Revels officer known to hold a patent, 'our welbeloued Iohn ffarlyon,' was appointed on 20 November 1534 to 'the office of yoman or Keper [of] our vestures or apparaill of all and singuler our maskes Revelles and disguysing*es* And also of the apparill and trappers of all and singuler our horses … for our iustes and turneys' to him 'and his sufficient Deputie or Deputies for the term of his lif' with wages of 6*d.* a day and one livery coat 'such as yeomen officers of our houshold haue' as well as 'oon sufficient house or mansion to be assigned vnto the same Iohn for the sure better/ and safe keping' of those properties.[3] Whether Gibson ever held the patent as Yeoman of the Revels is not certain, but the fact that Farlyon's appointment was made even before the vacancy in the Sergeantship of the Tents was filled suggests the possibility. Gibson was indeed Sergeant of Arms and Sergeant of the Tents, but since there was no appointment of a Sergeant of the Revels in 1534, it is unlikely that he formally held such a position.

These new appointments demonstrate that from at least 1534 the production of revels had an official status in the royal household. The Yeoman of the Revels continued to be closely attached to the Office of the Tents. Just how close is indicated by the fact that Farlyon was appointed to succeed Parker as Sergeant of the Tents on 28 August 1538 with an annual fee of £20 and livery.[4] Farlyon actually assumed the duties of Sergeant shortly before the date of his patent, for Richard

Longman, appointed Yeoman of the Tents on 19 August 1538, was to serve under John Farlyon.[5] The administrative structure of the establishment is not entirely clear. We do not know exactly how much control was exercised by the Sergeant of the Tents over the Yeoman of the Revels. However, when Cromwell made payments for his masks, they were issued to Farlyon or his servants, not to Parker, and when Sir Anthony Browne communicated the king's instructions for the 1541 New Year's revel it was to the Yeoman of the Revels, not to the Sergeant of the Tents.[6] Probably the Sergeant was chief administrator of the office, but did not directly supervise the revels duties of the Yeoman, although cooperation among the officers on their various projects was probably the rule rather than the exception. The connection between the Revels and Tents appears clearly to have been a matter of compatibility and convenience based on the precedent set by Richard Gibson.

Our evidence of court entertainments comes from random notices in the Works accounts, in ambassadors' reports, in Cromwell's accounts, and in a few of the comments Hall makes amid his descriptions of betrayals, rebellions, attainders, divorces, beheadings, hangings, and burnings, which occupy most of his attention. So few records survive from the decade of the 1530s that it is impossible to say who acted as Master of the Revels. An unnamed Lord of Misrule was appointed for Christmas 1534–5. The Clerk of the Works was paid to dig holes and set boughs 'for the makyng of an forreste' in an exterior court at Greenwich where the Lord of Misrule and his company hunted 'the wylde bore with his hounds to shew the Kyng and the quene pastym.'[7] No accounts survive for the year 1535, but there is no reason to suppose that the king did not keep his traditional Christmas festivities. Katherine of Aragon died on 8 January 1536, and by May the king had what he considered sufficient proof of Anne Boleyn's adultery. At a joust held on May Day he left suddenly with six of his closest advisors, arrested Anne on the following day, had the marriage declared invalid on the 17th, executed her on the 19th, and married Jane Seymour on the 30th.[8]

Jane died on 24 October 1537, after giving birth to Edward on the 12th. It is possible that *Thersites* was performed to celebrate the birth of the prince between 12 and 24 October. The play is conjecturally dated between 1530, when its source appeared – a Latin dramatic dialogue in hexameters – and October 1537, since it concludes with a prayer for the queen's recovery. References to Christmas in the play suggest that it may have been written somewhat earlier and revived and adapted for this occasion, and, from the evidence of the epilogue, the play was written for child actors. The allusions to Oxford and to the same characters of English fiction and legend as appear in *Ralph Roister Doister,* together with the fact that the character of Thersites is a rude sketch of the later, more famous Ralph, have been used as evidence to attribute the play to Nicholas Udall.[9] The combination of circumstantial evidence makes his appearance at court with a play for the birth of the prince within the realm of possibility.

The king and court went into mourning after Jane Seymour's death, according to Hall, which continued through the Christmas season to the day after Candlemas in 1538.[10] In a letter of 23 March 1538 to the Queen of Hungary, Eustace Chapuys, the Spanish ambassador, mentions that Henry 'has been masking and visiting the duchess of Suffolk,' but we have little information about entertainments in 1537–8.[11] The Chamber accounts, which resume in 1538, show that the king saw a full schedule of entertainments at Christmas in 1538–9. On New Year's Day, William Crane was paid for performing a play before the king with the Children of the Chapel. The King's Players, the Queen's Players, and the Prince's Players also were paid on this day for performances, as was Matthew de Johan the tumbler. That the entertainments shown at court in these years reflected Cromwell's reform campaign is suggested by the subject of the Thames water triumph held in June 1539. Two barges were prepared with ordnance,

as gonnes and dartes of reede, one for the Bishop of Rome and his cardinalles, and the other for the Kinges Grace, and so rowed up and downe the Thames from Westminster Bridge to the Kinges bridge; and the Pope made their defyance against England and shot their ordnaunce one at another, and so had three courses up and downe the water; and at the fourth course they joyned togither and fought sore; but at last the Pope and his cardinalles were overcome, and all his men cast over the borde into the Thames; howbeyt there was none drowned, for they were persons chosen which could swimme, and the Kinges barge lay by hoveringe to take them upp as they were cast over the borde, which was a goodly pastime.[12]

The Chamber payment to Sir John Dudley, Master of the Armoury, on a warrant of 13 June, for twenty-one armourers' doublets, gowns, and hose was probably made in connection with this event. Marillac, the French ambassador in England who reported the show to Montmorency, mentions that it was futile to give details of these entertainments, for there was no village or feast or pastime anywhere in which there was not something inserted to the derision of the Pope.[13] None of Farlyon's accounts survive for his revels productions during these years, but payments to him from 1537 to 1539 show that he produced masks in Cromwell's household which were later performed before the king at court.[14]

i   Cromwell's Revels

In his steady rise to power after Wolsey's fall, Cromwell accumulated a number of significant financial offices – Master of the Jewels in April 1532, Clerk of the

Hanaper in July 1532, and Chancellor of the Exchequer in April 1533. The Jewels was a department of the Chamber which invested in jewels, plate, cloths, and artwork. It was also a supplier of precious metals, cloths, badges, and other material for court revels and ceremonies.[15] Under Cromwell's Mastership the office became a major treasury, eventually surpassing the Chamber in its ability to finance ship building, royal works, garrisons, and even to support the expenses of embassies abroad.[16] This he accomplished by reassigning payments and income from existing treasuries and purses. Income to the Chamber, for example, was limited, and its payments were directed by Cromwell or his deputies. The major expenses which had been borne by the Privy Purse since the latter part of the 1520s were reassigned to other treasuries, and that purse reverted to a much smaller operation within the king's Privy Chamber under the control of the Groom of the Stool.

Cromwell also helped to set up new courts to administer the revenues pouring into Henry's coffers during the decade. The Court of First Fruits and Tenths, which collected those revenues from the dissolved monasteries, was set up on 7 May 1535, and though it was not ratified by Parliament until 1540, John Gostwyck administered the court as its Treasurer and General Receiver from its inception, making payments on Cromwell's warrants and on his verbal orders.[17] Cromwell created and personally controlled a massive financial network in which income and payments were assigned arbitrarily to various treasuries. After his fall in 1540, the government spent almost two decades untangling the bureaucracy. Cromwell's own accounts, which survive from 1536 to 1539, are remarkable for their range of payments, and resemble more the king's Chamber accounts kept by John Heron than those of a Lord Privy Seal.[18] The accounts consist partly of payments for public obligations associated with running the government and partly with the private luxuries of maintaining his estate. He made large payments in the amount of £1,000 and £2,000 to Gostwyck for the Court of First Fruits and other equally large payments to the king's privy coffers; many others were made to acting companies, to Farlyon, and to producers of entertainments, some for private performances at his own house, some for entertainments sent to the king's court, and others for the furtherance of his propaganda schemes.

Cromwell's Christmas schedule of revels was as full as any of the great nobles of the realm. Masks were held, and minstrels as well as playing companies made regular appearances. The Queen's Players performed on 10 February 1537. The King's Players, the Lord Chancellor's Players, and the Marquis of Exeter's Players were paid for performances on 26 December 1537. On 21, 22, and 23 January 1538 the Lord Warden's Players, the Duke of Suffolk's Players, and the Lord Chancellor's Players appeared, and on 4 February 1538 Lord Cobham's Players performed before him. What plays were performed by these companies is not recorded, but circumstantial evidence indicates that Cromwell's deep involvement in the reform movement in these years was reflected in some of the plays he saw. Wolsey's successes in international negotiations were the subject of some of the politically-oriented revels from 1518 to 1528. The focus of national policy in the 1530s shifted to domestic affairs, and it appears that, in his own way, Cromwell had an important influence on the revels at court. His key position in the government's financial bureaucracy put at his disposal vast sums of money with which to finance his reform schemes, some of it spent merely on his verbal orders. One of the methods he used to achieve his ends was the dissemination of propaganda, which has earned him a reputation as the first member of the English government to recognize its importance.[19] The reputation is somewhat exaggerated, for Henry VII, Henry VIII, and Wolsey all used entertainments and spectacles to advance their diplomatic causes, but Cromwell was the first to use the printing press together with the drama as political weapons in a large-scale publicity campaign. John Foxe praised him for this, noting that his tactics were furthered by the employment of a number of talented individuals whose industry and labour produced 'divers excellent both ballads and books' which were 'set abroad, concerning the suppression of the pope and all popish idolatry.'[20] John Rastell was one of these individuals in the early part of the decade, and Clement Urmeston aspired to be one. In the second part of the decade, the most prominent of them was Sir Richard Moryson, who wrote a number of tracts between 1536 and 1539 on the divorce, the supremacy, the Pilgrimage of Grace, and on Cardinal Pole. One of Moryson's relevant suggestions for disseminating propaganda was to use plays to show 'the abhomynation and wickednes of the bisshop of Rome, monkes, ffreers, nonnes, and suche like, and to declare and open to them thobedience that your subiects by goddes lawes and mans lawes owe unto your magestie. Into the commen people thynges sooner enter by the eies, then by the eares: remembryng more better that they see then that they heere.'[21]

There is clear evidence that Cromwell did patronize and otherwise lend his support to propagandist playwrights. Thomas Wylley, vicar of Yoxford, Suffolk, 'fatherlesse and forsaken,' wrote to Cromwell in 1537 for protection. Wylley had devised a play, 'A Reverent receyvyng of the sacrament as A lenton matter,' which was to be performed by six children 'representyng' Christ, the Word of God, St Paul, St Augustine, a child, and a nun named 'Ignoransy.' He claimed that most priests in Suffolk refused to allow him to preach in their churches since he had written a play against the Pope's counsellors: 'Error, Cole Clogger of Conscyns, and Incredulyte.' He also mentions that he had written another play, '*a Rude Commynaltie*,' and that he was now writing '*The Woman on the Rokke*.'[22] It may be that the payment in Cromwell's accounts on 12 April 1538 to Mr. Hopton's priest for performing with his children was for a play of this kind. It seems unlikely that Wylley's or Mr Hopton's priest's plays were as sophisticated as those by John Bale and Nicholas Udall. Bale, who adapted history to the morality tradition, and Udall, who adapted the new school of neo-Latin drama in which the structure and style of Terence was used to elucidate subject matter from religion, both presented plays before Cromwell. Even before this latter kind of drama was imported into England from Holland it had been turned to violent controversy, notably by Thomas Kirchmayer, whose most famous play, *Pammachius* (1538), was dedicated to Cranmer and translated by John Bale.

Bale had written a number of controversial plays during the 1530s. In his *Anglorum Heliades*, composed between 1536 and 1539 for his friend John Leland, Bale mentions that 'Eddi etiam in idiomate vulgari diuersas Comedias atque Tragedias. Sub diuerso metrorum genere, Presertim ad illustrissimum Dominum Ioannem Ver, Oxonie Comitem'[23] These plays, written in English for John de Vere, 15th Earl of Oxford, in support of royal supremacy included *De Sectis Papisticis, De Traditionibus Papistarum, Contra Corruptores Verbi Dei, De Traditione Thome Becketi*, and *Super Vtroque Regis Coniugo*. How many more of his twenty-four plays had been written by that time is difficult to estimate, but he had written some as early as 1534.[24] His abilities had come to Cromwell's attention in that year through the intercession of Leland when Bale had been summoned before Archbishop Lee of York to answer a charge that he had criticised the honouring of saints, and Cromwell arranged his release '*ob editas comedias.*'[25] Bale together with his 'fellows' later performed an unidentified play before Cromwell at St Stephen's, Canterbury, on 8 September 1538, and again, in London on 31 January 1539. Cromwell lent his support and encouragement to a number of controversial playwrights, and there is no evidence to show that this group is identical to the company known as Cromwell's Players.[26] It has been suggested that the play performed on 31 January was *King Johan*, based on a known performance of the play at Cranmer's during the Christmas season of 1538–9.[27] One witness to this 'enterlude concernyng King John' thought 'it was petie and nawghtely don to put down the Pope and Saincte Thomas.' Another thought King John one of the noblest of England's princes who 'was the begynner of the puttyng down of the Bisshop of Rome.'[28] *King Johan* celebrates Henry VIII in the way Sir Richard Moryson had suggested to Cromwell when he proposed a secular feast day to mark the delivery of England from the Pope. The occurrence of Bale's name in Cromwell's accounts in 1538 and 1539, the height of the campaign against ceremonies and images, suggests that Cromwell's propaganda had infiltrated entertainments even during the traditional holiday season and raises important questions about the kind of entertainments John Farlyon was producing for the king and about the entertainments Cromwell is known to have sent to court. There is no evidence of subsequent performances by Bale at Cromwell's or at court, and after Cromwell's fall in 1540, Bale fled to Germany, where he remained until Edward VI's accession.[29]

'Woodall' (Nicholas Udall), schoolmaster of Eton, was paid for performing a play at Cromwell's on 2 February 1538. Udall was involved in Protestant activities as early as 1528 when, along with other students, he was disciplined at Corpus Christi, Oxford, for reading Lutheran works and Tyndale's New Testament in English.[30] His associates at Corpus Christi in the 1520s included John Leland, with whom he later collaborated in producing a pageant for the reception of Anne Boleyn in May 1533, and Sir Richard Moryson, later one of Cromwell's propagandists. Udall's continuing support of the Protestant cause, which included translating the works of lecturers in England, earned Bale's praise, and the publication of his translation of *Apophthegmes, That Is to Saie, Prompte, Quicke, Wittie Saiynges. First Gathered by Erasmus* in September 1542 by his neighbour, the Protestant printer and chronicler Richard Grafton, led to patronage by Queen Catherine Parr, for whom he is also said to have written 'Comoedias plures' and to have translated 'tragoediam de papatu.' The queen arranged for him the benefice of the church of Hartyng, Sussex, in 1546, which he shared with three others, including his old school friend and propagandist Moryson.[31] His appointment as headmaster of Eton in 1534 coincided with the publication of his *Floures of Latine Spekynge Selected and Gathered Oute of Terence*, a popular school text for fifty years which taught grammar through idiomatic translation of the plays of Terence.[32]

Udall's *Thersites* may have been performed in October 1537 for the birth of Edward, but what play he performed with the boys of Eton before Cromwell in 1538 is uncertain. Several suggestions have been offered, the most plausible of which is that it was *Ezekias*.[33] *Ezekias* was written before 1545, since Udall refers to it in the preface to his translation of the paraphrase addressed to Henry VIII. Ezekias, or Hezekiah, was a revered biblical figure among Protestants because of the analogy to Henry VIII, who, like Hezekiah, destroyed idols and reformed religion. The story was still popular in Elizabeth I's reign. Sir Nicholas Bacon alludes to it in his address before the queen's first Parliament, and Elizabeth saw a production of the play on 8 August 1564 at Cambridge, probably because it accorded with her position in the controversy between moderate bishops and extremists over the preservation of images. Our only narrative evidence comes from a contemporary viewer. His testimony suggests that the play was in the tradition of Terentian thesis plays, on which subject Udall was a master. The play recorded:

that heroic deed of Hezekiah, who inflamed with zeal for the divine honor, crushed the brazen image of the serpent. From this sacred fount Nicholas Udall drew as much as he thought fitting for the proper magnitude of comedy, put it entirely into English verse, and gave it the name of *Ezechias*. It was truly amazing how much wit there was in it, how much charm in a subject so solemn and holy, and yet without once breaking off the definite sequence of reality.[34]

Plays were included among the entertainments in Cromwell's household during the holiday seasons along with masks, some of which were also shown at court. Cromwell paid John Farlyon 20 marks on 19 February 1537 for his 'part of the mask.' The wording of the payments suggests that the costs were shared by Cromwell and probably by some of the king's courtiers. From the date of the payment the mask appears to have been presented at Shrovetide (11, 12, 13 February), but there is no indication of its subject matter. In the following year, the court was in mourning for Jane Seymour's death from Christmas until 3 February 1538, but Cromwell sent a mask to court, probably again at Shrovetide (3, 4, 5 March), for on 4 March Robyn Drowne and his fellows were paid 20s. for waiting two nights at the time Cromwell 'made the king a maske.' There is no indication of subject matter, but John Portynare produced it, for on 5 March he was paid £25 11s. 5d. 'for the charges of the maske.' Portynare was a Florentine engineer, a Gentleman Pensioner, and one of the King's Spears in 1539, who was described as 'my lord Privy Seales man.'[35] There is no further evidence of his involvement in producing masks either at Cromwell's or at court. Portynare remained in favour, even after Cromwell's fall. He was still a resident of the precinct of Blackfriars in 1550, in possession of the keys to some of the Crown buildings which had been surrendered in 1538.[36] In 1539, Cromwell again had the help of Farlyon to produce masks, one of which by John Heywood was sent to court. Heywood was in royal service from as early as 1519 when he was listed as a singer in the Chamber account and by 1525 as a player on the virginals. He gave the king a New Year's gift in 1533, indicating that he was still in favour, but Heywood was married to Joan, daughter of John Rastell and niece of Sir Thomas More, and his influence at court must have waned in the later 1530s after Rastell's imprisonment and the execution of More.[37] There are only a few notices of his activities at court between 1528 and 1552, during which time he appears to have occupied himself with his writing and with devising and producing plays and masks. He became associated with John Redford and the Choristers of St Paul's, probably as early as 1537, for in this and the following year he appears as a payee in Princess Mary's accounts. His servant was paid for bringing 'regals' from London to Greenwich in January 1537, and Heywood himself appears to have been paid for 'playing an enterlude with his children before my ladyes grace' in March 1538.[38] The evidence suggests that Heywood associated himself with the Children of Paul's, producing occasional entertainments for the princess and for Cromwell.[39] He was still producing plays by the boys in 1551. On 13 February of that year, Princess Elizabeth paid Heywood and Sebastian Westcott 'towards the charge of the children with the carriage of the plaiers garments,' almost certainly a reference to Paul's Boys.[40] The Revels Office produced his unnamed play at court in 1552 which was performed by a group of twelve unnamed boys.[41] His fortunes rose higher during Mary's reign. He appeared in a pageant for the queen's entry procession into London in 1553, with the Children of Paul's School, in which he delivered an oration in Latin and in English; he was briefly involved in the planning for Philip's entry procession in 1554; and he received many benefits from the queen.[42] In 1559, he and Westcott produced a play by the Children of Paul's at Nonsuch before Elizabeth, but he was forced to flee from England on 20 July 1564 after the enforcement of the Act of Uniformity, and spent the rest of his life in exile.[43]

Bale and Udall were both Protestants whose work would have attracted Cromwell's attention, probably through Moryson, but it may seem puzzling that Heywood, a man of avowed Catholic sympathies, would have been asked to devise a mask at Cromwell's at the height of the reform campaign. After Cromwell's fall in 1540 and Bale's self-imposed exile, Heywood was involved in the attempt to convict Archbishop Cranmer of heresy, an attempt which resulted in a death sentence from which he escaped only after a public recantation. The age was a dangerous one which required many, like Heywood, to choose between temporizing personal belief and execution, but those choices were principally made over political stands, not over private conviction. Despite his reputation as a Protestant apologist, for example, Udall was a highly regarded playwright at Mary's court, and despite Heywood's reputation and political activities he was not barred from occasional employment in the households of the princesses, at court, at Cromwell's, and even at Cranmer's. Thomas Whythorne, later master of music to Archbishop Parker who spent over three years in Heywood's household beginning in 1545, records a play written by Heywood for Cranmer:

with mr haywood I remayned three yeer and mor, in the which tym I learned to play on the virginals, the liut, and to mak english ⟨verses. wh⟩y⟨ll I w⟩az with h⟨im, he mad div⟩r⟨z⟩ ditt⟨iez to⟩ bee sung vnto muzi⟨kal⟩ instrumen⟨ts⟩ (also hee ⟨caw⟩zed ⟨to⟩ be prin⟨ted A⟩ book mad vpon owr ⟨en⟩glysh proverbz) And also at the request of doktor ⟨Thos.⟩ Cranmer, lat a⟨rchb⟩yshop of Cantorbury, hee mad A sertayn enter⟨lude⟩ or play, the which waz devyzed vpon the parts of Man, at the end wherof hee lykneth and applieth the sirkumstans therof to the vniuersall estat of Chrystes church, all the which afforsaid befor thei wer published I did wryt owt for him, or had the yvs of them to read them. and I hav the copiez of most of them in A book at this present of myn own wryting.[44]

Whythorne's statement is the only evidence for this play on the *Parts of Man*, probably written to strengthen Cranmer's position in one of the theological controversies of the time. Later in the autobiography, in his philosophical discussion of reason and will, Whythorne has occasion to use Heywood's play as an illustration:

I will heer shew vnto yow *the* wurdz of my old master mr Haywood, *the* which he did wryt in A komedy or play *th*at hee mad of the parts of man, in *the* which after *th*at he hath mad Reazon to chaleng vnto himself *the* siuperiorite and government of all *the* parts of Man, and also to kommaund althings lyving vpon *the* earth, hee maketh reazon to say *th*us (in meeter) for him self. *And the diffrens between man the kommaunder, and beas(ts) being by man kommaunded, iz only Reazon in man, the disserner of good and ill, the good in man elekted by me, and th'ill in man by mee regected. man obeing mee shynth in exsellensy, and disobeing mee, shewth mans insolensy. Now sin(s I) reazon am th'(o)nly qu(a)lyte, tha(t q)ualifiet man (in s)uch A temp(er)ans az setteth man in plas of prinsipalite abov all beasts to stand in governans who but I over man shiuld him self advans, to govern lykwyz, sins I bring man therto, and keep man therin doing az I bid him do.* when reazon hath *th*us said for him self, *th*en kummeth in will, who dispiuteth with reazon for *the* siuprem government in man, whervpon in *the* end *th*ei both ar dryven to graunt *th*at man kan do nothing withowt will, and without reazon man kan do no good thing.[45]

Bale's summation of Heywood's work is fairly representative of the opinions of his contemporaries, 'pro choreis post commessationes & epulas hilariter ducendis, spectaculis, ludis, aut personatis ludicris exhibendis, aliisque uanitatibus fouendis, multum laborabat edititque,' for Heywood's wit and his voluminous writings were sometimes compared to Chaucer's. But when Bale goes on to give his own assessment of Heywood's work, 'in sua lingua studiosus ac sine doctrina ingeniosus,' he was probably speaking for his more radical Protestant contemporaries.[46] Heywood's dramatic work tends to be witty and to open up to a range of interpretations, and it is not difficult to imagine that the man who wrote *The Pardoner and the Friar*, with its satire of Roman church practices, and who wrote *The Parts of Man* for Cranmer, could have written an intellectual critique on a controversial subject for Cromwell which might have appealed to the king in the late 1530s. We know much less than we might wish about the factional manoeuvres over reform in this period, and it may well be that the king, Cromwell, and Cranmer sought out Heywood on certain occasions knowing full well that his work would be open to a variety of interpretations or in some cases would reflect conservative rather than radical views.

There are no narratives, and consequently neither the number nor the themes of the masks shown at Cromwell's in this year can be conclusively established. From entries in the accounts, it appears that at least two and possibly more were produced. The total cost of these masks was £109 17s. 4 1/2d., or an average of about £55, if we assume that two were produced, or about £36, if we assume three – the least estimate more expensive than the £26 Portynare's mask had cost in the previous year. If we assume that only one mask was produced, the cost would rival some of the most elaborate and expensive that the king himself put on in the early reign for the most important diplomatic occasions. Farlyon was employed on these masks, as is clear from entries in the accounts.[47] He was paid £3 8s. 6 1/2d. on 14 January for making Mr. Gregory's apparel,' and 57s. 9d. for making twelve doublets for 'the cornyshmen.' A saddler had been paid £11 12s. for Mr Gregory's horse harness on 11 January, a hosier was paid 57s. 4d. for Mr Gregory's bill on 20 January, Christopher Milliner was paid £10 for 'the charges of the maske,' and his servants were rewarded 7s. 6d. on 25 January. The payments here to Farlyon, and to the various merchants, particularly to Christopher Milliner, who supplied material, indicate full provision for a mask involving twelve Cornishmen.

More than one mask is indicated in the accounts for this season, not only from the number and dates of payments but also from the references to subject matter.[48] On 9 February, Farlyon's servants were paid 20s. for 'takyn paynes sundry tymes in maskes.' At least one of the masks in production was 'kinge Arturs knightes,' the title of which is mentioned in the 11 February payment of £10 17s. 11d. to Christopher Milliner and £3 for his labour and workmen. This is doubtless the same entertainment called 'my Lordes maske' in the payment to John Dymoke on 12 February for eleven copper plates and other necessaries. On 20 February more payments were made. A painter 'that made all the hobbyhorsses and the other thinges thereto belonging' was paid £33 17s. 6d.[49] John Heywood was paid £5 10s. 5d. for his costs and other necessaries. Mrs Vaughan, probably a silk woman, was paid £6 7s. 6d. for supplying other material 'for the maskes.' A barge man was paid on 22 February for carrying 'Heywodes maske to the court and home again.'[50] Heywood's mask is not identified by name. The only indication from Cromwell's accounts of the subject matter of an entertainment sent to court comes in the 28 February payment to Christopher Milliner of 21s. 2d. for 'trimmyng of Devine Providens when she played before the king.' The conclusion from this evidence is that Heywood's mask included the character of Divine Providence, and as in the past, it was probably sent to court for Shrovetide (16, 17, 18 February). We can only speculate on the rest. The evidence is inadequate to be certain what, if anything, was sent to court in addition to the show involving Divine Providence. However, it is adequate to make some general observations about Cromwell's influence in the revels.

We know that Cromwell sent masks to court probably in 1537 and certainly in 1538 and 1539. We know that subject matter of the June 1539 spectacle at court reflected Cromwell's reform campaign, and we can argue with reasonable certainty that plays on controversial subjects were produced at his house in these years. We know that as early as 1535 the king was personally interested in polemical plays on religious subjects. In a letter of 30 June 1535 to Cardinal Nicholas de Granvelle, Eustace Chapuys, the Spanish ambassador, reported that in June Henry walked ten miles at 2 a.m. and concealed himself within a house to see the performance of an outdoor pageant based on a chapter in the Apocalypse. He was so delighted to see himself represented as cutting off the heads of clergymen 'that in order to laugh at his ease, and encourage the people he disclosed himself,' and he sent word to Anne Boleyn that she ought to see the show, which was to be repeated on the eve of St Peter.[51] We also know that by 1538 such plays had become fashionable. John Husee, Lady Lisle's agent in London, wrote to her on 3 October 1538 that 'thes nyw ecclesiastycal maters wylbe hard to com by.' Two days later he had located an interlude called *Rex Diabole,* and then goes on to say that he will do his best to get some of these new plays, 'but they be very deare they askethe aboue xls. for an Enterlude.'[52] It seems probable, based on this evidence, that some of the revels at court from 1535 to 1539, reflected the subject matter of the Reformation. Like Wolsey's court in the previous decade, a more likely place than the king's to find innovative revels associated with diplomatic negotiations, Cromwell's household was now the likely place to find innovations in revels related to the Reformation.

ii

The last payment made to Farlyon from Cromwell's account in July 1539 was for making the coats and caps for the great muster in London in May of that year.[53] He died before he had held the post of Sergeant of the Tents for a full year. Thomas Thacker wrote to Cromwell on 26 July 1539 that 'this Last nyght Iohn ffarlian Sergeant of our souerayne lorde the Kinges tentes is departed oute of this world' and mentioned that he and the bearer of the letter, William Stone, went this morning 'to warwyk Inn where the Kinges tentes and your Lordshipes also lye. Stone and I haue locked vpp the doores and charged the keeper of the hous that no man come there.'[54] William Stone had charge of the Lord Steward's tents, and according to Thacker knew 'as moche in this busynes as any man in London,' but he was not granted Farlyon's position. On 28 September 1539 John Travers, Gentleman Sewer of the Chamber, received a grant of the office of Sergeant of the Tents with a fee of £20 per year.[55] There were several men with the name Travers appointed to the king's service from 1529 to 1544, but this John Travers was certainly the one who became Master of the Ordnance in Ireland in December 1544.[56] He is named in 'The First Institution' as one of the Masters of the Revels Office, but there is no evidence that he ever held this post, used this style, or performed any revels duties. In December 1539 he was in Ireland, for on the 20th he wrote from Waterford that his one hundred hackbuts had reinstated James Fitzmorris, Lord of Desmond, in possession of as many castles as he thought he could hold. He was in England in the summer of 1541, for he attended on the king's progress, but he was back in Ireland in 1544. When he was appointed Master of the Ordnance there in December 1544 after 'lately' surrendering his office of Sergeant of the Tents, he received a gift of frontier lands valued at 100 marks a year.[57] Travers's continuing duties in Ireland, dating from at least 1539, left the operation of the office to his yeomen, Bridges and Longman.

John Bridges was a citizen and merchant tailor of London. He was granted the patent as Yeoman of the Revels on 21 October 1539 with the same terms that had been granted Farlyon and with the same wages.[58] On 23 December 1546 he received a patent as the king's Tailor succeeding John Malte, 'deceased' with wages of 12d. a day payable from the previous Michaelmas.[59] Bridges continued in his post as Yeoman, but employed John Holt as his deputy to carry out those duties. Deputyships were not uncommon in this period. The deputy was recognized as the de facto officer to be paid in the accounts for his work, but the de jure officer continued to be paid from the Crown the annual fee specified in his patent. These deputyships were private arrangements between individuals, and the Crown was not bound to honour them with an appointment by patent. In this particular case, Holt eventually received a patent as Yeoman when Bridges resigned on 1 July 1550.[60] Bridges also received a patent in reversion with Longman as Yeoman of the Tents with a fee of £10 a year on 15 November 1541.[61] Longman was employed on Tents business in 1539 and in 1540, but, later, Bridges did most of the work in the office. He certainly did in 1546 when he was paid an imprest from the Court of Augmentations for conduct money for the charges of fifty-six men attending the tents from London to France.[62] There appears to have been something of a reorganization after Cromwell's fall in 1540, for on the same date that Bridges received the reversion to Longman's patent, Thomas Hale received a patent to the new post of Groom of the Tents with a fee of 6d. a day, later converted to £9 2s. 6d. a year.[63] Storage facilities for the office were also put in Bridges's hands, for in December 1540, as Yeoman of the Revels, he received a grant of the reversion of Warwick Inn in London, site of the Revels and Tents storehouse, and on 12 June 1542, as Yeoman of the Tents, he and Hale were granted the house and site of the late Charterhouse near London for the safe-keeping of the Tents.[64]

John Bridges's first season of 1539–40 as Yeoman of the Revels was dominated by the reception and entertainments for Anne of Cleves. Henry's marriage treaty was signed at Hampton Court in October 1539, and on 3 January 1540 Anne was formally received in London.[65] The Yeomen of the Tents and Revels probably supplied the pavilions for her progress and reception, the trappings for Henry's horse of estate at the Blackheath reception, and the coronation tournament held Sunday after Twelfth Night.[66] On New Year's Day the King's Players, the Queen's Players, the Prince's Players, and William Crane and the Children of the Chapel were paid for performances, as was Johan the tumbler. 'Bankettes, Maskes, and dyuerse dysportes' were held after supper on Twelfth Night as part of the wedding festivities.[67] On May Day the king and queen attended a tilt, tourney, and barriers at Westminster, and banquets were held at Durham Place.[68]

An inventory of Revels and Tents properties in the charge of John Farlyon, lately deceased, 'and now committed to one Brigges' taken by John Gostwyck, Treasurer of the Court of First Fruits and Tenths and servant to Cromwell, provides the only information we have about properties and costumes used in the revels between 1535 and 1540.[69] The inventory is misdated in *Letters and Papers,* but given the contents, it was likely done just after Cromwell's fall, for some of the material listed accords with the bits of information we have about the entertainments for Henry's wedding to Anne in January 1540. The first part of the inventory relates to Revels material stored in 'certain cofferes or standardes' at Warwick Inn in London. Some of the material was old. The pavilion made of twenty-six panes of cloth of gold and purple velvet embroidered with the letters H and K and lined with green sarcenet together with a variety of rich bases and bards for horses date from before 1533. Some of the material relates to jousts put on during Farlyon's Yeomanship, but given the elaborate and rich equipment listed some must have been made for Anne's reception and coronation. Under the heading of 'masking garments' are listed costumes for a total of nine masks, only one of which is named. The mask of palmers was supplied with eight short cloaks of scarlet with keys embroidered on the shoulders, eight hats of crimson satin with scallop shells embroidered on the front, and eight palmers' staves with clap dishes and beads. It is quite possible that this mask was on a Reformation subject, one suitable for a marriage which was to solidify a northern-European Protestant alliance. Further, the fact that Gostwyck listed it separately by title indicates that it was performed within recent memory. A few costumes in the eight other masks suggest subject matter: one of them used seven masking hats of yellow and red sarcenet, Tartary fashion; another employed eight satin mantles trimmed with silk, Irish fashion; a third used eight wooden falchions and eight wooden maces painted and gilded. While some of these masks were almost certainly used for the wedding and coronation tournament celebrations, others probably date from earlier in Farlyon's term of office, and argue that there were more masks produced between 1535 and 1539 than we can document.

Henry's marriage to Anne was annulled on 9 July, and Cromwell's execution in the summer of 1540 put an end to reform propaganda. The government turned its attention to suppressing the very kind of propaganda both in the press and in the drama and entertainments that Cromwell had been encouraging. In March 1542 the convocation of bishops petitioned the king to suppress public plays and comedies acted in London to the contempt of God's word, and in April Bishop Bonner issued an order banning 'common plays, games, or interludes' in churches or chapels.[70] The Act of Parliament for 'thadvauncement of true Religion and for thabolisshment of the contrarie' passed in January 1543 reprimanded seditious people who 'by printed bokes printed balades playes rymes songes and other fantasies' expressed false opinions about religion. Complaints about the 'licentious maner off playours' were discussed by the Mayor and aldermen of London in March and April 1543. On 10 April twenty joiners who put on a disguising on Sunday despite the king's intention to ban playing 'which was openly known' were committed to Newgate and the Tower, and four players of the Lord Warden were jailed for playing contrary to an order of the mayor of London.[71] Another proclamation against the performance of interludes and plays was issued in October 1544. In 1545 Bishop Gardiner issued an order at Christ College, Cambridge, restricting playing after a performance of Kirchmayer's *Pammachius,* the same year in which the king was thinking of using, among others, common players to serve in the war as galley slaves.[72] And on 6 May 1546 the council sent a letter to the mayor of London releasing five of the Earl of Bath's players who were jailed for ignoring a ban on lewd plays in the suburbs of London on the condition that they not play without license from the council.[73]

The relaxation of Reformation propaganda and the king's renewed interest in foreign policy led to the production of revels and spectacles between 1541 and 1546 which were calculated to support the new policies. The change in political climate was accompanied by attempts to untangle the financial bureaucracy that Cromwell had created. These financial reforms produced a number of positive results, not the least of which was a government-wide systematic approach to record keeping, the likes of which had not been done since Heron's retirement from the Chamber in 1521. Revels accounts survive beginning with the 1540–1 season.

Henry married Katherine Howard on 28 July 1540. No revels are recorded for her presentation at Hampton Court on 8 August, and it is probable that the festivities were postponed until Christmas 1540–1. In a letter of 31 December 1540 to Francis I, Marillac, the French ambassador, mentions that there is 'no other news these holidays but of mummeries and rejoicing.'[74] On 1 January the King's Players, the Queen's Players, and the Prince's Players were rewarded for performing before the king at Christmas, the Gentlemen of the Chapel were rewarded for their 'paines taking,' and the Duke of Suffolk's Players were rewarded 'for playing in the king*es* hall on twelfth even.' The king kept estate in the Hall on

Twelfth Night, and on New Year's Day the play by William Crane and the Children of the Chapel was outfitted by the Revels. Crane was paid on the same day along with the other playing companies for his performance, but while the other performances may well have been given any time between 26 December and 6 January, it is certain that the Children performed on New Year's.

Bridges's Revels account for Christmas 1540–1 is headed 'A Comaundement gevyn by the kinges grace vnto Sir Anthony browne And so vnto me Iohn bridges … the xxx Daye of Decembre to prepayre ordeyne & make in A Redynesse sertayne garmentes or Apparell for A play to be Don by the children of the chappell before the king on newe yeres Daye at his graycious honor of Grenwich After Supper.'[75] From the costumes listed in Bridges' account it appears that the performers in the play on New Year's 1541 included William Crane, who probably wore the long garment of red damask, and four of the boys costumes in jerkins and slops of white damask with caps and white feathers to match. It was a small affair, taking only four men's labour one day and costing in all £8 11s. 5d. We can document Crane's dramatic performances with the Children before the king for many of the years of his Mastership of the Chapel, but this is the first clear evidence since 1516 that the Yeoman of the Revels produced any of these plays.[76] We can only speculate that some of the many costumes and properties in the earlier Revels accounts may relate to such productions.

Sir Anthony Browne, Esquire for the Body from 1524, was appointed Master of the Horse after Sir Nicholas Carew's execution in 1539.[77] His personal friendship with Henry is evident from the fact that he stood as the king's proxy in the marriage to Anne of Cleves. He was appointed executor of the king's will and guardian of Prince Edward and of Princess Elizabeth. There is no evidence that Browne ever used the style, 'Master of the Revels,' and his name appears in no other Revels account. In this particular case, it is clear that Bridges was charged by the king to design and fabricate costumes to support a play. Such a production would not necessarily require the services of a Master of the Revels because nothing extraordinary was required. Beginning with the entertainments at Shrovetide 1542, however, the revels became increasingly complicated, and some of them would have required devising, artistic direction, coordination, and supervision. Whether the king along with his close associates in the Privy Chamber provided this or a temporary Master was appointed is not evident from the records. The issue was resolved in 1545 by the permanent appointment of Sir Thomas Cawarden as Master, who had certainly acted as Master beginning at Christmas 1544–5. Cawarden had been appointed to the king's Privy Chamber by 1540, and he may well have been acting informally as Master from 1542. Such an hypothesis would explain why he was eventually granted the Mastership by patent for life.

There is no record of festivities at court during Christmas 1541–2, but, despite the fact that Katherine Howard was executed on 13 February 1542, the king had masks produced for Shrovetide at Westminster. Bridges produced the mask shown after supper on Shrove Monday (20 February) with the help of eight men who worked half a day and half a night at a cost of £7 4s. 2 1/2d.[78] This does not represent the full cost of the production, for Bridges got eight long garments, half of satin and half of blue sarcenet set with flowers of gold and silver, from the king's store. There is no indication of the subject of the mask, but it appears that there were eight principals and four drummers who were costumed in blue sarcenet. Headpieces were made of felt and covered with red and white sarcenet. Hoods were also made, and twelve visors were ordered. The mask shown on Shrove Tuesday (21 February) was produced with the help of fifteen men who worked for one day at a cost of £18 13s. 11d., which did not include the eight long garments with sleeves of red satin and white silver sarcenet which Bridges obtained from the king's storehouse. These garments were embellished with white and gold sarcenet and lined with white cotton. There is no clear indication of the subject of the mask, but red sarcenet hoods were made, buttons were gilded, and twelve visors were covered with red and white gold sarcenet. Six pair of gold sarcenet slops were taken from the store, and eight pair of gold sarcenet buskins were made. Drummers were costumed in white and blue sarcenet, and the 'iiijor Gentlemen doyng servis wth Lyghtes' wore white sarcenet girdles.

On 12 July 1542 Henry married Catherine Parr. No Revels accounts or narratives survive to record the festivities, if any were held. Given the cost of the entertainments produced for Christmas, it is likely that festivities were postponed until then. This Christmas season inaugurates a period in Henrican revels which is reminiscent of the early reign. The similarity lies in the conception of most of the entertainments, not in the scale, for while Bridges began to spend more money on his productions than any we can document from the 1530s, the charges do not come near those of the first two decades of the reign. The costumes Bridges made beginning in 1542 suggest subject matter mainly from romance rather than domestic religious reform. The change in the subject matter of the revels is complemented by the shift from domestic to foreign policy in government. Henry's third war in France was conducted from 1542 to 1544, and the preparations for it, like those for the war of 1512–14, had an impact on the style of the revels.

For the Christmas revels of 1542–3 at Hampton Court, Bridges employed sixteen painters and other labourers at a cost of £112 17s. 8 1/2d., which does not reflect the total costs of the entertainments.[79] It is difficult to explain some of the details of the masks, for Bridges does not clearly distinguish all of his costs. For example, he paid the charges of a man and horse on Friday and Saturday before Christmas; on St Stephen's, St John's, and Innocent's Days; and the Wednesday after New Year's, that Thursday, and Friday. Whether this charge was part of the entertainments or for carriage of material or messages is not clear. Bridges made 'viij ffeltes lyck helmettes' gilded with gold and silver and 'Antique heddes sett on the knees sholders backs & brests of the men of Armys' all painted with gold and silver. Halberds, daggers, escutcheons, and other properties were painted by eight painters working for three days. He purchased 'xij vesardes with longe berdes' as well as eight others for 'mores' and eight more for torch bearers. Eight pair of buskins were made; eight straw hats, eight feathers, three dozen black lamb skins, eight pounds of wool, and six cowbells were bought. Whether the cowbells were used to teach dance steps or were stage properties for the mask is not clear. Obviously costumes for men-at-arms and for Moors were made, but how they were used is not certain.

For Shrovetide 1543 two masks were produced at Westminster, one of 'Alamains' and another of mariners.[80] The banqueting chamber was decorated with rosemary, some of it gilded with silver, and bays for the occasion. Bridges produced the first of the masks for Shrove Sunday (4 March) with the help of sixteen men who worked for eight days and nights at a cost of £64 5s. This appears to have been the 'Alamain' mask for which 'myters' were made. Eight 'brochis gilt' with gold were used on the hats for this mask, as well as eight staves embossed with roses and fleurs-de-lis and gilded with gold and silver. For the mariners mask on Shrove Tuesday (6 March), twelve ells of canvas were used for collars 'about the neck the cuffes at the handes & About the waiste & About the Small of the legges.' For the same mask, 'bodyes' were made, and there are charges for eight trunks with necks, eight pair of legs made with rods, eight breasts made with rods, and eight trunks standing on staves. This appears to be the same mask for which were bought eight hoods and visors for the 'monsterous torchbearers,' whose costumes included sixteen yards of horse mane and eight dog chains. The charge for 'dressing the wykers for viij monsters with lynen clothe & skalis' made with gold, silver, green, and red paper may be for pageant decorations, but they might also be connected to the mariners mask. It is probable that these wicker frames were the same 'certen fframes or pageantes' which were rented from the churchwardens of St Sepulcher's for 5s. He also rented garments from the King's Players.

Henry spent Christmas of 1543–4 at Hampton Court entertaining Ferdinand de Gonzaga and an embassy from the Emperor planning the invasion of France. Bridges produced two masks for the occasion at a cost of £88 10s. 9d., and from the dates of his payments for carriage it appears that they were performed on New Year's at night and on Twelfth Night.[81] The New Year's entertainment appears to have been a mask of women, for Bridges charges carriage 'to feche the ij woman mask' and for sixteen women's visors 'for the same mask.' Bridges also charged for 'a Whery to feche ye chyldrens gere,' but, as in 1541, it is more likely that these children were of the Chapel who performed in Crane's play before the king on New Year's. The Twelfth Night revel appears to have been a mask of Turks, for Bridges bought material for Turks' heads and ten yards of red satin, probably for their garments.

It is plain that revels of respectable though not lavish proportion were staged from 1534 to 1543. Cromwell sent masks to court in the late 1530s, one at least by a major playwright, and others, the remnants of which are recorded in Gostwyck's inventory, were put on by Farlyon. Gostwyck's inventory of revels garments, ca. 1540, shows that some material remained in the storehouse after Farlyon's death in 1539.[82] Bridges drew on this material to supply some of his masks up to 1543. But not much in the way of elaborate machinery or pageant frames had survived from Gibson's time, and not much in the way of garments either, for Bridges had to rent costumes from the King's Players and pageants from St Sepulchre's for his Shrovetide entertainments in 1543.[83] In fact, Bridges's accounts show that his revels were not nearly produced on the scale of those held before 1529. Between Christmas 1542–3 and Christmas 1543–4 he produced six masks at a cost of approximately £266, or roughly £45 each – more expensive than those Cromwell had sent to court in 1537 and 1538. Gibson, of course, not only spent more money than this but also had the resources of a storehouse packed with the remains of the great spectacles of the first decade of Henry's reign. Over the course of the 1530s the vast inventory of revels properties was depleted. Cromwell's Reformation schemes and personal control of finance did not encourage growth of the inventory, and this accorded well enough with the king's concern with domestic policy. When it is considered that Bridges's expenses included making all of the costumes and properties, these productions could not have come close to rivalling Gibson's. Even by the relatively conservative standards of the early reign of Elizabeth, who spent more nearly an average of £75 for her masks, Bridges's expenses – as indeed the expenses for the entire period from 1535 to 1543 – were 'a Taylers Bill.'[84]

7

The Offices of the Revels and Tents, 1542–1546

In the early 1540s Henry embarked on a course of war with France, and his revels began to reflect his renewed interest in international affairs. In 1542 revels once again drew their subject matter from romance, reminiscent of the great productions of the early reign. Around the same time Henry initiated changes in the organization for the production of revels. The man he chose to oversee this reorganization was one of his Gentleman of the Privy Chamber, Sir Thomas Cawarden. Cawarden's early life is not well documented. His father, William, was a citizen and fuller of London, and on 27 November 1528 Thomas was apprenticed to Owen Hawkins, citizen and mercer of London.[1] How Cawarden later became prominent enough to attract Cromwell's attention is not apparent. But along with Denny, Mewtis, Hoby, and Sadler – Protestants all – he was preferred to Henry's Privy Chamber by Cromwell.[2] By 1540 Cawarden was listed as one of the Gentleman, and in 1541 he received a New Year's reward of 40s. from the king.[3] Cawarden was in high favour to the end of Henry's reign. He had received license on 21 September 1545 to retain forty gentlemen and yeomen, and both he and his wife were listed among those ordinarily to be lodged at court.[4] There are many mentions of suits granted at his intercession, and he was left a legacy of £200 'in token of special love' in the king's will.[5]

Cawarden acquired significant landholdings and offices in Henry's service, chiefly in Surrey but also in Warwick, Berkshire, Sussex, and Kent. The more important grants made during Henry VIII's reign included the appointment on 25 June 1543 as Keeper of the castle of Donyngton, Berkshire, Keeper and paler of the park there, Steward and Bailiff of the lordship and manor, and also of all the lands in Berkshire acquired from Charles, Duke of Somerset.[6] In 1544 he was appointed Steward and Bailiff of the manor of Nonsuch and other manors in Surrey, and Keeper of the chief messuage, park, and gardens of Nonsuch. In August 1540 he had been appointed Keeper of the manor of Blechingly, Surrey, the little park there, and the great park there called the 'South Park,' Master of the Hunt of deer there, and Steward and Receiver of the manor and of other Crown lands. There were further grants of land in Surrey, and his yearly household expenses in 1548 at Blechingly, his principal residence, were a substantial £500, including charges of £45 for the liveries of one hundred servants.[7] Along with these grants came political responsibilities. He was a member of Parliament for Blechingly on 6 January 1542, and again on 16 October 1547. In the following month he was Sheriff of the County, and on 1 February 1553, 7 November 1554, and 23 December 1558 he was Knight of the Shire.[8]

Cawarden continued to prosper in Edward VI's reign. He was reappointed as Gentleman of the Privy Chamber to Edward VI, and received permission by signet letter on 18 June 1547 to maintain four horses and men for the king's service. He was Keeper of the king's chief messuage of his honour of Hampton Court, Chief Steward of the honour of Hampton Court and Bailiff of the lordship of Hampton Court, Steward and Bailiff of the manor of Nonsuch, and Keeper of the Wardrobe of the same manor. In 1550 he was appointed Keeper of the king's house of Nonsuch called 'le Banketyng House within the park there,' Keeper of the new gardens and orchards of the North, South, and New Park at Hampton Court, and Steward of all the king's manors in Newbury, Berkshire.[9] On 4 April 1548 he made formal application to the Crown for the site of the Blackfriars, which petition was granted on 12 May 1550 and included the entire precinct not already given away to others. Some of these buildings he was to develop for use as workrooms, storage facilities, and rehearsal halls for the Revels and Tents, and they continued to serve this purpose until 1560. At least by 1547, and probably much earlier, he made his own residence in the precinct, for on 28 October of that year he received a letter from Somerset requesting that Lord Cobham have the hall of his lodging at 'the blacke Freares' to use 'during his abode here at this instant parlement.'[10]

While John Travers, Sergeant of the Tents, returned to England occasionally to support the king's summer progresses, his absences from the office were frequent enough to justify the temporary assignment of Cawarden to some of his duties.[11] Cawarden's appointment to take inventory of the Tents and of the Revels, which he delivered to Bridges and Hale on 4 and 10 December 1542, suggests that plans to have him take over the office may have been made this early, probably in connection with preparations for the war.[12] While there is no evidence to confirm that he supervised revels productions before Christmas 1544–5, it is a reasonable hypothesis which explains his appointment to the Mastership by patent in 1545. It is certain that he was supervising in the Tents by the spring of 1543. Like the Blackfriars and the Charterhouse, Whitefriars, the former priory of the Carmelites which was dissolved and surrendered in 1538, was being used for government offices. Cawarden was occupied at the Whitefriars constructing the 'kynges lodgyng of tymber ffor the warres.'[13] The Tents checkbook beginning on 15 April shows that his servant, John Barnard, disbursed £139 16d. on projects which were not completed until summer, in addition to employing material confiscated from Cromwell's former house in London, which Cawarden and Nicholas Bristow had a commission from the king to sell.[14] He was also making a banqueting house there, probably fabricated for transport elsewhere, possibly to France. In the following year Cawarden was occupied in making tents and pavilions for the campaign in France, while John Bridges was employed in making patterns for coats and jerkins.[15] He accompanied the king to France in 1544 as Master of the Tents, attended by fifty-one horsemen, fifty archers, 150 billmen, pikes, and others, and on 30 September he was knighted at Boulogne.[16]

The Revels organization formed at the beginning of Henry's reign was influenced by preparations for the 1512–14 war. Now, at the end of the reign, the organization of the combined offices of the Tents and Revels was influenced by the preparations for the 1542–4 war. In early 1544 Cawarden was financed by Sir Richard Southwell, vice-treasurer for the war, to create a Tents organization for the campaign in France and to pay the army of carpenters, tailors, bricklayers, smiths, and other artisans and labourers who were to become part of it. Two surviving lists prepared for the French expedition, one dated 12 April 1544, show the administrative structure used to organize this Tents workforce.[17] A hierarchical bureaucracy was created in which ordinary duties were distributed among a number of officers, some of whom already held patents to their positions and others of whom were appointed for wartime service. Thomas Hale, who held the patent, served as Groom and was paid 18d. a day. John Bridges, who held the patent as Yeoman of the Revels and the reversion of the patent as Yeoman of the Tents, served as Yeoman and was paid 2s. a day. John Colyer was appointed Clerk at 18d. a day. John Barnard was appointed Clerk Comptroller at 2s. a day. Anthony Aucher was appointed Lieutenant at 10s. a day. And Cawarden, who adopted the style 'Master,' was paid 20s. a day. In addition to the officers, there were a number of wardens appointed to organize and to oversee the work of each group of artificers and labourers.

After the war, Cawarden was issued a patent as Master of the Tents, dated 11 March 1545, which was made retroactive to 16 March 1544, with a fee of £30 a year in survivorship with his former Lieutenant, Anthony Aucher.[18] Aucher, who became Master and Treasurer of the Jewels in 1545, died or resigned his reversion before 1559, for he did not succeed Cawarden.[19] On 11 March 1545, by separate patent, also made retroactive to 16 March 1544, Cawarden was appointed the first 'Magistri iocorum reuelorum et mascorum omnium et singulorum nostrorum vulgariter nuncapatorum Reuelles and Maskes' at a fee of £10 a year.[20] Cawarden, who had called himself 'Master' during the war, received confirmation of the style in his patents. An explanation for the style is given by the writer of 'The First Institution': 'Sir Thomas Carden ... did mislyke to be tearmed Seriaunt because of his better countenaunce of roome and place beinge of the kinges maiesties privye Chamber.'[21] Of course, there is historical precedent for using the style 'Master of the Revels.' Supervisors of the revels at court were so called at least as early as 1510, though none of them received a formal confirmation by patent. This was, however, the first use of the style in the Tents.

The organization that Cawarden had devised for the Tents during the war, with the exception of the Lieutenant, was used to structure the offices of the Revels and Tents. The Master and the Yeoman each held separate patents in the Revels and in the Tents, but the Clerk and Clerk Comptroller, because of the general nature of their functions, held joint appointments in both offices under single patents. The new office was composed of seven patent positions: a Master of the Revels, a Master of the Tents, a Yeoman of the Revels, a Yeoman of the Tents, a Clerk Comptroller of the Revels and Tents, a Clerk of the Revels and Tents, and a Groom of the Tents. A Porter, who did not hold a patent, was also employed, and a variety of chief artists and artisans, the equivalent of the wardens used during wartime, were hired on specific projects to direct crews of artisans and labourers. Basically, Cawarden formalized what had been ordinary procedure in the Revels and Tents from as early as 1513. The new changes involved the subdivision and distribution of mid-level supervisory and accounting duties – formerly done by the Yeoman and one of the king's clerks – among the Yeoman, the Clerk, and the Clerk Comptroller, and, of course, altering the status of the Master from appointee to permanent office holder.[22]

The seven patent positions in the office were based partly on tradition. Individuals had been performing the duties of Sergeant and Yeoman of the Tents for centuries, and those of Master and Yeoman of the Revels for at least thirty years. Cawarden's innovation was to create a centralized bureaucracy staffed by as few people as possible which could efficiently and economically serve the needs of the court. He held the patents to both Masterships. Bridges held a patent to one and the reversion of the patent to the other Yeomanship. When John Holt succeeded him as Yeoman of the Revels in 1550, he also received a reversion of the patent as Yeoman of the Tents. This put the seven patents in the hands of five people. Cawarden's tendency was also to absorb other compatible duties into his office, as can be seen from the title of the account he filed from 1550–5 for 'Thoffyces of the Tentes & revelles with the Toyles lorde of Mysryle Maskes Playes and other Pastimes tryumphes Banketinghowses and other preparacions actes & devices therto appartenente and accustomed made done furnished attended & setforthe of those offices.'[23]

Cawarden's office, tightened by the various ordinances he wrote to regulate it, reflects a general tendency in Tudor government around mid-century toward centralization. But Cawarden was wary enough of centralization to build a system of checks into his administrative structure. It is observed in 'The First Institution' that Cawarden wanted the officers of his organization to hold patents to their positions so that their chief obligation would be to the sovereign, not to the head of the Revels Office.[24] His organization provided a hierarchal structure and a clear chain of command, but at the same time the officers had specific responsibilities and perquisites – particular work to perform, artisans and labourers to supervise, and part of the inventory to control – which allowed them to supervise each other. Between 1559 and 1567, Richard Leys 'perceiving that in his conscience her maiestie hathe ben and is ouercharged in that behalf, hathe vtterlie refused according to his bounden dutie & othe to subscribe or consent to' the accounts.[25] His refusal to sign Sir Thomas Benger's accounts was followed by a petition to Lord Burghley asking that special surveyors be appointed to investigate the office. Leys could do this with impunity because his patent protected his position.

i

John Barnard was appointed by patent on the same day, and with the same retroactive pay as Cawarden, to the post of Clerk Comptroller of the Tents, Hales and Pavilions, and of the Revels, Masks, and Masking Garments, with a fee of 8 d. a day.[26] His patent included a life grant to a house called 'Egypt and Fleshall' and the adjoining house lately called 'le Garneter' with the chambers beneath it and a little garden called 'le Kitchen garden' nearby, situated within and upon the walls of the late Charterhouse near London. Barnard, who was a servant of Cawarden's, worked as supervisor in the Tents at Whitefriars in 1543, and as Clerk Comptroller of the Tents in the 1544 campaign, continued in office until his death on 4 September 1550.[27] Richard Leys, citizen and mercer of London, acted as Barnard's deputy from 1 September 1550. He was formally appointed to the office by patent on 17 March 1551 with wages of 8 d. a day, payable at the Exchequer half-yearly at Michaelmas and Easter, livery of four yards of woollen cloth from the Great Wardrobe at Christmas, and a life grant of a house with chambers, cellars, buildings, stable, yard, and garden for keeping the pavilions, hales and tents, and for a residence for himself and his family.[28] Leys, who died before 30 September 1570, spent a number of the last years of his life at odds with Sir Thomas Benger over the accuracy of the Revels bills. Leys's scrupulous attention to Elizabeth I's interests was at least one of Cawarden's motives in creating the position of Clerk Comptroller, as the writer of 'The First Institution' speculated:

Sir Thomas Carden havinge by all likelihoode mistrust of loose and negligent dealing*es* by Inferio*ur* officers or others in that office and because hym selfe coulde not be alwayes there p*re*sent to oversee the charge of the office procured at the king*es* handes That there shoulde be also a Clerke Comptroller of the said office who beinge the Princes sworne man and caryinge that name might with some countenaunce or aucthoritye stande hym in good steede for the better governement and direccion of the said office, and for the amendement of the loose dealing*es* both to his owne ease and the Princes good service.²⁹

The other motive, as it appears from Blagrave's description of duties in his 'Platte of Orders,' was supervision. The Clerk Comptroller

oughte to be of good experience and acquainted w*ith* thaffairs of the office, aswell for Deuise and settinge oute of the same, as for knowledge of the price and valewe of stuffe, and woorckmanshippe, shall vewe p*er*vse, and oversee the measure, weighte, tale, Rates and pric*es* and states of all p*ro*uisions and ympleament*es* and shall see all the busines of thoffice diligently wroughte & attended and the default*es* checked.³⁰

Cawarden regarded himself above the duties associated with the title of Sergeant, and so the Clerk Comptroller, the Master's former servant, assumed a supervisory role in the office.

John Colyer was the first Clerk of the office. His patent has not been discovered, but he was appointed Clerk during the 1544 campaign and was functioning in that capacity by 16 March 1544. He continued in the office after the war and signed the account for the Christmas revels of 1544–5.³¹ He did not sign the account for the following Christmas. It appears that a new Clerk was not appointed until, at Cawarden's suit, Thomas Phillips received a patent on 7 May 1546 with a fee of 8*d.* a day, 24*s.* a year for livery, and a house appointed in the precinct of Blackfriars.³² The Clerk's position was created, according to the writer of 'The First Institution,' because

Sir Thomas Carden after that beinge driven as it should seeme from tyme to tyme to have his bookes of accompte made vp by the Clerke of the King*es* woork*es* as the office might be vsed when it was kepte in the Princ*es* courte thought it expedient by reason of greate charge and expences daylie growinge by reason of the same office To have some necessarye person who beinge the Princes sworne servaunte and havinge office and wages or fee by Patent therefore might regester and enter the charges anye waye growen by reason of the said office from tyme to tyme who also might be a good witnes of the vpright service both of the masters and others dealing*es* in the said office, and to make vppe and perfitt the bookes reconyng*es* and accompt*es* of the said office with more readye vnderstandinge by reason of attendaunce then the Clerke of the work*es* beinge a straunger thervnto coulde doe.³³

Phillips held the patent until 1560, but as early as 1551 many of his duties were performed by Thomas Blagrave, who provides a summary of the Clerk's duties in his 'Platte of Orders.'

The Clerk oughte to be of like engine experience knoweldge and acquainetaunce [as the Clerk Comptroller] and noe lesse skilfull in Reconinges and accomptes for the cawses aforesaide shall take the entreye of all woorckes laboures attendaunces and other busines Done exercised or practized with in the office and likewise the measure weighte and tale of all Stoore provisiounes ymploymentes and remains of all that goeth into or oute of the office, or ys ymployed or altered in the same.[34]

Blagrave began his career as Barnard had, as personal servant to Cawarden. He was born about 1522, for he gave his age as fifty or thereabouts in an interrogatory of 1572, and therefore was about twenty-four years of age when he entered Cawarden's service in 1546.[35] Blagrave, who was from Wiltshire, was an important and trusted servant, and possibly was being groomed for the Mastership. He had only a semi-official status in the office, being assigned various tasks such as the receipt of money from the treasurers of the Court of Augmentations, the Court of Wards and Liveries, and the Exchequer along with Phillips. He served as deputy to Phillips from 1551, and when Phillips died Blagrave was granted the patent as Clerk on 25 March 1560 with a fee of 8d. a day, 24s. for livery, and a house appointed by the Master.[36] In about 1573 Blagrave took the opportunity in writing his 'Platte of Orders' to petition for the Mastership:

her Maiestie, shall haue more done, and bettre by a thirde parte for lesse chardge by a thirde parte then hetherto I haue knowen, and will yelde a iust and trewe accompte both of stuffe and money/ If it please her highnes to bestowe the Mastership of the office vpon me (as I trust myne experience by acquayntaunce with those thaffaires and contynuall dealing therein by the space of xxvij or xxviij yeres deserveth being also the auncient of the office by at the leaste xxiiij of those yeres otherwise I wolde be lothe hereafter to deale nor medle wyth it nor in it further then apperteyneth to the clerke.[37]

From 1573 until 1578 Blagrave received temporary commissions from the Lord Chamberlain to serve as acting Master of the Revels, but the appointment by patent of Edmund Tilney to the Mastership in 1579 was such a disappointment that he protested. Neither the Clerk nor the Clerk Comptroller, who apparently sided with Blagrave, signed the Revels accounts between 1579 and 1581, and Tilney noted on his account that 'there is no Clerke' in the office.[38] Beginning in 1582–3 Blagrave began to sign the accounts again, perhaps because he was promised the patent as Surveyor of the Works within the Tower and of her

Majesty's Houses of Access, which he received on 10 November 1586 after the death of Lewis Stockett.[39] Blagrave died between April and November 1590, and was buried at St John's, Clerkenwell, site of the Revels Office from 1560 to 1607.[40]

Feuillerat suggested that the Yeoman, who was a tailor, was not considered an officer of the Revels but rather a higher workman, since he was always listed with those workmen in Cawarden's accounts.[41] This is rather a reflection of the separation of duties in Cawarden's bureaucracy. The Revels Office designed and made many of the costumes and garments for court productions until well into Elizabeth's reign. The writer of 'The First Institution' specifically mentions that 'The cheife busynes of the office resteth speciallye in three poyntes In makinge of garmentes In makinge of hedpeces and in payntinge.'[42] The Yeoman, whose duties are the oldest and most basic to the revels, designed costumes and supervised tailors employed on projects. Most of the men who held this office achieved positions in the royal household which indicate their stature and reputation. Richard Gibson was Yeoman Tailor of the Great Wardrobe, John Bridges was Tailor to the king, and John Holt was Tailor to the prince. Further, the yeomen signed the Revels accounts along with the Master, Clerk Comptroller, and Clerk, and the various documents written to suggest reforms in the office in the early 1570s all charge the Yeoman with important responsibilities which clearly indicate that he was considered an officer. Blagrave, for example, writes of the Yeoman's duties in his 'Platte of Orders':

[The Yeoman] oughte to be of good Capacitie knowledge experience and acquaintaunce with thaffaires of the office aswell for vnderstandinge of devise and settinge fourthe of the same, as for castinge and ymployeinge of the stuffe to the furdeste stretche of sarvice and moste advauntaige/ Shall dow or cawse to be cutte oute made and furnishedd all the garmentes and vestures with theire peeces vtensilles and propertyes, Have take in chardge and sawfe keepe the same remaininge whole/ And see all the woorckes and busines of thoffice within his chardge diligentlye wroughte and attended.[43]

John Bridges, of course, was already Yeoman of the Revels by patent when Cawarden was appointed Master. After receiving a patent as king's Tailor on 26 December 1546, Bridges employed John Holt as his deputy.[44] In a book of expenses, 1–28 February 1547, Holt is styled Yeoman and also so styled in an inventory of masking garments and stuff 'delyueryd owte of the Custody of Iohn Bridges Late yoman of the same Revelles.' This document was signed by Cawarden and Barnard on 1 April of that year and shows that Holt was recognized, *de facto*, as an officer.[45] When Bridges resigned as Yeoman of the Revels, Holt received the patent on 1 July 1550, and shortly after, on 14 October 1550, he received the reversion to the patent as Yeoman of the Tents with Longman.[46] Holt, who was Sewer of the Chamber to Edward VI, for he is so styled in his patents, was also appointed by patent as Tailor to the prince in survivorship with Richard Neuport on 26 January 1547 with a fee of 6*d.* a day and livery.[47] This office gave him charge not only of making all garments, robes, and apparel for the prince, but also of making livery for the prince's gentlemen, henchmen, and footmen, and apparel for his stable. Connections between the posts of king's Tailor and Yeoman of the Revels had developed in Henry VIII's reign, if not earlier. Garments from the king's privy wardrobes were used for costumes, and surplus or outdated material from the Revels storehouse was occasionally used for footmen's jackets in the household. Bridges was paid under the terms of his patents for all three offices, for a warrant was issued in 1559 or 1560 for arrears unpaid since his appointment.[48] Holt exercised his duties as Yeoman of the Revels through a deputy, for sometime between 1–11 December 1570 William Bowle, one of the ordinary Yeomen of the Queen's Chamber, who had 'long tyme served as Deputye,' petitioned for the post, but he did not receive this appointment.[49]

The post of Groom of the Tents was established in 1540 with the appointment by patent to Thomas Hale who was later given a place in the combined office in 1545. John Broun succeeded Hale, and after his death in 1582 William Bowle, who served as deputy to the Yeoman and wanted the patent to that position, was appointed Groom of the Tents on 26 June 1582.[50] The main duties of the Groom of the Tents appear to have been purveying of material and arranging transportation. In Cawarden's time these duties, as well as those of the Porter, were performed for Revels business by the Master's personal servants. Thomas Vaughan, for example, was paid in the 1558–9 account for boat hire, for running errands, and for performing other business.[51] Another of Cawarden's servants, Thomas Tandall, was paid in the same account for running errands and for attending the gates. The functions of Groom and Porter were indispensable. As early as 1508, Wentworth hired a Porter, and under Tilney's Mastership a Porter was named as a regular employee in the accounts until the Revels were dispossessed of their quarters at St John's of Jerusalem, Clerkenwell.[52] A Groom is also named as a regular employee of the Revels at least by 1597. In the 1603–4 Revels account he is described as Purveyor, and, among other duties, was also paid for arranging transportation. Neither the position of Groom nor of Porter of the Revels was ever granted by patent, but they were recognized as important enough to the office to permit their fees to be charged in the accounts. This recognition did not prevent the Masters of the Revels from continuing to use personal servants. Tilney, who had the services of both Groom and Porter, still used four personal servants to attend him at court and charged their wages in the accounts.

'The First Institution' and Blagrave's 'Platte of Orders' provide the earliest doc-

umentation of the Master's qualities, position, and responsibilities. Blagrave notes
that the Master

oughte to be A man learned of good engyne inventife witte and experience aswell for vari-
etie of straunge devises delectable as to waye what moste aptlye and fitleye furnissheth the
tyme place presence and state; Shall haue the principall chardge of thoffice, to giue order
for that is there to be done & to see the hole affaires and orders of the same executed.[53]

His personal qualities should be such that he is 'neither gallant, prodigall, nedye,
nor gredye' and further that he 'be of suche learning wytt and experience as hable
of hym self to make and devise suche shewes and devises as may best fit and fur-
nisshe the tyme place and state with leaste burden.' Blagrave, who had served
Cawarden from the time of his youth and had worked under him in the office for
over ten years, thought little of Cawarden's successor, Sir Thomas Benger. It is
clear that the model for his description of the ideal Master of the Revels was his
old master and benefactor. Even the writer of 'The First Institution' imagines
Cawarden's accomplishment as the standard to which the office should aspire. In
addition to the ability to organize and to economize, Cawarden had the artistic
talent to invent devices for banqueting houses and masks, and to devise properties for plays, and the social stature to serve as liaison to the king. When the writer of 'The First Institution' suggests that a Sergeant be added to the staff of the
Revels Office, for example, he imagines that the new Master would be 'some one
of Countenaunce and of creditt with the Prince ... thought meetest to receyve her
highnes pleasure from tyme to tyme attendaunt in the Courte.'[54] The Sergeant
was to 'execute the devise receyved or to invente a new meete and necessarye with
the allowayunce of the Master.' Cawarden, of course, was of such 'good countenance' that he disdained the title of Sergeant, and is remembered by the writer of
'The First Institution' as 'skilfull and delightinge in matters of devise.'

These documents date from the early 1570s, fairly late in the history of Tudor
revels, and it is clear that the men who wrote them had no knowledge of the office
before the time of Travers nor of the revels before the time of Farlyon and Bridges.
They had no idea that the basic function of the Masters as devisers and supervisors of court revels reached back to the beginning of the Tudor period. Neither
were they aware that their conception of the Master's qualities and broad responsibilities could be traced to Sir Henry Guildford's time. Guildford devised revels
himself, negotiated performances by acting companies, contracted the services of
devisers and producers, drew on the services of Gibson for production, and had
the social stature to function as liaison to the king. There is an important difference, of course. For Guildford, the Mastership was only one of many appointed duties at court; for Cawarden, it was one among a prescribed set of duties in

the household, confirmed by patent. The duties and responsibilities of the Master were to expand, to contract, and to expand again over the course of the century and into the next, and many of the alterations in the position introduced beginning in the early 1570s can be traced to the analyses and recommendations contained in these two documents.

Cawarden's 'Constitucions howe the Kynges Revelles ought to be usyd' (ca. 1545) set out regulations and procedures for record keeping in the office.[55] Blagrave and the other writers of the 1573 Revels memoranda were influenced, if not by this document, at least by common practices in Cawarden's office, for their suggestions for reforms are modifications of the procedures Cawarden had put into effect. No material was to be bought for the office without the Master's or his deputy's approval. All such material was to be entered into a book of receipt. The inventory was to be stored in 'Fayr stonderdes or pressis and every presse or stonderd to have twoo lockes apece with severall wardes with ij keys thone for the master or clarcke and thother for the yoman so that non of them cum to the stuff without thothers.' Material issued out of the storehouse was to be entered by the Clerk into a book, which explained how it was to be used and was subscribed by the Master. The Clerk was also present at the cutting of all garments and entered into a book 'howe moche it Takyth of all kyndes to every maske, Revelles, or tryumphes,' which was subscribed by the Master. The Clerk also kept records of 'all daye men workyng on the premissis' and entered these into a book, one copy of which went to the paymaster and one copy to the Master. An inventory was to be made from time to time by the Clerk and Clerk Comptroller, which was to be signed by all of the officers, and no garments or material were to be lent out.

It is clear that an elaborate set of records was kept in the office. All bills submitted by merchants and contract artisans were kept. All materials brought into the office either purchased from merchants or delivered by certificates from the various wardrobes or other offices were entered into a book of receipt, and when material was issued an explanation was entered describing how it was employed.[56] The 'imploy books' recorded all material used in particular productions, and the 'day books' recorded the wages of artisans and labourers employed at the office. From these main records and various certificates, warrants, and bills, the 'ledger book' was made, which included charges for all work done in the office in a particular season. The auditors at the treasuries abstracted information from this book and preserved these records to justify their payments.

Blagrave recommends in his 'Platte of Orders' that 'Soe sone as anye Maske or other devise ys finished the patterne and platte of the same shalbe Drawne and putt in collers by A painter aswell for the witnes of the worcke, as for presidente to the office, to induse, Devise, and shewe, Difference, of that is to come frome that ys paste.' That Cawarden had these 'plats' or designs made to record his productions seems likely, as they continued to be made, at least on occasion, in Elizabeth's reign. All of these kinds of documents, except the 'plats,' survive among Sir Thomas Cawarden's papers. Yet, despite the fact that more and a greater variety of documents survive from this period than from any other up to 1642, we know less about Cawarden's productions than we do about Gibson's. The narrative quality in Gibson's early accounts, naive from an accounting standpoint, is exactly what historians four hundred years removed from the events need to understand the details of production. Cawarden's documents are financial accounts, prepared by specialized officers which can be interpreted only when all of the documents are read together. And, of course, not all of the documents survive for every entertainment.

ii

Cawarden remedied some of the long-standing problems associated with revels productions by centralizing the physical facilities of the office. Some government departments 'owtward' of the Chamber, like the Works, had permanent offices and work space.[57] Up to Cawarden's time the supervisors of the revels had only storage facilities. They had to contract work space, and the Revels accounts from 1508 to 1545 show that their procedures varied little. A facility large enough to construct the bulky pageants and lay out and cut material for costumes was required, as well as a location close enough to a wharf to conveniently transport materials to court. When Wentworth undertook to produce pageants and masks for the Christmas 1508–9 festivities, he rented one house 'at the Crane in the vintere for ij pagiauntes' and another at 'the bishop of harfordes place' for 'a pagiant cauled the mount.'[58] The Vintry was a ward in London 'so called of the vintners, and of the Vintrie, a part of the banke of the River of Thames, where the merchants of Burdeaux craned their wines out of Lighters, and other vessels ... in bredth this ward stretcheth from the Vintry north to the wall of the West gate of the Tower Royall.'[59] Its attraction to the producers of revels may have been the 'three strong Cranes of Timber placed on the Vintrie wharf by the Thames side, to crane vp wines there.' Wentworth loaded 'ij standardes and ij gret cofers' and transported them from London 'to Richmount banke' so that the king could inspect 'the disguising stuff' and again to transport the pageants and the costumes for the entertainment. Gibson used the Vintry to unload the pageant, *Shatew Vert*, built for the 3 March 1522 disguising at York Place before it was transported by cart to the Prince's Wardrobe for storage.[60] Gibson used Paul's wharf in 1515 to transport *The Pavyllyon vn the Plas Parlos* to Richmond for Twelfth Night. Bridges used Tower wharf to transport material to Greenwich during the war and for the Christmas entertainments of 1544–5.[61] The wharf at Scotland may have also been used by the Revels after 1550. Scotland was a parcel of land formerly belonging to the king of Scotland, an open space of about a thousand feet in length lying between York Place on the north and Rounceval on the south. It was granted to Wolsey on 10 November 1519 and so reverted to the Crown in 1529. After that date, the Works used it as a storage yard and built a wharf there in 1531–2.[62] Cawarden received a grant of the property in 1550, around the time he received a grant to the Blackfriars, and the Works rebuilt the wharf there in 1552.[63]

The house Wentworth rented in the Vintry was probably the one Stow describes as 'next ouer against S. Martins Church ... a large house builded of stone and timber, with vaults for the stowage of wines, and is called the Vintrie.'[64] Such a house with vaults would be required to construct pageants designed for the scale of the great halls of the royal palaces about London, and we have record of Gibson renting others. *The Golldyn Arber in the Arche Yerd of Pleyser* for the pageant-disguising of 13 February 1511 at Westminster was constructed at the Bishop of Hertford's place in Blackfriars. *Le Fortresse Dangerus* was constructed at Sir Edward Borrow's house in London for the disguising held on New Year's 1512 at Greenwich. And the mount and the unicorn for the *Castle of Loyalty* held at Greenwich in 1524 was constructed at the Prince's Wardrobe, outside the walls of Blackfriars.[65]

Wentworth worked from 8 to 22 January 1509 to make up his accounts and to store the pageants and costumes in the Prince's Wardrobe.[66] Gibson refers often to the Prince's Storehouse or Wardrobe in his accounts. An inventory was housed there, garments were occasionally cut, and pageants were sometimes built. This was probably the building in the parish of St Andrew on Warwick Lane, sometimes called Warwick Inn because it was built by Thomas Beauchamp, Earl of Warwick (d. 1379).[67] The building was granted to Sir Roger Cotton, Knight of the Body, on 15 February 1488, and a Privy Seal writ was issued for payment to Richard Doland, Clerk of the Works, for repairs to it over a three-year period: 'Where as oure place called the princes warderobe within our citie of London, which we have appointed vnto our derrest wif the quene for the sauf keeping of such her stufs as belong vnto hur, is greatly decayed and soo ruynous that withoute the souner remedie bee hade the said place within short tyme wilbe at thextreme point of desolacion, whiche we ne wold.'[68] The keepership of the building was granted to John Tourner, Sergeant of the Tents, and Robert Browne in 1513, and, again, on 16 October 1541, to John Bridges, Yeoman of the Revels.[69] The Tents inventory was probably stored there as early as 1513 but certainly by July 1539, for when John Farlyon died, Thomas Thacker wrote to Cromwell that he went to Warwick Inn 'where the king*es* tentes and yo*ur* Lordship*es* also lye' and locked the doors. The Revels inventory was probably stored there as early as 1510 but certainly by 1540, when an inventory shows a variety of material stored at

Warwick Inn, including masking garments in certain 'cofferes or standardes.'[70] The inventory was still here in 1543–4, for Bridges charges in his Christmas account for 'caryage from *the* wattr syd to warwyk in.'[71] While Warwick Inn was the main Revels and Tents storage facility, it did not contain all of the inventory. Wentworth kept material in his own custody, for when Gibson received the keys to the storehouse in November 1510 he also received 'two war chests and a standard' containing revels garments and properties.[72] Caring for some revels properties became the charge of the Yeoman in Henry VIII's reign. Farlyon's patent of 1534 assigns him a house suitable to store and care for the properties.[73]

In 1542 the Tents and Toils were assigned a new storehouse at the Charterhouse, the House of the Salutation of the Mother of God, founded by the Carthusians at Smithfield in 1371. It was surrendered to the Crown on 15 November 1538 and its buildings were divided among Sir Anthony Darcy, Dr. Crane, and William Dale until 12 June 1542, when it was granted for life to John Bridges and Thomas Hale for the Tents.[74] The officers had houses appointed to them here, and used 'the Southside of the Church in a Chapell' and also the north side to store tents until at least 1544.[75] The Charterhouse did not provide good access to the river, and the Tents, particularly in wartime, was mainly concerned with shipping materials by water to the front.[76] On 14 April 1564 the buildings were sold to Edward, Lord North, but there is evidence that at least some of the Tents had already been moved to their new quarters at Blackfriars as early as 1545.[77]

Under Cawarden's direction some Tents projects were undertaken in 1543 at Whitefriars, the former priory of the Carmelites located between Fleet Street and the river, east of Sergeant's Inn and west of Water Lane, which was surrendered in 1538. Some of the buildings were used to store seventy-seven bows and sheaves of arrows and javelins conveyed there from the Tower and from the king's fletchers for use by the Yeomen of the Guard on the king's progress.[78] The Tents were using some of the buildings or yards to make the 'kyngs lodgyng of timber ffor the warres' and a banqueting house.[79] It is possible that the Tents was stationed there temporarily to cannibalize materials, such as lead, timber, and hangings. There is no indication that they continued here, either because these were wartime projects and were completed or, possibly, because they were evicted after the buildings were granted to Lord de la Warr in 1544.[80] Whatever the reason, the evidence indicates that by 1545 the office, under Cawarden's leadership, was beginning to move into the Blackfriars.

Blackfriars, an approximately five-acre tract composed of a variety of buildings, was the former priory of the Dominicans, located between St Paul's and the river and east of Fleet ditch, and was surrendered on 12 November 1538. It was a liberty, quasi-independent of the city, situated conveniently to Puddle Wharf and

Blackfriars landing.[81] The buildings were convenient to Westminster as well. They had been used for a number of Parliaments, to house foreign dignitaries, as a meeting place for the king's council, and as a favourite residence of courtiers. The Tents certainly occupied some of the buildings at Blackfriars between March 1545 and March 1546. Some of the tents had already been taken from the Charter-house and 'layd up' in unidentified buildings at Blackfriars between November 1544 and March 1545. These buildings were leased from Sir Thomas Cheyne, for he later sued and won judgment in the Court of Augmentation for rental of £5 a year and arrears from 1545 to 1550 'for a house in Blackfryers to laye the kings tents in.'[82] The room that Cheyne claimed to have rented to the Tents was the paved hall under the fratery. There is some controversy over the exact location, for Sir William More mentioned that the room was never used by the Tents, and Sir John Portynare, who had the keys to the building, testified that it had remained empty until Cawarden took possession of it in 1550.[83]

Preparations to move the Revels were made as early as 1546. Hugh Losse, Surveyor of the Works, advanced money to John Barnard, acting as temporary surveyor for repairs at Blackfriars, to make a storehouse for the Revels and Tents.[84] The Revels inventory was transferred to Blackfriars in early 1547, for charges are included in the 1547–8 Revels account for moving the material from Warwick Inn.[85] Which buildings were used for the purpose is not clear, but by 4 April 1548 Cawarden had leased the buttery, the fratery, the kitchen, and a chamber.[86] The fratery, which measured 107 x 52 feet, was used as a storehouse.[87] On 12 March 1550, all of the buildings in the precinct not already owned were granted to Cawarden. He set about developing the precinct by building new roads and repairing or rebuilding houses.[88] The officers of the Revels who had previous grants of lodgings elsewhere were moved to Blackfriars. John Barnard lived in the Porter's lodge; John Holt had a house north of the churchyard; Thomas Phillips, who had a little chamber west of the fratery and who used the paved hall under it for a wood store, moved in 1552 to the Ankerhouse. Thomas Blagrave took Phillips's old quarters and rented an adjoining chamber from Sir Thomas Cheyne.[89]

As long as the Crown owned the buildings, the Revels paid no rent. After the grant to Cawarden in 1550, he charged the Crown rent in the accounts for the buildings and living quarters. In 1555 Cawarden was allowed six years' arrears, from Michaelmas 1549, at £3 6s. 8d. for each of the officer's dwellings, £6 13s. 4d. for his own house, an identical sum for the Tents buildings, and the same for the five great rooms used for the Revels store and work houses. By 1559 the rent had increased to £5 for the officers' dwellings and £10 for his own house.[90] Cawarden, of course, profited from the arrangement, but it was a logical one. For the first time, the Tents and Revels storehouse, workhouses, and officers' dwellings were all located in appropriate buildings near one another, near Westminster, and with convenient access to the river and a loading dock.

Despite a central storehouse, revels equipment and paraphernalia continued to be scattered among several offices. The Clerk of the Stable, answerable to the Master of the Horse, took charge of the saddles, reins, spurs, and other equipment relating to the horses, and the Master of the Armoury took charge of weapons relating to the martial exhibitions. Gold, silver, precious stones and cloths issued by the Master of the Jewels were returned to him after an entertainment. The Works dismantled their degrees and stages and stored the timber in their yards or reemployed it. The Masters of the Revels had access to properties and garments which were not connected to the main storehouse. Cawarden, for example, was Keeper of the manor of Nonsuch and of the wardrobe there. Occasionally he was ordered to supply the court with furnishings from its wardrobe, and, at his death, an inventory was taken of the tents, pavilions, swords, broad spears, and other equipment he had left at Westminster.[91]

iii

Henry besieged Boulogne and entered the city in a triumphal procession on 18 July 1544 with his retinue attired in the coats and jerkins made by John Bridges. The triumphs in France in that year and the creation of the Revels Office in 1545 provided both the impetus and the means to produce the spectacles and entertainments at home culminating in the Anglo-French peace negotiations of 1546 which recall, if only briefly, the grandeur of the early reign. Cawarden and his officers – including John Barnard, John Bridges, and John Colyer – in the newly reorganized Tents and Revels, yet without official status, produced the Christmas entertainments of 1544–5 at Greenwich. The accounts are not detailed enough to guess the theme of the revels, but they are sufficient to suggest that Cawarden and his officers worked for twelve days to produce a mask for eight men and eight women.[92] Nicholas Lizard, the king's Painter, was charged to gild with gold and silver the white and blue undergarments for the eight women. Eight long headpieces made of paste and gilded with gold and silver were also made for women, while eight round headpieces, eight hoods, and broad caps made of 'like stuff' were made for men. Twenty-four feathers of various colours, eight staffs with snakes, and sixteen gold and silver visors were used, as well as twelve dozen hawk bells – possibly for a morris – two dozen women's gloves, and hair, probably for the headpieces.

At Christmas 1545–6 the Revels officers worked for sixteen days to produce masks at Hampton Court at a cost of £82 9s., 'Ouer & besyde suche stuff as was spent of his majesties owne Store.'[93] One of the revels was a mask of Egyptians, possibly on the subject of Moses. At least two Egyptian women and two Egyptian 'babes' were outfitted, along with two Moors. The Moors were costumed in girdles, gloves, and caps all made of black velvet, and the crimson slops also appear to belong to their costumes. Headpieces were made for the Egyptian women and also 'Italyon coyffes of gold and siluer.' The Egyptian 'babes' also had headpieces and 'ij lytle coyffes of venys gold & siluer.' Most of the material, with the exception of that Cawarden had from the king's store, including forty-two capon's feathers trimmed with gold, twenty-seven pair of gloves, and eight and one-half dozen visors, was bought from Christopher Milliner who had supplied Cromwell's masks in 1539. John Payne, skinner, was paid for furring two caps with 'Cattes skynnes and gennettes tayles.' Anthony Toto, later the king's Sergeant Painter, painted eight staves with red and white. William Bayard, another painter, made eight chains of cord painted with gold for the torch bearers. Richard Lee, mercer, supplied four dozen yellow feathers as well as spangled capon feathers. Eight 'sockettes of white plates' were bought from a wire drawer to hold the feathers.

In the spring of 1546 Cawarden was assigned to several temporary projects. In April 1546 he was engaged on some unidentified project which required the services of Severn watermen. The council had sent a letter to Sir Anthony Kingston, Sir George Baynham, and Sir Nicholas Poynz to take up four hundred of these watermen and send them to Cawarden within twelve days for an important business.[94] Possibly in this connection some misfortune befell him. A note by Paget attached to a letter of Sir Edward Seymour, Earl of Hertford, concerning the flag of St George and the banner of the king's arms – no doubt having to do with the St George celebration on 23 April – mentions that 'Mr Carden (god comfort hym) was spoken unto it.'[95] Lisle wrote to the king about his bad time crossing the channel, of which he 'dyd aduertise Sir Thomas Cardeyn (god comfort hym) not knowing then of his misfortune.'[96]

Whatever calamity befell Cawarden in April did not deter him from participating in the grandest spectacles of the later reign, the reception and entertainments at Hampton Court in August–September 1546 for Claude d'Annebaut, Admiral of France, who was in England to formalize the Anglo-French treaty of peace. In addition to overseeing the revels Cawarden was designated to provide horses and foot cloths for the Admiral, and he also attended the court banquet as a member of the Privy Chamber.[97] For the reception and entertainments, Cawarden and his officers worked for fifty-one days, 'from the xvj*th* Daie of Iulij … vnto the v*th* Daie of Septembre next' on the banqueting houses, which were especially built for the occasion, and on the masks.[98] Hall mentions that 'To tel you of the costlye banquet houses … you woulde much maruel, and skant beleue.'[99] The council's letters of 13 and 15 September suggest a level of distress over the cost.

They had taken order to pay £4000 for the banqueting houses which 'disfurnished' all of the king's treasurers.[100] There were a number of banqueting houses in this period. At least three of them had already been constructed by 1546. One was a timber structure designed by Nicholas Bellin of Modena, and installed in the Privy Garden (later called the Preaching Place or Sermon Court) at Whitehall. A fragment of an account listing ranging line, 'by him occupied at sondry usis to and for the said bancket-house,' dates the construction between 1537 and 1547. Charges in the Tents account, 1544–6, for setting up the tents at Westminster for the banqueting house 'on the trilles there,' may refer to this structure. Another banqueting house was constructed at Nonsuch, probably sometime between 1541 and 1545. Nicholas Bellin was engaged in decorating Nonsuch palace with carved slate work during this period and he may well have designed this banqueting house as well. Charges in the Tents account show that the tents were set up at Nonsuch in 1546 and 'hangings' (tapestries?) were transported from Westminster to Nonsuch 'when thmbasadors' were there. Charges in an undated Tents account show delivery of tents to 'hyde parke for the bankett house ther' and transport back to the Charterhouse. There was also a banqueting house at Hampton Court which Robert Trunckwell claimed to have designed.[101] The activities of the Office of the Tents from July to September 1546 at Hampton Court, where some of the entertainments for the Admiral were certainly held, and at Oatlands and Cobham, suggest that the structures built there are the banqueting houses mentioned in the council's letters. Charges are listed in the Tents account for deliveries of tents and other material on 14 August 'to the banquettyng house on the hyll aboue otlandes.' Further deliveries from Oatlands to Hampton Court are recorded on 21 August, and the Revels account for 24 August – 5 September includes charges for decorating the banqueting house at Hampton Court.[102] In September material was transported from Oatlands to Cobham where the officers of the Tents were occupied with setting up and 'new Edyfyeng' a great timber house.[103] This great timber house was used 'for a quadrante to Ioyne the tymber houses together.' It appears that the king's timber tents were set up to form something like a temporary palace. Carpenters made stages and 'terrystes' for them and painters were hired to complete the decoration.[104] The preparations suggest full provision for a major entertainment. The Revels bills for the event, £570 5 1/2d., suggest a scale that rivals productions from the 1520s, particularly when it is remembered that the accounts do not indicate full provisions, only those extra charges for material or workmanship which could not be had from government or household departments.

In London, the Admiral was received with salutes of ordnance and entertained with banquets and ceremonies before his reception at Hampton Court. He was lavishly entertained there for ten days, beginning on 24 August when he dynned that daie at the Kinges bord, and so remayned in the court, with banqueting and huntinge, and riche maskes everie night with the Queene and ladies, with dauncinge in tow (sic) new banqueting howses, which were richlie hanged, and had ryche cubbordes of gold plate all gild, and sett with rych stones and perles.[105]

Although Cawarden's accounts do not preserve details of rich masks every night, we know that he was responsible for the cloth hangings and decorations in the revels chamber of one of the banqueting houses and that he produced several masks. Christopher Milliner supplied eight pair of velvet gloves, nineteen 'felts' and linen cloth to line headpieces, masks decorated with gold and silver, and eight great chains for torch bearers. Nicholas of Modena was paid for gilding these chains and for making eight garments of hair for wild men, and for clubs. Twenty-four falchions, twelve of which were supplied with gilded hilts and scabbards, were also used. The details do not permit a reconstruction of the masks, although apparently the subject of one of them was a tourney or barriers between wild men and knights, typical of the early reign.

No accounts survive for it, and given the fact that the king was seriously ill, it is unlikely that the Revels Office produced entertainments at Christmas 1546–7. Henry VIII died on 28 January 1547 after thirty-eight years on the throne. His last wars in France, and his last revels which again drew their inspiration from romance and developed the theme of princely magnificence, concluded his reign in much the way it had begun.[106] The story of the early Revels Office in the mid 1540s is one of an attempt to rebuild the organization along the lines of the Guildford-Gibson era. Cawarden actually bettered it for organization, and by 1546 the Revels was a major establishment, ordering material by the cart-load from the Great Wardrobe, hiring artists and artisans with international stature, and contracting for expensive materials, properties, and workmanship. For a brief period at the end of Henry VIII's reign Cawarden was producing spectacles in elaborate banqueting houses which were reminiscent of those of the 1520s.

8

The Revels - Tents - Toils Organization 1547–1553

The Revels Office cooperated with city authorities by supplying certain garments for Edward's coronation entry into London on 19 February 1547. The entry is based on Lydgate's poem describing the 1432 entry of Henry VI on his return from France. It has been suggested that city officials were pressed for time and so turned to Lydgate in desperation, but it is more likely that an entry for a child king was thought appropriate inspiration for another child king.[1] The interconnections among the entry pageants, coronation ceremony, and revels suggest that the collaboration between city and court extended beyond the loan of garments. Two themes which appear in all three events were the continuity of Henry VIII's reform policies and the projection of a suitable image for a boy-king. Cranmer's address in lieu of a sermon at the coronation ceremony on Shrove Sunday (20 February) focused on the Reformation by comparing Edward to 'Josias,' the biblical child-king of Judah famous for his reformation of religion according to ancient law.[2] Henry VIII had been compared to biblical figures, most notably to Ezechias, known for his destruction of idols and his attempt to reform religion. Now the analogy to biblical reformers was applied to Edward, and this time even more apt in the parallel, for Josiah and Edward were about the same age when they came to the throne.[3] The theme of religious reform had been introduced the previous day in one of the city's coronation entry pageants. As Edward passed before the great conduit in Fleet Street, a child attired as Truth, flanked by two others as Justice and Faith, informed him that

> auncynet trouth which longe tyme was Suppressed
> *with* hethen right*es* & detestable Idolatry ...
> by god*es* sarvant my defender kinge Henry ...
> hath made me free ...
> Wherefore yf ye wyll me lykewyse embrace

as did your father ...

then shall the god of Truth gyve you hys grace.[4]

   In addition to supplying garments for the entry, the Revels Office constructed
a visual centrepiece for the coronation, a mount which was used both in the ceremony and in the revels.[5] This mount was designed by Nicholas Bellin of Modena,
Italian artist in service to Henry VIII.[6] Bellin's bill for making the moulded work
for the mount with the assistance of twenty-two carvers shows that it consisted
of cast plaster-of-Paris figures and ornaments.[7] The figures probably included the
twenty-four antique heads which John Simpson painted along with the rest of the
mount. The timber work was completed at Blackfriars by twenty-seven joiners
and two sawyers as well as several other artisans. It was carried by water to 'tholde
palayce at westm*minster*' and installed there in the 'Seintory' for the coronation.[8]
The use of this mount in the coronation and in the revels suggests the extent to
which the planners had gone to provide an image for the new reign. The throne
of St Edward was installed atop the mount, echoing the coronation entry pageant
at the little conduit in Cheap representing the 'State of king Edward the con-
fessere.'[9] Bellin's mount recalls another pageant from the coronation entry. Near
Cheap was a mount with a 'Sumptuous throne' on which a child, representing
Edward, sat attired in cloth of gold and crimson satin.[10] The throne was supported
by four children representing Regality, Justice, Truth, and Mercy, and 'behynde
the throne the golden fleece was kept by two bulles and a serpent casting out of
their mouthes flaming fire, according to the story of Jason.' The devisers of the
pageant emphasized the story of Orpheus among the Argonauts.[11] When Jason
and his heroes tired, Orpheus used his musical skill to inspire them to row in uni-
son; when dissension threatened their unity, he used his lyre to bring peace and
harmony; and when the Sirens attempted to enchant the Argonauts with their
song, Orpheus played forcefully to drown out the temptation. The mount and the
coronation ceremony employed imagery which had been introduced in the royal
entry connecting Edward's Reformation to biblical history, to English history, and
to classical myth.
   The Revels and Tents accounts document some aspects of the coronation spectacles and revels at Shrovetide. The Tents delivered two long 'hales' from Blackfriars to the tilt-yard at Westminster for the coronation joust and tourney held on
Shrove Monday and Tuesday (21 and 22 February).[12] We have little other information about it. An undetermined number of masks were presented on Sunday,
Monday, and Tuesday nights, for the Revels charge for 'iij wheries' to be used 'in
Caring mask*es* to & from the Cow*rt*e.'[13] There was also a mask held after the joust
on the following Sunday, 27 February.[14] The descriptions of the properties for the
masks on Sunday and Monday are vague. Eight javelin staves, four pilgrims'

staves, and twenty 'ffachels' were painted and gilded by the Revels Office, suggesting that costumes were made for pilgrims and probably men-at-arms. The
Shrove Tuesday entertainment employed the mount which had been used at the
coronation. The Revels charge for dismantling the mount, carrying it to Whitehall, and installing it in the Hall.[15] It was designed to be moved about the Hall,
for a blacksmith was paid to install wheels at Blackfriars while it was under construction. John Simpson was also paid for gilding three ropes as part of his work
on the mount. It was obviously meant to be pulled by several costumed men
around the Hall, as so many of these pageants had been in the past. A mask was
shown in conjunction with the pageant, and according to an anonymous herald's
narrative, there was 'a goodly enterlude played in the said hall, where was also
made a mounte, with the story of Orpheus ryght conyngly composed/ At the
which play' the king was present.[16] The herald's description is ambiguous, and has
led to suggestions that the 'story of Orpheus' was a play produced on this evening.
Plays were performed that evening after the tourney. The French ambassador
mentions them, but he does not elaborate.[17] However, it is equally if not more
plausible to take the herald's description of 'the story of Orpheus ryght conyngly
composed' to refer to the mount, for such designs would have picked up on the
coronation entry pageant near Cheap.

It is difficult to say how many plays were shown for the coronation revels. John
Holt and forty-five other tailors were employed by the Revels to make costumes
for the masks and the plays.[18] Gray material was ordered to make friars' garments
'for a pley,' a doublet and hose was made for an Italian player, cardinals' hats were
made 'for players,' three caps of crimson and black satin were made 'for prestes
in pley,' 'crownes & Crosse for the poope in pleye' were supplied, as well as 'a lytle
hedpece for a pleyer of Syluer lawne.' Circumstantial evidence suggests that the
Gentlemen of the Chapel performed one of these plays. The Revels inventory of
1 April 1547 shows that some of the garments made for the coronation were in
the possession of Robert Stone, Gentleman of the Chapel.[19] Since costumes were
made for a Pope, cardinals, and priests, the subject of one or more of the plays was
anti-papal, which would have been consistent with a main theme of the coronation festivities.[20] Whether the Gentlemen themselves performed an anti-papal play
is not certain.[21]

The document used to argue that Edward performed in one or more of the
plays at his coronation along with the Gentlemen of the Chapel is included in
Feuillerat's edition of the Revels accounts under the inventories of 1547 and
1548.[22] The document may well have been used to produce the inventories of
April and May, but it is not itself an inventory. It is an 'imploy book,' like others of its kind in the Loseley collection, signed by Bridges, showing material delivered into the office and how it was employed. Cloth of gold, for example, was 'cut

for players for the king,' cloth of silver was 'Cutt for a long gowne for a prest for the Kinges grace to pley' along with a cap. It is possible that some of these garments were used at the coronation, but it appears clearly that some were used after 26 March. The document concludes with Bridges's receipt dated 26 March for deliveries of material by John Phylpot, Groom of the Privy Chamber, 'for the making of pleyers garmentes for the Kinges person the duke of Suffolke/ & my lorde straunge.' Clearly, the 'imploy book' lists material delivered into the office to be cut into garments, and the 26 March delivery by Phylpot was the material needed to finish some of the costumes. In all probability this last item in the document relates to a play on 11 April, the day after Easter, for another closely allied document shows garments delivered to court for it. In a list of remains of material stored at the Blackfriars in 1547, Thomas Blagrave notes deliveries 'to be brought vnto the covrte at grenewich the xjth daye of Apryll,' followed by a list of garments.[23] The evidence indicates that the king did perform in a play or a mask with several of his young friends and perhaps the King's Players on an anti-papal subject, probably on 11 April, the day after Easter.[24]

While it is not possible to specify the details of the masks and plays at the coronation, the interconnections of subjects and themes in the coronation entry and ceremony, the fact that the Revels Office was involved in all of the events, and the fact that religious costumes were prepared suggests that similar subjects and themes characterized the revels: masks and plays on the Orpheus myth, or on the story of Josiah, or on the evils of Popery. The coronation festivities reintroduced Reformation subjects, absent since the late 1530s, and such subjects continued to characterize the revels at court for the next two years. Clearly they were intended to express publicly the policies of the new government. Radical Protestants, exiles since the early part of the decade, responded by returning home. Reformation propaganda of the type Cromwell had sponsored appeared again in evangelical sermons, pamphlets, and plays.[25] Anti-Reformation propaganda was also being written, for on 6 August 1549 a proclamation forbidding performances until November was issued regarding some 'tendyng to sedicion,' and the Act of Uniformity passed in that year forbade 'depraving and despising' the *Book of Common Prayer.* By 1551, the same year in which the Venetian ambassador reported comedies 'in demonstration of contempt for the Pope,' a proclamation was issued requiring a license from the king or council for the printing or acting of plays.[26]

The accounts documenting Edward's first Christmas revels in 1547–8 are incomplete, but an abstract of the Revels accounts shows that the office produced masks and a pageant Tower of Babylon at Hampton Court.[27] One of the masks was on the subject of Prester John. Eight long cassocks were made for this 'maske of pretter iohns;' the upper garments were 'of Tynssyll beyng great mantells and the Reast to for viij capes for turckes.'²⁸ That friars as well as Turks were characters in this mask is suggested by a 3 January bill from Robert Fletcher for 'vj Turkyshe garmentes blewe Satten vj vpper shorter garmentes purple clothe Syluer vj hedpeces viz. ij grene satten ij yelowe Satten ij golde Sarcenit vj vezars iiijor ffryers with their huddes ij white ij Russat vellett' and other material 'lent' to Sir William Paget, Comptroller.²⁹ Prester John, remembered in legend as the priest-king who ruled in Ethiopia despite the fact that he was surrounded by pagans, was an apt analogy for England in Edward's reign and one which remained in the popular imagination throughout the century. Nash wrote in his *Lenten Stuff* that 'Not any where is the word seuerer practised, the preacher reuerentlier obserued and honoured, iustice sounder ministered, and a warlike people peaceablier demeanourd betwixt this and the Grand Cathay, and the strond of Prester Iohn.'³⁰ Other gowns were delivered to Somerset on the same day by R. Faylwaye, obviously for another of the masks, but it is impossible to guess the subject from the description of the garments. The bill included garments for 'vj Torcheberers blew Satten stripid with clothe Syluer & grene dornix. vj hedpeces to the same gre[ne] Satten trymyd with Antique heddes' and 'viij gownes clothe of golde gardyd with Antique garde Black vellett ... viij hedpeces' with other garments and properties.³¹ The pageant Tower of Babylon was made for a play, according to one of the summary accounts of the Revels, and the imagination does not have to stretch to guess the adaptability of this subject to the Reformation.³² It is possible that it was made for Edward's own lost comedy, *De Meretrice Babylonica*. Feuillerat conjectures that the date of the performance was Twelfth Night, but the Chamber account shows that the Children of the Chapel, under the direction of Richard Bower, and the King's Players performed on New Year's Day.³³ It is more likely, as in the past, that the Revels outfitted one or the other of these troupes for the performance, for they charge for making players' garments in one of their accounts.³⁴

The great spectacle of 1548 was a 'triumph,' held at Shrovetide (12, 13, 14 February) at Greenwich, which included an assault on a fortress, the first such recorded since the Castle of Loyalty in 1524–5. Six gentlemen challenged all comers at joust, tourney, barriers, and in defending a fort with thirty against one hundred or fewer men.³⁵ Construction was ordered by the council and completed by the Office of the Works.³⁶ Stow describes the structure as a 'Castle or fort' and notes that the spectacle was intended to 'shew the king the manner of warres.'³⁷ The accompanying Shrovetide revels were produced by Cawarden and his officers, but it is difficult to tell from the accounts whether they dealt with Reformation subjects. There were four masks held on Sunday, Monday, and Tuesday nights, for the Revels charges include 'Caring maskes of men & women' from Blackfriars to Greenwich, and for waiting there on those nights.³⁸ In addition, at least one play was produced. Thirty-one tailors headed by John Holt were employed to make the costumes. They altered a number of masking garments and made four new masks, one of men, two of women, and one of young Moors. Designs for the masks were made by Anthony Toto, the king's Sergeant Painter, and Nicholas Bellin designed and executed six of the headpieces for women, and lined and trimmed sixteen visors for the Moors. Mark Milliner made another six of the headpieces for women 'with here and fflax.' The mask of Moors was probably held on Shrove Sunday.[39] That the king participated in this mask is clear in a letter from Stanhope to Cawarden pointing out that the Lord Protector wanted six masking garments made 'whereof the kinges maiestie shalbe oon and the residue of his stature, and vi other garmentes of like bignes for torchebearers ... so as the same be in aredynes against sondaye next at the vttermost.'[40] Costumes for these Moors included black velvet gloves above the elbows, nether stocks of black leather, black goatskins for hose, caps made with 'Cowrse budge,' 'xij dossen belles to hange at the skyrtes of the mores garmentes,' darts, and swords. Like the theme of the masks at Shrovetide, that of the play produced by the Revels at Greenwich and performed by the King's Players is obscure. A property made by Robert Aras, joiner, for the production was a timber frame and canvas 'oven,' but there is no indication in the accounts of the subject.[41]

For Christmas 1548–9 Cawarden and his officers produced two masks. One employed 'Alamain' costumes, but there is not enough evidence from the accounts to specify the theme. Thirteen tailors, headed by Thomas Claterbouk and John Holt, were employed to alter torch bearers' costumes and to border 'one whole maske' with sarcenet. The eight torch bearers' costumes were of red satin and were tufted 'Rounde abowte with white, yellow, purple and red.' Eight long garments, probably for the 'Alamains,' were also tufted.[42] The King's Players and Richard Bower and the Children of the Chapel were rewarded on New Year's Day for performing before the king, but what support if any was provided by the Revels is not clear.[43]

For Shrovetide (3, 4, 5, March) 1549, Cawarden and his officers produced a play by the King's Players at Westminster. From the fact that only eight tailors were employed and that the officers attended for only four days, it appears that this was their only production. The garments made – 'Albes Surplyces and heade clothes,' six caps for priests 'with heare and Shave crownes of budge,' seven hermits' heads, and sheets of paper gilded silver, green, and red for a king's crown and a 'typped crowne' – and the major property, 'a dragon of vij heades,' leave little doubt as to the subject of the play.[44] Hangings were also transported from Blackfriars to the court and back again.

The masks and one or more plays produced by the Revels at Westminster for Christmas 1549–50 apparently were on Reformation subjects. Twenty-one tailors, headed by Thomas Claterbouk, and other contract artisans produced costumes and properties for 'Alamains,' who were probably the lance knights; for palmers, who are also called 'pylgryms;' and for friars and hermits. Eight feathers were bought for the lance knights who, no doubt, also used the 'gold skynes and gold and sylver paper ffor gyrdelles.' The hermits were equipped with lanterns, with bags stuffed with straw upon which was sewed canvas with painted inscriptions, and with ears made of 'whip Corde and paste.' The pilgrims, or palmers, were equipped with staves tipped with hilts, and the friars were supplied with painted girdles.[45] It appears that one mask was of lance knights and friars and another of hermits and pilgrims. How the nine painted globes, the gilt bowls, and the 180 'great beades stones coloread' were used is not certain.

Personal participation was the hallmark of Henry VIII's court spectacles and revels in which he developed the image of magnificence as the warrior prince. Now Edward expressed his own image as England's Josiah, child-leader of England in the struggle against Rome. There is every indication that Cawarden, reappointed as a Gentleman of the King's Privy Chamber, cooperated with Somerset and the council in an enterprise consistent with his own religious and political leanings.

i

The revels in Edward VI's reign were closely overseen by the leaders of the young king's government. From 1547 to 1549, when Somerset was Lord Protector, revels on Reformation subjects were produced. This focus began to change near the end of the war with France. Partial military successes by the French at Boulogne and Calais and the worsening political situation in England in late 1549 made a negotiated settlement attractive to both parties.[46] Somerset fell from power in October 1549, and peace was proclaimed on 25 March 1550. From 1550 to 1553 the council was dominated by Northumberland. Receptions, revels, spectacles, and entertainments reminiscent of the chivalric and romantic spectacles under Henry VIII were resurrected for the entertainment of the French hostages in England from April to June 1550 and of the French embassy in July 1551.

There were no entertainments at court for Shrovetide 1550, in anticipation of the acceptance of the peace treaty in March and of the reception of the French hostages in April and May.[47] The hostages were received at Blackheath on 27 April 1550 and were entertained at dinner on the 29th 'with much music.' This dinner initiated a two-month-long series of ceremonies, martial exhibitions, and entertainments which the king followed closely, for our main source of information about them is the entries in his journal. When the ambassadors arrived a month later, they were saluted with cannon at Woolwich, Deptford, and the Tower, and on 25 May they were received at court, where they witnessed the king's oath of acceptance of the treaty.[48] After dinner there was 'a pastime of ten against ten at the ring.' In keeping with the spirit of amity, the groups of ten were composed of both French hostages and English nobles. The Duke of Suffolk, the Vidame of Chartres, Lord Lisle, and seven others were on one side 'appareled in yellow,' and Lord Strange, Hunaudaye, and eight others were on the other in blue. The following five days before the departure of the ambassadors on the 30th were filled with entertainments. The ambassadors saw bear- and bull-baiting on the 26th, hunted and dined with the king on the 27th, visited Hampton Court and hunted on the 28th, and on the 29th they were given a banquet by Somerset and saw a bear 'hunted in the Thames,' 'wildfire cast out of boats,' and 'many pretty conceits.'

The revelry continued into June. The king was present at the marriage of John Dudley, Lord Lisle, on 3 June. After dinner and dancing 'the King and the ladies went into two chambers made of boughs' from which he watched a joust and tourney.[49] First, 'six gentlemen of one side and six of another' ran the course of the field twice over. 'Afterward came three masquers [disguised knights] of one side and two of another, which ran four courses apiece.' Lastly, 'The Count of Rangone' and three other Italians 'ran with all the gentlemen four courses and afterward fought a tourney.' The following day the king attended the wedding of Sir Robert Dudley, later Earl of Leicester, and, probably, the joust and tourney he attended on the 5th was part of these festivities. The tourney was on foot and the joust was with 'great staves as they [could] run withal on horseback.'[50] On the 8th, the Vidame of Chartres held a banquet for the Duke of Somerset and William Parr, 'with divers masques and other conceits.'[51] On the 16th, Northumberland held a banquet for the Vidame of Chartres, Hunaudaye, William Parr, and 'divers other gentlemen,' who on the following day ran at the ring.[52] On the 19th, the last recorded entertainment of this festive two-month period is recorded. The king and the hostages were invited to a banquet at Deptford by the Lord Admiral, Lord Clinton. Before supper the king 'saw certain [men] stand upon the end of a boat without hold of anything and ran one at another until one was cast into the water.'[53] The Vidame of Chartres and Hunaudaye dined with the king while Clinton was arranging the spectacular display afterwards, which consisted of a naval assault. Cawarden and his officers had no part in this production. Probably the support came from the Navy and, possibly, from the Works. This is one of only two sieges held during the reign, both of which, judging by the detailed descriptions he entered in his journal, impressed the king.

Plays and other entertainments, probably given in connection with the festivities in May 1550, are included in the king's Privy Purse account.[54] The rewards to the Vidame of Chartres's Master of the Horse and his 'antiques,' Chastillon's musicians, the French king's musicians, and the reward to the Sergeant of the

Bears – probably for the baiting of bulls and bears on 26 May before the ambassadors – all point to May 1550 as the date of the rewards for the first part of this itemized list of payments. Included there are payments of £12 13*s*. 4*d*. to the Children of Paul's, of £4 to the Duchess of Suffolk's players, of £4 to Somerset's players, and of £7 to the Marquis of Northampton's players.[55] Neither the number of plays nor their titles are recorded, but some of them were probably concentrated between 25 and 29 May 1550 during the formal reception and entertainments of the ambassadors, and others during the festivities in July 1551.

The Revels account for Christmas 1550–1 covers the period up to the end of July 1551, during which month entertainments were held for the French embassy, this time in England to install Edward into the Order of St Michael. The main Revels account records that 'The Maskes servinge at Christmas in Anno quarto and Shrovetide in Anno quinto of his Reigne/ and the plaies and other pastimes [were shown] aswell then as at diuers and sondry times with*in* those yeres.'[56] One of Cawarden's certificates makes it clear that there were 'v maskes made betwene the xxiiij*th* of December anno quarto and the laste of Iuly Anno quinto.'[57] The entertainments for Christmas were held at Greenwich, and for Shrovetide (8, 9, 10 February) at Westminster.[58] At least one of the masks shown on Twelfth Night was of Irishmen. John Holt charges for carriage on that day, and he hired an Irish bagpiper for the performance. Materials for this mask included 'ij womens heares,' 'vij heares for men made with horsehear,' and 'vij heares made with flaxe.' John Carrow made twenty-four Irish swords and targets, and painted lockram with flesh colour.[59] Headpieces and hose were made for the Irishmen from linen cloth. Costumes for Moors were also prepared, requiring twelve gloves 'longe & blak for mores,' and small lambskins. Will Somers, Henry VIII's fool, appears to have participated in some performance at Christmas, and the king performed as well, for the Revels Office made garments 'in his p*er*sone, as his yonge lordes and diuers plaiers and other p*er*sones for plaies and pastymes.'[60] More equipment for Irishmen was made for Shrovetide, and hose and gloves were made for Will Somers. Holt charged for carriage on four separate nights between Blackfriars and Westminster, suggesting four separate entertainments, but whether all of the material was used at Shrovetide or at other times is not certain, for many other entertainments were presented before the ambassadors in July.

It was no doubt in connection with this reciprocal installation of Henri II into the Order of the Garter and of Edward VI into the Order of St Michael that the king issued a challenge on 31 March 1551. Edward, with sixteen members of his Chamber would run at base, shoot, and run at the ring against any seventeen gentlemen of the court.[61] The challenge was answered on 1 and 6 April and on 3 May. The court was made ready in May for the reception of the French ambassadors, who were to conduct the investiture. Edward was informed of his election on 3

June, and on 11 July Jacques d'Albon, Seigneur de St Andre, Marshall of France, with his entourage of four hundred, was received in London with a salute from about fifty of the king's ships furnished with ordnance from the Tower.[62] He was met by the Lord Admiral with forty gentlemen at Gravesend and brought to Durham Place. Because of plague the king removed from Greenwich to Hampton Court and St Andre was lodged at Richmond, where on the 13th he hunted at night with over four hundred gentlemen.[63] On the 14th, St Andre was received at Hampton Court, where he dined with the king. The investiture ceremony was conducted on the 16th by St Andre and Francois de Rohan, Seigneur de Gye, and after a banquet they 'saw some pastime.'[64] St Andre dined with the king and 'saw a dozen courses' on 19 July, then toured the king's Chamber. He saw an archery exhibition on the 20th and hunted on the 26th.

The main celebration was held on 28 July in the banqueting facilities at Hyde and Marylebone parks. The council issued an imprest of £300 to Cawarden on 8 December 1550 and £133 6s. 8d. to Lawrence Bradshaw, Surveyor of the Works, on the same date. Cawarden was charged with overseeing the entire project, and complains in one of the documents that Bradshaw was usually absent. The surviving accounts show that Bradshaw's and Cawarden's work was divided along the lines of their offices. Bradshaw's crews worked from 28 June to 29 July and Cawarden's from 6 July to 2 August on the project. Bradshaw's crews undertook basic construction of the buildings. A standing (covered pavilion, 40' x 18') was constructed in Marylebone Park. Its floor was joisted and boarded, but the rest was made of scaffold poles. Six smaller standings (10' x 8') were constructed, three in Marylebone Park and three in Hyde Park. They constructed the banqueting house in Hyde Park, the pale around it, along with three ranges of brick for roasting and furnaces for boiling as well as tables, forms, trestles, and dressers. Cawarden's crews worked on the gatehouse, the tower, and in the carving, painting, gilding, garnishing, and decorating with flowers in the banqueting house. Robert Trunckwell and James Marcady headed the crew of joiners; Anthony Toto and John Leeds headed the crews of painters; Jasper Arnold the basket makers; and John Holt the tailors.

While the standings were perfunctory structures, the banqueting house had some architectural pretensions. Robert Trunckwell claimed to have designed it, and he was certainly employed as chief joiner on the gatehouse. Unfortunately there are no narrative descriptions, but the documents show that the building was 62' long and 28' wide. It had an 'halpace' and stairs which are described on one document as having a turret over them. It had pillars on the inside. Given the material ordered and the decorations provided, roof construction was probably of the open hammer-beam type, and given the 225 ells of canvas ordered it appears that the roof covering was of canvas. Peter Nicholson, Master Glaiser of the Works, installed the windows. Plasterwork was under the direction of Patrick Kellie, later Master Plasterer of the Works. The walls or some part of them were of lath and plaster, but other parts may simply have been covered with tapestries judging from the 2000 lbs. of great tenterhooks and 1000 lbs. of smaller ones ordered. Flowers supplied by James Harness the King's Gardner at Westminster were transported by barge from London. Those which could not be used in Hyde Park were sent to Hampton Court to decorate the banqueting house there.[65]

St Andre 'saw the coursing' in Hyde Park, probably from the various standings constructed for the purpose.[66] What other entertainments were offered is not certain. Some of the five masks made between Christmas and July were probably produced for the occasion. Payments from the king's Privy Purse were also made for entertainments in connection with these festivities. The French trumpeters who brought the Order of St Michael, St Andre's jester, the French ambassadors' musicians, and one that played a coronet were rewarded along with others of the ambassadors' men who played on 'flutes, Shawmes, Sackbuttes' and also one who 'Dawnsed on the Rope and vaulted' and a boy that 'tombled' before the king.[67] It is also probable that some of the plays mentioned in connection with the May 1550 reception were performed at this time.[68]

ii

The accounting cycle in the Revels Office was altered during Northumberland's administration as part of the financial rearrangements which were being made at all levels of government. The Revels bills were three years in arrears on 7 January 1550 when the council issued a warrant to pay them.[69] Then, beginning on 6 June 1550, the office was put on a five-year accounting cycle. Cawarden oriented this new method of accounting to the rhythm of the work year in his office. Each yearly account began with preparations for Christmas productions and ended with the June airing – the cleaning, refurbishing, and storing of the costumes and properties. The documents prepared by the office now consisted of bills, receipt books, 'imploy' books, day books, journals, and other records which were used to make up the office ledgers. These, in turn, were used to make up the five-year comprehensive accounts. The province of Cawarden's responsibilities was also expanded to include the Toils, the banqueting houses, and the production of the Lord of Misrule's entertainments, the last of which was certainly inspired by political motives.[70]

The Toils, an office concerned with making and maintaining the toils for hunting, was absorbed on 2 June 1552.[71] The decision to combine the Toils with the Revels and Tents was probably suggested by the hunting excursions for the French hostages in May and June 1550. Cawarden not only understood how to entertain dignitaries, but he also controlled the Tents, from which the Toils was supplied

with much of its canvas and equipment. The responsibility for banqueting houses came about in a similar way. The Revels had been employed in the decoration
of banqueting houses and temporary buildings from at least as early as 1520, and
the Tents supplied the tents for the workmen and material and the canvas for
roofs and sometimes walls.[72] Two of these offices were already under Cawarden's
control, and one of the many offices he held was as Keeper of the Wardrobe of
Nonsuch, and on 12 March 1551 he was granted the office of Keeper of the Banqueting House at Nonsuch.[73] This grant came at virtually the same time that
Cawarden was supervising the construction of the banqueting facilities at Hyde
and Marylebone Parks, and it seems clearly to have been another of the reorganizations of Northumberland's administration to centralize compatible duties.

Other changes in the method of financing court entertainments were made in
Northumberland's administration. The Chamber accounts do not survive after
1549, and it is probable that none were prepared after that year. The 1552 commission to inquire into the state of finances in the realm found that the Chamber had declined to such an extent that its treasury was bankrupt and that most
of its traditional payments had been reassigned.[74] The ordinary payments of the
Chamber had included rewards to the Gentlemen and Children of the Chapel and
to the king's and other playing companies for performances. The question of how
these entertainments were now funded cannot be answered satisfactorily. Like the
rest of the Chamber's traditional payments they were probably transferred to other
treasuries, but the chaotic state of the records makes it difficult to trace them. On
some occasions plays were funded by the Groom of the Stool who had charge of
the Privy Purse, but whether these payments covered all of the previous ones paid
by the Chamber cannot be determined.

Several accounts of the Groom of the Stool survive from 1541 to 1552.[75] Before
1541, Sir Thomas Henage, and from 1541 to 1548, Sir Anthony Denny, made
the kind of payments one would expect from the Privy Purse: the wages of scholars, gardeners, gentlemen-at-arms, keepers of bears and dogs, annuities due to
Princess Mary, alms, debts, riding charges, hire of horses, purchase of apparel for
Will Somers, the king's fool, New Year's gifts and rewards.[76] Payments for plays
were normally included in the category of rewards, but unfortunately Denny's
payments are neither itemized nor dated. The account filed by Sir Michael Stanhope from 1547 to 1549 also lumps payments together, but he does note that he
paid rewards to minstrels and to players.[77] The account is important because it
encompasses a period also covered by an extant Chamber account, and shows that
payments for dramatic and musical performances were paid from at least two
sources: the ordinarily scheduled performances by the Chamber, and the extraordinary ones as well as supplementary rewards from the Privy Purse. The most
detailed of these accounts, filed by Sir Thomas Darcy, Lord Chamberlain, which

includes the accounts of the Groom of the Stool, dates from 1550 to 1552, and includes all payments 'as have been vsuallye paide by Sir Anthony Denny knight Deceased and other late occupying the Rome or office of the gromeship of the Stoole.'⁷⁸ Traditional privy payments are made, in addition to payments to indi-. viduals and companies of musicians, players, and acrobats. The account not only itemizes payments but clearly indicates that these were usual from the time of Denny in 1541, and probably from much earlier.

The demise of the Chamber accounts makes it impossible to fully document appearances by the royal and other invited playing companies at court after 1549. During William Crane's tenure as Master of the Children of the Chapel from 1523 to 1545, we have the testimony of seven Chamber accounts and one Revels account to show that the Children continued to perform their customary plays before the king on or around New Year's Day. We know less about Crane's successor, Richard Bower, than about any other of the early Tudor Masters of the Children. Bower served from 30 June 1545 until his death in 1561, under three monarchs during some of the most turbulent years of the century.⁷⁹ Only two Chamber accounts survive from his Mastership, those for 1547–8 and 1548–9. In both of these years Bower was paid for performing a play with the Children before the king. This is a small amount of evidence to stretch over a sixteen-year period, but Wallace and Hillebrand both thought that the Children continued their customary performances around New Year's.

As weak and inconclusive as it is, the evidence for performances by the Children at court from 1550 to 1553 is better than that for other playing companies. The Revels accounts specify the preparation of plays in every season from 1550–1 to 1552–3, but we can assign titles, companies, and dates to only a few of them. The King's Players performed unnamed plays on Christmas Day and on Twelfth Night in 1551–2. They performed *Self Love* on 29 February 1552, and they probably performed *Aesop's Crow* at Christmas 1552–3, the same season in which Baldwin and Ferrers presented several unnamed interludes by unnamed companies.⁸⁰ In the spring of 1553, Baldwin's play of *The State of Ireland* by an unnamed company and Heywood's unnamed play acted by twelve unidentified children were performed. Other than this, there were performances of unnamed plays by the Children of Paul's, the Duchess of Suffolk's Players, Somerset's Players, and Northampton's Players in connection with the reception of the French hostages in May 1550 and with the reception of the French embassy in July 1551. Fortunately, the revels are better documented.

iii

The revels for Christmas 1551–2 and 1552–3 were under the direct control of

Northumberland and the council. Cawarden and his officers furnished masks, plays, triumphs, and pastimes as usual and, in addition, supported the production of an elaborate series of entertainments ordered by the council and devised by George Ferrers and his associates. Preparations for the revels in both of these Christmas seasons were the most elaborate of the entire reign. The Revels accounts in earlier years ran as high as £150 for Christmas 1547–8 and as low as £11 for Christmas of the following year, but the bills associated with Christmas 1551–2 were over £500, in the following year over £400, and those scheduled for Shrovetide and postponed to Easter and May Day 1553 another £165.[81] Richard Grafton thought that the Christmas revels of 1551–2 were designed to distract the king's and the court's attention from the fate of Somerset, who had been arrested in October 1551, tried for treason and felony in December, and was now scheduled to be executed:

The Duke beyng condempned as is aforesayd, the people spake diuersly and murmored against the Duke of Northumberlande, and against some other of the Lordes for the condempnation of the sayd Duke, and also as the common fame went, the kinges maiestie tooke it not in good part: wherfore aswell to remooue fond talke out of mennes mouthes, as also to recreate and refreshe the troubled spirites of the yong king, it was deuised that the feast of Christes Natiuitie, commonly called Christmas then at hand, should be solemply kept at Greenewiche with open houshold, and franke resorte to the Court, (which is called keping of the Hall)[82]

The council's main device to distract attention was to appoint a Lord of Misrule. Grafton points out that when the hall is kept

what time of olde ordinarye course, there is always one appoynted to make sporte in the Courte, called commonly Lorde of Misrule, whose office is not vnknowne to such as haue bene brought vp in Noblemens houses, and among great house keepers, which vse liberall feasting in that season.[83]

Because so few records and narratives survive, it is difficult to say what the Lord of Misrule's entertainments were ordinarily like. The mock hunt conducted in the Privy Garden at Greenwich in 1534 and the antics of Ferrers and his company in 1551–2 and 1552–3 suggest that his entertainments were parodies and burlesques of the pastimes, privileges, and power of the court and nobility. Such a burlesque was intended to have the effect of rendering the real struggles at court seemingly harmless.

George Ferrers, 'both wise and learned' according to Grafton, was appointed Lord of Misrule 'by order of the counsaile,' and because he was 'of better calling then commonly his predecessors had bene before, [he] receyued all his commissions and warrauntes by the name of the Maister of the kinges pastimes.' Ferrers 'so well supplyed his office, both in shew of sundry sightes and deuises of rare inuention, and in acts of diuers enterludes and matters of pastime' that he not only satisfied the 'common sorte' but also the 'counsayle and other of skill in the like pastimes.' Best of all he satisfied 'the yong king himselfe.' The success of the Christmas diversions, particularly those by the Lord of Misrule, are taken by Grafton to be the reason that the 'mindes and eares of murmorers were meetely well appeased,' and that it was 'now good to proceede to the execution of the iudgement geuen against the Duke of Somerset.' The execution was carried out on 22 January 1552.[84]

George Ferrers had a well-established reputation as a writer and courtier when Northumberland recruited him for the Christmas entertainments in 1551. Ferrers was a Cambridge graduate who entered Lincoln's Inn in 1531 and who published an English translation of *Magna Carta* and other statutes in 1534. Like Cawarden, Ferrers was promoted to the royal household by Cromwell in 1539. He had a knack for allying himself with the winning sides in the tumultuous upheavals of mid-century politics. He became one of Somerset's gentlemen, whom he accompanied in 1547 in the Scottish campaign, and he later served for a time in Ireland. Despite his sympathy for Somerset, Ferrers accepted Northumberland's invitation to devise revels for the Christmas seasons of 1551–2 and 1552–3, the former of which were instrumental in the council's plans for the Lord Protector's execution.[85] After Northumberland's fall, Ferrers helped Mary's government put down Wyatt's rebellion in 1554.[86] He supplied information in the council's investigation of the use of divination by Dr John Dee and Princess Elizabeth in 1556, and then, in 1575, he supplied verses for Queen Elizabeth's entertainment at Kenilworth. William Baldwin records that Ferrers admired Lydgate's *Fall of Princes*, and it was no doubt due to this work and to his checkered career that Ferrers owed the inspiration for *A Mirror for Magistrates*, one of the best-known and most influential works of the century.[87] The collaborative nature of that work, like the Christmas revels he devised at court, derived from Ferrers's belief that 'moe wits are better than one, & diversity of devise is always most pleasante.'[88]

To help devise these entertainments, Ferrers recruited other literary talents, among them Sir Thomas Chaloner and William Baldwin, both of whom were later associated with Ferrers in the *Mirror* project. Chaloner, also a graduate of Cambridge, was a diplomat who had established a reputation by the early 1550s as a translator and poet. His most important works up to this time included translations of *A Book of the Office of Servants* (1543), of Cheke's translation from Greek into Latin of *An Homilie of Saint John* (1544), and of Erasmus's *Praise of Folly* (1549). Chaloner also accompanied Somerset to Scotland in 1547, where he was knighted. How William Baldwin came to be associated with Ferrers and Chaloner is not known. Baldwin had acquired a reputation as a poet even before his graduation from Oxford in January 1533. By 1547 he had published the first sonnet in England in an edition of Christopher Langton's *A Very Brief Treatise*, and early in the following year Baldwin's *Treatise on Moral Philosophy*, one of the genuinely popular works of the late century, was published by Whitchurch, a noted Protestant printer and associate of Grafton. This, and his *The Canticles or Balades of Salomon*, dedicated to Edward VI in 1549 at a time when Baldwin was working as a servant to Whitchurch, may explain his recruitment by Ferrers.[89] His most well-known works, *A Mirror for Magistrates*, *Funerals of King Edward VI*, and *Beware the Cat* grew out of his association with Ferrers and Chaloner at court in 1552–3.[90]

Northumberland sent a letter to Cawarden ordering him to support Ferrers's entertainments as well as to produce the entertainments the Revels Office had already planned. This order was followed by warrants from the council authorizing the work.[91] Ferrers's appointment was a direct affront to Cawarden who had collaborated in devising and producing propaganda under Somerset between 1547 and 1549. Cawarden's displacement by Ferrers in 1551–2 and 1552–3 suggests that he was not one of Northumberland's supporters in the factional struggles over the removal of Somerset. While the additional duties and offices which the Revels and Tents acquired beginning in 1550 were part of a widespread reorganization of the government, they may also have been tactics used by Northumberland and the council to keep Cawarden overburdened with work.

There is no indication of open hostility between Ferrers and Cawarden, but plenty of evidence of frustration.[92] Cawarden was unprepared to meet the demands placed on the office. The letter he received from Northumberland, 'scriblide in haste this monday [21 December] at *vth* in thevening,' was delivered by Ferrers himself, in which Northumberland acknowledges that time was short and that Ferrers did not have the opportunity to prepare for his productions as well as he might have if he had been informed earlier.[93] The problems were laid at Cawarden's doorstep: 'I haue thought good to require *you* to Confer *with* him in the bett*er* setting fourthe of the matt*er*.' The letter was followed by a warrant from the council, dated Christmas Day, to furnish Ferrers with Revels properties and costumes 'as *yourself* shall thyncke convenient to serue the turne accordingly.'[94] Cawarden also received a warrant from the council to supply the King's Players with 'soche apparell and other fornyture as theye shall have nede of, for their playeng before the kinge*s* mai*e*stie this Christmas.'[95] Another warrant was issued by the Lord Chamberlain on 5 January – delivered by John Birch and John Browne, two of the King's Players – to supply garments for the company to perform an interlude on Twelfth Night.[96] The office had already been ordered by the king on 24 November to supply garments and properties for the tournament which was scheduled for 3 and 6 January, and the officers were at work producing four masks for the season.[97]

The council sent a warrant to Cawarden on 30 December 1551 to order a second livery for Ferrers and his entourage which required fourteen more tailors to accomplish.[98] After he received the garments, Ferrers wrote to Cawarden on 2 January complaining that those for his councillors were insufficient: 'you have mistaken the persons that sholde were them as Sir Robert Stafforde & Thomas wyndeham with other gentlemen that stande also apon their reputacion and wolde not be seen in london so torchebererlyke disguysed.' Ferrers reminded Cawarden that this livery was for use in the 4 January entry into London, and excuses himself by making it clear that he too was under pressure: the London entry 'was not of our device but of the Counseills appoyntement.'[99] The flurry of warrants and letters associated with these productions is accounted for by the unusual demand that the office support Ferrers's entertainments, by the shortness of time available to prepare them, and by the enormous expense. Cawarden was careful to copy all of the warrants into the heading of his account for the season to justify his expenditures. The warrants and letters surviving for Christmas 1552–3 indicate that arrangements went more smoothly. The council appointed Ferrers in time to make proper arrangements for his entertainments.

While complete documentation is lacking, there is a marked structural similarity in the arrangement and scheduling of Ferrers's entertainments and of the revels in the Christmas seasons of 1551–2 and 1552–3. Examining the evidence day by day for both Christmas seasons in concert provides a clearer conception of events. While Ferrers did not have the time to confer with Cawarden in advance about his entertainments for 1551–2, he wrote a letter outlining his plans for 1552–3:

this yeare I Imagin to cum oute of a place caulled *vastuum vacuum*. I. the great waste/ asmoche to saie as a place voyde or emptie withoute the worlde where is neither fier ayre water nor earth/ and that I haue bene remayning there sins the Last yeare And bicause of Certaine devisis which I haue towching this matter/ I wolde yf it were possyble haue all myne apparell blewe the first daie that I present my self to the kinges Maiestie.[100]

On Christmas Day in 1552, the Lord of Misrule's 'solempe ambassade,' including a herald, a trumpeter, 'an orator speaking in a straunge language,' and an interpreter, all of whom were to be costumed as Cawarden saw fit, were to appear at court to ask for an audience. On the 26th the Lord of Misrule himself was to be received at court. His journey was to be by water to Greenwich, for which purpose the king's brigantine, the 'poope ... covered with white and blewe,' and other

vessels were prepared. Ferrers was to be accompanied by 'one to plaie vppon a ket-
tle drom with his boye and a nother drome with a fyffe whiche must be apparelled
like turkes garmentes according to the patrons I send you herwith.' Sir George
Howard, the Lord of Misrule's Master of the Horse, was to meet him at Greenwich with a spare horse and 'iiij pages of honour one carieng my hedpece a nother
my Shelde/ the thirde my sword and the fourth my axe.' Ferrers was not sure how
he would enter the court, 'whether vnder a Canepie as the last yeare, or in a chare
trivmphall, or vppon some straunge beast that I reserve to you/ But the serpente
with sevin heddes cauled hidra is the chief beast of myne armes./ and wholie
bushe is the device of my Crest/ my worde is *Semper ferians.* I. alwaies feasting or
keping holie daie.'

Ferrers's 'device' for Christmas 1551–2 was to come from 'oute of the mone,'
and for 1552–3 from *'vastuum vacuum,'* where he had been dwelling since the last
season.[101] Since he sent an embassy together with an interpreter to announce his
presence on Christmas Day in 1552 and was received at court on the 26th, it is
likely that he kept the same schedule in the previous year. He entered court under
a canopy in 1551. In 1552, he travelled to court by boat. The fact that the King's
Players performed at court on Christmas Day in 1551 under the authority of the
council's warrant and the fact that Cawarden had a blanket warrant for the ordinary entertainments in 1552–3 suggest that the company may well have performed again.

Ferrers was not certain of all his entertainments or his schedule when he wrote
to Cawarden in December 1552. He mentions feats of arms, for which a challenge
was to be proclaimed for a joust of hobby-horses, another entertainment of hunting and hawking, and the rest were to be announced. He did require five suits of
apparel, one for his entry into court which was to double for his entry into London, 'two other sutes for the two halowed daies folowing,' and one for New Year's
and one for Twelfth Night.[102] By 27 December 1552, Ferrers had settled on more
of his entertainments. On that day Cawarden received a warrant from the council
for a fool's coat with a hood for John Smith – one of the King's Players who was
to act the part of the Lord of Misrule's heir apparent – because the costume Smith
had been issued was 'nott fytt' for the purpose. Ferrers also ordered hobby horses,
hunting apparel, a costume for his juggler, 'Clarinse,' for three other councillors,
for two disards, as well as maces for his Sergeants-at-Arms and Irish apparel for
a man and a woman.[103]

Ferrers gave an unnamed entertainment on New Year's Day 1552 which
involved his entourage, for Cawarden received a warrant from the council on
30 December to supply a livery for this day.[104] In 1553, the joust of hobby-
horses was held at Greenwich on New Year's Day at night. John Carrow made
these hobbies, one of which had three heads for the Lord of Misrule, and the

Office of the Tents supplied a toil to be used as the list.[105] On 2 January 1552 Ferrers performed a 'drunken' mask at court for which he required eight swords, eight vizards, two clubs full of spikes, and headpieces with serpents for eight men and one woman.[106] We do not know the schedule of shows in 1553 between 1 and 5 January, but at some point the Lord of Misrule conducted a mock hunt. The Revels Office furnished a coat of cloth of gold figured with red and green checkerwork and a hat of cloth of gold garnished with green leaves for the Lord of Misrule, and six sets of garments and horns for his attendants.[107]

One of the major spectacles at Christmas 1551–2 was the joust – called the 'Tryumphe of horsemen' in the Revels account – the challenge for which had been issued on 17 November, and the king's warrant to the Revels Office to furnish it had been issued on 24 November. Warwick, Henry Sidney, Sir Harry Gates, and Sir Henry Neville were the challengers, outfitted by the Revels with twelve bards for great horses and caparisons for eight light horses, with other furniture and equipment from the store. The Revels cannibalized some of the 'Riche hang*inges* that longyde to the kinges Tymber howses,' which were cut up for the coverings of bards.[108] Eighteen answerers ran six courses apiece against the four challengers. Ferrers's entertainment on this occasion was a mock Midsummer Night festival which may have included the combat devised by the king for Will Somers.[109] The properties prepared by the Revels Office included 'Counterfett harnesses & weapons ... and hoby horses.' Whether the show included a burlesque of the jousts held on that day is not certain. Kempe thought that the show was an imitation of 'the great procession of the Civic Guard, customarily held in London on the eve of St John the Baptist, attended by maskers as giants, morris-dancers, and pageants.'[110] A similar entertainment was given in 1553, possibly also on 3 January, called a Midsummer Sight. A combat appears also to have been included in this show as well, for which six great wooden 'squertes ... lyke vnto dragons' were made for Ferrers.[111]

A mock midsummer watch on the eve before the Lord of Misrule's entry into London, which occurred in both years on 4 January, is perhaps appropriate, for both parody the traditions of city in its relation to the court. The parody of the traditional royal entry into London is made clearer by Machyn's description of the event:

The iiij day of Januarii was mad a grett skaffold [in Ch]epe hard by the crosse, agaynst the kynges lord of myss[rule] cumyng from Grenwyche; and landyd at Towre warff [and with] hym yonge kynghts and gentyllmen a gret nombur on [horseb]ake sum in gownes and cotes and chynes abowt ther nekes, every man havyng a balderyke of yelow and grene abowt ther neckes, and on the Towre hyll ther they [went in] order, furst a standard of yelow and grene sylke with Sant Gorge, and then gonnes and skuybes, and trompets and bagespypes, and drousselars and flutes, and then a gret compeny all in yelow and gren, and doctures declaryng my lord grett, and then the mores danse dansyng with a tabret, and afor xx of ys consell on horsbake in gownes of chanabulle, lynyd with blue taffata and capes of the sam, lyke sage (men); then cam my lord with a gowne of gold furyd with fur of the goodlyest collers ... and after cam alff a hundred in red and whyt, tallmen [of] the gard, with hods of the sam coler, and cam in to the cete; and after cam a carte, the whyche cared the pelere ... [the] jubett, the stokes, and at the crose in Chepe a gret brod s[kaffold] for to go up; then cam up the trumpeter, the harold, and the doctur of the law, and ther was a proclamasyon mad of my lord('s) progeny, and of ys gret howshold that he [kept,] and of ys dyngnyte; and there was a hoghed of wyne [at] the skaffold, and ther my lord dranke and ys consell, and [had] the hed smyttyn owt that every body mytht drynke, and [money?] cast abowt them, and after my lord('s) grase rod unto my lorde mer and alle ys men to dener, for ther was dener as youe have sene; and after he toke his hers, and rod to my lord Tresorer at Frer Austens, and so to Bysshopgate, and so to Towre warff, and toke barge to Grenwyche.[112]

The Revels Office prepared seventy canvas jerkins 'paynted lyke mayll' for the Lord of Misrule's 'hakbuters,' and properties including rounded clubs hollowed out for 'squibbs'; joints, locks, hasps, and staples for the stocks; a pillory, prisons, manacles, keys for jailors; and a block and beheading axe. Similar costumes and equipment were prepared for the entry in 1553. In this year, the Lord of Misrule's entourage was dressed in his livery of white and blue, Ferrers himself 'gorgyusly a[rrayed in] purprelle welvet furyd with armyn, and ys robe braded with spangulls of selver full.'[113] In addition to the sumptuous costumes for his massive number of attendants, he had 'ys trympeters, taburs, drumes, and flutes and fulles and ys mores dansse, gunes, mores-pykes, bagpypes; and ... ys gayllers with pelere, stokes, and ys axe, gyffes, and boltes, sum fast by the leges and sum by the nekes.' The Lord of Misrule met with the Sheriff of London's Lord of Misrule, to whom he gave gifts and knighted in a mock ceremony, 'and after thay dran[k one to t]hodur a-pon the sakffold, and ys cofferer castyng gold and sylver in every plase as they rod, and [after his co]fferer ... hys gayllers and ys presonars.' The two lords went to the Mayor's for dinner. There was a pause at the Sheriff's house, a banquet at the Lord Treasurer's house, and a final send-off at Tower wharf.

The Lord of Misrule's entry is partly a parody of the entries the city of London had accorded to royalty for centuries and partly a burlesque of the power vested in royalty to dispense justice. Tower Hill is not mentioned in Machyn's description of the 1553 itinerary, even though the Lord of Misrule had prisoners, bound in chains and other restraining devices, hauled in carts behind the procession. In 1552, however, Tower Hill was the first place which the Lord of Misrule visited, along with his prisoners and engines of execution. Machyn does not record a mock execution there, but on the scaffold at the cross in Cheapside, where, after the proclamation of his style and progeny, the Lord had the head cut from a cask of wine for all to drink, and then cast money about in the crowd.[114] Machyn records the execution of Somerset on Tower Hill, immediately after his description of the entry, making Ferrers's entry into London one of the most cynical uses of the revels from the entire period.

The king himself recorded the schedule of entertainments on Twelfth Night 1552 in his journal. The second part of the challenge of 17 November, a tourney, was held during the day. That evening there was first an unnamed play by the King's Players furnished on the previous day with apparel and properties by the Revels Office. After that was 'a talk between one that was called Riches, and the other Youth, whether [one] of them was better. After some pretty reasoning there came in six champions of either side.' On Youth's side came 'Sir Anthony Browne, Lord Fitzwalter, Ambrose Dudley, Sir William Cobham' and two others, and on Riches's side, 'Lord FitzWarren, Sir Robert Stafford,' and four others.

All these fought two to two at barriers in the hall. Then came in two apparelled like Almains. The Earl of Ormonde and Jacques Granado, and two came in like friars, but the Almains would not suffer them to pass till they had fought. The friars were Mr. Drury and Thomas Cobham. After this followed two masques: one of men, another of women. Then a banket of 120 dishes. This was the end of Christmas.[115]

The entertainments are reminiscent of earlier revels. *Youth and Riches,* clearly a variant of *Love and Riches* in 1527, although the combat between 'Alamains' and Friars gives a Protestant overtone to the barriers. The entertainment is attributed to Sir Thomas Chaloner, who is named in a council warrant to Cawarden of 5 January 1552 informing him that '[Chaloner] shall declare vnto yow the rest of the matter how they ar to be trymmed whome we pray yow credite.' Chaloner, one of the clerks of the council, is connected with other dramatic activities during this period. He rewarded the King's Players for their performance of *Self Love* on Shrove Monday (29 February 1552) and others for playing 'amonges the maskers at dynner' on the same occasion.[116] According to the king, the two masks devised and produced by the Revels for Twelfth Night to accompany Chaloner's *Youth and Riches* were of men and women. The former was probably the mask of Argus and the latter either Moors or Amazon women of war.[117]

The list of entertainments provided in the king's journal entry for 1552 suggests that the revels may have been arranged similarly for Twelfth Night 1553. Circumstantial evidence indicates that the King's Players performed *Aesop's Crow,* possibly as the first of the series of entertainments. In an undated anecdote, William Baldwin mentions that he was rooming at court with George Ferrers, M.

Willet and M. Streamer – 'the one his [the Lord of Misrule's] astronomer, the other his devine' – which date the event in the Christmas season of 1552–3.[118] Baldwin, who is the best candidate for the Lord of Misrule's 'poet' in this season, mentions that he was also working with Ferrers 'about setting foorth of sertain Interludes, which for the Kings recreation we had devised & were in learning.' On the night of 28 December, Baldwin and Streamer had a discussion 'whether Birds and beasts had reason,' the occasion of which was prompted by the play of 'Esops Crow' which the King's Players were then learning, 'wherin the moste part of the actors were birds.' Baldwin thought that 'it was not Comicall to make either speechlesse things to speeke: or bruttish things to common resonably' in a play, although he did allow that it was acceptable in a fable. Several unnamed interludes were being readied by Baldwin for presentation by unnamed players this season, as well as *Aesop's Crow* by the King's Players.[119]

The main entertainment for Twelfth Night 1553 was a 'triumph' of Venus, Cupid, and Mars. Cawarden had received a council warrant on 31 December, ordering him to produce the revel and informing him that Sir George Howard would write to him with further details. In his undated letter, Howard requests that Cawarden 'furneshe venus in a chaire trivmfall,' which was to be carried on the backs of four male torch bearers, accompanied by three ladies.[120] Mars, who was to be costumed either in armour or in canvas painted like armour, was to have a naked sword in one hand and a shield painted with his arms in the other. He was to enter in 'a chaire ffurneshed *with* torche and men ffor the carrien of hime ffurneshed acordenge as yow shall thinke gode.' Mars was to be accompanied by three gentlemen having swords and shields painted with his arms. Cupid was to be 'a letell boy,' blindfolded and carrying a bow and arrows. Howard was diffident about his abilities to devise the revel and writes apologetically that he 'beenge not experte' in the matter will leave 'the hole Device of the thinge to your Desskression/ whow his better abull to Dow hit then I cane thinke hit or wryt hit.' Ferrers had to write to outline the revel, and to request that Cawarden furnish it accordingly. The letter is endorsed 'the lorde Myserabell,' indicating that despite the stresses of his duties, Ferrers had not lost his sense of humour. The revel was to include the Lord of Misrule, his Chancellor, Treasurer, Comptroller, and Vice-Chamberlain: Idleness and Dalliance as 'two Ladies straungely attyred'; Cupid as 'a small boye/ to be cladd in a canvas hose and doblett sylverd over/ *with* a payre of wing*es* of gold/ *with* bow and arowes/ his eyes bended'; Venus 'to come in *with* a Maske of ladies and to reskue Cupide from the Marshall'; Mars 'to come in very triumphantly/ Brett shalbe mars they must haue three fayre targettes/ the rest shalbe their owne armure'; and a herald, 'cuoeur ardant To haue a fayre short garment and a cote armour painted with burning hartes persed with dart*es*.'[121]

The Revels Office constructed two pageants for this triumph, one for Mars and

another for Venus.[122] John Carrow did the moulded work, including the dragon
for the seat of the pageant of Mars. A dragon's head and a mouth of 'plate with
stoppes to burne like fier' were also constructed. He fashioned an image of Cupid
to stand over the pageant of Venus, and made leaves for the headpieces of her
torch bearers. Enid Welsford suggested that the show involved a triumphal entry
of Venus in her chariot along with a mask of ladies, and that the main action was
in the form of a mock combat, but there are still a number of loose ends.[123] We
do not know what parts were played by the Lord of Misrule and his attendants,
nor do we know exactly what function Mars performed. All we know of the action
is that Cupid was rescued by Venus from the Marshall. As in the previous year's
Youth and Riches, Venus, Cupid, and Mars probably began with a debate of some
sort which came to a deadlock. This is made plausible by the personifications,
'Ydelnes' and 'Dalyance,' and the herald, 'cuouer ardant,' – all straight out of the
romantic disguisings produced early in Henry VIII's reign – and the fact that
Mars' attendants supplied their own armour. The failure of debate was probably
referred to a tourney or barriers.

There is no indication that any of the masks produced by the Revels for the
season were incorporated into *Venus, Cupid, and Mars*. Welsford correctly understood that the term 'mask' in the Revels account for this season refers to a set of
costumes and furniture for one band of maskers, not to an entire entertainment.[124]
From the accounts it is clear that there was a 'mask' of women of Diana hunting
together with a 'mask' of matrons as their torch bearers, a 'mask' of 'pollenders'
together with a 'mask' of soldiers as torch bearers, and a 'mask' of covetous men
together with a 'mask' of baboons as torch bearers.[125] As in 1551–2, it is likely
that two of these revels were produced for Twelfth Night.[126]

iv

The council kept tight control over the revels throughout the rest of the reign.
Cawarden was ordered by the council on 28 January to furnish 'all suche necessarie apparell' for a play by William Baldwin for Candlemas.[127] In addition, the
office was preparing a number of other plays, masks, and pastimes for Shrovetide.
Baldwin's play was postponed, and the preparations for Shrovetide 'surceased the
seide xiij*th* of ffebruary & were lefte of by commaundment the kinge then beinge
syck.'[128] Work resumed at the end of the month 'by specyall commaundement
vpon a newe determynacion of the kinges pleasure,' and the entertainments were
now scheduled for Easter (2 April) and May Day.[129] The Revels pay book which
runs from 28 February to 2 April includes charges for two plays, one by Baldwin
and one by Heywood. Heywood's unnamed play was to be performed by twelve
children, but other than this we know nothing about it.[130] John Carrow had been

contracted under the council's original warrant in January to make an Irish halberd and other properties for Baldwin's 'play of the state of Ierland.'[131] Further
preparations were now undertaken by Anthony Toto, Sergeant Painter, and by
Baldwin himself. Toto painted the halberd, put silver foil on its blade, made an
Irish sword and a 'prage' [spear], and painted a 'cote and a Cap with Ies tonges
and eares for fame.' Baldwin was paid for making, painting, and pasting a crown
of gold paper, for buckram for headpieces, and for an Irish headpiece. He also
rented 'heares, beards and devells apparel' and other material, suggesting that the
devil was one of the characters. While it is possible that he did not construct the
properties, it is certain from the account that Baldwin carried the material to and
from the court and superintended the performance himself.[132]

The Revels Office prepared five masks. One was a mask of bagpipes. The properties consisted of hoops and wicker over which canvas was stretched and painted to resemble bagpipes. They were 'made holowe and the pypes so great that the
men [bagpipe players] myght putt theyr pypes within them & blow & pype in the
same.'[133] John Carrow did the moulded work for six 'counterfett Apes,' covered
with grey rabbit skins, which were designed 'to syt vpon the topp of them [the
bagpipes] as thowghe they did play.' Carrow also made properties for the mask
of 'Medyoxs half man half deathe.' Doublets and hose were made for the six principals in this mask, as well as 'doble vizaged' headpieces, 'thone syde lyke a man
and thother lyke deathe.'[134] They carried 'long dartes' and shields of 'bord Ioyned
with deade beastes heddes in them.' They were accompanied by six torch bearers
for whom six frocks of canvas were made like 'deaths,' as was the 'tabretter' who
led them in.

For the mask of tumblers, Carrow made eight pair of legs and half-bodies with
leg pieces which were fashioned with arms and hands joined together. The principals who wore these costumes appeared to be walking on their hands.[135] Thirty dozen cats gave their all for the 'vj great tayles of wycker' which were furred for
the mask of cats, and thousands of pieces of glass and stone were used to make
imitation gems for their headpieces.[136] The principals in the mask of Greek worthies were accompanied by six satyrs as torch bearers costumed with 'oxens legges
and counterfett feete.' Carrow made the headpieces for the principals which were
'mowlded lyke Lyons heddes the Mowthe devowringe the mannes hed helmetwise.'
These costumes were among the garments listed in a Revels inventory of 26 March
1555, which explains that they had 'on the backes & brestes [of the costumes] the
names of hercules Iason percius Pirothus Achilles & Theseus writen,' lettered no
doubt with the pens and quills bought by the Revels 'to write vpon sylver & sylk
names.'[137] Remnants of the costumes survived into the early part of Elizabeth's
reign.

These masks are the most striking of the reign. Earlier writers wondered about the inspiration behind these and the others shown at Christmas and have thought of Ferrers.[138] As Lord of Misrule, Ferrers would not have been involved in any entertainments after Twelfth Night except by separate appointment from the council. There is no record of such an appointment. Further, if an appointment had been made, Cawarden would have been careful to copy the authorizing warrants for production into his account, as he had done for the previous Christmases. Finally, there is clear evidence in the Revels account that Cawarden devised these masks. Anthony Toto, Sergeant Painter, was paid 'for certen patrons by him drawen after the Masters device for maskes & other parcelles of the premisses in paper for syte & shewe of the forme in colours before the woorkemanshipp began.'[139] It is perhaps ironic that political manoeuvring and the grim reality of the young king's approaching death lay behind some of the most imaginative revels produced at court. As unlikely as it may appear from events in his political career, Northumberland managed to inspire court revels to new heights of innovation and to enlist in this service some of the best literary talent available.

Northumberland's desperation over the question of the succession might well have prompted him to authorize the mask of *Medioxes* to remind the king of his approaching death and to prepare him for arguments about altering the succession.[140] His attempts to persuade Edward were preceded by arrangements to marry his own son, Lord Guildford Dudley, to Lady Jane Grey, daughter of the Duke of Suffolk, and granddaughter of Mary, Henry VIII's younger sister. He also arranged to marry another of Suffolk's daughters, Lady Catherine Grey, to Lord Herbert, son of the Earl of Pembroke, and one of his daughters, Lady Catherine Dudley, to Lord Henry Hastings at the same time. The triple ceremony was held at the Bishop of Durham's palace in London on Thursday 25 May: 'the French ambassador was present, and most of the English nobility dignified the ceremony with their attendance.'[141] On 20 May, Northumberland wrote to Cawarden 'to apoynt out a couple of fayre maskes, oon of men and another of women' to show before the nobility at the wedding celebrations.[142] Immediately after the festivities Northumberland, Suffolk, and Pembroke went to the king at Greenwich to inform him 'of the prestigious marriages which had been solemnized with such general approval.'[143] The multiple wedding was the general background for the more particular arguments Northumberland was to use to convince the king 'that it would be right for the country and agreeable to the Word of God' to alter his will.[144] Cawarden's compliance in supplying masks was instrumental in Northumberland's plans, for it was not only the fact of the alliances but that the greater part of the nobility attended the elaborate celebrations, and consequently gave their approval, which helped to persuade the king. When Edward died on 6 July 1553, Northumberland had Lady Jane Grey proclaimed queen and over the next two weeks tried to maintain her on the throne.

9

Our Master of the Revels 'for the tyme beinge,' 1553–1559

Mary was proclaimed queen on 19 July 1553.[1] She made her triumphal entry into London on 3 August, and her coronation procession, in which she was accompanied by Princess Elizabeth and Lady Anne of Cleves, was held on 30 September. As in the past, some of the pageants in the entry drew analogies between the monarch and biblical and classical figures. Edward VI had been a Josiah and an Orpheus, unifying his people in renewed emphasis on the Reformation. Now Mary was a Judith and a Tomyris, defeating Holofernes and Cyrus in the person of Northumberland and freeing her subjects from tyranny.[2] Her coronation, held on 1 October, was a traditional ceremony for which the chrism had been sent by Charles V from Brussels. But in contrast to her brother's and, later, her sister's coronations there were to be no thematic connections made between the entry pageants and the revels. In fact there were to be no revels at all.

On 21 September, the queen sent a warrant to the Revels Office: 'Wee will and commaunde yowe vpon sighte herof forth with to make and delyuer owte of owre Revells vnto the gentillmen of our Chappell for a playe to be played before vs at the feastes of owr coronacyon as in tymes paste haithe ben accustomed to be done by the gentillmen of the Chapell of owr progenitours.'[3] Cawarden and his officers began work on 22 September for 'newemakinge translatinge allteringe garnysshinge and fynisshinge of dyuers and sondry garments apparell vestures and properties for one play or enterlude by the gentillmen of the Chapell,' but on 28 September, 'vpon newe determynacion,' they 'surceased and lefte of as ageane wrowght vpon fynysshed and serued att the christemas nexte ensuying by some woorkemen and thofficers of the reuels with there attendaunce att the courte theron.'[4] There are no other notices of revels or entertainments for the coronation, and why this play was postponed until Christmas can only be surmised.

Northumberland and his adherents were executed, beginning with the duke himself on 22 August, and perhaps it was felt that revels would hinder the serious business of forming a new government and initiating a counter-Reformation. Because of the proliferation of plays and books 'concerning doctryne in matters now in question and controversye, touchynge the hyghe poyntes and misteries of christian religion,' Mary issued an act on 16 August, very much like the proclamation issued by Edward VI in 1551, prohibiting the performance of plays without licence from her. It was not particularly effective, and her council issued further orders and kept close vigilance over players during the rest of the reign.[5] While the play prepared by the Revels Office for the Gentlemen of the Chapel does not seem particularly controversial, the queen may have wanted to reinforce the message that plays were to be discouraged at this time.

The play was shown at Christmas, however. The Wardrobe warrant authorizing material for costumes sent to Sir Edward Walgrave on 30 September provides a partial list of the cast.[6] It was a morality, including the character of Genus Humanum who wore a gown of purple satin, five Virgins costumed in white satin cassocks, Care in a green satin cassock, 'Skarcitie' in a woman's cassock of russet satin, 'Disceate' in a red satin cassock; Sickness, Feebleness, and Deformity in three long satin gowns – one ash-coloured and another black. Good and Bad Angel were supplied with wings, and Good Angel was costumed in white kersey. Reason, Verity, and Plenty were supplied with unidentified costumes – unless these were three of the five Virgins – and the Epilogue had a cassock of black satin and a long gown of purple damask. We can only guess the plot and theme from this incomplete list of characters, but it appears to have employed a standard temptation plot. Genus Humanum was probably first led through the temptations of Bad Angel to meet 'Disceate,' Care, 'Skarcitie,' Feebleness, Sickness, and Deformity and eventually to follow the counsel of Good Angel and become acquainted with Reason, Verity, and Plenty.

The Revels Office was not given specific instructions about entertainments at Christmas other than to produce *Genus Humanum*. For the rest, the officers prepared 'soche thinges' as they thought 'most behovable and lykely to be called vpon.'[7] They worked from 21 December to prepare unidentified garments and properties and attended at court for the traditional twelve days, but there is no clear indication what, if anything, might have been requested by the queen. *Respublica* is assigned to this season. Wallace and Hillebrand thought that it was performed by the Children of the Chapel.[8] They also thought, and Feuillerat agreed, that the Children performed parts in *Humanum Genus*. These are guesses, and some work well enough. There appears to have been enough parts in *Humanum Genus* to include some of the Children along with the Gentlemen. The arguments for *Respublica* are more complicated. The prologue to this play indicates that it was performed by boys as a Christmas diversion. The title page dates it 1553, and the epilogue addresses a prayer to Mary, not to Philip and Mary. It is attributed to Udall on internal evidence, and when the queen sent a warrant to the Revels Office in 1554 for production support of Udall's work, she mentions that he had shown plays at court before that.[9] While the play may have been performed at court in this year, the Revels account is not detailed enough to confirm its production by the office.

The small scale of Mary's 1553–4 Christmas festivities may be accounted for by the political uncertainty of the time. The commons were rebuked personally for their resolution urging the queen to marry an Englishman, and Mary's intention to accept the extremely unpopular proposal from Philip was announced on 15 January.[10] Grafton traced the tension in London to fear that Mary would not only 'bring in the Pope, but also by the mariage of a straunger, to bring the Realme into miserable seruitude.'[11] The Spanish delegation which arrived in this month to negotiate the marriage treaty was the spur which pricked unrest into open rebellion. Wyatt's rebellion was crushed by early February. In the ensuing reprisals Lady Jane Grey, Guildford Dudley, Suffolk, Wyatt, and a host of others were put to death in a series of executions lasting from February to April, which turned London into a charnel house. The dismembered quarters of those executed were displayed throughout the city, and the gibbets remained standing until June, when they were removed in preparation for the entry procession of Philip and Mary.[12]

i

The distance between the Revels Office and the council, observable during Northumberland's administration, increased in Mary's reign. When Henry VIII chose Cawarden as Master of the Revels, he was following a practice used as early as his father's reign. Cawarden's position as Gentleman of the Privy Chamber permitted the king close, personal contact with the planning and production of revels. This worked well enough when the appointment was made by word-of-mouth and held during pleasure. However, Cawarden's appointment by patent for life effectively undermined such personal control when the political climate changed. Cawarden's production of revels on Reformation subjects under Somerset indicates that the arrangement was still functional, but signs of strain appear later when Northumberland and the council chose Ferrers rather than Cawarden to devise the most important revels at court in 1551–2 and 1552–3. Personal oversight of revels from within the Privy Chamber was impossible to effect for a woman monarch. Her personal attendants were female, none of whom headed government or household offices. Discussions with the men who did hold such offices were conducted in more formal meetings, and the relationship between the sovereign and the Master of the Revels lost the intimacy by which it had been characterized. Instructions ordinarily were given to the Master second hand. But more importantly, Cawarden's religious and political commitments were radically different from the queen's, and such lack of sympathetic agreement must have had an impact on any plans for counter-Reformation revels.

Some of the lack of energy in Mary's court revels may be attributed to the fact that Cawarden found himself in deep trouble with the Crown beginning early in 1554. Cawarden's religious opinions were staunchly Protestant, and he had a history of involvement in Reformist causes. He was preferred to his position in the Privy Chamber by Cromwell along with a number of other noted Protestants at the height of the reform campaign. He had received a pardon in 1543 for heresy, of which he and his wife had been accused before the council and before the Bishop of Salisbury and other commissioners in Berkshire. They had aided, abetted, favoured, counselled, and consented with Anthony Person, who was burnt for heresies against the sacrament of the altar.[13] Cawarden's treatment of the parishioners of St Anne's after he had been granted the Blackfriars property showed little sensitivity for their religious convictions.[14] He used the old church for stabling horses and later pulled down the walls, leased the site for tennis courts, and used the cemetery for a carpenter's yard. He also pulled down the little church of St Anne. The parishioners objected, and Cawarden was ordered to rebuild the church. He did not. Rather, he simply provided them with 'a lodging chamber above a stair which in 1597 fell down.'[15] He devised revels on Reformation subjects from 1547 to 1549, and he supplied the masks for Jane Grey's wedding. Cawarden was also a supporter of Elizabeth, and had a letter from her signed 'Your lovinge friende,' thanking him for his gentle treatment of her servant and for his readiness to do her good service.[16] None of this would have endeared him to the new queen or her council, and their suspicions about his loyalty to the Crown in 1554 and again in 1556 threatened his position as Master of the Revels.

On 25 January 1554, Cawarden was arrested at his house at Blechingly and brought before the council in the Star Chamber. After questioning he was released, but was arrested again on his return to Blechingly and brought before the council at St James. He was ordered to reside at Blackfriars and to remain there until summoned again by the council.[17] He was freed a month later, but in the meantime Lord William Howard had issued a warrant to the Sheriff of Surrey to confiscate the large quantity of horses, armour, arms, and munitions, which included sixteen cannon, at Blechingly. The council was never able to prove complicity in Wyatt's rebellion, for there is no record of specific charges against him. It is possible that his store of munitions at Blechingly was regarded as an intent to support the rebellion, or he may have been lax in the matter of defence of the Crown as specified in the queen's letter to him to put your selff in full ordre with as many of your servauntes and tenauntes as ye can make both on horsseback and foote to be in a redines to marche and set forward uppon howers warning ether against the sayd rebelles [i.e.,'Thomas Wyat and sume others'] or such other wayes as shalbe signifyed unto you from us. And in the mean tyme to have good regarde to the quiet ordre of the parties where ye dwell, causing all suche idel and lewde person-es as shall ether by spreading abrode of untrue rumors or by any other meanes attempt to stirre or disquiet our loving subiectes, to be apprehended and punisshed as the qualitie of theyr offences shall deserve.[18]

Tension between Cawarden and the Crown did not end here. He was sum-moned before the council again on 24 July 1555 to answer the charge of being indebted to the queen for £1000. The debt and his reply to the summons is not extant. In 1556 Cawarden was implicated in a conspiracy to seize the treasure of one Brigham, a Teller of the Exchequer. Cawarden is named in March 1556 in the confession of Thomas White who in one of his depositions says that 'if the quenes maiestie had sent any treasure ouer to the Kinges maiestie that Sir Thomas Car-den with other A number of gentlemen shold haue taken the Treasure with fforce.' The council pursued the investigation. Later that month a list of questions was drawn up including one which specifically inquired about Cawarden's role in the plot. In April, John Dethicke's reply to this question was that he had heard that Cawarden was one of the principals in the affair.[19] The council did not get the evi-dence it needed to proceed against Cawarden, but enough to keep him under investigation. On 3 May 1556, he was required to sign a bond to 'contynually abyde and kepe within his dwellinghouse in the Citie of London' and not depart until it was 'signified unto him by the Lords of the Privie Counsell.'[20] It was not until 7 July that he was licensed to leave his quarters in Blackfriars and to return home, but in order to do so he was forced to enter into a recognizance for £4000 to 'neverthelesse within tenne daies warnyng make his personall apparaunce before the Lords of the Counsaill whensoever he shall, betwixt this and Allhallontide next.'[21] The council never let up in its investigation. On 25 May 1557 he was committed to Fleete prison, and the council sent a letter to the Warden to keep him in safe custody. He was still there on 14 June and his answers could not have been satisfying given the council's decree which was communicated by letter to the Warden:

Whereas Sir Thomas Cawarden, knight, hathe byn heretofore for his ill Misbehaviour to the State committed to the Fleete, forasmoche as the saide Sir Thomas having nowe for a good tyme remained there hath made no manner of submission nor knowleaged his offence, which sorte of obstinacie is not to be passed over without reformacion, the Lords considering the same this daie toke ordre that the said Sir Thomas Cawarden shuld be committed to the close prison of the Fleete, having, oone servant onlie to be with him, in like manner shut upp.[22]

The council relented at its meeting of 16 July and sent another letter to the Warden allowing Cawarden the freedom of the prison until a further determination was made, 'which shalbe shortlye.' How long Cawarden spent in prison beyond the obvious two-month period is not certain. It is evident that Mary's reign, from January 1554 until very near its end, was a trying experience for the aging knight. In his eulogy for Cawarden, William Browne mentions his courage not only in the field but in facing the council's harassment: 'for godes worde in tyme paste twyse did he skape godes enemyes, in pryson though he weare full faste.'[23] From 24 January 1554 until at least July 1557 Cawarden was under investigation, interrogation, house arrest, or in prison by order of the council. Through it all he managed to retain his position as Master of the Revels. His difficulties with the council did not bar him from payment in the Revels accounts each year, but it does not appear that he was in complete charge of the schedule of revels in 1554 and 1555.

Philip arrived in England on 19 July 1554, and the royal wedding took place at Bishop Gardiner's palace in Winchester on 25 July.[24] When the council requested Cawarden's plans for furnishing the banqueting houses and other devices of pleasure for the celebration, he pleaded illness and promised to send a deputy. The Office of the Tents sent two hales and six long houses to Winchester for Philip's reception.[25] No Revels accounts survive. It is unlikely that the Catholic interludes and pageants, which Holinshed records as part of the festivities, were produced with their help.[26] The king and queen spent the next few days in 'triumphing, bankating, singing, masking.' The royal couple delighted spectators by performing many styles of dancing. In his narrative of the festivities, John Elder records that describing the brilliant apparel or devices shown were 'but a phantasie and losse of paper and ynke.'[27]

Philip and Mary remained ten days at Winchester before moving on to Windsor by 3 August, where Philip was installed as Knight of the Garter and prepared for his entry into London. The well-documented pageant series produced mainly by foreigners was oriented toward welcoming the king.[28] Philip considered the entry a success, but, as historians have pointed out, even at this early date there was hostility towards the Spaniards, who were present in London in large numbers.[29] The hostility and disappointment was made worse over the next year or so by the installation of old practices in religious services and sermons, by the intensification of religious persecution, and by the proposal to crown Philip King of England.

Cawarden was paid in the Revels account for his work from 17 to 21 October

1554 – nine months after his first arrest by the council – on a mask of eight mariners to be shown in November. The costumes for this mask, which were listed in the inventory of March 1555, consisted of eight jerkins of purple cloth of gold 'barde over with gardes of clothe of greene Syluer' with sleeves of the same and hoods of blue cloth of gold edged with red silk lace. The slops were parted, one leg of blue cloth of gold and the other of green cloth of gold. The headpieces were of red satin striped with gold and white cloth of silver with 'Tarcells of cullen goowld' and feathers of white and black.[30] The entertainment was held late at night, which appears to have been the custom at Mary's court, for the officers charge for 'attendinge the same aswell in the after none as very late in the night for the recariage therof from the court.'[31] It does not seem, however, that Cawarden devised this mask. In a letter to Sir William Cecil, Francis Yaxley mentions that the mask of mariners in November 1554 was devised by William Lord Howard of Effingham: 'the Kinges and Quenes Majesties be in helth, and meary, whom I did see daunce togethers vppon Sunday at night at the Court, where was a brave maskery of cloth of gold and sylver, apparailed in maryners garmentes, the chief doer wherof I thinke was my Lord Admirall.'[32]

Another mask was produced at court, probably at Whitehall on 30 November. Revels were being held for Cardinal Pole who had arrived in London on the 24th and was received at court by the king and queen.[33] The following day the king participated in a martial exhibition, and on the 27th the cardinal addressed Parliament. On the 29th the Bishop of London proclaimed a mass throughout the diocese with a procession and bell ringing for 'thankes of owr [gracious] quen of her qwyckenyng with chyld.'[34] On the 30th the king attended mass at the Abbey:

for the Spaneards [sung], and ther mett ym at the cort gate a C. He-Alman in hosse and dobeletes of whyt and red, and yelow welvet cotes [trimmed], with yelow sarsenet, and yelow velvet capes and fethers … and drumes and flutes in the sam coler, and with gylt [halbards], and C. in yolow hosse, dobelets of welvett, and jerkens of [leather] gardyd with cremesun velvett and whyt, fether yelow and red; and thos be Spaneards; and a C. in yelow gownes of velvett with (blank) And the same nyght my lord cardenall cam to the courte, and whent to the chapell with the Kyng, and ther *Te Deum* songe.[35]

The occasion was the congruence of the reconciliation of England with the Church of Rome, the celebration of the queen's supposed pregnancy, and the cardinal's visit. Cawarden and his officers worked from 23 to 30 November to produce 'A Mask of vj hercules or men of war comynge from the sea with vj Maryners to their torcheberers.'[36] It appears that some of the garments and material were altered from the mask of Greek worthies which had been shown before Edward VI in the spring of 1553. Eight targets, six falchions, and six 'doble holberts' were made and painted. John Carrow made eight headpieces 'like morien helmettes the frountes like griffons heddes with cerbrerus in forme of a greyhound with iij heddes stondinge on the reast.' Sixteen lion's faces were used for the breast and backs of the maskers. No pageants or other properties are mentioned.

Cawarden and his officers worked from 13 December 1554 to 6 January 1555 to produce revels for Christmas. While he appears to have devised the two masks in this season, he had little control over the 'plaies set forth by [Nicholas] vdall' which were produced by the office under orders from the queen.[37] The warrant, which was issued on 12 December, was addressed 'To the Master and yeman of the office of our Revelles for the tyme beinge & to either of them & to their deputie or deputies ther & to euery of them,' indicating that Cawarden was not always in the office and suggesting that there may have been plans to remove him. The responsibilities of the officers in producing Udall's plays consisted in altering garments for 'his Actours from time to tyme' and in providing 'their incydentes.' We do not know exactly how many plays were produced or which companies performed them, but the wording of the warrant indicates that Udall had already performed some plays at court. The first of the two masks produced by the officers was of eight patrons of galleys 'like venetian Senatours with vj gally slaves for their torchebearers.' Only a few properties are mentioned in the accounts. John Carrow made the daggers carried by the patrons, and wicker served for the shackles and chains of the slaves.[38] The second mask was of six 'venusses or amorous ladies' with six cupids as torchbearers. For the cupids quivers containing three arrows were made, along with bows 'with Arrowes fastened in them and goinge thorowe the bowes.' Silk flowers were used in the headpieces of the amorous ladies and six 'fruterers baskettes' were made.[39] There are two other accounts for this mask. In one the torchbearers are described as 'vj matrons,' and in another as 'vj Cupides & women torchberers.'[40] It is impossible to be precise about the dates on which they were shown, but New Year's and Twelfth Night are probable.

Two more masks were produced at Shrovetide (24, 25, 26 February 1555). Cawarden and his officers worked from 26 January to 26 February to prepare a mask of six Turkish magistrates with six archers as their torch bearers.[41] The Turks carried 'six turkeye fawchens of woode' in green velvet scabbards. Their headpieces were made of 'Asshen hoopewood in queynte and straunge fassion' covered with white sarcenet, the tops of which were red gold sarcenet with tassels of gold. The torch bearers had similar headpieces in different colours and carried 'turkey bowes' and 'turkey quevers of arrowes' garnished with gold and silver foil. The second mask was of eight 'Goddesses Huntresses' with eight Turkish women as torch bearers.[42] They carried 'turkey' quivers and bows and their torch bearers carried 'dartes.' The extent of Cawarden's role in devising these masks is unclear. By Christmas

1555–6 he was certainly discharging all of his duties as Master, but given the continual harassment by the council and at least one more period of imprisonment, it is difficult to imagine how he could have given full attention to them.

ii

Philip spent about two and a half years in England at two different times. He was in residence from 19 July 1554 to 4 September 1555 and from 20 March 1556 to 5 July 1557. There was a considerable number of martial spectacles concentrated during the period from December 1554 to March 1555 which were more interesting than any since Henry VIII's reign. Barriers were held 'before the court gate,' possibly at Greenwich on 4 December 1554, and on the 18th there

was a grett tryhumph at the court gatte, by the Kyng and dyvers lordes boyth English-men and Spaneards, the whyche the Kyng and his compene [were] in goodly harnes, and a-pon ther armes goodley jerkyns of bluw velvett, and hosse in-brodered with sylver and blue sarsenett; and so they rane on fott with spayeres and swerds at the tornay, and with dromes and flutes in whyt velvet [drawn] owt with blu sarsenett, and ther wher x aganst [the Kyng] and ys compene, the wher xviij in odur colers.[43]

On 24 January 1555 there was a 'grett ronnyng at the tylt at Westmynster with spayres, both Englys men and Spaneards.'[44] March was filled with martial sports. On the 5th, the king saw an exhibition by the Master of Fence. On the 19th, 'the Kyng('s) grace rune at the tylt a-gaynst odur Spaneards, and brake iiij stayffes by viij of the cloke in the mornyng.' And on the 25th,

ther was as gret justes as youe have sene at the tylt at Vestmynster; the chalyngers was a Spaneard and ser Gorge Haward; and all ther men, and ther horsses trymmed in whyt, and then came the Kyng and a gret mene all in bluw, and trymmyd with yelow, and ther elmets with gret tuyffes of blue and yelow fether, and all ther veffelers and ther fotemen, and ther armorers, and a copene lyke Turkes red in cremesun saten gownes and capes, and with fachyons, and gret targets; and sum in gren, and mony of dyvers colers; and ther was broken ij hondred stayfffes in a-boyff.[45]

There were no recorded martial exhibitions in connection with the peace negotiations between France and the Empire, which were conducted by Cardinal Pole, but the Tents did work in May and June to supply five 'houses' for the ambassadors.[46] It appears that most of the garments and material for these events were simply borrowed from the Revels Office, for in the inventory taken in March 1555 the officers still list bards and bases.

Philip introduced something new to the martial exhibitions – the cane game. It was exhibited at the wedding festivities of Lord Strange and Lady Cumberland on 12 February 1555: 'after a grett dener, and justes, and after tornay on horsbake with swordes, and after soper *Jube the cane*, a play, with torch-lyght and cressett-lyghtes, lx cressets and C. of torchys, and a maske, and a bankett.'[47] It had been shown before the king and queen at Smithfield in early November and again on 25 November when 'the Kyngs grace and my lord Fuwater and dyvers Spaneards dyd ryd in dyvers colars, the Kyng in red, and some [in] yellow, sum in gren, sum in whyt, sum in bluw, and with targets and canes in ther hand, herlyng of rod on at a-nodur.'[48] The sport, which was brought to England by the Spanish, had been witnessed by Lord Berners, ambassador to Spain in 1518, who described such a game in which the king of Spain participated: 'the king, with xxiij with him, well apparelled in cootes and clokes of goulde and gouldsmythe work, on horsback, in the said marketplace (at Saragossa), ranne and caste canes after the countrye maner ... Assoone as the cane is caste, they flye; wherof the Frenche ambassador sayd, that it was a good game to teche men to flye.'[49] It was also little appreciated by the English. Count Langosco de Stroppiana mentions that it left 'the specta-tors cold, except for the fine clothes of the players, and the English made fun of it.'[50] There are no recorded martial exhibitions during Philip's second stay in Eng-land.

It is difficult to estimate the grandeur of these spectacles. Machyn, our prin-cipal source for the events, is no Edward Hall, and while his descriptions suggest a scale of magnificence for some of them, his narratives do not do them justice. It is clear, however, that they did not catch the imagination of the citizenry. Machyn did not know the names of many of the champions. He refers to them generically as 'Spaneardes,' and it is clear that the martial exhibitions had not recaptured the excitement of those in which Henry VIII and his courtiers per-formed.

iii

At Christmas 1555–6 Richard Bosum, Warden of the painters in the Revels Office, made patterns of masks and 'other draughtes of woorkes,' probably based on Cawarden's device. One of these was a mask for which twelve wicker heads were made, these to be garnished with 160 flowers of 'shredds & sleved sylke.'[51] Robert Trunckwell made six falchions and 'targettes of paper and cloth.' The sketchy evidence suggests one mask of six persons and six torch bearers, who were supplied with Spanish gloves. The subjects of the revels cannot be identified from the records, but it is certain that Mary was reviving traditional ceremonies. The Boy Bishop was legalized by this year, for example, and the child bishop of

St Paul's and his company had performed before the queen on 6 December.[52] At Candlemas (2 February 1556) Cawarden and his officers produced a mask of six persons with eight torch bearers, and at Shrovetide there was another entertainment, although it is not certain that it was a mask, for the officers charge for carriage to court only once.[53]

Cawarden produced a play by William Baldwin during the Christmas season of 1555–6 or 1556–7. There is no evidence of Baldwin's work at court since the production of his play of *The State of Ireland* in the spring of 1553. Baldwin wrote to Cawarden about a new play he had written called *Love and Lyve*, 'a Comodie concernyng the way to lyfe, mete as it is supposed to be played before the Quene.'[54] The letter provides conclusive evidence that Cawarden was discharging all of his duties as Master at this time. The letter is dated Tuesday, 24 December, and then endorsed 1556, creating a dating problem. Christmas Eve fell on a Tuesday in 1555. Further, Baldwin mentions that Cawarden had offered to produce some of his work at court 'now thre yeres passed,' probably a reference to the Christmas season of 1552–3, when Baldwin and Ferrers were setting forth certain interludes at court. Despite the endorsement of 1556, it appears that the letter was written in anticipation of the 1555–6 Christmas season.[55] Since Baldwin mentions that the play was to be ready for performance within ten days, it could have been shown between 4 and 6 January 1556.

'Love and Lyve' was Baldwin's motto. It appears on the first page of *Beware the Cat* (1570) and in the address to the reader in *The Funerals of King Edward VI.*[56] The play was about

a yong man whome I name Lamuel who hath a servant called Lob, these two will attempt the worlde to seke theyr fortune, they mete with Lust lucke and love, Lust promiseth them lecherie, Lucke lordship, Love Lyf, they folow lvst and through lechery be lost, than through Lucke they recover, Luck bringeth them to lordship from whiche through Larges and larracine they cum to Lacke/ Than through Love, they go to Light & therby attayne Lyfe/ All the players names begin with .L.[57]

The actors, who were to play the fifty-two parts of what Anglo described as 'almost inspired lunacy,' are not mentioned. They were rehearsing when Baldwin wrote to Cawarden and would 'be ready within these .x. dayes' to perform the play. *Love and Lyve* was in demand at the time: 'there be of the Innes of court that desyer to have the setting furth therof.' Because Cawarden had asked 'now thre yeres passed' to produce his work, Baldwin offered the Master of the Revels first choice of the play. The Revels accounts are too sketchy to determine what costumes or properties may have been used in it.

During Philip's second period of residence in England from 20 March 1556

to 5 July 1557, revels were held at Christmas, Candlemas, Shrovetide, and on
St Mark's Day (25 April 1557). At Christmas, Cawarden and his officers worked
from 11 December 1556 to 8 January 1557 to produce unidentified masks, plays,
and pastimes shown before the king and queen between Christmas Day and
Twelfth Night.[58] At least one new mask was devised by Cawarden, for Robert
Trunckwell was paid for 'a patron of a devyce of a maske.' The officers also
worked from 8 January to 2 February to produce entertainments at Candlemas.
There is no clear evidence of what was shown.[59] Trunckwell was paid again for
working and framing 'of to dyuers patrons of Maskes devysed by the Master,' but
there are no carriage charges included in the account. For Shrovetide, the officers
worked from 2 to 25 February.[60] Carriage charges are listed, but there are no
details of the preparations, and, probably, the patterns that Carrow worked on at
Candlemas also included the masks at Shrovetide.

Cawarden and his officers worked again from 9 to 26 April on the most elaborate mask of Mary's reign, the great mask of 'Alamains,' pilgrims, and Irishmen
which was held on St Mark's Day (25 April) at Whitehall, and the last Philip was
to see in England. The office was not well enough furnished to undertake the production, according to Cawarden. He expressed his concern to the queen through
Sir Henry Jerningham, Master of the Horse, who

declareyd to the quens hynes how that you haue no other maskes thene suche as has byne
shewyd all Redy before the kynges hynes & for that he hathe syne meny fayer & Ryche be
yend the seys you thynke yt not honorab[le] that he shuld se the lyeke here.[61]

Jerningham's reply was that 'sche knowes Ryght well that you cane make a schyffte
for ned Requeryng you so to do.' The great mask was put on by ordering non-
chargeable material from the Wardrobe, such as red and carnation velvet; purple,
gold, yellow, red, and white sarcenet; and cloth of silver.[62] Cawarden hired six
masking garments and their furniture from Christopher Milliner and altered them
for the pilgrims, and remade six old visors. The great mask of 'Alamains,' pilgrims,
and Irishmen was furnished partly from the store, partly by the Great Wardrobe,
and partly with garments made for the occasion by the officers who charged £42
11s.[63] In the following month Cawarden was committed to Fleete prison.

When Philip departed England on 5 July 1557, it was for the last time. Mary's
last revel for him in April 1557 was put together by 'a schyffte for ned,' and those
for the following Christmas, when she was alone, were meagre. The Revels
account for 1557–8 is even sketchier than earlier ones. It appears that some masks
were produced, for John Carrow was paid for working at home 'vpon certeyne the
Masters devices.'[64] Since there were no carriage charges at Candlemas it is possible that no entertainments were given, despite the attendance of the Revels offi-

cers. They did hire a boat for Shrovetide, but it is not certain what entertainments were produced.

It is a matter of regret that we have so few narratives of Mary's revels. Concessions were no doubt made to continental tastes when Philip and his entourage were in residence, and, of course, Mary herself had been intimately acquainted with English revels from early childhood. Her father paid for the upkeep of her household and made supplementary payments for her Christmas diversions. Her household accounts from 1 October 1520 to 30 September 1522 illustrate how elaborate those entertainments were even when she was a child.[65] Occasionally she spent Christmas at court with her parents, as she did in 1520–1. In other years she spent the holidays in her own household, as she did in 1521–2 at Ditton Park, Buckinghamshire. Oliver Hunt and others were paid to decorate a boar's head for the traditional Christmas ceremony, as well as to make costumes for entertainments. These, along with other properties, were no doubt used by John Thurgoode, a valet in Mary's household, who was appointed Lord of Misrule and paid 40s. for garments, properties, and 'pro diuersis interludes.' Thurgoode's account of expenses shows that he provided an undetermined number of entertainments for which he required changes of garments 'at sondrie tymes.'[66] At least one disguising was produced for which 'a paynter of Wyndesore' made 'vysors' and painted 'fases, Coote Armors, hattes,' and used 'xiij Quayers of paper in dyuerse Colors.' 'Garmentes/ herys/ and hattys' were rented and carried from London, and straw was bought 'that xij men war Couered with in a disgysyng.' There may have been other disguisings, for 'ffrayler at Wyndesore' was paid 'to make garmentes & other dysgysynges.' This may refer to the 'diuersis interludes,' but it appears that at least one of the others was for a morris dance for which 'Clateryng Stavez' and 'Marys pykes' were bought, and 'ix morres Cotes' and ten dozen bells – twenty-two of which were lost – were hired. Collier thought that the entry for 'mendyng of Adams Garmentes' indicated that a miracle play of the creation was put on, but conceded that Adam may have been a player's name, as in the entry for 'Jakes, when he pleyed the Chypman.'[67] Jakes must have played another part as well, for he also had a 'blewe garment made lyke harnes for the same Jakys and a nother garment for mayster Pennyngton.' Another unnamed person played 'the ffryer afore the Prynccesse.' How the other items in the account were used is not clear. Four gunners were hired, and firearms were discharged, possibly in connection with the Lord of Misrule's shows: the horse was also trimmed 'in dyuerse ffachyons at Sondre tymez.' Gold foil, rabbit skins and tails, and twelve crossbows were employed, as well as 'ij Tabrettes' hired 'all the tyme of Christemas.'[68]

Lavish entertainments continued to be held in the princess's household. Three years later, on 17 November 1525, six members of the princess's council wrote to Wolsey wondering whether 'We shall appoynte any lord of mysrule' and to 'provide for enterlud*es* disgysyng*es* or pleyes in the said fest/ or for banket on twelf nyght.'[69] The reply is not extant, but enough evidence survives from earlier and later Christmas celebrations to imagine that they were elaborate. Mary's Privy Purse accounts from 1536 to 1544 reveal many payments for musical performances by singers, minstrels, and musicians as well as occasional Christmas and New Year's rewards to the King's Players and to the Children of the Chapel. She was entertained by Lady Elizabeth's minstrels in April 1537, and in 1540 both Mary and Elizabeth were entertained by the Prince's minstrels. In March 1538 John Heywood was paid for performing an interlude 'with his children' before Mary. Heywood, who was to be involved in the initial planning for Philip's entry in 1554, had a prominent role in one of the pageants for Mary's coronation procession in 1553. Outside of the schoolhouse at St Paul's 'one master Heiwood sat in a pageant vnder a vine, and made to hir an oration in Latine and English.'[70] Not only was Mary used to full-scale productions in her own household, but she had, when only eleven years old, performed in one of the great pageant-disguisings of her father's reign – the revel of 6 May 1527, which celebrated the results of a year of negotiations by the French for Mary's hand in marriage. Very little evidence survives from her reign to suggest that her revels were produced on the same scale as her father's, her brother's, or even her sister's.

The charges of the revels in Mary's reign seldom exceeded £50.[71] Cawarden drew on the resources of the storehouse and various wardrobes to produce his revels, and cost alone is not proof of lack of variety or distinction. Nevertheless, there is sufficient evidence to support suspicions raised by the slender charges. An inventory prepared by the Revels officers from 9 to 26 March 1555 shows the remains of fragments of garments and material dating at least from Edward VI's reign, together with complete outfits for eleven masks of men and five of women.[72] Eight of these had been made since Mary's accession, and they were subsequently altered for new masks to disguise the fact that they had been shown before. When Cawarden expressed his concern about this in relation to the great mask for St Mark's Day in 1557 the queen replied that he could make do with what he had. This attitude toward one of her most elaborate revels, suggests the economic constraint placed on the Revels Office throughout the reign.

There are several reasons to explain why Mary's long tradition of holiday entertainments and Philip's importation of Spanish sports failed to produce inspiring revels. The social climate of an English court populated by Spaniards together with the domestic turmoil characteristic of the period simply was not conducive to a festive atmosphere. Further, Sir Thomas Cawarden was not one of the queen's most loyal supporters, and the differences in their religious and political views must have been taken into account in terms of what could be expected from the Revels Office. Finally, as her sister Elizabeth was to be later in the century, Mary was concerned about the state of the treasury. Revels were luxuries, and the level of display was calculated to achieve economy even when Philip was in residence. When he was not at court, revels were scaled down considerably. The Revels bills for the seasons of 1555–6 and 1557–8 when the queen was alone totalled about £100 and £90 respectively, and in both of these seasons the officers charged for the production of plays, pastimes, and masks at Christmas, Candlemas, and Shrovetide. Cawarden must have drawn heavily on support from the Wardrobe, and his tailors must have had to alter older garments as a matter of course to manage on such a budget. All of this changed with the accession of Elizabeth, who, like her brother Edward, spent a considerable amount of money on her first set of revels to create a new image for her reign.

iv

Sir Thomas Cawarden was restored to favour immediately after Elizabeth's accession on 17 November 1558. He was appointed on 24 November with others to the charge of the Tower, where he prepared the coronation lodging, and he produced many of the revels during the first year of her reign.[73] Cawarden and his officers began preparing for the coronation entertainments in conjunction with their Christmas productions, which they worked on from 11 December 1558 to 8 January 1559.[74] The hopes of many of her subjects for Protestant leadership were confirmed in Elizabeth's first Christmas revels. For the third time in twenty-five years revels were used in the service of religious propaganda.

At least one, possibly two, masks and one play were produced on Twelfth Night at court.[75] The Revels officers prepared swords, darts, 'dagges,' targets, six-foot staves, four cardinals' hats, six priests' caps, twenty other headpieces, four 'crogerstaves,' two great bells, and thirteen other bells for masking garments. The bill of Thomas Dachan for Christmas and Twelfth Night indicates delivery of cardinals' and bishops' costumes to the office for 'the firste mask,' and other garments for the 'pathway to perfect knowledge.'[76] Whether the 'pathway' was the title of the play, which may have been performed by the Queen's Players, or, more likely, the title of another mask, is not certain. The Revels also prepared 'vij visars with byrdes vpon them.' The latter were probably for the anti-Catholic mask mentioned by Schifanoya in his letter of 23 January 1559 to the Castellan of Mantua:

As I suppose your Lordship will have heard of the farce performed in the presence of her Majesty on the day of the Epiphany, and I not having sufficient intellect to interpret it, nor yet the mummery performed after supper on the same day, of crows in the habits of Cardinals, of asses habited as Bishops, and of wolves representing Abbots, I will consign it to silence.[77]

Like Marillac in the late 1530s, Schifanoya refuses to describe in detail 'the levities and unusual licentiousness practised at the Court in dances and banquets,' as well as the masquerade of friars in the streets of London and the outrages done by iconoclasts to statues of saints.[78] The evidence indicates that Elizabeth's first Christmas revels go back in subject and theme to those produced at the opening of Edward VI's reign. Like those at her brother's coronation, Elizabeth's first revels were also related to the coronation entry. By warrant from the queen dated 3 January, the Revels Office provided garments to John Gresham and John Elyot, citizens of London, to put on pageants for this entry.[79] As with Edward VI's coronation, cooperation between court and city appears to have gone beyond the loan of garments. The pageants shown on 19 January, prepared by a committee which included Richard Grafton, veteran of the 1554 entry for Philip II, dealt with a variety of subjects. Relief at having escaped the perils of Mary's reign, the expulsion of foreign influence, and advice on how to govern were the subjects of some of the pageants, but most, as Grafton points out, were presented in the context of the theme of religious reform.[80] Grafton interpreted the pageant at Gracechurch street depicting the uniting of the houses of Lancaster and York as 'the coniunction and coupling together of our Soueraigne Lady with the Gospell and veritie of Goodes holy woorde, for the peaceable gouernement of all her good subiects.' At Cornehill, Pure Religion tread on Superstition and Ignorance, which Schifanoya interpreted as meaning that 'religion had been misunderstood and misdirected, and that now it will proceed on a better footing.' In the pageant at the little conduit in Cheap, a child delivered a book, inscribed *Verbum veritas*, to Elizabeth, who held up the book and kissed it. The proper interpretation of the pageant, according to Grafton, was that 'Tyme had now once againe restored vnto us Goddes veritye whereby the dregges of Papistry might bee put away, and so the Mounteyne myght become all freshe.' The pamphlet describing the series explains that the pageants were all interconnected: 'The mater of this pageant [at the little conduit in Cheap] dependeth of them that went before.' It was also connected to the next pageant at the conduit in Fleete Street, which like the previous two coronation entries compared the sovereign to biblical figures. The pageant represented the queen enthroned in her parliament robes with the motto: 'Debora the iudge and restorer of the house of Israel.' Elizabeth was encouraged in these pageants to embrace the Reformation. She had anticipated the hopes of her subjects in her Christmas revels which publicly announced a new Protestant reign, and the effect was immediate. Not only did the citizens of London express their hostility to Mary's counter-Reformation but the Protestant exiles of Mary's reign began to return home.

There are important differences between Elizabeth's and Edward's use of the revels to further the Reformation. Under Somerset, Edward personally performed in anti-Catholic revels during the first few years of his reign. Elizabeth did not perform in such revels herself, nor did she continue to have them produced at court after the first Christmas. Edward VI put the royal image directly in the service of the Reformation; Elizabeth did not. Rather, she projected an image of encouraging it. She attended plays out of court, such as the performance of Udall's *Ezechias* at Cambridge in 1564. Examples of her interest in Protestantism contrast sharply with Edward's reforming zeal. Further, while Edward VI had used the royal playing company to stage plays dealing with Reformation subjects, Elizabeth did not. The Queen's Players may have performed at court once at Christmas 1558–9, but they were never invited again. The reasons for this are not entirely clear. Perhaps the royal company was too closely identified with Mary after having performed at her court for six years. The tradition, dating from Henry VII's reign, was to use the royal company to dominate the schedule of plays in the revels. Not using the royal company ran the risk of obscuring the queen's image as patron. In fact, this is precisely what happened, and it was not until 1583 that Elizabeth created a new company of players.[81] Given the difficulty of unifying a country violently torn by religious and political divisions, Elizabeth announced the continuation of the Reformation in her first revels, but then adopted a moderate course.

Cawarden and his officers worked from 8 January to 2 February to produce revels for the coronation on 15 January and for Candlemas (2 February). They produced a mask on the 16th in conjunction with the coronation tournament, held on the 16th and 17th, as well as another mask on the 22nd.[82] Chambers suggested that the subject of the mask on the 16th was of conquerors, dressed in white cloth of silver, and that the next mask on Sunday the 22nd was of Moors.[83] The mask of Moors was apparelled with cloth of gold and blue velvet, with sleeves of silver sarcenet. The Moors had curled hair, made of black lawn and wreathed with red gold sarcenet and silver lawn. Their arms and faces were covered with black velvet. They carried darts, and since the Revels officers ordered bells and staves as well as 37,000 spangles, it is likely that a morris dance was part of the same mask. One of the Yeoman's bills indicates the use of hoods and caps for monks and friars which were probably used for the Moorish friars who served as torch bearers.[84]

Cawarden and his officers worked again from 2 to 28 February to produce at least two entertainments for Shrovetide. On Shrove Sunday there was a double-mask which included an assault. Schifanoya briefly notes that

Last evening [5 February] at the Court a double mummery was played: one set of mummers rifled the Queen's ladies, and the other set, with wooden swords and bucklers, recovered the spoil.

Then at the dance the Queen performed her part, the Duke of Norfolk being her part-
ner, in superb array.[85]

One group of maskers were eight 'Swartrutters,' costumed in black and white
jerkins and long breeches, with hats and 'dags.' The other groups may have been
Hungarians, costumed in blue and purple cloth of gold, and the torch bearers
were six 'Alamains.'[86] On Shrove Tuesday there was another double-mask. The
first was a mask of fishermen and fisherwives, and the second was a mask of
marketwives.[87] It is possible that the dozen 'foxnettes' ordered by the Revels officers were used in the first mask. The officers also charge for carriage back and
forth between the office and court on Shrove Monday, just as they did on Sunday and Tuesday, indicating that an entertainment may have been given on that
day.[88]

In May Cawarden and his officers worked from the 2nd to the 25th to produce
a mask of astronomers on the 24th in a banqueting house at Westminster built
for the entertainment of the Duke of Montmorency, Constable of France, and
the French embassy.[89] The astronomers appear to have been costumed in long
robes of Turkey red cloth of gold, and their torch bearers in green damask. How
the canvas arms and legs stained flesh colour were used is not clear. Robert
Trunckwell had been working on 'toe modells of the Masters device for arowfe and
A cobboorde of a bancketinge howse' since Christmas.[90] This banqueting house
was probably intended for the coronation but not used. Trunckwell was back at
the task in February, altering the models he had made, which were 'nowe ageane
turnede to Another purpose.'[91] This house could not have been elaborate. Cawarden's charges for it were only £96 3s. 1d. Only the cupboard and roof are mentioned, and it appears clear that it was intended for installation in one of the
galleries at Westminster, rather than as a free-standing structure.[92]

Another banqueting house was erected at Greenwich on 10 July 1559, although there is no evidence that Cawarden and his officers were in charge. It was
made of fir 'powlles, and deckyd with byrche and all maner [of flowers] of the feld
and gardennes, as roses, gelevors, [lavender, marygolds,] and all maner of
strowhyng erbes and flowrs. [There were also] tentes for kechens and for all offe-
sers agaynst [the morrow,] with wyne, alle, and bere.'[93] On the following day, the
queen and ambassadors saw a tournament put on by her pensioners and then after
supper saw a mask at the banqueting house, which lasted until midnight. The
Revels Office did not contribute to the joust held at court on 2 July nor to the
entertainment given to the queen by the Earl of Arundel on 6 August at Nonsuch
with 'soper, bankett, and maske, with drumes and flutes, and all the mysyke that
cold be, tyll mydnyght.'[94] This was followed on the 7th by a play by the Children
of Paul's and 'ther master Se[bastian], master Phelypes, and master Haywod' with

a banquet and music. But the Revels officers did design and decorate the banqueting house at Lord Admiral Clinton's place at West Horsley, which had a second storey and a gallery, later in the summer. Richard Bosum, Sergeant Painter, and his brother were both paid in the Revels account 'for makinge of pyctures vpon clothe in the frunte and the gallerye.'[95] These charges derive from Lewis Stocket's bill in which Bosum was paid for working 'of the clothe' in the second storey with the 'counterfeits' of Henry VIII, Edward VI, and Elizabeth I.[96] The Revels officers worked there from 24 July to 30 September to produce a double-mask of shipmen and maids of the country. The shipmen were costumed in blue cloth of gold, and Chambers suggested that the two 'grasyers or gentillmen of the cuntrye,' whose black damask gowns appear in one of the inventories, may have acted as presenters.[97]

Cawarden did not personally help to produce the entertainments at West Horsley. He was active in the office through late June, however. He certainly worked on the Christmas revels, for Trunckwell's models of the banqueting house to be used in May were being built according to Cawarden's device.[98] He was still active in the spring of 1559, when he petitioned the council for redress of injuries suffered in Mary's reign, and, on 3 May, he filed suit at common law against Sir Thomas and William Saunders for detaining horses and armour which had been confiscated in 1554.[99] He continued with his Revels duties through the airing in June, for he received a letter from the council, dated 6 June 1559, requesting an estimate of debts in the office and a projection of expenses during the coming year, which he responded to on the 7th.[100] In early July, Cawarden broke his leg, and this may explain why the Revels officers did not charge for decorating the banqueting house at Greenwich early in that month.[101] By late July, the Revels officers were working again on the revels at West Horsley. But construction of the banqueting house was in charge of Lewis Stocket, Surveyor of the Works, and the revels work on the mask and decoration of the banqueting house was probably under Blagrave's supervision.

Cawarden never returned to the office. He died in August 1559 and was buried in Blechingly church.[102] His wife, Elizabeth, and his friend, Sir William More, were executors of his will.[103] He remembered the officers of the Revels and Tents in the will. To Brian Dodmer he left an annuity of 20 marks from his Blackfriars property. To the indefatigable Richard Leys he left an annuity of 20 marks and 'all such ofal stuff and lumber of tents and other old howses and timber as is now remaining within the Tents.' To Thomas Blagrave, 'my late servant,' who was one of the overseers of the will, he left crossbows, armour, bows, sheaves of arrows, two geldings, and a colt. Cawarden was paid for work on all of the Revels productions from Christmas 1558–9 through 30 September 1559 in the account prepared after his death and filed by Sir William More.[104] More had quite a bit of difficulty settling the estate, especially the affairs of the Office of the Revels about which he was still being harassed by creditors in 1571.[105]

Postscript

The Revels Office after 1559

Chambers observed that the practice of having all the Revels officers hold patents from the Crown after 1545 'bore the promise of administrative complications when the personal relation with the Master had terminated.'[1] There was good evidence of this from the squabbles which erupted all too frequently among the officers in Elizabeth I's reign, but Chambers did not note the more problematic complications which developed when the Master's personal relation with the sovereign had deteriorated.

Cawarden presided over an office from 1544 to 1559 which exhibits both the best and the worst aspects of the Revels organization as it had developed over the course of the century. Early in his reign, Henry VIII created a workable, semi-formal organization by locating production duties in the Tents under the supervision of Richard Gibson and by centring control in his Privy Chamber through the informal appointment of his friend, Sir Henry Guildford, as Master of the Revels. The creation of the Revels Office in 1545 was calculated to centralize compatible duties under Sir Thomas Cawarden. Despite his appointment by patent, Cawarden's position as Gentleman of the Privy Chamber permitted the king's personal oversight of planning and production of the revels. The problems which were later to develop could not have been anticipated at the end of Henry VIII's reign. Changes in the political climate around mid-century and the fact that the Privy Chambers from 1547 to 1603 were different from any imagined in Henry VIII's reign would alter the relations between the sovereign and the Master for the rest of the century. When the structure of the inner circle of the court changed, it became impossible for the sovereign to control the revels in the way that Henry VIII had.

During the reign of Edward VI, actual power was wielded by the king's chief ministers. The centre of power shifted from the Privy Chamber to the council and to the factions which grouped around Somerset and Northumberland. A minister could not control the Revels by word of mouth in the way a king could, but only by letters and warrants from the council. As a result the Revels Office came increasingly to be regarded as other household departments rather than as the chief personal public relations and propaganda instrument of the sovereign. The centralizing tendencies during Northumberland's administration expanded Cawarden's offices into a complex organization in which the Master was preoccupied with coordinating details in offices which worked year-round. By 1552 the office had as its province the production of all scheduled masks, plays, triumphs, and pastimes, the preparations for hunting, the support of receptions and martial exhibitions, the supervision and construction of banqueting houses, and the production of the Lord of Misrule's shows. It was as large and centralized an organization as it was ever to be.

The writer of 'The First Institution' mentioned that Cawarden took the style 'Master' because 'Sergeant' was beneath his dignity as a Gentlemen of the King's Privy Chamber.[2] As the issue itself suggests, the position Cawarden held by patent was one for which the title Sergeant was appropriate, and Northumberland simply capitalized on this by resurrecting the tradition of appointing a Lord of Misrule at Christmas and by ordering the Revels Office to produce Ferrers's entertainments in addition to their own Christmas revels. Ferrers produced revels which accorded with Northumberland's and the council's political agenda and Cawarden and the Revels Office were pushed to the sidelines.[3] Cawarden dutifully complied with Northumberland's requests thereafter.

The accession of two female monarchs, whose reigns dominated the rest of the century, made personal control of the revels from the Privy Chamber impossible. The queen's body servants were women who headed no household offices and wielded no direct power at court. Casual conversations about revels of the kind which undoubtedly characterized Henry VIII's Privy Chamber were now impossible. Discussions with the queen's male attendants in the outer Chamber were conducted in more formal circumstances. Also, the political problems were more complicated in Mary's reign than they were in Edward VI's. Cawarden's politics were radically different from the queen's, and he was under investigation and interrogation by the council or in prison during much of the reign. When he was at court, the queen kept him at a distance. She communicated with him by warrant, letter, or through her Master of the Horse, Sir Henry Jerningham, who was himself not one of her most trusted advisors.

It is unlikely that anyone at the opening of Elizabeth's reign assessed the problems of administering the revels accurately. The breakup of the bureaucracy after Cawarden's death in 1560 appears motivated not so much by an attempt to bring the office closer to the queen as partly by a desire for economy and partly by an attempt to find positions for Elizabeth's supporters. Henry Sackford and John

Tamworth, appointed Masters of the Tents and of the Toils respectively, were members of the queen's Privy Chamber. Sir Thomas Benger, a former auditor at Hatfield, was appointed Master of the Revels.[4] Probably it was hoped that a Master with an accounting background might achieve the economy which had been sought for the past six years, and Benger's difficulties with Mary's council and his unquestioned loyalty to Elizabeth and to high officials in her government probably appeared to be a comfortable enough solution. Despite Benger's initial claims of economy, he did not operate the office as carefully or as scrupulously as Cawarden had.[5] The expenses of the office grew during his tenure as Master. Suspicion and hostility developed between Benger and his under-officers, and his Clerk Comptroller refused to sign his accounts for five years because of what he claimed were overcharges to the queen.[6] The agenda of establishing a new government made it unlikely that attention would be paid to the problems of appointing another Master of the Revels by patent in 1560. However, such attention appears clearly to have been given in 1572.

In the summer of that year Benger died shortly before Burghley was appointed Lord Treasurer and Sussex succeeded as Lord Chamberlain. Internal dissension in the Revels Office, the fact that no economy had been achieved, and charges about Benger's mismanagement were apparently behind the initial decision to postpone the appointment of a new Master.[7] Memoranda were written in 1573–4 by interested officers which identified problems to be redressed in the office. Two of these memoranda, 'The First Institution' and Blagrave's 'Platte of Orders,' appear to have provided the basis for reform experiments throughout the rest of Elizabeth's reign. Several ideas were offered for reorganization. The writer of 'The First Institution' suggests, for example, that if the Revels were rejoined to the Tents and Toils, as they had been under Cawarden, some economy could be expected. It is possible that a variant of this suggestion had already been tried when in 1572–3 the office was administered jointly by Henry Sackford, Master of the Tents, and Sir John Fortescue, Keeper of the Great Wardrobe, supervised by Sussex and Leicester.[8] However, the traditional ties among these offices and the pressure to produce respectable revels for the French embassy in that year made this the most obvious temporary arrangement.

Between 1573 and 1578 the office was overseen by Sussex and administered by Thomas Blagrave, Clerk of the Revels, who was appointed to the 'execucon of the Masters office' by yearly commissions.[9] This appears to have been an experiment in reorganization rather than simply the result of postponing a decision on the appointment of a new Master. No Lord Chamberlain had taken such a personal interest in the office before. Blagrave was required to 'thoroughly' advertise Sussex of everything he did.[10] The appointment of an acting Master of Blagrave's status under these conditions meant, in effect, that the revels were controlled by the Lord Chamberlain.[11] The line of control is only superficially similar to that in Mary's reign when the Master of the Horse relayed messages between Cawarden and the queen. In contrast to Jerningham, Leicester and Sussex were members of Elizabeth's inner circle of advisors. The fact that Sussex and Leicester were overseers of the office in 1572 and that Sussex supervised the revels from 1573 to 1578 suggests that these changes were designed to effect more direct control by the queen's advisors who were also members of the council. The production function, earlier assigned to Yeoman level supervisors like Gibson, Farlyon, and Bridges, was vested in Blagrave and the quasi-political function, performed by Sir Henry Guildford and Sir Thomas Cawarden, was vested in Sussex.

Because of his suspicion of the motives of the officers in writing the memoranda of the early 1570s, Chambers misunderstood the point of the recommendation by the writer of 'The First Institution' to add a Sergeant to the office. He was convinced that the weak point in the organization was the Master because he was a courtier who knew less about the operation of the office than his staff. This seems to have been the opinion of Blagrave who wanted the Mastership for himself, but it was not shared by the writer of 'The First Institution.' His suggestion to add a Sergeant was intended to separate the Master entirely from production duties, a measure which hardly promised economy. He wanted a Master with 'Countenaunce and creditt with the Prince,' for he understood that economy was only one problem and that the main purpose of the revels was to serve the interests of the sovereign. The problem from his point of view was not that the Master was a courtier, but that he was not enough of a courtier. The Master had become too closely identified with his bureaucratic position and too distant from the centre of power. However potentially economical such an arrangement might be, it was deficient in satisfying the central aim the office was created to serve.

Changes in the Revels Office from the late 1570s to the end of Elizabeth's reign were oriented toward achieving economy, toward making practical political use of the Master, and toward bringing him closer to the centre of power. Edmund Tilney, who was appointed Master in 1579, derived his 'countenance' from his family connections. He was raised in the household of Lord William Howard, first Lord Chamberlain of Elizabeth I. He was connected to the Howards through the marriage of his grand-aunt, Agnes, dowager Duchess of Norfolk. He was a cousin of Charles Howard, later Lord Admiral and Earl of Nottingham, who preferred him to the position of Master. And, he was a distant cousin of Elizabeth I.[12] The fact that Tilney dealt directly with Sussex, Leicester, Burghley, Walsingham, and the queen in discussing plans for reorganizing the office reflects his credit at court.

The moves in the direction of bringing the Master closer to the centre of power are evident from the fact that the names of Elizabeth's circle of advisors as well as her own keep cropping up in relation to Tilney's appointment and in approving his plans for the reorganization of the office and of the revels at court. The moves in the direction of economy had the effect of making the Revels Office responsible for a set number of entertainments at court each year, principally plays which had always been far less expensive to produce than masks.[13] In contrast to other Tudor and Stuart monarchs, Elizabeth began to order very few masks after 1583. Her image as patron of the revels at court from 1583 to 1591 was principally established through the use of her new royal acting company which had been chosen by Tilney at Walsingham's instigation. This company was not invited to court after 1591, and by 1595 the acting companies of Elizabeth's cousins and close advisors, Henry Carey, Lord Chamberlain, and Charles Howard, Lord Admiral, dominated her revels until the end of the reign. Tilney was obligated to both of these men. The Lord Chamberlain supervised the Revels Office, and, as his cousin and benefactor, Howard had personal claims to Tilney's loyalty. Such personal control appears as the concomitant of plans to make practical political use of the Master. By the commission of 1581 the Master was made responsible for censoring plays for public performance, for licensing theatrical companies, and, by 1606, for licensing plays for publication. The minor officers of the Revels had no part in these duties. The Master issued licenses and injunctions himself or with the help of deputies and servants, and he derived a considerable income from these activities. Since the Master answered directly to the queen's circle of advisors, censorship of the public drama was concentrated close to Elizabeth. The commission as censor and licenser was issued to Tilney shortly before the creation of the new Queen's Players. Both appear to have been part of a move to assert the queen's image at court and at the same time to control criticism on the public stage.[14] Not all went smoothly. Tilney was at odds for years with his underofficers in the Revels over the imposition of Burghley's 'composition,' as it is called, which allotted a fixed sum of money for the ordinary production expenses and wages in the office. There is also evidence that Tilney was at odds with at least one of the Lords Chamberlain over an uncertain matter.[15]

By the opening of James I's reign, the role of the Revels Office in court entertainments had been restricted to producing a set number of plays each year and to contributing support for other entertainments and spectacles. The Master had been drawn closer to the centre of power by his ties to Elizabeth's advisors and given the political job of controlling the public theatres and drama.[16] The accession of a male to the throne once again made possible personal control of the revels through the kings' close associates in the Privy Chamber. And James did just that. The king's style of government was reminiscent of Henry VIII's, and he projected his image as the centre of the court and government immediately. He took over patronage of the Lord Chamberlain's acting company and Prince Henry took over that of the Lord Admiral's company. The Revels Office was mainly concerned with producing plays by the new King's Players, Prince's Players, and other royal companies at court and with contributing production services to masks and other entertainments. The masks, however, were now under the supervision of high-ranking courtiers who were personally close to the king, and the Office of the Works was more intimately involved in their production than the Revels. This new organization for the production of revels at court, of course, did not promote economy. Quite the reverse. The Jacobean masks were the most expensive revels to be mounted at court since the 1520s, and were part of a pattern of extravagant expenditure which precipitated a financial crisis in 1617. Both the expense and the means of production of the revels were reminiscent of the early part of Henry VIII's reign, although the Master of the Revels did not have the same status. There was an attempt to draw the Master somewhat closer to the centre of power. Within a month of the grant of his patent, George Buck was knighted and made a Gentleman of the Privy Chamber. Sir Henry Herbert, deputy and later Master of the Revels from 1623, was also appointed to the king's Privy Chamber, but by this time the real centre of power was James's Bed Chamber.[17] During the Stuart period the Masters were censors and licensers of the drama and producers of many of the revels at court, but none were on personal terms with the king and none had the status of Guildford or of Cawarden under Henry VIII.

PART II

Calendar of Court Revels, Spectacles, Plays, and Entertainments

The following calendar consists of notices of the revels, spectacles, plays, and entertainments held to celebrate traditional feasts, dynastic, state, and other occasions. The calendar is constructed principally from financial records, for a discussion of which see Principal Sources in Appendix 1. The financial records are supplemented by information from a variety of manuscript and printed sources, the citations for which are included within each entry (see Abbreviations). Dates listed in the calendar are mainly those on which payments were made from treasuries or purses, not those of performances. Exceptions are noted and cross-referenced. Regular payments as part of salary to performers (the royal troupes of players, minstrels, etc.), payments for performances by minstrels, tumblers, jugglers, fools, and singers (with the exception of certain performances by the Chapel Royal), and payments by the sovereigns for private recreation (gaming, gambling, sports, etc.) have been excluded.

Extracts from the financial accounts and records of the various purses and treasuries provide only a skeletal framework for a calendar of court entertainments, and it is by no means a complete skeleton. Accounts do not survive to document all of the years in the period, and because of the complicated changes in finance there is always the possibility that entertainments were put on which are not documented in any of the extant records. Further, there is a more specific problem in extracting information from these accounts.

While payments for revels and spectacles are usually unambiguous, payments for the performance of plays are not. The word 'play' is used in a variety of senses in the Chamber accounts. In Henry VII's Chamber accounts, for example, there are payments to 'mynstrels that pleyed,' 'to the 'pleyer' at tennis, to the king to 'pley at cards' and 'at dice,' and to those for 'pleying the mourice daunce.' Probably because the king read and signed them himself, the entries in Henry VII's Chamber accounts are not elaborate, since the king or one of his high officers would have been personally acquainted with the reasons for the payment. Payments for performances usually are entered in the following forms: for 'ij pleyes in the hall,' to the 'kinges pleyers' or 'princes pleyers,' to 'them that pleyed afore the king,' to 'pleyers in the hall.' Even these entries are not without ambiguity, and it is desirable to use corroborating evidence.

Later in the period, entries in the Chamber accounts tend to be more specific. Perhaps the reason for the specificity is that Henry VIII did not personally review and sign his accounts, and so more explanation would be needed to justify the expenses to the bureaucrats who processed the records but who may not have personally attended performances. The entry in the Chamber account in January 1520, for payment 'to Mr Cornisshe for playing two interludes with his children before the king,' is about as clear and unambiguous as these entries get. Other entries, while specific in some details, are ambiguous in others. For example, in January 1512 a payment is entered to four players that came out of Suffolk and played 'afore the lorde Steward in the kinges hall on Monday nyght.' The entry does not make it absolutely certain that what we would call drama is indicated. There are other occasions in which entries take similar forms. In January 1548, an entry was made for payment 'to Richard Bower for playing before the Kinges Maiestie with the Children of the Chappel,' and in January 1541 an entry was made for payment to 'Mr Crane for playing before the King with the Children of the Chapel.' Corroborating evidence in the form of a Revels account exists to show that the latter entry does refer to a play, which was produced by the Revels Office (Folger Library, MS. Lb 41, fol. 1). On that same day, entries for rewards are also made to the King's Players, the Queen's Players, to the Prince's Players, and to the Duke of Suffolk's Players 'for playing in the kinges hall on Twelfth Even.' On those occasions for which there is corroborating evidence, entries in the Chamber accounts in one or another of the above forms have proved to indicate the performance of a play.

Caution is nevertheless advised in handling this evidence. It would be prudent not to assume that what we would call drama is indicated every time the word 'play' is used in the Chamber accounts. However, given the correspondence between entries for such payments and evidence from other sources in particular instances, it is reasonable to conclude that a reward to one of the royal or other recognized playing companies at the major feasts and at dynastic and state occasions is more than likely an indication of the performance of drama. There are other occasions when narrative evidence exists to document the performance of plays at court which is not corroborated by evidence from the financial accounts. Because rewards were occasionally paid from a variety of purses and treasuries, the lack of such corroboration does not necessarily indicate that the narrative is incorrect.

No text, musical score, choreography, or design survives for any court revel in the early Tudor period. We are dependent for our understanding of some of their details on Revels accounts. Richard Gibson's accounts, one of our principal sources of information for much of Henry VIII's reign, are the most detailed and descriptive accounts from the entire century. Such accounts, however, resist precise interpretation, and care must be exercised in evaluating the evidence based on an understanding of the purpose of the documents. It must be kept in mind that accounts of this kind are concerned principally with justifying expenses, not with a careful exposition of form and theme.

We are dependent for our understanding of form and theme principally on narrative evidence. Narrative descriptions of revels, spectacles, plays, and entertainments are provided by ambassadors' letters, by heralds' reports, by chroniclers, and by a few other miscellaneous sources. It is rare to have more than one narrative to document an entertainment or spectacle, and bias or ignorance takes its toll in the reliability of these reports. As with the primary documents, it is important to consider the purpose behind the narrative to assess the weight to be attached to the observations. Heralds are concerned with order and form in ceremony and the martial exhibitions, not in the revels. Edward Hall, to whom we owe most of the narratives of Henry VIII's revels that have come down to us, and who may have had access to Gibson's Revels accounts, was a court chronicler writing for the king. He cared little about precise terms and definitions. His descriptions of the revels are illustrations of the magnificence of Henry VIII's court, not a treatise on the development of form and theme. Ambassadors are concerned with intelligence information, and while their perspective may be helpful in viewing court entertainments from the outside, their tendency is to describe entertainments by using terminology familiar from their own experience in continental courts, and to interpret them in political and diplomatic terms. To complicate matters further, the interplay between recognizable form and innovation which characterized the revels during this entire period prompted contemporary English witnesses to grasp at a variety of imprecise terms to describe them.

Because of the variety of entertainments listed in the calendar and the differences in the sources which document them, some inconsistencies in the entries are unavoidable. The entries are arranged chronologically by year, month, and day. Locating payments for revels, spectacles, plays, and other entertainments is facilitated by bold face type. Each entry abstracts or summarizes the primary source(s) which document the event(s). The formulaic quality of many of the entries reflects that quality in the original sources, as does the spelling of proper nouns even though these do not always appear in quotation marks. When documentary evidence exists to locate an event the place name is listed in the entry. Calendars, abstracts, extracts, and printings of the primary documents listed below can be found in Appendix 1.

HENRY VII
1485

October

23   Sir Richard Guildford, Master of the Armoury, was issued an imprest of 100 marks for the coronation jousts: PRO, E404/79, no. 90.

30   The tradition of a play by the Gentlemen of the Chapel at coronations mentioned in a warrant from Queen Mary on 26 September 1553 (Loseley Manor Documents, vol. V, no. 6) cannot be verified for Henry VII's coronation. *The Divill and Rychard,* an interlude supposedly performed by Paul's clerks and boys for the coronation is a forgery by William Ireland: J.W. Robinson, 'An Interlude or Mystery Play by William Ireland, 1795,' *Comparative Drama,* 13 (1979): 235–1.

November

13   **Coronation tournament** at Westminster: BL, Egerton MS. 985, fols. 46v–8 (articles). See 23 October and 9 December 1485.

18   Richard Pudsey was issued £20, presumably an imprest for the Twelfth Night disguising: PRO, E404/79, no. 72.

December

9   Sir Richard Guildford was paid £50 2*s.* 2*d.* for the coronation joust: PRO, E404/79, no. 58.

Christmas

25 Dec.⟨ ⟩ 6 Jan.   The play by the Gentlemen of the Chapel mentioned by Wallace, *Evolution,* pp. 12–13, is probably an overzealous interpretation of Collier's remarks, *HEDP* (1831), I: 36.

1486

January

6   **Disguising.** See 18 November 1485 and 3 March 1486.

18   No narratives of the 'magnificent festivities' for the wedding of Henry VII and Elizabeth of York survive: Bernardus Andreas, *De Regalibus Conviviis et Torneamentis in ipsa coronatione regio luxu celebratis,* printed in *Memorials,* pp. 36–7, survives as an introductory fragment.

March

3   Richard Pudsey was paid a reward of £10 for his labour and in repayment for material provided for the Twelfth Night disguising: PRO, E404/79, no. 31.

March–June
The king was entertained on his progress from 13 March to 5 June with receptions, pageants, and plays at Bristol, Hereford, Worcester, and York: BL, Cotton MS. Julius B. XII, fols. 8v–21, printed in *Collectanea* IV: 185–203. For other sources see McGee and Meagher, 'Checklist,' pp. 35–6.

September
21 **Joust**. Sir Richard Guildford was paid £16 19*s*. 10*d*. for 'oure last Iustes' (place name obliterated in writ): PRO, E404/79, no. 4; E403/2558, fol. 4v [for the birth of Arthur in September? for the Scots ambassadors at Eltham in June?].
24 **Play**. Warton, *HEP,* pp. 456–7, records that *Christi Descensus ad Infernos* was performed by the choir boys of St Swithun's and Hyde Abbey on Sunday (24th) at dinner for the christening of Arthur at Winchester Cathedral.

November
22 Richard Pudsey was paid £40 for 'thordaynyng and preparing of disguysing*es*' for Christmas: PRO, E404/79, no. 13.

Christmas
25 Dec.⟨ ⟩ 6 Jan. **Disguisings** at Greenwich: BL, Cotton MS. Julius B. XII, fol. 24. See 22 November 1486 and 23 March 1487.

1487

March
23 Richard Pudsey was paid £7 on his balance for the production of 'certeyn Disguysing*es* for our pleasur and for Rewarding of players': PRO, E404/79, no. 109.

October
5 Sir Richard Guildford was issued an imprest of 100 marks to prepare jousts for the queen's coronation in November: PRO, E404/79, no. 38.

November
25? **Coronation joust**. See 5 October 1487.

Christmas
25 Dec.⟨ ⟩ 6 Jan. 'many And dyue*rs* Playes' at Greenwich: BL, Cotton MS. Julius B. XII, fol. 46v.

1488

January
1   **Disguising** at Greenwich: BL, Cotton MS. Julius B. XII, fol. 46v.
6   Banquet and carolling by the Chapel Royal in the Hall at Greenwich: BL, Cotton MS. Julius B. XII, fol. 47v.

Christmas
25 Dec.⟨ ⟩ 6 Jan.   No entertainments are recorded at Shene where the king and queen kept Christmas: BL, Cotton MS. Julius B. XII, fol. 52v.

1489

Christmas
25 Dec.⟨ ⟩ 6 Jan.   **Abbot of Misrule** and **plays** at Greenwich: BL, Cotton MS. Julius B. XII, fols. 63, 64r–v.

1490

February
2   **Play** at Whitehall at night before the king and queen: BL, Cotton MS. Julius B. XII, fols. 64v–5.

Michaelmas Term.
Richard Pudsey was issued £40 in two instalments to produce disguisings at Christmas: PRO, E36/124, pp. 162, 167.

Christmas
25 Dec.⟨ ⟩ 6 Jan.   **Disguisings.** See Michaelmas Term 1490.

1491

December
24   William Ringley was issued an imprest of 100s. as **Lord of Misrule:** BL, Additional MS. 7099, fol. 2.

1492

January
1   **Players.** The 'Lorde of Oxon pleyers' were rewarded 20s.: BL, Additional MS. 7099, fol. 2.

May

1–2   **Tournament:** BL, Cotton MS. Vitellius A. XVI, fol. 145v, printed in C. L. Kingsford, ed., *Chronicles of London* (Oxford: Clarendon Press, 1905), 197; Guildhall Library, London MS. 3313, fol. 224, printed in *Great Chronicle,* p. 247; BL, Harleian MS. 69, fols. 3v–4 (articles and names of participants), fol. 7 (challenge). See 7 May and 17 June 1492.

7   The Clerk of the Works was paid £24 10s. 2d. for making the lists at Shene: BL, Additional MS. 7099, fol. 4.

June

17   'Master Gyfford' [Sir Richard Guildford] was paid £9 6s. for arms for the jousts [those held in May?]: BL, Additional MS. 7099, fol. 5.

July

8   **Maygame.** The maidens of Lambeth were paid 10s. for 'a May': BL, Additional MS. 7099, fol. 6.

October

2   The minstrels that 'pleyed in the Swan' [the ship in which Henry VII travelled to Calais where he remained from 2 October to 17 November or December] were paid 13s. 4d.: BL, Additional MS. 7099, fol. 7.

24   William Ringley was issued an imprest of 100s. as **Abbot of Misrule:** BL, Additional MS. 7099, fol. 8.

1493

January

6   **Musical performance?** William Newark, Master of the Children of the Chapel, was paid 20s. for making a song: BL, Additional MS. 7099, fol. 8.

7   **Players.** The 'Lorde of Northumberlande pleyers' were rewarded 20s.: BL, Additional MS. 7099, fol. 8.

March

2   **Cock-fighting.** A reward of 20s. was made to those who brought 'cokkes' at Shrovetide to Westminster: BL, Additional MS. 7099, fol. 8.

June

Henry VII saw the Corpus Christi plays at Coventry: Bodleian Library, MS. Top. Warwickshire d.4 (31431), fol. 13b, printed in R.W. Ingram, ed., Records of Early English Drama: *Coventry* (Toronto: University of Toronto Press, 1981),

77; William Dugdale, *The Antiquities of Warwickshire Illustrated*, 2nd ed. William Thomas (London, 1730), I: 149, col. a.

September

24   **Bull-baiting.** A reward of 10*s.* was paid to 'hym that had his bull baytedd': BL, Additional MS. 7099, fol. 12.

November

12   **Prophecy.** A reward of 13*s.* 4*d.* was paid to 'one Cornysshe for a prophecy' [in connection with the disguising on Twelfth Night?]: BL, Additional MS. 7099, fol. 13.

16   Walter Alwyn was paid £13 6*s.* 8*d.* for the 'revells at Estermes' [an imprest for the Twelfth Night disguising?]: BL, Additional MS. 7099, fol. 13.

1494

January

1   **Players.** 'iiij pleyers of Essex' were rewarded 20*s.* and the 'pleyers of Wymbone Mynystre' were rewarded 20*s.*: BL, Additional MS. 7099, fol. 13.

2   **Morris dance.** 40*s.* was paid for 'pleying of the mourice daunce': BL, Additional MS. 7099, fol. 14.

6   **Pageant-disguising** *(St. George and the Dragon).* BL, Additional MS. 6113, fols. 168–9; BL, Cotton MS. Vitellius A. XVI, fol. 148v, printed in C.L. Kingsford, ed., *Chronicles of London* (Oxford: Clarendon Press, 1905), 200; Guildhall Library, London MS. 3313, fols. 229v–31v, printed in *Great Chronicle*, pp. 251–2; PRO, SP46/123, fol. 56. Richard Doland, Clerk of the Works, was paid £28 3*s.* 5 3/4*d.* for building degrees or scaffolds in Westminster Hall for the disguising: PRO, E405/79, memb. 1d, transcribed in *King's Works*, IV.ii: 286. See 16 November 1493 and 15 February 1494.

Players. The French players were rewarded 20*s.* and the King's Players were rewarded 53*s.* 4*d.*: BL, Additional MS. 7099, fol. 14.

February

15   Walter Alwyn was paid £14 13*s.* 4*d.* 'in full payment for the disguysing made at Christenmes': BL, Additional MS. 7099, fol. 15.

June

1   **Disguising.** 'Peche' [Sir John Peche?] received £26 14*s.* 'for the disguising': BL, Additional MS. 7099, fol. 18.

October

31 A payment of £66 13*s.* 4*d.* was paid to the challengers and the same amount to the defenders at the jousts honouring Prince Henry's creation as Duke of York: BL, Additional MS. 7099, fol. 20. See 9 November 1494.

November

9, 11, 13, 22 **Tournament** at Westminster honouring Prince Henry who had been created Duke of York on 29 October: BL, Cotton MS. Julius B. XII, fols. 91–110, printed in *LP Richard III and Henry VII,* I: 388–404; BL, Cotton MS. Vitellius A. XVI, fols. 150–2, printed in C.L. Kingsford, ed., *Chronicles of London* (Oxford: Clarendon Press, 1905), 201–3; BL, Additional MS. 33735, fols. 5v–6 (copy of challenge); Guildhall Library, London MS. 3313, fols. 234–5v, printed in *Great Chronicle,* pp. 254–6; BL, Harleian MS. 69, fols. 6r–v (copy of challenge), fols. 7v–8 (articles), fols. 21v–2 (copy of challenge); College of Arms, MS. M 6, fols. 58v–9, printed in *Antiquarian Repertory,* I: 146–8. See 31 October 1494.

29 Jaques Haulte was paid £20 'for the disguysing': BL, Additional MS. 7099, fol. 21.

December

31 **Players.** 'iij pleyers of Wycombe' were rewarded 13*s.* 4*d.*: BL, Additional MS. 7099, fol. 22.

Christmas

25 Dec. ⟨ ⟩ 6 Jan. **Disguising.** See 29 November 1494 and 13 February 1495. The king kept Christmas at Greenwich: BL, Cotton MS. Vitellius A. XVI, fol. 152.

1495

January

4 **Players.** The French players were rewarded 40*s.*: BL, Additional MS. 7099, fol. 22.

February

13 Jaques Haulte was paid £13 10*s.* 6*d.* 'in full payment of his bille for his disguysings': BL, Additional MS. 7099, fol. 23.

November

27 Jaques Haulte received £10 'in *part*ye of payment for the disguysing*es*': PRO, E101/414/6, fol. 9.

December

23   Jaques Haulte received £10 for the disguisings: PRO, E101/414/6, fol. 13.

31   **Plays.** 26*s.* 8*d.* was paid for 'ij pleyes in the hall': PRO, E101/414/6, fol. 13v.

Christmas

25 Dec.⟨ ⟩ 6 Jan.   **Disguisings.** See 27 November and 23 December 1495, 24–9 January 1496.

1496

January

1–2   **Players.** The 'pleyers of Oxon.' were paid 13*s.* 4*d.* The 'pleyers of Essex' were paid 20*s.* The 'pleyers on Saterday at night [2 January]' were paid 13*s.* 4*d.*: PRO, E101/414/6, fol. 14v.

3–8   **Players.** The 'pleyers on monday [4 January]' were rewarded 13*s.* 4*d.* The King's Players were rewarded 13*s.* 4*d.*: PRO, E101/414/6, fol. 15.

10–15   William Ringley was rewarded 40*s.* as **Lord of Misrule**: PRO, E101/414/6, fol. 15v.

24–9   Jaques Haulte received £6 17*s.* 6*d.* 'in full payment for the disguysing at Cristenmes': PRO, E101/414/6, fol. 16v.

February

1–24   **Play?** Henry Medwall's *Fulgens and Lucrece* was probably performed, at Cardinal Morton's before the Flemish and Spanish ambassadors: Kipling, *Honour,* p. 21

7–9   **Disguising.** £40 was paid to 'my lorde Suffolk my lorde Essex my lorde William and otheres for the disguising' [at Candlemas?]: PRO, E101/414/6, fol. 18.

April

1   **Players.** The King's Players were paid 20*s.*: PRO, E101/414/6, fol. 25v.

June

29   **Revels?** According to Collier, *HEDP* [1831], I: 39–40, Hugo Standish, notary, was paid 'ad certos revelliones' at Westminster.

December

2   Jaques Haulte was paid £10 'for the disguysing': PRO, E101/414/6, fol. 54v.

31   **Musical performance?** The Children of the Chapel were paid 40*s.*, their ordinary reward for singing *Gloria in excelsis Deo* on Christmas Day, and

'Cornyshe of the Kinges Chapell' was paid 40*s.* for an unspecified service or performance: PRO, E101/414/6, fol. 56v.

Christmas
25 Dec. ⟨ ⟩ 6 Jan. **Disguising.** See 2 December 1496 and 27 January 1497.

1497

January
2–5 **Players.** The 'pleyers in the hall' were paid 13*s.* 4*d.* and, again, the 'pleyers in the hall' were rewarded 20*s.* 6*d.*: PRO, E101/414/6, fol. 58.
7 **Players.** The King's Players were rewarded 20*s.*: PRO, E101/414/6, fol. 58v.
27 Jaques Haulte was paid £8 17*s.* 8*d.* 'in full payment for the disguysing': PRO, E101/414/6, fol. 60.

February
19–23 **Players.** The King's Players were rewarded 20*s.*: PRO, E101/414/6, fol. 61v.

March
17 One of the King's Players was rewarded 20*s.*: PRO, E101/414/6, fol. 63v.

December
3–5 Jaques Haulte was paid £13 6*s.* 8*d.* 'for the disguysing': PRO, E101/414/16, fol. 7.
31 **Players.** The Players of London were paid 13*s.* 4*d.* and the 'pleyers of Essex' were rewarded 20*s.*: PRO, E101/414/16, fol. 10.

Christmas
25 Dec. ⟨ ⟩ 6 Jan. **Disguising.** See 3–5 December 1497 and 1 February 1498.

1498

January
1 **Players.** The King's Players were rewarded 20*s.*: PRO, E101/414/16, fol. 10v.
12 **Players.** The 'lorde of Oxon pleyers' were paid 13*s.* 4*d.* The 'pleyers of Essex' were rewarded 13*s.* 4*d.* The 'pleyers of Wycombe' were paid 13*s.* 4*d.* The King's Players were rewarded 20*s.*: PRO, E101/414/16, fol. 12.

February

1   Jaques Haulte was paid £14 14*s.* 2 1/2*d.* 'for the disguysing': PRO, E101/414/16, fol. 15.

17   **Musical entertainment?** 'Streme of the Kinges Chapell' was paid 40*s.*: PRO, E101/414/16, fol. 17.

August

5–11   **Bear-baiting.** The 'lorde of Oxon bereward' was paid 4*s.*, and 'one that held my Lorde of Oxon bere' was paid 6*s.* 8*d.*: PRO, E101/414/16, fol. 23.

November

11–16   Jaques Haulte was paid £20 'for the disguising': PRO, E101/414/16, fol. 47.

December

28   **Players.** The Players of London were rewarded 10*s.*: PRO, E101/414/16, fol. 51.

31   **Players.** The 'pleyers of Essex' were rewarded 10*s.* and the 'pleyers of Wicombe' were rewarded 10*s.*: PRO, E101/414/16, fol. 51v.

Christmas

25 Dec. ⟨ ⟩ 6 Jan.   **Disguising.** See 11–16 November 1498 and 3–5 March 1499.

1499

January

2–4   **Players.** The Prince's Players were rewarded 13*s.* 4*d.*: PRO, E101/414/16, fol. 52.

5–11   **Players.** The 'lorde of Essex pleyers' were paid 13*s.* 4*d.*: PRO, E101/414/16, fol. 53.

February

15   **Players.** The Prince's Players were rewarded 13*s.* 4*d.*: PRO, E101/414/16, fol. 56.

March

3–5   Jaques Haulte was paid £32 18*s.* 6*d.* 'in full payment for the disguysing at Cristenmes': PRO, E101/414/16, fol. 58.

24   Vincent, the armourer, was paid 100*s.* 'in party of payment for v jousting harnesse': PRO, E101/414/16, fol. 76v.

May

23   **Barriers** at Greenwich? (See 23 May 1504).

June

6   **Maygame, puppet players.** 4s. was paid 'for the maygame at Greenwich.' The players 'with mamettes [puppets]' were paid £4: PRO, E101/414/16, fol. 65.

December

29   [William] Ringley was rewarded 20s. [as **Lord of Misrule?**]. **Players.** The Players of London were rewarded 10s.: PRO, E101/415/3, fol. 4.

Christmas

25 Dec. ⟨ ⟩ 6 Jan.   **Disguising.** See 14 February 1500.

1500

February

1   **Players.** The King's Players were rewarded 40s.: PRO, E101/415/3, fol. 11.

14   Jaques Haulte was paid £8 10s. 6d. 'for the disguising in Cristenmes last passed': PRO, E101/415/3, fol. 12.

March

13   **Musical entertainment?** The Gentlemen of the Chapel were paid 40s. William Cornish was paid 40s. in reward: PRO, E101/415/3, fol. 14v.

May

8   The king was in Calais from 8 May to 16 June.

September

30   Jaques Haulte was paid 22s. 8d. 'opon his bill.' Jaques Haulte was paid 13s. 4d. 'for ij mynystrelles': PRO, E101/415/3, fol. 33.

December

31   **Musical or dramatic entertainment?.** William Newark, Master of the Children of the Chapel, was paid 53s. 4d. 'for Saint Nicholas' [a performance in connection with the Childrens' annual St Nicholas Bishop ceremony?]: PRO, E101/415/3, fol. 40.

1501

January

8   William Ringley was paid 100*s*. 'for hym and his company' [as **Lord of Misrule?**]. **Players.** The King's Players were rewarded 40*s*.: PRO, E101/415/3, fol. 42.

Undated payments this month made during the king's progress: **Players.** The King's Players were rewarded 13*s*. 4*d*. and the Prince's Players were rewarded 20*s*.: PRO, E101/415/3, fol. 48.

April

9   The Duke of Buckingham was paid £133 6*s*. 8*d*. for the jousts: PRO, E101/415/3, fol. 50.

11   The Earl of Suffolk was paid £50, the Earl of Essex £33 6*s*. 8*d*., Lord Harington £25, and Lord William of Devonshire £25 for the jousts: PRO, E101/415/3, fol. 50.

23   Sir Roland [Vielvill] was paid £40 for the jousts. PRO, E101/415/3, fol. 51.

May

21   Sir George Herbert was paid £40 for the jousts: PRO, E101/415/3, fol. 53v.

28   Sir Edward Darell was paid £40 for the jousts: PRO, E101/415/3, fol. 54.

Tournament or practice? at the Tower: Thomas Warley's Works account, BL, Egerton MS. 2358, fols. 12–23, records construction of a balcony within the ordnance house for royal spectators.

June

30   Lord Berners was paid £50 for the jousts. Jaques Haulte was paid 53*s*. 7 1/2*d*. 'opon ij billes.' John Atkinson was paid £20 'for certain stuff to be bought for Jakes Haulte': PRO, E101/415/3, fols. 57v–8.

July

16   John Atkinson was paid £10 'for silkes to be bought for the disguysing': PRO, E101/415/3, fol. 59v.

23   John Atkinson was paid £34 17*s*. 4*d*. 'in full payment of his Rekenynges for the disguysinges': PRO, E101/415/3, fol. 60.

31   John Atkinson was paid £24 10*s*. 8*d*. 'opon his boke': PRO, E101/415/3, fol. 60v.

August

6   £10 was paid to 'Cornyshe for a disguysing.' **Players.** The 'pleyers at myles Ende' were paid 3*s*. 4*d*.: PRO, E101/415/3, fol. 61v.

18 John Atkinson was paid £10 'apon a prest': PRO, E101/415/3, fol. 62v.

22–3 William Cornish was paid £10 'for disguysing.' John Atkinson was paid £20 'for an other disguysing': PRO, E101/415/3, fol. 63v.

31 John Atkinson was paid £6 13s. 4d. 'for John Englishe.' 66s. 8d. was paid 'for the frame of the tentt that Sir Charles and Master Comptroller [Sir Richard Guildford] hath devised': PRO, E101/415/3, fol. 64v.

September

8 John Atkinson was paid £25 'for the tentt.' Cornish was paid £10 for the 'disguising.' John English was paid £6 13s. 4d. for a 'pagient.' John van Delf was paid £40 18s. 8d. for 'The Rest of the Iacquettes' and £25 16s. 2d. 'for the brodering of the same' [for a disguising?]: PRO, E101/415/3, fol. 65v.

20–1 Cornish was paid £10 for 'his pagent.' John Atkinson received £79 9s. 8d. 'in full payment of his rekenyng vnto this day': PRO, E101/415/3, fols. 67r–v.

October

5 John Atkinson was paid £73 6s. 8d. 'by bille': PRO, E101/415/3, fol. 69.

15 **Morris dance.** 6s. 8d. was paid 'to theym that daunced to mores daunce': PRO, E101/415/3, fol. 70.

29 John Atkinson was paid £53 3s. 10 1/2d. 'apon a bille for the disguysinges': PRO, E101/415/3, fol. 72.

November

3 Cornish was paid £20 'for his iij pagenttes.' John English was paid £6 13s. 4d. 'for his pagent': PRO, E101/415/3, fol. 72v.

18, 22, 24, 25 **Tournament (joust, tourney, barriers, pageant-cars)** at Westminster to celebrate the wedding of Arthur and Katherine on 14 November: College of Arms, MS. M 13bis, fols. 51–60, printed in Kipling, *Receyt,* pp. 52–68, and in *Antiquarian Repertory,* II: 296–311; College of Arms, MS. Vincent no. 25, fols. 108–42v (copy of M 13bis); BL, Harleian MS. 69, fols. 28v–35 (copy of M 13bis); College of Arms, MS. M 3, fol. 24v, printed in Kipling, *Receyt,* pp. 97–102; College of Arms, MS. M 3, fol. 25v (tournament cheque); Archives of Simancas, MS. P.R. 54–14, fols. 5–8, collated with BL, Additional MS. 46455, fols. 4–6, printed in Kipling, *Receyt,* pp. 103–7; BL, Cotton MS. Vitellius A. XVI, fols. 197–9, printed in C.L. Kingsford, ed., *Chronicles of London* (Oxford: Clarendon Press, 1905), 250–3; Guildhall Library, London MS. 3313, fols. 288v–92, printed in *Great Chronicle,* pp. 312–15. £250 was spent by the Office of the Works in laying out the tiltyard and in building the scaffold for the king and queen: BL, Egerton MS. 2358, fols. 24–42.

19   **Pageant-disguising** (ship, castle, and mount): College of Arms, MS. M 13*bis*, fols. 52v–3v, printed in Kipling, *Receyt*, pp. 55–8; BL, Harleian MS. 69, fols. 29v–30 (copy of M 13*bis*). See payments June 1501 – January 1502.

20   Whiting was paid £6 13*s*. 4*d*. 'for the Kinges standing in the Chepeside' [the scaffold from which the king viewed Katherine's entry into London on the 12th]: PRO, E101/415/3, fol. 74.

21   **Interlude and pageant-disguising** (lantern and arbour): College of Arms, MS. M 13*bis*, fols. 54v–5, printed in Kipling, *Receyt*, pp. 59–60; BL, Harleian MS. 69, fols. 30v–1v (copy of M 13*bis*). See payments June 1501 – January 1502.

25   **Pageant-disguising** (fertile mount and arid mount): College of Arms, MS. M 13*bis*, fols. 58v–60, printed in Kipling, *Receyt*, pp. 66–8; BL, Harleian MS. 69, fols. 33v–4 (copy of M 13*bis*). See payments June 1501 – January 1502.

28   **Pageant-disguising** (chapel): College of Arms, MS. M 13*bis*, fols. 64–5, printed in Kipling, *Receyt*, pp. 75–6; BL, Harleian MS. 69, fols. 34v–5. See payments June 1501 – January 1502.

1502

January

7   **Players.** The 'pleyers opon xij*th* eve' were paid 13*s*. 4*d*. The King's Players were rewarded 40*s*. John English 'the pleyer' was paid 10*s*. John Atkinson was paid £100 'vpon his rekenyng.' William Ringley was paid £6 13*s* 4*d*. as **Abbot of Misrule:** PRO, E101/415/3, fols. 79v–80.

8–28   **Players.** The King's Players were paid 20*s*.: PRO, E101/415/3, fol. 80v.

24, 27   **Tournament** to honour the proxy marriage in London of Princess Margaret and James IV of Scotland: College of Arms, MS. M 1*bis*, fols. 84v–9 (contemporary narrative of the 'fiancialles'); College of Arms, MS. M 1*bis*, fols. 90–5 (another contemporary narrative); Houghton Library, Harvard MS. English 1095 (17th century copy of M 1*bis*), printed in *Collectanea*, IV: 258–64. Hall, p. 494.

25   **Morris dance, pageant-disguising** (lantern at Richmond): College of Arms MS. M 1*bis*, fols. 84v–9, 90–5 (contemporary narratives); Houghton Library, Harvard MS. English 1095 (17th century copy of M 1*bis*), printed in *Collectanea*, IV: 263. See 4 and 18 February 1502.

February

4   **Morris dance.** 'one Lewes [Lewis Adam?]' was paid 53*s*. 4*d*. for a morris dance [in connection with the disguising on 25 January?]. PRO, E101/415/3, fol. 82.

18 John Atkinson was paid £52 10*s*. 9 1/2*d*. 'in full payment of all his Reke-nynges vnto xij*th* tide.' John English and John Atkinson were paid £14 16*s*. 4*d*. 'in full payment of all their rekenynges from xij*th* tide to this day': PRO, E101/415/3, fol. 83.

March
31 William Pawne was paid £328 13*s*. 2*d*. in full payment 'of thexpenses of thembassadores of Scotland ... at their last being here': PRO, E101/415/3, fol. 90.

April
2 Death of Prince Arthur.

May
13 John Atkinson was paid 31*s*. 7*d*. 'opon a bille.' John Atkinson was paid £12 10*s*. 8*d*. 'opon a bille': PRO, E101/415/3, fol. 94v.

June
11 William Antyne, coppersmith, was paid 56*s*. 8*d*. from the queen's Privy Purse 'for spangelles settes square peces sterrys dropes and pointes after silver and gold for garnisshing of jakettes against the disguysing': PRO, E36/210, p. 40.

October
16 **Player.** Lady Bray was paid 3*s*. 4*d*. from the queen's Privy Purse 'for money by hure geven in rewarde to a disare [story teller] that played the Sheppert before the Quene' [probably at Ewlme, Oxford]: PRO, E36/210, p. 57.

December
9 Robert Marchene, tailor, was paid 8*s*. from the queen's Privy Purse 'for making of iiij Cotes of White and grene sarcenet for iiij of the kinges mynstrelles against the dysguysing in the yere last passed': PRO, E36/210, p. 76.
Disguising. Queen Elizabeth was paid £10 'for the kinges Disguysyng': PRO, E36/123, p. 93; BL, Additional MS. 59899, fol. 6.
25 13*s*. 4*d*. was paid from the queen's Privy Purse to 'Cornisshe for setting of a Carralle vpon Cristmas day in reward.' 13*s*. 4*d*. was paid in reward to the Children of the King's Chapel 'Upon Cristmas day' [for singing Cornish's carol?]: PRO, E36/210, p. 80.
31 **Players.** The Prince's Players were rewarded 6*s*. 8*d*. The 'pleyers of saint albones' were paid 10*s*.: BL, Additional MS. 59899, fol. 8v.

Christmas
25 Dec. ⟨ ⟩ 6 Jan.   **Disguising.** See 9 December 1502.

1503

January
1   The **Lord of Misrule** [the king's?] was paid 20*s.* from the queen's Privy Purse: PRO, E36/210, p. 85.
2–4   **Players.** The Players of London were rewarded 20*s.* Lord Burgavenny's Players were rewarded 13*s.* 4*d.* The 'pleyers of Essex' were rewarded 20*s.* The King's Players were rewarded 40*s.* The **Abbot of Misrule** was rewarded £6 13*s.* 4*d.* **Morris dance.** A payment of 66*s.* 8*d.* was made for 'Dauncyng of mores Daunce': BL, Additional MS. 59899, fol. 10.

February
11   Death of Queen Elizabeth.

April
12   **Disguising.** [for Palm Sunday?] Lewis Adam 'that made Disguysinges' was paid £10: BL, Additional MS. 59899, fol. 19.

August–September
Players. The King's Players accompanied Princess Margaret on her progress to Edinburgh (27 June – 13 August) and performed at least twice at the court of James IV of Scotland as part of the wedding entertainments: College of Arms, MS. M 13*bis*, fols. 76–115v; Houghton Library, Harvard MS. English 1095 (17th century copy of M 13*bis*), printed in *Collectanea,* IV: 265–300; see especially pp. 267, 289, 296, 299. Hall, p. 498.

December
31   **Players.** The Prince's Players were rewarded 20*s.* The 'pleyers in the hall' were paid 6*s.* 8*d.* **Musical entertainment?.** 'Cornyshe of the Chapell' was paid 40*s.*: BL, Additional MS. 59899, fol. 41v.

1504

January
5   **Players.** The Prince's Players were rewarded 13*s.* 4*d.*: BL, Additional MS. 59899, fol. 43v.
13   **Musical entertainment.** 'Iohn Sudbury of the Chapell' was paid 20*s.* 'Cornyshe of the Chapell' was paid 40*s.*: BL, Additional MS. 59899, fol. 44.

March

31   **Musical entertainment?** 'Iohn Sudborough' was paid 20s. for a song: BL, Additional MS. 59899, fol. 52. **Play.** Warton, *HEP,* pp. 557–9, records a performance of John Skelton's interlude, *The Nigramansir,* before the king at Woodstock on Palm Sunday. See R.S. Kingsman and T. Young, *John Skelton: Canon and Census* (New York: Renaissance Society of America, ca. 1967), 28–9.

May

23   **Barriers** at Greenwich: BL, Harleian MS. 69, fol. 5v (challenge and articles). May 23 occurred in Henry VII's reign in 1493, 1499, and 1504. Payments to the armourer on 24 March and for a may game at Greenwich in June suggest the year 1499, but the absence of mention of the Queen (d. 1503) suggests 1504. See Kipling, *Honour,* p. 132n. Anglo, *Tournament Roll,* I: 21n, 138, dates it 1510. See also McGee and Meagher, 'Checklist,' pp. 43–4.

December

31   **Players.** The Prince's Players were paid 10s. The 'pleyers in the Hall' were paid 10s.: BL, Additional MS. 59899, fol. 73.

1505

January

2–3   **Players.** The Players of London were rewarded 5s.: BL, Additional MS. 59899, fol. 74.

11   **Players.** The Players of the King's Chapel were paid 100s. The King's Players were rewarded 40s. An unnamed **Abbot of Misrule** was paid £6 13s. 4d.: BL, Additional MS. 59899, fol. 75.

February

7   **Musical or dramatic entertainment?** 'ix ffrenshemen that pleyed' were paid £4: BL, Additional MS. 59899, fol. 77v.

July

25   **Joust.** £8 was paid to 'Sir Bartelmew Rede for iiij oz. of gold made in Rynges for the Iustes at Richemond': BL, Additional MS. 59899, fol. 93v.

1506

January

1   **Players.** The players 'that played afore the Lorde Stewarde in the hall vpon

sonday nyght [28 December]' were paid 6s. 8d. The Prince's Players 'that played in the hall vpon Newyeres Even' were paid 10s.: PRO, E36/214, p. 25.
10   **Players.** The 'iiij pleyers of the kinges Chapel' were paid £6 13s. 4d. An unnamed **Lord of Misrule** was rewarded £6 13s. 4d.: PRO, E36/214, p. 28.

February
Entertainments and **joust** for Philip of Castile [at Richmond?]: Guildhall Library, London MS. 3313, fols. 306v–7, printed in *Great Chronicle*, pp. 330–1; BL, Cotton MS. Vespasian C. XII, fols. 236–44, printed in *Memorials*, pp. 282–303; Hall, pp. 500–1. See 20 February and 3 April 1506.
20   'Moryce Seint John, John Car, William Par, Charles Brandon, Edwarde Nevile, Sir Rowland [Vielvill], Christofer willoughby, George Bower, Walter Bawmefeld, and Griffeth Don' were each paid £6 13s. 4d. for jousting before the king: PRO, E36/214, p. 41.

April
3   Edward Guildford was paid £20 6s. 8d. 'vpon his bill signed for certein spere staves spent at the Kinges justes lately kepte at Richemounte': PRO, E36/214, p. 49.

May
14–21   **Jousts of May:** BL, Harleian MS. 69, fols. 2v–3 (challenge and articles); on the date, see Kipling, *Honour*, p. 132n.
22   **Maying.** 6s. 8d. was paid for 'settyng vppe of the may pole at Westmynster': PRO, E36/214, p. 63.

December
30   The players 'that played affore the lorde steward in the hall vpon tewesday nyght [29 December]' were paid 10s.: PRO, E36/214, p. 119.

Christmas
25 Dec. ⟨ ⟩ 6 Jan.   The king spent Christmas at Richmond: *Memorials*, p. 103.

1507

January
1   **Players.** The 'iiij players of the Chapell that played affore the Kinges grace' were rewarded £6 13s. 4d.: PRO, E36/214, p. 124.
16   **Players.** The 'kinges iiij players that played affore the king vpon xijth day at nyght [6 January]' were paid 40s.: PRO, E36/214, p. 128.

23   An unnamed **Lord of Misrule** was paid £6 13*s*. 4*d*. 'for his besynes in
Cristenmes': PRO, E36/214, p. 130.

May
10   William Creswell was paid 5*s*. 12*d*. for mending the tilt: PRO, E36/214,
p. 155.
· 11   **Bear-baiting.** The 'berwarde' was rewarded 6*s*. 8*d*.: PRO, E36/214, p. 155.
Jousts of May and June at Greenwich: College of Arms, MS. R 36, fols. 124–5
(challenge and articles); College of Arms, MS. SML 29 (Ceremonials 2), p. 21
(articles); *STC* 3543, *Here begynneth the iustes of Maye* [1507]; on the dating
see *Notes & Queries*, 225 [1980]: 386–9, and *Notes & Queries*, 229 [1984]:
158–62.

December
20   Henry Wentworth was paid £13 6*s*. 8*d*. 'to make a dysguysing for a moryce
daunce': PRO, E36/214, p. 222.
31   Henry Wentworth was paid 100*s*. 'towarde the making of a disguysing for
a moryce daunce': PRO, E36/214, p. 226.

Christmas
25 Dec. ⟨ ⟩ 6 Jan.   **Disguising for morris dance.** See 20 and 31 December 1507.

1508

January
7   **Players.** The 'v Gentlemen of the king*es* Chapell that played in the hall vpon
xij*th* nyght [6 January] afore the king*es* grace' were rewarded £6 13*s*. 4*d*.: PRO,
E36/214, p. 231.
14   **Players.** 'iiij Children *tha*t played afore *the* king' were paid 3*s*. 4*d*.: PRO,
E36/214, p. 232.
23   An unnamed **Lord of Misrule** was paid £6 13*s*. 4*d*. 'for his busynes in
Cristenmes holydays': PRO, E36/214, p. 234.

December
19   William Wynnsbury was issued 66*s*. 8*d*. 'vpon a prest toward*es* the king of
his Lordship of Mysrule': PRO, E36/214, p. 306.
25   **Betrothal** of Princess Mary and Archduke Charles. **Tournament:** *STC* 17558,
Petrus Carmelianus, *The solempnities & triumphes doon at the spousells of the*

kyngs doughter to the archeduke of Austrige, [London, 1508]; *STC* 4659: English translation.
Disguising and **morris dance** with three **pageants** (a castle, a tree, and a mount): PRO, LC9/50, fols. 149–53v. See 2 September 1509.
Players. 'M*aster* Kyte Cornysshe and other of the Chapell *that* played affore *the* king at Richemounte' were paid £6 13*s.* 4*d.*: PRO, E36/214, p. 308.

1509

January
2   **Players.** The 'Lorde of Buckinghams pleyers that playd in the hall at Grenewyche' were rewarded 6*s.* 8*d.*: PRO, E36/214, p. 316.
7   **Players.** 'diu*er*se of the king*es* Chapell that playde afore the king vpon xij*th* nyght' were paid 53*s.* 4*d.* The King's Players were rewarded 40*s.* The **Abbot of Misrule** (William Wynnsbury) was paid 66*s.* 8*d.* in full payment for his 'besynes in Cristenmes tyde': PRO, E36/214, p. 316.

April
21   Death of Henry VII

HENRY VIII

1509

May
1   £12 was paid for making a tilt at the Tower: PRO, E36/215, p. 8.

June
24   No revels recorded are recorded for the coronation of Henry VIII. The tradition of a play by the Gentlemen of the Chapel cannot be verified. See 30 October 1485.
25–7   **Coronation tournament** at Westminster: Guildhall Library, London MS., 3313, fols. 318–20, printed in *Great Chronicle,* pp. 341–3; Hall, pp. 510–12. Chamber payments relating to the events are found in PRO, E36/215, pp. 10–22.

July
17   In a letter to his father-in-law, Henry mentions that he has been occupying himself in **jousts:** *CSP Spanish,* III, no. 19.

August

Running at the ring: Sanuto, *Diarii,* IX. 149, calendared in *CSP Venetian,* II. 5, no. 11.

September

2 Sir Andrew Windsor, Keeper of the Great Wardrobe, was paid £60 17*s.* 11*d.* for 'disguising*es* afore th*ambassadors of* fflaunder*es*': PRO, E36/215, p. 23. See 25 December 1508.

December

9 William Wynnsbury received an 100*s.* imprest as **Lord of Misrule:** PRO, E36/215, p. 36; E101/417/2, pt. i, no. 2.

30 **Players.** The players in the Hall on Thursday and Sunday nights [27 and 30 December at Richmond] were paid 20*s.*: PRO, E36/215, p. 38.

1510

January

6 **Lord of Misrule.** William Wynnsbury received 100*s.* in full payment for his business at Christmas. **Players.** The Gentlemen of the Chapel were paid £10 for playing 'in the hall opon xij*th* nyght.' The King's Players were paid 53*s.* 4*d.*: PRO, E36/215, p. 43; BL, Additional MS. 21481, fol. 22.

12 **Joust.** The king and William Compton disguised themselves to participate in a joust at Richmond: Hall, p. 513.

18 **Private disguising.** The king and eleven companions costumed as Robin Hood's men and a woman as Maid Marian presented a 'gladness' [informal disguising] to the queen in her Chamber at Westminster: PRO, E36/217, fols. 1–2, 15; Hall, p. 513.

February

10 William Wynnsbury was paid 66*s.* 8*d.* for his business at Christmas as **Lord of Misrule.** Various payments were also made in connection with the **jousts:** PRO, E36/215, p. 46.

24 Robert Amadas was paid £451 12*s.* 2*d.* for 'plate of gold stuff bought of him for the disguising*es*.' William Bottry was paid £133 7*s.* 5*d.* for silks for the **disguisings:** PRO, E36/215, p. 46.

28 **Double disguising and mummery** in the Parliament Chamber at Westminster, in which the king participated: PRO, E36/217, fols. 3–12, 15–25; Hall, pp. 513–14. See 24 February 1510.

March
17   **Running at the ring** in which the king participated: PRO, E36/217,
fols. 13–14, 25–6; Hall, p. 514.

May
1   **Maying**. The king, his nobles, guard, and yeomen apparelled in white went
'to fetche May or grene bows' and to exercise at archery: Hall, p. 515.

May – June
23, 27, 1, 3, 6   **Barriers at Greenwich** in which the king participated: College
of Arms, MS. L 12b, fols. 10–11 (names of participants); Hall, p. 515.

June
23, 28   Henry disguised himself to see the **Midsummer Watch** at the King's
Head in Cheap on the 23d and, with the queen, saw it again on the 28th: John
Stow, *Annals* (London, 1592), p. 815.

July
Players? The schoolmaster and boys of Eton were rewarded 66s. 8d.: PRO,
E36/215, p. 60.

October
6 〈 〉 13?   **Joust and Tourney** at Oking in which the king, presumably, participated: Hall, p. 515.
14 〈 〉 31?   **Foot combat** at Greenwich in which the king participated: Hall,
p. 515. **Torchlight procession** by the gentlemen who participated in the foot
combats at Greenwich, who presented themselves to the king at the Tower:
Hall, pp. 515–16.

November
13–14   **Joust, tourney, and/or running at the ring** at Richmond in which the
king participated (See next item).
14   **Disguising and mummery** at Richmond in which the king participated:
PRO, E36/217, fols. 30–6; E36/229, fols. 1–6; Hall, p. 516.

December
15   An unnamed **Lord of Misrule** was issued an imprest of £6 13s. 4d. for his
business at Christmas: PRO, E36/215, p. 91.

1511

January

6   **Players.** The Gentlemen of the Chapel were paid £10 for playing before the
king: PRO, E36/215, p. 100. The King's Players received a reward of 66s. 8d.:
BL, Additional MS. 21481, fol. 50v.
Disguising at Richmond with a **pageant** of a mountain and a **morris dance:**
PRO, E36/217, fols. 38–45; E36/229, fols. 8–15; Hall, pp. 516–17.

February

12–13   **Tournament** at Westminster for the birth of Prince Henry in which the
king participated: BL, Harleian Charter, 83. H. 1, calendared in *LP,* I.i, p. 379,
no. 698 (1); BL, Additional MS. 6113, fols. 201v–2, calendered in *LP,* I.i,
no. 710; BL, Additional MS. 12514, fol. 136 (17th century copy of challenge);
BL, Harleian MS. 69, fols. 4v–5, calendared in *LP,* I.i, no. 698 (2); BL,
Harleian MS. 6079, fol. 36v, calendared in *LP,* I.i, no. 698 (4); Bodleian
Library, Ashmole MS. 1116, fols. 109–10, calendared in W.H. Black, *Catalogue of the Manuscripts Bequeathed unto the University of Oxford by Elias Ashmole* (Oxford, 1845); BL, Additional MS. 11826, fol. 16, calendared in *LP,* I.i,
no. 700; College of Arms, MS. The Westminster Tournament Roll, printed in
Tournament Roll, II; College of Arms, MS. Tournament Cheques, 1a, 1b,
printed in *Tournament Roll,* I: 112–15; Guildhall Library, London MS. 3313,
fols. 341v–8, printed in *Great Chronicle,* pp. 368–74; PRO, E36/217,
fols. 46–60, printed in *Tournament Roll,* I: 116–33; PRO, E36/229,
fols. 15–30; Hall, pp. 517–18. See 23 February and 19 April 1511.

13   **Disguising** and **pageant** ('the golldyn arber in the arche yerd of pleyser')
in the White Hall, Westminster, in which the king participated. In connection
with this, the Gentlemen of the Chapel performed an **interlude:** PRO,
E36/217, fols. 61–76; E36/229, fols. 31–47; Hall, pp. 518–19; Guildhall Library, London MS. 3313, fols. 347v–8, printed in *Great Chronicle,*
pp. 375–6. See 19 April 1511.

23   Fifteen trumpets at the **jousts** on 12–13 February were paid £26 13s. 4d.
and the heralds at the **jousts** were paid £40: PRO, E36/215, p. 105.

April

19   John Daunce was paid £4371 11s. 2d. for the **jousts** and **disguisings** held
at Westminster on 12–13 February: PRO, E36/215, p. 114.

May

1   **Joust, tourney, shooting,** and other sports with a **pageant** (a ship) at Green-

wich in which the king participated: Hall, p. 520; Guildhall Library, London MS. 3313, fol. 348v, printed in *Great Chronicle*, pp. 375–6.

15   **Joust:** Hall, p. 521.

December

21   An imprest of £6 13*s.* 4*d.* was paid to the **Lord of Misrule:** PRO, E36/215, p. 151.

26   John Crotchet, the king's armourer, and William Heywood, the king's joiner, were paid for spear heads and other equipment used in the jousts from 29 September 1510 to June 1511: PRO, E36/1, fol. 46v, calendared in *LP*, I.ii, no. 3608 (iii).

1512

January

1   The **Lord of Misrule** received a reward of 40*s.*: PRO, E36/215, p. 156. **Disguising** and **pageant** ('Le Fortresse Dangerus') at Greenwich in which the king participated: PRO, E36/229, fols. 91–106; SP2/ Fol. A, no. 4; Hall, p. 526. See 4 April 1512.

6   The **Lord of Misrule** was paid £6 13*s.* 4*d.* **Players.** The King's Players were rewarded 66*s.* 8*d.* Four players that came out of Suffolk were paid 13*s.* 4*d.* for playing 'afore the lorde Steward in the king*es* hall on Monday nyght [29 December]': PRO, E36/215, pp. 157–8; BL, Additional MS. 21481, fol. 79v.

Mask 'after the maner of Italie' in which the king participated: PRO, E36/229, fols. 91–106; SP2/ Fol. A, no. 4; Hall, p. 526. See 4 April 1512.

March

6   **Players.** The Gentlemen of the Chapel were paid £6 13*s.* 4*d.* for playing on Shrove Sunday (22 February): PRO, E36/215, p. 167.

April

4   A payment of £583 10*s.* 8*d.* was made for silks, embroidery, and other material and workmanship to William Bottry, Elizabeth Philip, Robert Amadas, and Richard Gibson for the disguisings the previous Christmas: PRO, E36/215, p. 174.

June

1   **Joust** at Greenwich in which the king participated: PRO, E36/217, fols. 177–83; Hall, pp. 533–4. William Bottry was paid for silks for the jousts and triumph

in May and June in the account of Edward Guildford and Sir Edward Howard: PRO, E101/417/7, no. 10. See 20 June 1512.

2   **Players.** The Gentlemen of the Chapel were paid £6 13*s*. 4*d*. for playing before the king on Wednesday of Whitsun week [2 June]: PRO, E36/215, p. 190.

20   Richard Gibson was paid £60 13*s*. 11 1/2*d*. for material for the jousts at Greenwich held on 1 June: PRO, E36/215, p. 190.

December

19   William Wynnsbury was issued an imprest of £10 for his business as **Lord of Misrule** at Christmas: PRO, E36/215, p. 216; E101/417/7, no. 25.

1513

January

6   **Disguising** and **pageant** ('the ryche movnt') at Greenwich, in which the king participated: PRO, E36/217, fol. 186–201; Hall, p. 535. See 15 March 1513.

William Wynnsbury was paid 66*s*. 8*d*. for the 'his Revelles' [as **Lord of Misrule**?]: PRO, E36/215, p. 223.

Players. The King's Players were rewarded 66*s*. 8*d*.: BL, Additional MS. 21482, fol. 112.

March

15   John Daunce made payments for 'our dysguysing on twelue nyght last': £7 13*s*. 4*d*. to Sir Henry Guildford, as Master of the Revels, for his diets; £134 7*s*. 6*d*. to William Bottry for silks, cloth of gold, etc.; £118 5*s*. 6*d*. to Robert Amadas for silver and gold; £72 3*s*. 11*d*.; to Richard Gibson for the 'Goldewyre drawer'; £6 2*s*. 2*d*. to Elizabeth Philip for silks; £36 13*s*. 8*d*. for the 'paient' [pageant]; and others: PRO, E36/1, fol. 58v, abstracted in *LP* I.ii, no. 3608 (v).

June

30   The King's Players accompanied the king to France from 30 June to 22 October: PRO, E101/62, no. 31, calendared in *LP* I.ii, no. 2053 (ii).

July

1   A payment of £857 8*s*. 6*d*. was made to Robert Amadas and to William Mortemer for gold stuff and silver. £2000 was paid for horses' harnesses and trappers of goldsmith's work, presumably for the **jousts** at Tournai: PRO, E36/215, p. 261.

September
18–20 'bankettes, playes, commodies, maskes and other pastymes' were presented at a reception and entertainment for Henry VIII at Lille by Charles Prince of Castile, Lady Margaret, his governess, and others of the court of Burgundy: Hall, p. 553.

October
18 **Joust, banquet, and mask** at Tournai in which the king participated: PRO, E36/217, fols. 79–83; SP1/7, fols. 134–6; BL, Stowe MS. 146, fol. 101 (13 October warrant to Sir Edward Guildford to prepare jousts at Tournai); *CSP Milan*, I, no. 669; Hall, pp. 566–7. See 1 July 1513.

December
4 William Wynnsbury was issued an imprest of £13 6s. 8d. as **Lord of Misrule** for Christmas: PRO, E36/215, p. 277.

1514

January
6 **Interlude** (*Venus and Beauty*) with a **morris dance** at Richmond: PRO, E36/217, fols. 81–3; SP1/7, fols. 136–9. See 15 and 28 March 1514.
Players. The King's Players were rewarded 66s. 8d.: PRO, E36/215, p. 283; BL, Additional MS. 21481, fol. 142. According to Collier, *HEDP* (1879), I: 68–70, Medwall's 'fyndyng of troth' was performed by the King's Players.

March
15 Warrant dormant to Sir Henry Guildford to pay for **disguisings** on the previous Twelfth Night last: PRO, E101/417/7, pt. i, no. 76; *LP,* I. 5720, pp. 952–8.
28 Payment issued to Gibson on account: PRO, E101/417/2, pt. i, no. 78.

May
Joust at Greenwich in which the king and Suffolk were disguised as hermits: Hall, p. 568.

December
William Wynnsbury was issued an imprest of £13 6s. 8d. for his business at Christmas as **Lord of Misrule:** PRO, E36/215, p. 348.

1515

January

1   **Disguising or mummery** in the queen's Chamber at Greenwich in which the king participated: PRO. E36/217, fols. 204–6; SP2/ Fol. A, no. 5; Hall, p. 580.

   Players. The Earl of Wiltshire's Players who 'shulde haue played in the king*es* hall oppon thursday [28 December] at nyght' were paid 13*s*. 4*d*. PRO. E36/215, p. 355; BL, Additional MS. 21481, fols. 177r–v.

6   **Disguising** and **pageant** at Greenwich ('the pavyllyon vn the plas parlos') with indoor **tourney:** PRO, E36/217, fols. 209–18; SP2/Fol. A, no. 6; Hall, p. 580.

   Players. The King's old Players were rewarded £4. The King's [new] Players were rewarded 66*s*. 8*d*.: PRO, E36/215, p. 356; BL, Additional MS. 21481, fols. 177r–v. A payment of £247 12*s*. 7*d*. was made to Leonard Friscobald for velvets and silks for the disguising on Twelfth Night and Gibson was paid £28 4*s*. 4*d*. for making garments: PRO, E36/215, p. 357.

February

2   **Play.** See 25 February 1515.

3   **Joust** at Greenwich for Candlemas [2 February] in which the king participated: PRO, E36/217, fols. 219–23; SP2/Fol. A, no. 7; Hall, pp. 580–1. See March 1515.

4   Richard Gibson was paid £137 14*s*. 1/2*d*. for the disguisings last Christmas: PRO, E36/215, p. 360.

25   **Play.** John Haryson, Yeoman of the queen's Chamber, was paid £28 13*s*. 6*d*. for stuff for a play on Candlemas night [2 February]: PRO, E36/215, p. 362.

March

Payments were made for bards and harnesses. A payment of £363 9*s*. 2*d*. was made for velvets and silks [for the February or April **jousts?**]. Richard Gibson was paid £40 on a warrant authorizing £200 for the king's business [in connection with the jousts in February or April or for the pageant begun 19 March?]: PRO, E36/215, p. 366.

19   Richard Gibson began work on a **pageant** ('pallys marchallyn') for a joust, which he abandoned on 9 May: PRO, E36/217, fols. 227–46; SP2/Fol. A, no. 8.

April

19   **Joust** at Richmond in which the king participated: PRO, E36/217, fols. 224–6; SP2/Fol. A, no. 8; Guistinian, I: 75–6. See March and 20 May 1515.

May

1   **May festival** at Greenwich **(athletic contest, disguise, pageants, procession, joust)** in which the king participated: PRO, E36/229, fols. 66–72; Hall, p. 582; Sanuto, *Diarii,* XX. 264–8, calendared in *CSP Venetian,* II. no. 624; Guistinian, I: 79–81, 90–2. See September 1515.

20 A payment of £466 10*s.* 9 1/2*d.* was made to Richard Gibson for velvets, silks, embroidery, garments, and saddles which he provided for the 19 April **jousts:** PRO, E36/215, p. 378.

September

A payment of £3202 16*s.* 8*d.* was made to Leonard Friscobald and Anthony Cavelary for velvets, silks, and cloth of gold [for the May Day celebration?]: PRO, E36/215, p. 399.

December

11 Sir Henry Guildford was issued money for payments to William Bottry for material and to others for skins and furs: PRO, E101/417/12, no. 8.

1516

January

1   **Players.** The Earl of Wiltshire's Players were rewarded 13*s.* 4*d.* The King's 'olde' Players were rewarded £4. PRO, E36/215, p. 422; BL, Additional MS. 21482, fol. 211.

6   **Comedy** *(Troylus and Pandor),* **barriers, disguising,** and **pageant castle** at Eltham: PRO, E36/229, fols. 73–82. Hall, p. 583. See 2 February 1516.
    Players. The King's [new] Players were rewarded 66*s.* 8*d.*: PRO, E36/215, p. 423; BL, Additional MS. 21481, fol. 211.

29 **Running at the ring** at Greenwich in which the king participated: PRO, E36/229, fols. 83–7. See 3 March 1516.

February

2   Richard Gibson was paid £139 2*s.* 4*d.* for 'the disguysing ayenst xij*th* tyde': PRO, E36/215, p. 427.

4   Letter from Knight to Wolsey. Guildford had [unsuccessfully?] invited Hans Nagle to play before the king [at Christmas 1515–16?]: PRO, SP1/12, pp. 137–9, calendared in *LP,* II.ii, no. 1478.

5   **Running at the ring** at Greenwich in which the king participated: PRO, E36/229, fols. 87–90. See 3 March 1516.

March

3 Richard Gibson was paid £172 3s. 10 1/2d. for velvet, damask, satin, sarcenet, and workmanship for the king's **running at the ring** on 29 January and on 5 February: PRO, E36/215, p. 432.

April

13, 27 Forster was paid £40 to repair the tilt at Greenwich. William Cornish was paid £100 for repairs at Greenwich. Robert Amadas was paid £481 5s. 1 1/4d. for four saddles and fourteen harnesses wrought with spangles and tassels of silver [in preparation for the jousts at Greenwich in May?]: PRO, E36/215, pp. 442–3.

May

19–20 **Jousts** in honour of Margaret, Queen of Scots, at Greenwich in which the king participated: PRO, E36/217, fols. 249–68; BL, Harleian MS. 69, fol. 16v (Tournament Cheque for 20 May); College of Arms, MS. Tournament Cheques, 1c; Hall, pp. 584–5. See 13 and 27 April and 8 and 24 June 1516.

20 **Play** to conclude the jousts [by Cornish and the Children of the Chapel]: PRO, E101/418/7, fols. 1–7.

June

8, 24 William Cornish was paid £36 10s. for 'paving gutters of lead for urinals' at Greenwich in connection with the **jousts** in May: PRO, E101/417/2, pt. ii, no. 117. John Crotchet, the king's Armourer, and William Haywarde were paid £35 18s. 6d. for spears and other equipment and for workmanship and carriage of material for the **jousts** in May: PRO, E101/417/2, pt. ii, no. 154. Richard Gibson was paid £281 15s. 11d. for apparel for the jousts and play at Greenwich in May. A payment of £972 2s. 2d. was made to Guydo Portinary for velvets, silks, etc. for the **jousts** at Greenwich in May: PRO, E36/215, pp. 453–4.

December

7 Richard Pole was issued an imprest of £13 6s. 8d. as **Lord of Misrule:** PRO, E36/215, p. 482.

1517

January

4 **Players.** William Cornish and the Children of the Chapel were rewarded £6 13s. 4d. for playing before the king. The King's 'olde plaiers' were rewarded £4.

The King's [new] Players were rewarded 66s. 8d.: PRO, E36/215, p. 493; BL, Additional MS. 21481, fol. 246.

6   **Disguising** and **pageant** ('Gardyn de Esperans') at Greenwich: PRO, E36/217, fols. 269–78. Hall, pp. 585–6.

March

8   William Cornish was rewarded £6 13s. 4d. for performing a play with the Children of the Chapel on Shrove Tuesday [24 February]: PRO, E36/215, p. 503.

July

6   William Cornish was paid for two pageants shown before the king and ambassadors. See 8 August 1518.

7   **Jousts** for the Flemish ambassadors and a banquet with representations at Greenwich in which the king participated: PRO, E36/217, fols. 86–97, 303–6. Hall, pp. 591–2. *CSP Venetian*, II, no. 918. Giustinian, II: 97–8, 101–3. See 19 July and 2 September 1517 and 8 August 1518.

19   Sir Edward Guildford was paid £4 14s. 10d. for vices and rings for saddles and steel saddles and Guydo Portinary was paid £426 14s. 4 1/2d. for velvets and silks [for **jousts**?]: PRO, E36/215, pp. 529, 531.

September

2   Sir Henry Guildford, now Master of the Horse, was paid £752 14s. 11 1/4d. 'for **jousts** lately holden at Greenwich': PRO, E36/215, p. 534.

Christmas

25 Dec. ⟨ ⟩ 6 Jan.   Because of the 'Swetyng sickenes' the king kept a small court and 'no solempne Christmas': Hall, p. 592.

1518

January

3   The King's [new] Players were rewarded 66s. 8d.: BL, Additional MS. 21481, fol. 280; the amount of the reward is not entered in PRO, E36/215, p. 561.

August

8   William Cornish was paid £18 2s. 11 1/2d. 'opon a Warrant for ij pagentes with all thinges & necessaries as were made for the same whiche was shewed before the king with other nobles and gentilles vjto die Iuly anno ixno [6 July 1517]': PRO, E36/216, fol. 11v.

15   Richard Gibson, now Sergeant of the Tents, was paid £26 13s. 4d. either in
     connection with Cornish's pageants or with the next entry. Undated payments:
     Sir Edward Guildford was paid £66 13s. 4d. for stuff for the jousts to be held
     at Greenwich before the ambassadors of France: PRO, E36/216, fols. 11v, 13.

September
12   Payment to Sir Edward Guildford for **jousts** to be held at Greenwich for the
     ambassadors of France: PRO, E101/417/12, no. 49.

October
5   'Mommery' at Wolsey's (York Place) in which the king participated: Hall,
     pp. 594–5. See 7 October 1518.
6–7 **Tournament** to celebrate the Treaty of Universal Peace at Greenwich in
     which the king participated: PRO, E36/228, fols. av, 1–5; *CSP Venetian*, II,
     no. 1088; Guistinian, II: 233–4; Hall, p. 595. See 15 August, 12 September,
     and 7 October 1518.
7   **Disguising** and **pageant** *(The Rock of Amity)* at Greenwich to celebrate the
     proxy marriage of Princess Mary; **political disguising** *(Report and Pegasus)*;
     indoor **tourney**: *CSP Venetian*, II,. no. 1088; Guistinian, II: 224–5, 228–35;
     Hall, p. 595.
     Three harnesses 'with peces of advantage for the tylt' and other equipment were
     purchased for £50. Sir Edward Belknap was paid £21 for 'making of an hall
     place in the bodye of powles Churche for the mariage of the princes.' Richard
     Gibson was paid £230 4s. 4d. for a 'mommery holden at my lorde Cardinalles
     place at Westmynster [on 5 October],' and for the 'disguysyng helde at green-
     wyche the vij day of October': PRO, E36/216, fols. 18r–v.

December
9   Edmund Travore was issued a reward of £13 6s. 8d. as **Lord of Misrule:** PRO,
     E36/216, fol. 23v.

1519

ca. **1519**   Richard Gibson's account for a **joust or revels:** PRO, SP1/32,
fols. 182r–v.

January
2   **Players.** The King's 'olde players' were rewarded £4. The **Lord of Misrule** was
     rewarded 40s.: PRO, E36/216, fols. 27v–8.
6   **Players.** William Cornish was paid £6 13s. 4d. for playing 'afore the king

opon new yeres day [1 January] at night' with the Children of the Chapel. The King's [new] Players were rewarded 66s. 8d.: PRO. E36/216, fol. 28.

March

3, 8   **Jousts** for the French hostages at Greenwich in which the king participated: PRO, SP1/18, fols. 52–7. Hall, p. 598. See 13 March 1519.

7   **Entertainment** for the French hostages at Greenwich including a **comedy of Plautus** [same as Cornish's interlude? See 1 May 1519] and a **mask** after the 'maner of the Contry of ettally': PRO, SP1/18, fols. 52–7. Hall, p. 597.

13   John Crochet, the king's Armourer, was paid £25 8s. 4d. for spears and other equipment for the **jousts** at Greenwich on 3 and 8 March: PRO, E36/216, fol. 33.

April

21   Richard Gibson was paid £60 7s. 3d. for garments for 'maskelers and many other thing*es* ... as apperith by a boke of the *par*ticulers of the same': PRO, E36/216, fol. 38.

May

1   William Cornish was paid £6 13s. 4d. for playing an **interlude** before the king on Shrove Monday [7 March] with the Children of the Chapel: PRO, E36/216, fol. 41.

September

3   **Entertainment** for the French hostages at Newhall, Essex, including a **pastime** (Summer and Winter) by Cornish and the Children of the Chapel, and a **double mask** of youth and age in which the king participated: PRO, E36/217, fols. 100–8, 123–9. Hall, p. 599. See 11 December 1519.

October

21, 27, 28   **Jousts** at Greenwich for the wedding [20 October] of the Earl of Devonshire: PRO, E36/217, fols. 108–11, 129–32; See March 1520.

December

4   William Wynnsbury was issued an imprest of £13 6s. 8d. as **Lord of Misrule:** PRO, E36/216, fol. 65.

11   Richard Gibson was paid £207 5s. 1d. for the '**maskelyn** at newhall in Essex [3 September]': PRO, E36/216, fol. 65v.

31   '**Meskeller or mummery'** at Greenwich: PRO, E36/217, fols. 111–14, 132–5.

1520

January
5   **Revels.** The king and nineteen gentlemen went in 'meskellyng apperell' to revels at Wolsey's (York Place): PRO, E36/217, fols. 114–15, 135.

6   **'dysguysyng** *with* **A pagent'** at Greenwich: PRO, E36/217, fols. 115–16, 136.

   Players. William Cornish and the Children of the Chapel were paid £6 13*s.* 4*d.* for playing before the king. The King's [new] Players were rewarded 66*s.* 8*d.* The King's 'olde' Players were rewarded £4. The **Lord of Misrule** was rewarded 40*s.*: PRO, E36/216, fols. 71–2.

8   **'Meskeler'** at Greenwich: PRO, E36/217, fols. 116–19, 136–39.

February
1   **Challenge** to a joust with disguise and pageant, a 'tryke' or 'spell' wagon. See 19 and 25 February 1520.

5   William Hayward was paid £34 15*s.* for spears and other equipment for the jousts: PRO, E36/216, fol. 74.

19   **Joust** in which the king participated: PRO, E36/217, fols. 119–21, 139–41. Hall, pp. 600–1. See 1, 5, and 25 February 1520.

25   William Buttry was paid £233 3*s.* 1*d.* for velvets and silks, presumably for the challenge in disguise and jousts: PRO, E36/216, fol. 75.

March
Undated payment: Richard Gibson was paid £200 4*s.* 9*d.* for the **jousts** at the wedding of the Earl of Devonshire the previous October: PRO, E36/216, fol. 80.

April
1   **Players.** William Cornish was paid £13 6*s.* 8*d.* for playing two interludes with the Children of the Chapel before the king at Greenwich: PRO, E36/216, fol. 81v.

22   John Browne, King's Painter, was paid £333 6*s.* 8*d.* for gilding and garnishing the roofs of the temporary palace at Guisnes: PRO, E36/216, fol. 84v.

May
1 George Lovekyn made an **inventory** of embroidered coverings of bards at the armoury in the tilt-yard at Greenwich: PRO, SP1/29, fols. 191–205.

   The French herald who proclaimed the **jousts** to be held at the Field of Cloth of Gold was rewarded £40. Henry Smith was paid £66 13*s.* 4*d.* for impressing 100 carpenters, 50 glaziers, 24 painters, and materials for the building projects associated with the temporary palace at Guisnes. Clement Urmeston and Henry Addler were paid £366 13s. 4d. for making buttons and other garnishing for the temporary palace at Guisnes. These and other payments relating to preparations for the Field of Cloth of Gold between April and August are to be found in PRO, E36/216, fols. 81–100.

31   The king was in France from 31 May to ca. 16 July.

June

3   **Pageant** (mount with a whitethorn tree) for the jousts at the Field of Cloth of Gold: PRO, E36/217, fols. 293–302. See other payments relating to preparations for the spectacles and entertainments at the Field of Cloth of Gold, April – August 1520 and February 1521.

11–22   **Jousts** at the Field of Cloth of Gold in which Henry VIII and Francis I participated, between Guisnes and Ardres: PRO, E36/9, fols. 1–18 (Sir Edward Guildford's account); E36/217, fols. 142, 145–74 (Richard Gibson's account); Sanuto, *Diarii*, XXIX: 466–650, calendared in *CSP Venetian*, III, no. 50, pp. 14–31; College of Arms, MS. M 6*bis*, fols. 69v–73 (challenge and names of participants); College of Arms, MS. M 9, fols. 1–7 (proclamation); College of Arms, MS. Tournament Cheques, 2; Bodleian Library, Ashmole MS. 1116, fols. 105–7v (proclamation and articles); *Lordonnance et ordre du tournoy/ ioustes/ & combat/ a pied/ et a cheval* [Paris, 1520], fols. a1–a4v, e2–f2v (articles and participants), abstracted in *LP,* III.i, no. 869, pp. 307–14; *La description et ordre du camp festins et ioustes* [Paris, 1520], fols. a1–b2v, abstracted in *LP,* III.i, no. 869, pp. 303–6; *Chronicle of Calais,* pp. 86–90; Hall, pp. 605–20. See payments April – August 1520 and February 1521.

17   '**Maskellers**' (young Russlanders, ancient maskers, and princely apparel) at Ardres in which the king participated: PRO, E36/229, fols. 48–65, 101; Hall, p. 615. See payments April – August 1520 and February 1521.

24   '**Maskellers**' (ten Genoese ladies, ten Milanese ladies, ten men in crimson satin, and nine men as the 'nine worthies' and Henry VIII as Hercules) at Ardres: PRO, E36/229, fols. 48–65, 101; Hall, pp. 618–19. See payments April – August 1520 and February 1521.

July

11   **Mask** for Charles V in the Staple Hall at Calais in which the king and fifteen of his companions participated: PRO, E36/229, fols. 48–65, 101; *CSP Venetian*, III. no, 50, pp. 31–4; College of Arms, MS. M 6*bis*, fols. 7–12 (entertainments of the Emperor at Gravelines and Calais), 73v–4v (text of dialogue in French and Latin between King Arthur and his servants); Hall, p. 621. See payments April – August 1520 and February 1521.

12   'Maskellers' and pageants for the entertainment of Charles V in the Exchequer at Calais [because the banqueting house built for the occasion was disabled by inclement weather]: PRO, E36/229, fols. 48–65, 101; Hall, p. 621; *Rutland Papers*, pp. 56–7. See payments April – August 1520 and February 1521.

August
1   William Cornish was paid for diets of ten of the Children of the Chapel from 29 May to 31 July during the king's journey to France: PRO, E36/216, fol. 98.

November
3   'Maskeller' at Greenwich with six friar's habits and six costumes from the store at Greenwich: PRO, SP1/29, fol. 212v.

December
1   William Tolly was issued an imprest of £13 6s. 8d. as **Lord of Misrule:** PRO, E36/216, fol. 110.
9   **Revels** at Greenwich employing mariners' frocks and friars' hoods: PRO, SP1/29, fol. 213; E36/217, fol. 314.

1521

January
1   The **Lord of Misrule** was rewarded 40s.: PRO, E36/216, fol. 116.
1 or 4   **Revels** at Greenwich in which the king participated: PRO, SP1/29, fols. 213v–14; E36/217, fols. 314–15.
3   **Revels** at Wolsey's court (York Place): PRO, SP1/29, fol. 214v; E36/217, fol. 315.
6   **Players.** William Cornish was paid £6 13s. 4d. for performing 'his play,' presumably with the Children of the Chapel. The King's [new] Players were rewarded 66s. 8d. The King's 'olde players' were rewarded £4: PRO, E36/216, fol. 116v.

February
11–12   **Joust and tourney** at Greenwich in which the king participated: PRO, SP1/29, fols. 215–18v; E36/217, fols. 316–18; Hall, p. 622.
11   'Maskeller' at Greenwich with friars' habits: PRO, SP1/29, fol. 219; E36/217, fol. 318.
12   'Maskeller' at Greenwich: PRO, SP1/29, fol. 219r–v; E36/217, fol. 319.
   Undated payment: Richard Gibson, William Mortemer, and others were paid £3007 16s. 11d. for clothes and other necessaries for the king and others at the

jousts and 'maskellers' held at the Field of Cloth of Gold: PRO, E36/216, fol. 122.

December
29 'Maskeller'. The king participated in this revel or the one held on 1 January.

Christmas
25 Dec. ⟨ ⟩ 6 Jan.   There were many 'goodly and gorgious Mommeries' at court this year and 'many sumptuous and gorgious disguisynges, enterludes and bankettes' for the Imperial ambassadors at Christmas: Hall, p. 628.

1522

January
1 'Maskeller'. The king participated in this revel or the one held on 29 December: PRO, SP1/29, fols. 220–3v.

March
2 Joust for the Imperial ambassadors at Greenwich in which the king participated: PRO, SP1/29, fols. 223–8; Hall, pp. 630–1.
3 Play by the Cardinal's Gentlemen, and a maskeller at Wolsey's court (York Place): PRO, SP1/29, fol. 237; Hall, p. 631.
4 Disguising and pageant ('Schatew Vert') at Wolsey's (York Place), in which the king participated: PRO, SP1/29, fols. 228v–37; Hall, p. 631–2.

June
4–5 Joust and Tourney at Greenwich in which Henry VIII and Charles V participated: PRO, SP1/24, fols. 226–30; CSP Spanish, II. no. 422; Hall, pp. 635–6.
4 'Maskeller' at Greenwich in which the king participated: Hall, p. 635.
5 'Maskeller' at Greenwich: PRO, SP1/24, fols. 230v–3v; Hall, p. 637.
5–8 Tents were pitched and removed for the king's and emperor's entry: PRO, SP1/24, fols. 236v–7.
15 'meskeller at the Kastell of Wyndsor': PRO, SP1/24, fols. 231v, 234–6; Hall, p. 641; CSP Spanish, II, no. 437.

Christmas
25 Dec. ⟨ ⟩ 6 Jan.   The king kept Christmas at Eltham: Hall, p. 651.

1523

Christmas
25 Dec. 〈 〉 6 Jan.   The king kept 'Christmas solempnely' at Windsor: Hall, p. 672.

1524

March
10   **Joust** in which the king was nearly injured: Hall, p. 674.

November
6   Richard Gibson was ordered to assist Lord Leonard Grey in producing the martial exercises associated with the **Castle of Loyalty** from December through February: PRO, SP1/32, fol. 256.

December
Challenge to martial exercises at the **Castle of Loyalty**: BL, Additional MS. 33735, fol. 4v (rules for assault); BL, Harleian MS. 69, fols. 20v–1 (copy of challenge); College of Arms, MS. M 6, fols. 57v–8 (challenge); Hall, pp. 688–89. See 6 November 1524.
Pageant, (mountain and unicorn) for the tournament at the Castle of Loyalty: PRO, SP1/32, fols. 256–61; Hall, p. 689. See 6 November 1524.
29   **Joust** in which the king and Suffolk participated as disguised knights at the **Castle of Loyalty**, Greenwich: PRO, SP1/32, fols. 258–9v; Hall, p. 689. See 6 November 1524.
'maskeler' in which the king participated: PRO, SP1/32, fols. 260–1; Hall, pp. 689–90. See 6 November 1524.

1525

January
2–3   **Assaults** on the **Castle of Loyalty** at Greenwich: Hall, p. 690. See 6 November 1524.
5   **Barriers** with swords at the **Castle of Loyalty** at Greenwich in which the king participated: Hall, p. 690. See 6 November 1524.

February
8   **Tourney** on horseback with swords at the **Castle of Loyalty** at Greenwich in which the king participated: Hall, pp. 690–1. See 6 November 1524.

June

18   **Disguisings** for the creation of the Duke of Richmond and Somerset: Hall, p. 703.

Christmas

25 Dec. ⟨ ⟩ 6 Jan.   Because of plague, the king kept a 'still Christmas' at Eltham while Wolsey kept an open court at Richmond and celebrated with disguisings and plays: Hall, p. 707.

1526

January

14   Gibson's day-book contains the dates 14 January and 17 February and lists costumes and materials for **barriers**, a **joust**, **'maskellers'**, and a **pageant** at Greenwich: PRO, SP1/37, fols. 7–15.

February

13   **Joust** at Greenwich in which the king participated: Hall, pp. 707–8. See 14 January 1526.

December

30   **Joust and tourney** at Greenwich: Hall, p. 719.

Christmas

25 Dec. ⟨ ⟩ 6 Jan.   The king kept a solemn Christmas at Greenwich with banquets, revels, masks, and disguisings: Hall, p. 719.

1527

January

3   **Joust:** Hall, p. 719. Following the joust, the king and fifteen companions went in masking apparel to Wolsey's (York Place) where they played **mumchance** before joining the banquet during which there was a **play**, Plautus's *Menaechmi* in Latin by the Cardinal's Gentlemen, followed by a **pageant-disguising** of Venus and elderly lovers: Sanuto, *Diarii*, XLIII: 703–4, calendared in *CSP Venetian*, IV, no. 4; Hall, p. 719; *STC* C1618: Cavendish, *The Life and Death of Thomas Wolsey, Cardinal* (London, 1667), pp. 25–30.

14   Gibson and some of his crews of artisans and labourers worked from 14 January to 7 May on the **Long House** at Greenwich: PRO, SP2/ Fol. C, fols. 106–38v.

Gibson and some of his crews worked from 14 January to 7 May on the pageant for the revels held on 6 May: PRO, SP1/41, fols. 221–53v.

February

6 Sir Henry Guildford's and Sir Thomas Wyatt's crews of artisans and labourers worked from 6 February to 7 May on the **Long House** at Greenwich: PRO, E36/227, fols. 1–36v (fols. 4–17v: a general account from 6 February to 7 May for two triumphal arches; fols. 19–23: Browne's account for painting and gilding; fols. 24–5v: Demyans's account; fols. 26v–9: Urmeston's account; fols. 30r–v: Lovekyn's receipt of material for the arches; fols. 31v–5v: Rastell's account for a pageant, lions, dragons, and greyhounds holding candlesticks).

16 Gibson filed a day book of workmanship and wages from 16 February to 12 April for some of his crews who worked on the **Long House** at Greenwich: BL, Egerton MS. 2605, fols. 1–10.

March

5 **Joust** on Shrove Tuesday in which the king participated: PRO, SP1/41, fols. 165–8. Hall, p. 719. See the payments in January and February 1527.

May

6 **Jousts** at Greenwich to celebrate the Anglo-French treaty negotiations, and a banquet in the **Long House** at Greenwich with a **dialogue** *(Love and Riches)*, **barriers, disguising, pageant** (mount with a cave), and two **masks** in which the king participated: BL, Egerton MS. 2605, fols. 11–14; PRO, SP1/41, fols. 203–6v; SP1/ Fol. C, fols. 106–38v; Sanuto, *Diarii*, XLV: 265–70, calendared in *CSP Venetian*, IV. no. 105; Hall, pp. 722–4. See the payments in January and February 1527.

October

11 Sir Henry Guildford's and Richard Gibson's crews of artisans and labourers began renovations on the **Long House** at Greenwich for the November revels: PRO, E36/227, fols. 48v–61 (Lovekyn's account from 12 October to 9 November); SP1/45, fols. 20–33 (Gibson's account from 11 October to 10 November).

24 John Rightwise was paid 40s. by the City of London for making 'the proposicion to the ffrenshe ambassadors' [in connection with Wolsey's reception and entertainments?]: Corporation of London Record Office, Repertories VII, fol. 224v.

November
10   **Joust** to celebrate the Anglo-French Treaty together with a banquet in the
Long House at Greenwich with a politico-religious **Play** [*Cardinalis Pacificus*, by John Rightwise] performed by the Children of Paul's and a **disguising**,
pageant (a fountain with a mulberry and a hawthorn tree),and four **masks**, in
one of which the king participated: BL, Egerton MS. 2605, fols. 16–43; PRO,
SP1/45, fols. 21–40; *CSP Spanish*, III.ii, no. 240; Hall, pp. 734–5; *STC:*
C1618, Cavendish, *The Life and Death of Thomas Wolsey, Cardinal* (London,
1667), pp. 76–7. See the payments in October and November 1527.

Christmas
25 Dec. 〈 〉 6 Jan.   Unspecified revels at Greenwich and Richmond: BL, Egerton
MS. 2605, fol. 15 (heading of account only).

1528

January
7   Entertainment of the papal legate and ambassadors at Wolsey's (York Place)
to celebrate the Pope's escape from imprisonment with a **play**, Terence's *Phormio*,
and a politico-religious **dialogue** [by John Rightwise], both performed by the
Children of Paul's: Sanuto, *Diarii*, XLVI: 595–7, calendared in *CSP Venetian*,
IV, no. 225. In a letter of 9 January du Bellay wrote to Francis I of **farces** performed in Latin [same as the play and dialogue?]: *Ambassades en Angleterre de
Jean du Bellay. La prèmiere ambassade*, ed. V.L. Bourrilly and P. de Vaissière
(Paris: A. Picard, 1905), 89, calendared in *LP,* IV.iii, Appendix, no. 140.

Christmas
25 Dec. 〈 〉 6 Jan.   The 'Kyng kepte his Christmas at Grenewiche, with muche
solempnitie … [and] shewed great pleasures, bothe of Iustes, Tornay, Bankettes, Maskes and disguisinges … but the Quene shewed to them no maner
of countenaunce, and made no great ioye of nothing, her mynd was so
troubled': Hall, p. 756.

1529

January
1   **Players.** William Crane was paid £6 13s. 4d. for playing before the king with
the Children of the Chapel. The King's Players were rewarded £6 13s. 4d. for
a play before the king. The Princess's Players were paid £4 for playing before
the king: PRO, E101/420/11, fols. 13v, 16.

December

31 The Master of the Bears was paid 40s.: BL, Additional MS. 20003, fol. 8.

Christmas

25 Dec. ⟨ ⟩ 6 Jan. The king and queen kept Christmas at Greenwich 'in great triumph: with great plentie of viaundes, and diuerse disguisynges and Enterludes': Hall, p. 768.

1530

ca. 1530 Fragment of Richard Gibson's account for joust: PRO, SP1/58, fols. 253–4).

January

1 **Players.** William Crane and the Children of the Chapel were paid £6 13s. 4d. for playing before the king: PRO, E101/420/11, fols. 72, 74.
Undated payment. Certain players of Coventry were paid 20s. for playing at court during Christmas: PRO, E101/420/11, fol. 76.

Christmas

25 Dec. ⟨ ⟩ 6 Jan. Following Wolsey's death the king and queen kept Christmas at Greenwich 'and on the twelfe night he satte in the halle in his estate, where as were diuers Enterludes, riche Maskes and disportes, and after that a great banket': Hall, p. 774.

1531

ca. 1531? In an undated petition, John Rightwise reminds the king of his service in making comedies and other pleasures which were shown before ambassadors and other strangers: PRO, SP 1/236, fol. 380, calendared in *LP,* Addenda, I.i, no. 717.

January

1 **Players.** William Crane and the Children of the Chapel were rewarded £6 13s. 4d. for playing before the king. The King's Players were rewarded £6 13s. 4d. for playing before the king. The Princess's Players were paid £4 for playing before the king: PRO, E101/420/11, fols. 146v, 149.
21 John Rightwise, Schoolmaster of St Paul's, was paid £13 9s.: BL, Additional MS. 20003, fol. 55v.

Christmas
25 Dec. ⟨ ⟩ 6 Jan.   The king kept Christmas at Greenwich 'with great solempnitie, but all the men sayde that there was no myrthe ... because the Queene
and the Ladies were absent': Hall, p. 784.

1532

January
10   **Bear-baiting.** The Sergeant Bearward was paid 40*s.*: BL, Additional MS.
20003, fol. 97.

October
25–7   **Bull- and Bear-baiting** at Calais before Henry VIII and Francis I.
27   Banquet and **Mask** for Francis I at the Staple Hall in Calais in which Anne
Boleyn participated. Banquet given by the Duke of Norfolk for French nobles
at the castle at Calais with 'sportes and pastymes': College of Arms, MS.
M 6*bis,* fols. 1–25 (reception, interviews, and retinue of Henry VIII); College
of Arms, MS. M 6*bis,* fols. 148–9v, printed in *STC* 4350, *The maner of the trymphe at Caleys and Bulleyn* (London, 1532); Nicholas Camusat, *Meslanges His-
toriques ou recueil de plusiurs actes, traités et lettres missives depuis 1390 jusqu'en
1580* (Troyes: N. Moreau, 1619), p. 106, calendared in *LP,* V, no. 1485; Hall,
pp. 793–4; *Chronicle of Calais,* pp. 44, 116–23. See 2 November 1532.

November
2   Richard Gibson was paid £11 3*s.* 1*d.* for supplying masking gear when the
king was in Calais: BL, Additional MS. 20003, fol. 139.

Christmas
25 Dec. ⟨ ⟩ 6 Jan.   The king kept Christmas at Greenwich: Hall, p. 795. Edward
Lord Herbert of Cherbury writes that one of the reasons for the Pope's refusal
to grant Henry his divorce was that 'there was a Comedy presented at Court,
to the no little defamation of certain Cardinalls' [At Christmas 1532–3?]:
Edward Lord Herbert of Cherbury, *The Life and Raigne of King Henry the
Eighth* (London: E.G., 1649), p. 368.

1533

May
31   **Coronation joust** for Anne Boleyn at Whitehall: Wriothesley, *Chronicle,* I:
22; Hall, p. 805; BL, Harleian MS. 41, fol. 2, printed in *Holinshed's Chron-*

icles of England, Scotland, and Ireland (London: J. Johnson, 1808), III: 786; BL, Harleian MS. 543, fol. 119 (brief mention of the jousts); BL, Additional MS. 6113, fol. 31v (brief mention); BL, Egerton MS. 985, fol. 58 (brief mention).

Christmas
25 Dec. ⟨ ⟩ 6 Jan.   The king kept Christmas at Greenwich 'with great solempenitie': Hall, p. 808.

1534

Christmas
25 Dec. ⟨ ⟩ 6 Jan.   **Lord of Misrule's mock hunt** at Greenwich: Bodleian Library, Rawlinson MS. D. 777, fol. 182v.

1535

June
30   In a letter to Granvelle, Chapuys mentions that on the eve of St John Henry walked ten miles at 2 a.m. to see an interpretation of a chapter from the Apocalypse: PRO, SP31/18, abstracted in *LP,* VIII, no. 949.

1536

January
8   Death of Katherine of Aragon.
24   In a letter to Granvelle, Chapuys mentions that on the 'eve of the conversion of St. Paul' Henry sustained a fall in running 'at the lists' [probably an exercise]: PRO, SP31/18, abstracted in *LP,* X, no. 200; *CSP Spanish,* V.ii, no. 21.

May
1   **Joust** at Greenwich which the king attended: Hall, p. 819.
19   Execution of Anne Boleyn.
30   Wedding of Henry VIII and Jane Seymour.
31   In a letter to Lord Lisle about the king's marriage on the 30th, John Husee mentions that the king intended to see the watch on midsummer night: PRO, SP3/12, abstracted in *LP,* X, no. 1000.

July
11   In a letter to Empress Isabella, Dr. Ortiz mentions that the king ordered

festivities on proclaiming his marriage to Jane Seymour seven days after the fact: printed in *Notes & Queries*, 4th ser., 3 (1889): 52, abstracted in *LP,* XI, no. 64.

1537

February
10   **Players.** The Queen's Players were rewarded 20*s.* from Cromwell's account: PRO, E36/256, fol. 84v.
19   **Mask.** John Farlyon, Yeoman of the Revels, was paid £13 6*s.* 8*d.* from Cromwel's account 'for my Lord's [Cromwell's] part of the mask' [for Shrovetide? – 11, 12, 13 February]: PRO, E36/256, fol. 85.

October
12 ⟨ ⟩ 24   **Play?** *Thersytes* [by Nicholas Udall? performed by children? for the birth of Prince Edward (b. 12 October)?]: STC: 23949 *A new enterlude called Thersytes.*
24   Death of Jane Seymour.

December
26   **Players.** The King's Players were rewarded 22*s.* 6*d.*, the Lord Chancellor's Players 20*s.*, and the Marquis of Exeter's Players 15*s.* from Cromwell's account: PRO, E36/256, fol. 114v.

Christmas
25 Dec. ⟨ ⟩ 6 Jan.   'The kinges maiestie kept his Christmas at Grenewich in his mournyng apparell [because of the death of Jane Seymour], and so was all the Courte till the morow after Candlemas day': Hall, p. 825.

1538

January
21   **Players.** The Lord Warden's Players were paid 20*s.* from Cromwell's account: PRO, E36/256, fol. 119.
22   **Players.** The Duke of Suffolk's Players were paid 20*s.* from Cromwell's account: PRO, E36/256, fol. 119.
23   **Players.** The Lord Chancellor's Players were paid 10*s.* from Cromwell's account: PRO, E36/256, fol. 119v.

February

2 **Play.** 'Woodall' [Nicholas Udall], schoolmaster of Eton, was paid £5 for performing a play with his children before Cromwell: PRO, E36/256, fol. 119v.

4 **Players.** Lord Cobham's Players were paid 20s. from Cromwell's account: PRO, E36/256, fol. 120v.

March

4 **Mask.** Robyn Drowne and his fellows were paid 20s. 'for their waitting ij nyghtes the same tyme my Lord [Cromwell] made the king a Maske' [for Shrovetide? – 3, 4, 5, March]: PRO, E36/256, fol. 122. See next entry.

5 John Portynare was paid £25 11s. 5d. from Cromwell's account for the charges of the mask: PRO, E36/256, fol. 122.

23 **Mask.** In a letter to the Queen of Hungary, Chapuys mentions that Henry was reported to be 'masking' [ca. 18 March] and visiting the Duchess of Suffolk [Mary, his younger sister]: *CSP Spanish*, V.ii. no. 220.

April

12 **Play.** Mr. Hopton's priest was paid 22s. 6d. for performing a play with his children before Cromwell: PRO, E36/256, fol. 125v.

July

Joust? Derike Dethike, Yeoman of the Armoury, was paid £16 13s. 4d. on a warrant of 25 April for 200 staves by him made for jousts, by the king's commandment: BL, Arundel MS. 97, fol. 29.

September

8 **Players.** John Bale and his 'fellows' were rewarded 40s. for playing before Cromwell at St Stephen's, Canterbury: PRO, E36/256, fol. 140.

1539

January

1 **Players.** William Crane was rewarded £6 13s. 4d. for 'playing with the children before the king'; the King's Players were rewarded £6 13s. 4d.; the Queen's Players, £4, and the Prince's Players, £4, 'for playing before the king this Christmas': BL, Arundel MS. 97, fols. 53–6.

14 **Mask?** John Farlyon, Yeoman of the Revels, was paid £3 8s. 6 1/2d. from Cromwell's account for making Mr Gregory's apparel, and 57s. 9d. for twelve doublets for 'the cornyshmen' [for a mask on New Year's or Twelfth Night?]: PRO, E36/256, fol. 152. See 25 January, 9 February, and 20 March 1539.

25   Christopher 'the Mylyoner' was paid £30 from Cromwell's account for 'the charges of the maske' and 7s. 6d. in reward for his servants: PRO, E36/256, fol. 153v. See 14 January 1539.

31   **Players.** John Bale and his fellows were paid 30s. for performing a play before Cromwell [possibly *Kyng Johan* which was performed at Cranmer's house in London at Christmas 1538–9: *Kyng Johan*, ed. J.H.P. Pafford and W.W. Greg ([London]: Malone Society, 1931), p. xvii]: PRO, E36/256, fol. 153v.

February

9   John Farlyon's servants were paid 20s. from Cromwell's account 'for takyn paynes sundry tymes in maskes': PRO, E36/256, fol. 154. See 14 and 25 January and 11 and 12 February 1539.

11   **Mask.** Christopher the Milliner was paid £10 17s. 11d. from Cromwell's account for the 'stuff of the maske of Kinge Arturs knightes' and £3 for his labour and workmen [at Candlemas?]: PRO, E36/256, fol. 154. See next entry.

12   John Dymoke was paid £9 2s. 6d. from Cromwell's account for 11 copper plates and other necessaries for 'my Lordes maske' and for comfits when the lords dined with Cromwell [at Candlemas?]: PRO, E36/256, fol. 154v.

20   From Cromwell's account a painter 'that made all the hobby horsses and other thinges thereto belonging' was paid £33 17s. 6d. John Heywood was paid £5 10s. 5d. for his costs and 'other necessaries by him layed out.' Mrs Vaughan was paid £6 7s. 6d. for the things bought of her for the masks: PRO, E36/256, fol. 155v. See next entry.

22   **Mask.** A bargeman was paid 16s. 8d. from Cromwell's account for carrying Heywood's mask to court and home again [at Shrovetide? 17, 18, 19 February]: PRO, E36/256, fol. 155v. See next entry.

28   Christopher the Milliner was paid 21s. 2d. from Cromwell's account 'for trimmyng of Devine Providens when she played before the king': PRO, E36/256, fol. 156.

March

20   John Farlyon, Yeoman of the Revels, was paid £6 13s. 4d. from Cromwell's account for ten yards of crimson satin occupied at the masks: PRO, E36/256, fol. 158. See other payments for masks in January and February 1539.

June

18   **Water Triumph** on the Thames (Henry VIII vs. the Pope): Wriothesley, *Chronicle*, I: 99–100; J. Kaulek, *De Chastillon et de Marillac: correspondance politique* (Paris: F. Alcan, 1885), 105, calendared in *LP* XIV, no. 1137; see also July 1539.

July

Sir John Dudley, Master of the Armoury, was paid £27 6s. for twenty-one armourer's doublets, gowns, and hose on a warrant of 13 June: BL, Arundel MS. 97, fol. 85.

September

15 **Mask.** In a letter to Cromwell, Sir Francis Brian mentioned that last night [14 September] the king had a fair mask at Ampthill: PRO, SP1/153, p. 132, calendared in *LP,* XIV.ii, no. 176.

December

4 Nicholas Gibson was paid £22 13s. 4d. on a warrant of this date for 440 mast poles delivered to Richard Longman, Yeoman of the Tents [for the **Reception** of Anne of Cleves?]: BL, Arundel MS. 97, fol. 103.

1540

January

1 **Players.** William Crane and the Children of the Chapel were rewarded £6 13s. 4d., the King's Players were rewarded £6 13s. 4d., the Queen's Players were rewarded £4, and the Prince's Players were rewarded £4, all for playing before the king this Christmas season: BL, Arundel MS. 97, fols. 108–12v.

6 **Banquets, masks,** and **'dyuerse dysportes'** for the wedding of Henry VIII and Anne of Cleves: Hall, p. 836–7.

11 **Joust** for the coronation of Anne of Cleves: Hall, p. 837.

March

10 Derike Dethike, Yeoman of the Armoury, was paid an imprest of £135 8s. 4d. on a warrant of 10 March for provisions to be made for the **jousts, tourney**, and **barriers** against May Day next. Richard Longman, Yeoman of the Tents, was paid £20 17s. 10d. for the wages of divers artificers for setting up of the king's tents upon Blackheath for receiving of the queen: BL, Arundel MS. 97, fol. 121.

May

1, 3, 5 **Joust, tourney, and barriers** at Westminster, after a banquet attended by the king and queen at Durham Place: PRO, E36/113, fols. 38–41v, abstracted in *LP,* XV, no. 616; BL, Harleian MS. 69, fols. 18r–v, abstracted in *LP,* XV, no. 617; College of Arms, MS. Partition Book I, fol. 80v; College of Arms, MS. Tournament Cheques 1d; W. Segar, *The Book of Honor and Arms*

(London, 1590), 93; John Stow, *A Survey of London,* ed. C.L. Kingsford (Oxford: Clarendon Press, 1908), II: 99; Hall, p. 838. See 10 March 1540.

July
9   Marriage of Henry VIII and Anne of Cleves annulled.
28   Wedding of Henry VIII and Catherine Howard.

December
30   Sir Anthony Browne communicated the king's commandment to John Bridges, Yeoman of the Revels, to prepare apparel for a play by the Children of the Chapel on New Year's Day at Greenwich: Folger Library, MS. Lb 2, fol. 1.
31   In a letter to Francis I, Marillac notes that the Christmas season was filled with 'mummeries and rejoicing': J. Kaulek, *De Chastillon et de Marillac: correspondance politique* (Paris: F. Alcan, 1885), 253, calendared in *LP,* XVI, no. 373.

1541

January
1   **Players.** William Crane and the Children of the Chapel were rewarded £6 13*s.* 4*d.* (See 30 December 1540). The King's Players were rewarded £6 13*s.* 4*d.* The Queen's Players were rewarded £4. The Prince's Players were rewarded £4. All of these rewards were for 'playing before the king' at Christmas: BL, Arundel MS. 97, fols. 164v, 167v.
6   **Players.** The Duke of Suffolk's players were rewarded 20*s.* 'for playing in the king*es* hall on Twelfth Even': BL, Arundel MS. 97, fols. 119r–v.

1542

February
13   Execution of Catherine Howard.
20   **Mask** on Shrove Monday at Westminster: Folger Library, MSS Lb 262, Lb 2, fols. 1v–2.
21   **Mask** on Shrove Tuesday at Westminster: Folger Library, MSS Lb 262, Lb 2, fols. 1v–2.

Christmas
25 Dec. 〈   〉 6 Jan.   **Masks** (men at arms and Moors) at Hampton Court: Folger Library, MSS Lb 259, Lb 2, fols. 2v–3.

1543

February

4 **Mask** ('Alamains') on Shrove Sunday at Westminster: Folger Library, MSS Lb 260, Lb 2, fols. 3v–4.

6 **Mask** (mariners and monstrous torch bearers) on Shrove Tuesday at Westminster. John Bridges prepared a **banqueting chamber** decorated with rosemary and bays and borrowed **'pageants'** [frames?] from St Sepulchre's and rented garments from the King's Players: Folger Library, MSS Lb 260, Lb 2, fols. 3v–4.

July

12 Wedding of Henry VIII and Catherine Parr.

Christmas

25 Dec. 〈 〉 6 Jan. **Masks** (one of women and one of Turks) and **entertainments** for Ferdinand de Gonzaga and the Imperial embassy at Hampton Court: Folger Library, MSS Lb 153, Lb 154, Lb 2, fols. 4v–5; Guildford Muniment Room, MS. LM 59/68.

1544

January

1 **Players.** William Crane was paid £6 13*s.* 4*d.* for playing before the king with the Children of the Chapel: BL, Additional MS. 59900, fol. 68v.

February

17 **Bear-baiting** for Don Manriques de Lara, Duke of Najera: BL, Additional MS. 8219, fol. 130v, abstracted in *LP,* XIX.i, no. 296.

July – September

16 From 16 July to 30 September the king was in France.

Christmas

25 Dec. 〈 〉 6 Jan. **Mask(s)** (one for eight men and eight women) and **entertainments** at Greenwich: Folger Library, MSS Lb 258, Lb 2, fols. 6v–7.

1545

Christmas

25 Dec. 〈 〉 6 Jan. **Masks** (Egyptians, Moors, others) and **entertainments** at Hampton Court: Folger Library, MSS Lb 266, Lb 267.

December 1545 ⟨   ⟩ August 1546. Play *[Old Custom?]* Cast list among Sir Thomas Cawarden's papers listing the characters of Virtue and/or Zeal as scholars, Insolence and/or Diligence as gentlemen, Old Blind Custom as a priest, Hunger for Knowledge as a London apprentice, and a collier as Thomas of Croydon: Guildford Muniment Room, MS. LM 17, abstracted in A. Feuillerat, 'An Unknown Protestant Morality Play,' *Modern Language Review*, 9 (1914): 94–6; C.A. Baskerville, 'On Two Old Plays,' *Modern Philology*, 14 (1916): 16, who suggest that the possible dates of performance are December 1545 – August 1546 and May 1547.

1546

August

24–31   **Masks** (wild men, knights, others) and **entertainments** for Claude d'Annebaut, Admiral of France, to celebrate the Anglo-French peace treaty in the **banqueting house** at Hampton Court: Hall, p. 867; Folger Library, MSS Lb 5, Lb 116; Guildford Muniment Room, MSS LM 59/98, LM 59/142, LM 59/143, LM 59/144. Wriothesley, *Chronicle*, I: 173, reports 'riche maskes everie night' and 'daucing in tow (sic) new banqueting howses.' Hall, p. 867. See 13, 15 September 1546.

September

13, 15   The council at Westminster wrote to the council attending the king that they had authorized the expenditure of £4000 'for the banquett houses': PRO, SP1/224, fols. 139–40, 150–2, abstracted in *LP*, XXI.ii, nos. 82, 96. In his undated petition [ca. 1575–88] to Elizabeth I for the pension granted him by Henry VIII, Robert Trunckwell claims to have designed, among other things, the banqueting house at Hampton Court: BL, Additional Charter, no. 1262.

1547

January
28   Death of Henry VIII.

EDWARD VI

1547

February

19   The Revels Office lent garments to the city of London for the **coronation entry** of Edward VI: Folger Library, MS. Lb 268.

20   The Revels Office supplied a 'mount' by Nicholas Bellin of Modena for the **coronation** ceremony of Edward VI at Westminster: Guildford Muniment Room, MS. LM 59/34. See also 22 February 1547.

20, 21, 22 (Shrovetide)   **Mask(s)** and **play(s)** [at least one on an anti-papal subject] at Westminster: Folger Library, MSS Lb 8, Lb 9, Lb 270, Lb 271, Lb 272.

21, 22   **Coronation tournament** at Whitehall: College of Arms, MS. I 18, fols. 92v–4; College of Arms, MS. I 7, fol. 43v (draft of I 18), printed (rather freely from I 18 and I 7) in *Literary Remains,* I, pp. ccc–ccciii; BL, Egerton MS. 3026, fols. 1–33 (imperfect copy of I 18 and I 7); Wriothesley, *Chronicle,* II: 183; Guildford Muniment Room, MS. LM 30.

22   **Pageant, interlude:** There was 'a goodly enterlude played in the said hall where was also made a mount [also used on 20 February at the coronation ceremony at Westminster] with the story of Orpheus ryght conyngly composed/ At the wh*ich* play' the king was present: College of Arms, MS. I 18, fol. 94, printed in *Literary Remains,* I, p. cccii. **Plays** [identical to the pageant and interlude?] after the tourney in the evening: G. Lefèvre-Pontalis, ed. *Correspondance Politique de Odet De Selve Ambassadeur de France en Angleterre (1546–1549)* (Paris: F. Alcan, 1888), 105.

27   **Joust:** College of Arms, MS. I 18, fols. 94–5, printed in *Literary Remains,* I, p. ccciii. **Mask:** Folger Library, MS. Lb 269.

March

26   Material was delivered to the Revels Office and cut into playing garments for the King's Players and other gowns for the king (including a long priest's gown) and his young friends: Guildford Muniment Room, MS. LM 59/145. See April 1547.

April

?   **Play.** Outline for a morality play including the characters of a pope, friar, and priest: Guildford Muniment Room, MS. LM 128/12.

11   **Play** or **mask** at Greenwich by the king [in a priest's gown?], Suffolk, Strange [and the King's Players?]: Guildford Muniment Room, MSS LM 59/145, LM 59/146.

ca. May
Play? *[Old Custom]*. See December 1545 – August 1546.

Christmas
25 Dec. ⟨ ⟩ 6 Jan.   **Pageant** (Tower of Babylon) for a **play** *[Comediam de meretrice Babylonica?* by Edward VI] at Hampton Court [by the King's Players for New Year's?]: Folger Library, MS. Lb 274. **Mask(s)** (Prester John, with costumes for Turks and friars, and others?) at Hampton Court [for Twelfth Night]: Folger Library, MS. Lb 274.

1548

January
1   **Players.** Richard Bower was paid £6 13*s.* 4*d.* for playing before the king with the Children of the Chapel. The King's Players were rewarded £6 13*s.* 4*d.*: PRO, E101/426/5, fols. 63v–4r.
3   Masking garments sent to the Lord Protector: Guildford Muniment Room, MS. LM 59/64. Bill for masking gear, including six Turkish gowns and blue satin and four costumes for friars were lent to Secretary Paget: Guildford Muniment Room, MS. LM 56/65.

February
12, 13, 14 (Shrovetide)   **Triumph** at Greenwich in which six gentlemen challenged all comers at a **joust, tourney, barriers**, and **assault** on a castle defended by thirty against up to a hundred men: BL, Cotton MS. Nero C. X, fol. 13v, printed in *Literary Remains*, II: 22; *APC*, II: 171 (warrant to Bradshaw for the construction); PRO, E351/3326, memb. 6 (Bradshaw's account); John Stow, *Annals* (London, 1615), 595.
Masks (one of men, two of women, and one of young Moors in which the king performed) and a **play** by the King's Players at Greenwich: Folger Library, MSS Lb 7, Lb 6, Lb 274; Lb 290 (see Christmas 1547).

Christmas
25 Dec. ⟨ ⟩ 6 Jan.   **Masks** ('Alamains,' and one on an unidentified subject) at Westminster: Folger Library, MS. Lb 11, fols. 1r–v; Guildford Muniment Room, MS. LM 59/63.

1549

January
1   **Players.** Richard Bower was paid £6 13*s.* 4*d.* for playing before the king with

the Children of the Chapel. The King's Players were rewarded £6 13s. 4d. The Gentlemen of the Chapel were rewarded £13 6s. 8d.: PRO, E101/426/6, fol. 30v.

March
3, 4, 5 (Shrovetide) **Masks** (one of Hermits and others), **pageant** (dragon with seven heads), and a **play** performed by the King's Players at Westminster: Folger Library, MS. Lb 11, fols. 2r–v.

Christmas
25 Dec. ⟨   ⟩ 6 Jan. **Masks** (costumes were made for hermits, Lance Knights [same as 'Alamains'?], friars, and pilgrims) and **play(s)** at Westminster: Folger Library, MSS Lb 12, Lb 113; Guildford Muniment Room, MS. LM 59/156.

1550

ca. 1550 **Dramatic fragment**, with a note in Sir Thomas Cawarden's hand, 'Parte of a play': Folger Library, MS. Lb 554, printed by L.A. Cummings, '"Part of a play": A Possible Dramatic Fragment (c 1550) from the office of the Master of the Revels,' *Records of Early English Drama Newsletter*, 2, no. 2 (1977): 2–15, and G.R. Proudfoot, 'Five Dramatic Fragments from the Folger Shakespeare Library and from the Henry E. Huntington Library,' *MSC*, IX (1977), 52–7.

January
18 In a letter to the Earl of Rutland on this date, Robert Constable describes a **barriers** with a 'device' in which defenders protected Lady Love from ascending a gallows to hang and mentions that Lord Fitzwater, Sir George Howard, Sir Anthony Browne, and Henry Neville had issued a challenge for a **joust, tourney, and 'trandon'** to he held at Shrovetide: H.C.M. Lyte, *The Manuscripts of His Grace the Duke of Rutland preserved at Belvoir Castle* (London: HMSO, 1889), Part I: 55, in *RCHM*, XII, appendix, part iv.

May
25 **Pastime** of ten against ten at the ring following a banquet for the reception of the French ambassadors: BL, Cotton MS. Nero C. X, fol. 22, printed in *Literary Remains*, II: 272.
26 **Bear- and bull-baiting** for the French ambassadors: BL, Cotton MS. Nero C. X, fol. 22, printed in *Literary Remains*, II: 272.
29 **Banquet** for the French ambassadors by the Duke of Somerset, after which

entertainments included seeing a **bear hunted in the Thames**, 'wildfire' cast out of boats, and 'many pretty conceits': BL, Cotton MS. Nero C. X, fol. 22, printed in *Literary Remains,* II: 273.

Mask: Wriothesley, *Chronicle,* II: 40.

Undated payments from the King's Privy Purse relate to the reception and entertainments of the French embassies in May 1550 and in July 1551. Gifts were given to the king by the French hostages and other visitors which he acknowledged by gift payments from his Privy Purse. He also rewarded French musicians, trumpeters, drones, and fifes: PRO, E101/426/8.

Bear-baiting. The king rewarded the Sergeant of his Bears £11 [for the baitings before the ambassadors in May]: PRO, E101/426/8.

Players. The Duchess of Suffolk's Players were rewarded £4, the Duke of Somerset's Players £4, the Marquis of Northampton's Players £8, and the Children of Paul's £12 13*s. 4d.* [for performances in May 1550 and/or in July 1551]: PRO, E101/426/8.

June

3   **Joust** and **tourney** for the marriage of John Dudley, Lord Lisle, and Anne, daughter of the Duke of Somerset, which the king attended: BL, Cotton MS. Nero C. X, fols. 22r–v, printed in *Literary Remains,* II: 273–5.

5   **Joust** with great staves and **tourney** on foot, probably in connection with the wedding of Sir Robert Dudley, later Earl of Leicester, and Amy, daughter of Sir John Robsart, on the 4th which the king attended: BL, Cotton MS. Nero C. X, fol. 22v, printed in *Literary Remains,* II: 275.

8   **Masks.** The Duke of Somerset and William Parr were banqueted by Francois de Vendome (Vidame of Chartres), at which banquet were shown 'divers masques and other conceits': BL, Cotton MS. Nero C. X, fol. 22v, printed in *Literary Remains,* II: 275–6.

17   **Running at the ring.** William Parr, Herbert, Francois de Vendome (Vidame of Chartres), and Jean d'Annebaut (Baron de la Hunaudaye) and 'divers other' gentlemen hosted this in return for the banquet given by the Earl of Warwick on 16 June: BL, Cotton MS. Nero C. X, fol. 23, printed in *Literary Remains,* II: 279.

19   The king was banqueted at Deptford by Lord Clinton, where before supper he saw an **exhibition** of men running at one another on the sides of boats until one was cast into the water; after supper he saw a fort or castle made 'upon a great lighter' on the Thames, defended by forty or fifty soldiers and a galley armed with men and munitions assaulted by four pinnaces armed with men, fireworks, and artillery: BL, Cotton MS. Nero C. X, fols. 23r–v, printed in *Literary Remains,* II: 279.

Christmas

25 Dec. 1550 ⟨ ⟩ 31 July 1551   The Revels account covers the period from Christmas to 31 July for the production of five **masks** (Irishmen, Moors, others), **plays**, and **pastimes** shown for Christmas at Greenwich, Shrovetide (8, 9, 10 February), and at other times, some of which were given in the banqueting houses at Hyde and Marylebone Parks in July. The account includes playing garments made for the king, his young lords, Will Somers and other players: Folger Library, MSS Lb 41, fols. 22–4v, 87–9; Lb 324.

1551

March

31   The king issued a **challenge** that he with sixteen of his chamber would 'run at base' (running), shoot (archery), and run at the ring (on horseback with lance) with any seventeen gentlemen of the court: BL, Cotton MS. Nero C. X, fol. 31, printed in *Literary Remains*, II: 310; Machyn, *Diary*, p. 5.

April

1   The first part of the king's challenge, to **'run at base,'** was answered: BL, Cotton MS. Nero C. X, fol. 31v, printed in *Literary Remains*, II: 311.

6   The second part of the king's challenge, **'rounds'** (shooting at targets placed at fixed distances from the archer) and **'rovers'** (shooting at targets selected at random), was answered: BL, Cotton MS. Nero C. X, fol. 31v, printed in *Literary Remains*, II: 312; Machyn, *Diary*, p. 5.

May

3   The third part of the king's challenge, **running at the ring**, was answered. A **tourney** fought with swords by six against six followed at Greenwich: BL, Cotton MS. Nero C. X, fols. 33r–v, printed in *Literary Remains*, II: 317; Machyn, *Diary*, p. 5.

June

28   Between 28 June and 24 July work progressed on the **banqueting house** and other facilities constructed at Hyde Park for the reception of the French embassy in July and flowers were also bought and arranged in the banqueting house at Hampton Court. For the many documents associated with the construction see Appendix 1, Principal Sources, below.

July

6   **Running at the ring** at Blackheath: Machyn, *Diary*, pp. 6–7.

16   **Investiture** of Edward VI into the Order of St Michael by Jacques d'Albon,

Seigneur de St Andre, Marshall of France, at Hampton Court. (Henri II had been elected on 23 April and installed on 20 June into the Order of the Garter; in return, Edward was elected to the Order of St. Michael on 3 June.) Following the ceremony there was a **banquet** after which the king 'saw some pastime': BL, Cotton MS. Nero C. X, fol. 38, printed in *Literary Remains*, II: 331–2.

19   St Andre dined with the king and after supper 'saw a dozen courses': BL, Cotton MS. Nero C. X, fol. 38v, printed in *Literary Remains*, II: 333–4.

26   St Andre dined with the king and saw an archery **exhibition**: BL, Cotton MS. Nero C. X, fol. 39, printed in *Literary Remains*, II: 335.

28   St Andre was entertained in the **banqueting house**, built under the supervision of Sir Thomas Cawarden, at Hyde Park where he saw 'coursing': BL, Cotton MS. Nero C. X, fol. 39v, printed in *Literary Remains*, II: 335.

Undated payments from the King's Privy Purse relate to the reception, ceremonies, and entertainments in July 1551. French trumpeters, St Andre's jester, and the ambassador's musicians were rewarded along with men who played on flutes, shawms, sackbuts, one who danced on a rope and vaulted, and a boy who tumbled before the king. Plays may also have been performed. See 29 May 1550.

October

31   **Reception** of Mary of Lorranie, Dowager Queen of Scotland, at Hampton Court: 'this night, and, the next day al was spent in dauncing and pastime': BL, Cotton MS. Nero C. X, fols. 45v–6, printed in *Literary Remains*, II: 359.

November

17   **Challenge** issued by the Earl of Warwick, Henry Sidney, Sir Harry Neville, and Sir Harry Gates to all comers at a **joust** on 3 January and a **tourney** on 6 January: BL, Cotton MS. Nero C. X, fol. 48v, printed in *Literary Remains*, II: 368. See 24 November 1551, 3 and 6 January 1552.

24   Warrant from the king to Cawarden to furnish the 'triumph': Folger Library, MS. Lb 16.

December

24   Letter from Northumberland to Cawarden, dated Monday before Christmas day, requesting that he furnish George Ferrers's entertainments as **Lord of Misrule**: Folger Library, MS. Lb 257.

25   **Play**. Warrant from the council to Cawarden to furnish a play by the King's Players: Folger Library, MSS Lb 278; Lb 41, fol. 41. Warrant from the council to Cawarden authorizing him to furnish the **Lord of Misrule**: Folger Library, MS. Lb 277.

30 Warrant from the council to Cawarden authorizing a second livery for the **Lord of Misrule's** entertainments: Folger Library, MS. Lb 281. Warrant from the council to Cawarden specifying certain parcels to be delivered to George Ferrers as **Lord of Misrule**: Folger Library, MS. Lb 284.

Christmas
25 Dec. 〈 〉 6 Jan. Letter from George Ferrers to Cawarden requesting that he send carpenters and painters to help prepare properties for the **Lord of Misrule's** entertainments: Folger Library, MS. Lb 282. The Revels Office produced four **masks** (Argus, two of women [Moors and Amazons], and one unnamed). The Revels Office also supplied the costumes and properties for the entertainments of George Ferrers, who received an appointment from the council as 'Master of the King's Pastimes': *Grafton's Chronicle*, ed. Sir Henry Ellis (London, 1809), 526–7; Folger Library, MS. Lb 41, fols. 41–8.

1552

January
[2] Letter from George Ferrers to Cawarden mentioning his **'drunken mask'** to be performed that evening: Folger Library, MS. Lb 285. Letter from Ferrers to Cawarden ordering certain garments for his entertainments: Folger Library, MS. Lb 500.
3 **Joust** at Greenwich: BL, Cotton MS. Nero C. X, fol. 51, printed in *Literary Remains*, II: 384; Folger Library, MS. Lb 80; Guildford Muniment Room, MS. LM 59/147. See 17 November 1551.
George Ferrers's **mock Midsummer Night's watch** together with, or identical to, a **combat** devised for Will Somers by the king: Folger Library, MS. Lb 285.
Warrant from the council to Cawarden authorizing the replacement of costumes for the Lord of Misrule's councillors: Folger Library, MS. Lb 286.
4 Lord of Misrule's **entry** into London: Folger Library, MS. Lb 285; Machyn, *Diary*, pp. 13–14; *Grafton's Chronicle*, ed. Sir Henry Ellis (London, 1809), 526–7.
5 Warrant from the council to Cawarden to furnish Chaloner's *Riches and Youth* for 6 January: Folger Library, MS. Lb 288.
Letter from Ferrers to Cawarden about Chaloner's *Riches and Youth*: Folger Library, MS. Lb 299.
6 **Tourney** at Greenwich. See 17 November 1551 and 3 January 1552.
Play. Warrant from the Lord Chamberlain to Cawarden to furnish a play by the King's Players: Folger Library, MS. Lb 282.

Dialogue with **barriers** (*Riches and Youth* [by Sir Thomas Chaloner]) and **masks:** BL, Cotton MS. Nero C. X, fols. 51v–2, printed in *Literary Remains,* II: 387–8.

17   **Joust** at Greenwich: BL, Cotton MS. Nero C. X, fol. 52, printed in *Literary Remains,* II: 389.

March

Play and mask. In March Sir Thomas Chaloner paid 20s. 'gevyn on Shrove monday [29 February] to the kinge*s* players who playd the play of Selflove' and further paid 10*s.* to them 'who playd amonge*s* the maskers at dyn*ner*': BL, Lansdowne MS. 824, fol. 17.

May

12   **Running at the ring** by the king and others after a progress with his guard through Greenwich to Blackheath: Machyn, *Diary,* p. 18.

December

21   Warrant from the council to Cawarden to furnish Ferrers's entertainments as Lord of Misrule: Folger Library, MS. Lb 291.

25   **Embassy** from the Lord of Misrule received at court: Folger Library, MS. Lb 292, fols. 1r–v. In this letter to Cawarden, Ferrers mentions a number of entertainments he had planned. In addition to those listed below he mentions hunting and hawking, and other devices to be given on unspecified days.

26   Lord of Misrule's **progress** by water, **entry, reception,** and an unnamed entertainment at Greenwich: Folger Library, MS. Lb 292, fol. 1v.

27   Ferrers ordered a suit of apparel from Cawarden for this day and planned to give an unnamed entertainment: Folger Library, MS. Lb 292, fol. 1v. Ferrers ordered twelve hobby-horses, hunters' apparel, and other costumes from Cawarden: Folger Library, MSS Lb 289, Lb 295; Guildford Muniment Room, MS. LM 128/13.

31   Warrant from the council to Cawarden to furnish the mask on 6 January: Folger Library, MS. Lb 294.

Christmas

25 Dec. ⟨ ⟩ 6 Jan.   The Revels Office made six 'masks' [sets of costumes] and produced at least three **masking entertainments** (covetous men with baboons as torch bearers; women of Diana with matrons as torch bearers; and 'pollenders' with soldiers as torch bearers): Folger Library, MS. Lb 41, fols. 61–2. The Revels Office also produced **pastimes,** in addition to producing the entertainments of George Ferrers who was again appointed 'Master of the King's

Pastimes' and served as **Lord of Misrule**, and Sir George Howard's '**triumph**' of *Venus, Cupid, and Mars:* Folger Library, MS. Lb 41, fol. 51. The King's Players were rehearsing the **play** of *Aesop's Crow,* and William Baldwin and George Ferrers were preparing certain **interludes**. See 6 January 1553.

1553

January

1   Ferrers ordered a suit of clothing from Cawarden for his entertainments this day at court: Folger Library, MS. Lb 292, fol. 2.

Lord of Misrule's **joust with hobby-horses** at Greenwich: Folger Library, MS. Lb 295.

4?   Lord of Misrule's **entry into London**: Machyn, *Diary,* pp. 28–9; Folger Library, MSS Lb 292, Lb 293.

5   Letter from Sir George Howard to Cawarden attempting to describe his *Venus, Cupid, and Mars:* Folger Library, MS. Lb 256.

Letter from Ferrers to Cawarden explaining the characters, properties, and costumes needed for *Venus, Cupid, and Mars:* Folger Library, MS. Lb 501.

6   Ferrers ordered a suit of clothing from Cawarden for this day at court: Folger Library, MS. Lb 292, fol. 2.

Play? [*Aesop's Crow* by the King's Players? William Baldwin, *Beware the Cat,* ed. W.P. Holden, Connecticut College Monograph, No. 8 (New London, Conn., 1963), 27–8].

'**Triumph**' of *Venus, Cupid, and Mars* with **pageants**. See Christmas 1552.

28   Letter from the council to Cawarden to furnish William Baldwin's play for Candlemas night [2 February]: *APC,* IV: 210.

February

2   William Baldwin's play scheduled for Candlemas was postponed: Folger Library, MS. Lb 41, fol. 64. See 2 April 1553.

13   Revels Office productions scheduled for Shrovetide (12, 13, 14) were postponed due to the king's illness: Folger Library, MS. Lb 41, fol. 64.

28   Revels Office productions were resumed and rescheduled for Easter and May Day: Folger Library, MS. Lb 41, fol. 64.

April

2 (Easter)   The Revels Office produced five **masks** (great bagpipes played by apes; cats; 'Medioxes' [half-men and half-death]; Greek worthies; and tumblers who walked on their hands): Folger Library, MS. Lb 41, fols. 64–71, 72.

Plays. William Baldwin's *The State of Ireland,* postponed from Candlemas;

John Heywood's unnamed play for twelve boys; and other plays and pastimes were performed on this day and on 1 May: Folger Library, MS. Lb 41, fol. 72.

May
1 **Plays** and **masks.** See 2 April 1553.
20 Letter from Northumberland to Cawarden 'to apoynt out a couple of fayre maskes, oon of men and another of women' for the weddings scheduled for 25 May. Loseley MS. [not located], calendared in *RCHM*, VII: 608b, reprinted in Feuillerat, *Edward VI and Mary,* p. 306.
25 Triple **wedding** of Guildford Dudley and Lady Jane Grey, Lord Herbert and Catherine Grey, Lord Hastings and Catherine Dudley. See 20 May 1553.

July
6 Death of Edward VI. Accession of Jane Grey.
19 Deposition of Jane Grey. Accession of Mary.

MARY

1553

September
26 **Play.** Warrant from the queen to the Revels Office to furnish a play by the Gentlemen of the Chapel 'to be played before vs at the feastes of owr coronacyon as in tymes paste haithe bene accustomed to be done by the gentillmen of the Chappell of owr progenitours': Loseley Manor Documents, vol. V, no. 6; Folger Library, MSS Lb 25 (copy), and Lb 41, fol. 73 (copy entered into Cawarden's account). Warrant to Sir Edward Walgrave, Keeper of the Great Wardrobe, to furnish material for the costumes: PRO, E101/427/5, no. 9. The play was scheduled for 1 October but then postponed until Christmas.

Christmas
25 Dec. ⟨ ⟩ 6 Jan. **Play** *(Humanum Genus)* by the Gentlemen of the Chapel; **masks**; and other **entertainments**: Folger Library, MS. Lb 41, fols. 73–5. See 26 September 1553.
Play? *Respublica?* [by Nicholas Udall?] performed by a children's company. W.W. Greg, ed., *Respublica,* Early English Text Society, o.s., vol. 226 (London: Oxford University Press, 1952), pp. viii–x.

1554

July

25   **Wedding entertainments** for Philip (who arrived in England on the 19th)
and Mary at Winchester, with 'triumphing, banquetting, singing, masking, and
daunsing,' some of which apparently were held in a banqueting house: *Chronicle of Queen Jane and Queen Mary*, p. 143.
Catholic interludes and pageants [probably public rather than court plays]:
Holinshed's Chronicles of England, Scotland, and Ireland, ed. Sir Henry Ellis
(1808), IV: 61.

November

(?)   **Jugo de cane** [cane game] exhibited before the king and queen at Smithfield:
Chronicle of Queen Jane and Queen Mary, p. 143.
Lawrence Bradshaw charged £41 16s. 1 1/4d. in the Works account for making a frame at Smithfield: PRO, E351/3326, memb. 8d.

1(?)   **Mask** (mariners): Folger Library, MS. Lb 41, fols. 78–85v.

11   Henry Lord Maltravers, after Earl of Arundel, and John Lumley requested
'one maske' of 'Alamains' or 'sume other' from Cawarden for a **mask** at Arundel place: Folger Library, MS. Lb 499.

25   Martial exhibition, including **jugo de cane**, in which King Philip participated: Machyn, *Diary*, pp. 75–6.
Challenge to a tournament by the Marquis of Berghes and three others: *CSP Venetian*, XIII. no. 111.

30(?)   **Mask** (Hercules with mariners as torchbearers) to celebrate the reconciliation of England to the Church of Rome, the queen's supposed pregnancy,
and Cardinal Pole's visit: Folger Library, MS. Lb 41, fols. 78–85v.

December

4   **Barriers:** College of Arms, MS. M 6*bis*, fols. 59–62 (challenge by Spanish
knights to fight on foot at barriers); College of Arms, MS. M 6*bis*, fols 60v–1
(list of winners at barriers); BL, Harleian MS. 69, fols. 22v–3v (articles); BL,
Additional MS. 33735, fols. 6v–7 (challenge); College of Arms, MS. Tournament Cheques, 3a, 3b.

8   Warrant from the queen to the Revels Office concerning Nicholas Udall who
had already shown 'dialogwes and Enterludes before vs' and 'myndeth herafter
to shewe' more of them. The Revels were ordered to furnish his productions
'at all & euery soche tyme and tymes so ofte and when so euer he shall neade
& requier it': Loseley Manor Documents, vol. VI, no. 7; Folger Library, MSS
Lb 26 (copy), Lb 27 (draft), Lb 41, fol. 78 (copy entered into Cawarden's
account).

18   **Running** 'on fott with spayers and swerds at the tornay': Machyn, *Diary*, p. 79.

Christmas
25 Dec. 〈 〉 6 Jan.   **Masks** (Venetian senators with galley slaves as torch bearers, and six Venuses or amorous ladies with six Cupids as torch bearers) and **plays** at Christmas and other times by Nicholas Udall and others: Folger Library, MS. Lb 41, fols. 78–85v.

1555

January
24   **Joust** at Westminster: Machyn, *Diary*, p. 80.

February
12   **Joust, tourney, jugo de cane, and mask** for the marriage of Lord Strange and Lady Cumberland: Machyn, *Diary*, p. 82.
24, 25, 26   **Masks** for Shrovetide (six Turkish magistrates with archers as torch bearers and eight women as goddesses-huntresses with Turkish women as torch bearers): Folger Library, MS. Lb 41, fols. 78–85v.

March
19   **Joust** in which King Philip participated: Machyn, *Diary*, p. 83.
25   **Joust** in disguise at Westminster: Machyn, *Diary*, p. 84.
   In 1–2 Philip and Mary, Lawrence Bradshaw charged £79 9s. 2d. for repairing the tilt at Westminster and Greenwich: PRO, E351/3226, memb. 9d.

December
6, 28   '*The Song of the Chyldbysshop as it was songe before the queenes maiestie in her priuie chamber at her manour of saynt Iames in the Feeldes on saynt Nicholas day [6 December] and Innocents day [28 December] this yeare nowe present, by the chyld bysshop of Poules churche with his company:*' printed in Thomas Warton, *History of English Poetry*, ed. William C. Hazlitt (London: Reeves & Turner, 1871), IV: 237, reprinted in Feuillerat, *Edward VI and Mary*, p. 202.
24   Letter from William Baldwin to Cawarden outlining his **play** – *Love and Lyve:* Folger Library, MS. Lb 298.

Christmas
25 Dec. 〈 〉 6 Jan.   **Masks, entertainments, and plays:** Folger Library, MS. Lb 42, fols. 19–21.

1556

February
2   **Masks** at Westminster for Candlemas: Folger Library, MS. Lb 42, fols. 21v–2v.
11(?)   **Mask.** Secretary Paget requested that Cawarden loan masking garments for the use of the Venetian ambassador: Folger Library, MS. Lb 296.
16, 17, 18 (Shrovetide)   **Entertainments:** Folger Library, MS. Lb 42, fols. 23–4.

Christmas
25 Dec. ⟨ ⟩ 6 Jan.   **Masks** and **plays:** Folger Library, MS. Lb 42, fols. 27–8v.

1557

February
2   **Masks** at Candlemas: Folger Library, MS. Lb 42, fols. 29r–v.

February – March
28 February, 1, 2 March (Shrovetide)   **Masks:** Folger Library, MS. Lb 42, fols. 30r–v.

April
(?)   Letter [n.d.] from Sir Henry Jerningham to Cawarden requiring him to prepare **masking entertainments:** Feuillerat, *Edward VI and Mary,* p. 245.
(?)   Warrant from the queen to the Keeper of the Great Wardrobe to supply Cawarden with material for the **mask** to be shown on 25 April: Bodleian Library, MS. Engl. Poet. d. 13, fol. 15.
(?)   Material delivered to Cawarden for the **mask** on 25 April: Folger Library, MS. Lb 301.
25   **Great mask** of 'Alamains,' pilgrims, and Irishmen: Folger Library, MS. Lb 42, fols. 31–2v. See the payments in April 1557.

Christmas
25 Dec. ⟨ ⟩ 6 Jan.   **Masks, plays, and pastimes:** Folger Library, MS. Lb 42, fols. 35–6.

1558

February
2   **Masks, plays, and pastimes** for Candlemas: Folger Library, MS. Lb 42, fols. 37r–v.

20, 21, 22 (Shrovetide)   **Masks, plays, and pastimes:** Folger Library, MS. Lb 42, fols. 38r–v.

November
17   Death of Queen Mary

ELIZABETH I
1558

[17 Nov. ⟨ ⟩ 31 Dec.]   **Joust, tourney, barriers** at Whitehall: William Segar, *The Booke of Honor and Armes* (London, 1590), 94.

Christmas
25 Dec. ⟨ ⟩ 6 Jan.   **Revels and masks** (one with costumes for cardinals and bishops; another called 'the pathway to perfect knowledge'): Guildford Muniment Room, MS. LM 59/170; Folger Library, MS. Lb 42, fols. 41–3v.

1559

January
3   Order from the queen to the Revels to supply certain garments to the City of London for the **coronation entry:** Folger Library, MSS Lb 33, Lb 109.
6   **Farce** [play?] and **mummery** in which cardinals were costumed as crows, bishops as asses, and abbots as wolves: *CSP Venetian,* VII, no. 10, p. 11. See Christmas 1558.
16, 17   **Coronation tournament: jousts, tourney, barriers** at Whitehall: College of Arms, MS. Portfolio Book I, following fol. 126 (warrant for coronation joust); Machyn, *Diary,* p. 187; *CSP Venetian,* VII, no. 10, pp. 18–19; PRO, SP12/38/35, calendared in *CSP Domestic, 1547–1580,* p. 264; College of Arms, MS. Tournament Cheques, 4a, 4b, 4c, 4d, 4e, 4f.
Mask: Folger Library, MS. Lb 42, fols. 45–7v. The tradition of a play by the Gentlemen of the Chapel at coronations mentioned in a warrant from Queen Mary on 26 September 1553 (Loseley Manor Documents, vol. V, no. 6) cannot be verified for Elizabeth I's coronation.
22   **Mask** [and **morris dance?**]: Folger Library, MS. Lb 42, fols. 45–7v.

February
5   '**double mummery**' on Shrove Sunday [**mask** of 'swartrutters' and Hungarians?]: *CSP Venetian,* VII, no. 18; Folger Library, MS. Lb 42, fols. 49–52.

7 **Mask** (fishermen and fisherwives); and another **mask** (marketwives with mariners as torch bearers) on Shrove Tuesday: Folger Library, MS. Lb 42, fols. 49–52; Guildford Muniment Room, MS. LM 59/169.

May
25 **Mask** (astronomers) in the **banqueting house** at Westminster for the embassy of the Duc de Montmorency, Constable of France: Guildford Muniment Room, MS. LM 58; Folger Library, MS. Lb 42, fols. 53–5. The banqueting house was designed by Robert Trunckwell and constructed by the Works in the stone gallery at Westminster: PRO, E351/3332 (Works account); Folger Library, MSS Lb 187, Lb 188, Lb 189, Lb 196 (Revels bills).

July
3   **Joust** at Greenwich: Machyn, *Diary*, pp. 202–3.
11 **Joust** by the queen's pensioners followed by a **mask** in a banqueting house at Greenwich: Machyn, *Diary*, pp. 203–4.

August
6 **Mask.** The queen was entertained by the Earl of Arundel in the **banqueting house** at Nonsuch with 'soper, bankett, and maske, with drumes and flutes, and all the mysyke that cold be, tyll mydnyght': Machyn, *Diary*, p. 206.
7 **Plays.** The queen was entertained by the Earl of Arundel in the **banqueting house** at Nonsuch with a play by the Children of Paul's 'and ther master Se[bastian], master Phelypes, and master Haywod': Machyn, *Diary*, p. 206.

September
before the 30th **Mask** (shipmen and maids of the country) in the **banqueting house** at Lord Clinton's, West Horsley: Folger Library, MS. Lb 42, fols. 55v–6v. The banqueting house, apparently a free standing structure of two storeys, was built and decorated by the Works and Revels: Folger Library, MS. Lb 142.

Notes

INTRODUCTION

1   I use the terms found in the accounts and narratives to refer to court entertain-
     ments, no matter how imprecise they may seem from our point of view: revel,
     pleasure, pastime, mask, maskelyn, maskyr, disguising, mummery, play, interlude,
     comedy, barriers, tourney, dialogue, *farsa,* talk, and so on. I call attention to
     instances in which contemporary witnesses contradict themselves or one another
     in their use of terms. When referring to these entertainments in general contexts
     (as opposed to specific discussions of entertainments in which I use the terms
     found in the sources) I use 'play' to refer to entertainments which are composed
     largely, but not necessarily exclusively, of dialogue. I am well aware of the ambi-
     guity of the term 'play' in this period (see John C. Coldewey, 'Plays and "Play" in
     Early English Drama,' *RORD,* 28 [1985], 181–8), but it is preferable to the even
     more problematical term 'interlude' (see Nicholas Davis, 'The Meaning of the
     Word "Interlude": A Discussion,' and 'Allusions to Medieval Drama in Britain:
     Interlude,' *Medieval English Theatre,* 6 no. 1 [1984], 5–15, 61–91). I use
     'pageant' to refer to a structural device used to convey disguised persons into a
     Hall, or used as a scenic backdrop, or as a property, or as a display piece, or used
     to convey disguised knights into the tiltyard – never to refer to a 'play.' I use
     'pageant-disguising' to refer to a costumed entertainment employing a pageant in
     which music, dance, and symbolic action are the principal, but not necessarily the
     only, components. I use 'mask' to refer to a costumed entertainment in which
     informal dancing and interaction between participants and spectators and sur-
     prise revelation of identity are the principal, but not necessarily the only, compo-
     nents. These terms are adopted for convenience in general discussion only and
     should not be taken to imply generic distinctions among entertainments in a peri-
     od in which the conception of genre was flexible and inclusive.

2   A.P. Newton, 'Tudor Reform in the Royal Household,' in Robert W. Seton-Watson, ed., *Tudor Studies* (London: Longman, 1924), 231–56.

3   J.D. Mackie, *The Early Tudors, 1485–1558* (Oxford: Clarendon Press, 1952), 201. John Guy, 'The King's Council and Political Participation,' in Alastair Fox and John Guy, eds., *Reassessing the Henrican Age* (Oxford: Blackwell, 1986), 121–47, and David Starkey, 'The Privy Council: Revolution or Evolution?' in C. Coleman and D. Starkey, eds., *Revolution Reassessed* (Oxford: Clarendon Press, 1986), 59–85.

4   Chambers, *ES,* I: 66.

5   Altering texts presented in the revels appears to have been done informally in the early Tudor period. William Baldwin, for example, sent a cast list and an explanation of his new play *Love and Lyve* in 1556 for Sir Thomas Cawarden's perusal. By the 1570s the Revels officers met formally to select the plays and masks and to plan productions, but 'reforming' them is always listed as one of the Master's duties in the accounts. Beginning in 1581 the Masters became censors of plays, licensers of theatres and of acting companies, and, in 1606, licensers of plays for publication. The 1581 commission appointing Edmund Tilney as censor, PRO, C66/1606, memb. 34, no. 46, is printed in Feuillerat, *Elizabeth,* pp. 51–2. Evidence of their continuing duties in reforming texts for the revels is found in the accounts printed in Feuillerat, *Elizabeth,* and in *MSC,* XIII, *passim.*

6   Chambers, *MS,* I: 404–13.

7   Sir Lewis Lewknor's appointment in 1603 is recorded in PRO, E403/2561, fol. 4 (1603–11). A number of the council's orders for receptions and revels in the Tudor period survive which specify protocol and the duties of all officers involved. Draft of plans for the reception and marriage of Katherine of Aragon in 1501: BL, Cotton MS. Vespasian C. XIV, fols. 94–103v, printed in *LP Richard III and Henry VII,* I: 404–17. List of officers and servants and their duties together with a seating plan for the banquet of 12 July 1517: College of Arms, MS. M 8, fols. 61–5. Memoranda on seating at the banquet for the French ambassador on 25–6 April 1519 and on the reception and seating plan for the banquet for the Papal Legate on 4 August 1519: College of Arms, MS. M 8, fols. 66–7. 'Thordre of the hall by me John Stephens then marshall of the said noble hall' made for Anne Boleyn's coronation: College of Arms, MS. M 8, fols. 73v–85. 'Remembrances for Ambassadors' in connection with the reception and entertainments for the 1546 Anglo-French treaty: BL, Cotton MS. Vespasian C. XIV, fols. 80–8v.

8   Chambers, *ES,* I: 30–70.

9   'Articles devised by the kinges highness *with* thadvice of his Councell for thestablishment of good Order and Reformacion of sundry Errors and misuses in his most honourable houshold and Chamber,' (the so-called Eltham Articles): PRO, E36/231, fol. 158, SP2/B/12, fol. 165, abstracted in *LP,* IV.i, no. 1939 (1), p. 862. Other copies and versions: BL, Cotton MS. Vespasian C. XIV, fols. 249v–94v,

BL, Harleian MSS 610 and 642, the latter printed with alterations in *A Collection of Ordinances and Regulations for the Government of the Royal Household* (London: Society of Antiquaries, 1790). The Lord Steward's department is often called the *Household* in Tudor documents to distinguish it from the Chamber. In order to avoid inevitable confusion between references to the Household and to the royal household, I refer to this part of the household as the Lord Steward's department and use the term 'Hall' to refer to social centre of that department. When used for revels the Hall was supported by a number of offices within the Lord Steward's department.

10   *MSC*, I.iii: 260–1.

11   For a detailed treatment of the political impact of different organizations within the Privy Chamber, see David Starkey et al., *The English Court* (London: Longman, 1987).

12   BL, Harleian MS. 642, fol. 209, printed in *A Collection of Ordinances and Regulations for the Government of the Royal Household* (London: Society of Antiquaries, 1790), 111. The ceremonial orders for the household of Henry VII are preserved in several early copies. For a discussion of these see Ian Lancashire, 'Orders for Twelfth Day and Night circa 1515 in the Second Northumberland Household Book,' *English Literary Renaissance*, 10 (1980): 44–5, and Louise Campbell and Francis Steer, *A Catalogue of the Manuscripts in the College of Arms Collections* (London, College of Arms: 1988), I: 123–5. The edited versions differ in important readings from the manuscripts.

13   BL, Additional MS. 38174, fol. 20, printed in *Antiquarian Repertory*, I: 313; Wickham, *EES*, I: 282.

14   The suggestion, Wickham, *EES*, I: 40, that the Comptroller had charge of tournaments is based on a passage from BL, Cotton MS. Vespasian C. XIV, fol. 94, printed in *LP Richard III and Henry VII*, I: 405: 'And esfor Iustes torneys and suche other Cerymonyes thei be remytted to the said Mr Comptroller Sergeant of the Kinges armory.' The only individual in this period to hold both offices was Sir Richard Guildford who was Master of the Armoury and the supervisor of preparations for tournaments long before he became Comptroller of the Household. The key office referred to in this document is that of Master of the Armoury.

15   John Stow, *A Survey of London*, ed. C.L. Kingsford (Oxford: Clarendon Press, 1908), II: 117.

16   The building projects at Westminster and Whitehall in this period are discussed in *King's Works*, IV.ii: 286–343.

17   *Great Chronicle*, pp. 286, 295. The building projects at Richmond in this period are discussed in *King's Works*, IV.ii: 222–34.

18   The building projects at Hampton Court in this period are discussed in *King's Works*, IV.ii: 126–47.

19   The building projects at Greenwich in this period are discussed in *King's Works,*
       IV.ii: 96–123.
20   On the banqueting houses at Hampton Court, see *King's Works,* IV.ii: 138, and
       Wyngaerde's sketch (1558), plate 8. It is there suggested that one or more of these
       may have been Robert Trunckwell's Tower of Babylon, but this was a pageant
       tower for a play staged at court by the Revels; the account is printed in Feuillerat,
       Edward VI and Mary, p. 26. The banqueting houses at Calais in 1520 and at
       Greenwich in 1527 are described in Anglo, *Spectacle,* pp. 159–68, 212–24. One
       at Nonsuch is described in *King's Works,* IV.ii: 201–2.
21   Hall, p. 867.
22   PRO, SP1/224, fols. 139–40, 150–2, abstracted respectively in *LP,* XXI.ii, nos.
       82, 96.
23   *Liber Niger.* PRO, E36/230, copied in BL, Harleian MS. 642, fol. 78, and printed
       in *A Collection of Ordinances and Regulations for the Government of the Royal House-
       hold* (London: Society of Antiquaries, 1790), 54.
24   *King's Works,* III.i, IV.ii, *passim.*
25   The Surveyors traditionally had the surplus of building materials as a perquisite.
       This was discontinued in the later part of the century. BL, Lansdowne MS. 6, no.
       4 (Windsor Orders [1564]), direct that some of the materials formerly taken by
       the Surveyor from old houses to his own use be set aside for the Revels. PRO,
       SP14/44, no. 101 (Orders of April 1609), specify that all material was to be re-
       employed by the Works: *King's Works,* III.i: 81, 113, item 18.
26   *MSC,* X; John Orrell, *Records of Early English Drama Newsletter,* 4, no. 1 (1979):
       1–9; W.R. Streitberger, *Records of Early English Drama Newsletter,* 7, no. 2 (1982):
       1–8; *King's Works,* III.i, IV.ii, *passim.*
27   On the masques, see C.H. Herford and P. and E. Simpson, eds., *Ben Jonson*
       (Oxford: Clarendon Press, 1925–52), X: 406–697. On the Office of the Works
       under the Surveyorship of Jones, see *King's Works,* III.i: 129–59.
28   Richard Doland, Clerk of the Works, built the lists at Shene in May 1492: BL,
       Additional MS. 7099, fol. 4, abstracted in Anglo, 'Henry VII,' p. 27. He also
       built the scaffolds in Westminster Hall for the 1494 Twelfth Night revel: PRO,
       E405/79, memb. 1d, abstracted in *King's Works,* IV.ii: 286.
29   Bodleian Library, MS. Rawlinson D. 775, fols. 55, 56v; *King's Works,* IV.ii:
       106.
30   Hall, p. 723, says that the chamber was raised with stages 'v. degrees on euery
       syde,' but the Venetian ambassador describes three: 'Dalli lati della sala erano dis-
       posti tre ordeni et dedili motlo comodi, ciascun di quali havea uno trabe per el
       longo dove si apogiavano li spectatori, ne l'uno era all'altro di impedimento. Spora
       quaesti tre ordeni erano collocati parimenti tre ordent de torzi, cosi ben disposti
       et intesi che non impedivano ne el veder nel luoco ne li spectaori.' Sanuto, *Diarii,*

XLV: 266–7, calendared in *CSP Venetian*, IV, no. 105. On the seating at the Calais banqueting theatre, see *Chronicle of Calais*, p. 29.

31   BL, Additional MS. 18825, a collection of warrants from 1486 to 1506, shows the Yeoman of the Robes purchasing material from London mercers, directly from ships in port, and ordering material from the Great Wardrobe on occasion for musicians at Christmas. He also issued material for the revels on occasion in Henry VIII's reign. Some of John Parker's accounts survive from 1509 to 1527: PRO, E101/418/18, E101/425/2, E101/425/3. Gibson's account, PRO, E36/229, fols. 82, 87, for example, shows some costumes and garments used in revels and jousts returned to the Yeoman of the Robes. On the early history of the privy wardrobes, see T.F. Tout, *Chapters in the Administrative History of Mediaeval England* (Manchester: University of Manchester Press, 1920–33), IV: 439–84.

32   BL, Lansdowne MS. 83, art. 58, fol. 157; printed in Feuillerat, *Elizabeth*, p. 17.

33   See T.F. Tout, *Chapters in the Administrative History of Mediaeval England* (Manchester: University of Manchester Press, 1920–33), IV: 349–437, on the early history of the Great Wardrobe.

34   PRO, LC 2/4 (2),(3); *King's Works,*, III.i: 56.

35   PRO, E36/215, p. 23, abstracted in *LP,* II.ii, p. 1443.

36   Sir Richard Guildford, Master of the Armoury (1485–1506), whose father, Sir John, was Comptroller of the Household to Edward IV, joined Henry's cause after Richard III's usurpation. Sir Richard was with Henry at his landing at Milford Haven where he was knighted. He received many grants and important offices at court: Master of the Ordnance and of the Armoury (29 September 1485: PRO, C66/561, memb. 19, calendared in *CPR Henry VII*, I: 18) which grant was reissued on 1 December 1493 in survivorship to him and to his son, Edward (PRO, C66/575, memb. 28, calendared in *CPR Henry VII*, I: 467); Chamberlain of the Exchequer (2 October 1485); king's council and Sheriff of Kent (1494); Knight Banneret at Blackheath (17 June 1496); Knight of the Body (1497); Comptroller of the Household (1498); K.G. (1500). Sir Richard prepared all of the tournaments to which we can attach a name early in Henry VII's reign. He died on 6 September 1506 on a pilgrimage to Jerusalem, and his will, dated 7 April 1506, was proved on 10 May 1508: Sir Henry Ellis, ed., *The Pylgrymage of Sir Richard Guylforde*, Camden Society, vol. 51 (London, 1851), pp. i–xvi. Sir Henry Herbert, Master of the Revels from 1623 to 1673, named Sir Richard as one of the early Masters of the Revels with the qualification, 'not on record': BL, Additional MS. 19256, printed in J.O. Halliwell-Phillipps, *A Collection of Ancient Documents Respecting the Office of Master of the Revels* (London: T. Richards, 1870), 97. Herbert confused him with Sir Henry, Sir Richard's son by his second wife Joan, who became Henry VIII's Master of the Revels and produced a number of revels from 1511

until his death in 1532. Sir Edward, Sir Richard's son by his first wife Anne and who succeeded him as Master of the Armoury, prepared a number of tournaments at court from 1506 until his death in 1534. The Masters of the Armoury in the early Tudor period following the death of Sir Edward Guildford on 4 June 1534 were Sir John Dudley, patent of 29 June 1534 (PRO, C66/664, memb. 27, calendared in *LP,* VII, no. 1026 [15]); Sir Thomas Darcy, patent of 9 June 1544 (PRO, C66/758, memb. 40, calendared in *LP,* XIX.i, no. 812 [30]); and Sir Richard Southwell, patent of 19 September 1553 which he surrendered on 21 July 1559 (PRO, C66/871, memb. 5, calendared in *CPR Philip and Mary,* I: 199. The connection between the production of tournaments and the Master of the Armoury continued in Elizabeth I's reign. Sir Henry Lee supervised the annual accession day tilt from the early 1570s until his retirement in 1590. On Lee's position as Master of the Armoury, see E.K. Chambers, *Sir Henry Lee* (Oxford: Clarendon Press, 1936), 106–44.

37   An exception is Neville Williams, 'The Master of the Royal Tents and his Records,' *Journal of the Society of Archivists,* 2, no. 2 (1960): 37–51.

38   Neville Williams, 'The Master of the Royal Tents and his Records,' *Journal of the Society of Archivists,* 2, no. 2 (1960): 47.

39   The Tents accounts from 1555 to 1675 are PRO, E351/2935–2959; AO1/2292/1–2297/40. Gibson's earlier accounts are discussed in Chapter 3, below.

40   *La description et ordre du camp festins et ioustes* [Paris, 1520], abstracted in *LP,* III.i, no. 869, p. 306. College of Arms, MS. M 16*bis,* fols. 74v–6 (specifications for the tents at Therouanne and Tournai in 1513 for the royal household); Hall, pp. 606–8. See also Chapter 7, below.

41   Letter dated 6 June 1545 from Secretary William Paget to Lord Cobham, Deputy of Calais, 'requiring my lord to send no mo strangers into england': BL, Harleian MS. 283, fols. 305r–v, abstracted in *LP,* XX.i, no. 877.

42   The earliest patent on record was issued to John Stratford: *CPR Edward IV,* p. 15. John Searle, who was king's Painter by patent in 1473, was reappointed in 1486. He appears regularly in the Chamber accounts as a payee for painting heraldic insignia for weddings and funerals and for decorating the royal carriage for Princess Margaret's progress to Scotland in 1503. His last recorded work is for Queen Elizabeth's funeral in 1503. Maynard Wewyck (1501 ⟨ ⟩ 1508) and Richard Rowanger (1508 ⟨ ⟩ 1527) were in the king's service, but it is not certain that they held patents. John Browne held the patent from at least 1511 to 1532. During his term of office, the title was changed from king's to Sergeant Painter. Browne was succeeded as Sergeant Painter by Andrew Wright (1532–44); Anthony Toto, an Italian (1544–54); and Nicholas Lizard or Lysory, a Frenchman (1554–71). Auerbach, *Tudor Artists,* pp. 54–6, 144–6, 183–4, 185.

43   Auerbach, *Tudor Artists,* pp. 7–8, 49–51; Kipling, 'Patronage,' pp. 135–6.

44   See the discussion in *King's Works*, IV.ii: 24–8, and in Auerbach, *Tudor Artists*, pp. 4–101.

45   On the careers of Rowangre and the rest, see Auerbach, *Tudor Artists*, pp. 144–94.

46   'Of the first Institution of the Revels with a Draught of certain Rules to be Observed for the better Management of the Office': BL, Lansdowne MS. 83, no. 59, fols. 158–61, printed in J.O. Halliwell-Phillipps, *A Curious Paper of the Time of Queen Elizabeth Respecting the Office of the Revels* (London: T. Richards, 1872); Feuillerat, *Elizabeth*, pp. 5–15; and Chambers, *Tudor Revels*, pp. 1–3, 31–42. BL Additional MS. 19256, Sir Henry Herbert's copy, is printed in J.O. Halliwell-Phillipps, *A Collection of Ancient Documents Respecting the Office of the Master of the Revels* (London: T. Richards, 1870). Collier, *HEDP* (1831), I: 290, attributed the document to Thomas Blagrave, Clerk of the Revels. Chambers, *Tudor Revels*, p. 49, *ES*, I: 82–4, attributed it to Buggyn, the Clerk Comptroller. Feuillerat, *Elizabeth*, p. 426, originally assigned it to Blagrave, but later settled on one of the high officers of the Tents, Works, Wardrobe, or Tower. The document is one of three memoranda which were probably prepared for Lord Burghley in considering reforms of the office. The other two are BL, Lansdowne MS. no. 56 and 58, fols. 155–7, printed in Chambers, *Tudor Revels*, pp. 31–42, and Feuillerat, *Elizabeth*, pp. 16–17, 411.

CHAPTER 1

1   BL, Additional MS. 7099, fol. 10, abstracted in Anglo, 'Henry VII,' p. 28.

2   PRO, E404/79, no. 72, abstracted in Streitberger, *RORD* (1983): 39.

3   The evidence of Pudsey's problems in the north on the king's business, PRO, C82/10, no. 224, is abstracted in Campbell, I: 441. Various payments, rewards, and grants to him are abstracted in Streitberger, *RORD* (1983): 39–42, and Campbell, I: 129, 297, 437. He was one of those appointed to attend the king in France in 1492: BL, Cotton MS. Julius B. I, fols. 93v–4v, printed in *LP Richard III and Henry VII*, II: 291.

4   PRO, C66/579, memb. 3, and C66/586, memb. 8, calendared respectively in *CPR Henry VII*, II: 85, 201.

5   The Privy Seal writs to Sir Richard Guildford for the jousts are PRO, E404/79, nos. 58, 90, abstracted in Campbell, I: 97–8, 206–7, 230, 232, and Streitberger, *RORD* (1983): 39. The payments to four men to watch the stuff in the king's standing for the jousts is PRO, LC9/50, fol. 147v. Sir Robert Willoughby's list of 'empcions and prouisions' for the coronation and the payments for constructing the stage at Westminster, PRO, LC9/50, fols. 140–8v, is printed in Campbell, II: 1–19. Sir Richard Croft, Treasurer of the Household, was paid £233 6s. 8d. for the feast: Campbell, I: 225. Sir Reginold Bray was paid £358 23d. for material

purchased for the coronation, including the delivery of some material to John English, later one of the King's Players, to be made into clothing for the king, his gentlemen, and horses: PRO, E404/79, nos. 108 and 109. Narratives of the coronation and the joust are 'The coronacion of the most noble king Henrie the Seventh,' BL, Egerton MS. 985, fols. 41v–8; and 'Here followth vnder correction a little device of the coronacion of the most high and mightie christian Prince henrie the vijth,' BL, Harleian MS. 985, fols. 1–11. For a discussion of the sources documenting the coronation, see Anglo, *Spectacle,* pp. 10–17.

6   A warrant from Queen Mary dated September 1553, copied into Folger Library, MS. Lb 41, fol. 73r, printed in Feuillerat, *Edward VI and Mary,* p. 149, states that a play by the Gentlemen of the Chapel was customary at the coronations of 'owr proginitours.' There is no evidence to confirm such a performance at Henry VII's coronation. Wallace, *Evolution,* pp. 12–13, cites Collier, *HEDP* (1831), I: 46, as his source for the suggestion that they did perform. Chambers, *ES,* II: 28, was of the opinion that Collier did not refer to the year 1485. Collier says nothing of the matter in his discussion of events in 1485 on p. 46. I think that Wallace's reference is to the general remark on p. 36 where Collier mentions that the King's Players and the Gentlemen of the Chapel 'appear to have performed always during the festivities of Christmas and perhaps at other seasons.' *The Divill and Rychard,* a play supposedly performed at the coronation by Paul's clerks and boys, is a forgery by William Ireland. See J.W. Robinson, 'An Interlude or Mystery Play by William Ireland, 1795,' *Comparative Drama,* 13 (1979): 235–51; *Dramatic Records,* p. 341.

7   *Memorials,* pp. 36–7.

8   Bernardus Andreas's narrative of the wedding is *De Regali ejusdem conjugio,* printed in *Memorials,* p. 38. Piers Curteis held several offices under three monarchs, the most important of which was Keeper of the Great Wardrobe from 11 October 1480: PRO, C66/546, memb. 23, calendared in *CPR Edward IV and Richard III,* p. 222; see also pp. 95, 196, 231, 255, 346, and BL Harleian MS. 433, fol. 67v, printed in *LP Richard III and Henry VII,* I: 73. His sympathies were with the Tudors, and the reissue of a life grant as Keeper of the Privy Palace of Westminster and of its Wardrobe on 24 September 1486 was made 'in consideracioun of his the trewe hert and service' and of 'the gret persecucioun imprisonments, and lossis of his goodes' he had suffered 'for oure sake,' having 'long tyme kept saintuary at Westmynstre': PRO, C66/561, memb. 26, calendared in *CPR Henry VII,* I: 26. He was granted the patent as Henry's Keeper of the Great Wardrobe on 25 May 1487: PRO, C66/566, memb. 11, calendared in *CPR Henry VII,* I: 176. Some of his accounts survive: PRO, LC 9/50, fols. 5–78, E101/413/1, E361/8; BL, Harleian MS. 4780, printed in N.H. Nicolas, ed., *The Privy Purse Expenses of Elizabeth of York; Wardrobe Accounts of Edward VI* (London: W. Pickering, 1830), 113–70. His principal residence seems to have been in Leicester, but he resided at Kingston-

Upon-Thames while at court: PRO, C66/576, memb. 19, calendared in *CPR Henry VII,* II: 13. His will of 25 February 1504 (PRO, PROB 11/14, fol. 232v) was proved on 26 April 1509. The Privy Seal writ for £95 3*s.* 6 1/2*d.* (PRO, E404/79, no. 46, abstracted in Campbell, I: 324) was issued on 28 February 1486. Richard Doland, Clerk of the Works by patent on 22 September 1486 (PRO, C66/576, memb. 24), also received a Privy Seal writ in Michaelmas 1486 to procure material for the wedding: PRO, E404/79, no. 105, recorded in the Privy Seal Book, E403/2558, and abstracted in Campbell, I: 233.

9   PRO, E404/79, no. 46, abstracted in Streitberger, *RORD* (1983): 39; see the lists of material printed from the bills attached to the Privy Seal writs abstracted in Campbell, I: 262–4, 265–6, 281–2, 324.

10 PRO, E404/79, nos. 31, 72, abstracted in Streitberger, *RORD* (1983): 39, and in Campbell, I: 165, 337.

11 Nicholas Warley was paid £143 19*s.* 4 1/2*d.* on 28 January 1486 for delivering jewels for use at Christmas, New Year's, and for the wedding, and on the 30th he was paid £181 14*s.* 8*d.* for delivering furs to the king: PRO, E404/79, nos. 52, 53, abstracted in Campbell, I: 265. Nicholas Flynte and Edmund Shaw were paid £30 7*s.* 7*d.* for making and mending gold and silver jewels for Christmas, New Year's, and Twelfth Night: PRO, E404/79, no. 30, E403/2558, abstracted in Campbell, I: 232, 281–2. Robert Drope, alderman of London, was paid £57 6*s.* 8*d.* for delivering gold jewels on New Year's Eve: PRO, E404/79, no. 95, abstracted in Campbell, I: 264.

The king was entertained on his northern progress from 13 March to 5 June with receptions, pageants, and plays at Bristol, Hereford, Worcester, and York: McGee and Meagher, 'Checklist,' pp. 35–6. A pageant of rose trees was planned by the city of York for Henry VII's reception, but it is not certain that it was used: Alexandra F. Johnston and Margaret Rogerson, eds., *Records of Early English Drama: York* (Toronto: University of Toronto Press, 1979), I: 137.

12 BL, Cotton MS. Julius B. XII, fol. 24, printed in *Collectanea,* IV: 207. On the inadequacies of this edition, see Kipling, *Receyt,* pp. liv–lvii. Another version is printed in *Antiquarian Repertory,* I: 353–7. The event is described in J. Gairdner, ed., *Three Fifteenth Century Chronicles,* Camden Society, n.s. vol. 28 (London, 1880), 104–5. The privy seal to Nicholas Kynston for preparation of the ceremony was issued on 1 October 1486: PRO, E404/79, nos. 45, 46, abstracted in Streitberger, *RORD* (1983): 40, and Campbell, II: 38–9, 82.

13 Warton, *HEP,* pp. 456–7, records that 'In the year 1487, while Henry VII kept his residence at the castle of Winchester, on the occasion of the birth of prince Arthur, on a Sunday, during the time of dinner, he was entertained with a religious drama called Christi Descensus Ad Infernos, or *Crist's descent into hell.* It was represented by the Pueri Eleemosynarii, or choir-boys, of Hyde abbey, and St.

Swithin's priory, two large monasteries at Winchester …. The story of this interlude, in which the chief characters were Christ, Adam, Eve, Abraham, and John
the Baptist, was not uncommon in the ancient religious drama, and I believe made
a part of what is called the Ludus Paschalis, or Easter play. It occurs in the Coventry plays, acted on Corpus Christi day; and in the Whitsun-plays at Chester, where
it is called the Harrowing of Hell.'

14   PRO, E404/79, no. 4, abstracted in Streitberger, *RORD* (1983): 40. Since the
     place name is obliterated in the Privy Seal writ and there is no record of an imprest,
     it is difficult to determine the location or to estimate how elaborate it may have
     been. Guildford had also been charged to entertain the Scottish ambassadors at
     Eltham in May while the king was on his northern progress, and it is possible that
     the joust was held at this time: PRO, E403/2558, abstracted in Campbell, I: 229,
     494.

15   BL, Cotton MS. Julius B. XII, fol. 24, printed in *Collectanea*, IV: 207.

16   PRO, E404/79, nos. 13, 109, abstracted in Streitberger, *RORD* (1983): 40; PRO,
     E403/2558, fol. 6; E36/125, p. 47. During his summer progress in 1487 the king
     was entertained at Coventry where he attended the Corpus Christi plays and at
     York where he also saw the Corpus Christi plays: R.W. Ingram, ed., *Records of Early
     English Drama: Coventry* (Toronto: University of Toronto Press, 1981), 67–8;
     Alexandra F. Johnston and Margaret Rogerson, eds., *Records of Early English Drama:
     York* (Toronto: University of Toronto Press, 1979), I: 153–6.

17   BL, Cotton MS. Julius B. XII, fol. 35, printed in *Collectanea*, IV: 218. 'The
     Coronacion of Queene Elizabeth,' BL Harleian MS. 985, fols. 11v–26, is a simi-
     lar account.

18   Piers Curteis submitted a bundle of ten memoranda for payment in connection
     with the event: PRO, E101/425/19, printed in Campbell, I: 253–5, under the
     conjectural date of 1–18 January 1485/6. Curteis had also supplied the heralds
     with cloth for the coronation of Elizabeth, wife of Edward IV: BL, Additional
     MS. 46354, fol. 63v, printed in A.R. Wagner, *Catalogue of English Medieval Rolls
     of Arms* (Oxford: Oxford University Press, 1950), 120–1. Sir Roger Cotton, the
     queen's Master of the Horse, was also paid for supplying some material for the
     coronation: PRO, E403/2558, fol. 8, abstracted in Campbell, II: 84.

19   The coronation banquet is described in BL, Cotton MS. Julius B. XII, fols. 39v–45,
     printed in *Collectanea*, IV: 226–33. Morton's 'intronization,' celebrated at Canter-
     bury in January, is described in the same manuscript, fols. 24v–5, and printed in
     Collectanea, IV: 208. The imprest issued to Guildford is PRO, E404/79, no. 38,
     abstracted in Streitberger, *RORD* (1984): 41, and Campbell, II: 198, 232.

20   BL, Cotton MS. Julius B. XII, fol. 46v, printed in *Collectanea*, IV: 235. BL,
     Egerton MS. 985, fol. 28, incorrectly dates the festivities at Christmas 1485.

21   BL, Cotton MS. Julius B. XII, fol. 47v, printed in *Collectanea*, IV: 237. No record

of an imprest survives, and Pudsey's next reward of £10 was issued in Easter term 1488: PRO, E404/79, no. 142.

22   BL, Cotton MS. Julius B. XII, fols. 48r–v, printed in *Collectanea*, IV: 238–9. PRO, E404/79, no. 117, abstracted in Streitberger, *RORD* (1984): 41, and Campbell, II: 290, 296.

23   BL, Cotton MS. Julius B. XII, fols. 51v–2v, printed in *Collectanea*, IV: 244–6.

24   BL, Cotton MS. Julius B. XII, fol. 52v, printed in *Collectanea*, IV: 245. Pudsey was also rewarded £10 on 20 February and on 13 July 1489 for 'good and lawdable service': PRO, E404/80, nos. 180, 135, abstracted in Streitberger, *RORD* (1983): 41.

25   BL, Cotton MS. Julius B. XII, fol. 58–62v, printed in *Collectanea*, IV: 250–4. Ceremonies associated with the queen taking her chamber are printed in *Collectanea*, IV: 179–84, and *Antiquarian Repertory*, I: 313, 333–7.

26   Arthur was created Prince of Wales and Earl of Chester on 29 November by Charter delivered into Chancery on 1 December. He was invested with the Principality of Wales and the counties of Chester and Flint by signed bill of 27 February following. The creation grants are printed in Campbell, II: 541–2, 544–6. A description of the procession by water is contained in BL, Cotton MS. Julius B. XII, fol. 59, printed in *Collectanea*, IV: 250.

27   BL, Cotton MS. Julius B. XII, fols. 63, 64r–v, printed in *Collectanea*, IV: 254, 255–6. Margaret Beaufort, the king's mother, also received 50 marks by signed bill on 14 December 1489 'ayenst the fest of Cristemas': PRO, E404/80, no. 222, abstracted in Streitberger, *RORD* (1983): 42.

28   BL, Cotton MS. Julius B. XII, fols. 64v, 65, printed in *Collectanea*, IV: 256.

29   PRO, E36/124, pp. 162, 167, abstracted in Streitberger, *RORD* (1983): 42. Wallace, *Evolution*, pp. 13, 26, 29, takes the narrative in BL, Harleian MS. 69, fols. 34v–5, 'The Tenth Chapter of the disport*es*,' in which eight boys of the Chapel dressed as mermaids participated in a disguising, to refer to this Christmas season, but as Sydney Anglo, 'William Cornish in a Play, Pageants, Prison, and Politics,' *Review of English Studies*, n.s., 10 (1959): 35n, has pointed out, the narrative unquestionably refers to the entertainment of Sunday, 28 November 1501.

30   On evidence of court revels among Exchequer records from 1485 to 1491, see Streitberger, *RORD* (1983): 31–54.

31   PRO, E404/79, nos. 31, 72, abstracted in Streitberger, *RORD* (1983): 39, and Campbell, I: 165, 337.

32   PRO, E404/79, nos. 13, 109, abstracted in Streitberger, *RORD* (1983): 40.

33   The king did see the Corpus Christi plays at Coventry in June 1493: R.W. Ingram, ed., *Records of Early English Drama: Coventry* (Toronto: University of Toronto Press, 1981), 77. Craven Orde, a 19th-century antiquarian and collector, had possession of the original Chamber accounts from 1491 to the end of the reign –

the 1502–5 account, BL, Additional MS. 59899, bears his bookstamp. The accounts from 1491 to 1495 have yet to surface, which makes Orde's collection of haphazard extracts, BL, Additional MS. 7099, still valuable; see Anglo, 'Henry VII,' pp. 12–13. Collier's extracts from the accounts, *HEDP* (1831), I: 44; (1879), I: 50, may derive from the originals, but they are plagued by confusions. The payment Collier cites for 15 February 7 Henry VII to Walter Alwyn is repeated again under 8 Henry VII. I believe that these payments, which are listed in Orde's extracts as relating to the 1494 Twelfth Night disguising, are confusions in Collier's notes or misprints in his text.

34   W.C. Richardson, *Tudor Chamber Administration, 1485–1558* (Baton Rouge, La.: Louisiana State University Press, 1952), 463–6.

35   The Spanish ambassador, de Ayla, described Henry as writing all of his own accounts. Actually, he reviewed the accounts of several of his major officers. His sign manual on each page of the Chamber accounts indicates that he was acquainted with the receipts and expenditures of his government down to some of the smallest details. F.C. Dietz, *English Government Finance, 1485–1558*, University of Illinois Studies in the Social Sciences, IX, no. 3 (Urbana, Ill., 1920), 60.

36   G.R. Elton, *The Tudor Revolution in Government* (Cambridge: Cambridge University Press, 1953), 169; A.P. Newton, 'Tudor Reform in the Royal Household,' in Robert W. Seton-Watson, ed., *Tudor Studies* (London: Longman, 1924), 235.

37   BL, Additional MS. 7099, fol. 4, abstracted in Anglo, 'Henry VII,' p. 27; for the narratives, see the Court Calendar.

38   BL, Additional MS. 7099, fols. 2, 8, abstracted in Anglo, 'Henry VII,' pp. 27–8.

39   BL, Additional MS. 7099, fol. 12, abstracted in Anglo, 'Henry VII,' pp. 27–8.

40   BL, Additional MS. 7099, fols. 13–14; Anglo, 'Henry VII,' p. 28, abstracts these and other relevant payments for 1493–4.

41   BL, Additional MS. 7099, fol. 13, abstracted in Anglo, 'Henry VII,' p. 28. Chambers, *Tudor Revels*, p. 4, states that payments were made to Alwyn (d. by 1495) from 1491 to 1494, but I cannot find any before 1493. Wallace, *Evolution*, p. 27.

42   BL, Additional MS. 7099, fol. 15, abstracted in Anglo, 'Henry VII,' p. 28.

43   PRO, E405/79, memb. 1d, abstracted in *King's Works*, IV.ii: 286.

44   Guildhall Library, London MS. 3313, fols. 229v–231, printed in *Great Chronicle*, pp. 251–2, is the most detailed contemporary account. See Sydney Anglo, 'William Cornish in a Play, Pageants, Prison, and Politics,' *Review of English Studies*, n.s., 10 (1959): 348–50; Kipling, *Honour*, pp. 101–2.

45   BL, Additional MS. 6113, fol. 169; the writer also notes that 'all was donn by x of the clocke.' The narrative and two others deriving from the same archetype (see Court Calendar) differ markedly from Guildhall Library, London MS. 3313.

46   *Thus endeth the legende named in latyn legenda aurea*, translated by Caxton from

the French of J. de Vignay, first published in 1483, followed by another edition (in 1487?). The edition printed by Wynkyn de Worde in 1493 (*STC* 24875) was the only text to omit the Bible stories. The *Legenda Aurea* had already been plundered as source material by dramatists in France. See Grace Frank, *The Medieval French Drama* (Oxford: Clarendon Press, 1954), 142–3, 184, 189–90, 192. Of course, Cornish was not a prophet, but a composer, singer, and dramatist, and it is possible that his 'prophecy' of 12 November 1493 functioned something like the banns announcing a play to set up expectations for the St George revel. On the use of prophecy in Elizabethan tournaments, see Roy Strong, *The Cult of Elizabeth* (London: Thames and Hudson, 1977), 140. Prophecies were taken seriously in the Tudor period. Henry used them to create a myth of destiny and for propaganda purposes. See Alastair Fox, 'Prophecies and Politics in the Reign of Henry VIII,' in A. Fox and J. Guy, eds., *Reassessing the Henrican Age* (Oxford: Blackwell, 1986), 78. The most common of these, called the Galfridian or Merlin prophecies because they take their cue from Merlin's prophecies in *Historia Regnum Britanniae* and from the *Vita Merlini*, employ heraldic and totemic imagery linking prophecies to dynastic hopes or topical events. One of the 'Merlin' prophecies listed by R.H. Robbins, 'Political Prophecies,' in Albert E. Hartung, gen. ed., *A Manual of the Writings of Middle English, 1050–1500* (New Haven: Connecticut Academy of Arts and Sciences, 1975), V: 1516–36, 1714–25, for example, is entitled 'A dragun with a red rose that ys of grete fame.' Another, 'The Fall of London,' takes the form of two stanzas in rhyme royal.

47 Ballad royal, the earlier name for the rhyme royal stanza, had been in use from ca. 1400. Martin Stevens, 'The Royal Stanza in Early English Literature,' *PMLA*, 97 (1979): 63. It was regarded as an appropriate form of address to royalty, used, for example, in the pageants for Henry VII at York and Bristol. Heywood uses it for Jupiter's speeches in his *Play of the Weather* and Skelton uses it for the title character in *Magnificence*. Lydgate had used the French *balade* in his mummeries as descriptive or explanatory songs which were probably recited rather than sung. On the complicated permutations of the ballade form, see Albert B. Friedman, 'The Late Medieval Ballade and the Origin of Broadside Balladry,' *Medium Aevum*, 27 (1958): 95–110.

48 See Ian Lancashire, 'Orders for Twelfth Day and Night circa 1515 in the Second Northumberland Household Book,' *English Literary Renaissance*, 10 (1980): 34–6.

49 BL, Additional MS. 7099, fol. 18, abstracted in Anglo, 'Henry VII,' p. 28. Collier, *HEDP* (1831), I: 42, and Wallace, *Evolution*, p. 27, following him, thought that this was the same 'Pechie' or 'Pachye' the fool who was paid rewards in the Chamber accounts from 1492 to 1496 – see the payments abstracted in Anglo, 'Henry VII,' pp. 27–31. While there were many performances by fools at Henry VII's court, most were 'naturals,' incapable of caring for themselves, and payments

to their keepers occur regularly in the Chamber accounts. Sir John Peche, Knight for the Body by June 1509, answerer in the 1501 tournament, escort for Princess Margaret on her progress to Scotland in 1503, and participant in many of the jousts held at Henry VIII's court, is a far more likely candidate. See the various grants and other references to Peche in *CPR Henry VII*, II: 67, 249, 538, 645, *LP*, I, no. 140, and *Tournament Roll*, I: 37–8, 47–8.

50   PRO, C66/539, memb. 14, calendared in *CPR Edward IV and Richard III*, p. 13; BL, Additional MS. 43489, fol. 29, printed in A. Davis, ed., *Paston Letters and Papers* (Oxford: Clarendon Press, 1971–6), II: 397. Collier, *HEDP* (1831) I: 89–92, thought he was the Jaques who played the Shipman in Mary's revels of 1522–3, but this Jaques Haulte was dead by 1508.

51   PRO, C66/544, memb. 14, and C66/550, memb. 34, calendared respectively in *CPR Edward IV and Richard III*, pp. 169, 323.

52   PRO, C66/556, memb. 11, C66/561, memb. 16, C66/578, memb. 7, calendared respectively in *CPR Edward IV and Richard III*, p. 458, *CPR Henry VII*, I: 14; II: 57.

53   This Jaques Haulte may also have been Underkeeper of Kenilworth: Sir Nicholas Harris Nicolas, ed, *The Privy Purse Expenses of Elizabeth of York* (London: W. Pickering, 1830), 200.

54   PRO, PROB 11/16, fol. 121.

55   PRO, C66/607. memb. 35, calendared in *CPR Henry VII*, II: 607.

56   BL, Additional MS. 7099, fol. 21, abstracted in Anglo, 'Henry VII,' p. 29.

57   PRO, E101/414/6, fol. 40, abstracted in Anglo, 'Henry VII,' pp. 31–2.

58   Henry was created Duke of York on 29 October 1494; the tournament was held from 9 to 22 November. Four gentlemen issued a challenge for jousts royal at Westminster 'for the laude and honnor of the ffeast' and 'the exercise of feates and deedes of Armes': BL, Harleian MS. 69, fol. 6. For other sources, see Court Calendar. Payments related to the jousts are found in BL, Additional MS. 7099, fol. 21, abstracted in Anglo, 'Henry VII,' p. 29.

59   BL, Additional MS. 7099, fols. 22, 23, abstracted in Anglo, 'Henry VII', p. 29.

60   PRO, E101/414/6, fol. 18, abstracted in Anglo, 'Henry VII,' pp. 29–30. Edmund de la Pole, Earl of Suffolk (1485–1513), was attainted on 26 December 1502 and executed on 4 May 1513. There is no evidence of Suffolk's involvement in other court entertainments. Lord William, probably William 11th Lord Willoughby (d. 1526), was at the reception for Katherine of Aragon in 1501 and escorted Margaret as far as York in 1503. He was later at the Field of Cloth of Gold in 1520. Henry Bourchier, 2nd Earl of Essex (1483), was active in martial exercises, ceremonies, and revels at court through the early years of Henry VIII's reign.

61   See Chapter 3.

62   F.S. Boas and A.W. Reed, eds., *Fulgens and Lucrece* (Oxford: Clarendon Press,

1926), pp. xix–xx, suggest the date of Christmas 1497 based on a line of Flemish
and references in the play to 'the season' and the fire in the Hall. M.E. Moeslein,
ed., *The Plays of Henry Medwall* (New York: Garland, 1981), 60–7, dates it 1497
as well, and argues that the mumming and other references in the play are to the
Perkin Warbeck affair, but Warbeck had been a problem for Henry from about
1491. Kipling, *Honour,* pp. 21–2, argues for Candlemas 1496 on the basis of the
presence of the Flemish and Spanish ambassadors at court, there to negotiate
respectively the *Magnus Intercursus* and the marriage between Arthur and Katherine, and on a description of the weather in the *Great Chronicle* in which it is
recorded that on 'Candylmas evyn, the ffrost still endurynd.' Alan H. Nelson, ed.,
The Plays of Henry Medwall (Cambridge: D.S. Brewer, 1980), 17–18, objects to
the dating by Kipling and by Reed. Given the importance of the 1496 negotiations and the extraordinary disguising put on at Henry's court by the amateur
aristocrats, Kipling's dating for a performance appears the likely one. There may
have been another entertainment in June 1496. Collier, *HEDP* (1831), I: 39–40,
states that 'In a bound book' containing payments to the queen's minstrels occurs
a payment to Hugh Standish, notary, for assisting in the production 'ad certos
revelliones' at Whitehall on 30 June 1496, and that the book contained other
payments for silks and material. While I have little doubt that such a document
existed, I have not been able to locate it at the PRO. There is no evidence to confirm the suggestion by Leigh Winser, 'The Bowge of Courte: Drama Doubling as
Dream,' *English Literary Renaissance,* 6 (1976): 3–39, that Skelton's poem was
performed as a disguising on this or any other occasion. On the visual qualities of
the poetry written at Henry VII's court, see Kipling, *Honour,* pp. 11–30.

63   The play was performed at Chester 3–4 August, and the prince was received at
     Coventry on 17 October 1498: L.M. Clopper, ed., *Records of Early English
     Drama: Chester* (Toronto: University of Toronto Press, 1979), 21–2; R. W.
     Ingram, ed., *Records of Early English Drama: Coventry* (Toronto: University of
     Toronto Press, 1981), 89–91.

64   PRO, E101/414/16, fols. 47, 58, abstracted in Anglo, 'Henry VII,' p. 34.

65   PRO, E101/414/16, fols. 52, 56, abstracted in Anglo, 'Henry VII,' p. 34.

66   PRO, E101/415/3, fol. 12, abstracted in Anglo, 'Henry VII,' pp. 35–6.

67   BL, Cotton MS. Vitellius C. XI, fol. 125v, from which I here quote, is one of the
     early versions of the orders. On the relationship among the extant versions see
     Kipling, *Receyt,* pp. xi–xii.

68   Pawne was Surveyor of the Works at Calais on 12 March 1501: PRO, E36/285,
     fol. 6; C66/587, memb. 18, calendared in *CPR Henry VII,* II: 231. He was in
     England beginning in 1501 and was appointed to a number of duties associated
     with the Works as well as other jobs, such as a commission to collect the benevo-
     lence on 14 October 1505: PRO, C66/598, memb. 27, calendared in *CPR Henry*

VII, II: 458. Later, he was Master of the Works at Tournai. He died before 25 April 1524: *King's Works,* III.i: 340, 376–81. He was related by marriage to the family of Lovekyn: George, king's Tailor under Henry VII (PRO, E404/81); Arthur, Clerk in the Works under William Pawne (PRO, SP2/ Fol. A, no. 3), and George, Clerk of the Stable under Sir Henry Guildford. See Chapter 5, note 21.

69 College of Arms, MS. M 13*bis,* fols. 51r–v, printed in Kipling, *Receyt,* pp. 52–3; BL, Egerton MS. 2358 (Thomas Warly's Works account for work on the tilt-yard and the platform, fols. 24–42, and for the construction of a balcony at the Tower in the Ordnance House for royal spectators, fols. 12–23, which may have been for a practice for the great November tournament). See also *King's Works,* III.i: 264n, IV.ii: 287; Anglo, *Tournament Roll,* I: 34–40.

70 Pawne was paid in the Chamber accounts between November and December 1501 and in March 1502 for his services in connection with arranging lodgings for the Scots ambassadors. Between 16 May and 24 July 1505 he was paid for building highways: BL, Additional MS. 59899, fols. 87–95.

71 PRO, E101/415/3, fols. 33, 57v–8, abstracted in Anglo, 'Henry VII,' pp. 35–6.

72 Atkinson was Yeoman of the Armoury (PRO, C66/554, memb. 3, calendared in *CPR Edward IV and Richard III,* p. 423), and Clerk of the Ordnance (PRO, C66/587, memb. 22, calendared in *CPR Henry VII,* II: 225). His will was made on 28 March 1521: PRO, PROB 11/20, fols. 133r–v.

73 College of Arms, MS. M 13*bis,* fols. 29v–32v, printed in Kipling, *Receyt,* pp. 4–11. See also the discussion in Kipling, *Honour,* pp. 173–4. The large number of sources for the reception and other entertainments are listed in McGee and Meagher, 'Checklist,' pp. 44–8.

74 College of Arms, MS. M 13*bis,* fols. 33v–45, printed in Kipling, *Receyt,* pp. 12–38. See also the discussions in Kipling, *Honour,* pp. 72–110; Sydney Anglo, 'The London Pageants for the Reception of Katherine of Aragon: November 1501,' *Journal of the Warburg and Courtauld Institutes,* 26 (1963): 53–89; and *Spectacle,* pp. 56–97

75 See the discussion in Kipling, *Receyt,* pp. xxv–xxix. As in the past Sir Richard Guildford had charge of supervising the preparations. See also Kipling, *Honour,* pp. 118–19

76 Buckingham's challenge, College of Arms, MS. M 3, fols. 24v–6, is collated with Staffordshire County Record Office, MS. D 1721/1/1, fols. 425–7, and BL, Additional MS. 46455, fols. 6–8v, and printed in Kipling, *Receyt,* pp. 95, 97–102. Suffolk's challenge, Archives of Simancas, MS. P.R. 54–14, fols. 5–8, is collated with BL, Additional MS. 46455, fols. 4–6, and printed in Kipling, *Receyt,* pp. 95, 103–7. See also Kipling's discussion of the versions of the challenge, pp. lxxi–lxxiv, 95. Romantic literature, as Anglo, *Tournament Roll,* I: 35n, points out, is full of 'tree born challenges' which appear to take their inspiration from the fountain

episode in Chretien de Troyes' *Ivain*. Kipling, *Honour*, pp. 116–36, provides an extensive discussion of the Burgundian influence in this tournament.

77   College of Arms, MS. M 13 *bis*, fol. 52, printed in Kipling, *Receyt*, p. 54. Guildhall Library, London MS. 3313, fol. 289, printed in *Great Chronicle*, p. 313, describes it as a 'Chapell hangid or curteynyd ... set at every corner wyth a gilt pynnakyll ... drawyn upon lowe whelys.' See the discussion in Anglo, *Tournament Roll*, I: 36n.

78   College of Arms, MS. M 13 *bis*, fols. 52v–4, printed in Kipling, *Receyt*, pp. 55–8. See also Kipling, *Honour*, pp. 102–5, and Anglo, 'Evolution,' pp. 8–11.

79   Robert Withington, *English Pageantry* (Cambridge, Mass.: Harvard University Press, 1918), I: 23–32, discusses the figure of St George in pageantry.

80   Kipling, *Honour*, p. 105.

81   College of Arms, MS. M 13 *bis*, fols. 54v–5, printed in Kipling, *Receyt*, pp. 59–60. See the discussion in Kipling, *Honour*, pp. 105–9.

82   The revel is described in College of Arms, MS. M 13 *bis*, fols. 58v–60, printed in Kipling, *Receyt*, pp. 66–8. See the discussion in Kipling, *Honour*, pp. 109–11. Ogilvie's remarks are from National Library of Scotland, MS. Advoc. 33.2.24, p. 36, quoted by Kipling, *Honour*, p. 110n; *Receyt*, p. xiiin.

83   College of Arms, MS. M 13 *bis*. fols. 64–5, printed in Kipling, *Receyt*, pp. 74–6. See the discussion in Kipling, *Honour*, pp. 111–14. As he suggests, the revel probably took its cue from the Burgundian pageant tradition of the Throne of Honour.

84   PRO, E101/415/3, fol. 65v, abstracted in Anglo, 'Henry VII,' p. 37. Kipling, *Honour*, p. 99n. The fountain was under the supervision of Sir Reginald Bray and Sir Charles Somerset. The tent was 'devised' by Sir Charles Somerset and 'Mr Comptroller' [Sir Richard Guildford] in August 1501.

85   PRO, E101/415/3, fols. 65v, 67r–v, 72v, abstracted in Anglo, 'Henry VII,' p. 37.

86   Sydney Anglo, 'William Cornish in a Play, Pageants, Prison, and Politics,' *Review of English Studies*, n.s., 10 (1959): 353.

87   W.R. Streitberger, 'Henry VIII's Entertainment for the Queen of Scots, 1516: A New Revels Account and Cornish's Play,' *Medieval & Renaissance Drama in England*, 1 (1984): 29–35.

88   Kipling, *Honour*, pp. 176–7.

89   PRO, E101/415/3, fol. 65v, abstracted in Anglo, 'Henry VII,' p. 37.

90   Kipling, *Honour*, pp. 175–6.

91   College of Arms, MS. M 1 *bis*, fols. 84v–9 (copy of lost original), fols. 90–5 (another copy); Houghton Library, Harvard MS. 1095 (another copy; printed in *Collectanea*, IV: 263). On the relationship among these copies and the lost original in College of Arms, MS. M 13 *bis*, see Kipling, *Receyt*, pp. xxxiv–xxxvi. Payments for other entertainments this Christmas are found in PRO, E101/415/3, abstracted in Anglo, 'Henry VII,' p. 38.

92   PRO, E101/415/3, fol. 83, abstracted in Anglo, 'Henry VII,' p. 38. Kipling, *Honour*, pp. 176–7.

93   PRO, E101/415/3, fol. 82, abstracted in Anglo, 'Henry VII,' p. 38; BL, Additional MS. 59899, fol. 19, abstracted in Streitberger, *RORD* (1983): 44. On the continuing popularity of the morris dance throughout the century, see M.W. Thomas, '*Kempes Nine Daies Wonder*: Dancing Carnival into Market,' *PMLA*, 107 (1992): 511–23.

94   See McGee and Meagher, 'Checklist,' pp. 49–50, for the sources. 'The Maner of the Crying of ane Playe,' ca. 1480–1500 – Alfred Harbage, *Annals of English Drama, 975–1700*, rev. ed. S. Schoenbaum (Philadelphia: University of Pennsylvania Press, 1964), pp. 16–17 – also called 'The Droiches Part of the Play,' has been attributed to William Dunbar and conjectured to be part of the welcome for Margaret at Edinburgh in 1503. W.M. Mackenzie, *The Poems of William Dunbar* (Edinburgh: Porpoise Press, 1932), pp. xxii, 170–4, 240–4, provides evidence of Dunbar's presence in London in late 1501, presumably for the wedding negotiations, but points out that the surviving monologue makes it very difficult to ascertain what kind of a play this was. The mention of Robin Hood suggests a spring or summer play.

95   Glynn Wickham, *EES*, I: 289, estimates the cost of the outdoor pageants at about £120 each. Certain payments for the tournament totalling about £250 are found in PRO, E101/415/3, abstracted in Anglo, 'Henry VII,' pp. 36–8; but the total for all of the events must have run into the thousands of pounds. Not all of the expenses were born by the court; the City of London contributed substantially. See Kipling, *Receyt*, pp. xiv–xix.

96   PRO, E36/123, p. 93, and BL, Additional MS. 59899, fol. 9, abstracted in Streitberger, *RORD* (1983): 43, 48, where payments for other entertainments at Christmas 1502–3 are to be found.

97   PRO, E36/210, the Privy Purse account for the last year of the queen's life, 28 March 1502 – March 1503, is printed in Sir Nicholas Harris Nicolas, *Privy Purse Expenses of Elizabeth of York* (London: W. Pickering, 1830).

98   PRO, E36/210, p. 57, printed in Nicolas, *Privy Purse Expenses*, pp. 52–3.

99   PRO, E36/210, p. 40, printed in Nicolas, *Privy Purse Expenses*, p. 21.

100   PRO, E36/210, p. 76, printed in Nicolas, *Privy Purse Expenses*, p. 78.

101   BL, Additional MS. 59899, fol. 10, abstracted in Streitberger, *RORD* (1983): 43.

102   BL, Additional MS. 59899, fol. 19, abstracted in Streitberger, *RORD* (1983): 44.

103   Prince Arthur died at Ludlow castle on 2 April 1502. Funeral: College of Arms, MS. M 13*bis*, fols. 68–74v, printed in Kipling, *Receyt*, pp. lvii–lxiv, 80–93.

104   The queen was buried at St. Margaret's, Westminster. *Antiquarian Repertory*, IV: 654–63.

CHAPTER 2

1   Evidence of appearances by playing companies and of the joust is found in BL,
    Additional MS. 59899, fols. 43–100v, abstracted in Streitberger, *RORD* (1983):
    45–8. On the creations and ceremonies, see *Collectanea*, IV: 253–4; *Complete
    Peerage*, III: 443.

2   Guildhall Library, London MS. 3313, fols. 306v–7v, printed in *Great Chronicle*,
    pp. 330–1; BL, Cotton MS. Vespasian C. XII, fols. 236–44, printed in *Memorials*,
    pp. 282–303; Hall, pp. 500–1.

3   Sir Edward, son of Sir Richard with whom he held a grant to the office of Master
    of the Armoury in survivorship (PRO, C66/575, memb. 28, calendared in *CPR
    Henry VII*, I: 467), and half-brother of Sir Henry, later Master of the Revels,
    succeeded to the post on his father's death in 1506 (*Calendar of Inquisitions Post
    Mortem, Henry VII* [HMSO, 1955], III, no. 374), and held it until his own death
    on 4 June 1534 (PRO, SP1/84, p. 161, calendared in *LP* VII, no. 789). He was
    born in 1478 or 1479, was knighted at Tournai on 25 September 1513 (BL,
    Harleian MS. 6069, fol. 112), was made Marshall of Calais in May 1519 (PRO,
    C76/210, memb. 4), Constable of Dover Castle (PRO, C66/437, memb. 5) and
    Lord Warden of the Cinque Ports in November 1521 (BL, Egerton MS. 2092,
    fol. 303), calendared respectively in *LP*, I.ii, no. 2301; III.i, no. 230; III.ii, no.
    1791; IV.iii, Appendix, no. 91.

4   Payments related to the jousts are found in PRO, E36/214, pp. 41–9, abstracted
    in Anglo, 'Henry VII,' p. 41. The joust is mentioned in Guildhall Library, Lon-
    don MS. 3313, fol. 307, printed in *Great Chronicle*, pp. 330–1. See Kipling,
    Honour, pp. 132–3.

5   The style was revived by Sir Henry Lee, Elizabeth I's Master of the Armoury, in
    the early 1570s and dominated at court in the accession day triumphs through
    the 1580s. Kipling, *Honour*, pp. 116–36; Young, *Tournaments*, pp. 144–84.

6   See the discussion in Anglo, *Tournament Roll*, I: 19–21. On the development of
    romance in the tournament, see *Tournament Roll*, I: 21–34, and Richard Barber
    and Juliet Barker, *Tournaments* (Woodbridge, Suffolk: Boydell Press, 1989),
    107–37.

7   The jousts were important enough to inspire a 200-line poem on their magnifi-
    cence: *STC* 3543: *Here begynneth the iustes of Maye* [1507]; Kipling, *Honour*,
    pp. 133–6. Chamber payments relating to this joust are recorded in PRO, E36/214,
    p. 155, abstracted in Anglo, 'Henry VII,' p. 42. R.F. Green, *Notes & Queries*, 225
    (1980): 386–9, argues for the date of 1441; Kipling, *Notes & Queries*, 229 (1984):
    158–62, argues for the date of 1507.

8   PRO, E36/214, pp. 222, 226, abstracted in Anglo, 'Henry VII,' p. 43.

9   *STC* 4659: [Petrus Carmelianus], *The solempnities & triumphes doon at the spousells*

of the kyngs doughter to the archeduke of Austrige (London, 1508); *STC* 17558:
English translation; J. Gairdner, ed., '"The Spousells" of the Princess Mary
Daughter of Henry VII, to Charles Prince of Castile, A.D. 1508,' *The Camden
Miscellany IX*, Camden Society, n.s., vol. 53 (London, 1895), 30. Gairdner, p.
v, attributes the Latin narrative to Petrus Carmelianus, Henry's Latin Secretary, and
remarks that while the earlier parts of the English version are a close translation,
the later part is mainly a paraphrase. The English translation of the Latin description of the entertainments which I quote, for example, reads: 'There lacked no
disguysynges, moriskes nor enterludes made and appareilled in the beste and rich-
est maner.'

10   PRO, E36/214, p. 308, abstracted in Anglo, 'Henry VII,' p. 44.

11   PRO, LC9/50, fols. 149–53, printed in A.R. Meyers, *Bulletin of the Institute of
Historical Research*, 54 (1981): 120–9.

12   PRO, LC9/50, fol. 153r, printed in Meyers, p. 128.

13   On Rowanger's career, see Auerbach, *Tudor Artists*, pp. 7–9, 183–4.

14   PRO, LC9/50, fol. 151, printed in Meyers, pp. 125–6.

15   PRO, LC9/50, fol. 152v, printed in Meyers, p. 127.

16   PRO, E36/215, p. 23, abstracted in *LP*, II.ii, p. 1443.

17   Kipling, 'Patronage,' pp. 150–1.

18   Kipling, 'Patronage,' p. 154, paraphrases the Latin as 'performers of plays for the
King,' and points out that Chambers, *MS*, II: 187–8n, simply assumed that they
were a travelling troupe like those patronized by the nobility.

19   PRO, E36/131, p. 73, records the first known payment to the company on 27 May
1494.

20   College of Arms, MS. M 13*bis*, fols. 76–115; Houghton Library, Harvard Library
MS. English 1095 (17th century copy of M 13*bis*), printed in *Collectanea*, IV:
265–300; see especially pp. 267, 289, 296, 299.

21   Kipling, 'Patronage,' p. 152, thinks that English was employed by the Wardrobe.

22   Kipling, 'Patronage,' p. 153.

23   Their appearances at court are recorded in the Chamber accounts; see the Court
Calendar. For a list of their appearances in the provinces, see *Dramatic Records*,
pp. 374, 389.

24   For a list of their appearances in the provinces, see *Dramatic Records*, pp. 389,
396.

25   Hans von Hecht, 'Henry Medwall's *Fulgens and Lucrece*,' *Palaestra*, no. 148
(Leipzig, 1925): 102–3, suggested that the King's Players took lead parts in this
play. M.E. Moeslein, *The Plays of Henry Medwall* (New York: Garland, 1981),
102–3, thinks the suggestion as unlikely as I do. The references to players in Part
I, lines 50–1, 54–7 and Part II, lines 10, 43, are generic.

26   'Joannes Cornyssh senior' of St John Zacharie, London, left £20 and other gifts in

his will of 1474 to four named children: John, Anne, William, and Richard: Edward
Pine, *The Westminster Abbey Singers* (London: D. Dobson, 1953), 20.

27   Westminster Abbey Muniments 19087, 19089, 19091, 19092, 19093, 19095,
19096, 19098, 19099, show that William Cornish was the first Master in 1479–80,
when he was paid 6s. 8d. for a half year. The stipend rose to 13s. 4d. in the next
and succeeding years until 1490–1 when he was again paid 6s. 8d. for half a
year.

28   The Privy Seal writ for the 100s. reward in Michaelmas was issued to 'a Willmo
Cornysshe de Rege': PRO, E403/2558, fol. 41v.

29   On 13 July 1494 William Cornish received a grant as the king's servant to keep
one brewhouse and four other messuages in the parish of St Martin-in-the-Fields
by Charing-Cross in the possession of James Nichol, an idiot, and other lands in
England to hold from 29 May 1494 with the stipulation that he provide food and
vesture for Nichol and that he maintain the buildings. A William Cornish also
received a commission to impress sailors and soldiers for a barque called *Le
Cornyssh Pakker* of Rye on 24 January 1496 to be sent with armed power to Scotland: PRO, C66/575, memb. 34, C66/579, memb. 22, calendared respectively in
CPR Henry VII, I: 473; II: 91.

30   Guildhall Library, London MS. 3313, fol. 230, printed in *Great Chronicle*, p. 251,
refers to him on 6 January 1494 as 'oon of the kyngys Chapell,' and the Chamber
payment of 4–7 September 1496 was issued to 'Cornishe of the kinges Chapell':
PRO, E101/414/6, fol. 38, abstracted in Anglo, 'Henry VII,' p. 30.

31   Westminster, Victoria Library MS. E.1, p. 414 (account of the wardens of the
parish of St Margaret's from 4 June 1500 to 12 May 1502), lists 6d. for 'the knelle
of Willm Cornysshe wt the grete belle,' 4s. 'for iiij torches to hym,' 16d. for 'iiij
tapres,' 4s. for 'iiij torches,' and in the second year of the account, p. 418, they
received 6s. 8d. 'of Willm Cornyssh wyffe for the bequeste of hyr husband.' It
appears that this William Cornish died in 1500. Hugh Baillie, in a letter printed
in *Music and Letters*, 36 (1955): 310, notes that the name of this William appears
in the Bede Roll of the Fraternity of St Nicholas, citing James Christie, *Some
Account of Parish Clerks, more Especially of the Ancient Fraternity (Bretherne and
Sisterne), of S. Nicholas, known as the Worshipful Company of Parish Clerks* (London: J. Vincent, 1893), but I cannot find the item printed in this work.

32   Hugh Baillie, *Music and Letters*, 36 (1955): 310–11; Edward Pine, *The Westminster Abbey Singers* (London: D. Dobson, 1953), pp. 1–10; *Dramatic Records*,
pp. 388, 392. Earlier in my research I also held this view: 'Henry VIII's Entertainment for the Queen of Scots, 1516: A New Revels Account and Cornish's Play,'
Medieval and Renaissance Drama in England, 1 (1984): 32.

33   BL, Additional MS. 5465 (Fayrfax Manuscript), named after Dr. Robert Fayrfax,
organist of St Albans and Gentleman of the Chapel. On his career see Edwin B.

Warren, *The Life and Works of Robert Fayrfax* (Dallas, Texas: American Institute of Musicology, 1969). Cornish's contributions are transcribed in John Stevens, *Music & Poetry in the Early Tudor Court* (London: Methuen, 1961), pp. 4, 370, 379, 380.

34   BL, Additional MS. 31922 (Henry VIII's Manuscript). On the manuscript and Cornish's contributions to it, see John Stevens, *Music & Poetry in the Early Tudor Court* (London: Methuen, 1961), pp. 386, 390, 395, 401–8. See also Michael Preston, *A Complete Concordance to the Songs of the Early Tudor Court* (Leeds: W.S. Maney and Son, 1972).

35   Henry C. De Lafontaine, ed., *The King's Music: A Transcript of Records Relating to Music and Musicians (1460–1700)* (London: Novello & Co., n.d. [ca. 1909–10]), 2. The name following Cornish's in this list is John Prate, and if the name John is a mistake for William it would be easy to explain how the scribe made this rather common error. William's name appears in the 1509, 1510, and 1520 lists, but not in that of 1526: PRO, SP1/19, p. 275; SP1/37, p. 103, calendared respectively in *LP,* III.i, no. 704, p. 245; IV.i, no. 1939, pp. 870–1.

36   PRO, C66/569, memb. 27; C66/592, memb. 15; C66/593, memb. 11; calendared respectively in *CPR Henry VII,* I: 285; II: 314, 338, 398. Hugh Baillie, *Music and Letters,* 36 (1955): 310–11, also lists a Patrick Cornish who joined the Fraternity of St Nicholas. Henry Littlehales, *The Medieval Records of a London City Church (St Mary at Hill) A.D. 1420–1559,* Early English Text Society, o.s., vols. 125, 128 (London, 1905), 98, lists priests' wages from the churchwardens' account of St Mary at Hill in 1479–80 in which 5s. was 'payd to syr Richarde Cornysshe for the space of ij wykes.'

37   BL, Additional MS. 5665 (Ritson's Manuscript); see John Stevens, *Music & Poetry in the Early Tudor Court* (London: Methuen, 1961), 338.

38   Chambers, *ES,* II: 29–30, made this conjecture.

39   The full title of the poem, BL, Royal MS. 18. D. II., fols. 163–4, and BL, Harleian MS. 43, fols. 88–91 (imperfect), is 'In the Fleete made by me William Cornysshe otherwyse called Nysshewhete, chapelman with the moost famoust kyng Henry the vij*th*, his raigne the xix*th* yere, the moneth of July, a Treatise bitwene Trowth and enformacion.' 'Nysshewhete' is a pseudonym which plays on Cornish's name by reversing the syllables and substituting the synonym wheat for corn. The poem, written in rhyme royal, consists of four introductory verses which complain that a man may be convicted by false information. This is followed by sixteen stanzas of *A Parable between Information and Music* which argue by musical metaphors that the author had been wrongfully accused. On this poem and its association with Sir Richard Empson (executed 17 August 1510), and on *O mischievous M,* a satirical poem attributed to Cornish by Stow, see Sydney Anglo, 'William Cornish in a Play, Pageants, Prison, and Politics,' *Review of English Studies,* n.s., 10 (1959): 353–7, and Wallace, *Evolution,* p. 35.

40   Cornish was still active late in 1522. Westminster Abbey, Muniments 33301
      records 10s. paid 'in reward to master Cornysh on seynt Edwardes day in October
      anno xiiij.' Cornish's will, PRO, PROB 11/21, fols. 96v–7r, was made on 10 Jan-
      uary 1512. Hillebrand, *The Child Actors*, p. 51n, speculates unconvincingly that
      the will should be dated 1522. Cornish wished to be buried in the Chapel of the
      Rood in East Greenwich, and left money for a tomb of brick to be built over him
      with a stone border for people to kneel on. His wife, 'Iohane,' was his sole executrix,
      to whom he left all of his lands, tenements, and money for her life, then to his
      son Henry, and, in default, to his son William. The will was proved on 14 October
      1524, not 1523 as Wallace, *Evolution*, p. 61, has it. Payments in the parish record
      of St Margaret's, Westminster, (Westminster, Victoria Library, MS. E.2) continue
      to be made to William Cornish for the hire of clothes for the choir from 1522
      until 1530. Since these payments continue well after the death of the famous
      composer, they may refer to his son William.

41   Important studies on the early Tudor Chapel Royal appeared in E.F. Rimbault,
      The Old Cheque-Book ... of the Chapel Royal, Camden Society, n.s., vol. 3 (Lon-
      don, 1872); Wallace, *Evolution*, pp. 13–32; Chambers, *ES*, II: 23–61; N.H.
      Hillebrand, 'The Early History of the Chapel Royal,' *Modern Philology*, 18 (1920):
      65–100, and *The Child Actors*, pp. 40–64. The earliest notice of the Chapel is
      found in the *Liber Rubeus Scacarii* of Henry II (1100–35). Up to the Tudor peri-
      od the number of Gentlemen varied between twenty and thirty and the number
      of Children between eight and twelve. BL, Harleian MS. 642, fols. 71–3, printed
      in *A Collection of Ordinances and Regulations for the Government of the Royal
      Household* (London: Society of Antiquaries, 1790), 49–51; Chambers, *ES*, II: 26,
      prints their fees and allowances. The first Master of the Children in the Tudor
      Chapel was Gilbert Banaster, who served from 1478 until some time before 1486.
      A poet of some note in his time, Banaster is credited with an interlude in 1482
      and may have written three Latin tragedies. He died in 1487, but by 29 Septem-
      ber 1486 Laurence Squier, Clerk of the Chapel and Chaplain to Henry VII, had
      become Master, though John Melyonke may have served from 1483 to 1485.
      Whether Banaster or Squier involved the Chapel in secular entertainments is not
      clear. Squier died in 1493 and was succeeded either in this year or in 1495 by the
      noted composer, William Newark, who had been one of the Gentlemen from at
      least 1480. During Newark's Mastership, the first quasi-dramatic performance of
      the Gentlemen is recorded for Twelfth Night 1494 and of the Children for 28
      November 1501. Collier, *HEDP* (1831), I: 46, and Wallace, *Evolution*, p. 26,
      both err in giving 1490 as the date of the latter performance. When Newark died
      in 1509, he was succeeded by the most famous of all the early Tudor Masters,
      William Cornish, who devised and participated in court interludes and revels and
      during whose career both the Gentlemen and the Children developed into play-

ing companies. Cornish retired in 1523, and was replaced by William Crane, member of the Chapel from at least 1509, who had been closely associated with Cornish in court revels during the second decade of the century. Crane was replaced by Richard Bower by 30 June 1545, Gentleman of the Chapel from at least 1526. Bower died in 1561 and was replaced by Richard Edwards. On the careers of the early Tudor Masters, see Wallace, *Evolution*, pp. 24–32, 61–4, 67–77; the supplementary information in Chambers, *ES*, II: 27n; and Nan Carpenter, 'Thomas More and Music: Stanyhurst's Translation of the Abyngdon Epitaph,' *Moreana*, 16 (1979): 63–8. On the late Tudor Masters, see Hillebrand, *The Child Actors*, pp. 74–104.

42   BL, Harleian MS. 642, fol. 72, printed in *A Collection of Ordinances and Regulations for the Government of the Royal Household* (London: Society of Antiquaries, 1790), 50.

43   On the fees and performances of the Children, see Hillebrand, 'The Early History of the Chapel Royal,' *Modern Philology*, 18 (1920): 73. Boy Bishop ceremonies surfaced in every cathedral, collegiate church, school, and parish church where there were choristers. The origin of the ceremony is obscure, but it was fully developed in England by 1263 when statutes were devised to regulate it. The ceremonies were quasi-dramatic, involving disguise, enacting ceremonies, recitation of prepared parts, and masquerade. Traditionally the boy bishop was elected by his companions on 6 December, the feast of St Nicholas, and he reigned until 28 December, the feast of the Holy Innocents. During the period, the boy bishop wore the elaborate regalia of a bishop. These outfits were rich ceremonial garments preserved from generation to generation. Edward Pine, *The Westminster Abbey Singers* (London: D. Dobson, 1953), 49–50, transcribes the dissolution inventory of the Abbey which includes a list of the regalia used by the choristers, some of which appear to date from 1388 and were, on occasion, lent to the king for use at court. The Children of the Chapel received a reward for their boy bishop each December, even though the ceremony was forbidden by royal proclamation on 22 July 1541 (David Wilkins, *Concilia Magna Britanniae et Hiberniae* [London, 1737], III: 859, abstracted in *LP*, XVI, no. 1022). It is doubtful that they enacted the ceremony after that date, until it was briefly revived under Queen Mary. Chambers, *MS*, I: 336–71; Karl Young, *Drama of the Medieval Church* (Oxford: Clarendon Press, 1933), I: 104–11; and A.P. Rossiter, *English Drama from Early Times to the Elizabethans* (New York: Hutchinson's University Library, 1950), 56–61, treat the ceremony as a burlesque. V.A. Kolve, *The Play Called Corpus Christi* (Stanford: Stanford University Press, 1966), 135–8, and R.L. de Molen, 'Pueri Christi Imitato: The Festival of the Boy Bishop in Tudor England,' *Moreana*, 12 (1975): 17–28, treat it as a serious ceremony.

44   BL, Harleian MS. 642, fol. 216, printed in *A Collection of Ordinances and Regula-*

tions for the Government of the Royal Household (London: Society of Antiquaries, 1790), 121.

45   Wallace, *Evolution*, pp. 37–40, thought that this annual reward was for dramatic performances. Chambers, *ES*, II: 28n, insists that even the rewards for their 'pains taking' at Christmas were for musical performances. There is no clear evidence, and the truth probably lies somewhere between these extremes.

46   BL, Additional MS. 59899, fol. 75, abstracted in Streitberger, *RORD* (1983): 47. Streitberger, 'William Cornish and the Players of the Chapel,' *Medieval English Theatre*, 8 (1986): 3–20.

47   Kipling, 'Patronage,' p. 154, draws important parallels between the two royal companies, but they were not chartered or organized in quite the same way.

48   Hugh Baillie, 'A London Church in Early Tudor Times,' *Music and Letters*, 36 (1955): 56.

49   Henry Littlehales, *The Medieval Records of a London City Church (St. Mary at Hill) A.D. 1420–1559*, Early English Text Society, o.s., 125, 128 (London, 1905), 270, 275, 281, 288, 309, 316, 323, 344, 396; Hugh Baillie, *Music and Letters*, 36 (1955): 55–7.

50   The Gentlemen performed at St Mary's on Corpus Christi 1521, St Barnabas's Day in 1523, again in 1523–4, in 1524–5, and in 1527–8; on St Martin's Day (11 November) in 1554, the Queen's Chapel sang a Mass. See note 49.

51   There are also settings for the *Magnificat* by Cornish and Prents in the Caius Choir Book: Hugh Baillie, 'A London Church in Early Tudor Times,' *Music and Letters*, 36 (1955): 56.

52   When quoting the financial accounts and narratives, I employ the term found in the documents. When referring to these entertainments in general contexts I use the term 'play.'

53   M.E. Moeslein, ed., *The Plays of Henry Medwall* (New York: Garland, 1981), 5.

54   Alan H. Nelson, ed., *The Plays of Henry Medwall* (Cambridge: D.S. Brewer, 1980), 14–15. On the interconnections between plays and Tudor revels, see Thomas Pettitt, 'Tudor Interludes and the Winter Revels,' *Medieval English Theatre*, 6, no. 1 (1984): 16–27.

55   *Fulgens and Lucrece*, Part II, lines 379–80.

56   Nelson, *Medwall*, pp. 19–20, observes that the bass dance was performed by one couple at a time, two dances to a set, and suggests that this was 'la basse daunce de Spayne,' whose forty-six steps are described in the Salisbury Cathedral MS.

57   *Fulgens and Lucrece*, Part II, lines 389–93. F.S. Boas and A.W. Reed, eds., *Fulgens and Lucrece* (Oxford: Clarendon Press, 1926), p. xviii, did not know what to make of these 'wylde Irissh Portyngales.' Moeslein, *Medwall*, pp. 60–7, tries not altogether convincingly to connect them to Perkin Warbeck.

58   See the discussion of dating in Greg Walker, *Plays of Persuasion, Drama and Politics at the Court of Henry VIII* (Cambridge: Cambridge University Press, 1991), 62–72.

59 Nan Carpenter, *John Skelton* (New York: Twayne Publishers, 1967), 78.
60 On the songs in Skelton's play see Nan Carpenter, *Skelton*, pp. 114–22. *Votre tres douce*, a song by Gilles Binchois (d. 1460), is found in a two-part instrumental version in BL, Additional MS. 5665 (Ritson's MS.). 'Rutty bully' is a version of Cornish's 'Hoyda, hoyda, iolly rutterkin' which is preserved in BL, Additional MS. 5465 (Fayrfax MS.). See John Stevens, *Music & Poetry in the Early Tudor Court* (London: Methuen, 1961), 348, 380. See also Peter Happé, *Song in Morality Plays & Interludes*, Medieval English Theatre Monographs, I (Lancaster: Lancaster University, 1991) [reviewed by C.E. McGee, *The Early Drama, Art, and Music Review*, 14 (1992): 74–7].
61 *STC* 20722: *A new i[n]terlude and a mery of the nature of the iiij. elements* [1520] contains the earliest piece of music printed in England, *Time to pas with goodly sport*. Wallace, *Evolution*, p. 16n.
62 Alnwick Castle Archives, Letters and Papers, vol. 7, fol. 22r, ed. Robert J. Alexander, 'A Record of Twelfth Night Celebrations,' *Records of Early English Drama Newsletter*, 16, no. 1 (1991): 16. See Peter Happé, *Song in Morality Plays and Interludes*, Medieval English Theatre Monographs I, (Lancaster: Lancaster University, 1991), on the widespread use of song in the plays of this period.
63 M.E. Moeslein, ed., *The Plays of Henry Medwall* (New York: Garland, 1981), 11–29, 455–67.
64 Moeslein, pp. 4n, 38n. Collier, *HEDP* (1831), I: 68–70, claimed to have discovered a reference to an interlude by Medwall and acted by the King's Players in 1514: 'the fyndyng of troth, who was caryed away by ygnorance & ypocrasy.'
65 Warton, *HEP*, pp. 557–9. He also calls the play 'The Trial of Simonie,' and mentions that his friend 'Mr William Collins, whose Odes will be remembered while any taste for true poetry remains, shewed me this piece at Chichester, not many months before his death [12 June 1759].' By some opinions this account is considered a fabrication. Joseph Ritson, *Observations* (London, 1782), thought so, but Bliss, in his edition of Anthony à Wood, *Athenae Oxoniensis* (Oxford, 1813), I: 53, remarks, 'I have so frequently seen and handled volumes mentioned by Warton and denied to exist by Ritson, that I have no doubt as to the authenticity of the account.' Chambers, *MS*, II: 440–1, follows Ritson in denying its existence, and Ian Lancashire, *Dramatic Records*, p. 342, includes it among his doubtful records. R.M. Baine, 'Warton, Collins, and Skelton's *Necromancer*,' *Philological Quarterly*, 49 (1970): 245–8; and R.S. Kinsman and Theodore Young, *John Skelton: Canon and Census* (New York: Renaissance Society of America, 1967), 28–9, consider it a trustworthy account. I might instance the rediscovery of Medwall's *Fulgens and Lucrece* in this century to point out that losing Tudor interludes is not an altogether unheard of occurrence.
66 The poem, PRO, E36/228, fols. 7–8v, abstracted in *LP*, II.ii, p. 1518, is printed in *John Skelton, The Complete English Poems*, ed. John Scattergood (New Haven:

Yale University Press, 1983), 111–12. Scattergood does not include the Latin marginalia (which is written in the same hand as the text of the poem) nor does he mention them in his notes, pp. 419–20. Scattergood dates the poem shortly after the coronation on 24 June 1509, noting that the penultimate line of fol. 8, 'Deo (21) gracias' refers to Skelton's personal dating system in which the year 1 was the date he entered the service of the Tudors: October 1488. This gives us the date of composition, but the arrest of Empson and Dudley and the king's promise to redress wrongs was a topical issue until their execution in August 1510. Scattergood also suggests that the poem may be identical to 'The Boke of the Rosiar' mentioned in *Garland of Laurel*, line 1178. The handwriting of the English is fairly clear, but the Latin is difficult in places. I have enclosed conjectural readings in square brackets. It is also difficult to say exactly how these marginalia were designed to work. They may simply be glosses, though it is not clear why glosses would be needed for such a short poem, nor why each ends with &c. If this is the text which was recited before the king, it is possible that it was intended for two or more individuals with one reciting the gloss to announce the subject and another reciting the stanza.

[fol. 7]   The Rose both white and Rede
            In one Rose now doethe grow:
            Thus thorow every stede   Candida
            Thereof the fame dothe blow: punica &c
            Grace the sede did sow:
            England now gaddir flowris
            Exclude now all dolowrs

            Noble Henry the eight
            Thy loving souereine lorde
            Of kingis line moost streight Nobilis
            His tittle dothe Recorde: henricus &c
            In whome dothe wele Accorde
            Alexis yonge of Age
            Adrastus wise and sage:

            Astrea Iustice height
            That from the starry sky
            Shall now com and do Right: Sedibus
            This hundred yere scantly   [acherijs] &c
            A man kowd not Aspy
            That right dwelt vs Among
            And *that* was the more wrong:

Right shall the Foxis chare
The wolvis the beris also
That wrowght have moche care   Arcebit
And browght Englond in wo   vulpes &c
They shall worry no mo
[fol. 7v]   Nor wrote the Rosary
by extort Trechery:

Of this o*ur* noble King
The law they shall not breke
They shall com to rekaning   [Ne] tanti
No man for them wil speke   Regis &c
The pepil durst not creke
There grevis to complaine
They browght them in soche paine:

Therfor no more they shall
, The commouns ouerbace
That wonc wer over all   Ecce [platonis]
Both lorde and knight to face: sedaque &c
ffor now the yeres of grace
And welthe ar com Agayne
That maketh England fame:

Adonis of ffreshe colour
Of yowthe the godely flo*ur*
Our prince of high hono*ur*   Redijt iam
Our paves our succour   pulcher Adonis &c
Our king our emperour
Our *Priamus* of *Troy*
Our welth our worldly Ioy:

Vpon vs he doth Reigne
That maketh our hartis glad
As king moost soueraine
[fol. 8]   That ever Englond had   Anglorum
Demure sober and sad   Radians &c
And Martis lusty knight
God save him in his right
           Amen

Bien men souient

Deo (21) gracias
Per me Laurigerum Britonum Skeltonida vatem:

67   Chambers, *ES*, I: 72; Wickham, *EES*, I: 40, 277–8. High offices such as Master of the Horse or Comptroller of the Household held in combination with the Master-ship of the Revels were purely coincidental. Sir Henry Guildford was Master of the Henchmen two years after, Master of the Horse five years after, and Comptroller of the Household eleven years after he began to act as Master of the Revels.

68   See David Starkey, 'Intimacy and Innovation,' in David Starkey et al., *The English Court* (London: Longman, 1987), 71–118.

69   Folger Library, MS. Lb 42, fols. 11, 26, printed in Feuillerat, *Edward VI and Mary*, p. 222, and in *Elizabeth*, p. 81. The term 'device' has proved difficult to interpret in medieval literary contexts; see David C. Fowler, 'On the Meaning of Pearl,' *Modern Language Quarterly,* 21 (1960): 27–9. In the orders for Twelfth Night in the Northumberland Household book the ordering of the dances and devising the pageant are 'Alwaies reseruid' to an officer called the Master of the Revels and in another instance called the Master of the Disguisings. See Ian Lancashire, 'Orders for Twelfth Day and Night circa 1515 in the Second Northumberland Household Book,' *English Literary Renaissance*, 10 (1980): 36.

70   Chambers's reliance on this document, *ES*, I: 71–3, led him to generalize Holt's remark to describe the entire early Tudor period.

71   Kipling, 'Patronage,' pp. 155–8, discusses the circumstantial evidence for a connection between the Wardrobe and King's Players and the Chapel Royal.

CHAPTER 3

1   PRO, E36/215, p. 23, abstracted in *LP,* II.ii, pp. 1441–3. Windsor was Keeper of the Great Wardrobe from 20 April 1506 (PRO C66/599, memb. 14, calendared in *CPR Henry VII,* II: 470) until his death on 30 March 1543. Included among the documents subsidiary to his accounts is a warrant from the king (PRO, E101/416/7), dated 27 July 1509, to furnish jousts.

2   Guildhall Library, London MS. 3313, fols. 318–20, printed in *Great Chronicle*, pp. 341–3, which differs from the narrative given by Hall, pp. 510–12. Chamber payments relating to the event are found in PRO E36/215, pp. 17–23, abstracted in *LP,* II.ii, pp. 1441–6.

3   Hall, p. 510.

4   Anglo, *Tournament Roll,* I: 48.

5   Hall, p. 512.

6   Hall, p. 515–16. Henry VIII encouraged the martial exercises and on occasion provided subventions for them. In October 1510 'The kyng not mynded to se yong Gentlemen, vnexpert in marciall feats, caused a place to be prepared within

the parke of Grenewyche for the Quene and the ladies to stande and se the fighte with battaill axes that should be done there.' Henry himself fought with battle axes on this occasion and gave the rest of the young gentlemen 200 marks in gold to have a banquet in London afterwards.

7   Gibson's account is PRO, E36/217, fols. 1–2, 15, abstracted in *LP*, II.ii, p. 1490. Hall, p. 513.

8   Gibson's account is PRO, E36/217, fols. 3–12, 15–25, abstracted in *LP*, II.ii, pp. 1490–2. Hall, pp. 513–14, describes the revel.

9   Henry Bourchier, 2nd Earl of Essex (1483–1540), was bearer of the spurs at Henry VII's coronation and a member of his council. He bore the sword at Henry VIII's coronation and held a number of significant court posts, including Captain of the Gentlemen Pensioners (1509–40) and Captain of the King's Spears (1512–14). He was Marshall of the king's train at the Field of Cloth of Gold in 1520. *Complete Peerage*, IV: 138–39. His grandfather patronized a troupe of players as early as 1468–9 which this earl continued.

10   Anglo, 'Evolution,' p. 20, suggests that the game was mumchance.

11   PRO, E36/217, fols. 15, 25, abstracted in *LP*, II.ii, p. 1491. The abstract contains an important mistranscription: garments were 'dellyuerd' by Wentworth, not 'devised' by him. Chambers's observation (*MS*, I: 404n; *Tudor Revels*, p. 4; *ES*, I: 71) that the first notice of a Master of the Revels is in a Household Order of 1494 is also based on a mistranscription, as Wickham, *EES*, I: 275–6, has already shown. The item is transcribed from BL Harleian MS. 642, fol. 202, printed in *A Collection of Ordinances and Regulations for the Government of the Royal Household* (London: Society of Antiquaries, 1790), 113. An insertion in another hand in the manuscript reads 'and if the master of the Iuells be ther' rather than as it is transcribed 'master of the reuells.' A form of the 'I' is employed which is easily confused with minuscule 'r' as in the word 'Inprimis' on fol. 213 of the manuscript.

12   Gibson's account is PRO, E36/217, fols. 13–14, 25–6, abstracted in *LP*, II.ii, p. 1492. Hall, p. 514. On the relationship between Gibson's accounts and Hall's narratives, see Sydney Anglo, 'Financial and Heraldic Records of the English Tournament,' *Journal of the Society of Archivists*, 2 (1962): 185.

13   Hall, p. 516, mentions a joust and tourney. Gibson (PRO, E36/217, fol. 36) mentions running at the ring.

14   Gibson's account for the revel is PRO, E36/217, fols. 30–6; E36/229, fols. 1–6, abstracted in *LP*, II.ii, pp. 1492–3. Hall, p. 516.

15   Gibson's account is PRO, E36/217, fols. 38–45; E36/229, fols. 8–15, abstracted in *LP*, II.ii, pp. 1493–4. Gibson also lists costumes for minstrels and fools in his account, but how the latter figured in the revel is not clear. Hall, pp. 516–17.

16   Gibson says that out of the mount 'yssuyd A morys daunce by the kynges young gentyllmen as hynsmen': PRO, E36/229, fol. 8. Hall, p. 517, refers to them as the

'chyldren of honor called the Henchemen.' It appears that younger members of the court are here costumed as knights, as if they were the king's Henchmen.

17 Guildford was knighted by King Ferdinand on 15 September 1511 (*CSP Spanish*, II, no. 54) and by Henry VIII at Westminster on 30 March 1512 (BL Harleian MS. 5177, fol. 12, calendared in *LP,* I.ii, Appendix, no. 26). He retained his position as Esquire for the Body (PRO C66/619, memb. 24, calendared in *LP,* I.i, no. 1732 [47]) despite his knighthoods.

18 He was made King's Standard Bearer on 28 May 1513 (PRO, C66/620, memb. 12, calendared in *LP,* I.ii, no. 1948 [96]), Master of the Horse on 6 November 1515 (PRO, C66/626, memb. 10, calendared in *LP,* II.i. no. 1114), and succeeded Sir Edward Poynings as Comptroller of the Household by 1 September 1522. He is named Comptroller in a grant issued on that date (PRO, C66/641, memb. 18, calendared in *LP,* III.ii, no. 2587) and he filed his first account for the period 30 September to 30 September 13–14 Henry VIII (PRO, E101/419/6).

19 The original signatures to the articles for the joust are in BL, Harleian Charter 83. H. 1, calendared in *LP,* I.i, no. 698 (1). Payment for the 1517 jousts is found in PRO, E36/215, pp. 528, 529, 531, abstracted in *LP,* II.ii, p. 1476.

20 The letter is PRO, SP1/12, pp. 137–9, calendared in *LP,* II.i, no. 1478. Guildford is called Master of the Revels in Gibson's accounts from as early as 1511 (PRO, E36/217, fols. 38–45, E36/229, fols. 8–15) and as late as ca. 1530 (PRO, SP1/58, fols. 253–4).

21 The letters are translated in R.A.B. Mynors and D.F.S. Thompson, trans., *The Correspondence of Erasmus* in *Collected Works of Erasmus*, vol. 6 (Toronto: University of Toronto Press, 1982), no. 966, pp. 363–5; and in R.A.B. Mynors, trans., *The Correspondence of Erasmus* in *Collected Works of Erasmus*, vol. 7 (Toronto: University of Toronto Press, 1987), no. 1032, pp. 107–8.

22 Collier, *HEDP* (1879), I: 37, probably quoting PRO, E36/131, p. 73. He also mentions a receipt, probably a strip cut from what appears to be an Exchequer document, now BL, Egerton MS. 2623 (3), fol. 1, naming Gibson as a player. See also PRO, LC2/1, fol. 133, calendared in *LP,* I.i, no. 20; Chambers, *ES,* II: 78; and Wickham, *EES,* II.i: 116n.

23 PRO, C66/587, memb. 16 and C66/593, memb. 2, calendared respectively in *CPR Henry VII*, II: 221, 350; and C66/611, memb. 13, calendared in *LP,* I.i, no. 94 (48). It was probably from this information that Chambers, *ES,* I: 72, suggested that the permanent official who assisted the early acting Masters of the Revels belonged to the Wardrobe. See also Kipling, 'Patronage,' pp. 149–64.

24 PRO, SP2/ Fol. A, no. 1, calendared in *LP,* II.i, no. 2736; PRO, C66/630, memb. 2, calendared in *LP,* II.ii, no. 3257; PRO, SP1/21, pp. 60–3, calendared in *LP,* III.i, no. 999.

25 The commission is PRO, SP1/40, p. 194, calendared in *LP,* IV.ii, no. 2758; the

appointment to investigate foreign artificers is PRO, E163/10/15, calendared in *LP,* IV.ii, no. 4997; the grant is recorded in PRO, C66/652, memb. 12d, calendared in *LP,* IV.ii, no. 5083 (3); the appointment as Sergeant of Arms is listed in PRO, SP1/37, pp. 65–103, calendared in *LP,* IV.i, no. 1939 (8); and his election to parliament for Romney at the same time that Sir Henry Guildford and Sir Edward Guildford were members is mentioned in PRO, SP1/56, pp. 2–47, calendared in *LP,* IV.iii, no. 6043.

26   PRO, E36/217, fol. 30.

27   PRO, E36/217, fol. 37.

28   PRO, E36/217, fol. 38: 'perselles delyuered of garmentes of the kynges store to Iohn ynglyche.' These costumes included four satin garments for ladies, two satin garments in Spanish fashion for ladies, and a red satin garment for a lady; three green and white satin garments for men, a short garment of satin for a man, and an embroidered crimson satin garment of Spanish fashion for a woman. Also listed are 'vj garmentes for ladyes of reed saten of breges powdyrd with tasselles of sylk of kolen on delyured to Iohn ynglyche,' 'ij yong ladyes garments of yelow saten of breges betyn and staynd werke spanyche facyon dellyured to Iohn ynglych,' a garment of 'crymsyn saten of breges spanyche fasyun browdyred with koper stufe delyuerd Iohn ynclych,' and 'vj garments for men of saten of breges brodyrd with koper.' The Revels Office ordinarily made garments for the King's Players later in the century when they appeared in court performances; see Feuillerat, *Edward VI and Mary,* pp. 22–4, for examples. We have no evidence of the practice at Henry VII's court.

29   Gibson's first payment from the Chamber on 1 June 1512 was for the sum of £60 13s. 11 1/2d. for the jousts at Greenwich: PRO, E36/215, p. 190, abstracted in *LP,* II.ii, p. 1457.

30   PRO, E101/417/11, abstracted in *LP,* I.ii, no. 2349 (8 February to 11 October). Gibson was appointed to the Tents as part of wartime preparations, as his accounts show him preparing material for shipment abroad (PRO, E36/3, fol. 95, calendared in *LP,* I.ii, no. 2483) and signing receipts for material sent back to him by Garnesche (PRO, E101/56/25, calendared in *LP,* I.ii, no. 2480 [8]). Garnesche, a Gentleman Usher who participated in many of the tournaments at court, was satirized in John Skelton's poem, 'A Flyting' (ca. 1514): '... Sithe ye haue me chalyngyd, M Garnesche,/ Ruduly revilyng me in the kynges noble hall ....' Garnesche's reply is not extant.

31   Hall, pp. 539–40.

32   Walshe was granted his patent by Privy Seal on 12 November 1485: PRO, C82/4, no. 565, calendared in Campbell, I: 204, in which he is paid an allowance for a 'boy' or 'garçon.' Tournell was granted his patent on 6 November 1489: PRO, C66/570, memb. 6, calendared in *CPR Henry VII,* I: 293, in which he is allowed

4*d.* a day to pay a 'yeoman.' Morton was granted his patent on 28 November 1496: PRO, C66/579, memb. 10, calendared in *CPR Henry VII*, II: 72–3. He was allowed 4*d.* a day to pay a 'groom.'

33 PRO, E101/414/7 is Morton's account to 1513, but he held his patent until 1518. Certainly by August 1518, and probably by 15 May of that year when Morton surrendered the patent, Gibson was discharging the duties of Sergeant of the Tents: PRO, E36/216, fol. 11v, abstracted in *LP*, II.ii, p. 1479. He also continued to exercise his duties in the Revels. The Revels and Tents were thus functionally combined as early as 1513, and the ties were further strengthened in 1518.

34 Sir Richard complained to Wolsey in a letter of 26 March 1516 (PRO, SP1/13, p. 76, calendared in *LP*, II.i, no. 1708) about a sum of £13 6*s.* 8*d.* due to him from Gibson for four year's rent; again on 20 August of that year he requested that Wolsey summon Gibson and command him to pay (PRO, SP1/13, pp. 281–2, calendared in *LP*, II.i, no. 2228). Sir Richard was paid £23 for five years' rent in October 1518 for his house in Calais 'where the king*es* tent*es* lyeth' (PRO, E36/216, fol. 19v). This is probably the house used by Gibson during the war for storage and fabrication of tents (PRO, SP1/230, fol. 209, SP1/8, fol. 161, E36/3, fol. 72, calendared in *LP*, I.ii, nos. 3017, 3090, 3091).

35 PRO, SP1/71, pp. 179–94, calendared in *LP*, V, no. 1492 (ii).

36 Hall, pp. 517–18. For the many other sources see Court Calendar. Prince Henry was to die on 22 February, less than two weeks after the festivities.

37 PRO, E36/217, fol. 46.

38 Brandon's spectacle, disguise, and drama is modeled on the *Pas de l'Arbre d'Or* of 1468. The hermit in Elizabethan tournaments is discussed in Frances A. Yates, 'Elizabethan Chivalry: The Romance of the Accession Day Tilts,' *Journal of the Warburg and Courtauld Institutes*, 20 (1957): 20–2; Young, *Tournaments*, pp. 173–4; Anglo, *Tournament Roll*, I: 54.

39 Guildhall Library, London MS. 3313, fols. 347v–8, printed in *Great Chronicle*, pp. 373–4.

40 Hall, p. 520.

41 Gibson's account is PRO, E36/217, fols. 177–83, abstracted in *LP*, II.ii, pp. 1498–9. Hall, pp. 533–4.

42 PRO, E36/217, fol. 60, abstracted in *LP*, II.ii, p. 1495.

43 Hall, p. 553.

44 Gibson's account is PRO, E36/217, fols. 79–80; SP1/7, fols. 134–6, abstracted in *LP*, I.ii, no. 2562. *CSP Milan*, I, no. 654. Hall, p. 566. Henry had made formal entries into Therouanne on 24 August, and Tournai on 25 September. See Hall, pp. 552, 565–6, and BL, Cotton MS. Cleopatra C. V, fols. 64–95v, the diary of John Taylor, calendared in *LP*, I.ii, no. 2391.

45 Hall, p. 568. Marie Axton, 'The Tudor Masque and Elizabethan Court Drama,'

in M. Axton and R. Williams, eds., *English Drama: Form and Development* (Cambridge: Cambridge University Press, 1977), 27–8, ignores Hall's interpretation and suggests that the 'posye' expresses Henry's commiseration and Brandon's reconciliation to the marriage of the king's sister, Mary, to Louis XII of France. After Louis' death, Brandon married Mary without Henry's permission.

46   Gibson's account is PRO, E36/217, fol. 227–46; SP2/Fol. A, no. 8, abstracted in *LP*, II.ii, pp. 1503–4.

47   According to Hall, p. 585, 'the king lent to the Emperour Maximilian a great summe of money: wherof the company of Friscobalde, & Anthony Caueler Geneuoy vndertoke thexchange, but they paied not the Emperour at his day, notwithstanding thei had receaued the money of the king. This Friscobald & Anthony Caveler by means of rewardes, geuen to great lordes of the counsaill borowed of the king xxx. M. l. & had long dayes for the payment: but Friscobald was shortly consumed, & Anthony Caueler could not be sene & so the king was not payd at his dayes, & many English merchauntes were by those men undone, for they spent liberally of euery mans goodes.'

48   Marie Axton, 'The Tudor mask and Elizabethan court drama,' in M. Axton and R. Williams, eds., *English Drama: Form and Development* (Cambridge: Cambridge University Press, 1977), 28.

49   Hall, p. 582; Anglo, 'Evolution,' p. 25; David Wiles, *The Early Plays of Robin Hood* (Cambridge: D. S. Brewer, 1981), 11.

50   Gibson's account is PRO, E36/229, fols. 62–72, abstracted in *LP*, II.ii, pp. 1504–5. Sanuto, *Diarii*, XX: 264–8, calendared in *CSP Venetian*, II, no. 624.

51   Gibson's account is PRO, E36/217, fols. 61–76; E36/229, fols. 31–47, abstracted in *LP*, II.ii, pp. 1494–7. Hall, pp. 518–19. Guildhall Library, London MS. 3313, fols. 347v–8, printed in *Great Chronicle*, pp. 375–6. See also P.T. Hadorn, 'The Westminster Tournament of 1511: A Study in Propaganda,' *RORD*, 31 (1992): 25–45.

52   C.S. Lewis, *The Allegory of Love* (Oxford: Clarendon Press, 1936), 119, suggests that in Guillaume, the garden in the *Roman de la Rose* refers to the life of the court considered as the necessary sphere or field for love's operation. For a different perspective on the *hortus deliciarum*, see John V. Fleming, *The Roman de la Rose* (Princeton: Princeton University Press, 1969), 54–103, and on some other uses of the garden in medieval literature, see D.W. Robertson, *Essays in Medieval Culture* (Princeton: Princeton University Press, 1980), 21–50.

53   Hall, p. 519 (and see also Guildhall Library, London MS. 3313, fol. 348v, printed in *Great Chronicle*, p. 374) mentions 'a shipman of London' who sold some of these letters for £3 14s. 18d., indicating that the audience for these major revels included a mix of social classes. Guildford and Gibson were charged for such shortages of gold issued by Robert Amadas, Master of the Jewels. As part of a

household wide attempt at better record keeping in 1519, Gibson's and Amadas's accounts were viewed by Sir Thomas Boleyn, Sir Robert Dymoke, and Sir Henry Guildford: BL, Cotton MS. Titus B. I, fol. 189, calendared in *LP,* III.i, no. 576. Such a review may explain the narrative quality of Gibson's accounts and his concern to document how the material was used and what happened to it after the revels were produced. When Amadas died by 1533, commissioners were appointed to take inventory of the jewels and to examine his accounts. It was discovered that he owed the king £1771 19*s.* 10*d.* in plate, of which £306 8*s.* had been issued to Guildford and £200 to Gibson: PRO, SP1/78, pp. 64–5, calendared in *LP,* VI, no. 924.

54   The disorder surrounding souvenir distribution occurred at Henry VII's court as well: 'And ye shall undyrstand that upon every nygth ffoluyng these ffforesaid Justis was made at the kyngis cost a sumptuous banket In the white halle, where alsoo were shewid goodly dysguysyngs and othyr dysportis, By meane whereof many of the kyngis Subgectis were Relevid as well ffor the stuff by theym sold & werkmanshyp of the same, as by platis spangyllis Rosis & othyr conceytis of Sylvyr & ovyr gilt which ffyll ffrom theyr garmentys bothe of lordys & ladyes and Gentylmen whiles they lepyd and dauncid, and were gaderid of many pore ffolkis standyng nere abowth & presyng In ffor lucre of the same': Guildhall Library, London MS. 3313, fols. 45r–v, printed in *Great Chronicle,* p. 313. Such incidents invariably demonstrated what Gibson describes as the vulgarity of those 'rude' people.

55   Gibson's account is PRO, E36/229, fols. 91–106; SP2/ Fol. A, no. 4, abstracted in *LP,* II.ii, pp. 1497–8. Hall, p. 526.

56   PRO, E36/229, fols 99, abstracted in *LP,* II.ii, p. 1498.

57   Eugene Vinaver, ed., *The Works of Sir Thomas Malory,* 2nd ed. (Oxford: Clarendon Press, 1967), I: 315. On uses of the castle and the assault in religious literature, see Roberta D. Cornelius, 'The Figurative Castle' (PHD. diss., Bryn Mawr College, 1930), 11, 58–67.

58   Hall, p. 526. Sudden entrances at feasts are traditional in romance literature, as for example in *Gawain and the Green Knight* and in Chaucer's *Squire's Tale.* Gibson's account for preparation is mixed with that for his preparation of 'Le Fortresse Dangerus': PRO, E36/229, fols. 91–106; SP2/ Fol. A, no. 4.

59   Rudolph Brotanek, *Die Englishchen Maskenespiele* (Wein and Leipzig: W. Braunmüller, 1902), 67, referring to PRO, E36/229, fol. 175, thought that the novelty lay in the use of garments. His argument is dependent on an overly scrupulous analysis of the syntax of the Revels account in which Gibson mentions 'long govns and hodes and hats after the maner of messkelyng in etaly.' Even in the most carefully constructed sentences written in this period, modifying phrases and clauses are left dangling, and as any cursory reading of Gibson's accounts will show, they

are financial statements which are concerned with what material he used, not with defining the form of his revels. Chambers, *MS*, I: 401, mistakenly thought that the mumming of 1377 involved dancing between the performers and spectators. Welsford, *Court Masque*, pp. 130–8, who provides a convenient summary of the history of the controversy, followed Paul Reyher, *Les Masques Anglais* (Paris: Hachette, 1909), in believing that the novelty lay in dancing of disguised and undisguised persons. Chambers, *ES*, I: 153 later changed his mind and thought that the novelty was the 'commoning' of disguised and undisguised persons.

60 Anglo, 'Evolution,' pp. 4–8.

61 For the revel of 18 October 1513 at Tournai, Gibson refers to the entertainment as a mummery, although in his accounts he lists costumes for 'iiij meskellyers' (PRO, SP1/7, fol. 75; E36/217, fol. 73). Here the term indicates the persons in the revel, as it does again in his account for 5 January 1520 when he mentions 'the maskellyers apparel' (PRO, E36/217, fol. 104; PRO, SP1/18, fol. 53). On occasion, Gibson uses the word as if it referred to a type of entertainment, as in the coats prepared for 'a meskeler' in September 1519 or in his note that it was the 'kynges plesyr that meskelers and other plesyers schoulld be had' for Christmas 1524–5 (PRO, E36/217, fol. 89; SP1/32, fol. 275). He uses it to mean a visor or the person who wore it in 1524–5 when he records cloth used by 'vj maskelers that had heedes and berds' (PRO, SP1/32, fol. 274). He also uses it to refer to a type of garment and to an entertainment when he writes of a 'meskeler of vj gentylmen in govnes of cloothe of syllver and cloothe of goold' and of 'viij maskelers viij long govnes of taffata and viij hoodes' in January 1526 (PRO, SP1/37, fol. 14v). In his account for 31 December 1519 Gibson notes payments for a 'meskeller or mvmry,' treating both terms as synonyms (PRO, E36/217, fol. 100). The loose terminology is not unique to Gibson. Hall and Gibson both call the revels of 17 and 24 June 1520 at the Field of Cloth of Gold 'maskers' or 'meskelers,' but in College of Arms, MS. M 6 *bis*, fols. 10v, 12, and in other documents, the term used is 'mommery.' In his 10 November 1527 account, Gibson uses the term 'mask' in its late Tudor sense when he lists black sarcenet 'spent for iij meskelyng hodes for the gret maske' and 'vj gyrdylls for the black maskelers,' 'vj gyrdylls for the gret maske' and 'vj gyrdylls for the first maske' (PRO, SP1/45, fol. 34). In a letter of June 1527 describing entertainments at the French court, Viscount Lisle mentions that the king and some of the young lords 'went in a maskyr' and danced, and that there were several sorts of 'maskes,' two of which were 'after the turkys facion.' A play followed, after which the 'maskers daunsyd agen' (PRO, SP1/42, fol. 74). See also Anglo, 'Evolution,' pp. 6–7.

62 'Mask' is the usual term used by Edward VI's reign to describe revels, and the persons performing in them, as well as the costumes they wore, but old terms die hard, and 'mummery' and 'disguising' are still to be found in use late in the cen-

tury, particularly among the artisans and suppliers of material who submitted bills to the Revels Office.

63   Sir Thomas Hoby gives an account of a mask at Shrovetide 1549 when the Duke of Ferrandine visited Venice. The duke and his companions ran at the ring on horseback during the day, and at night, 'The Duke cumming in a braue maskerye with his companions went (as the maner is) to a gentlewoman whom he most fansied .... There cam in another companye of Gentlmen Venetiens in another maskerye: and one of them went in like maner to the same gentlwoman that the Duke was entreating to daunse with him, and somwhat shuldered the Duke, which was a great iniurie': BL, Egerton MS. 2148, fols. 17v–18v, edited by Edgar Powell, *Camden Miscellany, Volume the Tenth*, Camden Society, 3rd. ser., vol. 4 (London, 1902), 14. In the ensuing brawl, the duke was killed.

64   Hall, p. 535. Gibson's account is PRO, E36/217, fols. 186–201, abstracted in *LP,* II.ii, pp. 1499–1500. Payment for this shows in Daunce's account on a warrant dormant (PRO, E101/417/7, no. 76) to Guildford: PRO, E36/1, fol. 58v, abstracted in *LP,* I.ii, no. 3608.

65   Hall, p. 535, says it was drawn by 'foure wood houses.' The Anglo-Saxon, *wudewasa, wudewasan*, became *wodewose, wodehouse* by the late Middle Ages. Richard D. Bernheimer, *Wildmen in the Middle Ages* (Cambridge, Mass.: Harvard University Press, 1952), 42.

66   Gibson's account is PRO, E36/217, fols. 81–3; SP1/7, fols. 136–9, abstracted in *LP,* II.ii, no. 2562.

67   Collier, *HEDP* (1831), I: 68–70. Gibson (PRO, E36/217, fol. 81) says that Guildford devised it, but that would not have precluded his hiring Cornish to write the text or songs for it.

68   Wallace, *Evolution*, p. 46.

69   Reed, *Early Tudor Drama*, p. 96, observed that 'There is no trace of this paper in the bound volume, nor is anything known of it at the Public Record Office, where the documents have been recently subjected to a close scrutiny for the revision of the first volume of the *Letters and Papers of Henry VIII*. As it could not have any bearing on the business of receipts and payments of which the roll was a record, its insertion does not find a ready explanation. I would suggest, therefore, that it is wise to treat the story of the folded paper with suspicion.' Chambers, *MS*, II: 201n, also remarks that the paper is not calendered in *Letters and Papers*. When Reed and Boas edited *Fulgens and Lucrece* (Oxford: Clarendon Press, 1926), pp. xvii–xviii, they say that the paper probably never existed and that the transcript is a fabrication, though they offer less evidence here than Reed had in *Tudor Drama*. The only conclusion warranted by the evidence is the caution that Reed initially advised, but scholars continue to repeat the allegation found in the Boas-Reed edition of *Fulgens and Lucrece* as if the charge were substantiated.

Extant Revels accounts do not preserve information on all entertainments produced in this period, and Collier's explanation of how he came by this paper is plausible to anyone familiar with primary research in these documents. We did not know, for example, that a Revels account existed to document a play put on by Cornish in conjunction with the May 1516 jousts until my discovery in 1981 of Gibson's subsidiary account, which had been calendered as a tailor's account in the Public Record Office: Streitberger, 'Henry VIII's Entertainment for the Queen of Scots, 1516: Gibson's New Revels Account and Cornish's Play,' *Medieval and Renaissance Drama in England*, 1 (1983): 29–35. In an interesting study, Dewey Ganzel, *Fortune and Men's Eyes: The Career of John Payne Collier* (Oxford: Oxford University Press, 1982), has investigated the charges against Collier.

70   Hall, p. 580. Gibson's account is PRO, E36/217, fols. 204–6; SP2/Fol. A, no. 5, abstracted in *LP,* II.ii, pp. 1500–1.

71   PRO, E36/215, p. 362, abstracted in *LP,* II.ii, p. 1466. Harrison was Yeoman of the Queen's Chamber.

72   Hall, pp. 580–1. Gibson's account is PRO, E36/217, fols. 219–23; SP2/Fol. A, no. 7, abstracted in *LP* II.ii, pp. 1502–3.

73   Hall, pp. 580. Gibson's account is PRO, E36/217, fols. 209–18; SP2/Fol. A, no. 6, abstracted in *LP,* II.ii, pp. 1501–2.

74   Richard Bernheimer, *Wildmen in the Middle Ages* (Cambridge, Mass.: Harvard University Press, 1952), plates 31–7.

75   The payments are found in PRO, E36/215 and BL, Additional MS. 21481, abstracted as follows: Christmas 1509–10 (*LP,* II.ii, p. 1444); Christmas 1510–11 (*LP,* II.ii, pp. 1448–9); Christmas 1511–12 (*LP,* II.ii, p. 1454); Christmas 1512–13 (*LP,* II.ii, p. 1459); Christmas 1513–14 (*LP,* II.ii, p. 1462); Christmas 1514–15 (*LP,* II.ii, p. 1466).

76   PRO, E101/62/11, calendared in *LP,* I.ii, no. 2053 (ii).

77   PRO, E36/215, p. 355; BL, Additional MS. 21481, fols. 177r–v.

78   PRO, E36/217, fol. 38.

79   For records of the activities of the King's 'new' Players in the provinces see *Dramatic Records*, pp. 389–90.

80   Hall, p. 592.

81   Later monarchs also used the royal company to achieve status at court and to influence the dynamics of playing conditions in the city or the provinces. See Scott McMillin, 'The Queen's Men and the London Theatre of 1583,' in *Elizabethan Theatre X*, ed. C.E. McGee (Port Credit, Ontario: P.O. Meany, 1988), 9–15, on Elizabeth I's use of her royal companies.

82   *Dramatic Records*, pp. 388–92.

83   David Starkey, 'Intimacy and Innovation,' in David Starkey et al., *The English Court* (London: Longman, 1987), 71–118.

84   Hall, p. 515.

85   Sir Thomas Hoby, trans., *The Courtier*, ed. B. A. Milligan, *Three Renaissance Classics* (New York: Charles Scribner's Sons, 1953), 285–7, 348; see also the comments on apparel for tournaments, pp. 344–5. On the international character of Henry's court see David Starkey, *Henry VIII, A European Court in England* (New York: Cross River Press, 1991).

CHAPTER 4

1   Gibson's account, PRO, E36/229, fol. 73–82, is abstracted in *LP,* II.ii, pp. 1505–6, and partly transcribed in Hillebrand, *The Child Actors*, pp. 324–5. Hall, p. 583, is the main narrative.

2   PRO, E36/215, p. 427, abstracted in *LP,* II.ii, p. 1470.

3   It is possible that the source was Boccaccio because of the inclusion of Pandarus. Another sixteenth-century adaptation in a ballad focuses on the consummation at Pandarus's house: David C. Fowler, *A Literary History of the Popular Ballad* (Durham, N.C.: Duke University Press, 1968), 101–2. On the various handlings of the Troilus story see Hyder Rollins, 'The Troilus-Cressida Story from Chaucer to Shakespeare,' *PMLA*, 32 (1917): 383–429, and Piero Boitani, *The European Tragedy of Troilus* (Oxford: Clarendon Press, 1989).

4   Similar oppositions are found in *Love and Riches* (1527) and in *Riches and Youth* (1552).

5   Cornish was not involved in the Running at the Ring on 29 January and on 5 February 1516. Gibson produced these events by himself and was rewarded with the headpiece used by the king in one of the exhibitions; his accounts are PRO, E36/229, fols. 83–90, abstracted in *LP,* II.ii, pp. 1506–7.

6   Gibson's account for the joust is PRO, E36/217, fols. 249–68, abstracted in *LP,* II.ii, pp. 1507–9. Hall, pp. 584–5, says that Henry won this tournament, but his statement that the king bore Sir William Kingston to the ground is not supported by the jousting cheque: BL, Harleian MS. 69, fol. 16v; Anglo, *Tournament Roll*, I: 64.

7   PRO, E36/215, pp. 442, 453, abstracted in *LP,* II.ii, pp. 1471–3. Cornish received £100 for repairs at Greenwich in April, £36 10s. from Gibson for paving urinals there in June, and a reward of £200 on 30 November for an unspecified service. For the play, see next note.

8   Gibson's account for material used in the play and other material left out of the main account for the jousts is PRO, E101/418/7, abstracted in Streitberger, 'Henry VIII's Entertainment for the Queen of Scots, 1516: A New Revels Account and Cornish's Play,' *Medieval and Renaissance Drama in England*, 1 (1984): 30. Subsidiary accounts, such as this one for the play and left over bills for the jousts,

reveals the extent to which the Revels organization had become administratively complicated. So many details were being handled that Gibson could not keep track of them. By 1520, the accounting system evolved to the point at which general summary accounts were made for the year and a number of smaller, subsidiary accounts were made for each entertainment.

9   The details of Gibson's account, PRO, E36/217, fols. 269–78, abstracted in *LP*, II.ii, p. 1509, do not agree with the narrative in Hall, pp. 585–6, in describing the pageant.

10   Anglo, 'Evolution,' pp. 26–7, points out that three different costumes were made for Cornish in this revel.

11   Hall, pp. 591–2, gives the date as June. See Court Calendar for other sources. See also David Starkey, *The Reign of Henry VIII* (London: Collins & Brown, 1985), 81, who regards the dispostion of forces in this joust as clear evidence of the king's preference for his new 'minions': Nicholas Carew, Sir Francis Brian, Henry Norris, Anthony Knyvet, and William Coffin.

12   PRO, E36/216, fol. 11v, abstracted in *LP*, II.ii, p. 1479.

13   *Rutland Papers*, p. 56.

14   Anglo, *Spectacle*, pp. 124–31.

15   PRO, E36/216, fol 18v, abstracted in *LP*, II.ii, p. 1479. Hall, p. 594.

16   Hall, pp. 594–5.

17   PRO, E36/216, fol. 18v, abstracted in *LP*, II.ii, p. 1479.

18   Hall, p. 595, usually spells 'Dauphin' as 'Dolphin.' Francis I's son was an infant at this time.

19   *CSP Venetian*, II, no. 1088; Guistinian, II: 224–5, 228–35; Hall, p. 595.

20   Anglo, *Spectacle*, pp. 131–5.

21   Anglo, *Spectacle*, p. 134. In Chaucer, *The Squire's Tale*, line 207, (*The Complete Poetry and Prose of Geoffrey Chaucer*, ed. John H. Fisher [New York: Holt, Rinehart and Winston, 1977], p. 191) a knight enters the hall at a feast on a horse of brass which is capable of flying around the world. While the king and his court think this horse like Pegasus, it is not associated with Report. The most famous literary treatment of the spread of rumour is in the *Aeneid*, but Vulgar Fame has specifically negative associations in those passages. On the use of Turks in court festivals, see Anglo, *Spectacle*, p. 135n.

22   There may have been a joust or a practice on 3 March 1519 for the king's armourer was paid for supplying equipment: PRO, E36/216, fol. 33, abstracted in *LP*, III.ii, p. 1534.

23   Hall, pp. 597–8. Gibson's account, PRO, SP1/18, fol. 52–7, abstracted in *LP*, III.i, no. 113, records £66 7s. 4d. as the cost of the production. He was paid £60 7s. 3d. by the Chamber in April: PRO, E36/216, fol. 38, abstracted in *LP*, III.ii, p. 1535.

24   Cornish was paid on 1 May 1519 for performing an interlude with the Children of the Chapel before the king on Shrove Monday (7 March): PRO, E36/216, fol. 41, abstracted in *LP*, III.ii, p. 1536. Wallace, *Evolution*, pp. 39, 54, identifies the payment with the comedy of Plautus and wonders whether Cornish produced an authentic Latin play or an adaptation, as he had done with Chaucer's *Troilus* in 1516. Anglo, 'Evolution,' p. 30n, is sceptical, noting that Hall is not an infallible source of information on entertainments and Cornish's interlude may have been played in addition to the comedy of Plautus.

25   Gibson's account, PRO, E36/217, fols. 100–8, 123–9, abstracted in *LP*, II.ii, pp. 1550–1, was paid by the Chamber in December: PRO, E36/216, fol. 65v, abstracted in *LP*, III.ii, p. 1538. Hall, p. 599. David Starkey, *The Reign of Henry VIII* (London: Collins & Brown, 1985), 81, sees in the distribution of personnel in this mask, with the king's 'minions' who had been expelled from court in 1519 taking the roles of 'youth,' and the king's middle-aged Gentlemen who had replaced them – Wingfield, Weston, Jerningham, and Kingston – taking the parts of 'age,' a clear foreshadowing of future factional division in the Privy Chamber between a ministerial party and its court opponents.

26   See the discussion in Wallace, *Evolution*, p. 55.

27   Gibson's account is PRO, E36/217, fols. 108–11, 129–32, abstracted in *LP*, III.ii, p. 1551.

28   The summary account for the revels projects from 31 December 1519 through 19 February 1520 does not survive. The particular accounts for the revels are PRO, E36/217, fols. 111–14 (31 December 'meskeller' at Greenwich), fols. 114–15 (5 January 'meskellyng' at York Place), fols. 115–16 (6 January disguising and pageant), fols. 116–18 (8 January 'meskeller'), abstracted in *LP*, III.ii, p. 1552.

29   The particular accounts for the February revels are PRO, E36/217, fols. 119–21 (1 February disguise and 'tryke wagon'), and fol. 121 (19 February joust), abstracted in *LP*, III.ii, pp. 1552–53.

30   Hall, p. 608; Joycelyne G. Russell, *The Field of Cloth of Gold* (New York: Barnes & Noble, 1969), 94–6. The furnishing of the jousts and the temporary palace were committed to Gibson: PRO, SP1/19, fols. 237–8, abstracted in *LP*, III.i, no. 704.

31   Sir Edward Guildford's account is PRO, E36/9, fols. 1–18. On the tournament see Anglo, *Spectacle*, pp. 152–4; and Joycelyne G. Russell, *The Field of Cloth of Gold* (New York: Barnes & Noble, 1969), 105–41.

32   Gibson's account is PRO, E36/217, fols. 293–302, abstracted in *LP*, III.ii, p. 1553.

33   Hall, pp. 616–17; Anglo, *Spectacle*, pp. 153–6. The jousts cost at least £3007 16s. 1d., as the Chamber payments show: PRO, E36/216, fols. 81–100, abstracted in *LP*, III.ii, pp. 1540–2 (payments from April to August). See also Alan Young, *English Tournament Imprese* (New York: AMS Press, 1988).

34   *Rutland Papers,* pp. 28–49; Joycelyne G. Russell, *The Field of Cloth of Gold* (New York: Barnes & Noble, 1969), 32–46.

35   Hall, pp. 605–6; the building is also described in *Chronicle of Calais,* pp. 79–85; see Anglo, *Spectacle,* pp. 139–44, on the French and English encampments.

36   *Chronicle of Calais,* p. 83. Over £6000 was spent on this building alone. The commissioners were so frustrated by the difficulty of obtaining material and by problems with workmen and artisans that they petitioned Wolsey to threaten them with imprisonment.

37   Joycelyne G. Russell, *The Field of Cloth of Gold* (New York: Barnes & Noble, 1969), 33–4; Anglo, *Spectacle,* p. 143.

38   In his account for the 10 November 1527 revels, PRO, SP1/45, fol. 34v, Gibson mentions that he had 'translated' one of the garments used at Ardres. The original plan for the revels in June 1520 specified fifty noblemen and women in five companies: PRO, SP1/19, pp. 237–8, abstracted in *LP,* III.i, no. 704, pp. 239–40.

39   On the masses and formal banquets, see Joycelyne G. Russell, *The Field of Cloth of Gold* (New York: Barnes & Noble, 1969), 153–66, 172–7. A great silver organ with gold ornaments was used in the king's chapel: *CSP Venetian,* III, no. 83; John Stevens, *Music & Poetry in the Early Tudor Court* (London: Methuen, 1961), 241. The memorandum relating to devising pageants and mummeries states that 'devisyng of the pageants at the bankett is commytted to Cornyshe' but the device of the mummeries was to be left to the king: *Rutland Papers,* p. 56. In another document, PRO, SP1/19, pp. 237–8, abstracted in *LP,* III.i, no. 704, pp. 239–40, the apparel for the mummeries was to be left to the king's pleasure. Wallace, *Evolution,* p. 56, quoting PRO, SP1/20, pp. 38–41, abstracted in *LP,* III.i, no. 804, confuses the masks held at the banquets at the Field of Cloth of Gold in June with the banquets, pageants, and entertainments for Charles V at Calais in July. On the facilities, ceremonies, and entertainments see *CSP Venetian,* III, nos. 60–95.

40   Gibson's accounts for these revels and those held on the 24th are PRO, E36/229, fols. 48–65, abstracted in *LP,* III.ii, p. 1554. Hall. p. 615. See also Joycelyne G. Russell, *The Field of Cloth of Gold* (New York: Barnes & Noble, 1969), 167–8.

41   See previous note for Gibson's account. Hall, pp. 618–19. Joycelyne G. Russell, *The Field of Cloth of Gold* (New York: Barnes & Noble, 1969), 78–81.

42   The characters here, of course, are the Nine Worthies *(les neuf preux),* formulated in the early fourteenth century in Jacques de Longuyon's *Les Voeux du paon.* There were also nine female worthies. See *The Arthurian Encyclopedia,* ed. Norris J. Lang (New York: Garland Publishing, 1986), 407–8. The tradition of the Worthies was so diffused that it is difficult to point to a source, but Caxton mentions them in his preface to *Mort d'Arthur,* lines 9–24: *Caxton's Malory,* ed. J.W. Spisak (Berkeley: University of California Press, 1983), I.

43 Hall, p. 621. Gibson was appointed to provide the pavilion for the meeting between the king and emperor: PRO, SP1/20, p. 38, abstracted in *LP,* III.i, no. 804, p. 280. PRO, E36/229, fol. 101, lists 'Mr. norres, Mr. nycollas carrew, Mr. thomas chayney, Mr. artur polle, lord ferres, Mr. bryan, Mr. carre, lord lenard, Mr. frances poynes' among those attending. College of Arms, MS. M 6*bis,* fols. 73v–4v, includes part of a dialogue in French and Latin between a king speaking as King Arthur and his servants at the doors of his pavilion which possibly formed part of the entertainments for the emperor.

44 Hall, p. 621. Bodleian Library, Ashmole MS. 1116, fols. 103v–5 ('The poesies and writings that were in the Rowndhowse made at Calais for the feasting and banqueting of the Emperor Charles the vth'). For a more detailed description of the theatre see Anglo, *Spectacle,* pp. 159–63; Richard Hosley, 'The Theatre and the Tradition of Playhouse Design,' in *The First Public Playhouse, The Theatre in Shoreditch, 1576–1598,* ed. Herbert Berry (Montreal: McGill-Queen's University Press, 1979), 60–79.

45 *Chronicle of Calais,* pp. 29–30. All of the work was under the supervision of Belknap: PRO, SP1/20, p. 39, abstracted in *LP,* III.i, no. 804, p. 281.

46 Reed, *Early Tudor Drama,* p. 9; Anglo, *Spectacle,* pp. 165–8.

47 Wallace, *Evolution,* p. 56.

48 Hall, p. 622.

49 PRO, E36/217, fols. 314–19, SP1/29, fols. 212v–19v, abstracted in *LP,* III.ii, pp. 1556–7, is Gibson's summary account of the seven revels projects from 3 November 1520 to 12 February 1521.

50 Revels accounts and narratives survive for the entertainments at Ardres, not at Guisnes. Gibson is loosely using the place name.

51 PRO, E36/217, fol. 319, abstracted in *LP,* III.ii, p. 1557.

52 Streitberger, *RORD* (1984): 22–30.

53 See, for example, PRO, SP1/37, abstracted in *LP,* IV.i, no. 1888.

54 Hall, p. 628.

55 PRO, SP1/29, fols. 220–3, abstracted in *LP,* III.ii, p. 1557.

56 PRO, SP1/29, fols. 223–8, abstracted in *LP,* III.ii, pp. 1557–8. Hall, pp. 630–1.

57 PRO, SP1/29, fol. 237, abstracted in *LP,* III.ii, p. 1559.

58 PRO, SP1/29, fol. 228v.

59 Hall, pp. 631–2. Gibson's account is PRO, SP1/29, fol. 228v–37, abstracted in *LP,* III.ii, pp. 1558–9.

60 John Stevens, *Music & Poetry in the Early Tudor Court* (London: Methuen, 1961), 402–3. Anglo, 'Evolution,' p. 34.

61 Charles Dahlberg, trans., *Roman de la Rose* (Princeton: Princeton University Press, 1971), line 3267. Dorothy Owen, *Piers Plowman: A Comparison with some Earlier and Contemporary French Allegories* (London: Hodder & Stoughton, 1912), 82–5.

62 Marie Axton, 'The Tudor Mask and Elizabethan Court Drama,' in M. Axton and R. Williams, eds., *English Drama: Form and Development* (Cambridge: Cambridge University Press, 1988), 29–30.

63 For a discussion of the reception, see Sydney Anglo, 'The Imperial Alliance and the Entry of the Emperor Charles V into London: June 1522,' *The Guildhall Miscellany*, 2, no. 4 (October 1962): 131–55, and Gordon Kipling, '"A Horse Designed by Committee": The Bureaucratics of the London Civic Triumph in the 1520s,' *RORD*, 31 (1992): 79–89.

64 Gibson's account is PRO, SP1/24, fol. 226–30, 236v–7, abstracted in *LP*, III.ii, no. 2305: the tents were pitched on the 5th and taken down on the 8th. Gibson probably also set up the tent of cloth of gold for the two sovereigns before the royal entry on the 6th. Hall, pp. 634–7, describes the reception, spectacles, and entertainments.

65 Gibson's account is PRO, SP1/24, fols. 230v–5, abstracted in *LP*, III.ii, no. 2305. Hall, pp. 635, 637.

66 Hall, pp. 637–40.

67 PRO, SP1/24, fols. 231v. Gibson's account is mixed with the 'meskelers': PRO, SP1/24, fols. 230v–3v, abstracted in *LP*, III.ii, no. 2305.

68 A version of this allegory which probably derives ultimately from Plato's *Phaedrus* occurs in Piers Plowman: *The Vision of William Concerning Piers the Plowman*, ed. W.W. Skeat (Oxford: Clarendon Press, 1886), 102–3; A Text: IV, lines 18–21 (includes the use of the bridle to keep the horse's head low); C Text: IV, lines 20–3 (mentions the unruly behaviour of the horse). The allegory also may be derived from the emblem tradition.

69 *CSP Spanish*, II, no. 437; 'William Cornish in a Play, Pageants, Prison, and Politics,' *Review of English Studies*, n.s. 10 (1959), 357–60.

70 Hall, p. 641.

71 Hall, p. 690.

72 Gibson's account is PRO, SP1/32, fol. 256–60v, abstracted in *LP*, IV.i, no. 965.

73 Hall, pp. 688–9. Lord Leonard Grey (executed 28 July 1541) is never styled Master of the Revels in the documents. It is clear that his supervision was limited to the martial exhibitions. Included in the fifteen challengers were the poet Thomas Wyatt, Francis Poins, Lord John Grey, Sir George Cobham, William Carey, Sir John Dudley, Francis Sidney, Sir Anthony Browne, Sir Edward Seymour, Oliver Manners, Percival Harte, Sebastian Newdigate, and Thomas Carlen.

74 Hall, p. 689.

75 According to Hall, p. 689, the king's party included the Earl of Devonshire, Lord Montacute, Lord Roos, Sir Nicholas Carew, Sir Francis Brian, Henry Norris, Anthony Knyvet, and five other unnamed individuals who ran eight courses. Gibson's account, PRO, SP1/32, fols. 258–9v, shows that he prepared apparel for

only eight answerers including the king, along with the costumes for the ladies who led the 'ancient' knights. The jousting cheque names only eight answerers and indicates that six courses were run; see Anglo, *Tournament Roll*, I: 71–2.

76 Hall, p. 689.

77 PRO, SP1/32, fols. 260r–v.

78 Hall, p. 690.

79 Hall, p. 691.

80 Anglo, *Tournament Roll*, I: 69n.

81 Hall, p. 674.

82 Hall, pp. 707–8. Henri II of France lost an eye in a similar accident on 20 July 1559, and died as a result of this and other injuries shortly after: Machyn, *Diary*, pp. 204, 375.

83 Anglo, *Tournament Roll*, I: 73.

84 Hall, p. 703, does not describe these disguisings, and neither do any other of the documents associated with the formal creation and ceremonies: PRO, C66/646, memb. 42; SP1/35, pp. 23–30; BL, Additional MS. 6113, fols. 62r–v; all calendared in *LP*, IV.i, no. 1431; College of Arms, MS. M 16*bis*, fols. 68v–9.

85 Hall, p. 707.

86 PRO, SP1/37, fols. 7–15, abstracted in *LP*, IV.i, no. 1888.

87 Although Anglo, 'Evolution,' p. 35, and McGee and Meagher, 'Checklist,' p. 83, list it as such, it is not certain that 14 January is the actual date of an entertainment.

88 Hall, p. 719; Sanuto, *Diarii*, XLIII: 703–4, calendared in *CSP Venetian*, IV, no. 4; *STC* C1618: William Cavendish, *The Life and Death of Thomas Wolsey, Cardinal* (London, 1667), 25–30.

89 Wallace, *Evolution*, p. 64.

CHAPTER 5

1 Compare the lists of attendants in *Rutland Papers*, pp. 28–38, and *Chronicle of Calais*, pp. 19–27.

2 Anglo, *Spectacle*, p. 144. Wolsey was privy to the design of the palace: PRO, SP1/20, fol. 77. *La description et ordre du camp festins et ioustes* [Paris, 1520], describes the pomp and ceremonies.

3 Hall, p. 707.

4 *King's Works*, IV.ii: 126–32, 300–7.

5 PRO, SP1/16, fols. 173, 205v, abstracted respectively in *LP*, II.ii, no. 4024, 4055. Hillebrand, *The Child Actors*, p. 50.

6 Chambers, *MS*, II: 215.

7 Sanuto, *Diarii*, XLIII: 703–4, calendared in *CSP Venetian*, IV, no. 4. *STC* C1618:

Cavendish, *The Life and Death of Thomas Wolsey, Cardinal* (London, 1667), 25–30.

8   Hall, p. 719.

9   Anglo, 'Evolution,' p. 36. These neoclassical revivals occur in England only about forty years after the first such experiments in Italy where they were being staged using scenery constructed in perspective. Chambers, *ES*, III: 1–21; IV: 353–65. One might expect Spinelli to note significant differences if he found them.

10   Anglo, 'Evolution,' pp. 35–7.

11   Hall, p. 722.

12   Gibson's daybook, PRO, SP1/41, fol. 165–8, abstracted in *LP,* IV.ii, no. 3064, runs from 19 February to 25 April. He purchased seventeen yards of purple velvet from William Botre (Bottry, Butry), a mercer who had supplied material to the Wardrobe and for the revels for a number of years; from Mistress Elizabeth Philip, a silk woman with whom Gibson did business on many occasions, he purchased six ounces of silk and fifty-two ounces of yellow and white silk for points for the challengers' bards; he also purchased 23 1/2 ounces of gold for the joust.

13   *CSP Milan,* no. 804.

14   See Appendix 1: Principal Sources, below, for Gibson's daybooks, and drafts for accounts as well as Guildford's and Wyatt's account for work on the banqueting house. While some of the accounts contribute important details, none of them provides a coherent overview of the entertainments.

15   PRO, SP2/Fol. C, fol. 106, which account, fols. 106–38v, abstracted in *LP,* IV.ii, no. 3097, continues to 7 May.

16   Guildford's and Wyatt's account is PRO, E36/227, fols. 1–36v, abstracted in *LP,* IV.ii, no. 3104.

17   Hall, p. 722.

18   PRO, E36/227, fol. 27v. On Urmeston's work at Greenwich and at Calais, see Anglo, *Spectacle,* pp. 166–7, 213, 231.

19   Payments to wire drawers occur in the Revels accounts throughout the reigns of Elizabeth I, James I, and Charles I: *MSC,* XIII.

20   On John Demynas (Giovanni da Maiano) see Auerbach, *Tudor Artists,* p. 176. In PRO, E36/227, fol. 25v, he lists charges totalling £59 5s. 1d. for six antique heads, gilt, silvered, and painted.

21   PRO, E36/227, fols. 17v–24: Lovekyn's account for the arches and other work on the banqueting house from 6 February to 7 May, abstracted in *LP,* IV.ii, no. 3104, p. 1396. George Lovekyn was son of a former Sergeant Tailor in the Wardrobe (patent of 28 July 1486, PRO, C82/12, no. 1026, abstracted in Campbell, I: 526) and nephew to William Pawne, Master of the Works, who was appointed to help Jaques Haulte produce the 1501 and 1502 entertainments for the marriages of the Prince and Princess (see Chapter 1, note 69). George probably owed his posi-

tion in the household and his advancement to his father's and his uncle's influence. By 1509 George was Clerk of the Stable and was later appointed to bring a gift of certain hobbies to the emperor in 1516. He appears to have had a minor role in the revels of February 1520. He was at the Field of Cloth of Gold in that year as Clerk of the Stable, and he was Clerk in charge of building and then renovating parts of the banqueting house at Greenwich for the May and November 1527 revels. By March 1529 he was Comptroller of the Works. He died before 2 July 1535. There were complaints by his successors: 'the Offyce hathe byn heretofore abusyd by the neclygens of suche as have byn comptrollers as ffor wante of knowledge and skyll in there Offyce': PRO, SP1/162, pp. 113–14; *King's Works*, III.i: 9.

22   PRO, E36/227, fol. 11; Hall, p. 722.
23   Hall, p. 723; Sanuto, *Diarii*, XLV: 265–70; *CSP Venetian*, IV, no. 105.
24   PRO, SP1/41, fol. 212, abstracted in *LP*, IV.ii, no. 3098 (4).
25   Hall, p. 723.
26   PRO, SP2/Fol. C, fol. 112, abstracted in *LP*, IV.ii, no. 3097, p. 1390.
27   On the attribution of the ceiling to Nicholas Kratzner (d. ca. 1550), see Reed, *Early Tudor Drama*, p. 18; Anglo, *Spectacle*, pp. 218–19; and Paul Reyher, *Les Masques Anglais* (Paris: Hachette, 1909), 337.
28   PRO, SP2/Fol. C, fol. 138v, abstracted in *LP*, IV.ii, no. 3097 (ii), p. 1392. Anglo, *Spectacle*, pp. 217–19.
29   Sanuto, *Diarii*, XLV: 265–70; *CSP Venetian*, IV, no. 105.
30   Hall, p. 723.
31   Sanuto, *Diarii*, XLV: 265–70; *CSP Venetian*, IV, no. 105.
32   Hall, p. 723.
33   Wallace, *Evolution*, p. 67.
34   Hillebrand, *The Child Actors*, p. 63.
35   Reed, *Early Tudor Drama*, pp. 19–20. The bill is PRO, E36/227, fols. 31v–5v, inadequately abstracted in *LP*, IV.ii, no. 3104, pp. 1396–7.
36   Anglo, *Spectacle*, pp. 221–2.
37   PRO, E36/227, fol. 35. On Rastell's 1522 pageant see Hall, p. 639; Robert Withington, *English Civic Pageantry* (Cambridge, Mass.: Harvard University Press, 1918), I: 177; and Anglo, *Spectacle*, p. 197.
38   Hall, p. 723; Sanuto, *Diarii*, XLV: 265–70; *CSP Venetian*, IV, no. 105.
39   PRO, SP1/41, fol. 195, 213v, abstracted in *LP*, IV.ii, no. 3098 (ii. 4).
40   Hall, p. 723.
41   Anglo, *Spectacle*, pp. 223–4.
42   For a description of these revels and entries see Anglo, *Spectacle*, pp. 225–31.
43   PRO, E36/227, fols. 48v–61, abstracted in *LP*, IV.ii, no. 3563.
44   Hall, p. 734.

45   Hall, p. 735. Gibson's account is PRO, SP1/45, fols. 20–33, abstracted in *LP,*
      IV.ii, no. 3564, pp. 1604–5.
46   *CSP Spanish,* III.ii, no. 240.
47   Gibson's account for the masks is PRO, SP1/45, fols. 33v–6, abstracted in *LP,*
      IV.ii, no. 3564, p. 1605.
48   *STC* C1618: Cavendish, *The Life and Death of Thomas Wolsey, Cardinal* (London,
      1667), 76–7. His narrative agrees with Gibson's account and with Hall. Wallace,
      Evolution, p. 68, says that Cavendish reports that it was in French and Latin,
      which confusion is perhaps traceable to Cavendish's discussion of the mummery
      held in January 1527 in which French was spoken.
49   Hall, p. 735. In a letter of 15 November 1527 (*CSP Spanish,* III.ii, no. 240), Don
      Inigo de Mendoca, imperial ambassador in England, describes the play as a 'farsa.'
      He is probably using the term in its original sense of an entertainment 'inserted'
      into a larger group of entertainments.
50   Gibson's account is BL, Egerton MS. 2605, fols. 37v–42; PRO, SP1/45, fols.
      36v–40, abstracted in *LP,* IV.ii, no. 3564, pp. 1605–6.
51   PRO, SP1/45, fol. 39.
52   Corporation of London Record Office, Repertories VII, fol. 224v. This '*proposi-
      cion*' was probably made in connection with Wolsey's reception of the French
      ambassadors. Other business related to this is recorded on fol. 225.
53   Chambers, *ES,* II: 11–12. The *Dictionary of National Biography* confuses this per-
      formance of *Dido* with the play of 10 November 1527.
54   PRO, SP1/236, fol. 380, abstracted in *LP, Addenda,* I.i, no. 717. *Letters and
      Papers* dates the document ca. 1530, and Anglo, *Spectacle,* p. 237, dates it before
      24 October 1530. The petition which survives as a fragment is undated, but it is
      more likely to have been written near or after Rightwise's dismissal from St Paul's
      in 1531. In the petition he reminds the king of his years of service at St Paul's, of
      his entertainments for the French ambassadors, and of his illness.
55   Alfred Harbage, *Annals of English Drama, 975–1700,* rev. ed., S. Schoenbaum
      (Philadelphia: University of Pennsylvania Press, 1964), 22; Chambers, *MS,* II: 219.
56   Anglo, *Spectacle,* pp. 224–5.
57   Anglo, *Spectacle,* pp. 225–31. On the cardinal's trip to France see Cavendish, *The
      Life and Death of Thomas Wolsey, Cardinal* (London, 1667), 54–66. Wolsey was
      given the informal title, *Cardinalis Pacificus,* at the Boulogne reception in June
      1527, and the style was repeated by observers and chroniclers; see for example,
      Hall, p. 730, and Sanuto, *Diarii,* XLVI: 595–7, calendared in *CSP Venetian,* IV,
      no. 225.
58   For a discussion of Humanist writings on the subject see Robert P. Adams, *The
      Better Part of Valor: More, Erasmus, Colet, and Vives, on Humanism, War, and
      Peace, 1496–1535* (Seattle: University of Washington Press, 1962).

59   See Barry B. Adams, *John Bale's King Johan* (San Marino, Ca.: Huntington Library, 1969), 56–65, for a brief discussion of Bale's play in relation to Protestant historiography.

60   Campeggius was in England to investigate the validity of Henry's marriage to Katherine. He was 'sore vexed with the goute,' and Gibson was ordered to make a chair of estate to carry him: Hall, p. 753; John Stow, *Annals* (London, 1615), 909; PRO, E101/420/11, fol. 3, abstracted in *LP,* V, p. 303.

61   Sanuto, *Diarii,* XLV: 595–7, calendared in *CSP Venetian,* IV, no. 225. In a letter of 9 January 1528, du Bellay wrote to Francis I, 'une procession et honneste service, au partir duquel nos feit le festin beau et triomphant, et aprés feit jouer farces en latin': *Ambassades en Angleterre de Jean du Bellay. La première ambassade,* ed. V.L. Bourrilly and P. de Vassière (Paris: A. Picard, 1905), 89. He is probably using 'farces' in the same sense that de Mendoca was in 1527 (see note 49 above) and is referring to the play and the dialogue.

62   Anglo, *Spectacle,* pp. 235–6.

63   Anglo, *Spectacle,* pp. 207–8, 238–9.

64   A.F. Pollard, *Wolsey* (London: Longman, 1929), 220; Anglo, *Spectacle,* p. 238.

65   Hall, p. 719. On Roo, see J.C. Boswell, 'Seven Actors in Search of a Biographer,' *Medieval and Renaissance Drama in English,* 2 (1985): 51–6.

66   Anglo, *Spectacle,* pp. 240–3.

67   BL, Egerton MS. 2605, fol. 15, is headed 'Revelles at Richmond and Grenewiche in the tyme of Christmas' [1527–8].

68   Hall, p. 756.

69   Wallace, *Evolution,* p. 70, and Hillebrand, *The Child Actors,* p. 61, both thought that if more financial records had survived we would find evidence of performances of plays by the Chapel in every year. We would no doubt also find evidence of other dramatic performances and entertainments.

70   PRO, E101/420/11, fols. 13v, 16, abstracted in *LP,* V, pp. 307–8.

71   Hall, p. 768.

72   PRO, E101/420/11, fols. 72, 74, 76, abstracted in *LP,* V, p. 317. The payment to the Master of the Bears was made from the king's Privy Purse: BL, Additional MS. 20030, fol. 8, abstracted in *LP,* V, p. 748.

73   Hall, p. 774.

74   BL, Additional MS. 20030, fol. 54, abstracted in *LP,* V, p. 753.

75   PRO, E101/420/11, fols. 146v, 149, abstracted in *LP,* V, pp. 307, 317, 323.

76   Wallace, *Evolution,* pp. 28, 38, 65n, assumed that all such payments were for dramatic performances. Chambers, *ES,* II: 24n, 28n, insisted that they were for musical performances. As is clear from BL, Harleian MS. 642, fols. 69v–73, printed in *A Collection of Ordinances and Regulations for the Government of the Royal Household* (London: Society of Antiquaries, 1790), 49–51, their duties

were so varied and flexible that there is no way to determine the full extent of their service at Christmas without further evidence.

77   Wallace, *Evolution*, p. 61. Hillebrand, *The Child Actors*, p. 59.

78   Crane functioned as Master from the time of Cornish's retirement in 1523 but his patent was not granted until 12 May 1526: PRO, C82/574, no. 28, calendared in *LP,* IV.i, no. 2218 (12).

79   Crane's will of 6 July 1545 was proved on 7 April 1546: PRO, PROB 11/31, fol. 49. He was buried in the parish church of St. Elias in Greenwich. Hillebrand, *The Child Actors*, p. 60n.

80   On Crane's business interests see Wallace, *Evolution*, pp. 61–4.

81   Hall, p. 784. The king's Privy Purse account for the following year is filled with payments for Anne Boleyn and for members of her family: BL, Additional MS. 20030, fols. 96–143, abstracted in *LP,* V, pp. 757–61.

82   Hall, p. 793. College of Arms, MS. M 6*bis,* fols. 1–13, 148–9v, printed as *STC* 4350: *The maner of the trymphe at Caleys and Bulleyn* (1532).

83   Hall, pp. 793–4. *Chronicle of Calais,* pp. 44, 116–23.

84   BL, Additional MS. 20030, fol. 139, abstracted in *LP,* V, p. 761.

85   Hall, pp. 795, 808.

86   See the description in Anglo, *Spectacle,* pp. 246–61.

87   Hall, p. 805.

88   Auerbach, *Tudor Artists,* p. 145.

89   PRO, SP1/236, fol. 380, abstracted in *LP, Addenda,* I.i, no. 717.

90   Reed, *Early Tudor Drama,* pp. 22–8.

91   Anglo, *Spectacle,* pp. 264–5.

92   PRO, PROB 11/25, fols. 153–4, made 4 October and probated 19 December 1534. Thomas Buckworth was appointed to be Sergeant of Arms in the place of Richard Gibson, deceased, on 28 October 1534: PRO, C66/664, memb. 1, calendared in *LP,* VII, no. 1352 (23), p. 514.

93   Probably the priest whom Machyn, *Diary,* p. 157, mentions as having been burned at Smithfield on 13 November 1557.

94   PRO, C82/683, no. 1, abstracted in *LP,* VII, no. 589 (2).

CHAPTER 6

1   Machyn, *Diary,* pp. 157–8, which evidence was used by Collier, *HEDP* (1879), I: 63, to suggest that Gibson held patents to both offices as Sergeant. Chambers, *Tudor Revels,* p. 6, *ES,* I: 72, observes that no such patents have been discovered. I have not been able to find them at the PRO.

2   Buckworth's patent as Sergeant of Arms was granted on 28 October 1534: PRO, C66/664, memb. 1, calendared in *LP,* VII, no. 1352 (23). Malte's patent as Yeoman

of the Great Wardrobe was also granted on 28 October 1534: PRO, C66/664, memb. 20, calendared in *LP,* VII, no. 1498 (18). Parker's patent as Sergeant of the Tents was granted on 8 December 1534: PRO, C66/664, memb. 3, calendared in *LP,* VII, no. 1601 (19). In 1516 Parker is styled Yeoman of the Robes (BL, Royal MS. 7. F. XIV, fol. 100, calendared in *LP,* II.i, no. 2735, p. 873) and still held that position in 1534 (PRO, E101/421/13, calendared in *LP,* VII, no. 9 [ii]). Ralph Worseley succeeded Gibson as Porter of the Great Wardrobe on 12 November 1534: PRO, C66/664, memb. 20, calendared in *LP,* VII, no. 1498 [14].

3   Farlyon's patent as Yeoman of the Revels was granted on 20 November 1534: PRO, C66/664, memb. 25, calendared in *LP,* VII, no. 1498 (41). He received the first payment under his patent in Easter term 1534: PRO, E36/128, p. 347. Collier, *HEDP* (1879), I: 79, mistakes 6 for 26 Henry VIII in citing a payment to Farlyon: A. Feuillerat, *Le Bureau des Menus-Plaisirs* (Louvain: A. Uystpryust, 1910), 22; Chambers, *Tudor Revels,* p. 7, *ES,* I: 72. Custody of the properties mentioned in Farlyon's patent had been the responsibility of Gibson from the time he was given the keys to the storehouse in 1510.

4   PRO, C66/680, memb. 9, calendared in *LP,* XIII.ii, no. 249 (15).

5   PRO, C66/683, memb. 16, calendared in *LP,* XIII.ii, no. 249 (12).

6   PRO, E36/256, fols. 85, 152, 154, 158, abstracted in *LP,* XIV.ii, pp. 329, 340; these payments were made on 18 February 1537; 14 January, 9 February, 20 March 1539; other payments were made on 27 March and 3 July 1539. The king's commandments communicated to Bridges are recorded in Folger Library, MS. Lb 2, fol. 1.

7   Bodleian Library, Rawlinson MS. D. 777, fol. 182v; *King's Works,* IV.ii: 102.

8   Hall, p. 819.

9   The source, Jean Tixier, Seigneur de Ravisi (ca. 1480–1524), *Dialogi Aliquot Festiuissimi,* is printed by Marie Axton, *Three Tudor Classical Interludes* (Cambridge: D.S. Brewer, 1982), who also provides a discussion of the play, pp. 5–15. A.W. Pollard, *English Miracle Plays, Moralities, and Interludes,* 8th ed. (Oxford: Clarendon Press, 1927), 213–14, attributed it to Udall; F.S. Boas, *University Drama in the Tudor Age* (Oxford: Clarendon Press, 1914), 20–1, suggested that it was written for a performance at Magdalen College, Oxford; William L. Edgerton, *Nicholas Udall* (New York: Twayne Publishers, 1965), 24–5, 34, also thought it was written at Oxford and later produced at court.

10   Hall, p. 825.

11   *CSP Spanish,* V.ii, no. 220.

12   Wriothesley, *Chronicle,* I: 99–100. M. Kaulek, *Correspondance Politique de MM. de Chastillon et de Marillac* (Paris: F. Alcan, 1885), 105, calendared in *LP,* XIV.i, no. 1137.

13   M. Kaulek, *Correspondance Politique de MM. de Castillon et de Marillac* (Paris: F.

Alcan, 1885), 114–16, calendared in *LP,* XIV.i, no. 1261. In another letter to Montmorency, Marillac mentions that he had heard that the sports and follies on land were similar to the ones on the river: Kaulek, p. 111, calendared in *LP,* XIV.i, no. 1230. See also note 12, above.

14   PRO, E36/256, fols. 85, 152, 154, 158, abstracted in *LP,* XIV.ii, pp. 329, 340.

15   The department had been headed by Robert Amadas until his death in 1533. The commission appointed to review his accounts shows that Guildford and Gibson both were charged with several hundred pounds of losses in gold: PRO, SP1/78, fols. 64–5, abstracted in *LP,* VI, no. 924. The various payments to Amadas for gold used in the revels is found in the Chamber accounts: PRO, E36/215 and E26/216, some of them abstracted, *inter alia,* in *LP,* II.ii, pp. 1441–80; III.ii, pp. 1533–45.

16   G.R. Elton, *The Tudor Revolution in Government* (Cambridge: Cambridge University Press, 1953), 111.

17   Elton, *Tudor Revolution,* pp. 192–203.

18   PRO, E36/256, abstracted in *LP,* XIV.ii, no. 782.

19   See for example, W. Gordon Zeeveld, *Foundations of Tudor Policy* (Cambridge, Mass.: Harvard University Press, 1948), 170–84.

20   *Acts and Monuments,* V: 403.

21   *A perswasion to the Kyng that the laws of the realme shulde be in Latin:* BL, Royal MS. 18. A. L., fols 1–25; BL, Cotton MS. Faustina C. II, fols. 5–22 (draft), extracted in Anglo, *Spectacle,* pp. 266–7.

22   Letter of Thomas Wylley, February 1537: PRO, SP1/116, fols. 157–8, abstracted in *LP,* XII.i, no. 529. The court was also concerned to control public plays. Suffolk wrote to Cromwell on 16 May 1537 about a play performed on May Day last concerning 'a kinge how he shuld Rule his Realm.' The actor who 'playd hussbandry' said 'many things Agaynst gentillmen,' more than was in the book of the play, and Suffolk was actively looking for him: PRO, SP1/120, fols. 100–1, abstracted in *LP,* XII.i, no. 1212.

23   BL, Harleian MS. 3838, fols. 111v–12v; facsimile by Jesse W. Harris, *John Bale,* Illinois Studies in Language and Literature, vol. 25 (Urbana, Ill., 1940), 132–4, who also argues, pp. 68–71, that Bale's *De Triplice Dei Legibus* may have been written as early as 1531.

24   *The Complete Plays of John Bale,* ed. Peter Happé (Cambridge: D.S. Brewer, 1985), I: 8–9, prints a summary of the four lists Bale made of his plays: (Bodleian Library, Selden MS. Supra 4, fol. 195; Anglorum Heliades, fols. 112r–v; *Summarium,* fols. 243v–4; *Catalogus,* p. 704). Only five of Bale's plays survive. On Bale's use of the term 'compiled' to describe his writing, see John N. King, *English Reformation Literature* (Princeton: Princeton University Press, 1982), 69, and pp. 56–75 on Bale's place in the development of a Protestant literary tradition.

25   Bale's autobiography from the *Catalogus* (1557), I: 702–4, in which this state-
      ment appears, is translated in *The Complete Plays of John Bale*, ed. Peter Happé
      (Cambridge: D.S. Brewer, 1985), I: 147–8.

26   *The Complete Plays of John Bale*, ed. Peter Happé (Cambridge: D.S. Brewer,
      1985), I: 4n, in which it is stated that the Lord Privy Seal's or Cromwell's Men
      'could possibly be a troupe led by Bale,' but there is no evidence for a conclusive
      identification. See also *Dramatic Records*, p. 380. The troupe appeared in Norfolk
      in 1538: Richard Beadle, 'Plays and Playing at Thetford and Nearby,' *Theatre
      Notebook*, 32 (1978): 7.

27   John Bale, *Kynge Johan*, ed. J.H.P. Pafford and W.W. Greg (Oxford: Malone Soci-
      ety, 1931), p. xvii.

28   From an enclosure in Cranmer's letter to Cromwell of 11 January 1539, printed
      in J.E. Cox, ed., *Miscellaneous Writings and Letters of Thomas Cranmer*, Parker
      Society, [vol. 19] (Cambridge: Cambridge University Press, 1846), 388. Relevant
      passages are transcribed in *The Complete Plays of John Bale*, ed. Peter Happé
      (Cambridge: D.S. Brewer, 1985), I: 5. See also Greg Walker's discussion of the
      political context of *King Johan* in *Plays of Persuasion, Drama and Politics at the
      Court of Henry VIII* (Cambridge: Cambridge University Press, 1991), 178–221.

29   Leslie P. Fairfield, *John Bale: Mythmaker for the English Reformation* (W. Lafayette,
      Ind.: Purdue University Press, 1976), 146–9, documents Bale's dramatic activity
      up to the early 1560s. Bale became rector of Bishopstoke, Hampshire, in 1547, of
      Swaffham, Norfolk, in 1551, and Bishop of Ossory in Ireland in 1553. At Mary's
      accession he fled to Basle, but he returned after Elizabeth's coronation and pro-
      duced plays in the provinces until his death at Canterbury in 1563.

30   In 1527–8 Udall was described by Anthony Dalaber, a principal in the case, as
      one of his 'faithful brethren and fellows in the Lord,' but Udall appears to have
      been among the 'young and penitent' who were marched past a bonfire into
      which they were required to throw their heretical books: William L. Edgerton,
      Nicholas Udall (New York: Twayne Publishers, 1965) 23–4.

31   On Catherine Parr's patronage see James K. McConica, *English Humanists and
      Reformation Politics under Henry VIII and Edward VI* (Oxford: Clarendon Press
      1965), Chapter 7. John N. King, 'Patronage and Piety: The Influence of Cather-
      ine Parr,' in Margaret P. Hannay, ed., *Silent but for the Word, Tudor Women as
      Patrons, Translators, and Writers of Religious Works* (Kent, Ohio: Kent State Uni-
      versity Press, 1985), 48–9, and his more general discussion of Protestant patron-
      age in *English Reformation Literature* (Princeton: Princeton University Press,
      1982), 103–21. Under the queen's patronage Udall was appointed to the team of
      scholars who translated Erasmus's paraphrases of the New Testament: *New Testa-
      ment Scholarship; Paraphrase on Romans and Galatians*, ed. R.D. Sider et al., in
      Collected Works of Erasmus, vol. 42 (Toronto: University of Toronto Press, 1984),

p. xxxi. From 1549 to 1555 Udall worked as a tutor, first to Edward Courtenay, a royal prisoner in the Tower, and at some time during this period to the household of Bishop Gardiner. Chambers, *MS*, II: 451–2. By a warrant from Queen Mary in 1553 the Revels Office was ordered to produce whatever dialogues and interludes Udall thought fit for the court: Loseley Manor Documents, vol. VI, no. 7 (original), Folger Library, MSS Lb 26 (copy), Lb 41, fol. 78 (copied into Revels account), printed in Feuillerat, *Edward VI and Mary*, p. 159. In December 1555 he was appointed headmaster of St Peter's school, annexed to Westminster. He was buried at St Margaret's, Westminster, on 23 December 1556.

32   William L. Edgerton, *Nicholas Udall* (New York: Twayne Publishers, 1965), 68–72. Udall taught a number of students at Eton who went on to fame, such as Thomas Wilson, Richard Mulcaster, John Parkhurst, and Thomas Tusser, not all of whom remembered him with fondness.

33   William L. Edgerton, *Nicholas Udall* (New York: Twayne Publishers, 1965), 34, thinks it was *Thersites*. Marie Axton, ed., *Three Tudor Classical Interludes* (Cambridge: D.S. Brewer, 1982), p. 13n, thinks it was *Ezechias*. Chambers, *MS*, II: 451, mentions *Placidias, alias Sir Eustace (Placy Dacy, alias Sir Ewe Stacy)*, written in 1534 at Braintree at about the time Udall was there. Reed, *Early Tudor Drama*, p. 56n, also suggests this play as a possibility.

34   Translated in William L. Edgerton, *Nicholas Udall* (New York: Twayne, 1965), 83, who thinks it doubtful that Udall's work owes anything to the play of the same name by Sixt Brink, Master of the Gymnasium of St Anna, Augsburg, who also wrote eight other plays between 1530 and 1537.

35   He is named in a list of the Gentleman Pensioners in 1540 (BL, Royal MS. 7. C. XVI, fol. 123, calendared in *LP*, IV.i, no. 1939 [11]) and appears as a payee on occasion in Cromwell's accounts (PRO, E36/256, fol. 122, abstracted in *LP*, XIV.ii, p. 329).

36   When Sir Thomas Cawarden took possession of the fratery and the paved hall under it at Blackfriars in 1550, Portynare turned the keys over to him, on which occasion Sir Thomas, his wife, and Sir John had supper and saw a play there: Irwin Smith, *Shakespeare's Blackfriars Playhouse* (New York: New York University Press, 1964), 27, 108, 110, 121; *MSC*, II: 35.

37   William Roper, *The Lyfe of Sir Thomas Moore*, ed. E.V. Hitchcock, Early English Text Society, o.s., vol. 197 (London, 1935), 104, reports the incident in which Sir Thomas Elyot, ambassador to Charles V, conveyed the emperor's dismay over the execution of More to Heywood and other family members. Reed, *Early Tudor Drama*, pp. 37–8, 234–6, challenges earlier suggestions that Heywood was a chorister in the Chapel in 1515. In a letter to Burghley of 18 April 1575, Heywood describes himself as 78 years old. It has been suggested on internal evidence that some of Heywood's plays were performed at court in the late 1520s and 1530s as

a means of supplementing his income. See Greg Walker, *Plays of Persuasion* (Cambridge: Cambridge University Press, 1991), 133–4, who argues that the *Play of the Weather* was performed at court, probably before the king; and *Two Moral Interludes*, ed. Peter Happé (Oxford: Malone Society, 1991), 13–14.

38   BL, Royal MS. 17. B. XXVIII, fol. 42; printed in F. Madden, *Privy Purse Expenses of the Princess Mary* (London: W. Pickering, 1831), 61–2.

39   The collaboration probably dates from as early as Redford's time. His interlude of *Wit and Science*, a fragment of another, *Will and Power*, a number of songs, and many of Heywood's minor poems appear together in a manuscript which is probably a song book from St Paul's (BL, Additional MS. 15233) and which was still being supplemented in Westcott's time. This manuscript may have been the one presented at court to Mary at New Year's in 1557. Reed, *Early Tudor Drama*, pp. 55–7; Trevor Lennam, *Sebastian Westcott, the Children of Paul's, and the Marriage of Wit and Science* (Toronto: University of Toronto Press, 1975), 20–36. Westcott first appears at court in 1545, but by then he had already been acquainted with the circle of writer-musicians associated with Redford and Heywood.

40   Viscount Strangford, ed., 'Household Expenses of the Princess Elizabeth during her Residence at Hatfield, October 1, 1551, to September 30, 1551,' *The Camden Miscellany II*, Camden Society, vol. 55 (London, 1853), 40. Wallace, *Evolution*, p. 84n, transcribes the payments, but as Reed, *Early Tudor Drama*, p. 59, points out, this is paid on a single warrant, suggesting one rather than three separate entertainments. We do not know what play he may have performed for Mary or for Elizabeth in 1551. We also do not know whether these plays, the play he wrote for Cromwell, or the mask he produced at Cromwell's and at court in 1539 employed the boys.

41   On the basis of the fact that twelve coats were made for the occasion, Reed, *Early Tudor Drama*, p. 59, suggests the Children of the Chapel, which employed twelve children in this period, rather than Paul's, which employed only ten. The evidence is, of course, inconclusive.

42   J.G. Nichols, ed., *Chronicle of the Grey Friars of London*, Camden Society, vol. 53 (London, 1852), 82n; *Chronicle of Queen Jane and Queen Mary*, p. 30; John Stow, *Annals* (London, 1631), 617. There was a second pageant at Paul's 'against the Dean of Paul's gate' where the choristers of Paul's 'played on vials and sung,' suggesting that Heywood's pageant was produced by the school, not by the choir. Machyn, *Diary*, p. 206, records an entertainment of Elizabeth by the Earl of Arundel at Nonsuch in August 1559 when there was a 'play of the chyldren of Powlles and ther master Se[bastian], master Phelypes and master Haywod.'

43   Reed, *Early Tudor Drama*, pp. 63–71; Robert W. Bolwell, *The Life and Works of John Heywood* (New York: Columbia University Press, 1921), 64–74.

44   Bodleian Library, MS. Engl. Misc. C. 330, printed in James M. Osborn, ed., *The Autobiography of Thomas Whythorne* (Oxford: Clarendon Press, 1961), 13–14.

45   Bodleian Library, MS. Engl. Misc. C. 330, printed in James M. Osborn, ed., *The Autobiography of Thomas Whythorne* (Oxford: Clarendon Press, 1961), 74; for a modernized version see Osborn, ed., *The Autobiography of Thomas Whythorne*, pp. 6, 60.

46   John Bale, *Index Britannicae Scriptorum*, ed. Reginald L. Poole (Oxford: Clarendon Press, 1902), 217. Bale lists only three of Heywood's plays: *De aura comoediam, De amore tragoediam, De quadruplici P.* The first two were printed by William Rastell and attributed to Heywood in 1533. *The Pardoner and the Friar* and *Johan the Husband* were printed by Rastell with Heywood's other plays. *Gentleness and Nobility* and *Witty and Witless* have been attributed to him. Wallace, *Evolution*, pp. 50–3, 81–3, attributed the *Four P, The Pardoner and the Friar,* and *Johan the Husband* to William Cornish. For refutations see Reed, *Early Tudor Drama*, pp. 118–47, and Robert W. Bolwell, *The Life and Works of John Heywood* (New York: Columbia University Press, 1921), pp. 90–5. Reed assigned Heywood *Love, Weather, Witty and Witless,* probably the *Four P,* and possibly the *Pardoner* and *Johan the Husband. Gentleness and Nobility,* assigned by Bolwell to Heywood, is attributed by Reed to John Rastell. Richard Axton, ed., *Three Rastell Plays* (Cambridge: D.S. Brewer, 1979), 15–26, Rastell's latest editor, agrees with Reed but assigns *Gentleness* to Heywood, with Rastell's collaboration in the epilogue. See Greg Walker's discussion of the political context of Heywood's *Play of the Weather* in *Plays of Persuasion, Drama and Politics at the Court of Henry VIII* (Cambridge: Cambridge University Press, 1991), 133–68.

47   PRO, E36/256, fols. 152, 153v, abstracted in *LP,* XIV.ii, pp. 339–40.

48   Reed's suggestion, *Early Tudor Drama*, pp. 61–2, that Heywood's mask was shown on two occasions at Cromwell's in 1539 does not do justice to the structure or the wording of the entries in the accounts.

49   PRO, E36/256, fols. 154, 155. It has been assumed that the hobby-horses were made for the mask of *King Arthur's Knights* and that therefore it was a humorous treatment of the subject. This is not certain from the entries in the accounts, and the use of hobby-horses does not necessarily argue a humorous treatment. Hobby-horses were used for humorous purposes as by George Ferrers in the 1552–3 revels at court, but they were also included in more sophisticated masques such as *Chloridia* in 1631 in which the 'Dwarf-post from hell' in the anti-masque used a 'curtal.' Stephen Orgel and Roy Strong, *Inigo Jones and the Theater of the Stuart Court* (Berkeley and Los Angeles: University of California Press, 1973), II: 434. On the hobby-horse, see Violet Alford, *The Hobbyhorse and Other Animal Masks* (London: Merlin Press, 1978), 2–3, 25, 51–3. Hobby-horses ranged in sophistication from a simple stick covered with a carved horse's head to the 'tourney horse,'

made of basketwork or a light wooden frame which fit around the waist of the rider, who was occasionally armed with a lance or sword. The head of this horse was fashioned with hair for a mane, and the frame was hung with a curtain to conceal the rider's legs.

50   PRO, E36/256, fol. 155v. Reed, *Early Tudor Drama*, pp. 61–2, speculated that Heywood was the author of *King Arthur's Knights* and that this mask was sent to court. The speculation has been repeated as fact since that time.

51   PRO, SP31/18/2/2, fol. 217, calendared in *LP,* VIII, no. 949.

52   PRO, SP3/12, nos. 3, 7, calendared respectively in *LP, Addenda,* Part II, no. 1360 (3 October 1538), no. 1362 (5 October 1538).

53   PRO, E36/256, fol. 163, abstracted in *LP,* XIV.ii, p. 342.

54   PRO, SP1/152, fol. 188, calendared in *LP,* XIV.i, no. 1318. Farlyon's widow is mentioned in BL, Arundel MS. 97, fol. 170v, calendared in *LP,* XVI, no. 1489, p. 701.

55   PRO, C66/686, memb. 40; calendared in *LP,* XIV.ii, no. 264 (30).

56   PRO, SP60/11, no. 51, abstracted in *LP,* XIX.ii, no. 731.

57   He requested allowance for attending the king's progress from 20 June to All Saints in 1541: Guildford Muniment Room, MS. LM 25/33. The king was received at York on 15 September of that year: McGee and Meagher, 'Checklist,' p. 94. The letter from Waterford is Lambeth Palace, MS. 602, fol. 126, calendared in *LP,* XIV.ii, no. 710. The gift of frontier lands is recorded in PRO SP60/11, no. 51, abstracted in LP, XIX.ii, no. 731.

58   Bridges's patent as Yeoman of the Revels (PRO, C66/691, memb. 5, calendared in *LP,* XIV.ii, no. 435 [48]) was surrendered on 1 July 1550 so that it could be granted to John Holt.

59   PRO, C66/791, memb. 27, calendared in *LP,* XXI.ii, no. 648 (59). Bridges surrendered this patent on 21 April 1560.

60   Holt had been acting as deputy from about December 1546; his patent, PRO, C66/830, memb. 32, is printed in Feuillerat, *Elizabeth,* pp. 70–1.

61   Bridges's patent in survivorship with Longman as Yeoman of the Tents is PRO, C66/709, memb. 32, calendared in *LP,* XVI, no. 1391 (34). Longman was a citizen and Merchant Taylor of London: Guildford Muniment Room, MS. LM 41, fol. 7. When Bridges resigned in 1550, John Holt received a patent in survivorship with Longman as Yeoman of the Tents on 14 October: PRO, C66/828, memb. 12, calendared in *CPR Edward VI,* III: 227–8.

62   The payment to Bridges from the Court of Augmentations is PRO, E315/254, fol. 83, calendared in *LP,* XXI.i, no. 643.

63   Hale's appointment as Groom of the Tents is PRO, C66/709, memb. 32, calendared in *LP,* XVI, no. 1391 (33); his fee is recorded in BL, Lansdowne MS. 156, fol. 105v. Hale was also appointed '*serviens ad arma*' on 2 January 1555 by Queen

Mary. He was born around 1506, for he still held the post of Groom of the Tents in 1572 when he was 66 years of age: Feuillerat, *Elizabeth*, p. 438.

64   The grant of the Charterhouse is PRO, C66/709, memb. 38, calendared in *LP,* XVI, no. 1308 (21). In a few years, however, they were displaced. In April 1545 parts of the Charterhouse were granted to Sir Edward North (*LP,* XX.i, no. 620 [33]), and in September 1545 much of the rest was granted to Robert Lawrence (*LP,* XX.ii, no. 496 [12]).

65   BL, Cotton MS. Vitellius C. XI, fol. 213, calendared in *LP,* XIV.ii, no. 286; Hall, pp. 832–5. The Chamber account contains payments for making ready for the progress of Anne of Cleves from Dover to London: BL, Arundel MS. 97, fols. 108–13, abstracted in *LP,* XVI.i, pp. 178–80. The formal reception took place on 3 January: PRO, SP1/57, fols. 1–10; BL, Cotton MS. Vitellius C. XVI, fol. 271; J. Kaulek, *Correspondance Politique de MM. de Chastillon et de Marillac* (Paris: F. Alcan, 1885), 150, 151, calendared in *LP,* XV, nos. 10, 14, 18, 22, 23).

66   Hall, pp. 835–7.

67   Hall, p. 837.

68   PRO, E36/113, fols. 38–41v, calendared in *LP,* XV, no. 616; BL, Harleian MS. 69, fol. 18r–v, calendared in *LP,* XV, no. 617. Hall, p. 838.

69   PRO, E36/228, fols. 9–12, abstracted in *LP,* II.ii, p. 1517. The document is classed with others from 1518, but obviously it could not have been written before 25 July 1539 and probably dates from shortly after Cromwell's fall in 1540.

70   David Wilkins, *Concilia Magnae Britanniae et Hiberniae* (London, 1737), III: 861: 'Deinde episcopi consilium dederunt regiam majestate, supplicare, ut ludi publici et comoediae, quae Londini in verbi Dei magnum dedecus et contemptum aguntur, corrigantur.' Bonner's injunction is printed on p. 866.

71   At its March and April meetings the council was especially concerned with restraining plays: *APC,* I: 103–4, 109, 110, 122. Some of the joiners arrested were not released until the 14th, and those who had gone to the Tower not until the 28th.

72   Society of Antiquaries (Burlington House, Picadilly, London), Collection of Proclamations, II, p. 151, calendared in *LP,* XX.i, no. 812.

73   *APC,* I: 407.

74   J. Kaulek, *Correspondance Politique de MM. de Castillon et de Marillac* (Paris: F. Alcan, 1885), 254, calendared in *LP,* XVI, no. 373.

75   Folger Library, MS. Lb 2, fol. 1.

76   Wallace, *Evolution*, p. 69, did not have access to BL, Additional MS. 59900 when he wrote that 1541 was the last notice of Crane's dramatic activity. Crane was paid again for a play at Christmas in 1543–4: fol. 68v, abstracted in Streitberger, *RORD* (1984): 31.

77   There appears to have been no Master of the Revels appointed after Sir Henry
      Guildford's death in 1532. The king's instructions were communicated to the
      Yeoman of the Revels by members of the Privy Chamber as in 1541 or personally
      by the king himself as at Shrovetide 1542: 'A Commaundement gevyn by *the*
      kyngs grace vnto me Iohn brydges on Shrof monday,' Folger Library, MS. Lb 262.
      The choice of Browne to communicate instructions in 1541 suggests that from
      1532 to 1544 men of his stature in the Privy Chamber were used for this purpose.
      On the role of Henry's Gentlemen of the Privy Chamber see David Starkey, 'Court
      and Government,' in C. Coleman and D. Starkey, eds., *Revolution Reassessed*
      (Oxford: Clarendon Press, 1986), 29–58, and 'Intimacy and Innovation,' in
      David Starkey et al., *The English Court* (London: Longman, 1987), 71–118. By
      December 1542 one of the Gentlemen of the King's Privy Chamber, Sir Thomas
      Cawarden, was taking inventories of the Tents and Revels, suggesting that plans
      to appoint a new Master were being formulated.
78   Folger Library, Lb 2, fols. 1v–2; MSS Lb 262. The commandment was initiated
      by the king and communicated to Bridges by Browne.
79   Folger Library, MSS Lb 2, fols. 2v–3; Lb 259.
80   Folger Library, MSS Lb 2, fols. 3v–4; Lb 260.
81   Folger Library, MSS Lb 2, fols. 4v–5; Lb 153 and Lb 154.
82   PRO, E36/228, fols. 9–12, abstracted in *LP,* II.ii, p. 1517.
83   Folger library, MSS Lb 2, fols. 3v–4; Lb 260.
84   This is John Holt's opinion, repeated in the 'The First Institution' (BL, Lans-
      downe MS. 83, art. 59, fol. 157, printed in Feuillerat, *Elizabeth,* p. 5), of the
      expenses of the early Revels establishment.

CHAPTER 7

1   Guildford Muniment Room, MS. LM 345/22; Folger Library, MS. Lb 476, print-
     ed in Craib, 'Sir Thomas Cawarden,' p. 20.
2   David Starkey, 'Intimacy and Innovation,' in David Starkey et al., *The English
     Court* (London: Longman, 1987), 113–14.
3   Cawarden is named among the Gentlemen of the Privy Chamber in 1540: PRO,
     SP1/164, pp. 116–17, abstracted in *LP,* XVI, no. 394 (6). His wages are listed in
     1545: PRO, E36/231, p. 63, abstracted in *LP,* XX.ii, Appendix, no. 2 (v). The
     New Year's gift is recorded in BL, Arundel MS. 97, fol. 164v, abstracted in *LP,*
     XVI, no. 1489.
4   The license for his retainers is PRO, SP4/1, calendared in *LP,* XX.ii, no. 418 (48).
     BL, Cotton MS. Vespasian C. XIV, fol. 106, abstracted in *LP,* XXI.i, no. 969, lists
     Cawarden and his wife among those ordinarily to be lodged at court.
5   Some of the suits granted at Cawarden's request are recorded in PRO, SP4/1, cal-

endared in *LP,* XXI.i, no. 148 (38, 39, 109, 110, 111); no. 963 (79, 80, 81, 124, 154), no. 1165. The king's will, PRO, E23/4, is abstracted in *LP,* XXI.ii, no. 634. A draft of this clause of the will specified £40 rather than £200, but by warrant from the council of 3 June 1549, printed by Craib, 'Sir Thomas Cawarden,' p. 24, Cawarden was paid 200 marks, suggesting that he may have received the entire £200.

6   On this and his many other grants and patents see Craib, 'Sir Thomas Cawarden,' pp. 9–14, 20–8.

7   Folger Library, MS. Lb 81, printed in Craib, 'Sir Thomas Cawarden,' pp. 23–4, records Cawarden's yearly expenses at Blechingly. William Browne's eulogy for Cawarden, Folger Library, MS. Lb 519, records that he kept his house 'full bounteously.'

8   Craib, 'Sir Thomas Cawarden,' p. 9.

9   The patents are printed in Craib, 'Sir Thomas Cawarden,' pp. 22, 24.

10   Folger Library, MS. Lb 273, calendared in *RCHM,* VII: 605a.

11   As Sergeant of the Tents, Travers was paid £9 19*s.* 3*d.* for money laid out by him for the king's progress in 1539: BL, Arundel MS. 97, fol. 91, abstracted in *LP,* XIV.ii, p. 314. In 1541 he attended the king's progress from 20 June to 1 November, during which time Travers was paid 4*s.* 2*d.* a day and Bridges and Hale were paid 18*d.*: Guildford Muniment Room, MS. LM 25/33.

12   Guildford Muniment Room, MSS LM 4, LM 48 (copy), an inventory roll of the Tents delivered to Cawarden by Bridges and Hale on 4 December 1542; Folger Library, MSS Lb 325 (copy), Lb 326, an inventory of the Revels garments, costumes, and properties in the custody of Bridges delivered to Cawarden on 10 December 1542.

13   Guildford Muniment Room, MSS LM 3/1, LM 3/2 (payments by Thomas Hale and John Bridges between 23 July 1543 and 26 August 1543), LM 48 (inventory giving a detailed description of the new lodging of timber), LM 24/11 (checkbook dated 21 July 1543 for four weeks' work on the 'Tent of Tymber'); LM 128/1–11 (bills and receipts related to work at Whitefriars; no. 5 records deliveries 'to the bankett howse at Whyte fryers'); Folger Library, MS. Lb 3 (Tents checkbook), calendared in *RCHM,* VII: 602a.

14   Folger Library, MS. Lb 3.

15   Cawarden's accounts for the work are Guildford Muniment Room, MSS LM 15a (pay book from 15 July to 22 November), LM 15b (pay book from May to December). Bridges's accounts are Folger Library, MSS Lb 117, Lb 258, Lb 2, fols. 6r–v. Many documents in the Loseley collection relate to the Tents preparations for the war: Guildford Muniment Room, MS. LM 24/1–27 (pay books related to Cawarden's offices); Guildford Muniment Room, MS. LM 127 (Bartholomew Penne and Nicholas Lizard were employed at Whitefriars in July

1544 in painting in imitation of jasper and marble and in making moulds for the king's arms); Folger Library, MS. Lb 261 (Anthony Toto, Sergeant Painter, was employed in painting and making badges for the king's tents).

16 Guildford Muniment Room, MSS LM 24/16 (pay sheet for the army); PRO, SP1/185, fols. 1, 42, calendared in *LP,* XIX.i, no. 275, pp. 162, 164 (Cawarden's attendants in France); PRO, SP1/192, fol. 75, and BL, Additional MS. 5482, fol. 92v, calendared respectively in *LP,* XIX.ii, no. 223 and no. 334 (list of knights made at Boulogne); Hall, p. 862 (narrative of the king's entry into Boulogne on 18 July).

17 Guildford Muniment Room, MSS. LM 16a (number of officers and artificers employed in Tents and their wages, 1–31 July 1544), LM 16b (copy), LM 10 (money received from Sir Richard Southwell for payment to officers, artificers, soldiers in the Tents, 1 July–26 September 1544); PRO, SP1/185, fol. 55, calendared in *LP,* XIX.i, no. 275 (6).

18 Guildford Muniment Room, MS. LM 9 (Cawarden's patent with seal attached appointing him Master of the Tents in survivorship with Aucher). The enrolment, PRO, C66/752, memb. 36, is calendared in *LP,* XX.i, no. 465 (27).

19 Aucher was appointed Master or Treasurer of the Jewels on 18 November 1545: PRO, C66/784, memb. 9, calendared in *LP,* XX.ii, no. 910 (58).

20 Cawarden's patent as Master of the Revels, PRO, C66/753, memb. 23, calendared in *LP,* XX.i, no. 465 (28), is printed in Feuillerat, *Elizabeth*, p. 53. Collier, *HEDP* (1831) I: 134, who thought that an 'Edm. Tho.' held the Mastership by patent before Cawarden, misread BL, Lansdowne MS. 156, fol. 106. As Chambers, *Tudor Revels*, p. 9n, has pointed out, the Latin abbreviation Collier refers to expands to *eidem Thome*, 'the same Thomas' [Cawarden] mentioned in the previous entry.

21 BL, Lansdowne MS. 83, art. 59, fol. 148, printed in Feuillerat, *Elizabeth*, p. 5.

22 The writer of BL, Lansdowne MS. 83, art. 59, printed in Feuillerat, *Elizabeth*, p. 6, comments on the means of rendering accounts: 'It might seeme that in tymes past the same office beinge kept in the Kinges house The Clerke Comptrollers of the Kinges housold or one of theym hadde eye vpon the Princes charges in that behalfe.' He also mentions that Cawarden had his books made up from time to time by the Clerk of the Works. Other than in the special circumstances surrounding the construction of the 1551 banqueting house, I have found no evidence of the involvement of Clerks of the Works making up accounts for the office. Of the involvement of Nicholas Bristowe, one of the king's clerks, there is much evidence. Folger Library, MS. Lb 5, for example, is one of Cawarden's original accounts listing payments for work on the revels and entertainments for the reception of the Admiral of France from 16 July to 5 September 1546, headed 'A payment made by Nycholas Bristowe Esquyre for the Charges of the kinges

Revelles At Thonor of Hampton.' Many of the imprests for work in the Tents and some of the accounts of that office in the early 1540s were made up by Bristowe: Guildford Muniment Room, MSS LM 128/6, LM 128/11, and LM 2, for example. Bristowe was also appointed in 1543, along with Cawarden, to sell Cromwell's house in London. As late as 1552, in an estimate of charges and a bill for money past due in Cawarden's offices (Folger Library, MS. Lb 322, 323 [copy]), Bristowe is referred to as paymaster of the office 'as before this tyme he hathe Done.'

23 Folger Library, MS. Lb 324 fol. 1.
24 BL, Lansdowne MS. 83, art. 59, fol. 158, printed in Feuillerat, *Elizabeth*, pp. 5–6.
25 BL, Lansdowne MS. 12, no. 54, printed in Feuillerat, *Elizabeth*, p. 407.
26 PRO, C66/753, memb. 23, calendared in *LP,* XX.i, no. 465 (29).
27 *APC,* III: 117; Feuillerat, *Elizabeth*, p. 440.
28 PRO, C66/836, memb. 5, calendared in *CPR Edward VI,* IV: 49, and printed in Feuillerat, *Elizabeth*, pp. 56–7. Feuillerat, *Elizabeth*, pp. 435, 440, based on a council letter to Cawarden mentioning that the king would place one of his servants in the vacant office, thought that Leys never acted as Clerk Comptroller before his appointment by patent. However, the terms of his patent show clearly that he did. BL, Lansdowne MS. 156, fol. 107v, lists his pay at £12 3s. 4d. Collier, *HEDP* (1879) I: 140, misreads this document, thinking that he was the Clerk.
29 BL, Lansdowne MS. 83, art. 59, fol. 158, printed in Feuillerat, *Elizabeth,* pp. 5–6. His petition to Burghley, BL, Lansdowne MS. 12, no. 54, is printed in Feuillerat, *Elizabeth*, p. 407.
30 BL, Lansdowne MS. 83, art. 58, fol. 155, 'A Platte of Orders to be Observed for the Better Management of the Office,' is printed in Feuillerat, *Elizabeth*, pp. 16–17.
31 Guildford Muniment Room, MS. LM 5/5, fol. 3v (Tents book of payments beginning 16 March 1544 in which Colyer is listed and paid as Clerk). Colyer continued to be paid for his duties as Clerk in the Revels accounts: Folger Library, MSS Lb 2, fols. 6–7, Lb 258, is the account for Christmas 1544–5; the accounts for Christmas 1545–6 are Folger Library, MSS Lb 266, 267. BL, Lansdowne MS. 156, fol. 100v, lists his wages as £12 3s. 4d., exactly those of the Clerk by patent. Chambers, *Tudor Revels*, p. 10, mistakenly thought that he may have had no function in the Revels.
32 PRO, C66/787, memb. 16, calendared in *LP,* XXI.i, no. 970 (15), and printed in Feuillerat, *Elizabeth*, pp. 66–7. He was appointed at Cawarden's suit: PRO, SP4/1, calendared in *LP,* XXI.i, no. 963 (80). In the household books, the Clerk and the Clerk Comptroller are enrolled as members of the Tents, and after 1607 the Clerk Comptroller received his house rent in the Tents accounts: PRO, E351/2939–57.
33 BL, Lansdowne MS. 83, art. 59, fol. 158, printed in Feuillerat, *Elizabeth,* p. 6.
34 BL, Lansdowne MS. 83, art. 58, fol. 155, printed in Feuillerat, *Elizabeth*, p. 16.
35 Feuillerat, *Elizabeth*, pp. 441–2.

36   PRO, C66/962, memb. 40, printed in Feuillerat, *Elizabeth*, pp. 68–9. Blagrave
      was one of the overseers of Cawarden's will and was generously remembered in it.
      (On the details of his life, see note 40 below.) In addition, Blagrave was appointed
      treasurer of the commission appointed to pay the debts of Somerset which he was
      involved in until at least December of that year; the many letters relating to this
      are in BL, Additional MS. 5755, fols. 178–86, 311, 314, 319–22.

37   BL, Lansdowne MS. 83, art. 58, fol. 157, printed in Feuillerat, *Elizabeth*, p. 17.

38   PRO, A0/2045, no. 6 (Audit Office Declared Account from 1 Nov. 1580 –
      31 October 1581); Feuillerat, *Elizabeth*, p. 434.

39   PRO, C66/1273, memb. 5, calendared in *Draft Calendar of Patent Rolls, 28–29
      Elizabeth, Part 1*, List and Index Society, vol. 242 (London: Printed for Sub-
      scribers, 1991), 46. *King's Works*, III.i: 92–4. Feuillerat, *Elizabeth*, p. 443.

40   According to his will made 13 April 1590 (PRO, PROB 11/76, fols. 225v–6),
      Thomas Blagrave, 'alias T.B. of St. Iones Ierusalem,' originally of Grafton, Wilt-
      shire, was to be buried in the church at Clerkenwell. Since the will was proved on
      10 November 1590, Blagrave died between April and November 1590. BL, Harleian
      MS. 1551, fol. 59, printed in Sir G.J. Armytage, ed., *Middlesex Peerages*, Harleian
      Society, vol. LXV (London, 1914), 83, also gives the date of his death as 1590.
      Feuillerat, *Elizabeth*, pp. 441–4, gives a brief life, but errs in giving the date of his
      death in 1603 based on a literal reading of Honing's patent which he received 'on
      the death of Tho. Blagrave.' Chambers, *ES*, I: 99, follows Feuillerat and notes
      without giving evidence that the date in *Middlesex Peerages* is wrong.

41   Feuillerat, *Elizabeth*, p. 432.

42   BL, Lansdowne MS. 83, art. 59, fol. 160, printed in Feuillerat, *Elizabeth*, p. 11.

43   BL, Lansdowne MS. 83, art. 58, fol. 155, printed in Feuillerat, *Elizabeth*, p. 16.

44   Bridges patent of 23 December 1546 succeeding John Malte as king's Tailor,
      PRO, C66/791, memb. 27, is calendared in *LP*, XXI.ii, no. 648 (59). Chambers,
      Tudor Revels, p. 11, supposed for the wrong reasons that Holt succeeded Bridges
      at the end of Henry VIII's reign. Feuillerat, *Elizabeth*, pp. 426–77, has made it
      clear that Holt was only a deputy until his appointment by patent in 1550.

45   Folger Library, MSS Lb 8, fol. 3v, Lb 319, printed in Feuillerat, *Edward VI and
      Mary*, pp. 5, 9.

46   Holt's appointment as Yeoman of the Revels, PRO, C66/830, memb. 32, is print-
      ed in Feuillerat, *Elizabeth*, pp. 70–1. The reversions of the patent as Yeoman of
      the Tents with Longman is PRO, C66/828, memb. 12.

47   His patent as Tailor in survivorship with Richard Newport, PRO, C66/788,
      memb. 18, is calendared in *LP*, XXI.ii, no. 771 (27).

48   BL, Lansdowne MS. 156, fol. 107v, shows that Holt received £9 2*s.* 6*d.* as Yeoman
      of the Revels, £9 3*s.* 6*d.* as Tailor to the prince, and £10 as Yeoman of the Tents.
      Chambers, *Tudor Revels*, p. 25, suggested that Holt was possibly the 'momer' who

received a reward for attendance at a pageant given by the Westminster Boys before the Merchant Tailor's Company in 1561 and who was paid a fee of 10s. when they played at court during Christmas 1564. Given the fact that earlier and later Yeomen, like Gibson and Kirkham, were involved as advisors or entrepreneurs in theatrical activities, it is possible. Feuillerat, *Elizabeth*, p. 427, argues that the name is common and that Holt's signature was a mark, showing that he was a 'totally untaught man,' and that therefore he could not have been an actor.

49   PRO, SP12/20/101, calendared in *CSP Domestic, Addenda, 1566–1579*, p. 375, printed in Feuillerat, *Elizabeth*, p. 408.

50   PRO, C66/1218, memb. 32, calendared in *CPR Elizabeth*, IX, no. 1758. Bowle was appointed to succeed John Broun 'defunctus.' The elder Bowle surrendered his office to his son, Robert, in February 1593.

51   Folger Library, MS. Lb 42, fols. 29, 42, printed in Feuillerat, *Elizabeth*, pp. 84, 107.

52   *MSC*, XIII, pp. xii–xiv, 164–5.

53   BL, Lansdowne MS. 83, art. 58, fol. 155, printed in Feuillerat, *Elizabeth*, p. 16.

54   BL, Lansdowne MS. 83, art. 59, fol. 158b, printed in Feuillerat, *Elizabeth*, p. 8.

55   Folger Library, MSS Lb 263, Lb 264 (copy), printed in John Doebler, 'A Lost Paragraph in the Revels Constitution,' *Shakespeare Quarterly*, 24 (1973): 333–4; 25 (1974): 286–7. Chambers's transcription, *ES*, I: 74, omits a paragraph.

56   BL, Lansdowne MS. 83, art. 58, fol. 155, printed in Feuillerat, *Elizabeth*, p. 16, describes the books which were to be kept.

57   For example, Scotland Yard was being used as a Works storage yard from as early as 1532: PRO, E351/3326. John Stow, *A Survey of London*, ed. C.L. Kingsford (Oxford: Clarendon Press, 1908), II: 101, describes the yard. The Hospital of the Blessed Mary of Rounceval came to the Crown in 1543, but the Comptroller of the Works was using some of the facilities as a counting house as early as 1540, and the Surveyor also had his office there. The Almshouse at Rounceval had also been used as a playhouse in 1531, but I have not been able to find more information on it: PRO, E36/251, p. 164, calendared in *LP*, V, no. 952. *King's Works*, III.i: 22–4.

58   PRO, LC9/50, fol. 152v.

59   John Stow, *A Survey of London*, ed. C.L. Kingsford (Oxford: Clarendon Press, 1908), I: 238–9.

60   PRO, SP1/29, fol. 288v, abstracted in *LP*, III.ii, pp. 1559.

61   Folger Library, MSS Lb 153, 258.

62   M.H. Cox and P. Norman, eds., *Survey of London* (London, 1930), XIII: 8–9; XVI: 161–2. PRO, E351/3326, records £262 spent in making a wharf, brick wall, and two gates at Scotland Yard; work and store houses were built in 1552: *King's Works*, III.i: 22–4; IV.ii: 310.

63 Cawarden was granted the precinct on 12 March 1550: PRO, C66/830, membs. 32–3, calendared in *CPR Edward VI*, III: 336–7.

64 John Stow, *A Survey of London*, ed. C.L. Kingsford (Oxford: Clarendon Press, 1908), I: 239.

65 PRO, E36/217, fols. 46, 209–18, abstracted in *LP* II.ii, pp. 1497–8, 1501–2; IV.i, no. 965.

66 PRO, LC9/50, fol. 153.

67 John Stow, *A Survey of London*, ed. C.L. Kingsford (Oxford: Clarendon Press, 1908), II: 15–16.

68 The grant to Cotton, PRO, C66/567, memb. 22, is calendared in *CPR Henry VII*, I: 209. The Privy Seal writ to pay Doland 20 marks (Campbell, II: 282) is addressed to Lord Brooke, Receiver General of the Duchy of Cornwall.

69 The grant of Warwick Inn to Bridges is recorded in PRO, C66/709, memb. 38, calendared in *LP* XVI, no. 1308 (21).

70 PRO, E36/228, fols. 9–12, abstracted in *LP* II.ii, p. 1517. The document is misdated 1518 in *Letters and Papers*.

71 Folger Library, MS. Lb 153.

72 PRO, E36/217, fols. 37–8, abstracted in *LP* II.ii, p. 1490.

73 PRO, C66/664, memb. 25, calendared in *LP* VII, no. 1498 (41).

74 On the Charterhouse see, J.S. Cockburn, H.P.F. King, and K.G.T. McDonnell, eds., *A History of the County of Middlesex* (Oxford: Oxford University Press, 1969), I: 159–68, in *The Victoria History of the Counties of England*, gen. ed. A.B. Pugh.

75 Guildford Muniment Room, MS. LM 6, shows that 200 'houses' were stored in the Charterhouse after the king's return from Boulogne.

76 Guildford Muniment Room, MSS LM 15a, LM 15b are pay books ending 22 November 1544 for making tents, loading them on ships for transport to Boulogne, unloading them again at Tower wharf, and transporting them by cart to the Charterhouse.

77 The grant to Sir Edward North, Chancellor of the Court of Augmentations, of the reversion of the house and site of the Charterhouse is recorded in PRO, C66/752, memb. 6, calendared in *LP* XX.i, no. 620 (33). Guildford Muniment Room, MS. LM 1a, a book of payments from 26 March 1545 to 1 March 1546, lists charges for carrying tents and timber houses from the Charterhouse and storing them at Blackfriars, confirming that during this period Cawarden and his officers were establishing themselves in the precinct. LM 20a, LM 20b (copy), lists charges between 15 August and 26 September 1546 for moving the king's timber houses and tents from Blackfriars and setting them up at Cobham Park, confirming that by this period Blackfriars was the principal storage facility for the Tents. Chambers's speculation in *Tudor Revels*, p. 13, based on a generalized passage in John Stow, *A Survey of London*, ed. C.L. Kingsford (Oxford: Clarendon

Press, 1908), II: 84, that the Tents and Toils found facilities in the Priory of St John of Jerusalem during Henry VIII's reign can be dismissed. The Tents were at Warwick Inn from about 1513 until 1542, at the Charterhouse from 1542 to 1545 or 1546, and at Blackfriars from 1545 or 1546 until 1560 when the office was moved to St John's.

78   BL, Arundel MS. 97, fol. 27v, abstracted in *LP,* XIII.ii, p. 532.

79   Guildford Muniment Room, MSS LM 59/117; LM 127 (payments to painters for work for the Tents projects at Whitefriars); LM 128/1–11 (bills for work on Tents projects at Whitefriars, include mention of 'the bankett howse at the Whyte fryers').

80   Stow describes the buildings: *A Survey of London,* ed. C.L. Kingsford (Oxford: Clarendon Press, 1908), II: 46–7.

81   See the description of the precinct in Chambers, *ES,* II: 475–515, and the related documents transcribed or abstracted in *MSC,* II.

82   W.C. Richardson, *The Court of Augmentations* (Baton Rouge, La.: Louisiana State University Press, 1952), 403. Cheyne was principal Gentleman of the King's Privy Chamber, Warden of the Cinque Ports, and Treasurer of the Household from 1541 until his death in 1558.

83   *MSC,* II: 35.

84   Folger Library, MSS Lb 115, 163, 215. PRO, E351/3329, E351/3535 are the Works accounts for the renovations. Bernard was allowed 2*s.* a day as temporary Surveyor; *King's Works,* III.i: 15.

85   Folger Library, MS. Lb 8, fol. 1, printed in Feuillerat, *Edward VI and Mary,* p. 3.

86   *MSC,* II: 109.

87   Guildford Muniment Room, MS. LM 59/146.

88   *MSC,* II: 4, 6, 8, 109, 114. Folger Library, MS. Lb 389 is the survey of the Blackfriars taken by Blagrave for Cawarden on 12 October 1552.

89   *MSC,* II: 44, 53.

90   Folger Library, MS. Lb 390 is a rent roll of the precinct taken from 29 September 1553 to 29 September 1554 by Blagrave listing the charges of the various buildings rented to the Crown; Lb 410 is an estimate of rents and revenues within the precinct [ca. 1557], listing the various tenants, including the officers of the Tents and Revels. See the abstracts from Cawarden's accounts in Feuillerat, *Edward VI and Mary,* pp. 210, 230, 242, 301; *Elizabeth,* pp. 103, 107, which list the charges to the Crown for these offices and houses.

91   Folger Library, MS. Lb 496.

92   Folger Library, MSS Lb 117, Lb 258, Lb 2, fols. 6–7 (copy).

93   Folger Library, MSS Lb 266, Lb 267.

94   *APC,* I: 365.

95   PRO, SP1/217, fol. 49, abstracted in *LP,* XXI.i, no. 637.

96 *LP,* XXI.i, no. 682.

97 BL, Cotton MS. Vespasian C. XIV, fols. 80–8v, abstracted in *LP,* XXI.i, no. 1384, 'Remembraunces for the Ambassadores ... and pastime &c.'

98 Folger Library, MS. Lb 5. Guildford Muniment Room, MS. LM 18 contains a list of deliveries and of remains of material for Christmas and a list of garments that Bridges was in the process of making, some probably for Christmas 1545–6 and others for this reception. Folger Library, MS. Lb 116, an inventory of finished garments and material, is dated 31 July 1546.

99 Hall, p. 867.

100 PRO, SP1/24, fols. 139–40, 150–2, abstracted respectively in *LP,* XXI.ii, nos. 82, 96.

101 The fragment recording delivery of material to Modena at Westminster is Bodleian Library, MS. Engl. hist. b. 192/1, fol. 30. The Tents account, 1544–6, Guildford Muniment Room, MS. LM 1b, fol. 1, records setting up the tents for a banqueting house at Westminster 'on the trilles.' On the banqueting house at Nonsuch, see Martin Biddle, 'Nonsuch Palace, 1959–60: An Interim Report,' *Surrey Archaeological Collections,* 58 (1961): 1–20; and King's Works, IV.ii: 201–3. Guildford Muniment Room, MS. LM 1b, fol. 5, records work at Nonsuch when 'thmbasadors' were there. Robert Trunckwell's petition mentioning the banqueting house at Hampton Court is BL, Additional Charter, 1262 (ca. 1575–88). The undated Tents account recording deliveries to Hyde Park for the banqueting house, Guildford Muniment Room, MS. LM 43/1, fol. 13, must be dated ca. 1544, before Anthony Denny 'esquire' was knighted and before the Tents began to move from the Charterhouse to Blackfriars.

102 The Tents account, Guildford Muniment Room, MS. LM 59/50, fol. 1, lists garnishing material delivered to Hampton Court for a banqueting house. Fols. 2v–3 of the same document list deliveries to the banqueting house at Oatlands. The Revels account, Folger Library, MS. Lb 5, records charges for decorating a banqueting house at Hampton Court.

103 Guildford Muniment Room, MS. LM 2. MS. LM 22/1 records payments for moving the tents from Blackfriars to Hampton Court, to Oatlands, to Cobham and then back to Blackfriars between 15 July and 5 September 1546.

104 Guildford Muniment Room, MS. LM 22/2, fol. 5.

105 Wriothesley, *Chronicle,* I: 173; Hall, p. 867; *Spectacle,* p. 280.

106 Anglo, *Spectacle,* p. 280, remarks on the comparative poverty of Henry VIII's last revels. Most revels of the early 1540s were less expensive and less elaborate than those of the first two decades of the reign, although the 1546 entertainments for the Admiral of France did rival some earlier receptions. The importance of these revels is less their elaboration than their departure from Reformation subjects and return to romance and to the theme of princely magnificence.

CHAPTER 8

1   The loan of garments is recorded in Folger Library, MS. Lb 268, printed in
     Feuillerat, *Edward VI and Mary*, p. 249. A long history of city and court coopera-
     tion lies behind this example. The court supplied virtually everything from car-
     penters to musicians for the 1520 and 1533 entries. J.G. Nichols, *Literary Remains*,
     I, pp. ccciii–cccv, prints the order for the 1547 procession, the entry pageants,
     the coronation, and the notices of the jousts, drawing freely on College of Arms,
     MSS I 7, fols. 33–8v, and I 18, fols. 75–83. See McGee and Meagher, 'Check-
     list,' pp. 97–8, for other sources. The 1547 entry is discussed in Anglo, *Spectacle*,
     pp. 281–94, who considers it totally undistinguished, 'a work of terrible haste.'
     Lydgate's poem describing the 1432 entry (BL, Harleian MS. 565; BL, Cotton
     MS. Julius B. II; and BL, Cotton MS. Cleopatra C. IV) is printed in H.N.
     McCracken, ed., *The Minor Poems of John Lydgate*, Early English Text Society,
     o.s., vol. 192 (London, 1934), Part II: 630–48; *Chronicles of London*, ed. C.L.
     Kingsford (Oxford: Clarendon Press, 1905), 97–116. See also *Great Chronicle*,
     pp. 156–70.
2   Udall, Bale, and Foxe, among other writers, also developed the parallel between
     Edward and Josiah: *Literary Remains*, I, pp. ccli–cclv. See John N. King, *English
     Reformation Literature* (Princeton: Princeton University Press, 1982), 184–206,
     for a discussion of the development of Edward VI's image.
3   On Hezekiah, see 2 Kings 18, and on Josiah, 2 Kings 22–3.
4   College of Arms, MS. I 7, fol. 38, printed in *Literary Remains*, I, p. ccxci.
5   Folger Library, MS. Lb 8, fols. 4–5v, printed in Feuillerat, *Edward VI and Mary*,
     pp. 6–8. A near parallel to this mount exists in the one placed outside Westmin-
     ster Abbey during the wedding service of Prince Arthur and Katherine of Aragon
     in November 1501.
6   Nicholas Bellin (ca. 1490–1569) was *valet de garderobe* to Francis I from 1516 to
     1522. In 1533, when he was working at Fontainbleau, he was styled *sculpteur et
     faiseur de masques*. He escaped to England after a plot to defraud Francis I was
     discovered, and despite two requests for extradition, Henry VIII, who took him
     under his patronage by 15 August 1537, refused to return him to France. In addi-
     tion to architectural projects such as the banqueting houses at Whitehall and Non-
     such, Bellin designed or supervised a number of Revels projects. Martin Biddle,
     The Journal of the British Archaeological Association, 3rd ser., 29 (1966): 106–21.
7   Guildford Muniment Room, MS. LM 59/34. While not named in this bill, the
     details of the charges correspond to the coronation mount and are confirmed by
     payment to Bellin in the account: Folger Library, MS. Lb 8, fol. 5v; Lb 9, fol. 4v.
     The mount is described in College of Arms, MSS I 7 and I 18, printed in *Literary
     Remains*, I, p. ccxciv: 'there was made and oredyned a mountyng scaffold, with

stayres up to the same, and down to the altar, on the which there was a throne of
vij. staires, whereof iiij. of the vppermost were covered with fine bawdekyn, and
the other staires covered with carpettes; and vpon the middest of the throne there
was sett a great whyte chaire covered with bawdekyn, damaske, and gold, with ij.
coshyns; whereof one was blacke velvett embrodered with gold very richely, and
the other of clothe of tyssu. The said chair had ij. pillers. at the backe whereof
there stood ij. lyons of gold, and in the middest a turret with a flowre de lyce of
golde.'

8   Folger Library, MS. Lb 8, fol. 4, printed in Feuillerat, *Edward VI and Mary*, p. 6.

9   College of Arms, MS. I 7, fol. 37, printed in *Literary Remains*, I, p. cclxxxviii.

10   College of Arms, MS. I 7, fol. 36, printed in *Literary Remains*, I, pp. cclxxxvi–
      cclxxxvii.

11   The tradition of allegorizing parts of the Orpheus myth in the Renaissance appear
      in emblems where his musical power is broadened to include oratorical skill, hence
      his capacity to transform savagery into civility. See *The English Emblem Tradition*,
      ed. Peter M. Daly et al. (Toronto: University of Toronto Press, 1987), 287. There
      was, however, a long tradition of Christianizing the myth. See Patricia Vicari,
      '*Sparagmos*: Orpheus among the Christians,' in John Warden, ed., *Orpheus, the
      Metamorphosis of A Myth*, (Toronto: University of Toronto Press, 1982), 63–83.
      The part of the myth first elaborated by Apollonius of Rhodes in his so-called
      Argonautica was Christianized by Marsilio Ficino in his *Orphic Argonautica* (1462)
      in which adaptation Orpheus plays an important role as spiritual leader of the
      quest. See D.P. Walker, 'Orpheus the Theologian and the Renaissance Platonists,'
      Journal of the Warburg and Courtauld Institutes, 16 (1953): 100–20, and John
      Warden, 'Orpheus and Ficino,' in John Warden, ed., *Orpheus, the Metamorphosis
      of A Myth*, 85–110. It was this aspect of the Christianized myth that was empha-
      sized at the coronation of Edward VI.

12   Guildford Muniment Room, MS. LM 30, fol. 1. The joust on Monday and the
      tourney on Tuesday is recorded in College of Arms, MS. I 18, fols. 92v–94,
      printed in *Literary Remains*, I, pp. ccc–cccii.

13   Folger Library, MS. Lb 8, fol. 2v, printed in Feuillerat, *Edward VI and Mary*, p. 5;
      Folger Library, MS. Lb 272 is the bill for carriage; Lb 270 and Lb 271 are bills for
      material for the masks at the coronation and at Shrovetide.

14   Folger Library, MS. Lb 269 is the bill for material for a mask on the Sunday after
      the coronation (27 February). The joust is recorded in College of Arms, MS. I 18,
      fols. 94–5, printed in *Literary Remains*, I, p. ccciii.

15   Folger Library, MS. Lb 8, fol. 4. Feuillerat, *Edward VI and Mary*, p. 258, suggests
      that the reference to the bridge is probably to the stairs leading from the Privy
      Garden at Whitehall. The mount was later transported to Blackfriars for storage.

16   College of Arms, MS. I 18, fol. 94, printed in *Literary Remains*, I, p. cccii.

17   *Correspondance Politique de Odet de Selve Ambassadeur de France en Angleterre (1546–1549)*, ed. G. Lefèvre-Pontalis (Paris: F. Alcan, 1888), 105.

18   Folger Library, MS. Lb 8, fols. 1–2, printed in Feuillerat, *Edward VI and Mary*, pp. 3–4.

19   Folger Library, MS. Lb 319 (inventory of 1 April 1547 from which Lb 139 and various other copies derive, including Lb 10 which may be Phillips's personal copy), printed in Feuillerat, *Edward VI and Mary*, pp. 12, 259–60. The authorizing warrant is printed on p. 149. Subdean Gravesend also had possession of playing garments (pp. 13, 260).

20   Folger Library, MS. Lb 8, fol. 3v, printed in Feuillerat, *Edward VI and Mary*, p. 6.

21   The suggestion that the Gentlemen performed *The Story of Orpheus* is based on the wording of the herald's narrative in College of Arms, MS. I 18, fol. 94, printed in *Literary Remains*, I, p. cccii. The reference, however, is imprecise and is more likely to Bellin's coronation mount. There is no evidence to connect the Gentlemen specifically with the revel on Shrove Tuesday which also employed this mount.

22   The document is Guildford Muniment Room, MS. LM 59/145, printed in Feuillerat, *Edward VI and Mary*, pp. 22–4; see his discussion, pp. 256, 263. Henry Brandon, Duke of Suffolk, and Henry Lord Strange were two of the king's companions and school fellows.

23   Guildford Muniment Room, MS. LM 59/146, fols. 8r–v.

24   One of the possible dates for *Old Blind Custom*, the cast list for which is included in Guildford Muniment Room, MS. LM 17, is shortly before the May inventory of 1547. The other date is between December 1545 and August 1546. It appears from an inventory that Northumberland owned a play with this title in 1550. See John N. King, *English Reformation Literature* (Princeton: Princeton University Press, 1982), 274.

25   *Spectacle*, p. 296. For a discussion of patronage and propaganda in this period, see John N. King, *English Reformation Literature* (Princeton: Princeton University Press, 1982), 72–106.

26   *CSP Venetian*, V. no. 703, p. 347.

27   Folger Library, MS. Lb 274, printed in Feuillerat, *Edward VI and Mary*, p. 26. See John N. King, *English Reformation Literature* (Princeton: Princeton University Press, 1982), 168–80, on Protestant influence at court under Somerset's Protectorship.

28   Folger Library, MS. Lb 28, fol. 1, printed in Feuillerat, *Edward VI and Mary*, p. 190.

29   Guildford Muniment Room, MS. LM 59/65, which Feuillerat, *Edward VI and Mary*, p. 251, dates as 1547, but obviously the document belongs to early 1548 by modern dating.

30   R.B. McKerrow, ed., *The Works of Thomas Nash,* (London: Sidgwick & Jackson, 1910), III: 172.
31   Guildford Muniment Room, MS. LM 59/64, printed in Feuillerat, *Edward VI and Mary,* p. 251.
32   Folger Library, MS. Lb 274, printed in Feuillerat, *Edward VI and Mary,* p. 26. Robert Trunckwell claimed to have designed the Tower: BL, Additional MS. Charter, no. 1262.
33   Feuillerat, *Edward VI and Mary,* p. xii. PRO, E101/426/5, fol. 63v, abstracted in Streitberger, *RORD* (1984): 33.
34   Folger Library, MS. Lb 274, printed in Feuillerat, *Edward VI and Mary,* p. 26.
35   BL, Cotton MS. Nero C. X, fol. 13v, printed in *Literary Remains,* II: 221.
36   *APC,* II: 163: warrant of 28 January 1548 for payment of £60 8s. 10d. for pikes, lances, and other necessaries for the triumph at Shrovetide and for weapons at Twelfthtide. Possibly the weapons at Twelfthtide were for a practice. Lawrence Bradshaw's account for the construction is PRO, E351/3326.
37   John Stow, *Annals* (London, 1615), 595.
38   Folger Library, MS. Lb 6, fol. 3, printed in Feuillerat, *Edward VI and Mary,* p. 32.
39   Feuillerat, *Edward VI and Mary,* p. xii, distinguishes this mask of Moors from the mask of men and speculates that it was performed on Shrove Sunday.
40   Folger Library, MS. Lb 290, printed in Feuillerat, *Edward VI and Mary,* p. 33.
41   Folger Library, MS. Lb 6, fol. 2v, printed in Feuillerat, *Edward VI and Mary,* p. 31.
42   Folger Library, MS. Lb 11, fols. 1r–v, printed in Feuillerat, *Edward VI and Mary,* pp. 34–5.
43   PRO, E101/426/6, fol. 30v, abstracted in Streitberger, *RORD* (1984): 34.
44   Folger Library, MS. Lb 11, fols. 2r–v, printed in Feuillerat, *Edward VI and Mary,* pp. 39–40.
45   Folger Library, MS. Lb 12, printed in Feuillerat, *Edward VI and Mary,* pp. 41–3.
46   D.L. Potter, ed., 'Documents Concerning the Negotiation of the Anglo-French Treaty of March 1550,' *Camden Miscellany,* Camden Society, 4th ser., vol. 29 (1984), 59–60. W.K. Jordan, *Edward VI, The Threshold of Power* (Cambridge, Mass.: Harvard University Press, 1970), 119–24.
47   Feuillerat, *Edward VI and Mary,* pp. 270, 274n, wondered if there might have been entertainments at Shrovetide, even though he points out that no accounts survive. Given the elaborate reception and entertainments for the French hostages beginning in April, it is likely that the council simply did not order revels for Shrovetide, but rather concentrated on the entertainments from April through June: BL, Cotton MS. Nero C. X, fol. 20v, printed in *Literary Remains,* II: 263. The hostages who were received on 27 April included Jean de Bourbon, Comte de Soissons and d'Enghien; Francois de Lorraine, Marquis de Mayenne (son of Claude Duc de Guise); and Francois de Montmorency (son of the Constable of

France). They were later joined by Louis Tremoille, Seigneur de la Tremoille; Jean d'Annebaut (son of Claude, Baron de la Hunaudaye, Admiral of France); and Francois de Vendome, Vidame of Chartres: W.K. Jordan, ed., *Chronicle and Political Papers of King Edward VI* (Ithaca, N.Y.: Cornell University Press, 1966), 22n.

48   BL, Cotton MS. Nero C. X, fol. 22, printed in *Literary Remains*, II: 272. The ambassadors were Gaspard de Coligny, Seigneur de Chatillon; Andre Guillart, Seigneur de Mortier; Guillaume Bochetel, Seigneur de Sassy; Francois de Coligny, Seigneur d'Andelot; Henry de Montmorency; Jean Pot de Rhodes, Seigneur de Chemault (ambassador to England in 1551); and Philip Rhinegrave: W.K. Jordan, ed., *Chronicle and Political Papers of King Edward VI* (Ithaca, N.Y.: Cornell University Press, 1966), 31–2.

49   BL, Cotton MS. Nero C. X, fols. 22r–v, printed in *Literary Remains*, II: 273–5. The king provides the names of two of the combatants – Lord Edward Seymour and Sir John Appleby. Pallavicino Rangone, nephew of Count Guido Rangone, was in Edward's personal service: W.K. Jordan, ed., *Chronicle and Political Papers of King Edward VI* (Ithaca, N.Y.: Cornell University Press, 1966), 32–3. The king uses the term 'masquer' to describe a costumed knight in a martial exhibition rather than the older term 'disguised.'

50   BL, Cotton MS. Nero C. X, fol. 22v, printed in *Literary Remains*, II: 275. One of the activities the king records at the wedding celebration on the 4th was one in which 'certain gentlemen that did striue who shuld first take away a goses heade wich was hanged aliue on tow crose postes.'

51   BL, Cotton MS. Nero C. X, fol. 22v, printed in *Literary Remains*, II: 275–6.

52   BL, Cotton MS. Nero C. X, fol. 23, printed in *Literary Remains*, II: 279.

53   BL, Cotton MS. Nero C. X, fol. 23r–v, printed in *Literary Remains*, II: 279. The show consisted of 'a fort made upon a great lighter on the temps wich had three walles and a watch towre in the middes of wich Mr Winter [the King's Surveyor of Ships] was captain *with* forty or fifty other souldiours in yelow and blake. To the fort also apperteined a galey of yelow colour with men and munition in it for defence of the castel. Wherefor ther cam 4 pinnessis with their men in whight ansomely dressed wich entending to geve assault to the castel first drove away the yelow piness and after *with* cloddes, scuibes, canes of fire, dartes made for the nonce and bombardes assauted the castel and at length came with ther pices and burst the utter walles of the castill beating them of the castil in the second ward, who after issued out and drove away the pinnesses sinking one of them, out of wich al the men in it being more than twenty leaped out and swamme in the temps. Then came th'admiral of the navy with three other pinnessis and wanne the castil by assault and burst the top of it downe and toke the captain and undercaptain. Then the admiral went forth to take the yelow ship, and at length clasped

with her toke her and assautid also her toppe, and wane it by composicion and so
returned home.'
54   PRO, E101/426/8.
55   PRO, E101/426/8, abstracted in Streitberger, *RORD* (1984): 36–7. A company
of actors patronized by Edward Seymour (ca. 1500–52), Earl of Hertford (1537),
Lord Protector (1547–9), Duke of Somerset (1547), appear as early as 1536 and
ceased playing after Somerset's execution on 22 January 1552. They are referred
to as the 'late' Duke of Somerset's players because this account was declared after
the Duke's death. Katherine Willoughby (1519–80), wife of Charles Brandon,
Duke of Suffolk, was widowed in 1545 and remarried in 1553. Her step-daughter
Frances, wife of Henry Grey, Duke of Suffolk, held the title until her death in
1559. A company of players was patronized by the Duchess of Suffolk from 1547
to 1553. William Parr, Marquis of Northampton, patronized a group of players
from 1550 to 1553. On these companies, see *Dramatic Records*, pp. 399, 403–4,
408. The Children of Paul's grammar school had performed under the direction
of John Rightwise at court in 1527, but it seems more likely that the group of
Paul's boys giving this performance in 1550 or 1551 was from the choir school,
and was probably under Heywood's and Westcott's direction. The Children of
Paul's performed at Hatfield before Elizabeth in February 1552 and at Nonsuch
in August 1559, under the direction of Heywood and Westcott. It is possible that
these are the twelve children who acted at court in April or May 1553 in Heywood's
play, and they probably acted before Elizabeth and Mary at Hatfield in April 1557.
See Trevor Lennam, *Sebastian Westcott, the Children of Paul's, and the Marriage of
Wit and Science* (Toronto: University of Toronto Press, 1975), 55–7, and Reavley
Gair, 'The Conditions of Appointment for Master of Choristers at Paul's (1553–
1613),' *Notes & Queries*, 225 (1980): 116–19. A dramatic fragment with a note
in Cawarden's hand, 'Parte of a play,' ed. L.A. Cummings, *Records of Early English
Drama Newsletter*, 2, no. 2 (1977): 2–15, and G.R. Proudfoot, *MSC*, IX, which
deals with a theological disagreement, is dated about 1550.
56   Folger Library, MS. Lb 41, fol. 22, printed in Feuillerat, *Edward VI and Mary*,
p. 47.
57   Folger Library, MS. Lb 314, is the best and most complete of a series of certificates (each approximately 24 feet long) subsidiary to the declaration of the
account for all of Cawarden's offices for this period: Lb 315 (imperfect); Lb 316
(abbreviated version of Lb 314); Lb 317 (copy of Lb 316). Feuillerat, *Edward VI
and Mary*, p. 273, abstracts information from these documents about the number
of masks produced in this period.
58   Charges 'forgoten in the last booke' (i.e. Christmas) were included in one of the
books for Shrovetide 1551: Folger Library, MS. Lb 13, fols. 2r–v. The material
includes a dozen lambskin capes, probably for the mask of Moors, Irish swords,

targets, holmaces, and locram, all for the Irish mask, and headpieces, crowns, and mitres 'for playrs,' suggesting that the play in which the king performed on this occasion was on an anti-papal subject.

59   Locram: a linen fabric made in Locronan, Brittany.
60   Folger Library, MS. Lb 41, fols. 22r–v, printed in Feuillerat, *Edward VI and Mary*, pp. 47, 49.
61   BL, Cotton MS. Nero C. X, fol. 31, printed in *Literary Remains*, II: 310.
62   BL, Cotton MS. Nero C. X, fol. 37, printed in *Literary Remains*, II: 330.
63   BL, Cotton MS. Nero C. X, fol. 37v, printed in *Literary Remains*, II: 331.
64   BL, Cotton MS. Nero C. X, fol. 38, printed in *Literary Remains*, II: 331–2.
65   Robert Trunckwell claims to have designed this banqueting house: BL, Additional Charter, no. 1262. Lawrence Bradshaw's expenses were £223 8s. 10d., of which he paid £104 16s. 11 1/2d. and left £118 11s. 10 1/2d. for Cawarden to take care of. Cawarden was furious, and in his letter of 26 October 1551 to Cecil he complains about Bradshaw's handling of the £133 6s. 8d. imprest he had received. Bradshaw's docket did not agree with the particular book of charges he delivered to the Clerk of the Tents and Revels by over £9, and Cawarden had not been able to examine the rest of the particular books in Bradshaw's possession. The result was that the artificers and labourers were now appealing to Cawarden for payment as head of the project, but his imprest was not intended to cover any of Bradshaw's expenses. The matter dragged on for years. Folger Library, MS. Lb 42, fol. 42v, indicates that the bills were still not settled in 1559. For the many accounts documenting the construction of this banqueting house see Principal Sources (in Appendix 1).
66   BL, Cotton MS. Nero C. X, fol. 39v, printed in *Literary Remains*, II: 335.
67   PRO, E101/426/8, abstracted in Streitberger, *RORD* (1984): 37.
68   In October more entertainments were held. On her return from a state visit to France, Mary of Lorraine, daughter of Claude Duke of Guise and mother of Mary Queen of Scots was entertained by Edward at Hampton Court and at Westminster. The council summoned the nobility to attend on 25 October 1551. The king notes that Mary was received on 31 October at Hampton Court, 'which was all hanged with arras, and so was the hall and all the other lodgings of mine in the house finely dressed. And for this night and the next day all was spent in dancing and pastime, as though it were a court, and great presence of gentlemen resorted thither.' On 1 November the queen toured Hampton Court and saw the coursing of deer, and a banquet at which the king kept formal estate was held on the 4th at Westminster. On the 6th, Mary began her progress northward, escorted briefly by Northumberland and other nobles. BL, Cotton MS. Nero C. X, fols. 45v–7, printed in *Literary Remains*, II: 359–64.
69   Folger Library, MS. Lb 275, abstracted in Feuillerat, *Edward VI and Mary*, p. 269.
70   The comprehensive accounts for the combined offices to 1559 are Folger Library,

MSS Lb 41, Lb 42. The heading of the former, which lists Cawarden's offices and responsibilities, is abstracted in Feuillerat, *Edward VI and Mary*, pp. 271–2. On the Privy Chamber in Edward VI's reign see John Murphy, 'The Illusion of Decline,' in David Starkey et al., *The English Court* (London: Longman, 1987), 119–46.

71   Richard Gibson had lent his support to the Toils, ca. 1519: PRO, SP1/232, fol. 176, calendared in *LP, Addenda*, I.i, no. 272. A letter from the council to Cawarden, Guildford Muniment Room, MS. LM 59/1, fol. 1, records his appointment to the office. The council issued an imprest for work in connection with the Toils on 1 July 1552: *APC*, IV: 91.

72   See Chapter 7, notes 13 and 79.

73   Craib, 'Sir Thomas Cawarden,' pp. 22, 24, prints the grant.

74   BL, Additional MS. 30198, fol. 49v; W.C. Richardson, ed., *The Report of the Royal Commission of 1552* (Morgantown, W. Va.: West Virginia University Library, 1974) pp. 196–7.

75   See the discussion of these accounts in Streitberger, *RORD* (1984): 27–9.

76   BL, Lansdowne Roll, no. 14, abstracted in Streitberger, *RORD* (1984): 34–5.

77   PRO, E351/2932, abstracted in Streitberger, *RORD* (1984): 35–6.

78   PRO, E101/426/8, abstracted in Streitberger, *RORD* (1984): 36–41.

79   Bower's patent is dated 31 October 1545: PRO, C66/785, memb. 44, calendared in *LP,* XX.ii, no. 910 (11). His will (PRO, PROB 11/44, fols. 216r–v), dated 18 June, was proved on 25 August 1561. See Hillebrand, *The Child Actors*, pp. 64–73, on his biography.

80   Sir Thomas Chaloner rewarded the King's Players in March for a performance of *Self Love* on Shrove Monday [29 February] 1552 and paid another reward for the players who performed in the mask at dinner: BL, Lansdowne MS. 824, fol. 17.

81   Folger Library, MS. Lb 41, fols. 23–72, printed in Feuillerat, *Edward VI and Mary*, pp. 53–145. Cawarden was, of course, using material from the wardrobes and the Revels storehouse in all of these years, and so the actual cost of these revels was much greater. The extra expenses from December 1551 to May 1553 are the direct result of having to prepare the Lord of Misrule's shows, which required properties and costumes for an enormous number of people.

82   *Grafton's Chronicle*, ed. Sir Henry Ellis (London: J. Johnson, 1809), 526–7; *Spectacle*, p. 303. A similar observation was made in *STC* 15217.5: Thomas Lanquet, *An epitome of cronicles ... To the reigne of Quene Elizabeth*, ed. Robert Crowley (London: T. Marshe, 1559), sig. Eeee3. John N. King, *English Reformation Literature* (Princeton: Princeton University Press, 1982), 181; and see pp. 113–21 on Somerset's imprisonment and death.

83   *Grafton's Chronicle*, ed. Sir Henry Ellis (London: J. Johnson, 1809), 526–7.

84   J.G. Nichols, *Literary Remains*, I, p. clvii, remarks that there is no spark of pity or regret in Edward's entry into his journal about the execution of his uncle. W.K.

Jordan, ed., *Chronicle and Political Papers of King Edward VI* (Ithaca, N.Y.: Cornell University Press, 1966), pp. xxiii and 107, also interprets the absence of an entry in the journal as evidence of the king's lack of warmth and affection. John N. King, *English Reformation Literature* (Princeton: Princeton University Press, 1982), 184, cites BL, Harleian MS. 2194, to demonstrate that Edward was in fact moved by his uncle's death. This anonymous manuscript, written about 1630, entitled 'Lords High Stewards of England,' includes a section on Somerset's trial and execution: fol. 20. The writer notes that the point of the revels was to dispel the king's ill thoughts, because at the mention of Somerset the king would sigh and sometimes cry and express the opinion that his uncle was innocent.

85 On Ferrers's sympathetic treatment of Somerset, see Lily B. Campbell, 'Humphrey Duke of Gloucester and Elianor Cobham His Wife in the *Mirror for Magistrates,*' *Huntington Library Bulletin,* 5 (April, 1934): 119–55.

86 *Chronicle of Queen Jane and Queen Mary,* p. 187.

87 The *Mirror* project was begun before 4 June 1555, and its first edition was suppressed because of its reliance on the work of the Protestant chronicler, Hall. Lily B. Campbell, 'The Suppressed Edition of *A Mirror for Magistrates,*' *Huntington Library Bulletin,* 6 (November, 1934): 1–16.

88 A. Tahler, 'Literary Criticism in *A Mirror for Magistrates,*' *Journal of English and Germanic Philology,* 49 (1950): 8n. On Ferrers's biography, see William Page, ed., *The Victoria History of the County of Hertford* (London: A. Constable, 1908), II: 189–90, in *The Victoria History of the Counties of England,* gen. ed. H.A. Doubleday. On his poetry, see C.S. Lewis, *English Literature in the Sixteenth Century* (Oxford: Clarendon Press, 1954), 241–2. The *Dictionary of National Biography* tries to straighten out the confusion begun by Puttenham between George Ferrers and Edmund Ferris.

89 John N. King, *English Reformation Literature* (Princeton: Princeton University Press, 1982), 76–121, discusses patronage and propaganda in the period.

90 See John N. King, *English Reformation Literature* (Princeton: Princeton University Press, 1982), 358–406, for a discussion of *Beware the Cat.*

91 Cawarden copied the warrants into the heading of his account for these revels. See Folger Library, MS. Lb 41, fol. 40, printed by Feuillerat, *Edward VI and Mary,* p. 62.

92 Chambers, *MS,* I: 405, observed that there were jealousies and conflicts of authority. Welsford, *The Court Masque,* p. 145, and Anglo, *Spectacle,* p. 305, follow Chambers.

93 Folger Library, MS. Lb 257, printed in Feuillerat, *Edward VI and Mary,* p. 56.

94 Folger Library, MS. Lb 277, printed in Feuillerat, *Edward VI and Mary,* p. 57.

95 Folger Library, MS. Lb 278, printed in Feuillerat, *Edward VI and Mary,* p. 57.

96 Folger Library, MS. Lb 282, printed by Feuillerat, *Edward VI and Mary,* p. 86.

97   The officers' own work is mentioned in their account (Folger Library, MS. Lb 41, fol. 41, printed in Feuillerat, *Edward VI and Mary*, p. 62). The warrant from the king for the joust is Folger Library, MS. Lb 16, printed in Feuillerat, *Edward VI and Mary*, p. 56. The joust was held on 3 January, in which eighteen answerers ran six courses apiece against the four challengers. The tourney was held on the 6th, in which twenty answerers 'fought right well,' according to the king. Yet another joust was held on the 17th in which Warwick and five companions won against Ambrose Dudley and five of his companions. BL, Cotton MS. Nero C. X, fols. 48v, 51, 51v, 52, printed in *Literary Remains*, II: 368, 387–8, 389.

98   Folger Library, MS. Lb 281, printed in Feuillerat, *Edward VI and Mary*, pp. 58–9.

99   Folger Library, MS. Lb 285, printed in Feuillerat, *Edward VI and Mary*, pp. 59–60. The letter was followed by a warrant from the council dated the morning of 3 January: Folger Library, MS. Lb 286.

100   Folger Library, MS. Lb 292, fol. 1, printed in Feuillerat, *Edward VI and Mary*, pp. 89–90. An imprest of £100 against expenses was issued by the council to Ferrers on 30 November 1552: *APC*, IV: 181. This was followed by a warrant from the council to Cawarden on 21 December to furnish Ferrers and his band with all necessaries from the office and in addition 'what soeuer wanteth in *the* same to take order that it be prouided accordingly by your discretion': Folger Library, MS. Lb 41, fol. 51, printed in Feuillerat, *Edward VI and Mary*, pp. 95. The warrant was copied into the Revels account to justify Cawarden's expenses, which ran over £400.

101   Anglo, *Spectacle*, p. 311, suggests that the *moon* in 1551–2 and *vastuum vacuum* in 1552–3 may have been pageants, but there is no record of their construction in the Revels accounts.

102   Folger Library, MS. Lb 292, fols. 1v–2, printed in Feuillerat, *Edward VI and Mary*, pp. 89–90. However, Ferrers received only four costumes according to the list of garments sent by the Revels: Folger Library, MS. Lb 320, printed in Feuillerat, *Edward VI and Mary*, pp. 117–19.

103   Folger Library, MS. Lb 289, printed in Feuillerat, *Edward VI and Mary*, pp. 90–1.

104   Folger Library, MS. Lb 277, printed in Feuillerat, *Edward VI and Mary*, p. 58.

105   The date of the event is fixed by a letter from Ferrers to Cawarden requesting him to pay for the sixty staves which were used (Feuillerat, *Edward VI and Mary*, p. 94; see p. 113 for the carriage charges) and the Tents account which shows the repair and modification of a toil to serve for the Lord of Misrule's joust (Folger Library, MS. Lb 41, fol 61v).

106   Folger Library, MS. Lb 285, printed in Feuillerat, *Edward VI and Mary*, p. 59.

107   Folger Library, MS. Lb 289 and Guildford Muniment Room, MS. LM 128/13, printed in Feuillerat, *Edward VI and Mary*, pp. 90–1. Chambers, *ES*, IV: 140, took the phrase 'betwin Newers Day and Twelfe Day' found in the Jacobean

Revels accounts to indicate that accounts were made retrospectively, but it is
clear from the dates in the Revels accounts for this year that the retrospect could
be as short as the few months between making up the particular books and
incorporating them into the comprehensive ledgers. See also Feuillerat, *Edward
VI and Mary*, pp. 117–18.

108   Folger Library, MS. Lb 280 and Guildford Muniment Room, MS. LM 59/147,
printed in Feuillerat, *Edward VI and Mary*, pp. 82–4. The warrant from the
king of 24 November (Folger Library, MS. Lb 16) specifies that the Revels use
such 'olde stufe' as they had on hand to make the bases. Guildford Muniment
Room, MS. LM 59/147 is the list of the rich hangings which they took from the
king's timber houses to make the properties.

109   Feuillerat, *Edward VI and Mary*, pp. xii, 59, 277, who thinks that the combat
may be identical to the Midsummer Night Festival. See also Chambers, *MS*, II:
382–3.

110   Alfred J. Kempe, *The Loseley Manuscripts* (London: J. Murray, 1835), 87. The
incomplete warrant from the council (Folger Library, MS. Lb 293 and Guildford Muniment Room, MS. LM 59/151, printed in Feuillerat, *Edward VI and
Mary*, p. 92) must relate to 1551–2, as Feuillerat, p. 283, himself recognized,
and as Anglo, *Spectacle*, p. 307n, has pointed out.

111   Folger Library, MS. Lb 41, fol. 61, printed in Feuillerat, *Edward VI and Mary*,
p. 107.

112   Machyn, *Diary*, pp. 13–14.

113   Machyn, *Diary*, pp. 28–9. Folger Library, MS. Lb 327, printed in Feuillerat,
Edward VI and Mary, pp. 77–81, shows that the Revels Office used 10 1/2
pounds of silver and 34 pounds of gold to coin money for the Lord of Misrule.

114   Machyn, *Diary*, p. 14.

115   BL, Cotton MS. Nero C. X, fols. 51v–2, printed in *Literary Remains*, II: 387–8.

116   Folger Library, MS. Lb 288, printed in Feuillerat, *Edward VI and Mary*, p. 60.
Wallace, *Evolution*, p. 74, attributed *Youth and Riches* to Heywood, but Reed
and others have pointed out that there is no evidence for such an attribution.
As Feuillerat, *Edward VI and Mary*, pp. 268–9, also observes, the reference to
the 'playe of Yeowthe' found in the margins to one of the documents (printed,
pp. 190–4; Guildford Muniment Room, MS. LM 59/148 is an imperfect copy)
is probably a reference to *Youth and Riches*. Chaloner was one of the clerks of the
council and held a position in the Exchequer. On his reward to the King's Players in March for a performance of *Self Love* on Shrove Monday (9 February), see
note 80.

117   Folger Library, MS. Lb 41, fols. 48v–9v, abstracted in Feuillerat, *Edward VI and
Mary*, p. 85.

118   William Baldwin, *Beware the Cat and The Funerals of King Edward The Sixth*, ed.

William P. Holden, Connecticut College Monograph, No. 8 (New London, Conn., 1963), 9, 27. Streamer was probably Gregory Streamer, a clergyman, whom Baldwin satirized in *Beware the Cat*. See also *A Short Answer* printed in Holden, pp. 94–5.

119   Lily B. Campbell, 'The Lost Play of Aesop's Crow,' *Modern Language Notes*, 49 (1934): 454–7, points out a passage in Foxe in which the structure of the mass is said to be 'not much unlike the crow of Esope,' and concludes that the play was on the subject of the Mass.

120   Folger Library, MS. Lb 294, printed in Feuillerat, *Edward VI and Mary*, p. 93.

121   Folger Library, MS. Lb 501, printed in Feuillerat, *Edward VI and Mary*, pp. 93–4.

122   Folger Library, MS. Lb 41, fol. 55v, printed in Feuillerat, *Edward VI and Mary*, p. 107.

123   Welsford, *Court Masque*, p. 147. But the Marshall was not played by Ferrers, as is clear from the cast list. See also *Spectacle*, p. 313.

124   Welsford, *Court Masque*, p. 147. When Feuillerat, *Edward VI and Mary*, p. xiii, lists the masks for this season, he enumerates them as if each was a separate entertainment. Anglo, *Spectacle*, p. 311, lists even more from the references in the accounts. But it is clear that the masks listed by the Revels officers in this account were sets of costumes.

125   Feuillerat, *Edward VI and Mary*, pp. 286, identifies the 'pollenders' with the 'grasiers' mentioned in John Holt's expenses (p. 109), and also suggests that the 'savage heades' (p. 116) were used in this mask for their torch bearers based on the fact that there were six rather than eight of them made. The number of head-pieces, or any other properties listed in the accounts, rarely tallies with the num-ber of principals in the entertainments, as Anglo, *Spectacle*, p. 311n, recognizes. I do not think that the 'pollenders' can be identified with the graziers. The 'pol-lenders' were probably Polanders who had soldiers as torch bearers. The graziers are identified as 'Gentlemen of the Country' in an inventory of 1559: Feuillerat, *Elizabeth*, pp. 26, 28, 42; Chambers, *ES*, I: 157, suggested that they may have been used as presenters for the double mask at West Horsley in 1559. The gra-ziers more properly fit into a rural setting. They were probably the covetous men who had 'babions,' for whom the savage heads were made as well as the furred gloves 'like cattes fete & paws,' as their torch bearers (p. 106).

126   There is much that we do not know about the revels in both of these years. The Lord of Misrule had an ape for which costumes were made. He also had a num-ber of 'disards', as well as fools for his base sons, and one member of the King's Players acted the part of his heir apparent. The Revels accounts are detailed, but there are no narrative descriptions which would permit a full reconstruction. John Smith, King's Player in 1547, was the Lord of Misrule's disard. Elderton (William Elderton?, the ballad writer, d. ca. 1592), Parkins (John Parkyn?, one

of the Earl of Leicester's Players in 1572–3), and Seame were his base sons. A Henry Byrche (George and John Birche were King's Players at this time) picked up some of the material from the Revels Office for the Lord of Misrule.

127   *APC*, IV: 210.

128   Folger Library, MS. Lb 41, fol. 70v, printed in Feuillerat, *Edward VI and Mary*, p. 141. Holt's expenses (Folger Library, MS. Lb 23, fol. 1) show charges before Shrovetide for 'Hawad*es* play and the yryshe playe,' the former a reference to Heywood's play (but the temptation to read 'Herrod*es*' is strong; cf, *Catalog of Manuscripts of the Folger Shakespeare Library, Washington, D.C.* [Boston: G.K. Hall, 1971], II. 76), and the latter to Baldwin's.

129   Folger Library, MS. Lb 41, fol. 70v, printed in Feuillerat, *Edward VI and Mary*, p. 141.

130   Folger Library, MS. Lb 41, fol. 71, printed in Feuillerat, *Edward VI and Mary*, p. 142.

131   Folger Library, MS. Lb 41, fol. 65v, printed in Feuillerat, *Edward VI and Mary*, p. 134.

132   Folger Library, MS. Lb 41, fols. 70v–1v, printed in Feuillerat, *Edward VI and Mary*, pp. 142–3. Feuillerat, p. 288, took exception to Wallace's suggestion that Baldwin worked on the properties himself, arguing that he was simply paying for material and workmanship through the Revels Office.

133   Folger Library, MS. Lb 41, fols. 64, 67r–v, printed in Feuillerat, *Edward VI and Mary*, pp. 130, 135–6. Furrier's charges for the apes are contained in Folger Library, MS. Lb 162.

134   Folger Library, MS. Lb 41, fol. 65v, printed in Feuillerat, *Edward VI and Mary*, p. 133.

135   Folger Library, MS. Lb 41, fol. 66, printed in Feuillerat, *Edward VI and Mary*, p. 134. Folger Library, MS. Lb 124 is one of Carrow's bills for this mask.

136   Folger Library, MS. Lb 41, fol. 66, printed in Feuillerat, *Edward VI and Mary*, p. 134.

137   Folger Library, MS. Lb 41, fols. 65v–6, 68v, printed in Feuillerat, *Edward VI and Mary*, pp. 133–4, 138. For the inventory, see Feuillerat, *Elizabeth*, p. 20.

138   Wallace, *Evolution*, p. 76; Anglo, *Spectacle*, p. 316. Feuillerat, *Edward VI and Mary*, pp. 277, 287–8, rightly objected to Wallace's suggestion.

139   Folger Library, MS. Lb 41, fol. 65, printed in Feuillerat, *Edward VI and Mary*, p. 132.

140   See D. MacCullouch, ed., *The Vita Mariae Angliae Reginae of Robert Wingfield of Brantham, Camden Miscellany*, Camden Society, 4th ser., vol. 29 (London, 1984), 246–9, on Northumberland's manipulations of the king on the matter of the succession. See also Machyn, *Diary*, pp. 35–6. Documents relating to changes in the king's will are printed in *Chronicle of Queen Jane and Queen Mary*, pp. 85–102.

141 *Vita Mariae*, p. 245. See note 140.
142 Neither Feuillerat, who prints his excerpt from Jeaffreson's calendar in *RCHM*, VII: 608b, in *Edward VI and Mary*, p. 306, nor I could find the document among the Loseley papers.
143 *Vita Mariae*, p. 246. See note 140.
144 *Vita Mariae*, p. 246. See Note 140.

CHAPTER 9

1   See D. MacCulloch, ed., *The Vita Mariae Angliae Reginae of Robert Wingfield of Brantham, Camden Miscellany*, Camden Society, 4th ser., vol. 29 (London, 1984), 196–293, and *Chronicle of Queen Jane and Queen Mary*, pp. 1–13, on events surrounding Northumberland's failed attempt to place Lady Jane Grey on the throne and on Mary's accession.

2   *Chronicle of Queen Jane and Queen Mary*, pp. 27–30, is the most complete account of the pageants for the coronation entry. For other sources, see McGee and Meagher, 'Checklist,' pp. 104–5.

3   The warrant dated 26 September 1553 is Loseley Manor Documents, vol. V, no. 6, Folger Library, MS. Lb 25 (copy), which is copied into the main Revels account, Lb 41, fol. 73, printed in Feuillerat, *Edward VI and Mary*, p. 149. John Holt lists charges for this play twice: 'a playe for the gentyllmen of the chapell' and, then, 'the second charges of *that* play at xpenmas,' in addition to the charges for attendance at court for the usual twelve days: Folger Library, MS. Lb 23.

4   Folger Library, MS. Lb 41, fol. 73, printed in Feuillerat, *Edward VI and Mary*, p. 149.

5   PRO, SP11/8/50, calendared in *CSP Domestic, 1547–1580*, p. 82. *APC*, V: 234, 237–8; VI: 102, 110, 118–19, 148–9, 168, 169.

6   PRO, E101/427/5, no. 9, printed in Feuillerat, *Edward VI and Mary*, pp. 289–90.

7   Folger Library, MS. Lb 41, fol. 74v, printed in Feuillerat, *Edward VI and Mary*, p. 152.

8   Hillebrand, *The Child Actors*, pp. 65–9. Wallace, *Evolution*, pp. 96–7, would credit them with *Roister Doister* as well, but few would agree that play was performed at court in this season. Wallace suggests that *Respublica* and *Roister Doister* are indicated as productions superintended by the Revels Office, but the Revels account does not support such a suggestion. The dating of *Roister Doister* is problematical. William Peery, 'The Prayer for the Queen in *Roister Doister*,' *University of Texas Studies in English*, 17 (1948): 222–3, also dates the performance at Christmas 1553–4. William L. Edgerton, *Nicholas Udall* (New York: Twayne Publishers, 1965), 89–94, dates the performance at Windsor Castle

before Edward VI in September 1552. For other dates, see Edgerton, p. 123n. Feuillerat, *Edward VI and Mary*, p. 290, states that 'another document' (probably Folger Library, MS. Lb 302, fol. 5v), which records garments for a play by the Children of the Chapel, relates to *Humanum Genus*, and shows that 'Children' and 'Gentlemen' were used synonymously. I have not come across any evidence to confirm this interchangeable use of the terms. Moreover, this document is an office book which was used as a draft for part of Lb 41. The section in which the entry occurs is dated 'the first year.' However, the first item mentioned is the mask of mariners which was not shown until November 1554, after the marriage of Philip and Mary. It is followed by the entry about players' garments for the Children of the Chapel. It is entirely possible that the entry refers to Christmas 1554–5, the season in which the Revels staged Udall's plays, and not to Christmas 1553–4. See also Trevor Lennam, *Sebastian Westcott, the Children of Paul's, and The Marriage of Wit and Science* (Toronto: University of Toronto Press, 1975), 55–6.

9   The arguments for attributing *Respublica* to Udall are found in L.A. Magnus, ed., *Respublica*, Early English Text Society, e.s., vols. 94, 98, 99 (London, 1905), and W.W. Greg, ed., *Respublica*, Early English Text Society, o.s., vol. 226 (London, 1952). William L. Edgerton, *Nicholas Udall* (New York: Twayne Publishers, 1965), pp. 65–6, doubts the attribution.

10   Machyn, *Diary*, p. 51.

11   *STC* 12152: Richard Grafton, *Abridgement of the Chronicles of England* (London, 1572), fol. 181.

12   Wriothesley, *Chronicle*, II: 112–17. *Acts and Monuments*, VI: 549.

13   The pardon is PRO, C66/722, memb. 32, calendared in *LP,* XVIII.ii, no. 241 (6). The incident appears to have been a political plot undertaken by Stephen Gardiner, Bishop of Winchester, in the early 1540s to undermine the group of radical Protestants appointed by Cromwell to the king's Privy Chamber. Cawarden was praised by Foxe, *Acts and Monuments*, VIII: 558, as one of those who helped to preserve the brethren during this period and mentions the 'congregation at master Carden's house.' 'Sir Thomas Cardine and his wife' are also listed as among those 'persecuted' at Windsor in 1543: *Acts and Monuments*, V: 464. The victim in the plot was Anthony Person who was executed for preaching sermons aginst the sacrament, and Cawarden and his wife were accused as his chief 'aiders, helpers, and maintainers.' After the condemnation of Person, Cawarden undertook to delay and even to kidnap Robert Occam, one of the Bishop's messengers: *Acts and Monuments*, V: 473, 494–5. In an inquiry into the matter, the Earl of Warwick testified that the Bishop of Winchester was 'a secret worker' in the plot to indict Cawarden, as the chief Gentleman of the king's Privy Chamber, along with others for heresy and to conceal this information from the king: *Acts and Monuments*, VI: 179.

14 Following Stow's hints, George Chalmers, *A Supplemental Apology for Believers in the Shakespeare-papers* (London: T. Egerton, 1799), Appendix, p. 193, suggested that Cawarden's problems stem entirely from his treatment of the parishioners of St Anne's. Chambers, *Tudor Revels*, pp. 14–16; and Irwin Smith, *Shakespeare's Blackfriars Playhouse* (New York: New York University Press, 1964), 121–2, follow Chalmers and ignore A.J. Kempe, *The Loseley Manuscripts* (London: J. Murray, 1835), 17, and Craib, 'Sir Thomas Cawarden,' whose comments on the matter are based on their reading of the documents.

15 John Stow, *A Survey of London*, ed. C.L. Kingsford (Oxford: Clarendon Press, 1908), I: 341.

16 Folger Library, MS. Lb 4; Craib, 'Sir Thomas Cawarden,' p. 16. The Privy Council sent letters to gentlemen and officers in Surrey on 16 July 1553 affirming Lady Jane Grey's title to the throne (Guildford Muniment Room, MS. LM Correspondence 3/3). Cawarden's response to this is not extant; neither is his response to the letter of 19 July 1553 (Loseley Manors Documents, vol. XII, no. 139, calendared in *RCHM*, VII: 610b, printed in A.J. Kempe, *The Loseley Manuscripts* [London: J. Murray, 1835], 131–2) from Lord Abergavenny and others informing him that they had proclaimed Mary queen and had denounced Queen Jane. They required him to do the same.

17 Craib, 'Sir Thomas Cawarden,' pp. 16–17.

18 Craib, 'Sir Thomas Cawarden,' p. 26. The order to the Sheriff of Surrey to confiscate his arms and horses was issued on 26 January 1554: Folger Library, MSS Lb 58, Lb 70, Lb 74, printed in A.J. Kempe, *The Loseley Manuscripts* (London: J. Murray, 1835), 133–9.

19 The charge of being indebted to the Crown is Loseley Manor Documents, vol. III, no. 6, printed in A.J. Kempe, *The Loseley Manuscripts* (London: J. Murray, 1835), 139–40; Craib, 'Sir Thomas Cawarden,' p. 17. Thomas White's confession and deposition are PRO, SP11/7, fols. 87, 90, calendared in *CSP Domestic, 1547–1580*, p. 77. The list of questions posed to one 'Rosary' in March 1556 and the examination of John Dethick in April are PRO, SP11/7, fol. 111, SP11/8, fol. 23, calendared in *CSP Domestic, 1547–1580*, pp. 78–9.

20 *APC*, V: 372.

21 *APC*, V: 305.

22 *APC*, VI: 86, 103.

23 *APC*, VI: 123. Browne's eulogy is Folger Library, MS. Lb 519.

24 *Chronicle of Queen Jane and Queen Mary*, pp. 137–43. Wriothesley, *Chronicle*, II: 120–1. *CSP Spanish*, XIII, no. 11.

25 The council wrote to Cawarden about banqueting houses and other devices of pleasure on 18 June 1554: Loseley Manor Documents, vol. III, no. 3, calendared in *RCHM*, VII: 611a. There are no charges for Revels in the accounts, but the

Tents sent two hales and six round houses for Philip's reception. Folger Library, MS. Lb 41, fol. 14. See *Chronicle of Queen Jane and Queen Mary*, pp. 134–6, for other council orders.

26   The description in *Holinshed's Chronicles of England, Scotland, and Ireland*, ed. Sir Henry Ellis (London: J. Johnson, 1808), IV: 61, suggests popular entertainments.

27   *Chronicle of Queen Jane and Queen Mary*, p. 143. Machyn, *Diary*, p. 66.

28   On the sources for the entry, see McGee and Meagher, 'Checklist,' pp. 106–7, and for a discussion, see Anglo, *Spectacle*, pp. 327–39.

29   *CSP Spanish*, XIII, nos. 53, 56, 60, 148, 149, 161, 164. *Chronicle of Queen Jane and Queen Mary*, p. 81. Machyn, *Diary*, pp. 79, 86, 96.

30   Folger Library, MS. Lb 42, fol. 63, printed in Feuillerat, *Edward VI and Mary*, p. 180. The torch bearers were also costumed as mariners in silk, sarcenet, and taffeta.

31   Revels were occasionally held late at night in other reigns, but the Revels accounts make a particular point of noting the lateness of the revels at Mary's court. Around 11 November, a mask was also held at Arundel place. Henry Lord Maltravers and John Lord Lumley requested to borrow 'one maske' of 'Alamains' from Cawarden or, if not that, something else that he had in 'fayre' condition for the unspecified occasion: Folger Library, MS. Lb 499, printed in Feuillerat, *Edward VI and Mary*, p. 249.

32   BL, Lansdowne MS. 3, art. 44, printed in Feuillerat, *Edward VI and Mary*, p. 292. Lord Howard of Effingham was Lord Admiral from 20 March 1554 to 1558. Yaxly goes on to say that 'Vppon thursday next there shalbe in Smithfield *Giuoco di Canne* where the King and Quene wolbe.'

33   Machyn, *Diary*, pp. 75–6.

34   Machyn, *Diary*, pp. 76–7.

35   Machyn, *Diary*, p. 77.

36   Folger Library, MS. Lb 41, fols. 87–8, printed in Feuillerat, *Edward VI and Mary*, p. 292. Carrow's bill for the lions' heads and other material is Folger Library, MS. Lb 145.

37   The warrant, dated 8 December 1554, is Loseley Manor Documents, vol. VI, no. 7, and Folger Library, MS. Lb 26 (copy on skin), which is copied into the main account, Folger Library, MS. Lb 41, fol. 78, printed in Feuillerat, *Edward VI and Mary*, pp. 159–60. One of the drafts for the warrant (Folger Library, MS. Lb 27) is addressed to the Master of 'our revells for the tyme beinge and to his deputye or deputes,' suggesting either that Cawarden had not yet recovered from his illness of June 1554 or that the queen and council were considering removing him from office. The draft is significant, for it states that the Master was to use the royal right of purveyance. Udall was to be provided with whatever he needed to stage his plays 'not only of soche Store as ye have allredy remayninge within our offices

of revells and tentes butt also in the lacke therof to make *provision* bye or take vp in o*ur* name and for vs all that shalbe necessary.' The draft was altered in the final version, which omits mention of the right of purveyance. The Revels eventually spent £44 4*s.* 11*d.* to produce these plays.

38   Folger Library, MS. Lb 41, fol. 81v, printed in Feuillerat, *Edward VI and Mary,* pp. 168. A description of their costumes in included in the inventory printed on pp. 181, 183.

39   Folger Library, MS. Lb 41, fol. 81v, printed in Feuillerat, *Edward VI and Mary,* p. 168. A description of their costumes in included in the inventory printed on p. 185.

40   Folger Library, MS. Lb 28, fol. 4, printed in Feuillerat, *Edward VI and Mary,* p. 193; Lb 29 (copy), Guildford Muniment Room, MS. LM 59/148 (copy with different notes).

41   Folger Library, MS. Lb 41, fols. 83–5, printed in Feuillerat, *Edward VI and Mary,* pp. 172–7. Their garments are described in the inventory printed on pp. 181–2.

42   Folger Library, MSS Lb 140 and Lb 145 are property bills for these masks, and Lb 279 is a draft of an account for the 'mask' of Turks. Garments are listed in the inventory printed in Feuillerat, *Edward VI and Mary,* pp. 184–5.

43   Machyn, *Diary,* p. 79.

44   Machyn, *Diary,* p. 80.

45   Machyn, *Diary,* p. 84.

46   Folger Library, MS. Lb 41, fols. 16v–18, is the warrant and pay book for work by the Tents from 8 May to 15 June for setting up hales and supplying furniture for the negotiations by Cardinal Pole to achieve peace between France and the Empire.

47   Machyn, *Diary,* p. 82.

48   Machyn, *Diary,* p. 76.

49   Machyn, *Diary,* p. 401.

50   *CSP Spanish,* XIII, no. 111.

51   The Revels account for work during this period is Folger Library, MS. Lb 42, fols. 19–21, printed in Feuillerat, *Edward VI and Mary,* pp. 199–202.

52   Hugh Rodes wrote *The Song of the Chyldbysshop, as it was songe before the queenes maiestie in her priuie chamber at her manour of saynt James in the Feeldes on saynt Nicholas day [6 December] and Innocents day [28 December] this yeare nowe present, by the chyld bysshope of Poules churche with his company.* The document, first printed by Thomas Warton, *History of English Poetry,* ed. W. Carew Hazlitt (London: Reeves and Turner, 1871), IV: 237, and reprinted by Feuillerat, *Edward VI and Mary,* pp. 292–3, is dated 1555. There are three vestments for St Nicholas mentioned in one of the Revels accounts and in the inventory of May 1555

(cf. Feuillerat, pp. 190, 292–3). Chambers, *MS*, I: 367, suggests that 1554 is the earliest date for the revival of the ceremony, and it is possible that Mary saw it in December 1554 as well.

53   The accounts for Candlemas and Shrovetide are Folger Library, MS. Lb 42, fols. 21v–2v, 23–4, printed in Feuillerat, *Edward VI and Mary*, pp. 203–8.

54   Folger Library, MS. Lb 298, printed in Feuillerat, *Edward VI and Mary*, pp. 215–17.

55   Feuillerat, *Edward VI and Mary*, p. 302, points out that Christmas Eve fell on a Tuesday in 1555–6, but then argues that the endorsement of 1556 shows that the play was probably prepared by the Revels at Christmas 1556–7. As Anglo, *Spectacle*, p. 341n, observes, Feuillerat's argument is inconclusive. Baldwin offered first choice to Cawarden because of their earlier association at court. Cawarden had asked to produce more of Baldwin's work in 1552–3, approximately three years before the Christmas season of 1555–6. Further, the play was new and in demand by one of the Inns of Court, and the actors were rehearsing and would be ready to perform it within ten days, or by 3 January. The endorsement probably refers to the account for this year which ran from 11 December 1555 to June 1556. It is likely that Baldwin's play was produced for Christmas 1555–6, some time after 3 January.

56   William P. Holden, ed., *Beware the Cat and The Funerals of King Edward VI*, Connecticut College Monograph, no. 8 (New London, Conn., 1963), 9, 68, 91.

57   Folger Library, MS. Lb 298, printed in Feuillerat, *Edward VI and Mary*, p. 215.

58   Folger Library, MS. Lb 42, fols. 27–8v, printed in Feuillerat, *Edward VI and Mary*, pp. 218–20.

59   Folger Library, MS. Lb 42, fols. 29r–v, printed in Feuillerat, *Edward VI and Mary*, pp. 221–2.

60   Folger Library, MS. Lb 42, fols. 30r–v, printed in Feuillerat, *Edward VI and Mary*, pp. 223–4.

61   Guildford Muniment Room, Loseley Correspondence 2/5, printed in Feuillerat, *Edward VI and Mary*, pp. 245, 304, who dates this letter in the spring of 1557.

62   Bodleian Library, MS. Engl. Poet. d. 13, fol. 15, printed in George Chalmers, *An Apology for the Believers in the Shakespeare-papers* (London, T. Egerton 1797; reprint A.M. Kelley, 1971), 478n, and Feuillerat, *Edward VI and Mary*, pp. 302–3, the queen's warrant of 30 April 1557 to Sir Edward Walgrave, Master of the Great Wardrobe, for 'a notorious maske of Alamaynes pilgrymes and Irishemen,' orders the provision of silks and other material listed in the warrant for the Revels. On its authenticity, see Feuillerat, p. 303.

63   The main Revels account for their work from 9 to 16 April is Folger Library, MS. Lb 42, fols. 31–2v, printed in Feuillerat, *Edward VI and Mary*, pp. 225–8. The Revels hired some garments from Christopher Milliner, who was still in business at this late date, and altered them into costumes for pilgrims. For a description of

the costumes, see Feuillerat, *Elizabeth*, pp. 23, 24, 41. Folger Library, MSS Lb 134 and Lb 301 are bills for material delivered to Cawarden for this mask.

64   The account for Christmas 1557–8 is Folger Library, MS. Lb 42, fols. 35–6, printed in Feuillerat, *Edward VI and Mary*, pp. 235–6. Why the designers did not work at Blackfriars in the five great rooms rented by the office (Feuillerat, *Edward VI and Mary*, p. 210) is not clear.

65   PRO, E36/219.

66   The payment to Thurgoode is PRO, E36/219, fol. 71v. His account, fol. 78, for 1520–1 is transcribed by Collier, *HEDP* (1831), I: 89–91.

67   Collier, *HEDP* (1831), I: 91–2. Collier also thought that this Haulte was the same 'Master of the Revels' at Henry VII's court and in Elizabeth of York's household. That Jaques Haulte was dead by 1508.

68   PRO, E36/219, fol. 78, abstracted in *HEDP* (1831), I: 90.

69   BL, Cotton MS. Vespasian F. XIII, fol. 240.

70   *Holinshed's Chronicles of England, Scotland, and Ireland*, ed. Sir Henry Ellis (London: J. Johnson, 1808), IV: 6. Mary's Privy Purse accounts from December 1536 to May 1539, BL, Royal MS. 17. B. XXVIII, are printed by F. Madden, *Privy Purse Expenses of the Princess Mary* (London: W. Pickering, 1830).

71   Anglo, *Spectacle*, p. 340n.

72   The practice of translating garments was still an ordinary means of achieving economy, as is clear from Edward VI's warrant to the Revels to use old material for bards and bases for the joust at Christmas 1551–2. The inventory of 1555 (Folger Library, MS. Lb 42, fols. 63–8v, printed in Feuillerat, *Edward VI and Mary*, pp. 180–9), which was to be certified by the Comptroller, Lord Chamberlain, and other commissioners appointed for the purpose, shows that there was some concern at higher levels about expenses. The concern with economy continued under Elizabeth. Folger Library, MS. Lb 106, 4 February 1560, (Lb 305 and Lb 306 are documents related to the attempt to settle the demands of the inferior officers after Cawarden's death) is a careful analysis of the Revels accounts from 1557 to 1560, made for the purpose of reviewing the expenses of the office.

73   *APC*, VII: 6, 11–12. Loseley Manor Documents, vol. VI, no. 8, calendared in *RCHM*, VII: 614a, and A.J. Kempe, *The Loseley Manuscripts* (London: J. Murray, 1835), 173–4, is the signet letter of 1 November 1558 appointing Cawarden, Sir Edward Warner, and Sir Robert Oxenbridge to the charge of the Tower. PRO, SP12/1/127, calendared in *CSP Domestic, 1547–1580*, p. 116, lists Cawarden's charges for himself and one hundred men serving at the Tower from 19 November to 12 December 1558. Loseley Manor Documents, vol. VI, no. 9, calendared in *RCHM*, VII: 614b, is the warrant relieving Cawarden as Lieutenant of the Tower on 10 December 1558.

74   Folger Library, MS. Lb 42, fols. 41–3v (Christmas), fols. 45–7v (Coronation),

printed in Feuillerat, *Elizabeth*, pp. 79–84, 84–9, who does not list any of the masks produced at Christmas.

75   Chambers, *ES*, IV: 77.

76   Guildford Muniment Room, MS. LM 59/170, calendared in Streitberger, *RORD* (1986–7): 41.

77   *CSP Venetian*, VII, no. 10. John Carrow, property maker, made seven 'visars with byrd*es*' on them for one of the masks (Folger Library, MS. Lb 42, fol. 42, printed in Feuillerat, *Elizabeth*, p. 81. Feuillerat, p. 445, insists on glossing 'byrd*es*' as 'beards.' It is the usual formula in earlier accounts, but it seems likely in this case to refer to the face masks of the cardinals. John Carrow's property bill for these masks (Folger Library, MS. Lb 179) lists visors 'with bird*es* vppon them.'

78   *CSP Venetian*, VII, no. 10.

79   Folger Library, MS. Lb 33. The officers were to select garments which will 'take lest hurte by vse.' MS. Lb 109 is the indenture which lists the garments and properties in detail. Both documents are printed by D. Bergeron, *English Literary Renaissance*, 8 (1978): 4–5. MSS. Lb 119, 120 (drafts), and 121 are warrants to the Great Wardrobe for the coronation and for the triumph afterwards (i.e. the tournament on the 16th and 17th).

80   *STC* 12152: Richard Grafton, *Abridgement of the Chronicles of England* (London, 1572), fols. 195r–v. One of the main narrative sources for the coronation entry procession is a pamphlet printed by Richard Tottell entitled, *The Quenes maiesties passage through the citie of London* .... (London, 1559). On these and other sources, see McGee and Meagher, 'Checklist,' *RORD*, 24 (1981): 58–62, and for a discussion, see Anglo, *Spectacle*, pp. 344–59.

81   Scott McMillin, 'The Queen's Men and the London Theatre of 1583,' in *The Elizabethan Theatre X*, ed. C.E. McGee (Port Credit, Ontario: P.D. Meany, 1988), 1–17, discusses the uses of the newly created Queen's Players in the 1580s.

82   Folger Library, MS. Lb 42, fol. 47, printed in Feuillerat, *Elizabeth*, p. 88. There was a mask the day after and another seven days after the coronation. There is no indication that a mask was produced for Candlemas.

83   Chambers, *ES*, IV: 77, gives the date of the second mask incorrectly as 29 January, and correctly as 22 January in *ES*, I: 156.

84   Folger Library, MS. Lb 111 is the Yeoman's bill for work on 2 January for a mask at Shrovetide and for one at the coronation, in which hoods and caps for monks and friars are mentioned. Folger Library, MSS Lb 34 and Lb 148, are also related to work between 2 January and 8 February.

85   *CSP Venetian*, VII, no. 18. The Revels account for Shrovetide is Folger Library, MS. Lb 42, fols. 49–52, printed in Feuillerat, *Elizabeth*, pp. 90–6. The mask of 'swartrutters' on Shrove Sunday is mentioned on p. 94.

86   Chambers, *ES*, I: 156.

87   Guildford Muniment Room, MS. LM 59/169 is a bill for a mask of mariners and fisherwives on Shrove Tuesday. Folger Library, MS. Lb 42, fol. 51, printed in Feuillerat, *Elizabeth,* p. 94. Their costumes are listed in the employ book, printed on p. 28. Guildford Muniment Room, MS. LM 59/58 and Folger Library, MS. Lb 168 is the basket maker's bill for this mask.

88   Folger Library, MS. Lb 42, fol. 51v, printed in Feuillerat, *Elizabeth,* p. 95.

89   PRO, E351/3332; *King's Works,* IV.ii: 319.

90   Folger Library, MS. Lb 42, fol. 42, printed in Feuillerat, *Elizabeth,* p. 81. There are a number of bills relating to this mask and banqueting house: Folger Library, MSS Lb 187, Lb 188, Lb 189, Lb 196.

91   Folger Library, MS. Lb 42, fol. 50v, printed in Feuillerat, *Elizabeth,* p. 93. Robert Trunckwell is paid in the Revels accounts for his design work beginning at Christmas and finishing in May.

92   Folger Library, MS. Lb 42, fol. 55, printed in Feuillerat, *Elizabeth,* p. 101. This banqueting house in May 1559 was hardly more than a floral improvisation built into the open part of the great or long gallery in the Great Garden (called the Privy Garden in Elizabeth's reign) at Whitehall: *Kings Works,* IV.ii: 319; PRO, E351/3332.

93   Machyn, *Diary,* pp. 203–4. Other than this brief mention, we have no evidence of the joust nor of the mask held on the 11th in this banqueting house.

94   For evidence of the joust on 2 July see Court Calendar (above). Machyn, *Diary,* p. 206, records the entertainment at Nonsuch on the 6th.

95   Folger Library, MS. Lb 42, fol. 60v, printed in Feuillerat, *Elizabeth,* p. 106.

96   Lewis Stocket, Surveyor of the Works, was in charge of part of the construction at West Horsley. His bill, Folger Library, MS. Lb 142, shows the payments to Bosum which later were entered in the Revels account. Guildford Muniment Room, MS. LM 59/152, a packet of documents relating to material for a banqueting house, lists payments made in June but does not identify the place. The payments may refer to the May 1559 banqueting house at Westminster.

97   Chambers, *ES,* I: 157. The inventory is printed in Feuillerat, *Elizabeth,* pp. 26, 28.

98   Folger Library, MS. Lb 42, fol. 42, printed in Feuillerat, *Elizabeth,* p. 81.

99   *APC,* VII: 98. Folger Library, MS. Lb 518, is a draft of a document related to this legal action.

100   Folger Library, MSS Lb 300, Lb 125.

101   In a letter of 22 June 1559 to Sir William More, Cawarden indicates that he had broken his leg: Guildford Muniment Room, Loseley Correspondence, 3/21.

102   The date of his death in uncertain. The Inquisition Post Mortem (PRO, C42/126/90) gives 29 August, which is the date the Blechingly Parish Register gives for the burial. The epitaph on the tomb at Blechingly Church gives the

date of death as 25 August: Craib, 'Sir Thomas Cawarden,'pp. 18–19; G. Levenson-Gower, 'Manorial and Parliamentary History of Blechingly,' *Surrey Archaeological Collections,* 5 (1871): 234 and plate.

103   Cawarden's will is Guildford Muniment Room, MS. LM 2011/13/1 (original), abstracted in G. Levenson-Gower, 'Manorial and Parliamentary History of Blechingly,' *Surrey Archaeological Collections,* 5 (1871): 258–60.

104   Folger Library, MS. Lb 42, fols. 41–61v, printed in Feuillerat, *Elizabeth,* pp. 79–108, 445–6. The account filed by More was comprehensive from 15 June 1555 to 29 September 1560. Cawarden was owed £740 13s. 10 1/2d., which sum was paid on 28 December 1560.

105   There are many documents in the Loseley collection relating to More's attempt to settle Cawarden's estate. On 4 July 1571 a decree of the Court of the Exchequer (Folger Library, MS. Lb 353) exonerated More of liability for certain sums claimed against him as executor of Cawarden's estate.

POSTSCRIPT

1   Chambers, *ES,* I: 73.
2   BL, Lansdowne MS. 83, art. 59, printed in Feuillerat, *Elizabeth,* p. 5.
3   *Grafton's Chronicle,* ed. Sir Henry Ellis (London: J. Johnson, 1809), II: 526–7.
4   Feuillerat, *Elizabeth,* pp. 427–9.
5   PRO, SP12/7, fols. 89–90, calendared in *CSP Domestic, 1547–1580,* p. 143, printed in Feuillerat, *Elizabeth,* p. 111: 'Memorandum that the Chargies for making of maskes cam never to so little a somme as they do this yere.'
6   BL, Lansdowne MS. 12, no. 54, printed in Feuillerat, *Elizabeth,* p. 407.
7   Chambers, *ES,* I: 80, suggested that Burghley wanted to look into the affairs of the office.
8   PRO, A03/2045, nos. 1 and 2, printed in Feuillerat, *Elizabeth,* pp. 151–86.
9   This was the case in 1573–4 and in 1574–5, and it was probably continued until 1578: PRO, A03/2045, no. 3, 4, and 6. See Feuillerat, *Elizabeth,* pp. 191, 225, 298–9.
10   There is no evidence to show that any Lord Chamberlain before Sussex took such an active, personal interest in the Office. Sir Thomas Darcy had supervision at some level of the entertainments for the French hostages in May 1550 and for the ambassadors in 1551: PRO, E101/426/8, abstracted in Streitberger, *RORD* (1984): 36–7. He also sent a letter to Cawarden requesting costumes for the King's Players for a performance on Twelfth Night in 1551: Folger Library, MS. Lb 282, printed in Feuillerat, *Edward VI and Mary,* p. 86. But such concern was part of the ordinary duties of his office, and there is no evidence to indicate

that he exercised the kind of control that Sussex did. Cawarden's position as Gentleman of the Privy Chamber put the relationship between the Lord Chamberlain and the Master of the Revels on quite a different footing than between Sussex and Blagrave.

11   J. Leeds Barroll et al., *The Revels History of Drama in English,* ed. Clifford Leech and T.W. Craik (London: Methuen, 1975), III: 10–14.

12   *MSC,* XIII, pp. ix–xxiii.

13   Streitberger, 'On Edmond Tyllney's Biography,' *Review of English Studies,* n.s., 29 (1978): 22–3.

14   Marie Axton, 'The Tudor Mask and Elizabethan Court Drama,' in M. Axton and R. Williams, eds., *English Drama: Form and Development* (Cambridge: Cambridge University Press, 1977), 32–47, discusses some of the criticism of the queen even in her own revels. Scott McMillin, 'The Queen's Men and the London Theatre of 1583,' in *The Elizabethan Theatre X,* ed. C.E. McGee (Port Credit, Ontario, 1988), 9–15, discusses the use of the royal company as a means of gaining prestige and of checking the growth of the theatre industry.

15   In 'A Letter from Edmund Tilney to Sir William More,' *Surrey Archaeological Collections,* 71 (1977): 225–31, I transcribed the letter and gave my arguments for dating it 1595, which would have made the last Lord Chamberlain Lord Charles Howard. No one has liked the suggestion. See R.J. Fehrenbach, 'When Lord Cobham and Edmumd Tilney were at odds,' *Shakespeare Studies,* 18 (1986): 67–101, who dates the letter 1599 or 1600. The last Lord Chamberlain would then have been the elder Lord Cobham, and Fehrenbach wants to advance the idea that the issue was the Oldcastle-Falstaff name in Shakespeare's *Henry IV.* See also Richard Dutton, *Mastering the Revels, The Regulation and Censorship of English Renaissance Drama* (Iowa City: University of Iowa Press, 1991), 104–5.

16   The changes in the office at the beginning of James's reign are discussed by Richard Dutton, *Mastering the Revels, The Regulation and Censorship of English Renaissance Drama* (Iowa City: University of Iowa Press, 1991), 144. The promotion of a new Lord Chamberlain, royal patronage of the most successful acting company of the day, the staying and granting of reversionary patents for the post of Master of the Revels, the creation of a new post of Master of Ceremonies – all within seven busy weeks of each other – suggests that someone had given careful thought to the whole question of court ceremonies and theatricals in the new reign. See also his discussion of the complexities of censorship in the public drama after 1581, pp. 45–7.

17   On Sir George Buck see Mark Eccles, 'Sir George Buck, Master of the Revels' in *Thomas Lodge and Other Elizabethans,* ed. C.J. Sisson (Cambridge, Mass., Harvard University Press, 1933), 444–5. On the importance of the Bed Chamber in James's reign see Neil Cuddy, 'The revival of the Entourage: the Bed Chamber of

James I, 1603–1625,' in David Starkey et al., *The English Court* (London: Long-man, 1987), 173–225.

Principal Sources

Government financial records provide the most consistent and reliable information on court revels, spectacles, plays, and entertainments in the Tudor period. The most important classes of these records are the accounts of the major treasuries and purses which disbursed payments for government expenses, including payments to the producers and performers of revels and spectacles and sometimes the participants. Another important class of records is the accounts of the government offices – the Revels, the Works, the various wardrobes – which directly contributed to the production of revels and spectacles. These accounts record the materials and workmanship that went into actual productions. Many of these records for the period between 1558 and 1642 have been extracted, enabling scholars to construct a calendar of court entertainments and to reconstruct some of their details (Streitberger, 'Renaissance Revels Documents, 1485–1642,' RORD, 21 [1978]: 11–16). Radical changes in the financial structure of the government and the generally less well-preserved state of the documents contribute in their ways to the comparatively less complete information available from the earlier part of the period. Still, a calendar can be constructed from financial records, supplemented by miscellaneous documents and by narratives.

When Henry VII ascended the throne in 1485 the Exchequer was still the nation's dominant treasury and still retained its function of auditing royal expenditure, including expenditure for revels and spectacles. Once the court decided to authorize revels for an event, for example, the Crown would appoint a supervisor to prepare them. His formal instrument of authority was a writ stamped with the Privy Seal. It defined the nature of his responsibilities, the limits of his authority, and the amount of money authorized for his project. After his duties were completed the supervisor appeared as an accountant before the Auditor and his Clerk at the Exchequer and presented a bill of charges, vouchers for money already spent from any 'imprest' or advance of money made to him for the project, and the Privy Seal writ to show that the charges fell within the limits of his authority. From these documents Exchequer officials prepared a balance sheet, a 'compotus,' and signed it when payment was made as a record that the supervisor was no longer indebted to the Crown. This sheet, along with supporting evidence – the bill of charges and Privy Seal writ – was sent to the King's Remembrancer and to the Lord Treasurer's Remembrancer where information from these documents was abstracted and enrolled by various clerks. The original documents were then returned to the King's Remembrancer where they were filed. The audited compotus was taken by the accountant to one of the Tellers of the Exchequer who paid the charges and recorded them in the Teller's Rolls. Primary documentary evidence of court revels and spectacles between 1485 and 1491 derives from several classes of Exchequer records, now preserved mainly in the PRO (Streitberger, *RORD* [1983]: 31–2, 39–42; Campbell, *passim*). These include the original Privy Seal writs, the breviates and the abstracts of the Privy Seal writs made by clerks at the Exchequer, the Teller's rolls which record payments to accountants, the 'Rough-entry books' which preserve drafts made by the clerks for a variety of records, and the accountants' original bills of charges.

Exchequer finance was not only cumbersome and inconvenient but because it came under the jurisdiction of the Lord Treasurer, there were political as well as practical liabilities from the point of view of the king (Chambers, *ES*, IV: 131). To effect more personal control over his finances, Henry VII deposited royal revenue into his own Chamber treasury rather than into the Exchequer. By 1491 the Chamber treasury had become more substantial than the Exchequer's, and national finance was essentially under the personal control of the king (W.C. Richardson, *Tudor Chamber Administration, 1485–1558* [Baton Rouge, La.: Louisiana State University Press, 1952], 463–6; J.D. Alsop, 'The Structure of Early Tudor Finance, c. 1509–1558,' in C. Coleman and D. Starkey, eds., *Revolution Reassessed* [Oxford: Clarendon Press, 1986], 135–62). By this date, the chief officers of the royal household as well as other government officers and appointees were funded mainly by the Treasurer of the Chamber. Accountants now brought their bills to the Treasurer of the Chamber for audit and payment. The Treasurer kept account books organized by day, week, and month. He entered each payment as it was disbursed. Payments of thousands of pounds for expensive projects, such as renovations of royal buildings, the construction of ships, and the purchase of investment jewels, are entered along with payments for minor expenses amounting to a few shillings. The Treasurer recorded rewards to the playing companies who performed at court as well as payments to individuals appointed to prepare revels and spectacles. Henry VII's sign manual appears on each page of these accounts, indicating that he was personally acquainted with his revenue and expenditures down to some of the smallest details (F.C. Dietz, *English Government Finance, 1485–1558*, University of Illinois Studies in the Social Sciences, vol. IX, no. 3 [Urbana, Ill., 1920], 60).

Under the competent leadership of John Heron, Treasurer of the Chamber from 1492 until his retirement in 1521, Chamber finance continued to dominate the early reign of Henry VIII (G.R. Elton, *The Tudor Revolution in Government* [Cambridge:

Cambridge University Press, 1953], 43). Records surviving from this period are as full and detailed as they ever were to be. Though some changes are evident after Heron's retirement, the Chamber continued as the principal treasury until the early 1530s. John Mycklowe, from 1 June 1521 to 1 May 1522, and Edmund Peckham, from 1 May 1522 to 1 January 1523, served as interim treasurers before the appointment of Sir Henry Wyatt by 18 February 1523, who held the post until 13 April 1528.

The original Chamber accounts, containing payments for revels, spectacles, scheduled plays, and other entertainments, are preserved in the PRO and in the BL. The accounts from 1491 to 1495 are lost, but a haphazard collection of extracts from them by Craven Orde survives in manuscript at the BL (BL, Additional MS. 7099; Anglo, 'Henry VII,' pp. 12–13). The original accounts run consecutively from October 1495 to April 1521, after which date fragmentary accounts exist for the period from June 1521 to January 1523 and for Michaelmas 1525. None survive from 1525 to early 1528.

Elizabeth of York and Henry VII, like earlier kings and queens, both had privy purses. The Privy Purse was ordinarily a small 'purse' or account – as opposed to a 'treasury' – used to pay for private expenses such as rewards or payments for entertainments. After 1491 Henry VII's Privy Purse was financed by the Treasurer of the Chamber (Streitberger, *RORD* [1984]: 23–4; Coleman and Starkey, *Revolution Reassessed*, p. 38). Certain individuals were designated as overseers of this Privy Purse, making privy purchases, payments, and rewards, and they were required to submit their bills to the Chamber for audit and payment. None of the bills survive, but evidence of Chamber payments for these purposes indicates that the expenses averaged about £220 a year. Overseeing privy purchases in this period appears to have been an appointed duty rather than an office financed with a set amount of money. And, in Henry VII's reign, the overseer was not responsible for paying all of what is usually regarded as privy expenditures. Rewards to individuals who brought gifts, payments and rewards to musicians and fools, and even gambling money were sometimes charged directly to the Chamber. Such a system in which privy expenses intermingled with major government and military expenditures worked well enough for a monarch personally acquainted with his finances. It did not suffice for Henry VIII.

William Compton, protégé of the king, appears clearly to have acted as overseer of Henry VIII's Privy Purse from near the beginning of the reign. He received large payments from the Chamber and, at one point, from the Exchequer, reckoned in the thousands of pounds, but no mention is ever made of his bills or accounts and none have been discovered (The payments are abstracted in *LP,* II.ii, pp. 1461, 1464, 1466–7, 1473–4). In 1518 or 1519 plans were made to reorganize the royal household and to institute a stricter accounting system. Among other innovations, the plan called for the creation of a formal Privy Purse on the scale of a small treasury, financed by the Chamber with £10,000 per year (*LP,* II.i, no. 576; Elton, *Tudor Revolution*, p. 38n; Coleman and Starkey, *Revolution Reassessed*, pp. 38–40). William Compton, who held the post of

Groom of the Stool within the Chamber, was to be appointed keeper of this purse, and, along with other individuals who handled revenue, was to have rendered an account of his expenses. There is no evidence that this Privy Purse was established in 1519, and Compton continued to receive his large sums of money for the king's use without accounting for it until his resignation in 1526.

Henry VIII did institute a large, formal Privy Purse by 1529. The single extant account of this purse runs from November 1529, one month after Wolsey's fall, to December 1532, seven months after Cromwell's appointment as Master of the Jewels, suggesting that this was a plan of which neither of Henry's chief ministers approved. This unique account (BL, Additional MS. 20030) preserved in the BL, is structured very much like the Chamber account which covers the period from 1528 to 1531 (PRO, E101/420/11. Coleman and Starkey, *Revolution Reassessed*, pp. 40–2). While most payments for court entertainments were still made by the Chamber, there are payments from the Privy Purse to Richard Gibson for masking apparel and to John Rightwise, High Master of Paul's, who had presented plays at court in 1527 and at Wolsey's in 1528. The appearance of payments related to court entertainments in this account suggests that such payments were probably made from the same source earlier in the period, and there is evidence later in the period that such payments continued to be made.

The disappearance of the formal Privy Purse which existed from 1529 to 1532 appears to be connected to Cromwell's financial reforms. Large expenses associated with royal building projects and investment jewels, which were paid from this purse, were now reassigned to other treasuries. The Privy Purse reverted to a smaller operation within the Privy Chamber under the general supervision of the Lord Chamberlain and, most often, under the control of the Groom of the Stool – an office assigned to one of the Gentlemen of the Privy Chamber who personally attended the king. It is clear from the accounts of Sir Anthony Denny, Sir Michael Stanhope, and Sir Thomas Darcy that the Privy Purse was used to reward playing companies on occasion between 1541 and 1552 (Streitberger, *RORD* [1984]: 34–7).

During Cromwell's administration a number of new financial courts were set up to administer the revenues which were pouring into Henry's coffers from the dissolved monasteries and other sources (Elton, *Tudor Revolution*, pp. 111, 192–203; Coleman and Starkey, *Revolution Reassessed*, pp. 45–6). The sporadic accounts which survive from this period show that the main bills for court revels were paid from several treasuries. The Chamber accounts are missing between 1531 and 1537, but resume for the period between 1538 and 1542. The accounts show that the Chamber retained its traditional function of paying the minor expenses for scheduled plays, but not the major expenses for the revels any more (Streitberger, *RORD* [1984]: 25–6). Cromwell's personal accounts (PRO, E36/256), which are preserved in the PRO, show that he paid for revels in his household, some of which were sent to court, and Revels officers were enlisted to produce some of his masks. Cromwell himself was the unifying principle in the financial bureaucracy he created during the 1530s, and efficiency declined after his death in 1540.

The period from 1540 to 1559 was characterized by reforms designed to simplify the system of national finance. The chief architect of these reforms was William Paulet, Marquis of Winchester, who served as Lord Treasurer from 1550 to 1572. A commission was appointed to survey the state of finance, and its report, issued in 1552, provided the data and suggestions for reorganization (W.C. Richardson, ed., *The Report of the Royal Commission of 1552* [Morgantown, W. Va.: University of West Virginia Press, 1974]; Elton, *Tudor Revolution*, p. 224). The commission found that the Chamber had declined to such an extent that its treasury was bankrupt and that most of its traditional payments had been reassigned. Sir Anthony Rous, who succeeded to the post on 25 November 1545, and Sir William Cavendish, who replaced him in February 1546, were the last Treasurers of the old Chamber. The Chamber was not dissolved, however, and was to be reorganized later into a much smaller household treasury. By 1554 the new financial courts which had been created in the 1530s and 1540s were dissolved and merged with the Exchequer. While the Court of Wards and the Duchy of Lancaster remained independent, by 1554 most of the royal income was again deposited into the Exchequer.

Tracing payments for revels, spectacles, plays, and entertainments in this period is somewhat difficult due to the complexity of the reorganizations and to the chaotic state of the records which have survived. The Chamber continued to pay for some scheduled plays and entertainments until 1549 (PRO, E101/424/9; Elton, *Tudor Revolution*, pp. 186–9). Rewards and payments for some plays and other entertainments were also paid from the king's Privy Purse under the supervision of the Groom of the Stool, some of which are preserved in the PRO and the BL. The charges of the Revels Office were paid from several treasuries. Some Revels charges show up in Cromwell's accounts from 1537 to 1539, but it seems clear that the bulk of the expenses was charged to various treasuries. The comprehensive account of the Revels Office from 1550 to 1555, for example, was paid by the Court of Augmentation and by the Court of Wards (Feuillerat, *Edward VI and Mary*, p. 272).

The re-emergence of the Exchequer as the dominant treasury after 1554 did not quite signal a return to the system as it had existed at the beginning of Henry VII's reign, for by 1560 a new streamlined system of auditing had been introduced which greatly improved the Exchequer's ability to finance government offices more efficiently (M.D. George, 'Notes on the Origin of the Declared Account,' *English Historical Review*, 31 [1916]: 41–58). Two Auditors of the Prests were appointed to audit and pay accounts. Accountants were now not required to appear in person before an Auditor and his Clerk at the Exchequer. Rather, they submitted a Ledger or Office book for audit. One copy was signed after audit and returned to the accountants, the other was kept by the Auditors whose clerks abstracted information from it into the Declared account. The Declared account was prepared in duplicate. One copy was filed in the Audit department and the other in the Pipe office. The amount of information copied into the Declared account from the Office book varied. A comparison between the Office books and the Declared accounts for the Office of the Revels shows that the clerks produced only sketchy abstracts.

By 1560 the Treasury of the Chamber had also been reorganized into a small house-hold treasury under Sir John Mason. This new Chamber treasury was never to rival in wealth or in responsibility its earlier namesake. It was used to pay certain small desig-nated charges, including those for preparing rooms for entertainments and for rewarding players. The Exchequer paid the bills of the Revels Office. The division of responsibil-ity between the Exchequer and the Chamber was the system used to finance court enter-tainments, with the exception of the Stuart masks, until 1642.

We are dependent for our understanding of the particular details of early Tudor rev-els on the Revels, Works, Tents, and Wardrobe accounts and on narrative descriptions. The earliest Revels account to survive dates from Christmas 1508–9. Thereafter we have many but not all of the accounts, until 1527. From 1528 to 1540, only a few frag-ments survive. These accounts are preserved in the PRO and the BL. A great number of accounts and documents of the Revels Office from 1541 to 1559 survive, preserved in the Loseley collection at the Folger Shakespeare Library and in the Surrey County Record Office, Guildford Muniment Room (L. Yeandle and W.R. Streitberger, 'The Loseley Collection of Manuscripts at the Folger Shakespeare Library, Washington, D.C.,' *Shakespeare Quarterly,* 38 [1987]: 201–7). The range of documents, from small bills and receipts from merchants and artisans hired by the Revels to comprehensive drafts and accounts for five-year periods, makes this the best documented period for the office in the entire century. But, because the system of accounting had become more sophisticated by that time, the narrative quality of the earlier accounts is lost. These documents, which must be read in concert to make full use of them, are less helpful to scholars interested in the productions themselves, but very helpful in understanding the operation of the office.

The Revels accounts can occasionally be supplemented by other documents from government offices. Except in a few specific cases the Tents accounts are too sketchy to be of much help. The most important accounts are those of the Office of the Works and of the Great Wardrobe. The Works were frequently contracted to build large struc-tures, such as lists, standings, foundations for banqueting houses, and fittings for revels and spectacles. The accounts of the Works are sketchy before 1560, but a major study of the office and its records has been undertaken which helps to illuminate its role in supplying construction support for major entertainments and spectacles (*King's Works,* III, IV, *passim*).

The Great Wardrobe and many of the minor wardrobes of the royal household sup-plied the Revels with material for its productions. A full study of the Great and other

wardrobes in this period has not been undertaken, but a variety of documents which
have been identified by scholars over the past three centuries are helpful in supplementing information from other sources. Important studies on the Tudor tournament have
been written in the past twenty years which also identify relevant financial records and
narrative sources preserved in the College of Arms and elsewhere (Young, *Tournaments;*
Anglo, *Tournament Roll;* Anglo, 'Archives of the English Tournament: Score Cheques
and Lists,' and 'Financial and Heraldic Records of the English Tournament,' in *Journal
of the Society of Archivists,* 2, no. 4 [1961]: 153–62; 2, no. 5 [1962]: 183–95; Louise
Campbell and Francis Steer, *A Catalogue of Manuscripts in the College of Arms Collections* [London, College of Arms, 1988], I). All of these records can be supplemented on
occasion by other documents.

EXCHEQUER DOCUMENTS, 1485–1521

Privy Seal Writs. PRO, E404/79, E404/80 [22 August 1485 – 21 August 1491],
    abstracted in Campbell, *passim.* Streitberger, *RORD* (1983): 39–42.
Breviate of Privy Seal Writs. PRO, E403/2558 [22 August 1485 – 21 August 1489].
Abstract of Great and Privy Seal Writs. PRO, E407/6/137 [22 August 1485 –
    21 August 1491].
Teller's Rolls. PRO, E405/75, E405/76, E405/77, E405/78, E405/79 [22 August 1485
    – 21 August 1498].
Rough Entry Books. PRO, E36/124, E36/125, E36/130 [22 August 1485 –
    21 August 1492], abstracted in Streitberger, *RORD* (1983): 42.
Warrants and documents subsidiary to accounts. PRO, E101/417 [1509–21].

CHAMBER ACCOUNTS, 1491–1558

Abstract of the original Chamber accounts by Craven Orde. BL, Additional MS.
    7099, fols. 1v–96 [24 December 1491 – 27 September 1505], abstracted in S. Bent-
    ley, *Excerpta Historica* (London, 1833), 85–133 [unreliable]; Anglo, 'Henry VII,'
    pp. 27–9, 38–9.
Chamber account. PRO, E101/414/6, fols. 1–91 [1 October 1495 – 30 September
    1497], abstracted in Anglo, 'Henry VII,' pp. 29–32.
Chamber account. PRO, E101/414/16, fols. 1–78v [1 October 1497 – 30 September
    1499], abstracted in Anglo, 'Henry VII,' pp. 32–5.
Chamber account. PRO, E101/415/3, fols. 1–104v [1 October 1499 – 30 September
    1502], abstracted in Anglo, 'Henry VII,' pp. 35–8.

Chamber account. BL, Additional MS. 59899, fols. 1–101 [1 October 1502 –
30 September 1505], abstracted in Streitberger, *RORD* (1983): 43–9.

Chamber account fragment. PRO, E101/415/16, fols. 1–2 [22 August 1504 –
21 August 1505].

Chamber account fragment. BL, Additional MS. 21480, fols. 13v–28v [30 April –
27 September 1505], abstracted in Anglo, 'Henry VII,' pp. 39–40.

Chamber account. PRO, E36/214, pp. 7–351 [1 October 1505 – 23 April 1509,
including payments for July 1509 and those made by the executors of Henry VII's
will], abstracted in Anglo, 'Henry VII,' pp. 40–4; *LP,* II.ii, p. 1441.

Chamber account. PRO, E36/215, pp. 7–577 [1 May 1509 – 31 March 1518], inadequately abstracted in *LP,* II.ii, pp. 1441–77.

Chamber account. BL, Additional MS. 21481, fols. 1–288 [1 May 1509 – 31 March
1518].

**Payments made by John Daunce (Treasurer for the War) and John Heron 'for the
kynges Warres.'** PRO, E36/1, fols. 29–96, inadequately abstracted in *LP,* I.ii, no.
3608 (v).

Chamber account. PRO, E36/216, fols. 2–130 [1 April 1518 – 30 April 1521], inadequately abstracted in *LP,* II.ii. pp. 1477–80; III.ii, pp. 1533–45.

Chamber account fragment. PRO, SP1/26, fols. 237–9v [1 June 1521 – 1 January
1523], abstracted in *LP,* III.ii, pp. 1156–7.

Chamber war loans. PRO, E36/221, fols. 19–36 [29 September 1522 – 28 February
1523].

Chamber monthly and quarterly payments. BL, Egerton MS. 2604, fols. 1–6v
[before Michaelmas 1525].

Chamber account. PRO, E101/420/11, fols. 1–166v [1 October 1528 – 30 April
1531], abstracted in *LP,* V, pp. 303–26; J.P. Collier, ed., *Trevelyan Papers Prior to
A.D. 1558,* Camden Society, vol. 67 (London, 1857), 136–79.

Chamber account. BL, Arundel MS. 97, fols. 1–195v [February 1538 – June 1541],
abstracted in *LP,* XIII.ii, pp. 524–39; XIV.ii, pp. 303–17; XVI.i, pp. 178–95,
698–709.

Chamber account fragment. BL, Stowe MS. 554, fols. 11–44v [1 May – 30 September
1542], abstracted in *LP,* XVII, pp. 474–85.

Chamber account. BL, Additional MS. 59900, fols. 43–150 [October 1543 – September 1544], abstracted in Streitberger, *RORD* (1984): 31.

Chamber – abstract of quarterly payments. BL, Additional MS. 27404, fols. 17–32v
[December 1545], abstracted in *LP,* XX.ii, pp. 515–17.

Chamber certificate book. PRO, E101/424/9 [19 February 1546 – 24 October 1555],
abstracted in J.P. Collier, ed., *Trevelyan Papers, Part II, A.D. 1446–1643,* Camden
Society, vol. 84 (London, 1863), 1–12.

Chamber account. PRO, E101/426/5, fols. 11–111 [31 March 1547 – 1 October 1548], abstracted in J.P. Collier, ed., *Trevelyan Papers Prior to A.D. 1558*, Camden Society, vol. 67 (London, 1857), 191–205; Streitberger, *RORD* (1984): 31–3.

Chamber account fragment. PRO, E315/439, fols. 13–62v [31 March 1547 – 31 December 1547].

Chamber account. PRO, E101/426/6, fols. 14–79 [30 September 1548 – 1 October 1549], abstracted in J.P. Collier, ed., *Trevelyan Papers, Part II, A.D. 1446-1643*, Camden Society, vol. 84 (London, 1863), 13–38; Streitberger, *RORD* (1984): 33–4.

Declared account of the reorganized Chamber. PRO, E351/541 [1 April – 31 December 1557; September 1558 – September 1560; 1560–79].

PRIVY PURSE AND OTHER ACCOUNTS, 1502–52

Elizabeth of York's Privy Purse account. PRO, E36/210 [18 March 1502 – March 1503], printed by Sir Nicholas Harris Nicolas, *Privy Purse Expenses of Elizabeth of York* (London: W. Pickering, 1830).

Henry VIII's Privy Purse account. BL, Additional MS. 20030, fols. 1–149v [17 November 1529 – December 1532], printed by Sir Nicholas Harris Nicolas, *The Privy Purse Expenses of King Henry VIII* (London: W. Pickering, 1827); abstracted in *LP*, V, pp. 747–62; BL, Lansdowne MS. 737, fols. 109-31v [abstract by Peter Le Neve].

Cromwell's accounts. PRO, E36/256, fols. 1–181 [1 January 1537 – December 1539], abstracted in *LP*, XIV.ii, no. 782.

Accounts, including receipts of the Groom of the Stool. PRO, E315/160, fols. 1–280 [1542–7].

Declared account of the Groom of the Stool. BL, Lansdowne Roll, no. 14 [22 April 1541 – 28 January 1548], abstracted in Streitberger, *RORD* (1984): 34–5.

Declared account of the Groom of the Stool. PRO, E351/2932 [24 August 1547 – 25 March 1549], abstracted in Streitberger, *RORD* (1984): 35–6.

Declared accounts of the Lord Chamberlain, including those of the Privy Purse and the Groom of the Stool. PRO, E101/426/8 [10 January 1550 – 1 January 1552], abstracted in Streitberger, *RORD* (1984): 36–7.

REVELS ACCOUNTS

25 December 1508. Henry Wentworth's account for a disguising and morris dance with 3 pageants (castle, tree, mount) before the Flemish ambassadors at Richmond for the betrothal of Princess Mary and Archduke Charles. PRO, LC9/50, fols. 149–53v, printed by A.R. Meyers, 'The Book of the Disguisings for the Coming of the Ambassadors of Flanders, December 1508,' *Bulletin of the Institute of Historical Research*, 54 (1981): 120–9.

[June 1509 – August 1510]. Included among Richard Gibson's Revels accounts is John Skelton's 'a Lawde and prayse made for o*ur sove*rigne lord the kyng.' PRO, E36/228, fols. 7–8v, abstracted in *LP,* II.ii, p. 1518, and printed without the Latin marginalia in *John Skelton, The Complete English Poems,* ed. John Scattergood (New Haven: Yale University Press, 1983), 110–12.

18 January 1510. Richard Gibson's account for an informal disguising (Robin Hood and his band and Maid Marian) before Queen Katherine in her Chamber at Westminster. PRO, E36/217, fols. 1-2, 15, abstracted in *LP,* II.ii, p. 1490.

28 February 1510. Richard Gibson's account for support of Essex's disguisings and mummery for ambassadors in the Parliament Chamber at Westminster. PRO, E36/217, fols. 3–12, 15–25, abstracted in *LP,* II.ii, pp. 1490–2.

17 March 1510. Richard Gibson's account for running at the ring. PRO, E36/217, fols. 13–14, 25–6, abstracted in *LP,* II.ii, p. 1492.

13–14 November 1510. Richard Gibson's account for a joust, tourney, and/or running at the ring, and for a disguising and mummery at Richmond. PRO, E36/217, fols. 30–6; E36/229, fols. 1–6; abstracted in *LP,* II.ii, pp. 1492–3.

15 November 1510. Richard Gibson's brief inventory of revels garments and properties, including an itemized list of garments and properties given to the King's Players. PRO, E36/217, fols. 37–8; E36/229, fols. 7–8.

6 January 1511. Richard Gibson's account for a disguising and morris dance 'devysed by master Harry gyllforth' at Richmond with a pageant (a mountain). PRO, E36/217, fols. 38–45; E36/229, fols. 8–15; abstracted in *LP,* II.ii, pp. 1493-94.

12–13 February 1511. Richard Gibson's account for a tournament at Westminster with pageants (a forest and four pavilions). PRO, E36/217, fols. 46–60; E36/229, fols. 15–30; printed in Anglo, *Tournament Roll,* I: 116–36; abstracted in *LP,* II.ii, pp. 1494–5.

13 February 1511. Richard Gibson's account for a disguising in the White Hall at Westminster to conclude the jousts of 11–12 February with a pageant (*The Golldyn Arber in the Arche yerd of Pleyser*). PRO, E36/217, fols. 61–76; E36/229, fols. 31–47; abstracted in *LP,* II.ii, pp. 1495–7.

1 January 1512. Richard Gibson's account for a disguising in the Hall at Greewnich with pageant (*Le Fortresse Dangerus*). PRO, SP2/Fol. A, no. 4; E36/229, fols. 91–106; abstracted in *LP,* II.ii, pp. 1497–8.

6 January 1512. Richard Gibson's account for a mask 'after the maner of messkelyng in Etaly' at Greenwich. PRO, SP2/Fol. A, no. 4; E36/229, fols. 91–106; abstracted in *LP,* II.ii, pp. 1497–8.

1 June 1512. Richard Gibson's account for a joust at Greenwich with pageants. PRO, E36/217, fols. 177–83, abstracted in *LP,* II.ii, pp. 1498–9.

6 January 1513. Richard Gibson's account for a disguising with pageant (*The Ryche Mount*). PRO, E36/217, fols. 186–201, abstracted in *LP,* II.ii, pp. 1499–1500.

Joust and Revels at Tournai:

(1) **13 October 1513.** Warrant under sign manual to Sir Edward Guildford to prepare 'Tyltys And Iustyng placis Skaffoldis & other necessaries Ayenst our Ryall Iustes made at Tornay.' BL, Stow MS. 146, fol. 101.

(2) **18 October 1513.** Richard Gibson's account for a joust and mummery or maskeler at Tournai. PRO, E36/217, fols. 79–80; SP1/7, fols. 134–6; abstracted in *LP,* I.ii, no. 2562.

6 January 1514. Richard Gibson's account for an interlude (*Venus and Beauty*) containing a morris dance. PRO, E36/217, fols. 81–3; SP1/7, fols. 136–9; abstracted in *LP,* I.ii, no. 2562.

ca. 1514. Fragment of Richard Gibson's account for apparel for ladies and gentlemen maskers. PRO, SP1/231, fols. 219-23, calendared in *LP, Addenda,* I.i, no. 121.

1 January 1515. Richard Gibson's account for a disguising or mummery in the queen's Chamber at Greenwich. PRO, SP2/Fol. A, no. 5; E36/217, fols. 204–6; abstracted in *LP,* II.ii, pp. 1500–1.

6 January 1515. Richard Gibson's account for a disguising with tourney in the Hall at Greenwich with pageant (*The Pavyllyon vn the Plas Parlos*). PRO, SP2/Fol. A; no. 6; E36/217, fols. 209–18; abstracted in *LP,* II.ii, pp. 1501–2.

3 February 1515. Richard Gibson's account for a joust for Candlemas at Greenwich. PRO, SP2/Fol. A, no. 7; E36/217, fols. 219–23; abstracted in *LP,* II.ii, pp. 1502–3.

19 March – 9 May 1515. Richard Gibson's account for construction of a pageant ('Pallys Marchallyn') intended for use in a joust. PRO, SP2/Fol. A, no. 8; E36/217, fols. 227–46; abstracted in *LP,* II.ii, pp. 1503–4.

19 April 1515. Richard Gibson's account for a joust at Richmond. PRO, SP2/Fol. A, no. 8; E36/217, fols. 224–6; abstracted in *LP,* II.ii, p. 1503.

[22 April 1515 – 21 April 1516]. Document containing a list of 'Garmentes for players,' dated 'Anno vij hen[   ]iij.' BL, Egerton MS. 2623, art. 4.

1 May 1515. Richard Gibson's account for a May Festival at Greenwich, including athletic contests, disguises, pageants, procession, and joust. PRO, E36/229, fols. 66–72, abstracted in *LP,* II.ii, pp. 1504–5.

6 January 1516. Richard Gibson's account for a comedy (*Troylus and Pandor*) barriers, and disguising with a pageant (a castle) at Eltham. PRO, E36/229, fols. 73–82, abstracted in *LP,* II.ii, pp. 1505–6; Hillebrand, *The Child Actors,* pp. 324–5.

29 January 1516. Richard Gibson's account for running at the ring at Greenwich. PRO, E36/229, fols. 83–7, abstracted in *LP,* II.ii, pp. 1506–7.

5 February 1516. Richard Gibson's account for running at the ring at Greenwich. PRO, E36/229, fols. 87–90, abstracted in *LP,* II.ii, p. 1507.

Joust and Revels at Greenwich:
    (1) **19–20 May 1516.** Richard Gibson's account for a joust for Margaret, Queen of Scots, at Greenwich. PRO, E36/217, fols. 249-68, abstracted in *LP,* II.ii, pp. 1507–9; see next item.
    (2) **20 May 1516.** Richard Gibson's subsidiary account for the joust of 19–20 May and for a play at Greenwich. PRO, E101/418/7, fols. 1–7, abstracted in Streitberger, 'Henry VIII's Entertainment for the Queen of Scots, 1516: A New Revels Account and Cornish's Play,' *Medieval and Renaissance Drama in England,* 1 (1984): 29–35.

6 January 1517. Richard Gibson's account for a disguising with a pageant (*Gardyn de Esperans*) at Greenwich. PRO, E36/217, fols. 269–78, abstracted in *LP,* II.ii, p. 1509.

7 July 1517. Richard Gibson's account for a joust for the Flemish ambassadors at Greenwich and a banquet with 'representations.' PRO, E36/217, fols. 86–97, abstracted in *LP,* II.ii, pp. 1510. The banquet is described in BL, Additional MS. 21116, fol. 40, abstracted in *LP,* II.ii, no. 3446.

6–7 October 1518. Richard Gibson's account for a joust to celebrate the Treaty of Universal Peace. PRO, E36/228, fols. a, 1–5, abstracted in *LP,* II.ii, pp. 1515–17. The banquet is described in PRO, E36/217, fols. 303–6, abstracted in *LP,* II.ii, pp. 1514–15.

3, 7, 8 March 1519. Richard Gibson's account for entertainments for the French hostages at Greenwich: joust (3 and 8 March) and 'maskalyn *after the* maner of the Contrey of ettally' (on 7 March at night). PRO, SP1/18, fols. 52–7, abstracted in *LP,* III.i, no. 113.

ca. 1519. Fragment of Richard Gibson's account for cloth of gold used in revels. PRO, SP1/32, fol. 182, abstracted in *LP,* Addenda, I.i, no. 273.

3 September 1519. Richard Gibson's account for an entertainment for the French hostages at Newhall, including a 'pastime' (*Summer and Winter*) and a double maskeller. PRO, E36/217, fols. 100–8, 123–9, abstracted in *LP,* III.ii, pp. 1550–1.

21, 27, 28 October 1519. Richard Gibson's account for a joust for the wedding of the Earl of Devonshire. PRO, E36/217, fols. 108–11, 129–32, abstracted in *LP,* III.i, p. 1551.

31 December 1519. Richard Gibson's account for a 'meskeller or mvmmery' at Greenwich. PRO, E36/217, fols. 111–14, 132–5, abstracted in *LP,* III.ii, pp. 1551–2.

5 January 1520. Richard Gibson's account for supplying the king and nineteen gentlemen when they went in 'meskellyng apperell' to Wolsey's (York Place). PRO, E36/217, fols. 114–15, 135, abstracted in *LP,* III.ii, p. 1552.

6 January 1520. Richard Gibson's account for a 'dysguysyng *with* A pagent' at Greenwich. PRO, E36/217, fols. 115–16, 136, abstracted in *LP,* III.ii, p. 1552.

8 January 1520. Richard Gibson's account for preparing 'a new & an other meskeller' at Greenwich. PRO, E36/217, fols. 116–19, 136–9, abstracted in *LP,* III.ii, p. 1552.

1, 19 February 1520. Richard Gibson's account for a challenge to a joust in disguise and a pageant (a 'tryke' or 'Spell wagvn & Ther in A lady') on 1 February and for a joust on 19 February. PRO, E36/217, fols. 119–21, 139–41, abstracted in *LP,* III.ii, pp. 1552–3.

Field of Cloth of Gold (Guisnes and Ardres) and Interview with Charles V (Gravelines and Calais):

(1) **1 May 1520.** Inventory of coverings for bards, trappers, harnesses, saddles, base coats, etc. at the armoury in the tilt-yard at Greenwich in the custody of George Lovekyn, Clerk of the Stable. PRO, SP1/29, pp. 191-205, abstracted in *LP,* III.ii, pp. 1548–50.

(2) **13 May – 3 June 1520.** Richard Gibson's account for work on a pageant (a mount and a whitethorn tree) from 13 May to 3 June for the joust at the Field of Cloth of Gold at Guisnes-Ardres. PRO, E36/217, fols. 293–302, abstracted in *LP,* III.ii, p. 1553.

(3) **11–22 June 1520.** Richard Gibson's account for a joust at the Field of Cloth of Gold at Guisnes-Ardres. PRO, E36/217, fols. 142, 145–74, abstracted in *LP,* III.ii, pp. 1554–6.

(4) **June – July 1520.** Richard Gibson's account for 'maskellers' at Ardres and at Calais. PRO, E36/229, fols. 48–65, abstracted in *LP,* III.ii, p. 1554.

(5) **July 1520.** Richard Gibson's account for 'maskellers' at Calais. PRO, E36/229, fols. 48–65, 101, abstracted in *LP,* III.ii, p. 1554.

3 November 1520 – 12 February 1521. Richard Gibson's accounts and subsidiary documents for work on maskellers, jousts, and tourneys, as follows:

(1) **3 November 1520 – 12 February 1521.** Material received and used by Gibson in 'maskellers', jousts, and tourneys. PRO, E36/217, fols. 281–92.

(2) **3 November 1520.** 'Maskeller' at Greenwich with friars' habits. PRO, SP1/29, fol. 212v, abstracted in *LP,* III.ii, p. 1556.

(3) **9 December 1520.** Revels at Greenwich with mariners' frocks. PRO, SP1/29, fol. 213; E36/217, fol. 314; abstracted in *LP,* III.ii, p. 1556.

(4) **1 or 4 January 1521.** Revels at Greenwich. PRO, SP1/29, fols. 213v–214; E36/217, fols. 314–15; abstracted in *LP,* III.ii, p. 1556.

(5) **3 January 1521.** Revels at York Place. PRO, SP1/29, fol. 214v; E36/217, fol. 315; abstracted in *LP,* III.ii, p. 1556.

(6) **11–12 February 1521.** Joust and tourney at Greenwich. PRO, SP1/29, fols. 215–18v; E36/217, fols. 316–18; abstracted in *LP,* III.ii, pp. 1556–7.

(7) **11 February 1521.** 'Maskeller' at Greenwich with friars' habits. PRO, SP1/29, fol. 219; E36/217, fol. 318; abstracted in *LP,* III.ii, p. 1557.

(8) **12 February 1521.** 'Maskeller' at Greenwich. PRO, SP1/29, fol. 219r–v; E36/217, fol. 319; abstracted in *LP,* III.ii, p. 1557.

29 December 1521, 1 January 1522. Richard Gibson's account for two 'maskellers'. PRO, SP1/29, fols. 220–1v, abstracted in *LP,* III.ii, p. 1557.

2 March 1522. Richard Gibson's account for a joust for the imperial ambassadors at Greenwich. PRO, SP1/29, fols. 223–8, abstracted in *LP,* III.ii, pp. 1557–8.

3 March 1522. Richard Gibson's account for a 'maskeller' employing eighteen garments at York Place. PRO, SP1/29, fol. 237, abstracted in *LP,* III.ii, p. 1559.

4 March 1522. Richard Gibson's account for a disguising with pageant *(Schatew Vert)* at York Place. PRO, SP1/29, fols. 228v–37, abstracted in *LP,* III.ii, pp. 1558–9.

Entertainment of Charles V:

(1) **4–5 June 1522.** Richard Gibson's account for a joust and tourney at Greenwich for Emperor Charles V. PRO, SP1/24, fols. 226–30, abstracted in *LP,* III.ii, no. 2305.

(2) **5 June 1522.** Richard Gibson's account for 'a meskeller' and revels 'devysed by Master Wylliam Kornyche' at Greenwich for Emperor Charles V. PRO, SP1/24, fols. 230v–3v, abstracted in *LP,* III.ii, no. 2305.

(3) **5–8 June 1522.** Richard Gibson's Tents account for pitching and removing tents and pavilions for a tourney on 5 June in connection with the entertainments of Emperor Charles V. PRO, SP1/24, fols. 236v–7, abstracted in *LP,* III.ii, no. 2305.

(4) **15 June 1522.** Richard Gibson's account for 'a meskeler at the kastell of wyndsor' with a pageant, including the costs of Cornish's revels. PRO, SP1/24, fol. 231v, 234–6, abstracted in *LP,* III.ii, no. 2305.

[1525–1534]. Bill sent to Richard Gibson for eighteen pillars and knops to be set on posts 'for the kinges vse.' BL, Egerton MS. 2623, art. 2.

Castle of Loyalty Tournament and Revels:

(1) **29 December 1524.** Richard Gibson's account for a pageant (a mount and a unicorn) for *Castle of Loyalty* tournament and siege at Greenwich. PRO, SP1/32, fols. 256–61, abstracted in *LP,* IV.i, no. 965.

(2) **29 December 1524.** Richard Gibson's account for a joust at Greenwich for *Castle of Loyalty* tournament and siege. PRO, SP1/32, fols. 258–9v, abstracted in *LP,* IV.i, no. 965.

(3) **29 December 1524.** Richard Gibson's account for a 'meskeler' to conclude the joust at the *Castle of Loyalty* tournament and siege. PRO, SP1/32, fols. 260–1, abstracted in *LP,* IV.i, no. 965.

14 January – 17 February 1526. Richard Gibson's day book of material and wages for work on barriers, a joust, 'maskellers', and a pageant. PRO, SP1/37, fols. 7–15, abstracted in *LP,* IV.i, no. 1888.

19 February – 25 April 1527. Richard Gibson's day-book of material and wages for work on jousts held on 5 March. PRO, SP1/41, fols. 165–8, abstracted in *LP,* IV.ii, no. 3064.

Anglo-French Treaty Celebration, 7 May 1527. Accounts and subsidiary documents for the construction of a banqueting house (the Long House) and production of a joust, a 'dialogue' *(Love and Riches)*, a disguising with pageant (a mount), and mask:

(1) Richard Gibson's primary day-book for work on the entire project from 14 January to 7 May. PRO, SP1/41, fols. 221–53v, abstracted in *LP,* IV.ii, no. 3107.

(2) Richard Gibson's draft of an account for wages and material used from 14 January to 7 May. PRO, SP2/Fol. C, fols. 106–38v, abstracted in *LP,* IV.ii, no. 3097 (i, ii).

(3) Richard Gibson's day-book for wages and material used from 16 February to 12 April for the banqueting house. BL, Egerton MS. 2605, fols. 1–10.

(4) Richard Gibson's day-book for work on the joust from 19 February to 7 March. BL, Egerton MS. 2605, fols. 11–14.

(5) Richard Gibson's account for material and work on the banqueting house and pageant. PRO, SP1/41, fols. 212–13v, abstracted in *LP,* IV.ii, no. 3098 (4).

(6) Richard Gibson's draft of an account for the joust held on 6 May. PRO, SP1/41, fols. 203–16v, abstracted in *LP,* IV.ii, no. 3098 (2, 3).

(7) Richard Gibson's eight documents for material, work, and services. PRO, SP1/41, fols. 194–202, abstracted in *LP,* IV.ii, no. 3098 (i–ix).

(8) Sir Henry Guildford's and Sir Thomas Wyatt's account of money disbursed in connection with building the banqueting house. PRO, E36/227, fols. 1–36v, abstracted in *LP,* IV.ii, no. 3104.

(9) Fragment in Gibson's hand giving a summary of the charges of three other accounts [possibly for 1527]. PRO, SP2/Fol. C, fols. 104–5.

Revels for the installation of Henry VIII and Francis I into the Order of St Michael and the Order of the Garter, 10 November 1527. Accounts and subsidiary accounts for the renovation of the banqueting house (the Long House) and the production of a joust, a pageant (two trees), a Latin play *[Cardinalis Pacificus]*, and four masks at Greenwich:

(1) Richard Gibson's draft for an account for work on the banqueting house between 9 October and 10 November. BL, Egerton MS. 2605, fols. 16–33v. Fair copy of above signed by Guildford and Gibson. PRO, SP1/45, fols. 21–33, abstracted in *LP,* IV.ii, no. 3564.

(2) Richard Gibson's draft for an account for work on the revels to be held on 10 November. BL, Egerton MS. 2605, fols. 34–7. Fair copy of above signed by Guildford and Gibson. PRO, SP1/45, fols. 33v–6, abstracted in *LP,* IV.ii, no. 3564.

(3) Richard Gibson's draft for an account for work on the play 'in *the* latyn tong' *[Cardinalis Pacificus]*. BL, Egerton MS. 2605, fols. 37v–42. Fair copy of above signed by Guildford and Gibson. PRO, SP1/45, fols. 36v–40, abstracted in *LP,* IV.ii, no. 3564.

(4) Plan and elevation, probably for the 'Long House' at Greenwich in 1527. BL, Egerton MS. 2605, fol. 43.

(5) George Lovekyn's day-book for material and work in garnishing a portal and a fountain in the banqueting house from 11 October to 10 November at the command of Sir Henry Guildford. PRO, E36/227, fols. 48v–60, abstracted in *LP,* IV.ii, no. 3563.

(6) Sir Henry Guildford's, Sir Thomas Wyatt's, and Richard Gibson's account for garments and properties for four masks and a Latin play *[Cardinalis Pacificus].* BL, Egerton MS. 2605, fols. 16–45; PRO, SP1/45, fols. 33v–40; abstracted in *LP,* IV.ii, no. 3564.

[25 December 1527 ⟨ ⟩ 6 January 1528]. Heading of Richard Gibson's account for revels at Greenwich and Richmond for Christmas. BL, Egerton MS. 2605, fol. 15v.

[ca. 1530]. Fragment of Richard Gibson's account for a joust. PRO, SP1/58, pp. 282–3, calendared in *LP,* IV.iii, no. 6791.

1539–40. Inventory of revels properties formerly in charge of John Farlyon [Yeoman of the Revels, d.1539] and now committed to John Bridges [Yeoman, 1539]. PRO, E36/228, fols. 9–12, abstracted in *LP,* II.ii, p. 1517 (misdated 1518 in *LP*).

Christmas 1541 – Shrovetide 1542:

(1) 1 January 1541. John Bridges's account for making costumes for a play by the Children of the Chapel at Greenwich on New Year's day at night. Folger Library, MS. Lb 2, fol. 1, abstracted in A.J. Kempe, *The Loseley Manuscripts* (London: J. Murray, 1835), 69–70.

(2) 20, 21 February 1542. John Bridges's account for making garments and properties for masks on Shrove Monday and on Shrove Tuesday at Westminster. Folger Library, MSS Lb 262; Lb 2, fols. 1v–2; abstracted in A.J. Kempe, *The Loseley Manuscripts* (London: J. Murray, 1835), 70.

December 1542. Inventory of 4 December of the Tents taken by Sir Thomas Cawarden. Guildford Muniment Room, MS. LM 4. Inventory of 10 December of the Revels taken by Sir Thomas Cawarden. Folger Library, MSS Lb 325; Lb 326 (draft).

Christmas 1542 – Shrovetide 1543:

(1) 26 December 1542 – 6 January 1543. John Bridges's account for garments and properties for masks (men-at-arms and Moors) at Hampton Court. Folger Library, MSS Lb 259; Lb 2, fols. 2v–3; abstracted in A.J. Kempe, *The Loseley Manuscripts* (London: J. Murray, 1835), 70.

(2) 4, 6 February 1543. John Bridges's account for preparing a banqueting chamber and for renting pageants and making garments and properties for a mask ('Alamains') on Shrove Sunday and for a mask (mariners and monstrous torch bearers) on Shrove Tuesday, all at Westminster. Folger Library, MSS Lb 260; Lb 2, fols. 3v–4; abstracted in William Bray, 'Observations on the Christmas Diversions formerly given by the Lord of Misrule, and on the King's Office of the Revels and

Tents: Chiefly from the Papers preserved at Loseley, near Guildford,' *Archaeologia*, XVIII (1817): 325; A.J. Kempe, *The Loseley Manuscripts* (London: J. Murray, 1835), 71.

[1542–1546]. At some point during this period tents were carried to the banqueting house at Hyde Park and then to the Charterhouse for storage: Guildford Muniment Room, MS. LM 43, fol. 13.

[1543]. Cawarden and his crews of workmen in the Tents were at Whitefriars constructing a timber house for the king. One of the bills mentions deliveries to the 'bankett howse at the Whyte fryers.' Guildford Muniment Room, MS. LM 128/5.

Christmas 1543–44:

(1) [1543–4]. John Bridges's account for altering torch bearers' costumes and for carrying them to court on New Year's and Twelfth Night and a bill for tailors' work at court. Guildford Muniment Room, MS. LM 59/68.

(2) **1, 6 January 1544.** John Bridges's account for preparing [two] masks of women [for New Year's] at Hampton Court and possibly for outfitting a play by the Children of Chapel on the same day and for preparing a mask of Turks [for Twelfth Night] at Hampton Court. Folger Library, MSS Lb 153; Lb 154; Lb 2, fols. 4v–5, abstracted in A.J. Kempe, *The Loseley Manuscripts* (London: J. Murray, 1835), 71–3.

[1544]. Tents check-book including charges for carriage of tents to and from the Charterhouse to Hyde Park for a banqueting house. Guildford Muniment Room, MS. LM 43/1, fol. 13.

22 April 1544 – 21 April 1546. Tents account for setting up certain tents at Westminster 'for the banket howse on the *trilles* there' [possibly the banqueting house designed by Nicholas Bellin of Modena: Bodleian Library, MS. Engl. hist. b. 192/1, fol. 30]: Guildford Muniment Room, MS. LM 1b, fol. 1. Charges in this account, fol. 5, refer to setting up the tents at Nonsuch and transporting 'hangings' there from Westminster when 'thmbasadors' were there.

26 December 1544 – 6 January 1545. Revels Office account for Christmas revels. Folger Library, MSS Lb 258; Lb 2, fols. 6v–7.

26 December 1545– 6 January 1546. Revels Office account for masks (Egyptians and Moors) at Hampton Court. Folger Library, MSS Lb 266; Lb 267.

December 1545 – August 1546. Book of receipts of material from the Great Wardrobe between December 1545 and August 1546 including a list of masking garments for men and women and a cast list of the characters of Virtue and/or Zeal as scholars, Insolence and/or Diligence as gentlemen, Old Blind Custom as a priest, Hunger for Knowledge as a London apprentice, and a collier as Thomas of Croydon. Guildford Muniment Room, MS. LM 17, abstracted in A. Feuillerat, 'An Unknown Protestant Morality Play,' *Modern Language Review*, 9 (1914): 94–6; see also C.A. Baskerville, 'On Two Old Plays,' *Modern Philology*, 14 (1916): 16.

1545. List of silks delivered to Cawarden from the Great Wardrobe. Folger Library, MS. Lb 479.

Entertainments for the Admiral of France:

(1) **[1546].** Tents account listing garnishing material delivered to Hampton Court for a banqueting house. Guildford Muniment Room, MS. LM 59/50, fol. 1. Charges in this account, fols. 2v–3, also list deliveries to a banqueting house 'on the hyll aboue otlandes.'

(2) **29 July [1546].** List of cloth of gold and other material. Guildford Muniment Room, MS. LM 59/144.

(3) **July 1546.** John Bridges's and John Barnard's list of material ordered for the entertainment of the French embassy. Guildford Muniment Room, MS. LM 59/98.

(4) **July 1546.** List of masking garments and material. Folger Library, MS. Lb 116.

(5) **17 July – 23 August 1546.** Yeoman's Book showing material delivered to the Revels Office and what garments were made. Guildford Muniment Room, MS. LM 59/143.

(6) **16 July – 5 September 1546.** Revels Office account (24 August – 5 September) for decorating the banqueting house at Hampton Court and for preparing two masks, one of wild men and one of knights. Folger Library, MS. Lb 5, abstracted in A.J. Kempe, *The Loseley Manuscripts* (London: J. Murray, 1835), 73.

(7) **14 August 1546.** Cloth of gold, silver, and silks, etc. delivered to Hampton Court 'oute of the charge of Sir Thomas Henage,' Groom of the Stool, by the king's commandment to Sir Thomas Cawarden. Guildford Muniment Room, MS. LM 59/142.

(8) **[September 1546].** Tents account for setting up and 'new Edyfyeng' of a great timber house at Cobham 'for a quadrante to Ioyne the tymber houses together.' Guildford Muniment Room, MS. LM 2, LM 22/2, fol. 5.

Coronation of Edward VI, tournament, and revels; the revels at Shrovetide, and the revels a week after Shrovetide:

(1) **13 January – 24 February 1547.** Tents account including charges for the carriage of two long hales from Blackfriars to the tilt-yard at Westminster for a triumph. Guildford Muniment Room, MS. LM 30.

(2) **1–28 February 1547.** Revels Office account for (i) moving the office from Warwick Inn to Blackfriars; (ii) the Coronation of Edward VI; (iii) producing masks for Shrovetide; (iv) producing a mask a week after Shrovetide (27 February). Folger Library, MSS Lb 8; Lb 9; printed in Feuillerat, *Edward VI and Mary*, pp. 3–8.

(3) **February 1547.** Garments delivered by the Revels Office to the city of London for the coronation entry. Folger Library, MS. Lb 268, printed in Feuillerat, *Edward VI and Mary*, p. 249.

(4) **[February 1547].** Material used in a mask on the Sunday following the coronation (27 February). Folger Library, MS. Lb 269.

(5) **February 1547.** Material for masks at the coronation. Folger Library, MS. Lb 270.

(6) **February 1547.** Material for masks at Shrovetide. Folger Library, MS. Lb 271.

(7) **February 1547.** Boat hire and carriage for masks. Folger Library, MS. Lb 272.

(8) **[February 1547].** Bill from Nicholas of Modena for making the moulded work for the [coronation] 'mount'. Guildford Muniment Room, MS. LM 59/34.

[1547]. Outline for a morality play including a pope, friar, and priest. Guildford Muniment Room, MS. LM 128/12, printed in Feuillerat, *Edward VI and Mary*, p. 245.

March 1547. John Bridges's list of material delivered to the Revels Office up to 26 March cut for playing garments for the King's Players, for the king (a priest's gown), the Duke of Suffolk and Lord Strange. Guildford Muniment Room, MS. LM 59/145, printed in Feuillerat, *Edward VI and Mary*, pp. 22–4.

1 April 1547. Inventory of Revels Office garments and properties. Folger Library, MS. Lb 319, printed in Feuillerat, *Edward VI and Mary*, pp. 9–17; Lb 139 (one of the many office books used to make the inventory).

April 1547. List of remains of stuff stored in the fratery (at Blackfriars) and deliveries to Thomas Blagrave 'to be brought vnto the covrte at grenewich the xjth daye of Apryll' with a list of garments. Guildford Muniment Room, MS. LM 59/146.

May 1547. Inventory of Revels Office garments. Folger Library, MS. Lb 112, printed in Feuillerat, *Edward VI and Mary*, pp. 18–21.

14 September 1547. Inventory of Revels Office garments. BL, Harleian MS. 1419 (A), abstracted in Feuillerat, *Edward VI and Mary*, pp. 264–6.

Christmas – Shrovetide 1547–8:

(1) **Christmas 1547–8 – Christmas 1549–50.** Abstract of Revels Office accounts. Folger Library, MS. Lb 113, printed in Feuillerat, *Edward VI and Mary*, pp. 269–70.

(2) **26 December 1547 – 15 January 1548.** Abstract of Revels Office account for work on masks and entertainments at Christmas and for Shrovetide 1547–8 and for a pageant (the Tower of Babylon). Folger Library, MS. Lb 274, printed in Feuillerat, *Edward VI and Mary*, p. 26.

(3) **3 January 1548.** List of masking garments delivered by the Revels Office to the Lord Protector. Guildford Muniment Room, MS. LM 59/64, printed in Feuillerat, *Edward VI and Mary*, p. 251.

(4) **3 January 1548.** Bill of Robert Fletcher for masking garments sent to Paget including six Turkish gowns of blue satin and four friar's costumes. Guildford Muniment Room, MS. LM 59/65, printed in Feuillerat, *Edward VI and Mary*, p. 251.

(5) **5–15 January 1548.** Revels Office account for work at Shrovetide. Folger Library, MSS Lb 6; Lb 7; printed in Feuillerat, *Edward VI and Mary*, pp. 29–32.

(6) **5 February 1548.** Letter from Stanhope to Cawarden requiring six garments for maskers 'whereof the kinges maiestie shal be oon and the residue of his stature

and vj other garments of like bignes for torchebearers.' Folger Library, MS. Lb 290, printed in Feuillerat, *Edward VI and Mary,* p. 33.

Christmas – Shrovetide 1548–9:

    (1) **Abstract of Revels accounts.** Folger Library, MS. Lb 113, printed in Feuillerat, *Edward VI and Mary,* pp. 269–70.

    (2) **26 September 1548 – 26 September 1549.** Revels Office account for work on masks and entertainments at Christmas and for a pageant (dragon with seven heads) and costumes for a play by the King's Players at Shrovetide. Folger Library, MS. Lb 11, fols. 1–2v, printed in Feuillerat, *Edward VI and Mary,* pp. 34–5, 39–40.

    (3) **[February – March 1549].** John Holt's list of material for a mask involving 'Alamains.' Guildford Muniment Room, MS. LM 59/63.

Christmas 1549–50:

    (1) Revels Office account for making and altering costumes for masks and plays. Folger Library, MS. Lb 12, printed in Feuillerat, *Edward VI and Mary,* pp. 41–3.

    (2) **30 December 1549.** Bill for material and masking garments. Guildford Muniment Room, MS. LM 59/156.

    (3) **ca. 1550.** Fragment of a play with a note in Sir Thomas Cawarden's hand. Folger Library, MS. Lb 554, printed by L.A Cummings, '"Part of a Play": a possible dramatic fragment (*c* 1550) from the office of the Master of the Revels,' *Records of Early English Drama Newsletter,* 2, no. 2 (1977): 2–15, and G.R. Proudfoot, 'Five Dramatic Fragments from the Folger Shakespeare Library and from the Henry E. Huntington Library,' *MSC,* IX (1977), 52–7.

    (4) **7 January 1550.** Warrant for payment to Sir Thomas Cawarden for the Revels Office. Folger Library, MS. Lb 175 (draft); Lb 275, printed in Feuillerat, *Edward VI and Mary,* p. 269.

ca. 1550. Inventory of the Royal Household including the Revels in the charge of Sir Thomas Cawarden. BL, Additional MS. 46348, fols. 399–413.

6 June 1550 – 15 June 1555. Thomas Blagrave's brief description of charges in the Offices of the Revels and Tents. Folger Library, MS. Lb 41, fols. 87–91, abstracted in Feuillerat, *Edward VI and Mary,* p. 301.

6 June 1550 – 15 June 1555. Comprehensive account for the Offices of the Revels, Tents, and Toils (Cawarden had been appointed overseer of the Toils on 2 June 1550: Guildford Muniment Room, MS. LM 59/1). Folger Library, MS. Lb 41, abstracted in Feuillerat, *Edward VI and Mary,* pp. 270–3 (heading), 47–179 (text).

6 June 1550 – 15 June 1555. Revels Office declared account. Folger Library, MS. Lb 324.

6 June 1550 – 15 June 1555. Cawarden's certificate declaring the income and expenditures for his Offices of the Tents, Revels, Toils, as well as charges for the Lord of Misrule and for the banqueting house. Folger Library, MSS Lb 314; Lb 317 (copy); Lb 316 (abbreviated copy); Lb 315 (imperfect copy).

Christmas 1550 – August 1551:

(1) **1550–1.** Estimate of charges for the revels at Christmas 1550–1 and Shrovetide 1551, for the banqueting house, and for the Tents in 1550–1. Folger Library, MSS Lb 20, Lb 322, Lb 323.

(2) **24 December 1550 – 9 June 1551.** Revels Office account for work at Christmas (24 December – 7 January), Shrovetide (3–11 February), masks and the airing (3–9 June), and at other times in making costumes and properties for the king, his young lords, 'divers players and other persones for plaies and other pastimes.' Folger Library, MS. Lb 41, fols. 22–4v, printed in Feuillerat, *Edward VI and Mary*, pp. 47–55.

(3) **24 December 1550 – 9 June 1551.** Docket for Revels accounts. Folger Library, MS. Lb 41, fols. 25r–v.

(4) **28 December 1550 – 3 August 1551.** Revels Office book. Folger Library, MS. Lb 15.

(5) **3 February 1551 – 9 June 1551.** Revels Office book with charges for properties used in masks and plays omitted from the main account and for the airing. Folger Library, MS. Lb 13.

28 January 1551 – 27 January 1552. Declared account of the Offices of the Revels and of the Tents. BL, Harleian MS. 284, fol. 120.

The banqueting facilities at Hyde Park and Marylebone Park, July 1551:

(1) Lawrence Bradshaw's docket for construction between 28 June and 29 July. Folger Library, MS. Lb 18.

(2) Lawrence Bradshaw's pay books for work from 28 June to 10 July. Folger Library, MS. Lb 182.

(3) Copy of Lawrence Bradshaw's docket. *Calendar of the Manuscripts of the Most Hon. The Marquis of Salisbury, K.G., &c. preserved at Hatfield House, Hertfordshire* (London: Eyre and Spottiswoode, 1883), Part I: 92–3, in *RCHM*, IX. Printed in Mrs. Alec [Ethel Brilliana] Tweedie, *Hyde Park, Its History and Romance* (New York: Pott, 1908), 44–6.

(4) Copy of the council's letter of 8 December 1550 authorizing an imprest of £300 to Cawarden to begin the banqueting house. Folger Library, MS. Lb 47.

(5) Joiners, basket makers, sawyers employed by Cawarden on the project. Folger Library, MS. Lb. 165.

(6) Charges for material and for the artificers and labourers employed by Cawarden on the project. Folger Library, MS. Lb 135.

(7) Cawarden's pay book for work on the banqueting house. Folger Library, MS. Lb 21, fols. 1–10 (fair copy); Lb 17 (draft).

(8) Bills from John Leeds and Richard Lee. Folger Library, MSS Lb 150, Lb 151.

(9) Account of John Harness, the king's Gardener at Westminster, for flowers purchased for the banqueting houses at Hyde Park and at Hampton court. Folger Library, MSS Lb 276 (fair copy); Lb 155 (draft).

(10) Note of Cawarden's payments for flowers. Folger Library, MS. Lb 149.

(11) Various bills. Guildford Muniment Room, MSS LM 59/78, LM 59/153, LM 59/154.

(12) Charges of the banqueting house at Hampton Court in 1551. Guildford Muniment Room, MSS LM 713a, LM 713b (draft); LM 715 (pay book), LM 714 (draft).

(13) Revels Office ledger for the banqueting house and other facilities. Folger Library, MS. Lb 41, fols. 28-38v.

(14) Docket for the above. Folger Library, MS. Lb 41, fols. 39r–v.

(15) Cawarden's estimate of charges in the Revels and Tents in 1551 including those for the banqueting house. Folger Library, MS. Lb 20.

(16) Cawarden's letter of 26 October 1551 to Cecil complaining about Bradshaw's handling of the £133 6s. 8d. imprest granted to him. *Calendar of the Manuscripts of the Most Hon. The Marquis of Salisbury, K.G., &c. preserved at Hatfield House, Hertfordshire* (London: Eyre and Spottiswoode, 1883), Part I: 92–3, in *RCHM*, IX. Printed in Mrs. Alec [Ethel Brilliana] Tweedie, *Hyde Park, Its History and Romance* (New York: Pott, 1908), 44–6.

Christmas 1551–2:

(1) **24 November 1551.** Warrant from the king to Cawarden to furnish the triumph at tilt. Folger Library, MS. Lb 16, printed in Feuillerat, *Edward VI and Mary*, p. 56.

(2) **12 December 1551 – 7 January 1552.** Revels Office account for work at Christmas. Folger Library, MS. Lb 41, fols. 41–8, printed in Feuillerat, *Edward VI and Mary*, pp. 62–76.

(3) **12 December 1551 – 7 January 1552.** Revels Office book. Folger Library, MS. Lb 19.

(4) **25 December 1551.** Warrant from the council to Cawarden to deliver garments to the King's Players to perform before the king during Christmas. Folger Library, MS. Lb 278, printed in Feuillerat, *Edward VI and Mary*, p. 57.

(5) **Christmas 1551–2.** Revels charges related to the Lord of Misrule. Folger Library, MS. Lb 327, printed in Feuillerat, *Edward VI and Mary*, pp. 77–81.

(6) **Christmas 1551–2.** Revels charges related to the triumph at tilt. Folger Library, MS. Lb 280; Guildford Muniment Room, MS. LM 59/147; printed in Feuillerat, *Edward VI and Mary*, pp. 82–4.

(7) **Christmas 1551–2.** Docket for Revels accounts, including list of masks. Folger Library, MS. Lb 41, fols. 48v–9v, printed in Feuillerat, *Edward VI and Mary*, p. 85.

(8) **5 January 1552.** Warrant from the council, carried to Cawarden by Sir Thomas Chaloner, to furnish apparel for two people to play in a dialogue *[Riches and Youth]* before the king the next night. Folger Library, MS. Lb 288, printed in Feuillerat, *Edward VI and Mary*, p. 60.

(9) **6 January 1552.** Warrant from the Lord Chamberlain to Cawarden to furnish the King's Players with garments for a play 'to morrowe at night' before the king. Folger Library, MS. Lb 282, printed in Feuillerat, *Edward VI and Mary*, p. 86.

Documents relating to the entertainments of George Ferrers, Master of the King's Pastimes, at Christmas 1551–2:

(1) 24 December letter from Northumberland to Cawarden to confer with Ferrers, Lord of Misrule, to devise shows for Christmas. Folger Library, MS. Lb 257, printed in Feuillerat, *Edward VI and Mary*, p. 56.

(2) Letter from Ferrers to Cawarden requiring the services of carpenters and painters. Folger Library, MS. Lb 283, printed in Feuillerat, *Edward VI and Mary*, p. 61.

(3) 25 December warrant from the council to Cawarden to outfit the Lord of Misrule. Folger Library, MS. Lb 277, printed in Feuillerat, *Edward VI and Mary*, p. 57.

(4) 30 December warrant from the council to Cawarden to furnish Ferrers and his associates with a second livery. Folger Library, MS. Lb 281, printed in Feuillerat, *Edward VI and Mary*, p. 58.

(5) 30 December warrant from the council to Cawarden to furnish Ferrers with garments and properties. Folger Library, MS. Lb 284, printed in Feuillerat, *Edward VI and Mary*, p. 58.

(6) 2 January letter from Ferrers to Cawarden to deliver apparel for the Lord of Misrule's attendants. Folger Library, MS. Lb 500, printed in Feuillerat, *Edward VI and Mary*, p. 59.

(7) [2–3] January letter from Ferrers to Cawarden on the insufficiency of the garments sent for the Lord of Misrule's councillors. Folger Library, MS. Lb 285, printed in Feuillerat, *Edward VI and Mary*, p. 59.

(8) 3 January warrant from the council to Cawarden to furnish appropriately the Lord of Misrule's councillors. Folger Library, MS. Lb 286, printed in Feuillerat, *Edward VI and Mary*, p. 60.

(9) Incomplete warrants for garments and properties for the Lord of Misrule for an entry into London and for a mask. Folger Library, MS. Lb 293; Guildford Muniment Room, MS. LM 59/151; printed in Feuillerat, *Edward VI and Mary*, p. 92.

(10) 5 January letter from Ferrers to Cawarden concerning the properties to be used for the last day of the Lord of Misrule's reign. Folger Library, MS. Lb 299, printed in Feuillerat, *Edward VI and Mary*, p. 61.

[1551–2 or 1552–3]. Yeoman's book of garments including those for the Lord of Misrule. Guildford Muniment Room, MS. LM 59/149.

1552–5. John Holt's expenses as Yeoman of the Revels from 1552 to 1555. Folger Library, MS. Lb 23.

5 August 1552. Warrant for payment to the Revels and Tents for the period from 4 May 1550 to 2 August 1552. Guildford Munimnet Room, MS. 59/8.

Christmas 1552–3:

(1) **28 January 1551 – 27 January 1552.** Revels Office declared account. BL, Harleian MS. 284, fol. 120.

(2) **27 December 1552 – 7 January 1553.** Revels account for work at Christmas. Folger Library, MS. Lb 41, fols. 51–9, printed in Feuillerat, *Edward VI and Mary*, pp. 95–114.

(3) **18 December 1552 – 16 October 1554.** Warrant to pay Cawarden for charges, some associated with the Lord of Misrule's entertainments. Folger Library, MSS Lb 147, Lb 325.

(4) **27 December 1552 – 7 January 1553.** Revels Office estimate of charges for support of the Lord of Misrule's entertainments. Folger Library, MS. Lb 320, printed in Feuillerat, *Edward VI and Mary*, pp. 117–25.

Documents relating to the entertainments of George Ferrers, Master of the King's Pastimes, at Christmas 1552–3:

(1) Letter from Ferrers to Cawarden outlining his Christmas entertainments. Folger Library, MS. Lb 292, printed in Feuillerat, *Edward VI and Mary*, pp. 89–90.

(2) 21 December warrant from the council to Cawarden to furnish Ferrers for the Lord of Misrule's entertainments. Folger Library, MS. Lb 291.

(3) 27 December warrant from the council to Cawarden ordering a fool's coat for John Smyth. Folger Library, MS. Lb 287, printed in Feuillerat, *Edward VI and Mary*, p. 90.

(4) Letter from Ferrers to Cawarden to supply William Elderton 'a vyce Coate *with* a cappe and a dagger And a girdelle.' Guildford Muniment Room, MS. LM 59/168.

(5) 27 December letter from Ferrers to Cawarden ordering properties. Folger Library, MS. Lb 289, printed in Feuillerat, *Edward VI and Mary*, pp. 90–1.

(6) List of garments delivered to Henry Birch for the Lord of Misrule. Guildford Muniment Room, MS. LM 128/13, printed in Feuillerat, *Edward VI and Mary*, p. 91.

(7) Letter from Ferrers to Cawarden ordering garments and properties for New Year's night. Folger Library, MS. Lb 295, printed in Feuillerat, *Edward VI and Mary*, pp. 91–2.

(8) Letter from Ferrers to Cawarden ordering liveries for two footmen for the entry into London. Folger Library, MS. Lb 292, printed in Feuillerat, *Edward VI and Mary*, p. 92.

(9) Letter from Sir George Howard to Cawarden stating that the council has approved his triumph of *Venus, Cupid, and Mars* for Twelfth Night. Folger Library, MS. Lb 256.

(10) Letter from Sir George Howard to Cawarden outlining his pageant and mask, the triumph of *Venus, Cupid, and Mars*. Folger Library, MS. Lb 294, printed in Feuillerat, *Edward VI and Mary*, p. 93.

(11) Letter from Ferrers to Cawarden ordering garments for Howard's *Venus, Cupid, and Mars*. Folger Library, MS. Lb 501, printed in Feuillerat, *Edward VI and Mary*, pp. 93–4.

(12) Letter from Ferrers to Cawarden ordering payment to a joiner for sixty staves used in the mock joust on New Year's. Guildford Muniment Room, MS. LM 128/15, printed in Feuillerat, *Edward VI and Mary*, p. 94.

[1552–3]. Docket for Revels accounts, including list of masks. Folger Library, MS. Lb 41, fols. 61–2, abstracted in Feuillerat, *Edward VI and Mary*, p. 116.

[1552–3]. Bill sent to Cawarden for five items including four globes 'for the Revells at cryssenmes.' Guildford Muniment Room, MS. LM 25/32.

Shrovetide (revels postponed to Easter and May Day) 1553:

(1) **7 January 1553 – 7 June 1553.** Revels account for work at Shrovetide (7 January – 16 February), Easter, and May Day, charges for plays (28 February – 1 April), and the airing (31 May – 7 June). Folger Library, MS. Lb 41, fols. 64–71v, printed in Feuillerat, *Edward VI and Mary*, pp. 129–44.

(2) **7 January–16 February 1553.** Bills for the masks: payments for making counterfeit apes for a mask of bagpipes and for furring tails on wicker for a mask of cats. Folger Library, MSS Lb 162, Lb 124.

(3) **7 Edward VI [1553].** Docket for Revels accounts, including list of masks and plays. Folger Library, MS. Lb 41, fols. 72r–v, abstracted in Feuillerat, *Edward VI and Mary*, p. 145.

Letter from Northumberland to Cawarden, 20 May 1553. Requests a couple of masks, one of men and one of women, be appointed for the wedding of Lady Jane Grey. J.C. Jeaffreson calendared the document in *RCHM*, VII: 608b, but neither Feuillerat, *Edward VI and Mary*, p. 306, nor I could locate it.

1–7 June 1553. Revels account for the airing. Folger Library, MS. Lb 41, fol. 60r, printed in Feuillerat, *Edward VI and Mary*, p. 115.

February 1553 – 26 February 1555. Revels Office book. Folger Library, MS. Lb 302 (cf. Folger Library, MS. Lb 41, fol. 70).

Coronation of Mary, Christmas and Shrovetide revels 1553–4:

(1) **1553–4.** Revels account for work at the coronation of Queen Mary (22–8 September), Christmas (21 December – 6 January), and the airing (31 May –6 June). Folger Library, MS. Lb 41, fols. 73–5v, printed in Feuillerat, *Edward VI and Mary*, pp. 149–55.

(2) **22 September 1553 – 6 June 1554.** Docket for Revels accounts. Folger Library, MS. Lb 41, fol. 76.

(3) **26 September 1553.** Warrant from the queen to Cawarden to furnish a play, *Humanum Genus*, by the Gentlemen of the Chapel at the coronation. Loseley Manor Documents, vol. V, no. 6; Folger Library, MSS Lb 25 (copy); Lb 41, fol. 73 (copy entered into Cawarden's account), printed in Feuillerat, *Edward VI and Mary*, p. 149.

(4) **30 September 1553.** Warrant from the queen to Sir Edward Walgrave, Keeper of the Great Wardrobe, to furnish *Humanum Genus.* PRO, E101/427/5, no. 9, printed in Feuillerat, *Edward VI and Mary,* pp. 289–90.

Revels at All Hallows, Revels in November, Christmas, and Shrovetide 1554–5:

(1) **1554–5.** Revels Office account for work at All Hallows (17–21 October), the end of Parliament term (23–30 November), Christmas (13 December – 6 January), Shrovetide (26 January – 26 February), and the airing (9–26 March). Folger Library, MS. Lb 41, fols. 78–85v, printed in Feuillerat, *Edward VI and Mary,* pp. 159–79.

(2) **11 November 1554.** Letter from Maltravers and Lumley to Cawarden wanting to borrow Revels costumes for a mask of 'Alamains.' Folger Library, MS. Lb 499, printed in Feuillerat, *Edward VI and Mary,* p. 249.

(3) **8 December 1554.** Warrant from the queen to Cawarden to furnish all dialogues and interludes that Nicholas Udall will stage at court. Loseley Manor Documents, vol. VI. no. 7; Folger Library, MSS Lb 26 (copy); Lb 41, fol. 78 (copied into Cawarden's account), printed in Feuillerat, *Edward VI and Mary,* pp. 159–60, 290–2 (drafts).

(4) **Shrovetide 1555.** Revels Office book. Folger Library, MS. Lb 279 (copied in Folger Library, MS. Lb 41, fols. 84–5).

(5) **26 March 1555.** Revels Office inventory. Folger Library, MS. Lb 42, fols. 63–8v, printed in Feuillerat, *Edward VI and Mary,* pp. 180–9.

(6) **ca. March 1555.** Revels inventory of remains. Folger Library, MSS Lb 28, Lb 29; Guildford Muniment Room, MS. LM 59/148 (with different notes); the former printed in Feuillerat, *Edward VI and Mary,* pp. 190–4.

(7) **ca. March 1555.** Draft of warrant, 1 & 2 Phillip and Mary, to the Treasurer and Chamberlains of the Exchequer to pay Cawarden on his accounts. Guildford Muniment Room, MS. LM 128/14.

26 March 1555 – 29 September 1559. Copy of the declared account for the Offices of the Revels and Tents. Folger Library, MS. Lb 42, fols. 60–1v, abstracted in Feuillerat, *Edward VI and Mary,* p. 303 (summary of Revels charges).

[1554–5]. Docket for Revels Office accounts. Folger Library, MS. Lb 41, fols. 86r–v.

15 June 1555 – 29 September 1559. Revels Office declared account. PRO, E351/2935.

18 June 1555 – 30 September 1559. Comprehensive account for the Office of the Revels. Folger Library, MS. Lb 42, abstracted in Feuillerat, *Edward VI and Mary,* pp. 300 (heading), 195–242; *Elizabeth,* pp. 79–108.

18–30 June 1555. Revels Office account for the airing. Folger Library, MS. Lb 42, fols. 18r–v, printed in Feuillerat, *Edward VI and Mary,* pp. 195–6.

Christmas, Candlemas, and Shrovetide 1555–6:

(1) Revels Office account for work at Christmas (11 December – 8 January), Candlemas (8 January – 2 February), Shrovetide (2–25 February), and the airing (31 May – 12 June). Folger Library, MS. Lb 42, fols. 19–25v, printed in Feuillerat, *Edward VI and Mary,* pp. 199–211.

(2) **19 December [1555 or 1556].** Letter from the council to Cawarden requiring him to loan certain garments to the fellows and scholars of [New College? Trinity College?] Oxford to perform a tragedy at Christmas. Guildford Muniment Room, MS. LM 41, printed in Feuillerat, *Edward VI and Mary*, p. 250; On the date and college see J.R. Elliott, 'A "Learned Tragedy" at Trinity?' *Oxoniensia*, 50 (1985): 247–50.

(3) **Tuesday, 24 December [1555].** Letter from William Baldwin to Cawarden outlining his play for Christmas, *Love and Lyve*. Folger Library, MS. Lb 298, printed in Feuillerat, *Edward VI and Mary*, pp. 215–17 (he dates the letter 1556, p. 302).

(4) **11 February 1556.** Letter from Paget to Cawarden wanting to borrow masking garments for the use of the Venetian ambassador. Folger Library, MS. Lb 296, printed in Feuillerat, *Edward VI and Mary*, p. 250.

Christmas, Candlemas, Shrovetide, and Revels in April 1556–7:

(1) Revels Office account for work at Christmas (11 December – 8 January), Candlemas (8 January – 2 February), Shrovetide (2–15 February), St Mark's Day [25 April] (9–26 April), and the airing (31 May – 12 June). Folger Library, MS. Lb 42, fols. 27–34, printed in Feuillerat, *Edward VI and Mary*, pp. 218–31.

(2) **Shrovetide 1557.** Yeoman's bill. Folger Library, MS. Lb 111.

(3) **April 1557.** Warrant from the queen to Sir Edward Walgrave, Keeper of the Great Wardrobe, to provide Cawarden with material for the mask on 25 April. Bodleian Library, MS. Engl. Poet. d. 13, fol. 15, printed in Feuillerat, *Edward VI and Mary*, p. 302 (see p. 303 on its authenticity).

(4) **April 1557.** Revels bill for tailors' work and for material for the mask on 25 April. Folger Library, MSS Lb 134, Lb 301.

(5) **April [1557].** Letter from Jerningham to Cawarden requiring him to prepare masking entertainments. Guildford Muniment Room, Loseley Correspondence, 2/5, printed in Feuillerat, *Edward VI and Mary*, p. 245.

Christmas, Candlemas, and Shrovetide 1557–8:

Revels Office account for work at Christmas (11 December – 10 January), Candlemas (10 January – 3 February), Shrovetide (3 February – 3 March), and the airing (31 May – 12 June). Folger Library, MS. Lb 42, fols. 35–40, printed in Feuillerat, *Edward VI and Mary*, pp. 235–42.

18 July 1558. Letter from Thomas Copely to Cawarden asking him to secretly lend Revels garments for his wedding celebration. Folger Library, MS. Lb 303, printed in Feuillerat, *Edward VI and Mary*, p. 251.

Christmas revels, coronation of Elizabeth I, Candlemas revels, Shrovetide revels, revels in May, and revels in September 1558–9:

(1) **11 December 1558 – 30 September 1559.** Revels account for work at Christmas, New Year's, and Elizabeth's coronation (11 December – 8 January), Candlemas and Elizabeth's coronation (8 January – 2 February), Shrovetide (2–28 February),

on the banqueting house at Whitehall and a mask (2–25 May), at the airing (31 May – 14 June), and at a mask in a banqueting house at West Horsley (24 July – 30 September). Folger Library, MS. Lb 42, fols. 41–59, printed in Feuillerat, *Elizabeth*, pp. 79–108.

(2) **27 December 1558**. Warrant to the Great Wardrobe to furnish the coronation and the triumph afterwards. Folger Library, MSS Lb 121; Lb 119 and Lb 120 (drafts).

(3) **1558–9**. Account of Sir Edward Walgrave, Keeper of the Great Wardrobe, including deliveries for the coronation and the tournament. PRO, E101/429/4.

(4) **1558–9**. Silks delivered from the Great Wardrobe for use in the masks and revels. Folger Library, MS. Lb 152.

(5) **[1558–9]**. Draft of Revels account by Sir William More, as executor of Sir Thomas Cawarden, for masks in 1558–9. Guildford Muniment Room, MS. LM 58.

(6) **[1558–9]**. Thomas Dachan's bill to Cawarden (receipted June 1559) for masks at Christmas, cardinals and bishops for the first mask and for 'the pathway to *per*fecte knowledge.' Guildford Muniment Room, MS. LM 59/170.

(7) **3 January.** Order from the queen to Cawarden to furnish apparel to the city of London for the coronation entry. List of garments delivered to the city. Folger Library, MSS Lb 33, Lb 109, printed in D. Bergeron, 'Elizabeth's Coronation Entry (1559): New Manuscript Evidence,' *English Literary Renaissance*, 8 (1978): 58–62.

(8) **[February 1559]**. Bill for masks of mariners and fisherwives on Shrove Tuesday. Guildford Muniment Room, MS. LM 59/169. Bill for masks at the coronation and at Shrovetide. Folger Library, MSS Lb 34, Lb 111, Lb 148.

(9) **[May 1559]**. Bills and receipts for material for the masks and for the banqueting house at Westminster. Folger Library, MSS Lb 187, Lb 188, Lb 189, Lb 141, Lb 168, Lb 160, Lb 194, Lb 196; Guildford Muniment Room, MS. LM 58.

The banqueting house at Westminster, May 1559:

(1) Works account for the banqueting house in the gallery at Westminster. PRO, E351/3332.

(2) Declared account of the Office of the Works for the banqueting house at Westminster. PRO, E351/2935.

(3) Works account for the banqueting house at Westminster. PRO, E101/474/26.

(4) Packet of documents relating to the banqueting house at Westminster. Guildford Muniment Room, MS. LM 59/152.

(5) Robert Trunckwell's work in designing the banqueting house. Folger Library, MS. Lb 42, printed in Feuillerat, *Elizabeth*, pp. 81, 89, 93, 97–100.

August 1559. Lewis Stocket's bill for work on the banqueting house at West Horsley. Folger Library, MS. Lb 142.

Playing Companies at Court

ANONYMOUS. Unnamed companies of players performed before the court during the Christmas seasons of 1486–7, 1487–8, 1489–90, and on Candlemas (2 February) 1490. Other unnamed companies were paid on 31 December 1495 (for two plays in the Hall), 2 January 1496, 4 January 1496, 2–5 January 1497 (for two plays in the Hall), 7 January 1502, 31 December 1504 (in the Hall), 28 December 1505, 1 January and 30 December 1506 (before the Lord Steward in the Hall), 27 and 30 December 1509 (in the Hall) for court performances. An unnamed company performed possibly between Christmas 1486–7 and 23 March 1487. Warton records that Skelton's *The Nigramansir* was performed on 31 March 1504. John Harrison was paid for producing a play on 2 February 1515 in the queen's Chamber. Plays by unidentified companies were performed for the coronation of Edward VI on 20 and 22 February, during the Christmas seasons of 1549–50 and 1550–1, and at Shrovetide (8, 9, 10 February) 1551. Baldwin's *Play of the State of Ireland* was performed on 2 April or 1 May 1553. Heywood's unnamed play for twelve boys was also performed on one of these dates. A number of dialogues or plays by Nicholas Udall were produced with assistance from the Revels Office by order of Mary in 1554–5. Baldwin's *Love and Lyve* was apparently performed at Christmas 1555–6. Plays by unidentified companies were performed in the Christmas seasons of 1555–6, 1556–7, and 1557–8, as well as on 2 February 1558 and at Shrovetide (20, 21, 22 February) 1558.

BALE'S FELLOWS. John Bale (1495–1563) and his 'fellows' were paid on 8 September 1538 for performing a play at St Stephen's, Canterbury, before Cromwell. They were paid for a performance at Cromwell's on 31 January 1539, and they are probably the company which performed Bale's *Kyng Johan* at Cranmer's in London at Christmas 1538–9. It is not certain that this company is identical to the one patronized by Thomas Cromwell, Principal Secretary (1534), Lord Privy Seal and Lord Cromwell (1536), Earl of Essex (1540), called variously players of the Lord Privy Seal, of the Secretary, of Lord Cromwell. For references to the various companies associated with Cromwell see *Dramatic Records*, p. 380.

BUCKINGHAM. Edward Stafford (1478–1521), Duke of Buckingham (1485–1521). His company was paid on 2 January 1509 for a performance at court. For a list of appearances in the provinces see *Dramatic Records*, p. 405.

BURGAVENNY. George Nevill (? –1535), Lord of Burgavenny (1492–1535). His company was paid on 2–4 January 1503 for a performance at court.

CARDINAL WOLSEY. The Gentlemen of the Cardinal's Chapel performed a play before the court at Wolsey's (York Place) on 3 March 1522 and performed Plautus' *Menaechmi* in Latin at Wolsey's (York Place) 3 January 1527. They may have been the company (rather than the Children of the Chapel) who performed the comedy of Plautus at court on 7 March 1519.

CHAPEL ROYAL. While the **Children of the Chapel** participated in some of the major disguisings in Henry VII's reign, there are no dramatic performances certainly given by them as an acting company. The Chamber payment of 14 January 1508 is ambiguous (see under Child players). They performed in a number of the disguisings early in Henry VIII's reign. They are identified as a playing company under the Master of the Children in payments from the Chamber on 4 January 1517, 8 March 1517 (for a play on 24 February), 6 January 1519 (for a play on 1 January), 1 May 1519 (for a play on 7 March – possibly for the performance of the comedy of Plautus), 1 January 1520, 1 April 1520 (for two interludes), 6 January 1521, 1 January 1529, 1 January 1530, 1 January 1531, 1 January 1539, 1 January 1540, 1 January 1541 (produced by the Yeoman of the Revels), 1 January 1544, 1 January 1548, 1 January 1549. They also performed plays as part of revels: 6 January 1516 (comedy of *Troylus and Pandor*), 20 May 1516 (unnamed play produced by William Cornish at Greenwich), 3 September 1519 (pastime of *Summer and Winter*), 6 May 1527 (dialogue of *Love and Riches*, probably with some of the Gentlemen), probably 6 January 1552 (dialogue of *Youth and Riches*), probably 6 January 1553 (triumph of *Venus, Cupid, and Mars*), and possibly 15 June 1522 (political disguising or play at Windsor). Collier records their performance of *Venus and Beauty* on 6 January 1514. See also under Oxford, below, for a payment to the Earl's Chapel.

The supposed traditional performance of a play at coronations by the **Gentlemen of the Chapel** specified in a warrant of Queen Mary (Loseley Manor Documents, vol. V, no. 6, printed in Feuillerat, *Edward VI and Mary*, p. 149, from Folger Library, MS. Lb 41, fol. 73) cannot be verified for Henry VII's, Henry VIII's, and Elizabeth I's coronations. The Gentlemen apparently performed a play on 20 February 1547 for Edward's coronation, and a play (*Humanum Genus*) at Christmas 1553–4, postponed from Mary's coronation. They received an annual reward on New Year's of £13 6s. 8d., most often for unspecified services, although on a few occasions 'for their pains taking' at Christmas. For a list of members of the Chapel in the period see *Dramatic Records*, pp. 383–4, 388, 392–3, 397–8. For other performances by the Gentlemen, see under Players of the Chapel, below.

The **Players of the Chapel** were first paid on 11 January 1505 for a court performance. The payments for performances on 10 January 1506 and on 16 January 1507 mention that there were four members of the troupe. For the performance on 7 January 1508 there were five of them. They were paid for performances on 25 December 1508 (possibly in conjunction with Wentworth's disguising and morris dance), on 7 January 1509, on 6 January 1510 (in the Hall), on 6 January 1511, on 6 March 1512 (for a performance on 22 February), and on 2 June 1512. The most likely candidates for the company's personnel are William Cornish, John Kyte, John Sidborough, William Newark (to 1508), William Crane, and Henry Prents: Streitberger, 'William Cornish and the Players of the Chapel,' *Medieval English Theatre*, 8 (1985): 3–20. Members of this company performed in plays as part of revels and in court disguisings probably in Henry VII's reign in December 1508 and in Henry VIII's reign beginning by 13 February 1511.

CHILD Players. Four children were paid on 14 January 1508 for playing before the king. It is unlikely that these were the Children of the Chapel. Mr [Edward? Walter?] Hopton's priest's children were paid on 12 April 1538 for a performance before Cromwell. See also Children of the Chapel, St Swithens, Children of Paul's.

COBHAM. George Brooke (ca. 1497–1558), Lord Cobham of Cobham, Kent (1529). His players were rewarded on 4 February 1538 for a performance before Cromwell. For a list of appearances in the provinces see *Dramatic Records*, p. 377.

COVENTRY. The players of Coventry were paid on 1 January 1530 for a performance at court during Christmas 1529–30.

ESSEX. Henry Bourchier (c. 1473–1540), 2nd Earl of Essex (1483–1540), patronized a group of players who were paid on 5–11 January 1499 for a court performance. For a list of their appearances in the provinces between 1482 and 1527 see *Dramatic Records*, p. 376.

The **Players of Essex,** who may be identical to Henry Bourchier's players (q.v.), were paid on 1 January 1494, 1–2 January 1496, 31 December 1497, 12 January 1498, 31 December 1498, and 2–4 January 1503 for court performances. A company calling themselves the Players of Essex appeared in the provinces from 1525 to 1541. For a list of appearances in the provinces see *Dramatic Records*, p. 355.

ETON COLLEGE, Berkshire. The schoolmaster and boys of Eton were paid a reward in July 1510, possibly for a play. 'Woodall' [Nicholas Udall], schoolmaster of Eton, was paid on 2 February 1538 for a play before Cromwell.

EXETER. Henry Courtenay (ca. 1498–1539), Earl of Devon (1511), Marquis of Exeter (1525). His company was paid on 26 December 1537 for a performance before Cromwell. For a list of appearances in the provinces see *Dramatic Records*, pp. 379–80.

FRENCH Players. A company called the French Players was paid on 6 January 1494 and 4 January 1495 for court performances. The Chamber payment on 7 February 1505 to nine Frenchmen 'that played' may be for a musical performance.

HYDE ABBEY. See St Swithun's.

KING'S PLAYERS.

    Henry VII's (ca.1494–1509) company was paid for performances at court on 6 January 1494 (probably in conjunction with the *St George* pageant – disguising), 3–8 January 1496, 1 April 1496, 7 January 1497, 19–23 February 1497, 1 January 1498, 12 January 1498, 1 February 1500, 8 January 1501, again in January 1501, (probably on 21 November 1501), 7 January 1502, 8–28 January 1502 (probably for a play acted in connection with the lantern pageant-disguising and morris dance), 2–4 January 1503, August–September 1503 (for at least two plays acted at the court of King James IV of Scotland), 11 January 1505, 10 January 1506, 16 January 1507, 7 January 1509. In 1494 the members of the troupe included Richard Gibson, John English, John Hammond, and Edward Maye. In 1503–4, William Rutter and John Scott were added and Edward Maye dropped out. For a list of members see *Dramatic Records*, pp. 387–8.

    Henry VIII's (1509–47) company was paid for performances on 6 January 1510, 6 January 1511, 6 January 1512, 6 January 1513, and 6 January 1514; they also accompanied the king to France in 1513. Collier claimed to have transcribed a now lost document which records their performance of Medwall's lost *Finding of Truth* on 6 January 1514. The company was split into two groups by 1515. The King's 'olde' Players, which probably included John English, John Slye, William Rutter, Thomas Sudborough, and John Scott, were rewarded £4 on 6 January 1515, 6 January 1516, 4 January 1517, 2 January 1519, 6 January 1520, and 6 January 1521. When evidence from the Chamber accounts again becomes available in 1529, the 'olde' Players are not rewarded. The King's 'new' Players, probably including George Maller, Thomas Arthur, Richard Hole, and possibly John Roo and, after 1530, Thomas Sudborough, were a travelling troupe, but they received rewards for court performances on 6 January 1515, 6 January 1516, 4 January 1517, 3 January 1518, 6 January 1519, 6 January 1520, and 6 January 1521. No Chamber accounts survive to document the Christmas seasons from 1522 to 1528; thereafter the King's Players received rewards in every year for which a Chamber account survives: 1 January 1529, 1 January 1530, 1 January 1531, 1 January 1539, 1 January 1540, and 1 January 1541. They were also paid on 26 December 1537 for a performance at Cromwell's and on 1 January 1544 for a performance before Princess

Mary. By 1533 the company was led by Robert Hinstock and included George Birch and George Maller who was replaced ca. 1540 by Richard Parrowe. For a list of members and of appearances in the provinces see *Dramatic Records*, pp. 388–92.

Edward VI (1547–53). From 1547 to 1552 there were at least six members of the King's Players: Robert Hinstock and George Birch, leading figures in the King's Players near the end of Henry VIII's reign, Richard Cooke, Richard Skinner, Henry Harriot, who disappeared after 1552, John Birch, John Smith, who appeared in 1547 only and was replaced by Thomas Southey in 1548. John Browne and John Young (formerly of Jane Seymour's troupe; see under Queen's Players) are mentioned separately in 1552. For a list of members and of appearances in the provinces see *Dramatic Records*, pp. 381–3. The King's Players may have performed a play along with Edward VI and some of his young friends on 11 April 1547. They performed a play at court, possibly using the pageant Tower of Babylon made by the Revels Office, on 1 January 1548; a play at Shrovetide (12, 13, 14 February) 1548, using an Oven made by the Revels Office; a play on 1 January 1549; a play at Shrovetide (3, 4, 5 March) 1549, possibly using the pageant Dragon with Seven Heads made by the Revels Office; and a play on 6 January 1552. During the Christmas season of 1551–2, the company was practising the lost play, *Aesop's Crow*. Sir Thomas Chaloner rewarded them in March for performing the lost *Self Love* on 9 February 1552.

KINGSTON. There is no record of a performance at court by the players of Kingston, but they received a payment on 31 May 1505 'towardes the building of the Churche stiple in almns.' There were Easter plays at Kingston between 1505 and 1565. There was also a Maygame, Robin Hood game or gathering, or King game with Little John, Maid Marian, and the friar linked with the Lord of Misrule, morris dance, and fool from 1506 to 1539: *Dramatic Records*, pp. 162–3.

LONDON. A company or companies called the Players of London were paid on 31 December 1497, 28 December 1498, 29 December 1499, 2–4 January 1503, and 2–3 January 1505 for court performances. The Inns of Court and some of the London parishes had playing companies by Henry VII's reign. By the mid sixteenth century, the Players of London had come to mean any of the troupes acting within the city or suburbs rather than to one official city-sponsored troupe: *Dramatic Records*, pp. 361–2.

LORD CHANCELLOR. Thomas Audley (ca. 1488–1544), Lord Audley of Walden, Lord Chancellor (1533). His players were rewarded twice for performances on 26 December 1537 and 23 January 1538 for performances at Cromwell's. For a list of appearances in the provinces see *Dramatic Records*, p. 374.

LORD WARDEN.
    Henry Tudor (later Henry VIII) was patron of a travelling troupe, the Lord Warden's Players, from 1494 until 1502.

Arthur Plantagenet (ca. 1484–1542), Viscount Lisle (1523), Lord Warden of the Cinque Ports (1536) patronized a company (Lord Lisle's Players, Lord Warden's Players) paid on 21 January 1538 for performing before Cromwell. For a list of appearances in the provinces see *Dramatic Records,* pp. 400–1.

MILES END. The players at Miles End, Middlesex, received a payment on 6 August 1501 for a performance, possibly in connection with preparations for the reception of Katherine of Aragon.

NORTHAMPTON. William Parr (1513–1571), Earl of Essex (1543), Marquis of Northampton (1547–53, 1559). His company appeared at court in May 1550 or July 1551. For a list of provincial appearances see *Dramatic Records,* pp. 399–400.

NORTHUMBERLAND. Henry Algernon Percy (1478–1527), 5th Earl of Northumberland (1489–1527). His company was paid on 7 January 1493 for a court performance. For a list of provincial appearances see *Dramatic Records,* p. 400.

OXFORD. John de Vere (1442–1513), Earl of Oxford (1462–75, 1485–1513), patronized a group of players who were paid on 1 January 1492 and 12 January 1498 for court performances. The troupe appeared in the provinces from 1497 to 1499. For a list of provincial appearances see *Dramatic Records,* p. 407. The Children of the Earl's Chapel were paid on 15 May 1506 for a court performance and his 'jocular' and bearward were paid for entertainments in August 1498.

The **Players of Oxford,** who may be identical to John de Vere's players (q.v.), were paid on 1–2 January 1496 for a court performance.

PAUL'S, Children of. The supposed performance of *The Divill and Rychard* by Paul's Clerks and Boys for the coronation of Henry VII on 30 October 1485 is a forgery by William Ireland. Under John Rightwise, Master of St Paul's School, the children performed a Latin play *(Cardinalis Pacificus)* at court on 10 November 1527 as part of a revel. They were probably the same (rather than the Children of Paul's Choir School) who performed Terence's *Phormio* and a political-religious dialogue at Wolsey's (York Place) on 7 January 1528. The Children of Paul's (it is uncertain whether they were the Children of the Grammar or the Choir School) performed at court in May 1550 or in July 1551. [John] Heywood's Children (probably Paul's Choir Boys) performed before Princess Mary in March 1538. Sebastian [Westcott, Master of Paul's Choir School] performed a play with his Children in February 1553 [with John Heywood] before Elizabeth. Westcott and Heywood performed a play with the Children of Paul's before Elizabeth at Nonsuch on 7 August 1559. It is not certain whether Heywood's play for twelve children at court on 2 April or 1 May 1553 was performed by the Children of Paul's (see Anonymous Players).

PRINCE'S PLAYERS.

Arthur's (1486–1502) company was paid on 2–4 January 1499, 15 February 1499, and in January 1501 for court performances.

Henry (1502–9) had a company of travelling players when he was Lord Warden of the Cinque Ports (q.v.). The Prince's Players under his patronage were paid on 31 December 1502, 31 December 1503, 5 January 1504, 31 December 1504, and 31 December 1505 for court performances.

Edward (1537–47). There were at least four Prince's players led by Thomas Yely in 1539. This company was paid on 1 January 1539, 1 January 1540, and 1 January 1541 for court performances. They were paid for a performance before Princess Mary in January 1540.

For a list of provincial appearances by the Princes' companies see *Dramatic Records*, pp. 374 (Arthur), 388–92 (Henry), 381–3 (Edward). See also under King's Players, above.

PRINCESS'S PLAYERS. Princess Mary (1516–53) patronized a company of players who were rewarded on 1 January 1529, 1 January 1530, and 1 January 1531 for performances at court. In 1531 the company included William Slye and three others. See also under Queen's players.

PUPPETS. Players using 'mammets' [puppets] were paid on 6 June 1499 in connection with a May game at Greenwich.

QUEEN'S PLAYERS.

Elizabeth of York (1486–1503) had a company who may have been musicians rather than actors and who appeared in the provinces from 1492 to 1501. There is no record of their appearance at court.

Jane Seymour (1536–7), 3rd Queen of Henry VIII, had a company of players including John Young, John Slye, David Sotherne, and John Mounffeld who were paid on 10 February 1537 for a performance before Cromwell and on 1 January 1539 for a performance at court.

Anne of Cleves (1540), 4th Queen of Henry VIII, had a company of players who performed at court on 1 January 1540.

Catherine Howard (1540–2), 5th Queen of Henry VIII, had a company of players who performed at court on 1 January 1541.

Mary (1553–8) had a company of players when she was Princess (q.v.). The Queen's Players from 1553 to 1556 included John Birch, Richard Cooke, and Thomas Southey. Udall's *Roister Doister*, *Respublica*, and *Wealth and Health* are associated with the company.

Elizabeth I (1558–1603) inherited her sister's company. They possibly performed a play on 6 January 1559. Thereafter, the company appears to have been sent on tour.

After the death of the last member of this troupe, the queen created a new company of players in 1583.

For a list of personnel and appearances by the Queens' companies see *Dramatic Records*, pp. 384 (Elizabeth of York), 395 (Jane Seymour), 373 (Anne of Cleves), 378 (Catherine Howard), 396–7 (Mary); Chambers, *ES*, II: 83–5, 104–15 (Elizabeth I).

ST ALBANS. The players of St Albans were paid for a court performance on 31 December 1502. On the dramatic tradition at St Albans see *Dramatic Records*, p. 258.

ST PAUL'S. See under Paul's.

ST SWITHUN'S. Warton *HEP*, pp. 456–7, records a play, *Christi Descensus ad Infernos*, performed before the court at Winchester by the choir boys of St Swithun's and Hyde Abbey on 24 September 1486 for the christening of Prince Arthur.

SOMERSET. Edward Seymour (ca. 1500–52), Earl of Hertford (1537), Duke of Somerset, Lord Protector (1547). His company appeared at court in May 1550 or July 1551. For a list of provincial appearances see *Dramatic Records*, pp. 403–4.

SUFFOLK. Charles Brandon. (ca. 1484–1545), Duke of Suffolk (1514–45), patronized a group of players who were rewarded on 22 January 1538 for a performance before Cromwell and on 6 January 1541 for a court performance in the Hall. For a list of provincial appearances see *Dramatic Records*, pp. 376–7.

Katherine Willoughby. (1519–80), Baroness Willoughby de Eresby, widow of Charles Brandon, Duke of Suffolk (q.v.), styled Duchess of Suffolk from 1545 until at least 1553. Her company performed at court in May 1550 or July 1551. For a list of provincial appearances see *Dramatic Records*, p. 408.

Four players from Suffolk were rewarded on 1 January 1512 for playing in the Hall before the Lord Steward on 29 December 1511. For a list of provincial appearances see *Dramatic Records*, p. 369.

WIMBORNE. The players of Wimborne Minster, Dorset, were paid on 1 January 1494 for a court performance. On dramatic activities in Wimborne Minster later in the Tudor period, see R.C. Hays, 'Dorset Church Houses and the Drama,' *RORD*, 31 (1992): 13–23.

WILTSHIRE. Henry Stafford (ca. 1479–1523), Earl of Wiltshire (1510). His company was rewarded on 1 January 1515 for a scheduled performance on 28 December which was cancelled. They were rewarded on 1 January 1516 for a performance.

WYCOMBE. The players of High Wycombe, Buckinghamshire, were paid on 31 December 1494, 12 January 1498, and 31 December 1498 for court performances.

Abbots and Lords of Misrule, 1489–1553

Unnamed Abbots of Misrule: 1489–90, 1502–3, 1504–5.

Unnamed Lords of Misrule: 1505–6, 1506–7, 1507–8, 1510–11, 1511–12, 1534–5.

William Ringley: Abbot of Misrule 1492–3, 1501–2; Lord of Misrule 1491–2, 1495–6, 1500–1.

William Wynnsbury: Lord of Misrule 1508–9, 1509–10, 1512–13, 1513–14, 1514–15, 1519–20.

Richard Pole: Lord of Misrule 1516–17.

Edmond Travore: Lord of Misrule 1518–19.

William Tolly: Lord of Misrule 1520–1.

George Ferrers: Master of the King's Pastimes 1551–2, 1552–3.

Officers of the Revels and of the Tents

MASTER OF THE REVELS

1. Henry Wentworth (d. 1510?) produced disguisings and pageants at court from 1507 to 1510. He is called 'Master of the Revels' in Richard Gibson's account in 1510: PRO, E36/217, fol. 24, abstracted in *LP*, II.ii, p. 1492. No patent discovered.

2. Sir Henry Guildford (d. by 27 May 1532) is called 'Master of the Revels' in Richard Gibson's accounts as early as 1511 (PRO, E36/217, fol. 38) and as late as ca. 1530 (PRO, SP1/58, fol. 253). No patent discovered.

3. Sir Thomas Cawarden (d. 25 or 29 August 1559) was granted the patent as Master of the Revels on 5 March 1545, made retroactive to 16 March 1544: Folger Library, MS. Lb 40 (original), PRO, C66/753, memb. 23 (enrolment), calendared in *LP*, XX.i, no. 465 (28), printed in Feuillerat, *Elizabeth*, p. 7. See Master of the Tents.

SERGEANT (1485–1545), MASTER (1545–1559) OF THE TENTS

1. Thomas Walshe (d. 1489?) was granted the patent as Sergeant of the Tents on 8 December 1485: PRO, C66/565, memb. 13, calendared in Campbell, I: 204.

2. William Tournell (d. 1496?) was granted the patent as Sergeant of the Tents on 5 November 1489: PRO, C66/570, memb. 6, calendared in *CPR Henry VII*, I: 293.

3. John Morton (resigned 15 May 1518) was granted the patent as Sergeant of the Tents on 28 November 1496: PRO, C66/579, memb. 10, calendared in *CPR Henry VII*, II: 72–3.

4. Sir Christopher Garnesche is called 'Sergeant of the Tents' in Richard Gibson's account in 1513: PRO, E101/417/11, E101/56/25, abstracted in *LP*, I.ii, no. 2349, 2480 (8). No patent discovered; probably a wartime appointment.

5. Richard Gibson (d. 4–28 October 1534) is called 'Sergeant of the Tents' in a Chamber account payment in August 1518, suggesting that he was appointed to the post on Morton's resignation on 15 May: PRO, E36/216, fol. 11v, abstracted in *LP*, II.ii, p. 1479. No patent discovered. See Yeoman of the Revels and Yeoman of the Tents.

6. John Parker (d. 1539) was granted the patent as Sergeant of the Tents on 8 December 1534: PRO, C66/664, memb. 3, calendared in *LP,* VII, no. 1601 (19).

7. John Farlyon (d. 25 July 1539) was granted the patent as Sergeant of the Tents on 28 August 1538: PRO, C66/680, memb. 9, calendared in *LP,* XIII.ii, no. 249 (15). See Yeoman of the Revels.

8. John Travers (resigned 1543: PRO, SP60/11, no. 51, calendared in *LP,* XIX.ii, no. 731) was granted the patent as Sergeant of the Tents on 28 September 1539: PRO, C66/686, memb. 40, calendared in *LP,* XIV.ii, no. 264 (30).

9. Sir Thomas Cawarden (d. 25 or 29 August 1559) was granted the patent as Master of the Tents on 5 March 1545, made retroactive to 16 March 1544: Guildford Muniment Room, MS. LM 9 (original), PRO, C66/752, memb. 36 (enrolment), calendared in *LP,* XX.i, no. 465 (27). See Master of the Revels.

CLERK COMPTROLLER OF THE TENTS AND REVELS

1. John Barnard (d. 4 September 1550) was granted the patent on 5 March 1545, made retroactive to 16 March 1544: PRO, C66/753, memb. 23, calendared in *LP,* XX.i, no. 465 (29).

2. Richard Leys (d. before 30 September 1570) was granted the patent on 17 March 1551 after serving as deputy from 1 September 1550: PRO, C66/836, memb. 5, calendared in *CPR Edward VI,* IV: 49, printed in Feuillerat, *Elizabeth,* pp. 56–7.

CLERK OF THE TENTS AND REVELS

1. John Colyer (d. by 1546?) was paid in the accounts for his services as Clerk in 1544 and for the Christmas revels in 1544–5: Folger Library, MSS. Lb 258, Lb 2, fols. 6–7; *RCHM,* VII: 600a. No patent discovered.

2. Thomas Phillips (d. by 1560) was granted the patent on 4 May 1546: PRO, C66/787, memb. 16, calendared in *LP,* XXI.i, no. 970 (15), printed in Feuillerat, *Elizabeth,* pp. 66–7.

3. Thomas Blagrave (d. April – November 1590), who was active in the office from as early as 1546 and who served as deputy to the Clerk from 1551, was granted the patent on 25 March 1560: PRO, C66/962, memb. 40, calendared in *CPR Elizabeth,* I: 468, printed in Feuillerat, *Elizabeth,* pp. 68–9. He later served as acting Master from 31 October 1573 probably until February 1578: PRO, AO3/2045, no. 3, 4, 6, printed in Feuillerat, *Elizabeth,* pp. 191, 225, 298–9. He was granted the patent as Surveyor of the Works on 10 November 1586: PRO, C66/1273, memb. 5, calendared in *Draft of Patent Rolls, 28–29 Elizabeth, Part 1,* List and Index Society, vol. 242 (London: Printed for Subscribers, 1991), 46.

YEOMAN OF THE REVELS

1. Richard Gibson (d. 4–28 October 1534) served in this capacity between 1510 and 1534. No patent discovered. See Yeoman of the Tents and Sergeant of the Tents.

2. John Farlyon (d. 25 July 1539) was granted the patent on 20 November 1534: PRO, C66/664, memb. 25, calendared in *LP,* VII, no. 1498 (41).

3. John Bridges (resigned 1 July 1550) was granted the patent on 21 October 1539: PRO, C66/691, memb. 5, calendared in *LP,* XIV.ii, no. 435 (48). See Yeoman of the Tents.

4. John Holt (d. 1–11 December 1570) was granted the patent on 1 July 1550: PRO, C66/830, memb. 32, calendared in *CPR Edward VI,* III: 311, printed in Feuillerat, *Elizabeth,* pp. 70–1. See Yeoman of the Tents.

YEOMAN OF THE TENTS

1. Boy, Garçon, Groom, Yeoman: 1485–ca. 1513. No patents discovered.

2. Richard Gibson (d. 4–28 October 1534) is called 'deputy' and 'yeoman' in 1513: PRO, E101/417/11, E101/56/25, calendared in *LP,* I.ii, nos. 2349, 2480 (8); Hall, pp. 539–40. He served in this capacity from 1513 to 1518. No patent discovered. See Yeoman of the Revels and Sergeant of the Tents.

3. Richard Longman (resigned 14 October 1550 – PRO, C66/828, memb. 12, calendared in *CPR Edward VI,* III: 227–8 – to receive a grant of the office in survivorship with John Holt) was granted the patent on 19 August 1538: PRO, C66/683, memb. 16, calendared in *LP,* XIII.ii, no. 249 (12).

4. John Bridges (resigned 1 July 1550) was granted the patent in reversion with Richard Longman on 15 November 1541: PRO, C66/709, memb. 32, calendared in *LP,* XVI, no. 1391 (34). See Yeoman of the Revels.

5. John Holt was granted the patent in reversion with Richard Longman on 14 October 1550: PRO, C66/828, memb. 12, calendared in *CPR Edward VI,* III: 227–8. See Yeoman of the Revels.

GROOM OF THE TENTS

Thomas Hale (resigned 25 March 1575: PRO, C66/1123, calendared in *CPR Elizabeth,* VI, no. 2204) was granted the patent on 12 November 1541: PRO, C66/709, memb. 32, calendared in *LP,* XVI, no. 1391 (33).

Index